Politics and history in band societies

D1591269

frontispiece—Band societies discussed in this book
key: ○ DENE—ethnic group
   • Yellowknife—urban center affecting the
   lives of contemporary foragers

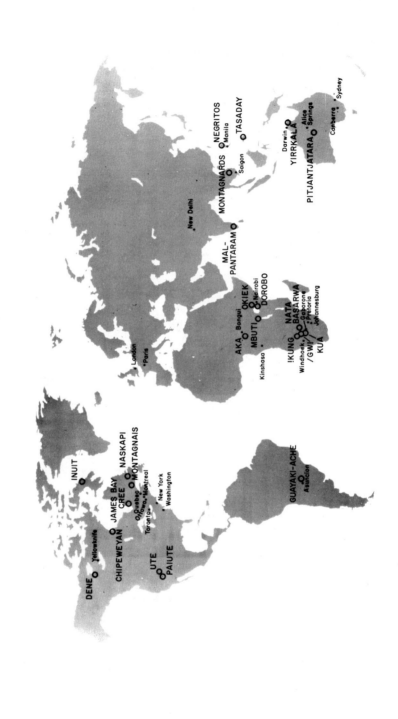

Politics and history in band societies

edited by

ELEANOR LEACOCK
City College, City University of New York

RICHARD LEE
University of Toronto

CAMBRIDGE UNIVERSITY PRESS

Cambridge
London   New York   New Rochelle   Melbourne   Sydney

& EDITIONS DE LA MAISON DES SCIENCES DE L'HOMME

Paris

Published by the Press Syndicate of the University of Cambridge
The Pitt Building, Trumpington Street, Cambridge CB2 1RP
32 East 57th Street, New York, NY 10022, USA
296 Beaconsfield Parade, Middle Park, Melbourne 3206, Australia

© Cambridge University Press 1982

First published 1982

Printed in the United States of America

Library of Congress catalogue card number: 81-18043

British Library cataloguing in publication data

Politics and history in band societies.
1. Society, Primitive   2. Hunting, Primitive
I. Leacock, Eleanor B.   II. Lee, Richard B.
306   GN388

ISBN 0 521 24063 8 hard covers
ISBN 0 521 28412 0 paperback
ISBN 2 7351 0019 7 (France Only)

Contents

Notes on the Contributors

MICHAEL I. ASCH (Ph.D., Columbia) is currently Associate Professor of anthropology at the University of Alberta, Edmonton. He has conducted research into various aspects of Dene life, and has advised on Dene economic history and change at a variety of hearings and enquiries. Among his publications are: 'The Dene economy' (1977) and 'The economics of Dene self-determination' (1979).

SERGE BAHUCHET (M.A., École des Hautes Études en Sciences Sociales, Paris) is currently Research Associate at the Laboratoire de Langues et Civilisations à Tradition Orale of the c.n.r.s., Paris. He is studying ecology and ethnoecology among the Aka Pygmies in the Central African rain forest. He is the author of *Introduction à l'ethno-écologie des Pygmées Aka* (1978) and a number of articles on the Pygmies.

RODERIC H. BLACKBURN (Ph.D., Michigan State) is currently Assistant Director of the Albany Institute of History and Art, Albany, New York where he is pursuing research on the ethnography of the colonial Dutch of New Netherlands. From 1968 to 1970 he carried out field work among the Okiek, a foraging society in Kenya, about which he has published a number of articles.

JEAN L. BRIGGS (Ph.D., Harvard) is currently Professor of anthropology at the Memorial University of Newfoundland. She has carried out research in Canadian Inuit communities, and has written a number of articles and two monographs on the Inuit. Her books are: *Never in anger: portrait of an Eskimo family* (1970), and *Aspects of Inuit value socialization* (1979).

CYNTHIA CHANG is presently working towards a Ph.D. in anthropology at the City University of New York Graduate Centre, New York, and is an adjunct lecturer at Baruch College. She has written several (unpublished) research papers directed towards expanding the unit of historical analysis to encompass a region.

PAUL CHAREST (Ph.D., l'École Pratique des Hautes Études, Paris) is currently Associate Professor of anthropology at Laval University, Quebec. After conducting fieldwork on the impact of development in Rwanda and Senegal, he has concentrated his research on the native peoples of the North Shore of the Gulf of St Lawrence. His works include *Les changements socio-culturels à St Augustin* (1969) which he co-authored, and many papers (in French) in various journals.

H. C. COOMBS (Ph.D., London) is currently Visiting Fellow at the Centre for Resource and Environmental Studies, Australian National University, Canberra. He served as Chairman of the Australian Council of Aboriginal Affairs between 1968 and 1976, during which time he became interested in the outstation movement, and he has since maintained contact with a number of outstation communities. His publications include: *Kalmma: listening to Aboriginal Australians* (1976) and 'Decentralization trends among Aboriginal Australians' (1973).

BARRIE G. DEXTER (M.A., Dip.Ed., Melbourne; CBE) is currently Australian High Commissioner in Canada. He has worked for the Council for Aboriginal Affairs, the Office of Aboriginal Affairs, and the Department of Aboriginal Affairs, and has been responsible for the financing of, and infrastructural provisions for, the outstation movement. Among his publications are various Reports of the Council for Aboriginal Affairs co-authored with H. C. Coombs and W. E. H. Stanner.

HARVEY A. FEIT (Ph.D., McGill) is currently Associate Professor of anthropology at McMaster University, Hamilton, Ontario. Since 1972 he has served as adviser to the James Bay Cree of Quebec on social issues related to legal proceedings, land-claims negotiations and implementation of the James Bay and Northern Quebec Agreement. Recently he has undertaken a study of the implications of the aboriginal rights negotiations process.

HENRI GUILLAUME (M.A., École des Hautes Études en Sciences Sociales, Paris) is currently a researcher at the Office de la Recherche Scientifique et Technique Outre-Mer, and a member of the Laboratoire des Langues et Civilisations à Tradition Orale of the c.n.r.s., Paris. His present work concerns the Aka Pygmies of the Central African Republic and the People's Republic of the Congo. He is currently preparing a general work on the transformation of their socio-economic organization brought about through their interaction with successive colonizers of the forest. Among his publications are: *Les nomades interrompus* (1974) and 'Les Liens de dependance, a l'époque précoloniale, chez les Touaregs de l'Imannen' (1976).

ANNETTE HAMILTON (Ph.D., Sydney) is currently a Senior Lecturer in anthropology at Macquarie University, New South Wales. She has conducted fieldwork among the Burarra people of Arnhem Land, and the Pitjantjatjara and Yangkuntjara-speaking people of the Western Desert. She is preparing a book on the relationship between racism and colonialism in British settler colonies. Her many articles on aboriginal life include *Nature and nurture* (1981) and 'Dual social systems: technology, labour and women's secret rites' (1980).

L. R. HIATT (Ph.D., Australian National University) is currently Reader in anthropology at the University of Sydney, and President of the Australian Institute of Aboriginal Studies. He has conducted fieldwork in Arnhem Land, including a visit in 1978 to make the outstation film 'Waiting For Harry'. Among his publications are *Kinship and conflict* (1965). He is also editor of *Australian Aboriginal mythology* (1975) and *Australian Aboriginal concepts* (1978). He co-edited *Anthropology in Oceania* (1971) with C. Jayawardena.

ROBERT K. HITCHCOCK (Ph.D., New Mexico) is currently Senior Rural Sociologist in the Ministry of Agriculture, Republic of Botswana. His research interests range from gatherer-hunter adaptations in arid lands to problems of the rural poor in the Third World. He has worked among several groups in the Kalahari, and is currently involved in monitoring the effects of livestock development projects on gatherer-hunters and small-scale pastoralists and agriculturalists. He is the author of *Kalahari cattle posts* (1979), 'Tradition, social justice and land reform in central Botswana' (1980) and 'Foraging and food production among Kalahari hunter-gatherers' (1981).

SUSAN HURLICH (M.A., Calgary) is completing a Ph.D. in anthropology at the University of Toronto, and she also works for Oxfam-Canada as Southern Africa Programme Development Officer. Her research interests include underdevelopment, liberation movements and native peoples' struggles in Canada. Her publications include 'Colonialism, apartheid and liberation: a Namibian example' with R. B. Lee (1979), 'Up against the bay: resource imperialism and native resistance' (1975) and numerous articles on Southern African liberation struggles.

ELEANOR LEACOCK (Ph.D., Columbia) is currently Professor of anthropology at the City College, City University of New York. She studied the Montagnais-Naskapi of eastern Canada. Other research interests are urban, applied anthropology and the cross-cultural study of women. Her publications include *North American Indians in historical perspective* (co-edited with Nancy Lurie), *Teaching and learning in city schools*, *The culture of poverty: a critique*, *Myths of male dominance: collected articles on women cross-culturally*, and introductions to Morgan's *Ancient society* and Engels' *The origin of the family, private property and the state*.

RICHARD LEE (Ph.D., Berkeley) is a Professor of anthropology at the University of Toronto. He has conducted field work in Canada and East Africa and since the 1960s has been involved in a long-term study of ecology and social change among the !Kung San of Botswana. He is a co-founder of the Kalahari Peoples Fund (KPF) and of Anthropologists for Radical Political Action (ARPA) and is active in the Toronto Committee for the Liberation of Southern Africa (TCLSAC). His edited works include *Man the hunter* (1968) and *Kalahari hunter-gatherers* (1976) with Irven DeVore and *The new native resistance* (1974) with Joe Jorgenson. His monograph *The !Kung San: men, women and work in a foraging society* (1979) recently received the Herskovits Award of the African Studies Association.

BRIAN MORRIS (Ph.D., L.S.E.) is currently a Senior Lecturer in anthropology at Goldsmith's College, University of London. His doctoral research was based on field work among the Hill Pandaram of south India. He is the author of a book on Epiphytic orchids, and a biography of Ernest Thompson Seton, the naturalist writer. He has recently undertaken ethnobotanical studies in Malawi.

NICOLAS PETERSON (Ph.D., Sydney) is currently a Senior Lecturer in anthropology at Australian National University, Canberra. His research interests include economic and ecological anthropology, territorial organization, social change and symbolic systems. The present paper arises from his position in 1973–4 as Research Officer to the Aboriginal Land Rights Commission that drew up the report on which the Northern Territory legislation is based. Among his publications are: *Tribes and boundaries in Australia* (1976), which he edited, and many other papers on the Australian Aborigines.

RENATO ROSALDO (Ph.D., Harvard) is currently a Fellow at the Center For Advanced Study in the Behavioral Sciences, Stanford, California, and has taught at Stanford University since 1970. He has carried out research among the Ilongots of northern Luzon, and in Ecuador and Mexico. He has particular interest in history, colonialism, and ideology. Among his publications are: *Ilongot headhunting 1883–1974* (1980); and a number of other articles on Philippine society.

GEORGE SILBERBAUER is currently Senior Lecturer in the Department of Anthropology and Sociology at Monash University, Australia. He has conducted research among the G/wi of Botswana and is now engaged in a wide-ranging comparative study of economic adaptation, social organization and religious belief among the San of the Central Kalahari and the Australian Aborigines of the Western Desert. He is the author of *Hunter and habitat in the Central Kalahari*.

COLIN TURNBULL (D.Phil., Oxford) is currently a Research Professor of anthropology at George Washington University in Washington D.C. He has done field work in India and the U.S.A. and has carried out a number of key studies of African peoples, particularly on the Mbuti pygmies of the Republic of Zaire. Most recently he has become involved in innovative research on the links between drama and anthropology. His many books include *The forest people* (1961), *The lonely African* (1962), *The Mbuti Pygmies* (1965), *Wayward servants* (1966) and *The mountain people* (1972).

DANIEL VACHON (M.A., Toronto) is currently serving as anthropologist for the Pitjantjatjara Council in South Australia, and completing his doctoral thesis at the University of Toronto. His research interests include kinship and social organization of Western Desert peoples, land rights, and mining on Aboriginal land. Among his publications are: *Mantaku: the struggle of the Pitjantjatjara Council for their land* (forthcoming, with P. Tyne) and several articles.

HELGA VIERICH (M.A., Toronto) is currently on the staff of International Crop Research Institute working in Upper Volta. During her field work among the Basarwa of Botswana she became involved in regional development planning, and in 1979 she worked for several months as a consultant to the Botswana government, assessing the impact of drought on rural populations. She has published a number of papers in the area of foraging ecology and social change.

POLLY WIESSNER (Ph.D., Michigan) is currently a Research Associate at the Max Planck Institut in the Federal Republic of Germany and a lecturer in archaeology at Aarhus University, Denmark. Her research interests include hunter-gatherer social organization, ethno-archaeology and human ethology. She carried out field work among the !Kung San of Botswana on traditional exchange systems and on the correspondence between style in artifacts and social organization. She has submitted a series of articles for publication.

Introduction

ELEANOR LEACOCK and RICHARD LEE

This book deals with a set of questions that are vital to our understanding of ourselves as human beings: what was human social life like when people lived directly from the fruits of the earth? How do people relate to each other under such circumstances? How do they make decisions about group activities? How do they handle disagreements and conflicts? How does 'human nature' in band societies differ from 'human nature' as we know it in urban industrial society?

During most of human history everyone helped, according to their age and sex and to the resources of their environment, in acquiring food, in making tools and utensils, in building shelters, and in obtaining and working materials for clothing in climates where it was needed. People foraged for wild fruits and vegetables, for roots and nuts, and for small animals and insects. They collected shell-fish, or caught fish with hook and line or in nets. They built stockades into which they drove large animals, used ingenious traps and snares to catch game, or hunted with bows and arrows or spears.

People shared food; there were no rich and poor. They made decisions collectively; some people were more influential than others, but there were no powerful chiefs. Foraging peoples worked hard, but, contrary to popular stereotypes, life was not a grim battle for survival. Instead, foragers had a great deal of leisure, and they made the most of it. They painted and carved and decorated their tools and utensils, their clothes, their bodies, and their sacred objects. They composed stories and songs and developed rituals to commemorate birth, puberty, marriage, and death. They had time to enjoy talking and joking and, after periods of strenuous work, had time to rest and laze about.

This much anthropologists know from living among people distant from urban industrial centers who still live close to the land and depend in good part on its wild products, and from studying reports on the

1

gathering-hunting peoples first encountered by European missionaries and explorers. However, beyond these generalizations are topics on which data are sparse, contradictory, or difficult to interpret. Early accounts by explorers and missionaries are few and threaded through with Western biases, while the lives of contemporary gathering-hunting peoples that anthropologists study have changed greatly over the past centuries to meet new circumstances. Therefore such questions as how social groups among foragers are composed; how decisions are made and serious disputes settled; and how relations between the sexes are structured are subjects for lively debate.

Such issues are important, for answers yield information on the boundaries of human nature and social forms. Anthropologists have always challenged the ethnocentric assumption so characteristic of Western attitudes – that the behaviour patterns of Western culture reflect basic 'human nature'. Anthropologists point out that Western behaviour reflects the developments of a particular place and time and a specific set of circumstances. Anthropologists have been particularly interested in knowing more about the behaviour of peoples in societies that are structured along cooperative lines, by contrast with the competitive structure of capitalism. That people have lived and therefore can live cooperatively contradicts a common assertion that humans are innately too aggressive and competitive to be capable of socialism.

Today the query about cooperative ways of life has been joined with another question, one urgent both to gatherer-hunters as peoples, and to humanity as a whole. What is the future of peoples who have maintained a direct and intimate connection with the earth in the period when industrial capitalism has become the dominant world system? Their future is part of an issue basic to modern times: how to achieve a peaceful world society designed for people, rather than for profits. It may well be the ultimate question for human survival, for if there is no place left in the world for foraging peoples, is there to be a future for humanity as a whole?

The first section of this book deals with ways in which a number of gathering-hunting peoples structure their lives and solve their daily problems. The second section places gatherer-hunters in history, as they have related to agricultural neighbours in times past and present. The last section deals with the struggles of foraging peoples to maintain their lands and their right to make their own decisions about their futures.

Background to the book

This book had its genesis at the Conference on Hunters and Gatherers, held in Paris on 27–30 June 1978. The conference was initiated by Maurice Godelier of the Ecole Pratique des Hautes Etudes and was sponsored by the Maison des Sciences de l'Homme. Some fifty people, in four close-packed days, presented their thinking on the organization of local groups and relations to land, on kinship and relations between the sexes, and on religion, values, and symbol systems among gatherer-hunters, as well as on their economic, political, and cultural relations with dominant nation-states.

The Paris conference followed up two earlier conferences on the cultural and social lives of foraging peoples. The first was organized by David Damas, then of the National Museum of Canada. It was held in Ottawa 30 August to 2 September 1965, and the proceedings were published in the *National Museums of Canada Bulletin* 228, 1969. Some fourteen ethnologists compared the nature of the band among foraging peoples of North America, Africa, and India and discussed similarities and differences among these. A major subject of interest was the flexibility of band structure, and the variability of seasonal patterns according to which groups either fragmented into smaller units or came together in larger units. Discussion made it clear that behind the great variability found in different areas lay the common principle of adaptive fission and fusion in order to take advantage both of changing animal and plant resources and of opportunities for socializing.

'Man, the Hunter', the second conference on foraging peoples, was initiated by Sol Tax of the University of Chicago and organized by Richard Lee of the University of Toronto and Irven DeVore of Harvard. Some seventy-five people came together from 6 to 9 April 1966, in Chicago, to hear and debate twenty-eight papers. Central issues included the nature of the foraging subsistence base, demography, marriage, and the composition of social units, and the interface between archaeological and ethnographic data. The conference's main findings were that gathering and fishing, not hunting, were often the mainstays of foraging subsistence, and that, in most non-arctic foraging societies, women's work provided a share of the food equal to or greater than that of men. The resulting book, *Man the hunter*, was therefore a misnomer and could have been titled with equal justice *Woman the gatherer*.

These two conferences from the mid-1960s in effect established the terms of reference for the study of foraging peoples in the decade following. Since then, field and historical studies have accumulated (e.g. Bicchieri 1972), and the problems of group structure and composition, and nature of ecological adaptation have been clarified and refined.

The present volume, however, adopts a different starting point. It focuses on a set of issues that were barely raised in the 1960s but were brought to the fore by research in the decade following and by the struggles and demands of foraging peoples themselves. The first is the question of the internal dynamics of social relations in foraging societies. What common structural features underlie the great variability found in different ecological and historical settings? The papers in Part I show how the central elements of sharing, communal ownership of land and resources, and egalitarian political relations serve to structure the cultural consciousness of foragers in settings as diverse as Australia, Africa, and North America.

The second issue raised in this book concerns the longstanding relationships that some foraging peoples have maintained with neighbouring agricultural peoples. In the case of the Southern San of Botswana such ties go back 300–500 years, and for the Mal-pantaram of South India links can be traced back over 1,000 years. In these cases foraging peoples provided crucial forest products for the market economy of farmers. The papers in Part II explore ways in which these and other peoples have maintained themselves as gatherer-hunters in a world of non-foragers.

The third and most crucial issue for the future survival of modern foragers concerns their political struggles against encompassing and encroaching state systems. The Dene of northern Canada (Asch), the James Bay Cree (Feit), and the Pitjantjatjara of South Australia (Vachon) all share a common predicament: how to preserve their land base and way of life in the face of expanding industrial capitalism. The papers in Part III explore the political mobilization of these people and document the skill and resilience with which they adapt to the world of courts, land claims, and lobbying in the struggle for their rights.

Before considering the issues underlying the three divisions of this book – foragers among themselves, foragers and farmers, and foragers versus capitalism – a few words are in order on the role of foraging peoples in contemporary anthropological theory.

Foragers and anthropological theory

Foraging peoples have played an important role in human history. They represent the original condition of humankind, the system of production that prevailed during virtually 99 per cent of human history. Having said that, it is important to make two caveats. First, contemporary or recent foragers are not living fossils, their history and their distance from humanity's ancestors are as long as those of all human groups. It is their economy and technology that make foragers so important for science. They represent a basic human adaptation without the accretions and complications brought about by agriculture, cities, states, advanced technology, and national and class conflict. Second, foraging people are not isolates, they are living in the twentieth century and are moulded in part by that context. For many centuries they have not been 'hunters living in a world of hunters' as Sahlins put it at the Chicago conference (Lee and DeVore 1968:4).

The crucial role of foragers in history has made their study into a contested domain of ideology in contemporary social theory. As subjects of study, the collective social arrangements of foraging peoples have been and continue to be used in ideological debates about the possibility or impossibility of achieving a future collectivist world. In the nineteenth century it was commonly assumed that gatherer-hunters were unfortunate and indigent peoples who had fallen from a previous state of grace. Anthropologists took issue with this assumption and argued that all humanity had once lived in such societies. In his theoretical outline for human social history, Lewis Henry Morgan (1974:561–2) stressed the 'liberty, equality and fraternity' of kin-based gathering-hunting and technologically simple agricultural societies; qualities that were lost when humanity embarked on 'a property career' that 'contains the elements of self-destruction' and, if not abandoned, would be likely to terminate in the 'dissolution of society'.

Morgan's work, taken up by Frederick Engels in his *Origin of the family, private property and the state*, generated lively dispute in the then young field of anthropology, while popular images of non-urban peoples as living in a state of unbridled 'savagery' served conveniently to rationalize European colonization. In recent years, thinly revised versions of such images reappear in a line of argument best known from the books of the science writer, Robert Ardrey (1961, 1966, 1970), that (erroneously as the following pages will show) assumes that hunting life encourages aggression and competition.

In the course of argument such as the above, the social forms of gatherer-hunters are typically presented either as polar opposites of exploitative hierarchical society, or as incipient forms of exploitative hierarchical society. Neither view does justice to the complexities of foraging life and the socio-economic relations intrinsic to it. The problem remains to reconstruct and understand the organization of foragers on its own terms. What are its common features in different parts of the world? What are its intrinsic contradictions? This book suggests some answers to these questions and probes the theoretical and empirical problems encountered along the way.

A major problem is posed by the fact that the lives of recent foraging peoples are inseparable from their relations with systems of predatory expansion. In order to resolve debates concerning their past and present social forms, it is necessary first to locate a people being studied in its full historical and socio-economic context, and second to agree on what constitutes essential data for settling a debated issue. Without such agreement, debates remain ideological ones, interesting enough but not susceptible of resolution.

The contributors to this volume share an interest in discovering the commonalities among gatherer-hunters, although they bring a range of theoretical perspectives to bear on their analyses. As editors, our own view is that anything less than a dialectical and historical-materialist view of society ends in distortion, a view we have each elaborated on elsewhere (Leacock 1972, 1975, 1978; Lee 1978, 1979, 1980). As we see it, the strength of the Marxist approach comes to the fore at the level of synthesis. Marxist methodology resolves the conflict between generalizing and particularizing emphases, for it both enables fine-grained analyses of underlying determinant relations in specific instances and articulates these analyses with a comprehensive general theory of human history. In so doing, it does not – or should not – exclude the insights drawn from other approaches, but is informed by the corpus of anthropological functionalist, ecological, and historical particularist studies.

While committed to the importance of historical and cultural specificity, a dialectical and historical-materialist approach requires the search for underlying regularities or 'laws'. While committed to the significance of functionalist social cohesion, the approach calls for definition of the basic disharmonies, conflicts, or 'contradictions' within socio-economic structures that impel change. While taking account of the fact that ideologies and rituals are in part shaped by the necessity for some measure of coherence in symbol systems, it seeks to understand these in more than formalistic terms by examining their relations to the ongoing social life of a group. And, while committed to the necessity of objective analysis, the Marxist approach recognizes these analyses are inextricably linked to identification with people who are engaged in struggles both to understand the conditions of their existence and to find ways of using this understanding to fight for control over their own futures.

A dialectical and historical-materialist approach situates a society's centre of gravity in the relations and forces of production – the ways in which people necessarily relate to each other in the course of producing and reproducing their life. It necessitates both placing a society fully in the historically specific context of its relationships with its social and geographical environment, and dealing with the complex interrelations and interactions within and between the relations and forces of production on the one hand and the social and ideological superstructures on the other. We see the dialectical and historical-materialist approach as realizing the full historical promise of the anthropological endeavour: 'the study of humanity'.

I: Dynamics of egalitarian foraging societies

What links together diverse peoples in Australia, Africa, the Arctic and elsewhere under the rubric of 'foragers'? The link is not only their common way of making a living through the hunting and gathering of wild game and plants and through fishing, nor is it the absence of domesticated plants and animals among them. A mode of subsistence *per se* is not a 'mode of production'. The latter includes not only the means for making a living but also the relationships involved: who owns these means, how is production organized, who controls the product and how is it distributed, and who consumes what part of it?

Is there a foraging 'mode of production'? In our view there *is* a core of features common to *band-living* foraging societies around the world. Extraordinary correspondences have emerged in details of culture between, for example, the Cree and the San, or the Inuit and the Mbuti. These features, however, differ from a number of cases such as California and the Northwest Coast of North America where relations of production, distribution, exchange, and consumption have more in common with many horticultural peoples than with other foragers.

Similarities among foragers include: egalitarian patterns of sharing; strong anti-authoritarianism; an emphasis on the importance of cooperation in conjunction with great respect for individuality; marked flexibility in band membership and in living arrangements generally; extremely permissive child-rearing practices; and common techniques for handling problems of conflict and reinforcing group cohesion, such as often-merciless teasing and joking, endless talking, and the ritualization of potential antagonisms. Some of these features are shared with horticultural peoples who are at the egalitarian end of the spectrum, but what differentiates foragers from egalitarian farmers is the greater informality of their arrangements. Foragers do not 'keep accounts' in as strict a sense. In Sahlins' (1972) terms, there is a greater emphasis among foragers on 'generalized' than on 'balanced' reciprocity.

A preliminary list of core features that characterize relations of production among foragers includes the following:

1. Collective ownership of the means of production – the land and its resources – by a band, 'horde', or camp. We use the term 'band' somewhat reluctantly, both here and in our title, since the image of a geographically fixed and socially precise group of people the word conjures up contradicts the flexibility of foraging life. However we feel it preferable to redefine an accepted term rather than to invent a new one.

2. The right of reciprocal access to resources of others through marriage ties, visiting, and co-production. The necessity of obtaining formal 'permission' to use the land of others in a crisis situation does not imply 'ownership' in the sense of being able to withhold access; granting permission often takes the form of hosts telling guests to help themselves. This changes, however, when the aboriginal right of all people to land and its resources is undercut by colonial usurpation of aboriginal lands which then have to be defended on new terms. Failure to recognize this has confused past anthropological writings on land rights.

3. Little emphasis on accumulation. The land is the larder and the emphasis is on mobility and adaptability to the land rather than on accumulation. There may be storage on racks and in caches and some food may be processed to be carried, especially in northern areas where seasonal shortages can be extreme, but such accumulation is very limited.

4. 'Total sharing' or 'generalized reciprocity' within the camp as well as with others who come to visit or to seek help if food shortages exist in their terrain. This does not mean that each item of food is divided, nor that all eat together out of a common pot. Indeed, eating may be quite individualized much of the time. However, it does mean that no one goes hungry if there is food in camp.

5. Access of all to the 'forces of production'. Virtually everyone possesses the skills for making essential tools. The sexual division of labour enables a degree of specialization and, presumably, greater productivity. The sharing of what they produce means the economic relations of the sexes are reciprocal and complementary.

6. Individual 'ownership' of tools. However, tools are easily lent and borrowed, and the fact that people generally possess the resources and skills necessary for replacing them means that such ownership does not divide haves from have-nots as it does in class societies. Yet tools and utensils do embody the time and skill put into making them, and in addition may be made from special materials more readily available in one area than another. Hence individual ownership forms the basis for individual gift-giving and for inter-band exchange systems that make possible farflung networks of reciprocity. By contrast, commodity trade, especially for metal tools, eventually reaches the point of undermining such reciprocity and opens the way for potential inequality of access to important resources, a point we shall return to shortly.

The foregoing does not mean that foraging societies are societies without problems or contradictions. All social life is fraught with contradictions and foraging life is no exception. But the nature of contradictions among foragers must be sought in the particular character of their relations of production. Highly valued by foraging peoples are the qualities of sharing, reciprocity, marrying out, hard work, political equality, sociability and even temper. Contradictions arise when individuals desire to hoard rather than share, to marry in, to be lazy and freeload, to try and lord it over others, to be sullen and isolate themselves, or to be quick to argue and fight. The ridicule, misfortune, or social isolation brought on a person habitually indulging in such behaviour are widespread themes in gatherer-hunter belief, mythology, ritual, childrearing practice, and daily life. The social life of foragers is in good measure the continual prevention or working out of potentially disruptive conflicts in accord with the particular cultural ways of each society. The measure of its success is its record as a viable way of life for by far the greater part of human history. As for the nature of contradictions that led to its transformation, we shall consider these in relation to Part ii below.

The papers presented in Part i reveal the complex and subtle nature of social dynamics among foragers; dynamics which must be accorded the same degree of attention that has already been given to their social organization and ecological adaptation. The subjects treated below are decision-making and conflict resolution, sharing and exchange, the allocation of rights to lands and resources, the socialization of children, and the ritualization of potential conflict between the sexes. Each chapter deals with a particular society, yet the principles spelled out ring true of other societies as well. The extent to which the findings presented can be generalized is a topic that invites comparative analysis.

Silberbauer describes ways in which the G/wi of Botswana seek to influence each other, to arrive at collective decisions and to resolve disputes without resort to institutionalized power or formal coercive force. His analysis parallels both Turnbull's (1962) descriptions of the Congo Mbuti and Jesuit descriptions of the seventeenth-century Montagnais-Naskapi (Leacock 1981). The point he makes in relation to the different meanings of *political* in different types of societies is telling: the 'consensus polity' of the G/wi is only possible in societies free from fundamental conflicts of interest among its constituents. The problem of how to adapt consensus politics to contemporary needs is now being directly confronted by gathering-hunting peoples as shall be seen in Part III.

In his paper on decision-making and economic responsibilities of women and men among the !Kung, Lee demonstrates that former assumptions that authority among them was held by chiefs or headmen do not stand up to further research. Like the G/wi, the !Kung arrive at group decisions and handle potential or actual interpersonal conflict through a variety of techniques that range from discussion, through 'rough humour' and 'put downs', to interpersonal fighting when these are not successful, and in extreme cases the execution through community decision of persistently aggressive and arrogant individuals. Lee indicates that both women and men participate in decision-making and conflict resolution and are influential in accordance with their age, experience, and wisdom.

Women and men both travel widely, and as Wiessner shows in her paper on !Kung exchange networks, they use gift exchanges to build and cement intergroup ties. However, Lee points out that it is men who take on the role of intermediaries in relation to non-!Kung outsiders. While any assumption of authority within their own group by such individuals leads to ridicule or anger among the !Kung, as has been recorded for the Mbuti (Turnbull 1962), the Hadza (Woodburn 1980) and the Montagnais-Naskapi (Thwaites 1906 VI:243), among others; nonetheless the role of intermediary with outsiders potentially accords men positions of recognized influence in what becomes an increasingly important 'public' sphere. The question is raised for further research as to what extent women of influence among gatherer-hunters also played such roles. For example, there are references to women as negotiators of intergroup disputes among the Andamanese (Radcliffe-Brown 1964:85–6), to powerful women shamans among the seventeenth-century Montagnais-Naskapi (Thwaites 1906 ix:113–17), to politically influential elder women among the Gippsland peoples of Victoria, Australia (Fison and Howitt 1880:212), and to an informal woman leader among the contemporary Batek of Malaysia (Endicott 1980).

Wiessner's paper on exchange networks for non-food items among the !Kung makes available detailed data of a kind rarely gathered on foragers. The contrast between exchange in market and non-market societies has been outlined by Mauss (1967) in his classic essay *The gift*, but Wiessner's material points up a further and most important distinction: that between gift giving in the Oceanic and Northwest Coast societies on which Mauss concentrates, where it is tied in with amassing and redistributing large amounts of goods, and gift giving in societies where wealth is not collected in any sizeable amount. Radcliffe-Brown (1964:84) wrote that among the Andamanese the purpose of exchange was more 'to produce a friendly feeling between the two persons concerned', than to procure goods. Wiessner explores the functions of this 'friendly feeling', to which Lorna Marshall (1961, 1976:ch. 9) also refers, in creating a kind of social insurance for a !Kung individual – a pool of exchange partners who can be turned to for help in times of personal need, and an inter-band network that enables people to deal with regional fluctuations of resources by visiting exchange partners in other areas when food or water are short in their own.

Wiessner speculates that, before metal tools were procured from outsiders, !Kung exchange may have served to distribute resources such as flint; and that the importance of gift exchange in ensuring sharing and smoothing social relations may have become increased at the time when these were threatened by the encroachments of a market economy. Her speculation suggests the need for comparative investigation of an important topic: the differential effects on internal social dynamics of exchange networks and of trade. Do internal exchange networks among foragers consistently reinforce interdependence and sharing? Does sustained trade with outsiders always lead to individuation and decreased intra-group dependence, as Morris' paper on the Mal-pantaram of South India in Part ii describes? Under what conditions are cooperative ties and values retained, and when do these break down?

Just as Wiessner's paper points up the necessity of interpreting !Kung exchange in terms of production relations specific to foraging society, so Hamilton's paper on land rights in Western Australia shows the inappropriateness of applying concepts of ownership derived from Western society to Aboriginal attitudes and practices. Disposition of rights and responsibilities in the West are bound up with a system whereby individual ownership of land subsumes the possibility of total alienation. By contrast, individual rights and responsibilities to lands are inalienable in Aboriginal society. Their disposition is inseparable from the entire structure of social and economic relations, and is elaborately reinforced through ritual and ideology. Hamilton demonstrates that the multiple and complex ties to land held by both women and men are distorted by extant assumptions of patrilineal inheritance. She also alludes to changing forms of human–land relations in the Australian Western Desert in the period preceding 'contact'. The subject calls for ethnohistorical as well as ethnographic analysis, and differentiation of ongoing developments in Aboriginal society from changes resulting from the influx of refugees fleeing from European colonization in the east.

Briggs and Turnbull both focus on ways in which egalitarian peoples attempt to deal with and head off conflict and aggression. Briggs treats socialization among the Inuit, and Turnbull the ritualization of potential antagonism between the sexes among the Mbuti. The cultural practices they describe are diverse, but underlying them is a striking commonality. Both societies recognize interpersonal rivalry straightforwardly as a feeling to be objectified and counteracted, rather than to be swept under the rug or guiltily 'repressed'. Turnbull describes ways in which potential antagonism between the sexes is ritualized and dissipated, whether in overt – but contained – acts of aggression or in riotously humorous play. Briggs details an episode in which a child is being taught to confront its jealousy of an infant brother.

Briggs and Turnbull both deal, as well, with ambiguities and contradictions in the values held by the groups on whom they are writing. Briggs elaborates on the importance of recognizing such contradictions, rather than trying to impose a false consistency on ideological data. Her discussion of the careful consideration Inuit give to alternative explanations for, and possible courses of action subsequent to, conflict situations parallels the examples Turnbull (1962) gives in his full account of the Mbuti, as well as the examples presented in the above papers on the San. What comes through all these accounts is the contextual and relativistic – indeed dialectical – manner in which behaviour is probed and judged. In place of an attempt to define a reified 'good' or 'bad', each person's particular interests and motives are carefully examined and weighed against those of others in a consideration of possible outcomes in a particular conflict situation. Yet all of this is only in part sober and serious. Not only is there great latitude for the expression of a wide range of feelings, but a truly theatrical sense of the comic is always close at hand to be drawn on when appropriate for easing tensions.

II: Forager–farmer relations

Placing foraging peoples in history means tracing long periods of contact between foragers and their farming neighbours. While, in subartic Canada and Australia, hunters lived in a world of hunters until recently, in other cases foragers show a thousand years or more of continual contact with horticultural and pastoral societies. The Aka pygmies here reported on by Bahuchet and Guillaume first contacted ancestors of the contemporary Bantu no later than 500 b.c. and have remained neighbours ever since, while the Malapantaram of South India here discussed by Morris have been trading forest products for the markets of their peasant neighbours for 1,500 years. Colin Turnbull (1962, 1965) has written at length on forager–farmer relations in his classic accounts of the Mbuti, and the subject has been discussed by Williams (1968) and Roy (1925) for the Birhor of India, Seligman and Seligman (1911) for the Veddas of Ceylon, Dentan (1979) for the Samai of Malaysia, and Peterson (1978) for various Agta groups in the Philippines. These are all cases in which foragers have not assimilated, but have maintained their ethnic identity and a separate economic base.

The papers on forager–farmer relations pose a diverse set of questions: How do foragers articulate with their tribal and peasant neighbours? What prevents their rapid assimilation? How are ethnic boundaries maintained? What impact has close proximity with farmers had on the lives of foragers and, conversely, how do farmers incorporate their relations with foragers into their own lives? What can be learned about the underlying dynamics of foraging societies by observing them in a state of partial transformation, suspended between two social and ideological centres of gravity? And finally, what light can answers to these questions throw on the origins of sedentism and of agriculture?

In a paper on relations of production among gatherer-hunters, Leacock stresses the importance of locating a society in the concrete specificities of its history and relations with other societies before drawing conclusions about the generalizability of its social arrangements. Writing on the Malapantaram or Hill Pandaram of south India, Morris develops the point that their family structure and band organization cannot be interpreted solely in terms of their ecological adaptation to the resources and conditions of their environment. Instead their social forms must be understood in terms of the Hill Pandaram role as providers of forest products for the markets of neighbouring farmers.

The Hill Pandaram contrast with the Andamanese as well as with the !Kung, the G/wi, the Mbuti and the Pitjantjatjara as described in the pages that follow, in the degree to which nuclear-family units have become economically independent. Nonetheless they are strongly cooperative, egalitarian, and anti-authoritarian. The same has been recorded for the near-by Paliyan (Gardner 1972) as well as the Birhors of north India (Sinha 1972). Morris draws the parallel between these instances and the individualization of family units that followed fur trading in eastern Canada (Leacock 1954) and rubber collecting among the horticultural Mundurucu (Murphy and Steward 1955).

The Aka of the Congo described by Bahuchet and Guillaume were long engaged in exchange relations with Bantu neighbours that, similarly to those practised by the Mbuti, did not undermine their economic interdependence. They traded meat for metal tools and some agricultural products without giving up traditional sharing patterns within their own villages. However, the recent history of the Aka has caused an increasing individualization of their social organization. The European demand for ivory, bush-buck skins and other luxury products of the forest tied them into an outside market at roughly the same time as colonial officials were encouraging them to become settled agriculturalists, 'free' of their dependence on trade with the Bantu. As the Aka became more settled, however, they depleted local game and other resources and took on new needs. Requiring cash to procure food and manufactured goods, they increasingly lost their economic autonomy and became a supplementary labour force on Bantu farms.

Papers by Vierich and Hitchcock on the Basarwa of Botswana bring to the fore a further dimension of foraging life: the fact that to move from foraging to farming and/or pastoralism does not constitute a simple one-way continuum. Instead, foragers who have become part- or full-time farmers and/or pastoralists may shift back to gathering-hunting as weather and other exigencies require. Hitchcock points out that Basarwa who were full-time foragers fared better during a drought period than did those with a mixed sedentary economy, thereby testifying to the viability of foraging life and hinting at some of the reasons why the pristine transitions to sedentism and agriculture as revealed by archaeological data were so slow and uneven. Hitchcock also gives a thoughtful and critical review of the literature on the causes of sedentism.

Chapters by Chang and Blackburn on the Okiek of the Rift Valley in Kenya and northeast Tanzania treat their relations with pastoral peoples living in the region. Chang reviews the complex history of inter-ethnic relations in Kenya and stresses the importance of examining the indirect effects of European colonization on relations among groups. She sees colonization as having caused a tightening of ethnic and territorial boundaries. Blackburn details the relations between one group of Okiek and both their environment and their powerful Maasai neighbours. Honey, the critical resource of the Okiek, is exchanged with the Maasai through the institution of individual trade partnerships. Interestingly enough, all wild food resources of their lands with the exception of honey are available to all members of an Okiek group. Honey, as a 'commodity' produced for exchange rather than use, is owned by members of a family or lineage just as furs in eastern Canada are privately owned as alluded to above.

On the one hand, the above cases of forager–farmer exchange demonstrate the persistence of collective arrangements among foragers despite the individualization of economic ties. On the other hand, however, they illustrate in microcosm the process whereby commodity production that develops through intergroup exchange ultimately undercuts this collectivity. In so doing, such cases pinpoint the basic contradiction that transforms egalitarian social-economic structure, as defined in classic Marxist terms of disjunctions between relations of production and developing forces of production. Commodity trade generates the intensification of production and a consequent tendency towards specialization, and these conflict with the relatively equal participation in production, distribution and consumption that characterizes egalitarian arrangements. Thus increasing trade and specialization militate against the reproduction of egalitarian social relations, and, with sedentarization, eventually lead to their transformation. The well-known rank societies of California and the Northwest Coast of North America exemplify the nature of this transformation.

III: Contemporary political struggles

When we look at gatherer-hunter groups in the advanced capitalist countries of Canada and Australia, we find an impressive resilience among them and a surprising commitment to living off the land. The

James Bay Cree are actually doing more foraging today than they were ten years ago and the same is true of some Aboriginal groups in central Australia. More important, contemporary foragers have made a successful transition to becoming effective political forces within their respective capitalist states. They have developed national organizations, have mobilized their people on a mass basis, and have learned to use the media and the courts in pursuing their goal of preserving or reclaiming their economic integrity and their land base. Foragers along with other 'Fourth World' native peoples are coming to understand the capitalist state and how to fight it.

Why have peoples like the Cree, the Dene, the Pitjantjatjara, and the San come to political prominence within their respective countries, when only a few years ago they were treated by the media as vanishing ethnographic curiosities? The answer is that foragers occupy one of the key battlegrounds of late capitalism: the last remaining resource frontiers in a world dominated by a profiteering system searching for energy and minerals. When foragers were first 'granted' occupation rights to lands that were rightfully theirs, the agents of capitalist states did not dream that these vast and remote desert, arctic and tropical forest areas would one day be worth billions in oil, gas, minerals, timber and hydroelectric potential.

A century ago expanding settler capitalism in the United States, Canada, South Africa and Australia simply appropriated the lands of foragers by right of conquest. Today such appropriation is not so simple. The laws of property upon which capitalist relations of production are based are a two-edged sword. On the one hand they defend the capitalist's economic power; on the other hand they confer a legitimacy on the natives' claims to their own lands. Major court decisions have gone in the natives' favour despite the efforts of the powerful business interests arrayed against them. In some cases such as among the Dene of Canada's Northwest Territories, discussed by Asch, the natives have fought big business to a standstill, at least for the moment. In others, such as the James Bay Cree reported on by Feit, the move to stop a development did not succeed and the James Bay Hydroelectric Project was built on native hunting lands. However, the impact of hydroelectric development on the native peoples of eastern Quebec, as documented by Charest, was well known; and the James Bay Cree procured a better settlement in terms of land, hunting and fishing rights and income security than would have been thought possible only ten years ago.

The political mobilization of foraging peoples is occurring on two fronts. They are building national and regional organizations to lobby governments, fight court cases and construct alliances with progressive non-native forces; and they are also revitalizing their local communities. As the chapter by Coombs, Dexter and Hiatt shows, the 'homeland' or 'outstation' movement in Australia is a back-to-the-land movement of aboriginal peoples, to reconstitute living groups on their traditional totemic lands and/or abandoned cattle or sheep stations. About 200 of these communities are now in existence. The people make a living from a combination of gathering and hunting, tourism, occasional wage-labour, and government subsidies. The homeland movement in Australia has rekindled aboriginal traditions and sense of community, has reduced alcoholism and *anomie*, and has brought a sense of political purpose that was lacking on the large welfare-supported government and mission stations that merely provided a pool of cheap labour for cattle stations and other enterprises.

The question has been raised, however, whether homeland settlements are not simply creating 'Bantustans', economically marginal rural enclaves that make it possible for governments to shed economic responsibility for the people whose lands have been largely usurped. The fact that the resurgence of hunting and gathering has reduced the number of Aborigines on welfare payments and has saved the Australian taxpayer's money is not lost on the governments involved. After some initial fears of 'renegade' Aborigines living on their own, the state and federal governments, with the exception of Queensland, have become supporters of the homeland movement. Similar government programmes are encouraging Canadian and Alaskan native peoples to go 'back to the bush'. Canada has found it much cheaper to service a family at a trapping camp than it is to keep them on welfare at the main settlement.

Although the 'back to the bush' and the homeland movements might seem to serve a policy of containment, their political content is at present a progressive one of struggle for valuable lands and the right to determine the uses to which these lands will be put. Peterson traces the history of Aboriginal land claims in the Northern Territory of Australia, and documents their successes and failures. Political autonomy is also an issue in the homeland movement, as is the right of Aborigines to retain their communal life-style and adapt it as they wish in choosing their own forms of participation in the larger society. Focusing on the Pitjantjatjara of southwestern South Australia, Vachon traces the genesis of their contemporary political consciousness in the dialectical interplay between their local culture and organization and the expanding economy of the state. He shows how the Aborigines were first drawn into the labour market and then periodically cast out at times of economic down-turn, and he analyses the extent to which the Pitjantjatjara retained both the forms and consciousness of labour as a collective rather than individual effort.

Despite some recent gains made by foraging peoples in Canada and Australia, in most of the world their situation has deteriorated. In his paper on the Tasaday and other foragers of the Philippines, Rosaldo documents the thinly disguised racism that continues to justify encroachment on their lands. Meanwhile the !Kung San of northern Namibia, foragers twenty years ago but now fully proletarianized, have been organized into military units by the South African army occupying Namibia. As described by Lee and Hurlich, the use of the San by South Africa is reminiscent of the American Special Forces' use of the Montagnard tribespeople in their Southeast Asian War. Facing South Africa and its puppet armies in Namibia is the South West African People's Organization (SWAPO), a liberation movement that is supported by the great majority of the people of Namibia. SWAPO is determined to stamp out the tribal competition encouraged by South African apartheid, and by its puppet armies, and seeks to build a united Namibia for the benefit of all its people . . . including the !Kung San.

The political mobilization of foraging peoples is part of a world-wide movement for justice and self-determination by peoples of former colonial possessions. The struggles of the Dene and the Cree for the right to control their own destinies are linked to similar struggles by the peoples of Namibia, Zimbabwe and South Africa. Native peoples themselves have come to see these links, and have forged connections between their own organizations and their counterparts in other countries, as well as with non-native student, environmentalist, union, and other support groups in their own metropolises.

The existence of broad coalitions such as these underlines the sharing of common goals and indicates an important path for progressive anthropologists to follow. Social scientists who have committed themselves to the goals of native organizations have made valuable contributions to their struggles by providing key research to back up land claims and contract negotiations; by helping to draft political manifestos; and by educating the wider public about the machinations of giant companies and the justice of native demands.

Foraging peoples now engaged in fights for their lands and for the right to decide on the course of their lives have long been told they are fighting a losing battle, that they are on a collision course with history, that they might as well 'adapt'. Until recently, despite the Western ethnocentrism of the position, assimilationism seemed justified even to liberals. Indeed, anthropologists have often felt it their responsibility to provide information to gathering-hunting people that might help them to conform. Today, however, the case looks otherwise. There is widespread recognition that a capitalist economy of waste is based both on the exploitation of human lives and abilities and on the destruction of the earth as a human habitat. The awareness is growing that urban 'development' in its present form must be contained if the delicate ecological balance necessary for life on this earth is to be maintained. Therefore the battle of erstwhile foragers has become part of a larger struggle. History has joined their fight with the struggle of all humanity to achieve a cooperative world system, in balance with the rest of nature.

Bibliography

Ardrey, Robert 1961. *African genesis*. New York: Dell
  1966. *The territorial imperative*. New York: Atheneum
  1970. *The social contract*. New York: Atheneum
Bicchieri, M. G. (ed.) 1972. *Hunters and gatherers today*. New York: Holt, Rinehart and Winston
Damas, David 1969. *Band societies*. National Museum of Canada Bulletin No. 229
Dentan, Robert Knox 1979. *The Samai, a nonviolent people of Malaya*. New York: Holt, Rinehart and Winston
Endicott, Karen Lampell 1980. 'Batek Negrito sex roles', paper given at the 2nd International Conference on Hunting and Gathering Societies, Ste-Foy, Quebec
Engels, Frederick 1972. *The origin of the family, private property and the state*. New York: International Publishers
Fison, L., and Howitt, A. W. 1880. *Kamilaroi and Kurnai*. Melbourne: Robertson
Gardner, Peter M. 1972. 'The Paliyans', in M. G. Bicchieri (ed.), *Hunters and gatherers today*. New York: Holt, Rinehart and Winston
Leacock, Eleanor 1954. *The Montagnais 'hunting territory' and the fur trade*. *American Anthropologist*, Memoir 78
  1972. 'Introduction', in Frederick Engels, *The origin of the family, private property and the state*. New York: International Publishers
  1975. 'Class, commodity, and the status of women', in Ruby Rohrlich-Leavitt (ed.), *Women cross-culturally: change and challenge*. The Hague: Mouton
  1978. 'Structuralism and dialectics: Review of Lévi-Strauss, *Structural anthropology, vol. ii*', in *Reviews in Anthropology* 5(1)
  1981. 'The seventeenth-century Montagnais: social relations and values', in

June Helm (ed.), *Subarctic. Handbook of American Indians* vol. 6, series ed. William Sturtevant. Washington, DC.: Smithsonian Institution

Lee, Richard Borshay 1978. 'A Marxist methodology for anthropology'. Paper presented at the 77th Annual Meeting of the American Anthropological Association, Los Angeles

   1979. *The !Kung San: men, women and work in a foraging society*. Cambridge and New York: Cambridge University Press

   1980. 'Existe-t-il un mode de production "fourrageur"?'. *Anthropologie et Sociétés* 4 (3):59–74

Lee, Richard B. and DeVore, Irven (eds.) 1968. *Man the hunter*. Chicago: Aldine

Marshall, Lorna 1961. 'Sharing, talking and giving: relief of social tensions among !Kung Bushmen'. *Africa* 31:231–49

   1976. *The !Kung of Nyae Nyae*. Cambridge, Mass.: Harvard University Press

Mauss, Marcel 1967. *The gift*. New York: Norton

Morgan, Lewis Henry 1974. *Ancient society*, ed. and intro. by Eleanor Leacock. Gloucester, Mass.: Peter Smith

Murphy, Robert F. and Steward, Julian H. 1955. 'Tappers and trappers: parallel processes in acculturation'. *Economic Development and Culture Change* 4:335–55

Peterson, Jean Treloggen 1978. 'Hunter-gatherer/farmer exchange'. *American Anthropologist* 80:335–51

Radcliffe-Brown, A. R. 1964. *The Andaman Islanders*. New York: Free Press

Roy, Sarat Chandra 1925. *The Birhors: a little-known jungle tribe of Chota Nagpur*. Ranchi: Loudon, Probsthain

Sahlins, Marshall 1972. *Stone Age economics*. Chicago: Aldine

Seligman, C. G., and Seligman, B. Z. 1911. *The Veddas*. Cambridge: Cambridge University Press

Sinha, D. P. 1972. 'The Birhors', in M. G. Bicchieri (ed.), *Hunters and gatherers today*. New York: Holt, Rinehart and Winston

Thwaites, R. G. (ed.) 1906. *The Jesuit relations and allied documents*. 71 vols. Cleveland: Burrows Brothers Co.

Turnbull, Colin 1962. *The forest people*. Garden City, New York: Doubleday

   1965. *Wayward servants: the two worlds of the African Pygmies*. Garden City, New York: Natural History Press

Williams, B. J. 1968. 'The Birhor of India and some comments on band organization' in Richard B. Lee and Irven DeVore (eds.), *Man the hunter*. Chicago: Aldine

Woodburn, James 1980. 'Hunters and gatherers today and reconstruction of the past', in Ernest Gellner (ed.), *Soviet and Western anthropology*. London: Duckworth

Part I: Dynamics of egalitarian foraging societies

1. Political process in G/wi bands

GEORGE SILBERBAUER

The 'ethnographic present' is 1958–66, the period I spent among G/wi-speaking Bushmen in the Central Kalahari Reserve of Botswana. At that time Bushmen were the only permanent inhabitants of this, the remote and arid heart of Botswana. The Clifford and Marshall expeditions of 1928 and 1955 traversed the area, the Marshall party staying two months with a G/wi band. Kgalagadi herdsmen customarily moved in from their wells and cattle-posts on the periphery of the centre, grazing cattle and goats in rare years of good rain, abundant pasture and pools of water in the pans. Mounted hunting-parties armed with century-old muzzle-loaders would make brief forays, living off the veld for a few weeks and then returning home, their horses and donkeys loaded with antelope biltong (strips of dried meat) and the hides of illicitly poached giraffe. In their turn, some Bushmen made expeditions to the ranches, cattle-posts and village trading-stores to visit friends and relatives and to trade dressed hides and pelts for tobacco, metal and enamel-ware. In times of drought some would temporarily remove to the ranches of the white farmers around Ghanzi. Attracted by wells and bores from which the cattle were watered, they lived off what their friends, kin and the farmers could or would spare in the way of food. When rain came and broke the drought, the Bushmen returned to the desert.

Apart from such incursion and excursions the G/wi, and other Bushmen of the central Kalahari lived as autonomous hunters and gatherers. When the decade-long drought broke in the late sixties these Bushmen were overwhelmed by a rush of Kgalagadi and Tswana pastoralists and their herds. Held back by the long drought, desperate for new grazing-lands because their stock had exhausted the pasture within reach of established wells and bore-holes, the cattlemen took advantage of the good rain. Without adequate government control, they effectively dispossessed many Bushmen bands of their territories and, hence, of their

23

livelihood and life-style. Exploration for, and exploitation of, minerals in parts of the central Kalahari will further disrupt the lives of the Bushmen. These developments will bring some material benefits but Bushmen, at the bottom of the socio-economic ladder, will gain least. Lately the Botswana Government has moved to do something for Bushmen but, for better or worse, the close-knit, self-sufficient organization of band society and the completeness of members' control of its political processes are gone. The 'ethnographic present' is now the past.

As hunters and gatherers, the G/wi do not manipulate their habitat to suit their society. They achieve the match the other way round – by manipulating society to conform with the availability of environmental resources. This is evident, for instance, in their territorial arrangements by which occupation and exploitation by bands are centred on the finite number of unevenly distributed nexuses of essential resources which occur in the central Kalahari. The same strategy is expressed in the alternation between joint and separated phases of band life which has the effect of altering localized population density to accord with seasonal rises and falls in biomass and, hence, of (principally) plant-food resources. For this strategy to succeed it is necessary that the bonds between the band's households be of such a nature as not to inhibit separation, yet of sufficient strength to bring the households together again when the time comes to resume living in joint camps. Political processes must, therefore, be integrative without creating interhousehold dependence which would cripple the autonomy which is essential to separation and isolation during winter and early summer.

The social and political community is the band. There are no exclusive formal qualifications for membership, but such attributes as marriage or close kinship to existing members, or birth into the band, are the basis of strong to absolute claims to membership. That these qualifications are not mandatory is shown by the fact that non-G/wi (e.g. G//ana) and even non-Bushmen (e.g. one Kgalagadi 'drop-out') have been accepted as members. The emphasis is on inclusion of individuals or families and not on the exclusiveness of their qualifications.

There is marked stability of the band in its conceptualized identity as a group of people living in a geographically specific territory and controlling the use of the resources of that territory. Membership of the band is somewhat less stable than is its identity. In the absence of structural restrictions – the lack of exclusive qualifications for membership – members are free to join other bands and are, therefore, free to leave the current band. Psychological factors (e.g. compatibility, or desire for

G/wi women and men discussing a camp move (G. Silberbauer)

variety) appear to be the most important motives for moving. These motives are subject to change from time to time, so minor and unpredictable alterations of membership occur in most years. Movement to a new community is facilitated by the importance of kinship as the basis on which relationships are ordered in the band. Kin links exist between an individual and most, if not all, of his G/wi acquaintances and can be further extended by the universalistic device of deeming as one's own kinsmen those who are kin of kin. The significance of kinship here is not that it is the vector of a body of rights – those of membership – but in its prescriptive, informational value in guiding the recruit's interaction and, hence, integration with, and adaptation to, other members of the new band. Incorporation of the newcomer is thus made much easier if he has ready-made kin status in the band or assumes a newly forged link. G/wi bands may, therefore, be seen as stable, but open, communities whose personnel may leave if they wish and which recruits may join if they are accepted. The size of the community is obviously limited by, *inter alia*, the state of its resources of food etc.; so, while it is an open community, it is nevertheless a finite one.

Decisions affecting the band as a whole are arrived at through discussion in which all adult, and near-adult, members may participate. Discussion seldom takes the form of a single, set-piece public debate. Much of the groundwork before decision is covered in the course of ordinary conversation between friends, neighbours and hunting-partners. If only one, clear-cut course of action merits serious consideration, the casual exchanges routinely lead to a decision, and perhaps function more as announcements of concurrence than processes by which agreement is reached (i.e. agreement is automatic but nevertheless requires some form of declaration in order that it be the basis of action). Where the matter is more contentious or confused, and factions emerge, protagonists will involve others by airing their views before a wider audience. The behaviour of the onlookers gives a more or less clear indication of the strength and inclination of sentiment in the band as a whole. This is both 'testing the wind' and influencing opinion. There are many ways of doing it: a quiet, serious discussion with one or two key individuals in the hearing of a few band fellows, or a long campaign of persuasion in which the case is put together piece by piece, allowing time for each to settle before placing the next. Or else a public, but ostensibly private, harangue is contrived by loudly addressing a friend, making sure that the whole camp can hear, i.e. talking-at, rather than talking-to. This ploy of the 'forced eavesdrop' avoids direct confrontation with the opposition who would be guilty of bad manners if they were to join in the conversation. However, opponents are free to resort to the same device. The band may then be treated to the occasionally comic spectacle of two sets of orators putting their conflicting arguments, each pointedly ignoring the other but striving desperately to avoid a breach of either logic or etiquette, trying to answer point with counter-point without being seen to attack directly.

The spectrum of audience responses to all of these preliminaries is equally broad. Some express their feelings tacitly, signalling assent, opposition or indifference to the speaker's argument by facial expression, bodily attitude or gesture. Others are more explicit and answer with murmurs and grunts, or echo the last phrase of the utterance to show support.

The time taken for discussion is naturally limited by the urgency of the matter under consideration; the need to arrive at conclusive agreement before the passage of time and events closes off an option is clearly recognized by the band. Less urgent matters can be debated for longer. Discussion is then intermittent with the subject cropping up from time to time until a satisfying solution to the problem is reached. The Dilemma of the Deserted Husband, for instance, took longer than two years before it was resolved:

/wikhwema was not very bright. He tried to mask his difficulty in understanding a mystifying world by a show of firmness – hastily expressing an opinion and being quite inflexible thereafter. His opinions were often wrong. Male vanity is an accepted G/wi value and /wikhwema would usually follow one of his *faux pas* with petulant pompousness or a storm of temper. The poor man came to be something of a standing joke in his band and it is perhaps not surprising that his wife, N!onag//ei, one day ran away with his recently widowed, best and closest friend, /amg//ao. /amg//ao, a dwarf, was a virtuoso dancer, a consistently successful hunter and was rumoured to be a bit of a demon as a lover. N!onag//ei was a morose and chronically discontented woman. Nobody could understand why /amg//ao had chosen her to run away with and people said she must have exploited his grief at being widowed.

G/wi marriages generally last but, when one does fail, it is usual for the deserted spouse to remarry within a few months or, at most, a year. But /wikhwema would not. He mourned the loss of his wife and of his friend with equal intensity. When the band camped together he lived at the bachelors' tree and his impatience at the young men's high spirits made him a nuisance. He carefully avoided other men's wives but his dreariness got on everybody's nerves. As an 'owner' of the territory he could not be expected to move to another band so his people were stuck with him. His daughter and his mother-in-law were as cross-grained as was N!onag//ei and gave him no comfort.

When, after more than a year had passed, it was clear that he would not remarry and people despaired at the prospect of living with his misery forever, word was passed to where /amg//ao and N!onag//ei were living, 'Would she return?' She missed her daughter and mother but was a proud woman and loath to leave /amg//ao and return to /wikh-wema who, in turn, could not bear to be without his friend – the necessary consequence of his wife's return. Intervening parties tried to resolve the dilemma but she remained steadfast and would not leave /amg//ao and /wikhwema was obdurate. Every time /wikhwema threw a tantrum, or was overtaken by despondency, the matter would be discussed again. Then some inspired lateral thinker proposed that as neither would have the other without /amg//ao, let them have each other *and* him. A polyandrous marriage. This was unprecedented in G/wi knowledge but long deliberation led to acceptance of the innovation. While the three did not exactly live happily ever after, /wikhwema was no longer a nuisance to his band fellows.

The pattern of the summer and autumn camps (i.e. as distinct from the isolated camps of single households during winter and early summer) is for groups of households to build their shelters next to each other, forming a pattern of clusters. The households making up such a cluster I have termed a clique. Cliques are nearly always unstable groups which are partially or wholly reconstituted whenever the band shifts to a new campsite, i.e. after three to six weeks. The only factor determining their composition appears to be a temporary preference among the constituent households for one another's close company. Interaction within a clique is significantly more intense than between cliques: most conversation is within, or between, clustered households; the women of a clique usually form a food-gathering gang: the men assist one another with tasks more often than they help men from other cliques, and the rate of exchange of goods and services is generally higher within the group. Cliques also function as a form of ephemeral segmentation of the band by becoming focuses of opinion and the level at which factionalization initially occurs. Progress towards decision is not, therefore, an even permeation of persuasion through the band. As the diverse strands of argument are ordered and simplified the cliques further function as sub-units of agreement and the balance of opinion shifts in larger-than-individual increments towards one or other of the poles of proposal.

Leadership in the band is apparent at all phases of decision-making. The process of reaching a decision is initiated by somebody identifying and communicating a problem which calls for decision. Leadership may be measured as the extent to which an individual's suggestion or opinion attracts public support and is thus exercised at the initial stage as well as during the subsequent steps toward final decision. In the main, leadership is authoritative, rather than authoritarian; knowledge, experience of the matter under discussion and firmness of personality are characteristics which win most support. In themselves these are prestigious qualities, and success in promoting a particular argument confers further prestige but never sufficient to occasion an 'overflow' into habitual success. Expertise in one field of activity may be seen as not at all relevant to another field and, even in matters which are quite closely related, leadership shifts unpredictably among acknowledged experts with the occasional inclusion of a 'dark horse'. The emotionally calm atmosphere of many discussions and the general lack of competitiveness partly explain the readiness to separate idea from identity. It often happens that the suggestion finally adopted is one which was initially voiced by somebody who has taken no further part in the proceedings, leaving it to others to take up, and 'push' his or her proposal.

This is not to say that passion is unknown: contentious matters do stir speakers to emotional oratory and a single dissenter can shift an apparently decided band to another way of thinking. But the band is reluctant to come to decision under the sway of strong feelings: if discussion becomes too angry or excited, debate is temporarily adjourned by the withdrawal of the attention of the calmer participants until things cool down. Withdrawal is not usually physical – to get up and move away is too explicit a gesture of rejection. It is, rather, an auditory withdrawal. Members signal their lack of sympathy with the heated mood by affecting preoccupation with other matters. It must indeed be frustrating to find one's fine flow of rhetoric washing unheeded round a woman busying herself with an apparently well-ordered cooking-fire, or wasted on a man suddenly absorbed in microscopic examination of an invisible thorn embedded in the sole of his foot, but such inattentiveness is not overtly rude. One cannot castigate this sort of absent-mindedness. One must simply 'chew the teeth inwardly', or try a more winsome appeal to straying minds. Auditory withdrawal is also made from a speaker who persistently pursues an unacceptable argument, leaving the bore high and dry with neither support nor legitimate cause for complaint.

Public decisions cover a wide field. Such matters as the allocation of wintering-ranges among households about to retreat into isolation during the seasonal dispersal of the band, or the location of the next campsite are obvious inclusions. A domestic dispute could perhaps be seen as properly concerning only the spouses and their close kin, yet the band as a whole may become involved over an issue of principle or if the other members feel themselves threatened or otherwise affected by the behaviour of one of the spouses. In a community as small and as intimate as the band, the parameter of affairs of public policy intrudes far into what a larger-scale society would regard as the domain of private, or personal decision. That which is not public is permitted to be private by a public conspiracy not to proclaim cognizance. There can be little of any individual's doings which escapes the vigilance, close concern and profound insight of his band fellows. The field of band decisions therefore includes much that is not considered as public in more complex, clearly differentiated social systems. Interpersonal conflicts and transgressions of norms commonly involve other band members in their settlement which is attained by judgement, arbitration and reconciliatory good offices preceded by discussion and decision. At the same time the scope for public decision-making is restricted in other directions by the narrow range of effective choice of action imposed on the band by the combination of environmental factors, rudimentary technology and the small scale of the social universe.

The question arises whether this decision-making constitutes political action and whether the band has any form of political organization. Max Weber's viewpoint (1966:154) was that an organization is political in character 'if and insofar as the enforcement of its order is carried out continually within a given territorial area by the application and threat of physical force on the part of the administrative staff'. This is partly paraphrased by Radcliffe-Brown's famous definition of political organization (1940:xxiii) as being that 'which is concerned with the control and regulation of the use of physical force'. Both definitions are, I think, too narrow and selective. Southall (1965:120) tones down their view by defining political action as that which is concerned with the use of power, ultimately sanctioned by the use of physical force, however remote and indirect its invoking may actually be. Leach (1973:29) takes the view that a man is engaged in political action whenever he behaves in such a way as to rally others to support a cause in which he is interested'. At first glance this appears to fit the band case. It helpfully implies the questions of competition and the overcoming of public inertia but, on the other hand, is open to pedantic misapplication to almost any interaction and is perhaps too broad to distinguish usefully that which is political. More specific 'modality of action' definitions of political organization (and, by implication, of politics) are exemplified by that of Morton Fried (1967:21) echoing M. G. Smith (1960): 'Political organization comprises those portions of social organization that specifically relate to the individuals or groups that manage the affairs of public policy or seek to control the appointment or action of those individuals or groups', or of David Easton (1965:50), who sees a political system as 'that system of interaction in any society through which binding or authoritative allocations are made and implemented'.

The two sets of definitions – those concerned with the use of force and those concentrating on modality of action – are complementary, rather than conflicting. Together they yield legitimacy, coercion and power as being the attributes of political action.

Band decisions are arrived at by consensus – a term in common use but without much common meaning. Consensus is *not* unanimity of opinion or decision. In much the same way as egalitarian does not mean equality, consensus is not a synonym of democracy. Democracy is about equality of opportunity of access to positions of legitimate authority and the limitations this imposes on the exercise of power. It is an organizational framework for the making and execution of decisions. Consensus is arrived at after a series of judgements made by people who all have access to a common pool of information. As the etymology of the word suggests, it is arrived at when people consent to judgement and decision. They may not all actually possess the information and may choose not to make the judgements themselves, but the opportunity must always be available. The shared information includes the criteria of judgement – the values, the objectives and the differentials in weight and priority accorded these, plus a common knowledge (or belief) about the logical and causal relationships between items of information.

As Elizabeth Colson (1974:5) notes, small, face-to-face communities (such as a G/wi band) share the attributes of dense social networks and the common expectation of continuity of relationships over time. A dense network, she points out (1974:54), is necessary to provide the context for frequent interaction among its participants at which they can both engender and communicate the requisite spectrum of information. Partridge (1971:95) imposes more rigorous limitations: that a consensus policy can only survive if a society is stable and free of the stress of radical internal conflict and that there is a need for other, widely extended areas of voluntary cooperation and agreement to buffer the specifically political aspects of the system from disruptive pressures. So, not only must there be access to a common pool of information but also there must be a shared set of standards of interpretation and evaluation of that information. Consensus can only operate as a mode of decision-making where there is general agreement about 'the rules of the game' – about the way decisions are made, the bases for making them, and what the foreseeable extent and nature of the consequences of decisions shall be for which individuals.

Activity in the band is goal-directed. Megan Biesele (n.d.) has described band politics as management-by-objective. Consensus is reached by a process of examination of the various proffered courses of action and rejection of all but one of them. It is a process of attrition of alternatives other than the one to which there remains no significant opposition. That one, then, is the one which is adopted. The fact that it is the band as a whole which decides (i.e. that each adult and near-adult member has the opportunity to participate in the process) is both necessary and sufficient to legitimize what is decided and to make the decision binding on all who are concerned with, and affected by, it.

This does not mean that consensus is arrived at by a mere sorting process which always identifies a single course of action among the proffered alternatives as being the correct one. If this were so then consensus would, indeed, be synonymous with unanimity. That it is not is because consensus is reached when there remains no significant opposition to the particular proposal. To explain what is meant by 'significant opposition' in this context it is necessary to consider the problems of coercion and of power.

Laswell and Kaplan (1950:98) state that coercion is present if the alternative courses of action are associated with severe deprivations or indulgences'. As political means coercion and consensus are apparently antithetical: the element of consent in consensus negates coercion, and vice versa. Furthermore, the egalitarian nature of G/wi society makes improbable a political style in which an individual or faction coerces the rest of the band into withdrawing opposition to a proposal. There is no means by which anybody could acceptably distinguish himself or herself from the others to rationalize the assumption of the differential needed to coerce them. It must also be considered that the openness of the band as a social unit would eventually bring about the defeat of a forceful faction when the other members exercised their freedom to move to another band in much the same way as auditory withdrawal is used to adjourn debate when feelings run too high. To move to another band would be to meet coercion with coercion. The loss of a substantial portion of the membership would be costly to those who decamp, but would prove ruinous to those remaining. It is also true that the band has the potential means of bringing a delinquent member or faction to heel by withdrawing the normal social facilities of cooperation, protection and fellowship. But, as I have indicated above, these threats make no sense while the conventions of consensus politics are adhered to. My argument is that the threats to withdraw members from the band, or to withhold benefits of the band commonwealth from members, constitutes coercion to uphold and abide by those conventions – coercion not to coerce, if you will. In the circumstances of hunter-gatherers in the Central Kalahari such threats carry far greater danger than the mere use of physical force. So coercion, although never explicit, is present as a concept of the G/wi political system but functions as a deterrent in nascent form to ensure compliance with a style of political action from which force and 'severe deprivations and indulgences' are excluded.

The lack of general agreement among political scientists on the precise definition of power (see Davies and Lewis 1971:131) is perhaps a reflection of the diversity of styles of exercising power and the subtlety of some who wield it. A Weberian concept of power as the capacity of an actor to impose his or her will on others is deficient in the context of a consensus polity and leads to the paradox that, as there is no locus of power, such a polity has no authority. This is, of course, nonsense for it is the very fact of consensus which lends authority to the decision.

A perspective of definition more fruitful than that of the actor's obtaining the results intended, despite the opposition of others, is that of Karl Deutsch (1963), who defined political power as the capacity for self-determination. He also introduced the notion of political creativity – the variety of means an actor is capable of devising, discovering and employing to achieve self-determination within the confines of the system of which he or she is part. In the context of band politics steering its course between the Scylla of excessive interdependence and the Charybdis of fragmenting anarchy, the exercise of power calls for considerable creativity.

Although a G/wi audience enjoys a bit of cut-and-thrust between orators this is no more than entertainment incidental to the progress of discussion. Scoring points may be fun for everybody but the victim, but is irrelevant to the decision. Power is not gained and used in the manner of the politicians of Fred Bailey (1969): band decisions are not the spoils of victory of the member who devises the craftiest stratagems to discountenance opponents. Power lies in what the band judges to be competent assessment of the gains and costs of following a particular course of action and the entries in that book-keeping include not only the material benefits but also the social balance-sheet. Power lies in the ability to persuade a body of people privy to the same information as that possessed by the actor. It comes through perceiving the mood of the band and by finding an acceptable pathway to the goal of consensus. Thus an individual or group may use political creativity by conceding an objective at one level in the interests of achieving some other object at another level – gaining power later by forgoing it now.

Political power seen in terms of self-determination implies the notion of responsibility, of accepting the consequences of one's actions or lack of action. Unanimity may not exist at the time of consensus but those who did not actively promote the adopted proposal will, in the interests of band solidarity, convenience or some other consideration, not press their opposition. 'Significant opposition', then, is the dissent of one or more band members to whom the proposal is not acceptable, who feel themselves unable to 'live with it' and who are not prepared to concede the decision.

The style of band politics is facilitative, rather than forceful, seeking ways of getting things done, means of accommodating dissent and transposing discord into harmony without drowning out the dissenter's distinctive melody. Leadership is authoritative, rather than authoritarian and what an individual strives for is cooperation in the activities he or she wishes to undertake. There is available a variety of means of gaining that cooperation and the exercise of political power and leadership are only two among them, to be resorted to when circumstances make these means the most suitable choice. Power and leadership are sought neither as ends in themselves nor as habitual attributes.

Acknowledgements

The research on which this paper is based was funded by Colonial Development and Welfare Scheme No. D.3721. My colleague, Dr Rashmi Desai, read a pre-conference draft of this paper and contributed to it a number of useful ideas. My thanks go to him, our departmental Guru, for his help and encouragement.

Bibliography

Bailey, F. G. 1969. *Stratagems and spoils*. Oxford: Blackwell
Biesele, M. n.d. 'Sapience and scarce resources: communication systems of the !Kung and other foragers'. Paper given at the Conference on Hunter-Gatherers, Paris, 30 June 1978
Colson, E. 1974. *Tradition and contract: the problem of order*. London: Heinemann
Davies, M. R. and Lewis, V. A. 1971. *Models of political systems*. New York: Macmillan
Deutsch, K. W. 1963. *The nerves of government*. New York: Free Press
Easton, D. 1965. *A systems analysis of political life*. New York: John Wiley
Fried, M. 1967. *The evolution of political society*. New York: Random House
Laswell, H. and Kaplan, A. 1950. *Power and society*. New Haven, Conn.: Yale U.P.
Leach, E. 1973. 'Buddhism in the post-colonial order in Burma and Ceylon'. *Daedalus: post-traditional societies* 102(1)
Partridge, P. H. 1971. *Consent and consensus*. New York: Macmillan
Radcliffe-Brown, A. T. 1940. 'Preface', in M. Fortes and E. E. Evans-Pritchard, *African political systems*. London: O.U.P.
Smith, M. G. 1960. *Government in Zazzau: 1800–1950*. London: O.U.P.
Southall, A. 1965. 'A critique of the typology of states and political systems', in *A.S.A. 2: Political systems and the distribution of power*. London: Tavistock
Weber, M. 1966. *The theory of social and economic organisation*. New York: Free Press

2. Politics, sexual and non-sexual, in an egalitarian society

RICHARD LEE

Among the !Kung San, hunter-gatherers of southern Africa, women play, an important role in production, in fact providing a greater proportion of the subsistence than do the men (Marshall 1960; Lee 1968). The same predominance of female over male work productivity has been observed among many other tropical and warm-temperate hunter-gatherers (Woodburn 1968; Lee and DeVore 1968; McCarthy and McArthur 1960). The economic importance of women has led observers to question the male-dominated 'patrilocal' model of hunting and gathering society and to revise and upgrade woman's role in human prehistory (Friedl 1975, Rohrlich-Leavitt 1975; Slocum 1975; B. Hiatt 1974; E. Morgan 1972; Tanner and Zihlman 1976; Reed 1975; Leacock 1972, 1978). The counterposing of 'Woman the Gatherer' to 'Man the Hunter' has been part of a welcome and long overdue re-examination of the implicit and explicit male biases in anthropological theory (Rosaldo and Lamphere 1974; Reiter 1975; Golde 1970; Voorhies and Martin 1975; Gough 1970, 1971; Lamphere 1977; Reiter 1977).

The re-evaluation of women's status in hunter-gatherer society raises the more general issue of the nature of politics in egalitarian societies. Is there a baseline of non-exploitative social relations in the small-scale societies of hunter-gatherers, or is this postulate in error, arising out of a romantic Rousseauesque image of the primitive (Diamond 1975)? Recent writings have sought to discern status inequalities in even the simplest small-scale societies, with males lording it over women and controlling their labour-power, and elder males controlling the labour-power and access to resources of younger males as well as females (Tiger 1969, Fox 1967, Rose 1968, Meillassoux 1975, Rey 1977). The issues raised are not simple and agreement has yet to be reached on even the question of what constitutes the data for resolving the questions.

The more modest purpose of this paper is to examine male–female

// Gumi, a !Kung woman orator (R. Lee)

relations and the problem of equality and inequality in general in hunter-gatherer societies, by using data on the !Kung San as an illustrative starting point. Three groups of problems are addressed:

1 By what kinds of criteria – economic, social, ideological – can we evaluate the equality of the sexes or lack of it among the !Kung, so that the results can be cross-culturally applicable? How representative are the !Kung of other hunter-gatherers?

2 What forms of leadership exist in !Kung society, and how do the people handle the apparent paradox of leadership–followership in an egalitarian society?

3 How does the equality in the political sphere correspond to the relations of production in the economic sphere and what are the key contradictions between and within these spheres that give to !Kung society a dynamic quality and the potential for change?

In answering these questions the area of male–female relations is addressed first, followed by an ethnography of !Kung leadership in the foraging and sedentary contexts, and finally the questions of relations of production and their contradictions are considered.

Men and women foragers: contemporary perspectives

Although debate continues on the question of the presence, absence or degree of male dominance in foraging societies happily the day is past when learned authorities could simply characterize hunter-gatherer societies as male-dominated and aggressive and contrast them with the female-dominated, fertility-obsessed cultures of the neolithic horticulturalists. It wasn't so long ago for example that Lewis Mumford could assert:

> Paleolithic tools and weapons mainly were addressed to movements and muscular efforts: instruments of chipping, hacking, digging, burrowing, cleaving, dissecting, exerting force swiftly at a distance; in short every manner of aggressive activity. The bones and muscles of the male dominate his technical contributions . . . Under woman's dominance the neolithic period is pre-eminently one of containers: it is an age of stone and pottery utensils, of vases, jars, vats, cisterns, bins, barns, granaries, houses, not least the great collective containers like irrigation ditches and villages. (Mumford 1961:25)

Schemes like these echo nineteenth- and early-twentieth-century sequences which equated hunters with patriarchy and horticulturalists with matriarchy (e.g. Bachofen 1861; Lubbock 1865; Freud 1919). However, given this long history of controversy, we should be wary of formulas that simply invert the previous sequences and grant all political power to women in early society, or for that matter which postulate a perfect equality between males and females in the pre-agricultural past. Rather than give a global assessment of male–female relations in !Kung society, I prefer to deal with the problem piecemeal by discussing in turn the various spheres in which men and women interact to show that dominance of one sex in one sphere does not necessarily lead to dominance in another.

Hunting versus gathering

!Kung men hunt and !Kung women gather; and gathering provides about two-thirds of the diet and hunting one-third. Behind this simple statement lie some not-so-simple qualifications. For example, there are at least three ways of calculating the relative contributions of hunting and gathering to the foraging diet: first by the weight or calorific content of food from each source, second by the amount of work effort and the productivity per person-hour, and third by the cultural evaluation the people themselves place upon the two kinds of subsistence. On the first count it is clear that gathered foods provide about twice the food value of hunted foods. In a July 1964 study of work, vegetable products yielded 69 per cent by weight and 71 per cent of the calories of the Dobe camp. At other seasons of the year such as the late-summer and fall camps in mongongo nut groves or tsin bean fields, the proportion of vegetable foods may go even higher, as high as 80 per cent. Is there ever a time when hunting predominates over gathering? In late-spring and early-summer hunting camps the proportion of meat may sharply rise. In one study, the four hunters of a small camp of 12 killed 29 animals in 17 days for a *per capita* consumption of almost two kilos of meat per day. These bursts of meat-eating tend to be of short duration, however, and overall I estimate that meat comprises between 30 and 40 per cent of the diet and vegetables between 60 and 70 per cent. Of course not all the plant gathering is done by women. Men gather as well, and their work provides almost a fifth of all the gathered food. Therefore when we sum up the overall contribution of each sex, the disparity is reduced. Men produce about 44 per cent and women 56 per cent of the weight and calories of the food brought into the camp.

Considering work effort and productivity next adds a further dimension to the differences between the sexes. Men put in a longer subsistence-work week than do women – about 2.7 days of work for men compared to 2.1 for women – but the productivity of women's work overall and per person-huur is higher than the productivity of men's. A man brings back one game animal for every four days of hunting for a success rate of 25 per cent, while the probability of a woman finding food during a day of gathering is 100 per cent. It is true that a single game animal may provide a very large input of food, as many calories as 50 days of gathering in the case of a large kudu. But such kills are few and far between and for the most part men have to content themselves with smaller kills. Overall each man-day of hunting brought in about 7,230 calories, compared to 12,000 calories for each person-day of gathering. These differences in productivity account for the fact that women provide a larger share of the food even while they do less of the subsistence work.

In light of the greatest importance of gathered food in the diet it is curious that all !Kung, both men and women, value meat more highly than plant food. When meat is scarce in the camp all people express a craving for it even when vegetable foods are abundant. And the occasions when large animals are killed are usually marked by feasting, dancing and the giving of gifts of meat as well. Since game animals are scarce and unpredictable compared to plant foods it is perhaps not so surprising that hunting is invested with more symbolic significance than gathering; and one should not lose sight of the fact that hunting provides essential nutrients such as high-quality protein, which are not as readily available from plant foods alone.

Women, men, and child-care

The question of child-care and how it should be divided between mother, father, and other caretakers is a key issue in the contemporary West. The saddling of the woman of the modern household with the great bulk of the child-care responsibilities has come to be regarded as a key symbol of woman's oppression in the capitalist system. In arguing for a more equitable distribution of household labour, feminist anthropologists have turned to data on non-Western societies for evidence of a more just set of child-care arrangements. In some ways the !Kung data offer little support for this point of view, since over 90 per cent of the work involved in caring for young children is borne by the mother aided by the other women (Draper 1976). This is not to say that !Kung fathers ignore their children; they are attentive and loving and spend part of their leisure hours playing with and holding the young infants. But the !Kung father rarely takes sole responsibility for the child while the mother is absent, while the opposite occurs every day (Draper 1975; West and Konner 1980).

For their part the women do not consider themselves to be oppressed by this state of affairs. They keenly desire children, are excellent mothers and often complain that they do not have as many children as they would like.

In interpreting these attitudes one should avoid projecting the negative features we associate with child-care on an entirely different cultural situation. The !Kung women consider child-birth and child-care as their sphere of responsibility and they take steps to guard their prerogatives in this area. For example, the fact that women go to the bush to give birth and insist on excluding men from the child-birth site is justified by them in terms of pollution and taboos; but the underlying explanation may be that it simplifies matters if a decision in favour of infanticide is made. Since the woman will commit a considerable amount of her energy to raising each child, she examines the newborn carefully for evidence of defects; if she finds any, the child is not allowed to live and is buried with the afterbirth. By excluding men from the childbed women can report back to the camp that the child was born dead without fear of contradiction. But if the child is healthy and wanted by the woman she accepts the major responsibility for raising it. In this way the women exercise control over their own reproduction.

Another important reason why the !Kung woman's share of the childcare is not oppressive is that she is not isolated from the community in the same way that modern urban mothers are. She is helped by all the other women in the camp and there is no necessity to divide her productive work from her child-care work. Gathering and food processing is carried out with her child on her hip and not left at home with babysitters. Also men do participate in the non-child-care aspects of housework: about 20–40 per cent of the housework of a four-person household is done by men (Lee 1979, ch. 9). For these reasons it is inaccurate to say that !Kung women are oppressed by the burden of child-care responsibilities.

Marriage, divorce and group structure

Their contribution to the food supply and their control over reproduction and child-care give !Kung women influence in other areas such as marriage and divorce. For a variety of reasons there is an imposed scarcity among the !Kung of women of marriageable age. Parents of a girl can afford to be selective about a prospective son-in-law. As a result men usually have to prove themselves worthy by demonstrating their competence in hunting and ritual activities. This task takes many years and men are often 7–15 years older than their wives at marriage. For example, the typical age of marriage for the Nyae Nyae !Kung during the 1950s was 14–15 for women and 22–25 for men (L. Marshall 1959), while in the Dobe area a decade later it was 16–17 for women and 23–30 for men. At marriage, the girl's people insist that the young couple live with them. The reasons given are of three kinds: they say, first, that it must be seen that the man treats the daughter well; second, that he must prove his hunting abilities by providing meat; and, third, that the female is too young to leave her mother. In the majority of cases, the husband leaves his own group and takes up residence with the wife's group, a stay that may last three, five or ten years, or even a lifetime. Bride service is found among many of the world's hunter-gatherers and occurs even in northern Australia, an area usually regarded as the heartland of the patrilocal band (Shapiro 1971; Burbank 1980).

Thus there is a central paradox in the idea of Lévi-Strauss that in simple societies women are a 'scarce good' and that they may have functioned as the original medium of exchange between men in early society (1967:62–5). Their very scarcity makes women more desirable and allows them considerable scope to dictate their own terms of marriage. The result is that though among the !Kung most first marriages are arranged, many break up soon after, and the break-up is usually initiated by the wife, not the husband. Furthermore, there is a feedback relationship between the demography of marriage and its ideology. The fewer the women available for marriage, the greater the pressure to marry-off girls at a younger age. However, the younger the girl, the longer will be the period of 'bride service' necessary for the husband. By the time his bride service is completed, the husband's own parents may be dead, and these men often decide to continue to stay with their wife's group.

The husband during the period of bride service is not exploited or treated as a menial by his wife's family (as was the daughter-in-law in the pre-revolutionary Chinese family). Precisely the opposite is the case. The atmosphere is made as congenial as possible to encourage the son-in-law to stay on after the period of bride service. Usually these men in fact form strong ties with other men in the group, especially brothers-in-law. Recruiting sons-in-law adds hunting strength to the group and means more meat for the members, a point to be discussed further below.

Bride service and age differences at marriage are two of the factors that explain why women comprise the core of !Kung living groups as frequently as do men (Lee 1976). Statistically, mother–daughter bonds predominate followed by sister–sister and brother–sister, but father–son and brother–brother bonds are also found. Thus it would be an overstatement to say that the !Kung group structure is a simple inversion of the patrilocal band model with females replacing males at the group's core. Instead we see that the genealogical core consists of males *and* females, and no single rule of uxorilocal or virilocal post-marital residence will account for the arrangements actually observed.

Women and political power

Does women's predominant role in production, their leverage in marriage, and their sharing of core group membership with men lead to power in the political arena as well? The answer in a broad sense is yes:

!Kung women's participation in group discussions and decision-making is probably greater than that of women in most tribal, peasant and industrial societies. But the level of their participation is not equal to that of men. The latter appear to do about two-thirds of the talking in discussions involving both sexes, and men act as group spokespersons far more frequently than do women.

This disparity between men and women comes into sharper relief when discussions and arguments turn to violence. In 34 cases of fights occurring in the period 1963–9 a man attacked a woman 14 times, while a woman attacked a man only once (Lee 1979, ch. 13). Since 11 of these 15 cases involved husband and wife it is clear that in domestic scraps the wife is the victim in the great majority of cases. Similarly in cases of homicide there were 25 male and no female killers (though it is worth noting that 19 of the 22 victims were males as well).

Remarkably, one major form of violence against women, rape, is rare among the !Kung. This kind of sexual violence so common in many state societies (Brownmiller 1975; Webster 1976) has been reported for the !Kung as extremely rare or absent (Marshall 1976:279).

In summarizing the evidence for male–female relations, we see that women predominate in some spheres of behaviour and men in others, while the overall sense of the relations between the sexes is one of give and take. Both sexes work equally hard, with men working longer hours in subsistence and tool-making and women working longer hours in housework and child-care. Women's subsistence work is more efficient and productive than men's so that they provide more of the food despite their shorter subsistence-work week. In marriage arrangements women exercise some control and they initiate divorce far more frequently than men. On the other hand, because the men are so much older than their wives at their first marriage this factor may tip the balance of influence within the marriage in favour of the males. However, in about one out of five !Kung marriages the woman is older than the man – up to 20 years older – and in these unions it is usually the woman's influence which predominates.

In the political sphere men do more of the talking than women and it is my impression that their overall influence in 'public' matters is greater, though I cannot present any data to confirm this point. Men exhibit more violent behaviour than women, though women are rarely the victims in serious conflicts; and rape, a primary form of violence against women in many societies, is rare among the !Kung.

On balance the evidence shows a relatively equal role in society for the two sexes, and there is certainly no support in the !Kung data for a view of women in 'the state of nature' as oppressed or dominated by men or as subject to sexual exploitation at the hands of males. However the comparative evidence suggests that the status of !Kung women may be higher than that enjoyed by women in some other foraging societies such as the Eskimo at least in modern times (Friedl 1975) and the Australian Aborigines (Gale 1974).

Leadership

We turn now from male–female relations to the general question of leadership. How group and individual decisions are made in a society without formal political or judicial institutions is difficult to discern. In egalitarian societies such as the !Kung we see group activities unfolding, plans made and decisions arrived at all without a clear focus of authority or influence. Closer examination, however, reveals that patterns of leadership do exist. When a waterhole is mentioned, a group living there is often referred to by the !Kung by a single man's or woman's name, for example Bon!a's camp at !Kangwa, or Kxarun!a's camp at Bate. These individuals are often older people who have lived there the longest or who have married into the owner group, and who have some personal qualities worthy of note as a speaker, an arguer, a ritual specialist, or a hunter. In group discussions these people may speak out more than others, may be deferred to by others, and one gets the feeling that their opinions hold a bit more weight than the opinions of other discussants. Whatever their skills, !Kung leaders have no formal authority. They can only persuade but never enforce their will on others. Even the !Kung vocabulary of leadership is limited. Their word for Chief, '//Kaiha', derived from the word '//Kai' (wealth), is applied to Black headmen and chiefs, and even to English kings and queens but only rarely do the !Kung use it of other !Kung and then usually in a derisory manner. One /Xai/xai man nicknamed //kaihan!a meaning 'Big Chief' told us it was a joking name since when he was young he tended to put on airs; people called him Big Chief to take him down a peg.

The suffix '-n!a' (old or big) is added to any person's name after the age of 40. When one person of a camp is singled out as 'n!a' from other age mates it usually means that he or she is the leader of the camp. Marshall calls the camp leader the 'K''xaun!a' meaning 'Big owner' (1976:191).

Paths to leadership

Analysing the attributes of the acknowledged leaders of the living groups of the Dobe area one finds a wide variety of skills, backgrounds and genealogical positions. Some people are powerful speakers, others say very little. Some leaders are genealogically central; others are male outsiders who have married a core woman. Some have many children and grand-children in the living group, others have few or no offspring. The majority of leaders are males but females as well take leadership roles. At least four attributes can lead to leadership and most leaders have several of these in varying degrees:

1. seniority in a large family
2. n!ore (land) ownership
3. marriage to a n!ore owner
4. personal qualities

Seniority – being the oldest member or surviving member of a sibling group puts one in a position of respect within the family, and if the family is large enough the entire camp could be made up of a person's descendants, his or her siblings' descendants and their spouses. Seniority alone, however, does not make a leader, since many of the oldest people do not take leadership roles.

N!ore ownership – This is an important criterion; people who are senior descendants of a long line of n!ore owners have a very strong claim to leadership. For example, Sa//gain!a who died in 1971 was a descendant of several generations of /Xai/xai owners and though she was a soft-spoken person she was the acknowledged leader of her camp, a position shared with her husband. Her niece Baun!a (d. 1966) had equal claim to n!ore ownership but since she was a strong forceful woman as well she was doubly a leader of her /Xai/xai group. Her son Tsau later became the chief spokesperson for the /Xai/xai San in their relations with the Blacks.

Marriage to a n!ore owner – This was the most frequent route to leadership positions among the !Kung. It usually involved an energetic, capable man from another waterhole marrying a woman of the n!ore-owning group. The best example of this kind of leader is ≠Toma n!wa, one of Lorna Marshall's main informants at /Gausha (Marshall 1960, 1976). He married !U, a woman of the n!ore-owning sibling group, and he became the leader of the /Gausha camp, while !U's older brother,

Gao, went to live in the Dobe area. ≠Toma is known to students of anthropology as the senior of the four giraffe hunters in John Marshall's classic film 'The Hunters' (1956). Another example of a leader who married in is ≠Toma//gwe at Dobe. He married //Koka of the n!ore-owning group and settled at Dobe to raise a family that by the 1970s had grown to consist of a group of four married children and their spouses and eight grandchildren. ≠Toma//gwe (d. 1978) was considered gruff and unreasonable by other !Kung but his large family plus his connection to the owner group validated his leadership role.

Personal qualities – Some leaders like ≠Toma n!wa of /Gausha have obvious leadership qualities, being excellent speakers and diplomatic mediators. Others like ≠Toma//gwe are gruff and unreasonable but have strong personalities. ≠Toma Leopard, the young leader of a group at /Xai/xai, is charming, but also short-tempered, feisty, and fiercely independent, while Kxaurun!a of Bate and Sa//gain!a of /Xai/xai are mellow, grandmotherly, and soft spoken. No single personality type or personality trait dominates the ranks of leaders. If anything, what the leaders have in common is *an absence of certain traits.* None is arrogant or overbearing, boastful or aloof. In !Kung terms these traits absolutely disqualify one as a leader and may lead to even stronger sanctions. Some extremely aggressive men have been killed by community agreement (Lee 1979, ch. 13).

Another trait emphatically not found among traditional camp leaders is a desire for wealth or acquisitiveness. The leaders of the 15 or so living groups not closely tied to Black cattle posts live in huts no larger, or dress in clothing or ornaments no more lavish than those of the other camp members. Whatever their extravagances in speech, their personal style of living is modest and their accumulation of material goods is minimal. Whatever their personal influence over group decisions they never translate this into more wealth or more leisure time than other group members. !Kung leaders therefore adhere closely to the image of the 'egalitarian redistributor' noted by Harris (1975:289) or the modest band leader noted by Fried (1967:82ff.) as characteristic of egalitarian societies.

San headmen?

The question of hereditary headmen or chiefs among the San has been a matter of dispute. The existence of San chiefs was stated clearly long ago by Fourie who wrote:

At the head of each group is a big man or chief. Though usually considered to be a chief in name only and without any authority over the members of the group, he in fact does exercise considerable influence in the life of the community because in him are vested certain functions, the performance of which is of vital importance to the welfare of his people. The family area with its food and water supply as well as the fire are all looked upon as belonging to him. Among the tribes of the Kalahari he is succeeded by a son or failing such, by the nearest male relative.

(Fourie 1928:86)

Lorna Marshall in her earlier writings also spoke of a hereditary headman in whom resided the ownership of the group's resources and who inherited his position patrilineally (1960:344–52), a view which Fried has questioned (1967:87–9). Marshall has subsequently altered her views and has more recently stated that ' "headman" was a misleading and unfortunate paraphrase' for 'K"xaun!a' meaning 'Big owner' (1976:191). Her revised thinking on the subject of headmen now brings the data on the Nyae Nyae !Kung into line with the data from the Dobe area, since in the latter case it is clear that the institution of the headman was completely absent among the pre-contact !Kung. Further there is good evidence that the concept of headmen only came into currency *after* the arrival of the Blacks.

After reading Marshall's 1960 article and the earlier writings of others, I made enquiries in the Dobe area in 1964 to find out who was the headman or chief (//kaiha) at each waterhole. The answers the people gave were almost entirely negative. The younger people didn't know who, if anyone, was the headman, and the older people were obviously puzzled by the question. Some people offered up a variety of names but most answered that the only headman they knew of was Isak, the Motswana headman appointed by the Paramount Chief. Finally I discussed the question with K"au, a senior /Xai/xai man originally from /Gam: 'Before the Tswanas came here,' I asked, 'did the San have chiefs?'

'No,' he replied. 'We had no one we set apart like a chief; we all lived on the land.'

'What about /Gaun!a? Was he a chief of /Xai/xai?' I asked, citing the name of a man whom the Hereros had mentioned as a former San headman.

'That is not true,' K"au responded. 'They are mistaken. Because, among the Bantu the chief's village is fixed; you come to him, speak, and go away. Others come, speak, and go. But with us San, we are here today, tomorrow over there, and the next day still elsewhere. How can we have a chief leading a life like that?'

'If San have no chiefs,' I asked, 'then how did /Gaun!a come to be labelled as the chief here?'

'I can tell you that. /Gaun!a was living at /Twihaba east of /Xai/xai when the Blacks came. They saw evidence of his many old campsites and so they called him //Kaiha. But they named him something that no !Kung person recognizes.'

'But even that is lies,' the old man continued, 'because /Gaun!a was not even the real owner of /Twihaba! His proper n!ore is N!umtsa, east of /Gam, /Twihaba properly belongs to the people of a ≠Toma whose descendants now live mostly in the east.'

Other !Kung informants corroborated K"au's statements about the absence of headmen among themselves, but the most striking confirmation of the point came from a conversation with K"au-Kasupe, a short lively Dobe resident who had originally come from the Nyae Nyae area. In her detailed discussion of the headman (1960:344–52) Lorna Marshall had used the /Gausha waterhole as a prime example. The leader of her /Gausha Band 1 was ≠Toman!wa, discussed above, who had married into the core group. But the headman at /Gausha was not ≠Toma, but his wife's younger brother, a crippled man named Lame ≠Gao. The real headman however should have been one Gao, who, according to Marshall, 'chose to renounce his headmanship and to live with his wife's people in Band 21 . . . However, should Gao change his plan and return to Band 1, the headmanship would automatically fall on him again, as he is the eldest son' (1960:350).

Marshall's Gao turned out to be none other than Kasupe living at Dobe. When I asked him how it felt to be the absent headman of /Gausha he expressed surprise, shock, disbelief, and then laughter. With a keen sense of the irony of the situation, Kasupe insisted that he was in no way the headman of /Gausha; that his shrimp of a kid brother Lame ≠Gao certainly wasn't the headman; that the !Kung don't even have headmen; if they did he, Kasupe, would be the headman of //Karu, not /Gausha since the latter was his father's true n!ore; and, finally, Kasupe asked, if he was such a headman how did it happen that he, the 'boss', was living in rags at Dobe, while underlings like his brother and sisters were living in luxury at the South African settlement scheme at Chum!kwe?

Kasupe's genuine surprise at being named the headman of /Gausha along with the abundant corroborating evidence from other informants convinced me that indeed the !Kung have no headman. Years later I was speaking with /Twi!gum, one of the owners of !Kangwa, and I casually asked him whether the !Kung have headmen.

'Of course we have headmen!' he replied, to my surprise. 'In fact we are all headmen,' he continued slyly, 'each one of us is headman over himself!'

!Kung leadership in the contact setting

Given the conflicting nature of the evidence on the headman question we may legitimately ask how the illusion of !Kung headmanship came into being. The answer must be sought in the contacts of the !Kung with Blacks and Europeans over the last 80 years. The Tswana were a hierarchically organized expanding people who brought under their rule a number of tribally based societies in western and northern Botswana. By the time they reached the Dobe area in the 1890s, the Tswana had already become part of the British colonial protectorate of Bechuanaland (Sillery 1952; 1965). Like the British the Tswana employed a system that combined elements of direct and indirect rule. Around the turn of the century the Tswana Kubu and Mhapa clans were given stewardship of the Dobe area by the Tswana paramount chief, but because the area was vast and their numbers were few they tried to recruit local !Kung to be the spokespeople for the San camps at the various water holes. Later when they moved their cattle up to /Xai/xai, /Gam and !Kangwa they put local !Kung men in charge of the livestock. Gradually a system of leaders came into being who were recognized as //kaihas by the Tswana but who had no equivalent standing among the !Kung themselves.

This contradiction between what we might call 'inside' leaders and 'outside' leaders continues up to the present day. Inside leaders achieve their status by being n!ore owners or spouses of n!ore owners in combination with personal qualities of leadership. The outside leaders excel in their ability to deal with Blacks and Europeans, and in their entrepreneurial skills. Rarely are the two kinds of attributes combined in a single person. For example at Dobe in 1973 there were two camps, the one led by ≠Toma//gwe who had lived there for many years, and a group led by !Xoma, a vigorous and able man who had long worked for Blacks and Europeans but who had no claim to the ownership of Dobe. Because of his knowledge of and sensitivity to the outside world !Xoma was highly regarded by government people, anthropologists and missionaries; but, whenever the outsiders were absent, !Xoma's !Kung neighbours would express hostility and resentment toward him.

This hostility came to a head in the mid-1970s over a government-sponsored project to dig a well at Dobe to improve and stabilize the water supply and thus make stockraising possible for the Dobe residents. When it came time to register the well in a leader's name, the outside agents favoured !Xoma who was fluent in Setswana and who could make a highly articulate case for the !Kung before the District Council's Land Board in Maun, the district capital. To the dismay of the outsiders the Dobe !Kung chose as their leader a quiet and unaggressive man named ≠Dau whose main claim to the role was the fact that he was the descendant of ≠Dauhwanadum (≠Dau licks the river bed), the senior owner of Dobe 50 years ago. At the long and contentious meetings held to discuss the issue of the well, ≠Dau would sit quietly to one side listening and only rarely would he interject a comment, compared to !Xoma who discoursed at length. The fact that the Dobe people chose the former man in preference to the latter indicated that they were not yet fully aware of the threats to the security of their land, and thus were not able to fully mobilize against it. Polly Wiessner has pointed out (personal communication) that at the Chum!kwe settlement across the border ≠Toman!wa (the /Gausha leader) was initially elected as the 'foreman' to represent the !Kung in their dealings with the South African authorities, but he was defeated at the next election, a fate which has befallen many of his successors as well.

The changing patterns of leadership among the San reveal the existence of two contradictory systems of politics among them. The old system based on genealogy and n!ore ownership favoured a leader who was modest in demeanour, generous to a fault, egalitarian, and whose legitimacy arose from long-standing n!ore ownership. The new system required a man who had to deny most of the old virtues. The political arena of District Councils, Land Boards and nationalist politics required someone who was male, aggressive, articulate, and wise in the ways of the wider world. As antithetical as these characteristics are to !Kung traditional values, the dynamic of their rapid incorporation into the national capitalist system of Botswana will make it inevitable that these new leaders will have to come to the fore.

Social relations of production

Central to the foraging mode of production is a lack of wealth accumulation and the social differentiation that accompanies it. This lack of accumulation, even though the means for it – free time and raw materials – are at hand, arises in part from the requirements of the nomadic life. For people who move around a lot and did not keep pack animals until very recently, it would be sheer folly to amass more goods than can be carried along when the group moves. Portability is the major design feature of the items themselves. The total weight of an individual's personal property is less than twenty-five pounds and can easily be carried from place to place.

The modest investment in capital goods and the lack of wealth disparities between individuals contribute to the distinctive style of San social relations. With personal property so easily portable, it is no problem for people to move as often as they do. There is a similar lack of investment in fixed facilities such as village sites, storage places, and fenced enclosures. When parties come into conflict it is simpler to part company than to remain together and resolve differences through adjudication or fighting.

A dynamic of movement informs the daily life of individuals and groups. Land ownership is vested, not in a single individual, but in a collective of k"ausi, both males and females, who form the core of the resident camp and who must be approached for permission to use the resources of the area. The right of reciprocal access to food resources is a fundamental principle of land use. If Group A visits Group B in one season, it is expected that Group B will repay the visit in the next. These visiting patterns tend to keep people in circulation from area to area providing a change of scene and change of company. An individual's primary kin and close affines are always distributed at several different waterholes, and through the far-reaching ties of the name relation s/he may establish close ties at a number of others. The outcome of these multiple options is that an individual may utilize the food resources of several waterholes as long as s/he observes the elementary good manners of sharing fully with the members of the local camp. Whether individuals will choose to join a given camp depends on the history of their relations with the long-term residents. Many men and women who have a reputation for good humour, industry, or curing skills have standing invitations at many different camps. Even less popular individuals nevertheless have strong primary kinship ties that make them welcome in at least two or three camps and tolerated in others.

This dynamic of movement coupled with the fact that both males and females form the core of groups leads to an emphasis in social relations on recruitment rather than exclusion. The older model of male-centred territorial bands (Service 1962; Fox 1967; Tiger 1969) assumed that the primary requirement of the foraging living group was the maintenance of exclusive rights to land, a task that was best fulfilled by a core of male sibling defenders. In contrast, it is clear that the maintenance of *flexibility* to adapt to changing ecological circumstances is far more important in hunter-gatherer group structure than is the maintenance of exclusive rights to land. Flexibility favours a social policy of *bringing in* more personnel rather than keeping them out, hence the emphasis on the social principle of *recruitment* rather than *exclusion*. Because of the nature of production in hunter-gatherer society, the principal way to increase output is to add personnel; therefore, a primary social strategy of many hunter-gatherers is to recruit sons- and daughters-in-law to augment the group's meat- and plant-food-getting capacity while at the same time trying to retain the sons and daughters. The net effect of this strategy is that many of the males in any group are outsiders and unrelated.

On the political level these characteristics of foraging life lead to a strong emphasis on egalitarian social relations. It is not simply a question of the *absence* of a headman and other authority figures but also a positive insistence on the essential equality of all people and the refusal to bow to the authority of others, a sentiment expressed in the statement: 'Of course we have headmen . . . each one of us is headman over himself.' Men and women whom we would call leaders do exist, but their influence is subtle and indirect. They never order or make demands of others and their accumulation of material goods is never more, and is often much less, than the average accumulation of the other households in their camp.

The ideology of equality and its contradictions

Two remarkable cultural practices at the level of consciousness accompany the egalitarian political ideal. They occur among the !Kung and among many other hunter-gatherers. The most serious accusations that one !Kung can level against another are the charge of stinginess and the charge of arrogance. To be stingy or 'far-hearted' is to hoard one's goods jealously and secretively, guarding them 'like a hyena'. The corrective for this in the !Kung view is to make the hoarder give 'till it hurts', that is to make her/him give generously and without stint until everyone can see that s/he is truly cleaned out. In order to ensure compliance with this cardinal rule the !Kung browbeat each other constantly to be more generous and not to set themselves apart by hoarding a little nest-egg. The importance of sharing and giving has been ably documented by Lorna Marshall (1961, 1976:287–312).

But, as serious as they regard the fault of stinginess, their most scathing criticisms are reserved for an even more serious shortcoming: the crime of arrogance (≠twi). While a stingy person is anti-social and irksome, an arrogant person is actually dangerous, since according to the !Kung 'his pride will make him kill someone'. A boasting hunter who comes into camp announcing: 'I have killed a big animal in the bush', is being arrogant. A woman who gives a gift and announces to all her great generosity, is being arrogant. Even an anthropologist who claims to have chosen the biggest ox of the year to slaughter for Christmas is being arrogant. The !Kung perceive this behaviour as a danger sign and they have evolved elaborate devices for puncturing the bubble of conceit and enforcing humility. These levelling devices are in constant daily use, minimizing the size of others' kills, downplaying the value of others' gifts, and treating one's own efforts in a self-deprecating way. 'Please' and 'thank you' are hardly ever found in their vocabulary; in their stead we find a vocabulary of rough humour, back-handed compliments, put-downs, and damning with faint praise. In fact the one area in which they are openly competitive is in recounting suffering. They try to outdo each other in tales of misfortune: cold, pain, thirst, hunger, hunting failure, and other hardships represent conversational gold, the obverse of the coin of arrogance, which they so strongly discourage.

To the outsider these cultural preoccupations are disconcerting. We admire the !Kung from afar, but when we are brought into closer contact with their daily concerns, we are alternately moved to pity by their tales of hardship, and repelled by their nagging demands for gifts, demands that grow more insistent the more we give.

These contradictions, generosity–stinginess, arrogance–humility, equality–hierarchy, sociability–withdrawal, are central themes in !Kung culture and they afford us a glimpse into the internal workings of a social existence very different from our own. The essence of this way of life is sharing, a practice that is extended more widely in the foraging mode of production than in any other. People share within the family and between families, and the unit of sharing extends to the boundaries of the face-to-face community and beyond. Visualize the kind of sharing that occurs around the dinner table in a Western household but expanded in scale to include a group of 15 to 30 people, and one has some idea of the nature of sharing in a !Kung camp.

The principle of generalized reciprocity within the camp, the giving of something without an expectation of equivalent return, is almost universal among foraging peoples (Sahlins 1965, 1972). In the case of the !Kung, food is shared in a generalized familistic way, while durable goods are changed according to the principle of balanced reciprocity; that is, transactions are expected to balance out in the long run. These kinds of reciprocities have their counterpoints in the political sphere. Egalitarian relations are a kind of balanced political reciprocity where giving orders and receiving them balances out. In the same way hierarchical relations correspond to a negative reciprocity at the level of exchange. To give orders from A to B but not from B to A is like taking goods from B to A but not giving anything in return. Conversely sharing of food and sharing of power seem to go hand in hand.

The fact that communal sharing of food resources and of power is a phenomenon that has been directly observed in recent years among the !Kung and dozens of other foraging groups is a finding that should not be glossed over lightly. Its universality among foragers lends strong support to the theory of Marx and Engels that a stage of primitive communism prevailed before the rise of the state and the break-up of society into classes (Engels 1972). One should add the proviso, however, that this communism does not extend, as far as we know, to include the institution of 'group marriage' as Engels, following Morgan (1877), originally believed.

Having declared that the foraging mode of production is a form of primitive communism, it would be a mistake to idealize the foraging peoples as noble savages who have solved all the basic problems of living. Like individuals in any society, the foragers have to struggle with their own internal contradictions, and living up to the demands of this strongly collective existence presents some particularly challenging problems. Sharing, for example, is not automatic; it has to be learned and reinforced by culture. Every human infant is born equipped with both the capacity to share and the capacity to be selfish. During the course of socialization each society channels these impulses into socially acceptable forms and every society expects some sort of balance between sharing and 'selfish' behaviour – between the needs of self and the needs of others. Among the foragers, society demands a high level of sharing and tolerates a low level of personal accumulation compared to Western capitalist norms. And living up to these demands, while it has its rewards, also takes its toll. I doubt whether any !Kung ever completely gives up selfish impulses; and the tension to conform continues through life. Elderly !Kung in particular give voice to the contradictions between sharing and keeping. On one occasion ≠Toma//gwe asked me for a blanket and, when I responded that he would just give it away, he replied: 'All my life I've been giving, giving; today I am old and want something for myself.' And similar sentiments have been expressed by other elders. Perhaps because they are old their departures from the cultural norm are tolerated more than they would be coming from younger adults.

Sharing food is accompanied by sharing space, and a second area of communal life that causes stress is the lack of privacy. Daily life goes on in full view of the camp. People rarely spend time alone and to seek solitude is regarded as a bizarre form of behaviour. Even marital sex is carried on discreetly under a light blanket shared with the younger children around the family fire. It is considered bad manners for others to look. Sullen withdrawn behaviour is regarded with concern and not allowed to continue. The person showing it is pestered and goaded until he or she loses his temper and the anger that follows helps to clear the air and reintegrate the outsider. When people are depressed or their feelings are hurt, they express it by awaking at night to compose sad songs which they play for themselves on the thumb piano. These poignant refrains form a counterpoint to the night sounds of the crackling sleeping fires and the calls of the nightjars, and no one tells the players to pipe down or shut up.

So it is clear that the demands of the collective existence are not achieved effortlessly, but rather they require a continuing struggle with one's own selfish, arrogant and antisocial impulses. The fact that the !Kung and other foragers succeed as well as they do in communal living, in spite of (or because of?) their material simplicity, offers us an important insight. A truly communal life is often dismissed as a utopian ideal, to be endorsed in theory but unattainable in practice. But the evidence for foraging peoples tells us otherwise. A sharing way of life is not only possible but has actually existed in many parts of the world and over long periods of time.

Acknowledgements

Field research among the !Kung was conducted in 1963–4, 1967–9, 1973, and 1980, with support from the National Science Foundation, the National Institute of Mental Health, the Canada Council and the Wenner-Gren Foundation. Much of this paper has been adapted from R. B. Lee, *The !Kung San* (Cambridge University Press 1979).

Bibliography

Bachofen, J. 1861. *Das Mutterrecht*. Basel: Benno Schwabe

Brownmiller, S. 1975. *Against our will: men, women and rape*. New York: Simon and Schuster

Burbank, V. 1980. 'Expressions of anger and aggression in an Australian Aboriginal community'. Ph.D. thesis, Rutgers University

Diamond, S. 1975. *In search of the primitive*. New York: Dutton

Draper, P. 1975. '!Kung women: contrasts in sexual egalitarianism in the foraging and sedentary contexts', in R. Reiter (ed.), *Toward an anthropology of women, 77–109*. New York: Monthly Review Press

   1976. 'Social and economic constraints on child life among the !Kung', in R. B. Lee and I. DeVore (eds.), *Kalahari hunter-gatherers*, 199–217. Cambridge, Mass.: Harvard University Press

Engels, F. 1972. *The origin of the family, private property and the state*, ed. and intro. by E. Leacock. New York: International Publishers (first published 1881)

Fourie, L. 1928. 'The Bushmen of South West Africa', in C. Hahn, H. Vedder and L. Fourie (eds.), *The native tribes of South West Africa*, 79–106. New York: Barnes and Noble

Fox, R. 1967. *Kinship and marriage*. Baltimore: Penguin

Freud, S. 1919. *Totem and taboo*. London: G. Routledge

Fried, M. H. 1967. *The evolution of political society*. New York: Random House

Friedl, E. 1975. *Women and men: an anthropologist's view*. New York: Holt, Rinehart and Winston

Gale, F. (ed.) 1974. *Woman's role in Aboriginal society*. Canberra: Institute of Aboriginal Studies

Golde, P. (ed.) 1970. *Women in the field: anthropological experiences*. Chicago: Aldine

Gough, K. 1970. 'Women in evolution'. Boston: New England Free Press. Pamphlet

   1971. 'The origin of the family'. *Journal of Marriage and the Family* 33:760–71

Harris, M. 1975. *Culture, people, nature: an introduction to general anthropology*. New York: Thomas Crowell

Hiatt, B. 1974. 'Woman the gatherer', in F. Gale (ed.), *Woman's role in Aboriginal society*. Australian Aboriginal Studies, No. 36. Social Anthropology Series No. 6, Canberra, 4–15

Lamphere, L. 1977. 'Anthropology' (Review article). *Signs* 2(3):612–27

Leacock, E. 1978. 'Women's status in egalitarian society: implications for social evolution'. *Current Anthropology* 19(2):247–75

Leacock, E. (ed.) 1972. *Engels' the origin of the family, private property and the state*. New York: International Publishers

Lee, R. B. 1968. 'What hunters do for a living, or, how to make out on scarce resources', in R. B. Lee and I. DeVore (eds.), *Man the hunter*, 30–48. Chicago: Aldine

   1976. '!Kung spatial organization: an ecological and historical perspective', in R. B. Lee and I. DeVore (eds.), *Kalahari hunter-gatherers: studies of the !Kung San and their neighbours*. Cambridge, Mass.: Harvard University Press

1979. *The !Kung San: men, women, and work in a foraging society.* New York and Cambridge: Cambridge University Press

Lee, R. B. and DeVore, I. (eds.) 1968. *Man the hunter.* Chicago: Aldine

Lévi-Strauss, C. 1967. *The elementary structures of kinship.* Boston: Beacon Press

Lubbock, J. 1865. *Prehistoric times, as illustrated by ancient remains and customs of modern savages.* London: Williams and Norgate

Marshall, J. 1956. 'The hunters' (Film). Somerville, Mass.: Center for Documentary Anthropology

Marshall, L. 1959. Marriage among !Kung Bushmen. *Africa* 29:335–65

1960. '!Kung Bushmen bands'. *Africa* 30:325–55

1961. 'Sharing, talking and giving: relief of social tension among !Kung Bushmen'. *Africa* 31:231–49

1976. *The !Kung of Nyae Nyae.* Cambridge, Mass.: Harvard University Press

McCarthy, F. and McArthur, M. 1960. 'The time factor in aboriginal society', in C. Mountford (ed.), *The Australian–American scientific expedition to Arnhem Land: vol. 3: Anthropology and nutrition,* 145–90

Meillassoux, C. 1975. *Femmes, greniers et capitaux.* Paris: Maspero. English translation 1981. *Maidens, meal and money: capitalism and the domestic community.* Cambridge: Cambridge University Press

Morgan, E. 1972. *The descent of woman.* New York: Stein and Day

Morgan, L. H. 1877. *Ancient society.* New York: World Publishing

Mumford, L. 1961. *The city in history: its origin, its transformations, and its prospects.* London: Secker and Warburg

Reed, E. 1975. *Woman's evolution from matriarchal clan to patriarchal family.* New York: Pathfinder Press

Reiter, R. 1977. Introduction to special issue on the anthropology of women. *Critique of Anthropology* 3(9–10):5–24

Reiter, R. (ed.) 1975. *Toward an anthropology of women.* New York: Monthly Review Press

Rey, P. P. 1977. 'Contradictions de classe dans les sociétés lignagères'. *Dialectiques* 21:116–33

Rohrlich-Leavitt, R. 1975. *Peaceable primates and gentle people.* New York: Harper and Row

Rosaldo, M., and Lamphere, L. 1974. *Women, culture and society.* Stanford: Stanford University Press

Rose, F. G. G. 1968. 'Australian marriage, initiations and land-owning groups', in R. Lee and I. DeVore (eds.), *Man the hunter.* Chicago: Aldine

Sahlins, M. 1965. 'The sociology of primitive exchange', in M. Banton (ed.), *The relevance of models in social anthropology.* A.S.A. Monographs No. 1. 139–236 London: Tavistock

1972. *Stone Age economics.* Chicago: Aldine

Service, E. R. 1962. *Primitive social organization: an evolutionary perspective.* New York: Random House

Shapiro, W. 1971. 'Wawilak: ontogeny, phylogeny and sexuality in Miwyt ("Murngin") thought'. Paper presented at 70th Annual Meeting of the American Anthropological Association, New York

Sillery, A. 1952. *The Bechuanaland Protectorate.* Cape Town: Oxford University Press

1965. *Founding a protectorate: history of Bechuanaland 1885–1895*. The Hague: Mouton

Slocum, S. 1975. 'Woman the gatherer', in R. Reiter (ed.), *Toward an anthropology of women*, 36–50. New York: Monthly Review Press

Tanner, N., and Zihlman, A. 1976. 'Women in evolution; Part I: innovation and selection in human origins'. *Signs* 1:585–608

Tiger, L. 1969. *Men in groups*. New York: Random House

Voorhies, B., and Martin, K. 1975. *Female of the species*. New York: Columbia University Press

Webster, P. 1976. 'The politics of rape in primitive society'. Paper presented at 75th Annual Meetings of the American Anthropological Association, Washington, D.C.

West, M., and Konner, M. 1980. 'The role of the father: an anthropological perspective', in M. Lamb (ed.), *The role of the father in child development*. New York: John Wiley and Sons

Woodburn, J. 1968. 'An introduction to Hazda ecology', in R. B. Lee and I. DeVore (eds.), *Man the hunter*, 49–55. Chicago: Aldine

3. Risk, reciprocity and social influences on !Kung San economics

POLLY WIESSNER

Introduction

Over the past years, many hunter-gatherer societies have been analysed within an ecological framework based on the underlying hypothesis that, because hunter-gatherers live directly off the land and are not food producers, their economy and social organization can be seen as the direct product of their interaction with the environment. But, although ecological studies provide many important insights into the hunting-gathering way of life, it has become increasingly evident that they yield only a partial understanding of hunter-gatherer economics and social organization. As Lee (1978) points out in summarizing the status of hunter-gatherer studies: 'Only part of the behavior of hunter-gatherers can be accounted for by even the most fine-grained ecological analysis.'

I would like to make two points about !Kung San organization which I hope will add a social dimension to present and past ecological studies of other hunting and gathering societies as well. The first is that the apparent flexibility of organization among the !Kung is not true flexibility in itself, but the product of a structured system of social relations operating according to certain principles. These social relationships open up a range of options to every family when it is confronted with the multitude of risks inherent in the hunting and gathering way of life. In the environments of many hunter-gatherers today, possible mean subsistence income may be high, but so is the variance around the mean, creating a high level of risk and uncertainty. Without a systematic way of ensuring that needs are regularly met, life is indeed precarious. The flexibility of organization can not simply result from spontaneous bending to meet the needs of others as they arise, but must be the product of a structured set of social relations. These relations ensure that a reliable means of reducing risk is always available and can be passed on from generation to generation.

The second point I am making here is that such a social system for reducing risk, and its accompanying ideology, permeate many areas of life, and have their own effects on the economy of hunter-gatherers, effects that can not be predicted from environmental variables alone. There is no justification for the view that, because hunter-gatherers live directly off the land, all aspects of their social organization and economy are more directly predictable from environmental variables than those of agricultural societies.

In the following pages, I will illustrate the above two points by describing the !Kung system of reciprocity called *hxaro* which is used to keep a wide range of contacts and possibilities open in the face of a highly variable environment, and by outlining how the hxaro system in and of itself affects !Kung work effort and distribution of wealth. First, however, it will be necessary to review certain elements of !Kung life.

The !Kung San

The !Kung San today live in northwest Botswana, northeast Namibia, and southeast Angola. Those included in this study are centred in the Dobe/Xai/xai area of Botswana and the Nyae Nyae area across the border in Namibia.[1] Their direct ties of reciprocity, however, extend to more distant !Kung San as well as San of other language groups living within a radius of about 200 kilometres.

The !Kung San are spread out over this region in areas of landrights called n!ores. Each n!ore has enough food and water to sustain at least one band throughout its seasonal rounds in the average year (Marshall 1976), although it is surprising how diverse resources are from n!ore to n!ore. Even adjacent n!ores within a relatively small area are known for certain localized plant and animal foods (Yellen and Lee 1976). Today, the presence of agriculturalists in the Dobe – /Xai/xai area, a settlement scheme in the Nyae Nyae area, and farms in more distant ones have added still more variations among n!ores, with differential access to domestic foods, wage-labour, opportunities to market crafts, schools, clinics, etc.

All persons inherit one n!ore from their mother and one from their father. They do not inherit the land itself, but rather the right to exploit the resources of the land along with others who inherit similar rights. Throughout a person's lifetime, he or she develops a strong hold on the n!ore chosen to live in and maintains a weak hold on that of the other

A !Kung woman, lavishly adorned with beadwork obtained through 'hxaro' (R. Lee)

parent (Marshall 1976; Wiessner 1977). Children, in turn, will inherit rights to the n!ores which each parent held strongly, although in some cases they may trace rights back to their grandparents. If a n!ore is left uninhabited because its owners have moved or died out, others can obtain rights to it by getting permission from those who hold it weakly, and subsequently living there for an extended period of time.

Because a !Kung generally holds rights to two n!ores, can live in a spouse's n!ore (or those of other close affinal relatives), or can obtain rights to a n!ore through prolonged residence, the population distributes itself over the existing n!ores with minimal conflict. Since a person will not utilize the n!ore of others, without having the correct ties to ask for permission, the system allows the !Kung to plan their seasonal rounds on the basis of accurate information about who has been utilizing which resources. A person will not arrive at a place and find the resources unexpectedly used up by others.

Those claiming rights to a n!ore (usually close consanguineous relatives) and their affinal relatives live together in one or more camps or bands. When a !Kung man and woman marry, they often spend several years deciding which camp they can best fit into, but, once established in a group, they are likely to remain in it for many years. Camp membership is rather stable although frequent extended visiting makes it seem most unstable to the short-term observer. During a ten-year period, from 1964 to 1974, there was a 15 per cent turnover in six camps originally totalling 130 persons. Twelve individuals emigrated for marriage and were replaced by nine who married into the area; nine others emigrated for other reasons (usually accompanying siblings or children who married out) and were replaced by seven immigrants. Not included in the above figure were ten other San who emigrated seeking wage-labour; it was not clear when or if they would return. Of course, cores of close relatives within the /Xai/xai area shifted camps during this time to compensate for demographic events and conflict. This attachment of the !Kung to their n!ores means that when persons form relationships of reciprocity with other adults, they do so with a good idea of where and with whom their partners will be living.

Within their n!ores, the !Kung can hunt and gather a high-subsistence income for moderate work effort. Lee (1969) has shown for the Dobe !Kung that in July–August, which is neither the best nor the worst time of year, the amount of time devoted to the food quest is 12–15 hours a week. Marshall (1976) worked in the Nyae Nyae area, which lacks rich groves of mongongo nuts, and estimated that the !Kung work a little longer – at least half of each week. Medical studies have verified that this work-week is sufficient to keep the !Kung generally well nourished, although they may suffer from a shortage of calories in the dry season (Truswell and Hansen 1976; Wilmsen 1978).

Risk and uncertainty in !Kung life

Although the Kalahari environment can and does provide excellent returns for work effort, it is highly variable from year to year. Drought makes many resources inaccessible for much of the year (Lee 1972), and there are fluctuations in the seasonal and yearly productivity of wild vegetable foods (Wiessner 1977; Wilmsen 1978; Yellen and Lee 1976) as well as variation in game movement and hunting success (Wilmsen 1978; Yellen and Lee 1976). Other risks that are not a product of the environment are compounded by the hunting and gathering way of life, especially demographic fluctuations in sex ratios in small populations (Howell 1979), and periods of individual disability (Wiessner 1977) and conflict.

Such risks are not necessarily greater than those in other societies, but for hunter-gatherers means of reducing risk commonly used in sedentary societies – prevention of loss, storage, transferal of risk – are not effective. The !Kung to some degree prevent variation in the productivity of wild foods by burning areas to attract game and promote new growth of plant foods, but, by and large, their control over the natural environment is minimal. After a hunting or gathering trip, they do keep a stash of food in their huts to tide them over for a few days, but on the whole storage is not practical; those foods which can be preserved during the dry season are often far from the location of camps. Risk cannot be transferred to any *one* other party, as no one family or band will constantly have the resources to cover the losses of another.

The most efficient method of risk reduction open to hunters and gatherers in environments like that of the !Kung, then, is a social method of pooling risk through storage of social obligations. The method encompasses many principles of any social insurance and hinges on the assumption that the population which pools risk is diverse enough to absorb the losses of any member. In pooling risk, small, certain losses or contributions are substituted for larger, uncertain ones. Among hunter-gatherers, the small contributions cannot be stored in a communal pool, so they must be stored in social obligations. A person creates relationships of mutual reciprocity with others in the population and thereby spreads losses over a unit much larger and more varied than the local band. In times of hardship, a person's losses can be absorbed by others in the population, if risk is well distributed. It might be added that if the system covers most risks in the society, the small contributions (or losses in income) can increase to the point where they lower mean income in exchange for assuring a lower variance around the mean.

The key factor in successfully pooling risk, then, is in distributing it over as many and as independent units as possible. The Kalahari environment is highly amenable to pooling risk, because resources are localized and conditions vary from n!ore to n!ore. Thus, if risk is well distributed, the regional population can absorb most losses. For adequate distribution of risk through storing coverage for losses in social obligations, it is essential for each family to place its social obligations carefully according to the profile of risk it wishes to minimize, depending on its area of residence, its composition, the abilities of its members and so on. For this reason the !Kung cannot rely on flexibility alone, but must have a structured system within which to place their obligations.

The hxaro relationship[2]

Through a system of mutual reciprocity called hxaro, the !Kung San organize themselves in such a way that each family creates ties which distribute its risk over the population and thereby assure that losses will be covered in bad years. In good years, it will have access to the abundant wild crops of other areas. The hxaro relationship involves a balanced, delayed exchange of gifts, whose continuous flow gives both partners information about the underlying status of the relationship – one of a bond of friendship accompanied by mutual reciprocity and access to resources. In addition, each partnership links a person to a broad network of hxaro paths.

A person initiates a hxaro relationship by giving a gift to a prospective partner, who is putatively a consanguineous relative of his mother or father. Approximately half of a person's partners are genealogically traceable (most of these being parents, children or siblings), while the rest are relatives with whom genealogical ties are unclear, but who have been remembered over the years as kindred members. With a few exceptions, hxaro is not done directly with affinal relatives, because a person does not 'know the hearts of his or her affines well enough to do hxaro with them appropriately'. Furthermore, if a quarrel does arise over hxaro between consanguines, the !Kung feel that their common relatives will unite and try to resolve the conflict, while if one arose between affinal relatives, that each person's respective kin would side with their relative and a serious fight would arise between the two kindreds. Therefore, people give a large proportion of the gifts they receive from relatives to their spouses who in turn pass them on to theirs, both spouses maintaining separate spheres of hxaro. This indirect hxaro plays an important role in sustaining a marriage and maintaining smooth relations with affines.

The prospective hxaro partner who receives a gift talks it over with his or her spouse and together they decide whether they are interested in the new relationship and are able to make another commitment. It is an important consideration, because once a relationship is firm, a person is said to '//hai' that person in his or her heart, meaning literally to hold and figuratively to be responsible for the person. A strong bond of friendship is solidified by the hxaro partnership, and, from then on, each partner can call on the other in times of need. If the relationship works out as expected, both partners will come out ahead because the value of goods, resources or assistance to the one who needs is often much greater than the burden that assistance places on the one who has. Relationships may be unbalanced for a few years but often even out over time. Nonetheless, misfortune does not strike all equally, and, in taking on a hxaro relationship, people realize that even if they do come out behind, they cannot drop the relationship without considerable conflict unless both parties lose interest. Thus, a person who does not wish to begin a new partnership will just keep the gift as a token of friendship and say that at the time he or she has nothing to give.

To accept a new relationship, a !Kung returns a gift of similar worth, and after a trial period of at least a year, during which several gift exchanges take place, the relationship is considered firm. Once secure, a balanced, delayed exchange of gifts will continue, but the underlying obligations of the partnership will remain loosely defined so that they can cover a wide range of needs. As Sahlins (1972) has noted for hunter-gatherer reciprocity, returns are not stipulated by quantity, quality or time, but one who has gives to one who needs, *need being relative to the means of both*. Hxaro is geared to unpredictability and returns are measured by their utility to the receiver, rather than by fixed quantity. A person who has given assistance has no desire for an immediate and fixed return that would even the relationship and make it possible for it to be cancelled. Rather, the aim is to store the debt until the situation of have and have not is reversed. Only then will unpredictable losses be covered. On the other hand, the terms of hxaro are so loose that, when partners live far apart, the status of the relationship can become ambiguous. Then a continual balanced flow of gifts is important to let each partner know that the relationship is still intact.

The actual content of a hxaro partnership depends on the abilities and location of both partners. If they are in the same camp, the hxaro relationship generally smooths over income differences with an intense flow of gifts and a strong commitment for mutual assistance. A hxaro partner is likely to be in the 'first wave' of meat sharing (Marshall 1976) and receive a large piece of meat. A person who for some reason cannot gather vegetable foods can count on a hxaro partner in camp to give sustained assistance, even though vegetable foods usually are regularly shared only with those in the nuclear family.[3] A disabled person will get some assistance from many members of a camp, but can only count on hxaro partners for sustained care.

Hxaro partnerships with those in neighbouring camps lead to frequent visits, a share of meat when a large animal is killed, access to a partner's n!ore which, although it may be adjacent, can have different resources, and an alternate residence if conflict breaks out. In a society where there are many potential partners in reciprocity and much jealousy over giving, the existence of hxaro partnerships justifies giving more to one than another. Few will seriously question what was given to a hxaro partner.

Hxaro relationships with people in different areas allow individuals and their families to make extended visits to a partner's camp lasting from two weeks to two years. While living there, they will have access to the resources of the area and the partner will integrate them into the reciprocal relations within the camp. For the first few days the visitors will be supported, but after that they will be expected to hunt and gather their own living and share any surplus with their host and others as they would in their own camp.

Census data collected by Richard Lee in 1968–9 and by myself in 1974 on the extended visits of 30 adults who were resident at /Xai/xai in both years give an illustration of the importance of hxaro ties for visiting. Of 86 visits made which lasted for more than two weeks, 45 in 1968 and 41 in 1974, to areas outside of persons' own n!ores or those of their spouses, 80 were to areas where nuclear family members had hxaro partners, while only six were to areas where they had none.

Because hxaro partnerships are not economic contracts with set terms, but rather bonds of mutual help, it can be difficult for a person to avoid exploitation. The loose terms of the relationship are well suited to covering a variety of needs, but working out who has and who is in need is the burden of the system. The means a person uses to avoid exploitation, and at the same time keep up the joking spirit appropriate to a relationship, are either to limit work effort so that s/he is not always a 'have', or to be very discreet about what s/he does have. The !Kung do both regularly. Lee (1972) notes that after a man has had a run of successful hunting, he pauses to enjoy some of the reciprocal obligations he has built up. Women gather enough plant foods to feed their family, but rarely more, unless they have some real obligation to a person outside the immediate family. Likewise, families are discreet about the food they have brought in, and it is not unusual to hear a person with a full belly complain that s/he has not had anything to eat and is 'dying of hunger'. Therefore, considerable time is spent in trying to establish who has and who is in need. About 60 per cent of the topics of conversations, recorded in a month, came down to who had what and did or did not give it to whom.

A person who feels badly exploited may turn to deceit, for a lie is a tactful way of telling another that s/he has taken too much and made little effort to reciprocate. If this tactic does not work, a person is free to drop the relationship with no further consequences than the conflict or bad feelings which arise between partners as well as others along their hxaro path.

Hxaro networks

A person who has established a new hxaro relationship ties it into existing networks and gifts frequently pass through two or three sets of hands in a camp before going on to another camp. A typical segment of a hxaro network for any one exchange would look like:

Camp 1	Camp 2	Camp 3
A ←——————→	B↔C↔D ←——————→	E↔?

The genealogical relationship of B, C, and D is typically very close with gifts passed to a spouse, sibling, parent or child. A person along the path who wishes to keep a particular gift may replace it with another.

After a period of two weeks to a year has elapsed, E gives a gift from a partner to D, who will give it to C and so on back to A. The flow of gifts along what the !Kung call 'paths for things' means that A's hxaro with B also creates a link between A and others two or three steps down the path. C and D do not feel any direct obligation to A, but, because they have been receiving A's gifts indirectly, they recognize A as a reliable and generous friend. Thus they feel at ease about including A in daily interactions of reciprocity within the camp when A comes to visit. Without this acceptance, it would be trying for A to stay long as a visitor. The relationship created by indirect hxaro works the other way as well, so that, if B goes to visit A, C or D can come too. In this way, hxaro paths extend the bond of a partnership to others in the camp.

Patterns of hxaro paths are highly variable because different relationships have different rates of interaction. Frequency of gift exchange tends to fall off with frequency of contact (although some gifts are sent via other visitors), and those in a camp exchange gifts more frequently than those in different areas. The flexibility in hxaro paths allows a !Kung to balance the need for reciprocating quickly when a relationship must be affirmed, with the need to direct gifts in a way which will make his or her other camp a comfortable alternate residence for a partner. So, if B feels s/he wants to give a gift to his or her spouse, C, in order to maintain good relations with his or her affines, and A lives far away and has been slow in reciprocating, B can take a gift from another source and immediately give it to c.

The previous discussion has suggested that close consanguineous relatives are almost automatically hxaro partners and that hxaro marks years of living together and helping one another. In the sample population of 59 !Kung adults, 93% of all parents, siblings and children were hxaro partners and 53% of all grandparents, half-siblings, parents' siblings and parents' siblings' children were hxaro partners. Because close consanguineous relatives are almost always hxaro partners and because they tend to live together hxaro can be best understood as a core of relatives reducing risk. Hxaro paths wind through both camps and cores of these close relatives, thereby making them into nodes in the hxaro network, and travel through many camps over hundreds of kilometres. The !Kung are very aware of this, even though they cannot trace paths more than two or three links in either direction. They give no reason as to why gifts travel so far, 'they just get passed on'. Despite extensive questioning and tracing of items, I also could find no apparent reason for the length of hxaro paths. They do not systematically bring new goods into the area, nor do they create ties beyond those already discussed. However, hxaro networks may have developed out of previous trade networks, speculation that would have to be tested by archaeological research.

Gifts for hxaro

Gifts for hxaro can be any non-food items – beads, arrows, ostrich eggshells, clothing, blankets, bowls, pots, etc. They constitute the bulk of a !Kung's material wealth and there is no non-food item which does not enter the hxaro system. For the 59 !Kung in the sample, 69 per cent of a person's possessions were obtained through hxaro while the remaining 30 per cent were recently made or purchased by the owner, but destined for the hxaro network. Out of over 1,000 possessions of the !Kung in the sample, only four were 'begged' from others who were not hxaro partners. Thus, even though the !Kung say that they can not refuse to give a gift if asked, they also stress that such a situation would rarely arise – a person without the appropriate hxaro ties would not ask, except for a few individuals who ask for everything.

A gift is private property for as long as a person wishes to keep it. A gift is passed on within anywhere from two weeks to two years, and a person who wishes to keep a gift for more than a few months will replace it with another item so as not to disrupt the chain. An item critical to daily life will be kept until a replacement comes along. Women can receive and pass on gifts, normally made and used by men, like arrows, while men can receive and pass on women's aprons.

Hxaro exchange is always delayed and it would be an insult to return a gift immediately. A person either waits quietly for a return, or, may enjoy joking with a partner about a debt. Reviewing the partner's possessions, a person may express an interest in something in particular, thereby establishing a claim on it, if the object is not already on its way to another.

Hxaro gifts are surrounded by an air of appreciation and expectation partially because many are either very pretty or useful and the !Kung enjoy having new things, and partly because they are expressions of a social relationship. An appropriate hxaro gift should be generous, but not overly generous so that it would arouse jealousy in others or indicate that the giver felt he or she was a 'bigshot'. It is said to 'enter a person's heart so that the person knows that he or she is also held in giver's heart'. An inadequate gift, however, with no promise of more to come is an outward sign of tension in a friendship which is brought to the surface by an argument over the gift.

A person plays on the inherent worth of a gift to express affection and concern for a partner, getting as much mileage out of it as possible. For example, a person who gives another a blanket might say that he or she did so out of concern that 'the beloved partner might freeze to death in the winter', ignoring the fact that it is spring and the blanket will probably be in others' hands by winter or that the partner already has four blankets. In asking for a return, one person will not hesitate to remind the other of a most timely, useful, or pretty gift in the past, a way of showing that he or she still cares.

Gifts for hxaro are manufactured in a social context – when !Kung make gifts, they sit in a group, slowly working on their gifts while talking, laughing, putting down their work from time to time to illustrate a story with their hands, picking them up again, stretching them out, admiring them and then beginning work once more. Hxaro gifts are completed in a few weeks or even months. It is as if they grow in social value through conversation after conversation. Others can later recognize their maker and know how much care was put into an item. The work pace contrasts with that when making items to sell, when a person works alone, quickly and with concentration, annoyed at any disturbances. After receiving an item via a hxaro path, a person often alters it in some way before passing it on – repairs or makes a hole in it, restrings beads, carves a design on an arrow shaft, etc. – anything that adds a personal touch. For instance, as trade-store, knitted caps make their way along hxaro paths, they are unravelled and reknit into different patterns again and again.

Hxaro and the !Kung lifecycle

A !Kung child is brought into the system of reciprocity by receiving his or her first hxaro beads from a maternal or paternal grandmother between the age of six weeks and six months. Subsequently many people follow suit and give presents to the child. Their collective effort is believed to promote the child's well-being by showing that many people care and thus 'God shouldn't take him or her away.' Although these gifts require no return, sometimes the mother gives a return to certain people she feels might later make good hxaro partners for the child. She carries out hxaro with them in the child's name until the child takes an interest in hxaro and decides for itself whether to continue the relationship.

Symbolic training for hxaro begins between six months and one year, when the grandmother cuts off the child's beads, washes them and puts them in the child's hand to give to a relative. She then replaces them with new ones. From this point on, whether the child agrees or not, the parents or grandparents periodically cut off the child's beads and encourage the child to give them to a grandparent, aunt, uncle or another person who takes an interest in the child. The parents continue to do so until the child does hxaro of its own accord, generally between the ages of five and nine. Although proud mothers give long lists of partners for their children, the children either are not aware of these or take little interest in them, listing four to five hxaro partners as their cryptic hxaro partners ($x = 4.4$, s.d. $= 2.2$, $n = 14$). These are usually parents, grandparents or mature siblings but occasionally more distant relatives. Although, objectively, giving is unbalanced with these partners, the children see themselves as helping their hxaro partners 'a lot'. Children develop hxaro partnerships with their peers quite separately during play. It seems that hxaro partnerships formed in early childhood in an atmosphere of giving freely maintain tolerance for imbalance throughout life.

Between the ages of 10 to 14, 'adolescents' expand their sphere of hxaro to include others both in their camp and in other camps. This hxaro is done with guidance of their parents who help them fit into the

Table 3.1 *Summary statistics of hxaro partners by age category*

Age category	Number of San interviewed	Mean number of hxaro partners per person		Mean number of other areas of hxaro ties		Mean number of hxaro partners in each other area of hxaro	
		x	s.d.	x	s.d.	x	s.d.
Adolescents	6	10	4	1	1.1	1	1.8
Marriageable young adults	4	16	5	2.5	0.6	2.3	0.5
Adults with small children	27	13	7	2.9	3.7	2.4	1.7
Adults with mature children	14	24	8	3.6	1.5	4.4	2
Old partially dependent adults	8	12	6	2.3	1	2.0	1.8

overall hxaro network. Only hxaro between peers is done independently and often a group of adolescents in an area develops its own hxaro chains. Hxaro ties increase gradually in number during adolescence. By marriage, an average person has somewhere between 10 and 16 hxaro partnerships (see Table 3.1) making up the greater part of the partnerships he or she will have during the next twenty years. This well-distributed set of hxaro ties before marriage is most important to both men and women, for it means that, if the marriage breaks up, each person has enough ties to stand on his or her own and can return to his or her group as an adult in a secure position.

With marriage, a son's parents consider him or her a true hxaro partner, and obligations to all relatives become more serious. Still, relatives are lenient with newlyweds and will often help out a couple by giving gifts which they do not expect to be reciprocated for years. The biggest change in hxaro that comes with marriage is the link formed with affinal relatives. Before marriage, an adolescent's gifts were squeezed into already existing chains and backed by parents. After marriage, a large percentage of gifts are supposed to pass to the spouse, and on to the spouse's relatives, creating new paths. These paths cannot be broken without much strife and nobody else can compensate for a person's failure to reciprocate gifts from the spouse's relatives.

As a San's children reach maturity, he or she enters a stage of great vitality, mobility and social influence which lasts as long as good health holds. A person doubles his or her number of hxaro partners from a previous mean of 13 to one of 24 (see Table 3.1). After visiting other areas for years, a person has made many contacts and can expand in hxaro, because, without the burden of small children, he or she has 'more things to give'. In addition, it is at this stage of life that a person picks up many of his or her parents' contacts. Their expansion of hxaro is not surprising as it coincides with the time in which San are concerned with finding spouses for their children and helping them out while their grandchildren are young.

By the time !Kung become old and partially dependent, they have helped their children through their hardest years, and, with declining strength and mobility, are happy to pass on many of their hxaro partnerships to their children, whom they rely on for necessary support. As one old lady said, 'Just as a medicine man gives over his medicine to a younger man, so we give over our hxaro partners. We are too old, we don't want them anymore. What would we find to give?' An older !Kung does maintain lifelong partnerships and sometimes one or two of those of a deceased spouse, beginning new ones only with grandchildren. When a person dies, some possessions are buried with him or her, but most are passed on to remaining hxaro partners by children with a request for return so that the hxaro network will not be broken.

Distribution of hxaro partnerships

In choosing hxaro relationships, a !Kung is more concerned with obtaining a well-rounded set of partners than a few particularly promising ones. In doing this, a person will be assured of coming out ahead in some, equal in most and perhaps behind in still others, but the set of partners as a whole should be sufficient to cover all critical risks.

Close relatives are almost always hxaro partners and those more distantly related are chosen for their merits. Hxaro relationships 'activate' some of the many potential relationships of reciprocity in the society, allowing certain kin ties to be 'remembered' and others conveniently 'forgotten'.

A person selects hxaro partners first for their personal qualities and then for their location and abilities, disregarding age and sex. Personal qualities are most important because hxaro solidifies a bond of friendship and mutual help, and if two people are not compatible, the hxaro bond is quickly broken.

Location of hxaro partners is important since a key role of hxaro is to give an individual an alternative residence in another area. Table 3.2

Table 3.2 *Distribution of hxaro partners by area for /Xai/xai !Kung*

Area	KM from /Xai/xai	Number of hxaro partners in area	Percentage of hxaro partners in area	Important resources of area
Own camp	—	91	18	—
/Xai/xai area	5–25	123	24	Hunting, gathering, subsistence-labour, possibility to market handicrafts
Nyae Nyae-Due areas	10–40	44	9	Hunting, gathering, wage-labour, steady supply of meal and sugar to workers, transport to points west
N/umsi area	30–40	82	16	Hunting, gathering, store (rarely stocked), school seat of local government, wage-labour (cattle trekking) subsistence-labour, transport to points east.
/Gam area	50+	17	3	Hunting, gathering, some wage-labour??, transport to points west?
Tsumkwe area	75	102	21	Clinic, store, school, agricultural projects, wage-labour (50–80 jobs), assistance for sick and old, handicraft market.
Nxau Nxau area	100+	1	0 (0.002)	Hunting, gathering, subsistence-labour.
Farms in Namibia	150+	12	2	Wage-labour, subsistence-labour, store, clinic, school?, transport
Sehitwa farms	150+	26	5	Store, school, clinic, wage-labour, subsistence-labour with good returns, transport
Ghanzi farms	190+	12	2	Store, school, clinic, subsistence- and wage-labour.
TOTAL		510	100	

gives the distribution of hxaro partners of the 35 /Xai/xai !Kung in the sample by area and by distance. Partners within the camp are usually close relatives who 'back' relationships by integrating the visitor into their camp. Those in a person's own area always live within five kilometres of the /Xai/xai well during the dry season, but have separate wet season n!ores with different resources. These critical contacts serve to open up access to a wide range of resources nearby.

Outside of the /Xai/xai area, hxaro partnerships are more a function of areal quality than of distance. The majority of the partnerships of the /Xai/xai !Kung in the sample were with others residing at Tsumkwe, a settlement scheme in Namibia. Tsumkwe offers wage-labour, a store, a school, and a clinic. Those working there have an ample, steady income so that domestic food is available to support visitors during the dry season. But Tsumkwe has its problems as well. Frequent conflict arises from many !Kung living in one place with no formal method of settling disputes. Therefore many /Xai/xai residents prefer to visit Tsumkwe for only one short season of the year. The Tsumkwe area is favoured over the /Gam area which like /Xai/xai has excellent hunting and gathering, but few other alternatives – a bad year at /Xai/xai is likely to be a bad one at /Gam as well. More partners are found at Tsumkwe than in the Nyae Nyae-Due or N/umsi areas because even though the latter two areas are preferred for living, they cannot guarantee resources to support a huge number of visitors in the dry season.

Of the more distant areas, more than 100 km from /Xai/xai, Nxau Nxau is the closest, but the least desirable, as its resources overlap with those of the /Xai/xai and N/umsi areas. Hxaro partnerships are most common with !Kung to the east in the Sehitwa area, as many of the /Xai/xai !Kung's relatives have recently moved there. In summary, the !Kung in the sample have approximately 70 per cent of their partnerships in their own area and in adjacent ones up to 50 km away, and 30 per cent in more distant ones between 50 and 200 km away. Looking at profiles of hxaro for individual families, rather than for the sample as a whole, there are very few which do not have at least one partner between 150 and 200 km away in an area which is likely to have sufficient resources when /Xai/xai does not.

Age and sex of partners are less relevant than the resources a person has to share and the willingness of a person to welcome visitors and share with them. The proportion of partners in each age category is not significantly different from their occurrence in the population, except for adolescents who are not considered true partners until marriage. Of the 961 hxaro partners of 59 Dobe, /Xai/xai and Tsumkwe residents, 53 per cent of the men's 424 partners are men and 47 per cent women, while 44 per cent of the women's 537 partnerships are men and 56 per cent other women. Some women express a slight preference for hxaro with other women because of a common interest in beadwork. Women have an average of 14.6 hxaro partnerships (s.d. = 7.7, n = 34), and men an average of 17.0 (s.d. = 9, n = 27). The difference is not statistically significant at the 0.05 level, but may be real today when young men are more mobile seeking wage-labour.

Through hxaro, risk is distributed so that, in the case of environmental failure, each family has its own alternatives. Thus the entire population of one area does not descend on any one other area, requiring that the resources be so widely shared that they will be of little use to anybody. A period of environmental failure in 1974 provided an excellent example of how the hxaro system works (Wiessner 1977). At that time, high winds had destroyed most of the mongongo nut crop in groves around /Xai/xai. Because of exceptionally heavy rainfall, game was scattered and gathering and snaring were difficult in the unusually high grasses. Plagues of insects and cattle disease made domestic foods scarce. By August, work effort had decreased as the !Kung said that there was nothing worth hunting or gathering. People spent much time sitting around, talking, making hxaro gifts and handicrafts, and eagerly gathering information about conditions in other areas from those who passed through /Xai/xai. Sharing broke down and those who found something to eat consumed it discreetly, as they knew there were too many others who would try to claim a share. By mid-September, families began to leave to visit relatives in other areas, 'because they missed them and wanted to do hxaro with them'. Within two weeks, 48 per cent of the population of /Xai/xai had scattered to the four winds, relieving the pressure on those who did remain.

Finally, through hxaro, means of reducing risk is effectively reproduced from generation to generation. Hxaro relationships are passed on in a family in a way which permits those who reciprocated well to be continued and those who did not to be quietly dropped and forgotten and still new ones added to meet changing needs.

The effect of hxaro on !Kung economics

Having argued that hxaro is a structured means of pooling risk – one of many possible ways of doing so – I will now return to the second point made at the beginning of this paper – that hxaro has its own effect on !Kung economics, one that cannot be predicted from environmental variables alone. As a thorough discussion of the effect of hxaro on !Kung life is beyond the scope of this paper, I will briefly discuss how hxaro affects work effort and division of wealth.

Lee (1969) has shown that the Dobe !Kung enjoy a relatively short work-week of 12–15 hours. Other !Kung in areas with different resources have a slightly longer one (Marshall 1976) but, nonetheless, Lee's point holds – the !Kung do not spend nearly as much time as they could in the food quest. Today, with the introduction of wage-labour and opportunities to purchase highly desired items, the !Kung continue to choose a work strategy which allows them ample 'leisure' time. If the environment had a strong determining influence on the economy, as is frequently hypothesized, then one would expect to find some limiting environmental factor which makes the !Kung 'underproductive'. For instance, a recent analysis of Lee's data by Blurton Jones and Sibly (1978) has shown that the average birth spacing of four years for the Dobe !Kung, in combination with a tempo of gathering one out of every two to three days, is optimal for an individual's reproductive success. However, they point out that their analysis does not explain why women do not gather more nuts at the end of the wet season and store them for the dry season, why the men do not help more with gathering when they are not hunting and so on. More detailed ecological studies may come up with an answer as to why the !Kung enjoy so much leisure all year round, but I doubt it. Instead, I argue that the limits on time the !Kung put into the food quest is partially the result of people preventing themselves from being exploited in their relationships of reciprocity, and is partially due to the amount of time put into the 'business of hxaro'.

First of all, it must be emphasized that, just because only 12–15 hours a week are put into procuring and preparing food, the remaining hours are not necessarily ones of leisure. Many hours are put into maintaining critical social relations. Participating adequately in hxaro involves taking the time to make or remake gifts (some pieces of beadwork take three to seven days of concentrated work), gathering information about who has and who is in need, and finally making sure that one gets one's fair share of goods and resources. Showing interest in a relationship involves collecting, as much as it does giving. The !Kung say that a person must make a debtor want to reciprocate. Thus, studies measuring how much time is spent in the food quest yield a short week, but if the hours spent in the business of social relations are added to these, a 14-hour work-week can quickly become a 40-hour one.

Secondly, in reciprocal relations, one means that a person uses to prevent being exploited, in a relationship whose terms are merely that the one who has gives to the one who needs, is to prevent him or herself from becoming a 'have' more than his or her share of the time. As mentioned earlier, men who have killed a number of large animals sit back for a pause to enjoy reciprocation. Women gather enough for their families for a few days, but rarely more. Those working for wages in Namibia today hold their jobs for a few months or even a few years, supporting others with their income, but eventually quit work and take time to sit back and 'rest' and let others support them.

And so, in deciding whether or not to work on a certain day, a !Kung may assess debts and debtors, decide how much wild-food harvest will go to family, close relatives and others to whom he or she really wants to reciprocate, versus how much will be claimed by freeloaders. A person may consider whether the extra effort is worthwhile, or if time would be better spent gathering more information about the status of partners and trying to collect from one of them. In the latter case, people will reduce their work effort and either enjoy their leisure time or put more effort into evaluating and reaffirming social relations. Limiting work effort over the long run can result in bringing in a lower-than-possible mean income in exchange for reaffirming a strong hold in social relations necessary for reducing the variance around the mean. Such a mean-variance contradiction would be less likely to occur in a society which depends primarily on private storage to reduce risk. There, an increase in work effort could at once secure a higher mean income with a lower variance.

Distribution of wealth, like work effort, is strongly influenced by hxaro. Today, even though !Kung families in one community make a living in a variety of ways, some having a cash income and others not, 'wealth' is still remarkably evenly distributed. 'Wealth' here is measured by number of possessions, since every person inherits rights to one or two n!ores. It might be added that number of possessions also closely reflects number of hxaro partners – 75 per cent of the variation in number of possessions can be accounted for by number of hxaro partners. Table 3.3 shows the number of possessions by category for each of 14 households in three camps at /Xai/xai. Comparison of number of possessions poses a problem as the !Kung have no set standards of equivalence. To avoid attaching meaningless monetary values to each item, a household's possessions are put into one of six categories – beadwork, clothing, blankets, hunting-gathering equipment, kitchen-ware and livestock. These categories are very general and contain goods of varying quality – store-bought and handmade goods, traditional and non-traditional goods, etc. – nonetheless, they should give the reader some approximate idea of the distribution of goods among !Kung households.

As can be seen in Table 3.3, differences in number of possessions among individual households in Camps A and F are minimal. Some of the small differences which do exist can be the result of making a survey at one point in time when some household may have many debts and others many debtors. The residents of both camps have a more tradi-tional life-style than those of other camps at /Xai/xai such as Camp B, whose members regularly engage in wage-labour, sale of crafts and some agriculture, thereby having much higher cash income. Members of Camp B have roughly twice as many items of clothing and blankets as those of A and F and four times as many head of livestock, but similar amounts of beadwork, hunting–gathering equipment and kitchenware. How-ever, Camp B had recently received many visitors from Tsumkwe, the settlement scheme in Namibia, and many items of clothing and blan-kets were recent gifts. Later these will probably filter out to the rest of the surrounding population.

Table 3.3 shows that many households have more possessions than they can carry (for example six heavy blankets!) and yet still spend four to eight months a year either at other sites in the bush or visiting other areas. When away, they either give away many possessions before leav-ing or, more frequently, store them with friends until their return. Mobility seems to be a deterrent to accumulating possessions only for members of Camp A who express a desire not to get used to sleeping with more blankets than they can carry into the bush. The most com-mon explanation given by a !Kung today for having a high cash income and an average amount of possessions is that 'my people kill me for things', in other words, my partners in reciprocity are merciless about asking for gifts. Even though exchange of hxaro gifts is supposed to be roughly equal, if one family has much more than others, demands on them increase and they are expected to be more generous than those who have less. (The exceptional case of livestock will be discussed below.)

It cannot be argued today for /Xai/xai residents that 'wealth is a bur-den' (Sahlins 1968), nor can it be argued that !Kung have little interest

Table 3.3 *Possessions of /Xai/xai and residents*

	Camp A							Camp F						Camp B					
Age category[a]	3	3	4	5	5	x	s.d.	3	3	4	5	x	s.d.	3	3	4	4	x	s.d.
I.D. no. of adult members of household	367 368	557 572	324 330	333 511	329[b]			536 103	404 405	563 534	429 406			518 519	188 341	520 521	512 513		
Items																			
Beadwork	13	11	17	12	12	13	2.4	15	15	15	8	13.3	3.5	11	11	26	12	15	7.4
Clothing	10	5	7	6	6	6.8	1.9	9	8	8	6	7.8	1.3	17	20	13	18	17	2.9
Blankets	2	3	2	2	2	2.2	0.5	4	5	2	4	3.8	1.3	4	6	6	2	4.5	1.9
Hunting and gathering equipment	4	6	4	4	3	4.2	1.1	3	3	8	2	4	2.7	0	2	3	9	3.5	3.9
Kitchenware	10	10	10	9	9	9.6	0.6	8	9	11	8	9	1.4	6	9	21	15	12.8	6.7
Livestock	3	0	0	0	0	0.6	1.3	3	2	0	0	1.3	1.5	3	4	9	4	4.3	3.4

[a] Age category 3 = adults with young children; 4 = adults with mature children; 5 = old, partially dependent adults.
[b] Possessions of 329 were multiplied by 150% to make them equivalent to those in a household with two adult members.

in material possessions. Most possessions, from traditional ostrich egg-shell beads, to shoes, to watches, are highly desired; and many !Kung are really torn between the desire to accumulate goods and the desire to remain within a secure system of mutual help. It is not uncommon to see a person work hard for a while, accumulate goods, come under more and more pressure to give them away in hxaro, and finally give in and redistribute them. The person inevitably gives in (or moves away for work), partially because risk is high and he or she needs to remain within the reciprocity system, and partially because the ideology of generosity and equality is such a strong force in !Kung life. A person who has been stingy for too long feels miserable. There are a few items that can bridge this conflict, like record-players which a person can keep while sharing the music.

The above discussion does not imply that a system like hxaro holds the !Kung society static and impervious to change. Quite the opposite. Today, as new opportunities and priorities are introduced with change, the !Kung are restructuring their means of confronting risk. As some /Xai/xai !Kung begin to engage in agriculture, storage is beginning to play a role in reducing risk. In the recent past when the !Kung first acquired some livestock, they would slaughter them so that the meat could be distributed. Today, livestock has moved out of the system of reciprocity and become an asset like the land. A person can own several cows (see Table 3.3) if milk is shared, can own donkeys if they are lent to others, or if the large nut harvest which can be carried in by donkeys is shared. Some !Kung are now regularly and successfully planting crops and do not meet with social disapproval if they do not share their harvest widely, as long as they maintain their reciprocal obligations in other ways. Thus, more items have moved into the realm of private property and storage exists side by side with hxaro as a means of reducing risk.

At Tsumkwe, the settlement scheme in Namibia, hxaro seems to be undergoing another transformation. Until 1976, the primary source of income for Tsumkwe residents was either welfare or wage-labour. The central problems that face the !Kung living there are insecurity of jobs and serious conflicts arising from many people living in one place with no formal mediation to settle differences. Consequently, many San maintain regular hxaro with relatives in Botswana to keep up alternate residences in times of conflict or unemployment. However, within Tsumkwe itself, the hxaro system appears to be developing into one in which people exchange gifts to smooth over relations rather than to gain access to goods and resources. The number of hxaro partnerships within the area has greatly increased among those frequently employed, who can not just pack up and leave in times of conflict. The flow of gifts between Tsumkwe residents is very intense, and, even though the residents have the cash and available store to purchase their own goods, 65 per cent of the possessions of Tsumkwe residents included in the sample had been received through hxaro. A person does not buy himself a blanket, but rather buys one, gives it to a partner and eventually will receive one in return. It is intriguing to think that hxaro may have changed from a trade network in the past, to a system for giving !Kung access to each others' goods, resources and assistance, and today is undergoing still another transformation at Tsumkwe to a gift exchange which smooths over social conflicts.

As change continues, hxaro, a system which has offered the !Kung security and leisure for generations, will probably continue to operate in more-and-more-limited spheres as the !Kung reorganize to take advantage of new opportunities. As this happens, so will its effects on other spheres of !Kung life be diminished.

Acknowledgements

I would like to thank all of the !Kung San who took the time patiently to discuss hxaro and regret my inability to reciprocate adequately. I am also grateful to the Office of the President and Ministry of Local Government and Lands in Botswana for being most helpful as well as continually extending my research permit.

The research for this paper was funded by the Ford Foundation and the Max Planck Institut für Humanetheologie, Seewiesen, W. Germany.

Notes

1 For excellent descriptions of the !Kung in these areas see Lee (1969, 1972), Lee and DeVore (1976) and Marshall (1976).
2 This paper is primarily based on discussions with 59 !Kung San adults and 14 children about hxaro in 1974–5. This sample consists of all cooperative members and visitors of three randomly chosen camps at /Xai/xai, and 14 more individuals selected from their lists of hxaro partners to cross-check the information. Each person was asked about how hxaro operates, how he or she feels about giving and receiving, balance in partnerships, etc. as well as to list each hxaro partner and give their age, sex, location, area of landrights, genealogical relation to ego, kin relation to ego, and intensity of relationship between the two. This information was then supplemented by taking a tally of each person's possessions and determining their origins. The data yielded information on 955 partnerships and 1483 possessions. Data on partnerships were checked again on a return trip in 1977 when people were asked to list

84   Polly Wiessner

their hxaro partners once more. The two lists were remarkably comparable with only a few alterations. For a more detailed analysis of the data see Wiessner (1977).

3 Here it is difficult to separate cause from effect – hxaro with close relatives in a camp usually marks a relationship of many years of friendship and mutual assistance while that with !Kung in other camps places specific obligations within a population of potential partners.

Bibliography

Blurton Jones, N. G., and Sibly, R. M. 1978. 'Testing adaptiveness of culturally determined behavior: do Bushmen women maximize their reproductive success by spacing births widely and foraging seldom?', in V. Reynolds and N. Blurton Jones (eds.), *Human behavior and adaptation*, 135–57. Symposium No. 18, Society for Study of Human Biology. London: Taylor and Francis

Howell, Nancy 1979. *Demography of the Dobe !Kung*. New York: Academic Press

Lee, R. B. 1969. '!Kung Bushman subsistence; an input–output analysis', in A. P. Vayda (ed.), *Environment and cultural behavior*, 47–79. New York: Natural History Press

1972. 'The !Kung Bushmen of Botswana', in M. Bicchieri (ed.), *Hunters and gatherers today*, 327–68. New York: Holt, Rinehart and Winston

1976. '!Kung spatial organization: an ecological and historical perspective', in R. B. Lee and I. DeVore (eds.), *Kalahari hunter-gatherers*, 73–97. Cambridge, Mass.: Harvard University Press

1978. 'Issues in the study of hunter-gatherers, 1968–1978'. Paper presented at the International Conference on Hunter-gatherers, Paris, June 1978

Lee, R. B., and DeVore, I. (eds.) 1976. *Kalahari hunter-gatherers*. Cambridge, Mass.: Harvard University Press

Marshall, Lorna 1976. *The !Kung of Nyae Nyae*. Cambridge: Harvard University Press

Sahlins, M. D. 1968. 'Notes on the original affluent society', in R. B. Lee and I. DeVore (eds.), *Man the hunter*, 85–9. Chicago: Aldine Publishing Company

1972. *Stone age economics*. Chicago: Aldine Publishing Company

Truswell, A. S., and Hansen, J. D. L. 1976. 'Medical research among the !Kung', in R. B. Lee and I. DeVore (eds.), *Kalahari hunter-gatherers*, 166–94. Cambridge, Mass.: Harvard University Press

Wiessner, Polly 1977. *Hxaro: a regional system of reciprocity for reducing risk among the !Kung San*. Ph.D. dissertation, University of Michigan. Ann Arbor: University Microfilms

Wilmsen, E. N. 1978. 'Seasonal effects of dietary intake on Kalahari San'. *Anthropology and the assessment of nutritional status, Federation Proceedings*, 37, 1

Yellen, J. E., and Lee, R. B. 1976. 'The Dobe–/Du/da environment: background to a hunting and gathering way of life', in R. B. Lee and I. DeVore (eds.), *Kalahari hunter-gatherers*, 1–46. Cambridge, Mass.: Harvard University Press

4. Descended from father, belonging to country: rights to land in the Australian Western Desert[1]

ANNETTE HAMILTON

In the many debates over allocation of people to land among hunters and gatherers, the Australian evidence has repeatedly been seen as problematic. Lee (1978) has already suggested the outlines of this debate, between proponents of the patrilineal territorial band and those of the flexibly organized bilateral band. He suggests that the 'patrilineal theorists . . . seek to impose an Australian model of clans on the rest of the world'. The purpose of the present paper is to show that the imposition of an Australian model of clans is by no means a *fait accompli* in certain parts of Australia itself, and that the anthropologists' theorizing (fetishing?) at the ideological level mirrors the efforts of Aborigines in certain areas to construct and impose a coherent theory of patrilineal inheritance to sites and to establish patrivirilocally organized local groups, at least at their own ideological level. Why this should be so, and the problems that stand in their way, form the main focus of this discussion.

Without wishing to bore everyone with the outlines of this debate yet again, it might be worthwhile to go back to Stanner's paper, 'Aboriginal territorial organization: estate, range, domain and regime' (1965). Stanner, replying to Hiatt's criticism of Radcliffe-Brown (Hiatt 1962), claimed that what Radcliffe-Brown had presented was an 'ideal-type' model. In spite of the Weberian overtones, we might note that this view is closer to that of Lévi-Strauss, who has repeatedly stressed that the proper concerns of anthropology are with the fundamental structures beneath the superficial distortions and apparent contradictions to be found at the level of mere empirical reality, or even in the 'native model' of reality (Lévi-Strauss 1963:281; 1968:350). He considers that observable phenomena, such as real 'hordes', are at best 'a series of expressions, each partial and incomplete, of the same underlying structure, which they reproduce in several copies without ever completely exhausting its reality' (Lévi-Strauss 1963:130). Notwithstanding the possible implications of this, the Hiatt–Stanner debate led to a crucial clarification – that is, the necessity to maintain a clear distinction between economic and ritual relationships to land – so that instead of a horde there is both a ritual group and an economic group. Stanner says:

> The evidence allows us to say that each territorial group was associated with both an *estate* and a *range*. The estate was the traditionally recognized locus . . . of some kind of patrilineal descent group forming the core or nucleus of the territorial group . . . The range was the tract or orbit over which the group, including its nucleus and adherents, ordinarily hunted and foraged to maintain life. The range normally included the estate . . . Estate and range together may be said to have constituted a domain, which was an ecological life space.
>
> (Stanner 1965:2)

Here Stanner has (a) described the patrilineal descent group as a 'nucleus' with adherents – so the horde now is no longer composed exclusively of clan agnates and their wives and children – and (b) shown that this reconstructed 'horde' uses land over and above that to which its patrilineal nucleus is exclusively connected.

Stanner's distinction between estate and range is apparently a distinction between the 'religious' and the 'economic' systems. The estate is defined by virtue of 'spiritual' ties between individuals and certain places in the landscape, whereas the 'range' is defined by the hunting and foraging activities of people in the landscape. The 'clan', that is, a group of people linked by agnatic ties, is the effective 'owner' of the estate. The 'horde' however does not own anything, but merely utilizes the products of a number of estates (as well as the territory in between estates, which may be only hazily defined as 'owned' in the religious sense, if at all). Analytically, the two domains are quite distinct. A concept analogous to 'property' may be applied to the religious sphere, but there is no equivalent concept in the 'economic' sphere. If we assume that products of the land are the basic 'means of production', we would appear to have arrived at the conclusion that Aboriginal society lacks any form of economic ownership of the means of production. This would seem to go beyond anything which Marx envisaged as 'primitive communism'.

Marx tended to view all societies which lacked heritable private property as cases of primitive communism, although he himself preferred the term 'tribal ownership' to the other usage, favoured by Engels (Marx and Engels 1973, 1:21; Engels 1973a, 2:401). He included all cases where

A contemporary Western Desert Aboriginal camp in South Australia (P. Hamilton)

'a people live by hunting and fishing, by the rearing of cattle or, in the highest stages, agriculture . . . The social structure is, therefore, limited to an extension of the family: patriarchal family chieftains, below them the members of the tribe, finally slaves' (Marx and Engels *ibid*). Engels included 'the German mark, the Celtic clan, and the Indian', as well as the Roman village, as communities with a 'primitive communistic order' (Engels *ibid*.) While the absence of individually held private property in these instances contrasts clearly with property-ownership under capitalism, from an anthropological perspective it lumps together forms of society which exhibit marked levels of internal differentiation and an extraordinary variety of forms of possession of property. The same tradition has been continued by Hindess and Hirst, in their recent reappraisal of pre-capitalist modes of production (Hindess and Hirst 1975). Without examining the implications of their theory here, it is necessary to note that, rather than looking at the ownership of property (or the means of production), they instead 'define primitive communism as a mode of production governed by a mode of communal appropriation of surplus labour' (Hindess and Hirst 1975: 22). Wherever the appropriation of surplus labour is collective, 'there are therefore no classes, no state and no political level' (*ibid*:27). All other modes of production involve non-collective appropriation of surplus labour, and a class of non-labourers. Hindess and Hirst, therefore, group together a number of 'archaic' societies, which would include both hunters and gatherers, and a number of horticulturalists. Admittedly they further subdivide primitive communism according to whether or not redistribution can be classed as 'simple or complex' (ibid:44ff.), but that also fails to distinguish along the lines which are at issue here.

The theoretical reasons for adopting these views of pre-state societies seem compelling when viewed from the contrasting perspective of modern capitalism. But to lump together all pre-state formations as cases of primitive communism is to obscure differences between them. If these differences cannot be derived from the concept 'mode of production' then we are left to conclude that they originate in the realm of the idea, and are the product of purely mental activities.

> For instance, if an epoch imagines itself to be actuated by purely 'political' or 'religious' motives, although 'religion' and 'politics' are only forms of its true motives, the historian accepts this opinion. The 'idea', the 'conception' of the people in question about their real practice, is transformed into the sole determining active force, which controls and determines their practice.   (Marx and Engels 1973, 1:43)

Marx and Engels show how German ideology is replete with the illusion that 'pure spirit', 'thought', 'consciousness', is the driving force of history. 'This conception is truly religious: it postulates religious man as the primitive man, the starting point of history; and in its imagination puts the religious production of fancies in the place of the real production of the means of subsistence and of life itself' (ibid:44).

This approach is apparent in Australian Aboriginal anthropology. Elkin, for instance, writes: 'The most important aspect of the local group, however, is spiritual in nature . . . From one point of view, the members who belong to the local group by birth own their subdivision of the tribal territory. But it is truer to say that the country owns them and that they cannot remain away from it indefinitely and still live. The point is, the Aborigines hold the doctrine of the pre-existence of spirits' (Elkin 1970:79). More recently, Maddock (1974:27) makes similar statements: 'Aborigines regard land as a religious phenomenon . . . The tie between men and land is taken back to the Dreaming . . . The Aboriginal theory is thus that rights to land have to do with the design of the world, not with alienable legal title . . . It would be as correct to speak of the land possessing men as of men possessing land.' Maddock recognizes the difficulties of reconciling this view with an 'economic' one:

'whether this is properly to be called ownership is debatable, for if there are owners there is nothing they can alienate'.

At one level, then, it would seem that Aboriginal society had no concept of economic ownership of land, although it would seem to have had the notion of inalienable spiritual connection between persons and particular pieces of land. Therefore it should be possible to say that all Aborigines had equal access to the means of production.[2] Strehlow would seem to agree.

> Here, then, was a land where men and women in a sense lived in those ideal communities envisaged by Karl Marx . . . where there were no social classes or castes, and where men could not be tyrannized by well organized central governments . . . Since the land rights of all tribal units and, where they existed in the Aranda form, even those of the local *njinanga section* areas were believed to have been laid down for all time by the supernatural beings, no organized wars of aggression or territorial conquest were possible in Central Australia. (Strehlow 1970:130)

And yet, while the literature frequently mentions the sharing of natural resources by people in one area with people from another, there is also mention of a rigidly possessive attitude towards one's own country and the refusal to share resources with non-kin, and even instances of armed conflicts over resources. For example, Meggitt gives an account of such a conflict between the Waringari and the Walbiri: 'the Waringari had claimed the ownership of the few native wells at Tanami and the country surrounding them, but in a pitched battle for the possession of the water the Walbiri drove the Waringari from the area which they incorporated into their own territory. By desert standards, the engagement was spectacular, the dead on either side numbering a score or more' (Meggitt 1962:42). Another example from the eastern part of the Western Desert itself concerns a massacre of the original inhabitants of Mount Chandler, overlooking Indulkana, for the rights to water in that area (Tindale 1974:10). Isobel White (personal communication) reports that the grandfathers of the oldest inhabitants of Indulkana in 1966 had told them about it, which suggests that it occurred in the 1880s.

Tindale has consistently stressed the point that areas of land were 'owned' and were inviolable except by specific permission to enter. 'Larger disputes often involved the defence of territories or their usurpation, and the taking of women. Occasional instances of all-out attack on a tribe of people and the usurpation of a tribal area by members of another tribe are matters of history. In some instances drought has been the impelling force and lack of immediate associations or contact the spur' (1974:33). He quotes (1974:77–8) a number of early observers, in diverse regions, such as Teichelmann (1841), J. D. Lang (1861), Gray (1878), Palmer (1884), all of whom indicate that 'tribal' areas are defined and subject to laws of trespass. It is clear however that these instances are concerned with 'tribal' areas, rather than the smaller segments ('clan estates', 'ranges') discussed earlier. Tindale views these 'tribal' arrangements as primarily economic. Discussing the temporary lapsing of territorial exclusivity when a particularly abundant resource was available, he says: 'The occurrence of such temporary abrogations of territorial rule in tribal distributions emphasizes the point that one of the principal factors determining the existence of tribal boundaries is economic. The ability [sic] of the tribal group, speaking a common language . . . enables it to arrange the distribution of land-use rights among its members, either as family or hordal units, so that they can . . . maintain themselves for the whole cycle of the year' (1974:80). Without considering how such land-use rights might be allocated by the tribal group, this leads us to conclude that 'the tribe' exercized economic rights over the land it occupied, while rights within it were held communally by the tribespeople and access to its products was held in common by all of its members. We have now reached a point where Marx's definitions of primitive communism would seem to apply.

Yet the fact remains that some notion of 'ownership' or exclusive possession over certain segments of tribal land by specific persons must be acknowledged, even if this cannot be considered by us to be 'economic' in character. For example, rights over sacred sites are owned by certain specified men; access to them is forbidden to all women, uninitiated men, and children, as well as to men who own other unconnected, sacred sites, except on specified occasions. These might be classed as 'religious' in character, and not 'economic', following Marx. But let us for a moment see these relationships not in Western European terms, as pertaining to two entirely separate domains, the one of which is based in reality (i.e. material) and the other in fantasy (i.e. religion), but from the perspective of the Aborigines themselves. At once the distinction is dissolved. The apparently non-economic aspect of the man–land relationship is only so to us: to the Central Desert Aborigines it is highly, almost entirely, economic; for it is by access to these pieces of land, these sacred sites, that the reproduction of species is controlled. Strehlow's account of this is excellent:

each Aranda local group was believed to perform an indispensable economic service not only for itself but for the population around its borders as well . . . the religious acts performed by the totemic clan members of all the inland tribes at their respective totemic centres were regarded as being indispensable for the continuation of all human, animal and plant life in Central Australia.

(Strehlow 1970:102–3)

The literal interpretation which Aborigines put on these powers of production is apparent from one of Strehlow's informants:

The Ilbalintja men are always taking and boasting about their bandicoot (*gura*) ceremonies. But their ceremonies are utterly useless. Euros are to be found everywhere, and it is we who created them. The bandicoots have vanished long ago. Even we old men can remember eating bandicoot meat only when we were still mere boys. Where they have gone to since, I do not know.   (Strehlow 1970:103)

The powers of a specific group of men to control the reproduction of a species, through their access to a sacred site and its associated paraphernalia, does not confer any advantages to them exclusively; indeed it is conceptualized as being for the advantage of all Aborigines in the area. But not everyone can so act, for no women can ever do so, and only those men who have fully conformed to the demands of the elders can hope to join them. We have chosen to call this 'religion', and yet the truly 'economic' nature of their religious action is apparent to Aborigines: why else do they use the English term 'business' for their ceremonial activities, and why else do they consider their entire structure of 'religious' belief 'the Law'? 'At a certain, very primitive state of the development of society, the need arises . . . to see to it that the individual subordinates himself to the common conditions of production and exchange. This rule, which at first is custom, soon becomes *law*' (Engels 1973, 2:365).

So within the Aboriginal perspective 'religious' property has an aspect of 'economic' property, since reproduction of species is held to depend on human actions over certain objects, jealously guarded and kept from all but their owners, at certain places from which all but the owners are excluded. What then is the nature of these human actions? Here we encounter one of the paradoxes of Central Australian Aboriginal society, for those who perform the actions are at one and the same time the 'owners' and the 'workers';[3] they themselves must perform the necessary actions, often using their own body products (blood, semen) from which procedures they would appear to obtain no exclusive benefit, but by virtue of which the entire Aboriginal community will gain a livelihood.[4]

In many Aboriginal languages (e.g. Bidjandjara)[5] there is no indigenous term for 'work', but the English word is used to refer to two activities only, copulation and ceremonial participation. Thus, in Aboriginal thought, the powers of production and reproduction are not held to reside in the 'real' world of material reality but in the 'religious' realm (which is, to them, no opposition at all). And so it follows that whatever ideas of property, exclusivity and control over productive forces are to be found in this society, will be found in the 'religious' rather than the 'economic' sphere, or in the interaction between them. Are we then, in reaching this conclusion, ignoring Marx and Engels, who were so vehement about the necessity to search for the well-springs of an epoch in its purely material aspects? I argue that although religious manipulations are themselves mystifications – that is, that rain would fall, plants grow, and animals be born, without the intervention of humans – nonetheless it is in the religious realm that changes in technology, articulation of man–land relationships and the elaboration of systems of exchange first come into existence, and are thereafter developed. I am arguing that it is in the sphere of the 'religious' that the first hints of truly 'economic' differentiation are to be found.

If this is true, then it becomes all the more crucial to ask, how do men come to have access to the 'religious' sector of production? In particular, how do men come to have access to sacred sites and to the symbolic acts which mediate their powers? I will return now to the eastern sector of the Western Desert, and examine in detail the situation in this area.

Traditional local organization in the Western Desert

The area of the Everard Ranges and its immediate surroundings is in the literature described as being part of Janggundjara country. Janggundjara is closely allied to Bidjandjara and, while a detailed discussion of the meanings and referents of these terms will occur below, it must be noted that these are names of dialectical variants of a single language which is spread right across the south-central portion of Australia, to the edges of Aranda and Walbiri country in the north east, to the Dieri in the south east, to the borders of the Bight in the south, and to the coastal tribes of Western Australia in the west. This language, nameless to the Aborigines, has been called various terms, among the best known being Kukatja and Luritcha or Loritja, a derogatory term used by the Aranda for their unsophisticated neighbours. Across this whole area there is a general continuity of language and cultural forms, including religious and ceremonial life. But there are also differences, the most striking being the absence in the furthest eastern areas of exogamous moieties or any form of the section system. The four-section system has been diffusing across the desert rapidly, and in 1970–1 had reached Amata Settlement where it was being utilized in ritual organization but seemed otherwise little understood (notably, not understood by women). Elkin (1938:40) has given an extensive account of kinship in South Australia, and has documented the passage of the section system and the necessary adjustments which different groups have made to it. It is of interest that even in 1930 local organization in this whole region was extremely difficult to describe. Elkin, like others, put this difficulty down to 'migration'.

> As I see it, the movement of the groups has been constantly from the (Musgrave and Everard and other) central ranges to the south . . . Under pressure of droughts and at best constant desert conditions the groups pressed towards the south, seldom if ever to return, lengthening the mythological tracks and cutting themselves off from the spread of new forms of social and kinship organization and terminology. Thus, there was not much intermarrying, and there was relative isolation.

In a footnote he adds:

> This constant migration too explains the difficulty of defining tribal boundaries in this desert region, for life was in a state of flux.
>
> (Elkin 1940:305)

Elkin implies that at least part of the motivation for such movement was indigenous, rather than solely the result of white contact.

Many other writers have commented on the confusing question of tribal boundaries and dialectical units in the Western Desert. (See especially Tindale 1972; Berndt and Berndt 1945.)

Nonetheless, all these writers imply that boundaries did indeed exist, and could at some time in the past have been fixed, but owing to movements of population such boundaries cannot now be established with any certainty. The difficulties of dealing with local organization in this area were discussed also by Yengoyan. 'The reconstruction of pre-contact local organization was the most frustrating phase of the overall study. Since local organization as manifest prior to European contact, is no longer functioning, data on this aspect were collected from the living memory of tribal elders. The exact composition of local groups could not be determined' (Yengoyan 1970:81–2).

Without wishing in any way to minimize the disruptive effects of white contact, the fact remains that other writers have been able to give accounts of local organization in other areas, all of which have been affected by white contact (see the discussion in Lee and DeVore 1968:147, 211). Such accounts may offer problems of interpretation, and be difficult to reconcile to one particular model, but accounts they are, in many cases detailed and exhaustive. Probably the best example is T. G. H. Strehlow's (1965) account of the 'Njinanga' section areas, but Meggitt (1962), Falkenberg (1962) and Hiatt (1965) as well as many earlier writers have, primarily from information gained from older informants and a bit of on-the-ground mapping, been able to reconstruct at least a plausible account. Yet, for the most part, writers on the Western Desert culture area have been hard put to offer any coherent ethnographic account of territorial organization at either the 'tribal' or the 'local group' level. This is to say, various writers have discussed theoretically the nature of tribal groupings, and the nature of smaller component groups, but have found it difficult to anchor these to any particular territorial space in reality, in terms which outline the area under discussion and specify which people actually have rights of what kinds over the area, or even which people actually lived there.

The sole exception to this is Tindale, who has held to a Radcliffe-Brownian model consistently. In 1972 he described and mapped the traditional and post-1915 territories of the Bidjandjara. He then said that

> the whole population of the Pitjantjara is divided into a series of smaller groups with patrilineal descent. These groups are called clans, the basis of their clan organization is a ceremonial one and is linked with a patrilineal and patrilocal inheritance of the totem of a particular locality, an inheritance shared by all men who are directly descended from a common ancestor.   (Tindale 1972:223)

The normal living unit or local group likely to be found exploiting the area around an important totemic locality is a different one than the clan and is to be known as a horde. It tends to be composed of male members of the clan minus the older girls and women who have been sent away as wives to other clans, but plus the girls and women who have been brought in as brides for local clansmen. To these persons may be added a few casual visitors and some odd persons who for one reason or another have become attached to the local group from other clans. Such persons through the passing of time may become a part of it.   (Tindale 1972:224)

This neat picture however cannot be substantiated in reality. 'The obtaining of accurate information on the number of such hordes present among the Pitjantjara has been difficult . . .' He estimates that there were some 30 hordal groupings and the 'remants of several less successful family lines' (*ibid.*). 'Pitjantjara tribespeople recognize five named regional units, which are separate and tend to live in different parts of their whole territory' (228). But he adds, 'It must not be considered that these are true sub-tribal groupings. Rather, they are generalized names associated with smaller regional groups within the whole tribal area' (*ibid.*).

I think Tindale has experienced as much difficulty in giving a coherent account of local organization in the Western Desert as anyone. Let us turn then to Strehlow and Berndt, who have both considered this problem.

Strehlow (1965, 1970) in contrasting the apparently rigid man–land relationship among the Aranda with that found in the Western Desert, has characterized the area as one of 'loose structure'. He points out that these groups among whom he includes the Matuntara, Andekerinja, Jankuntjatjara, Pitjantjara and Pintubi, originally had no subsection systems: 'they completely lacked the main structural element of the Aranda local-group organization – its *land-based* kin-group class system. According to Yengoyan the introduction into these tribes of subsection systems superficially resembling the Aranda-type class system in recent decades has not been able to do anything to rehabilitate the local groups' (Strehlow 1970:100). One might well dispute the relevance of 'rehabilitation' in this context, but Strehlow has pointed to a fundamental feature of Western Desert organization, which has tremendous significance for the understanding of many aspects of social organization in the area.

Berndt's contribution is of a different order. He challenges the applicability of the concept of 'tribe' throughout this area, and musters much data to support an alternative explanation (Berndt 1966). Berndt gives maps referring to 'tribes' in the eastern section in 1941 and 1944, and in the western section in 1957–9, but cautions that although the material is based on 'native information' it is inexact. Among the groups concerned are the Mandjindji, Bidnanda, Andingari, Gugada, Ngalia, Mara, Mangula and Janggundjara which have been called tribes. Elkin among others has commented on the numerous tribal names for this region, referring 'either to single hordes or to a group of hordes which could hardly be regarded as a tribe in the same way as the Aranda or Yantruwantra' (Quoted in Berndt 1966:37). He adds that it is difficult to fix boundaries and names. Berndt's contention is that 'these groups are not "tribes", that there are no strict boundaries, that movements were relatively frequent, and that what we are faced with is, rather, a cultural and social bloc' (1966:39). He enumerates the linguistic affiliation of people in different camps, and notes that every individual in such a camp might offer a different set of terms to describe his grouping. For instance, a person may claim to be Bidnanda-Ngalia, and another Bidjandara-Wolundara-Mandjili. All of these are differentiated dialects. On the other hand, at Wiluna Berndt found people who claimed to speak each of the following – Mandjilu, Mandjila, Mandjildjara, Mandjilijuwa, saying that each of these was different. Certainly these cannot be called 'tribes', and Berndt could not find any real territorial linkage to these terms. He concludes that such labels have nothing more than linguistic significance, and are 'ways of classifying groups of people according to dialect variations. This is done without emphasizing "anchorage" and has no territorial significance' (ibid.: 41).

Indeed, mutual intelligibility of language makes the situation of the Western Desert unusual, if not unique in Aboriginal Australia. If the boundaries of the tribe 'are the boundaries of intelligibility, then the Western Desert itself is the "tribal unit" and this involves a pre-contact population of as many as 10,000 people' (Berndt 1966:32). The amount of dialectical variation from the east to the west, and the north to the south, is still within the bounds of mutual intelligibility.[6] On the one hand, then, we have Berndt's assertion that dialectical variation is a means of classifying people and has 'no territorial significance' (1966:41). On the other, we have Tindale's assertion that each dialect group is indeed a tribe and has known territorial associations. Both writers have been in the field intermittently but frequently since the thirties (Tindale) and early forties (Berndt). There is no reason to assume bad faith on either of their parts; they are both careful and meticulous scholars, they are both familiar with Western Desert languages, they are both interested in 'the truth' about Aboriginal local organization. Why then should there be this disparity?

In my own field work I fluctuated between their two views. Berndt's reconstructions made intuitive sense, in the social context of the area where I was working. Nonetheless people repeatedly referred to the

Everards as 'Janggundjara' in everyday contexts, contrasting the area with Amata and Ernabella, which they said were 'Bidjandjara'. In addition they referred to people as having one or other language, and this did indeed seem to refer to an idea of 'ngura'.

Nguṛa ngaiyugu? Baṛari, weluṛara! Bidjiwanga tjuṭa!

Country mine?   Far,   west!   Bidjispeakers all!

Further questioning however elicited the fact that although everyone there spoke Bidjandjara, some also spoke Ngadadjara and some Mandjildjara, which were like Bidjandjara but belonged further west. The answers I received made it obvious that in some way both Berndt and Tindale were right, that there was indeed an association between dialect and territory, but that it was *independent* of any individual's or group's own territorial affiliations.

In order to consider this proposition more fully it is necessary to consider the social aspects of dialects in more detail. The prefix *bidja*-comes from the word *bidjani* – to go, while *janggun* – comes from *janani* – to go, and is the Janggundjara usage. The suffix – *tjara* means 'having'. The meaning, then is 'those people who say *bidjani* for going' and 'those people who say *janani* for going'. The initial 'j' sound is also significant. Janggundjara say *juwa* – give; Bidjandjara say *uwa*. Janggundjara say *jalindjara* for north. Bidjandjara say *alindjara*. Janggundjara-speakers maintain that their usage is more clear and precise, since it prevents elision, whereas the Bidjandjara consider it rather vulgar and unsophisticated. Although the two dialects are almost identical grammatically there are a number of nouns, the use of which is a marker of one's own linguistic affiliations, but which are merely alternative words for the same concept. The Bidjandjara say *mina* for water, the Janggudjara say *gabi*; the Bidjandjara say *buli* for rock, the Janggudjara say *jabu*. It would be misleading to treat these words as exclusive to one group or the other. In fact any speaker of either dialect knows and uses these alternative words as it suits him/her, and may know others. For instance, the Warburton people say *gumbuli* for water, while groups further west again say *juro*. The choice of one word rather than another depends not merely on what dialect the person speaks, but on the person spoken to, the place where the transaction occurs and recent social and ritual events. A concrete instance of this occurred in connection with the shortage of rain in 1971. A party of Everards men travelled to Warburton where they handed over sacred objects in exchange for the Warburton men's singing the rain songs which they had in their custody at the time. When the men returned they brought with them the word *gumbuli* for water, and this term replaced *gabi* until the rain fell a month later. The reason given for this was that since the rain songs used *gumbuli* for water the people had to follow suit if they were to be effective in their area. The dialect form used is also an indication of social relationships between the speaker and the person addressed. When visiting Ernabella on one occasion I was brought to task for failing to switch to the Bidjandjara vocabulary when talking to Ernabella people. On the other hand, if one wishes to express disappointment with members of another group, for their stinginess as hosts at a ceremony, for instance, one uses one's own dialect forms very ostentatiously in public.

The dialects of the Western Desert, then, are not separate manners of speaking handed down unconsciously from generation to generation, but are subject to conscious modification and manipulation by their speakers. A certain speech-style communicates more than just information of immediate interest – the words a speaker chooses also make statements about him/her, about the group where s/he customarily resides, and his/her situation *vis-à-vis* others. The customary rule of courtesy is that one uses the same dialect form as most others in the place where you happen to be. The 'Bidjandjara' men in the Everards used Janggundjara speech forms. In pre-contact times the customary distribution of people would have been such as to make great mixing and ambiguities, such as Berndt encountered (1966), unusual; instead there would have been scattered camps of people usually to be found within a particular area, whose customary linguistic form would have been Janggundjara, Bidjandjara or whatever. But the boundaries of such areas are not defined physiographically – instead they exist only by virtue of the linguistic behaviour of the people usually to be found there. This is why Ernabella is now considered a 'Bidjandjara' place. An individual's identity as a speaker of one dialect rather than another depends on which dialect he grew up speaking, before initiation in the case of men, before marriage in the case of women. Because the majority of people at any one location at any one time used one dialect form rather than another, there is a *de facto* relationship between a particular territory and a particular dialect. Nonetheless it is incorrect to describe someone as a member of the Bidjandjara tribe, the territory of which is to be found between A and B.

How then are people affiliated to territory, if not by tribal membership which conveys automatic territorial rights? I referred earlier to Tindale's view on Western Desert local organization, and discussed his opinion that the land was owned by patrilineal, patrilocal groups. Berndt would appear to follow this view:

Those persons united by common patrilineal descent, who share a given site or constellation of sites, constitute the local group; this is the land-owning group with special spiritual and ritual ties, of which the land itself represents the most obvious . . . focus . . . the female members of such a group move out of it at marriage but . . . they do not relinquish their totemic affiliations. We may therefore speak of this local unit as a patrilineal descent group.   (Berndt 1966:47)

Although Berndt describes this group as 'land-owning' he adds a puzzling footnote:

It is territorially based; but the local group country is defined not by boundaries explicitly demarcating it from similar units, but by the actual sites connected with the ancestral being and his acts. Such territory is, ideally, unalienable but members of other local groups are not debarred from entry or from hunting game or collecting food within its precincts, although they may be denied access to a sacred site where objects of ritual use are stored.   (Berndt 1966:47, note)

We may ask, among other things, in what sense it is 'land-owning' if others have free access to the land and there are no boundaries? How does a person 'join' such a group? The answer would seem to be: by virtue of patrilineal descent. On the other hand, all accounts of Western Desert social organization maintain that a person gains his/her totemic affiliation by being born at a particular place, near to a particular waterhole, which will be one among a number of such sites mythically associated with a particular ancestral being. 'Mentioning the waterhole at which he was born a person may say "that's my *gabi*, my country"; this is his most important tie with the land, and he is not as a rule articulate concerning any larger territorially-based unit' (Berndt 1966:46). The only way that the two means of territorial connection can be reconciled is if every man is born in his own father's country, which presumably means at or near the same waterhole-based area where his father was born. Yet what, given the exigencies of desert living, is the likelihood of this? Such 'countries' may be only 200 square miles (320 km) in an area where the carrying capacity is only 0.007 persons to the square mile (Berndt 1966: 32, note) – which gives a total of 1.4 persons. Berndt mentions that men have a desire to return to their own countries when a birth is imminent, but this is an ideal which may not be fulfilled in the majority of cases. While each country usually contains one fairly reliable supply of water, hard years would make even this doubtful, and in any case the country between where a pregnant woman happens to be as birth approaches and that where her husband was born may be virtually devoid of water. We may safely assume, then, that in many cases chil-

dren are not born in their father's totemic country. We will return to
the problem of how they gain rights in their father's estate in a moment.
But first, let us ask about the mother's totemic affiliations. All writers
on this area concur that local-group exogamy is necessary. That is, the
most important thing in arranging a marriage is that the wife should
come from an area away, but not too far away from her husband's (see
Berndt and Berndt 1945:152(56)). One might therefore assume that the
wife's totemic affiliations would be different from those of the husband,
in which case 'patrilineal descent' would be a possibility. But this is not
the case. In fact, the preferred marriage is where both husband and wife
are of the same totemic affiliations.

> By being born near his father's waterhole (and if his father has mar-
> ried a woman born in a particular country through which the ances-
> tral being associated with him has passed) the child, after initiation,
> becomes a full member of his father's cult lodge.
>
> (Berndt and Berndt 1945:23(327))

> The preference in the Ooldea region and in the Spinifex country to
> the north and north-west seems to be for a man to marry a wife of the
> same cult totem as himself, but born at a *ga:bi* outside his country.
>
> (127(373))

It should be noted that this is a preference, not a prescription. Marriages between members of different totemic associations are just as
acceptable as those between members of the same ones. However, the
reason for the preference is that it is only by such a marriage, and by
being born on the same track as both parents, that a son can be guaranteed a place in his father's totemic cult. Each of the three factors is
taken into account in such decisions; the presence of at least one such
association is an absolute necessity, two make the case stronger, but
only all three can operate as an automatic guarantee. Hence we see that
there are a number of factors operating to decide the affiliations of any
particular individual. The 'ideal' is that a son shall be born in his father's
country, near the totemic track on which both mother and father were
born. But birth at any place along the track nonetheless confers rights
to that totemic complex, even if it is not in the same area where the
father was born. The cult totem is the focus of ritual action for all men
born on its tracks.

> the Aboriginal assumption is that all those sharing a common totemic
> track do in effect constitute a unit . . . irrespective of their particular
> local groups they are members of the cult . . . this is not a closed unit

in the sense of being restricted to a specifically defined section of the common ancestral track. It is flexible enough to include, conceptually, more distant local groups having the same totemic identification.'

(Berndt 1966:48)

In what sense then can we talk of 'patrilineal descent' or of 'patrilineal descent groups'? It is true that provided a child is born on the same totemic track as his father, even if in a different 'country', then he may take up rights in the totemic complex associated with his father's country. But, if he is born both away from that country and off that totemic track, he must take the cult totem of the country where he was *born*, and restrictions will be applied to his participation in his father's ritual complex (see Berndt 1966:49, note).

It is therefore incorrect to speak of 'patrilineal descent' – rights do not accrue primarily by being born to a particular father, but by being born at a particular place. Further, the time-depth created by groups who have managed to fulfil the conditions for patrilineal descent is extremely short, no more than three or four generations. The taboo on the names of deceased persons, and the desire to erase their memory as soon as possible, ensures that no precise genealogical knowledge can be maintained. This shallow time-depth is accentuated further by the custom of naming children after their grandparents' deceased siblings; the taboo name of a dead person is revived, and handed on to someone of the appropriate sex two generations below, so that the precise identities of the deceased are obliterated and the names revived in the person of young children born on the same totemic track.

Indeed everything in Western Desert culture indicates a tendency to forget the deceased, which is in marked contrast to the situation in other parts of Australia, such as northern Arnhem Land, where a great deal of creative labour is employed in memorializing the dead, together with elaborate funeral ceremonies, double disposal in some cases, graveposts, and so on. These are also the areas where patrilineal descent is firmly articulated and socially embedded in one form or another. By comparison, Western Desert people dig shallow graves, place the corpse inside, and abandon the site until a year or two later, when they perform a brief ceremony to ensure that all spiritual traces of the dead have disappeared. No intense creative energies are devoted to the dead – concern is much more with the not-yet-living (increase rites) and with the already alive (especially initiations) (see Berndt and Johnston 1942). Peterson (1972) has noted that there are two common ways in Australia of establishing totemic affiliations – by the question 'from which water do you come?' or else 'where is your bone country?' The former implies conception or birth at a particular place, the latter means that, no matter where a person is born or conceived, the link with the father has a physical expression in the bones of the body. This indicates a comparison between place-based claims and father-based claims to sites; among the Bidjandjara a man's father can never represent his 'bone' but is always one of the 'flesh' (i.e. the named endogamous moieties, *ngan-andarga* (us bones) and *djanamildjan* (them flesh), mean that all members of a person's own and alternate generations are thought of as 'bones', while the father's or son's generations are the 'flesh').

In the eastern Western Desert then, a person's primary affiliation to land is not to a bounded territory, nor yet to a single specific site within a bounded area; and it is not achieved automatically by means of descent from a particular father. Instead, a person's location as a member of a cult group, as a person entitled to know, share and perform the secret rituals of that cult (if a man), and to receive certain benefits from this position, comes about as a result of being born at a particular place, near a waterhole on the track of a particular totemic ancestor. This automatically gives rights to the ceremonies connected with that ancestor, which properly speaking follow the tracks of that ancestor across the landscape, rather than being attached to specific bounded areas of land. Symbolically, this is a sort of patrilineal descent, but the 'father' is not the real father, but instead the totemic species whose essence is reincarnated in the individual born along his track. It seems as if the principle of patrifiliation to a real father is in opposition to the principle of filiation to a symbolic ancestor; in the former case it is the 'place' of the real father which counts; in the latter, the 'place' of the hypothetical ancestor, the country in which he left his marks. In this account, then, we cannot suggest that a system of matrilineal attachments precedes a patrilineal one; instead, a system of symbolic filiation to place precedes a real one to father. However, we might note that, if the allocation to totemic group and associated rites depends primarily on place of birth, then the decision of the mother as to her whereabouts is crucial for the child's future. There is the possibility that the shift to an ideology of patrifiliation is a *de facto*, although covert, method of removing any ambiguities regarding the father–son transmission of identity which might be introduced by the mother's choice of birth-site for her child.

In summary then, I am suggesting that the confusion surrounding the nature of Western Desert local organization is not simply caused by the 'degeneracy' of social institutions as a result of white contact, nor by the inability to make accurate observations on the part of observers, not even by a simple confusion between the 'ideal' model and the 'real' model. In defiance of Occam's Razor, the explanation is not the simplest explanation apparent. The whole of the Western Desert cultural area was, at the time of the arrival of the Whites, in a state of transition, in which indigenous cultural institutions were undergoing transformations without having yet achieved any kind of balance. A static model of social organization could not possibly account for the structural features found under these circumstances. Where such transitions had already occurred and been stabilized, a static account appears much more successful (see the Walbiri, the Aranda). It remains a moot point whether such a stabilization would indeed have been possible, given the ecological constraints of the area. Strehlow repeatedly attributes the social organization of the Western Desert to its extreme aridity and lack of resources. This question cannot now be decided empirically, since that particular trajectory has now ended for good, to be replaced by another of equally doubtful outcome. We may however construct an ideal model to account for the features of the system of local organization in the Western Desert as they might once have been, and another to describe the system as it was straining to become. Both models partake of 'crystalline structures', and could never account for any real observation of any real historical situation, but are nonetheless useful to provide a basic reference point.

The past

The Western Desert is socially defined by the tracks of ancestors. People are born on a particular track, and join the cult totem of that ancestor on initiation. Marriages are arranged between groups of people along the same track, but geographically distant from one another. Hence there is totem-group endogamy, local-group exogamy. Persons who marry thus are common children of the one ancestor, and symbolically 'brother' and 'sister' to each other. Choice of residence is not fixed, but in any lifetime many such choices along the same track will be made. A family group may live for a time with the wife's people, for a time with the husband's, for a time with other siblings. Ultimately choice of residence depends on interpersonal relations and individual preferences, not on rules. However, persons connected with one track associate with others on that same track wherever possible. 'Following the Dreaming' means literally 'following the tracks of the ancestor' in both real and symbolic terms. Religious activities are focused on the celebration of the actions of the ancestor, and on the replenishing of productivity of both man and animal species – and just as husband and wife are 'siblings', so are living people 'siblings' of the actual animal embodiments of the ancestor. Interdependence of groups is totally at the symbolic level – kangaroo people are responsible for the supply of kangaroos, emu people for emus and so on, and the well-being of the whole depends on each group carrying out its appropriate rituals. There is no sense in which 'patrilineality' is preferred to 'matrilineality' and there is no real system of human descent at all.

Differentiation between countries along the same track occurs at the level of dialect – that is, people who usually live in one particular segment of the track speak in a particular manner by which they can be differentiated from others who live in other segments. At some places tracks cross one another, and here there may be choice of totemic affiliation and some ambiguity. Initiations are all-important, but they are initiations into the world of men connected with one particular totem, and do not concern members of other cult groups.

The future

The totemic tracks of the ancestors remain. However, the 'countries' along them are now differentiated by more than dialect, for certain groups of men now claim to 'own' these countries whereas men born elsewhere on the track do not. Marriages are still arranged with distant groups, but the specification of totemic affiliation of the wife is of no importance, for all rights in cult activity are now defined wholly and solely by patrilineal descent. Persons who marry are no longer 'brother' and 'sister' to each other. Men take their wives to live with them at marriage in their own countries. Religious activities are no longer solely concerned with the actions of a particular ancestor by people born on that track, for other ceremonies celebrating new heroes have emerged, which ignore individual totemic affiliation and group together men of different totems in celebration of the activities of these 'species-neutral' heroes. Interdependence of groups is now articulated not in symbolic terms, but in terms of real exchange – of women, of ceremonies and of paraphernalia. The possibility of 'patrilineality' has emerged and solidified, and has overcome the possibilities of non-descent, or rather, symbolic ancestor-based descent. Dialectical differentiation remains, but is now unrelated to country or track, and has lost its socially differentiating functions. Initiations are now the concern of all men, not merely of men on the initiate's track, especially since marriages are now arranged through the initiation procedures. The likelihood is that a section or subsection system will be well integrated, on a model like that of the Walbiri or the Aranda.

Contradictions

Clearly neither of these systems can exist in reality. In the case of the 'past' system the ability to remain wholly on the track of a given ancestor is limited by seasonal factors and especially by any overall change in climate. But any leaving of the track introduces the question of totemic affiliation of children born while away. Intergroup communication is at a minimum. There are no means of integration of groups wider than the totemic cult group. Choice of marriage partners in particular is limited to those people of the same cult totem in distant but not too distant places. Such a system could have been a possibility at a time when the Western Desert had a greater carrying capacity than at present, with a greater population density and less need to exploit far-flung resources in drought times. A general decline in productivity would result in greater spreading of the population, greater ambiguity about cult-group affiliation, and a greater need to alter the principles of the social formation.

In the case of the second system, environmental constraints again militate against its successful integration. Ideally, it requires that all men live on their own 'country' and that all their children are born there. Certainly under present-day desert conditions this is absolutely impossible. A wider definition of 'country', and its articulation with a subsection system, as happens among the Aranda, might provide one possible avenue of resolution. The exigencies of drought and unreliability of food supplies mean that such 'countries' would have to be at least twenty to thirty times their present size, to allow this possibility to emerge. Alternatively, connections between men could be freed of precise connections to locality, and be articulated instead in terms of a ritual system that provided access to resources not in terms of land alone but in terms of obedience to certain ritual requisites, such access to be handed on from father to son as a matter of course. There is some evidence to suggest that this is the path which the Western Desert people were taking.

Conclusion

I have attempted to show in this paper that the question of patrilineal, patrilocal band structures is far from settled in Australia, not simply because the 'economic' unit is to be differentiated from the 'religious' unit, but because Aboriginal systems, at least in some areas, were themselves in a state of change. That these changes, in the case of the Western Desert from a place-based to a father-based system of defini- tion of rights, occur in 'religion' is apparently a confirmation that in 'archaic' societies the structures characteristic of distinct levels as found under capitalism cannot be identified in the same way. Instead we find a collapsing together of levels, in which structures usually considered appropriate to 'economic' organization are operating within the 'reli- gious' system. Furthermore, to the extent that these alterations in ide- ology (e.g. the introduction of sections through the movement of rituals between men in adjacent areas) become linked into the kinship system, the distribution of women and the nature of rights held by men over women is also altered. But here we must pause, and invoke again both Lévi-Strauss and Hindess and Hirst. For, although men act in the ritual sphere using means reminiscent of action in the economic world under capitalism, and attempt to find more and more secure ways of ensuring the transmission of rights to *ritual* property from fathers to sons, the material basis on which the male religious life rests is gained through the labour of the women. This 'real' base, however, does not appear anywhere at the ideological level; men continue to act as if ritual manipulations are the sole determinant of human production, and con- cern themselves exclusively with defining access to the rituals which constitute their 'business world', in which women feature mainly by their absence.[7]

Notes

1 The research on which this paper is based was carried out in 1970–1 at Ever- ard Park Station (now *Mimili*) in the north-west corner of South Australia. I am grateful to the Australian Institute of Aboriginal Studies for its financial support, and to Sally White, Dan Vachon and Nicolas Peterson for their help- ful comments. The whole question of local organization in the Western Desert remains unsettled in my mind, and the results of further research by male field workers now in the area may add a great deal to our understanding of the situation.
2 I am ignoring for the moment the argument regarding appropriation of sur-

plus labour, and exploring the simpler 'materialist' formulation here. The subject of surplus labour will be discussed elsewhere.

3 Certain Australian societies have introduced a division of labour into the religious sphere; the Dalabon for instance separate ownership and control (Maddock 1974:38), while in northeast Arnhem Land clansmen may go to their sacred sites only with the permission of their uterine relatives who are custodians, and who are the only people permitted food and water from the site (Peterson 1972:18–19). Evidence by Aborigines in recent land-claim cases has highlighted the great significance of this relationship. The theoretical implications of such a ritual division of labour require urgent exploration, since it suggests that the idea of division of labour between men is being elaborated within the ideological sphere while the economic division of labour operates primarily along sexual lines.

4 However, this 'ideologically correct' account of Aboriginal production obscures the fact that these 'owner/workers' do in reality receive disproportionate benefits as a result of their holding the key to the secrets of species reproduction. For example, over any given year they receive a great deal more hunted meat than do young men or women.

5 Or Pitjantjara, 'b' and 'd' being alternatives for 'p' and 't' in all Aboriginal languages. There is no orthographical agreement among Australian scholars at present.

6 That is to say, an adult person from any of these areas could, on moving to another such area for a short period of time, assimilate the necessary variations in dialect very rapidly. By contrast, a speaker of one of these dialects would have difficulty in learning Walbiri, or Aranda, as quickly, even though these areas abut that of the speaker.

7 The question of women's labour has been considered in Hamilton 1980. Since completing the present paper I have further considered Aboriginal land-*ownership* in the Western Desert as a relationship between men and land established through the possession of Sacred Objects as signifiers. This approach has been briefly outlined in my Ph.D. thesis 'Timeless transformation' (University of Sydney, 1979).

Bibliography

Berndt, R. M. 1966. 'The concept of the tribe in the Western Desert of Australia', in L. R. Hiatt and I. Hogbin (eds.), *Readings in Australian and Pacific anthropology*. Melbourne: Melbourne University Press

Berndt, R. M., and Berndt, C. H. 1945. *A preliminary report on fieldwork at Ooldea, South Australia. Oceania*, bound reprint: Sydney

Berndt, R. M. and Johnston, T. H. 1942. 'Death, burial and associated ritual at Ooldea, South Australia'. *Oceania* 12(3):189–208

Elkin, A. P. 1937. 'Beliefs and practices connected with death in north-eastern and western South Australia'. *Oceania* 7(3):257–99

1938–1940. 'Kinship in South Australia'. *Oceania* 8(4); 9(1); 10(2); 10(3)

1970. *The Australian Aborigines*. Rev. edn. Sydney: Angus and Robertson

Engels, F. 1973a. 'On social relations in Russia', in *The selected works of Marx and Engels* vol. 2. Moscow: Progress Publishers

1973b. 'Supplement on Proudhon and the housing question', in *The selected works of Marx and Engels* vol. 2. Moscow: Progress Publishers

Falkenberg, J. 1962. *Kin and totem*. New York: Humanities Press

Hamilton, A. 1979. 'Timeless transformation: women, men and history in the Australian Western Desert'. Unpublished Ph.D. thesis, University of Sydney

  1980. 'Dual social systems: technology, labour and women's secret rites in the eastern Western Desert of Australia'. *Oceania* 51:4–19

Hiatt, L. R. 1962. 'Local organisation among the Australian Aborigines'. *Oceania* 32:267–86

  1965. *Kinship and conflict*. Sydney: Angus and Robertson

Hindess, B. and Hirst, P. G. 1975. *Pre-capitalist modes of production*. London: Routledge and Kegan Paul

Lee, R. 1978. 'Issues in the study of hunter-gatherers: 1968–1978'. Paper presented at the Conference on hunter-gatherers, Paris, June 1978

Lee, R. B., and DeVore, I. (eds.) 1968. *Man the hunter*. Chicago: Aldine

Lévi-Strauss, C. 1963. *Structural anthropology*. New York: Basic Books

  1968. 'The concept of primitiveness', in Lee, R. and DeVore, I. (eds), *Man the hunter*. Chicago: Aldine

Maddock, K. 1974. *The Australian Aborigines: a portrait of their society*. Sydney: Allen Lane

Marx, K., and Engels, F. 1973. 'The German ideology', in *The selected works of Marx and Engels*. vol. 1. Moscow: Progress Publishers

Meggitt, M. J. 1962. *Desert people*. Sydney: Angus and Robertson

Peterson, N. 1972. 'Totemism yesterday'. *Man*, N.S. 7(1)

Stanner, W. E. H. 1965. 'Aboriginal territorial organisation: estate, range, domain and regime'. *Oceania* 36:1–26

Strehlow, T. G. H. 1965. 'Culture, social structure and environment in Aboriginal Central Australia', in R. M. Berndt (ed.), *Aboriginal man in Australia*. Sydney: Angus and Robertson

  1970. 'Geography and the totemic landscape in central Australia: a functional study', in R. M. Berndt (ed.), *Australian Aboriginal anthropology*. Nedlands: University of Western Australia Press

Tindale, N. B. 1972. 'The Pitjandjara', in M. Bicchieri, (ed.), *Hunters and gatherers today*. New York: Holt, Rinehart and Winston

  1974. *Aboriginal tribes of Australia*. Berkeley: University of California Press

Yengoyan, A. 1970. 'Demographic factors in Pitjandjara social organisation', in R. M. Berndt (ed.), *Australian Aboriginal anthropology*. Nedlands: University of Western Australia Press

5. Living dangerously: the contradictory foundations of value in Canadian Inuit society

JEAN L. BRIGGS

Introduction

The problems that presently concern me in my work with Canadian Inuit have to do with the affective dimension of values and with the role of emotional conflict in generating and maintaining those values. Social values may sometimes be adhered to merely because individuals wish to be approved of by their fellows, in which case the content of the value is irrelevant to the act of conforming. Often, however, a value has intrinsic meaning, and the motivations that produce conformity are specific to the value.

If values are not to remain extrinsically motivated 'oughts' or 'ought nots' they must be emotionally charged, created afresh for every individual, in emotionally powerful, consciousness-raising experiences of various sorts. My observations in Inuit society lead me to think that the emotions that motivate people to adhere to a socially approved value and to make it their own can be – and perhaps even must be – both complex and conflicting or ambivalent. I think that under certain circumstances the contradictory motives strengthen, rather than weaken, adherence to the values. My argument is that the incompatibility of a person's wishes arouses in him or her a sense of danger, which ultimately becomes a motive for conforming to that which is socially approved.

Although this idea is consonant with psychoanalytic thinking about the effects of inner conflict, I should like to emphasize that I did not enter the field with a psychoanalytic frame of reference. I had been observing Inuit interpersonal relations for about 12 years before I even began to notice the kinds of phenomena that I shall describe in this paper. My first conception of Inuit childrearing practices (Briggs 1970) was a great deal sweeter, simpler and more straightforward, and — I now see – extremely one-sided. My present orientation was forced upon me by a mass of field data which were too complex and contradictory to be explained in terms of simpler theories. In the course of analysing the data, I discovered that I was reinventing Freudian ideas.

In this paper I will briefly describe some of the ways in which Inuit manage one set of polar values: killing versus non-violence. I will describe some of the ways in which complex emotions concerning these values are aroused in Inuit children and will outline the circumstances that cause these contradictory motives to be supportive of the central values of Inuit society. But, in keeping with the theme of this volume, the ethnographic data will be used primarily to point up questions to which future research on value socialization in hunting and gathering societies might profitably be directed.

Background

My data, and consequently my hypotheses, derive from fieldwork[1] with two Canadian Inuit groups, the Utkuhikhalingmiut of Chantrey Inlet in the central Arctic and the Qipisamiut of Cumberland Sound in the eastern Arctic. The physical and social situations of these two groups are in some respects different, but in many important respects they are similar. Both groups are small and seasonally nomadic, and they live in camps remote from the settlements which most Inuit now inhabit. The major difference between them concerns their relative prosperity. The Utkuhikhalingmiut in their river environment live primarily on fish, and their small cash income comes from trapping foxes during the winter months. The inventory of their household goods is small, and shortages of fuel, ammunition, and store food are common. The living conditions of the Qipisamiut are much less austere than those of the Utkuhikhalingmiut. Whereas the Utkuhikhalingmiut live in snowhouses in winter, the Qipisamiut live in double-walled tents, insulated by a thick layer of Arctic heater between the two canvas walls. These tents can be heated up to 70° or 80°F with seal-oil lamps. The Qipisamiut have a more varied diet than the Utkuhikhalingmiut, too. They hunt seal and harp seal, beluga and caribou, as well as fish, birds, and eggs in season. Cash income comes from sealskins and is ordinarily sufficient to provide expensive items such as tape-recorders, phonographs, shortwave radios, and so on, in addition to the essentials: food, clothing, fuel, ammunition, snow-mobiles, boats, and boat motors. The

An Inuit two-year-old playing the game 'Shoot me, Bang!' (J. Briggs)

Utkuhikhalingmiut know about the more affluent conditions in which the eastern people live, but they do not appear to feel deprived. As one young man remarked: 'If I get twelve foxes this winter, I can buy everything I want.'

Apart from the above matters, the life-styles of the two groups are very similar. At the time my fieldwork was done, there were about 35 Utkuhikhalingmiut living in Chantrey Inlet and about 50 Qipisamiut in Cumberland Sound. Both groups are composed of bilaterally related kin – a core of close relatives together with a few other families who are related to the core in various ways. In both groups the core comprises an old man, widowed either before or during my fieldwork, his married daughters and their families, and his unmarried adult and adolescent children of both sexes. Numbers fluctuate from year to year as the less centrally related families join or separate from the main group. They also fluctuate seasonally, as families tend to disperse in spring and summer and rejoin one another in the autumn at a central winter camp. In the seasons of dispersal, the various families may live within sight of one another or at much greater distances, and the lines of division within the group are reflected in the camping patterns. Men from the various camps meet one another quite frequently while out hunting or fishing, but the women and children seldom see those camped far away.

Among the Qipisamiut, households tend to be nuclear whenever sufficient building material is available. Utkuhikhalingmiut households also tend to be nuclear during the summer, but in the winter, an occasional joint showhouse may be built, perhaps for added warmth as well as for increased sharing of food, work, and sociability.

Among the Utkuhikhalingmiut, there are no acknowledged group leaders. Each household-head directs his own household but no others. Among Qipisamiut, however, as among other eastern Inuit, sons and sons-in-law may continue to defer in certain matters to the wishes of their fathers and fathers-in-law even after they marry and set up their own households, especially if they live in the same camp. In the case of the Qipisamiut, the elder – the father of them all – is recognized as an authority of this kind by everyone in the camp. In everyday matters of whether or not to hunt and where and what, he exercises authority only over his own household members; but in long-range decisions, such as whether to move to Pangnirtung or not, people tend to defer to his wishes. No household head is sanctioned if he makes his own decisions in such matters; deference is voluntary, but, phrased as loyalty, it is nevertheless often there.

Both of these groups were chosen for research because their contact with the outside world is minimal. In both cases, the nearest settlements – and nearest neighbours – are about 100 miles away across open water. Women and children make this journey only rarely, though the men travel in to the settlement every month or so during the winter to trade skins for the store goods that they need in their camp life. Qipisamiut also trade during the summer. For them the round trip can easily be made in three or four days at any season, equipped as they are with snowmobiles and powered boats. The Utkuhikhalingmiut, on the other hand, travel by dog-sled in winter, and the round trip to the settlement may take up to twelve days. In summer they are cut off altogether for lack of suitable boats.

The trading trips are almost the only contact the two groups have with the outside world, except for occasional visitors: Inuit from the settlement who are out hunting; officials from the settlement on official visits; and, in the case of the Utkuhikhalingmiut, groups of sports fishermen who are flown in by charter airlines in July and August. Individuals from both groups have been sent out to hospitals, and a few of the children in both groups have had a little schooling. On the whole, however, the outside world plays a minor role in camp life. Both groups live quite self-sufficiently, adjusting minimally to Western culture, except for the practice of Anglicanism and the incorporation of such material goods as are useful to life in a hunting camp. As far as I can tell, the quality of interpersonal relations in the camp, and child-rearing practices in particular, are little, if at all, influenced by Western contact. In spite of the aforementioned differences in living conditions, the values of the two groups are variations on the same theme, and their ways of managing these values are also very similar.

The tangled web of contradictions

The most obvious sort of contradiction that one finds in social life – and perhaps even more dramatically in hunting societies than in others – is that potentially conflicting kinds of behaviour are socially constructive in different contexts. Society, valuing both or all of these behaviours, is presented with the problem of creating in its members motivations that will allow them to engage appropriately in the contradictory behaviours. An example in a hunting society is killing versus non-violence. Clearly, killing is essential in such a society: human life depends on it. It is useful also as a protective measure against the occasional dangerous human being in a society in which other means of protection, such as incarceration or removal of the offender, are unavailable. But, just as clearly, it is dysfunctional, in a hunting society as in other societies, if directed indiscriminately against fellow members of the society. So Inuit value both violence and non-violence.

Another example of opposite behaviours, both of which are socially constructive in a hunting society, is self-sufficiency versus nurturance. A man must behave in the self-sufficient, autonomous way that makes him a good hunter, but he must also be a socially responsible, generous, nurturant member of his group. Again, not surprisingly, both autonomy and nurturance are valued in Inuit society. (I am here phrasing these oppositions in Western terms for purposes of analysis and not as the Inuit conceptualize them.)[2]

The question is, how are these potentially conflicting values to be managed, cognitively and emotionally? What feelings underlie them, how are the feelings created, and how do they serve to motivate appropriate behaviour?

Let us take the cognitive level first. Different societies may manage conflicting values cognitively in different ways. They may be compart-mentalized, so that approval is given to each in its own proper context. In this case, ideally, conflict is abolished – or never existed except in the ethnocentric mind of the anthropologist. In its most extreme form, compartmentalization implies that the two potentially conflicting val-ues are never put into juxtaposition. Conflicting values may also be rationalized, for example, by saying that under certain circumstances exceptions may be justified, other values take precedence; or, more complicatedly, by interpreting behaviour appropriate to one value as an expression of the opposite value, for example, viewing killing as a nurturant act. It is also possible that societies may deal with contradic-tory values by developing a high degree of tolerance for inconsistency,[3] or even by valuing impulsive – that is, inconsistent – behaviour. Or the values might remain unreconciled and antagonistic to each other. In some societies one finds requirements for simultaneous adherence to contradictory values, so that whatever a person does – whether he is chaste or a Don Juan – is wrong and sanctionable (Paine 1971).

These various possibilities are, of course, theoretical abstractions. I doubt that any real society ever chooses neatly among them, and I shall presently describe the untidy state of affairs that I find among the Inuit. Nevertheless, societies do seem to vary in the way they combine these possibilities; and the question therefore arises whether individuals feel conflicted as a result of these different situational requirements under different conditions of social management; and what effects such con-flicts have on value maintenance.

So far what I have said sounds as though the problem of value conflict were largely cognitive and could be resolved by manipulating ideas appropriately. But valuing is an emotional activity, and a problem that exists on an emotional level cannot be solved entirely on a cognitive level, since ideas and feelings rarely manage to harmonize perfectly. One must expect to find other coping mechanisms, too, and other effects of the conflict on behaviour.

Moreover, feelings and values do not often fit neatly together, either, in such a way that each value is supported by a simple corresponding feeling. In Inuit society, the value placed on violence is not supported only by enjoyment of killing; the value placed on non-violence is not supported only by enjoyment of peacefulness or by fear of killing. The situation is much more complex than this. Not only do the behavioural values conflict, but the feelings underlying each value are themselves in conflict. Inuit refrain from injuring partly because they wish to injure and they injure sometimes because they feel loving. They behave self-sufficiently partly because they feel intensely dependent, and they are nurturant partly because they wish not to be. In other words, conflicts within individuals may be generated not only by imperfectly separated situations which demand contradictory behaviour, but also by contradictory psychological needs which predispose a person to behave in opposite ways in a given situation. It is the creation and management of these psychological conflicts that I find so fascinating in Inuit society and that leads me to argue, in psychoanalytic terms, that intrapsychic conflict about a value can create allegiance to it. Inuit dramatize – and perhaps even generate or intensify – in socialization rituals the value conflicts that occur in everyday life. The question that must be answered is whether conflict is essential to the creation and maintenance of value, or whether Inuit methods of creating value are exceptional. I will return to these questions in greater detail later. First let me illustrate the grounds for the questions by giving a fuller description of Inuit modes of managing aggression.[4]

The fact that Inuit themselves find aggression problematic is indicated by the Iglulik shaman whom Birket-Smith quotes as saying that 'life's greatest danger . . . lies in the fact that man's food consists entirely of souls' (1959:166). There is good evidence that Inuit both enjoy and fear killing. Ostensibly, they enjoy it when the object of the aggression is an animal and fear it when the object is human. Enjoyment is evident in the way a man tells a hunting story, dramatizing with shining eyes not only the pursuit but also the act of striking. It is evident also in the exclamations of women watching a hunt: 'Oh, how I wish I had a gun!' 'Brother, lend me your gun, let *me* shoot!' Chasing a lemming or smoking out a fox are sports engaged in by the whole camp, from the smallest child to the most staid elder. I have also seen an unwanted dog chased by snowmobile with great hilarity and repeatedly bumped until it died. On the other hand, when it is human life that is at issue, Inuit manifest a horror not only of killing but also of much milder forms of aggression, such as striking a person or even shouting.[5] Fear makes them exaggerate incidents of aggression and expect it when it does not occur.

Compartmentalization, then, is an important way of coping with aggressive feelings and behaviour in Inuit society. But in a hunting society it is not easy to keep men and animals comfortably compartmentalized. Men tend to identify with animals. They attribute souls to them; they hear words in a bird call; they recognize emotions and thoughts in an animal's behaviour; and sometimes they respond to animals emotionally as if they were human. Inuit children play with puppies as if they were babies, 'nursing', cuddling, and backpacking them; they may drag a seal foetus across the floor, crying 'maaaa maaaa' – the sterotypic rendition of a cry of pain – and I have seen women murmur to a wounded gull chick as it flutters toward the water the same sympathetic endearments they would murmur to an injured child.

This identification cannot help but create a sense of danger when violence is directed toward the creatures one identifies with, especially when, as often happens, the perpetrator of violence is oneself. Children not only 'adopt' and cuddle puppies, they also kill superfluous new-born pups with gusto, dashing them against boulders, dropping them off cliffs, or throwing them out to sea. And the wounded gull chicks to whom those endearments were murmured had been shot, for sport, by the same women who cooed at them sympathetically as they fell.

Other experiences, too, contribute to the creation of a sense that danger surrounds aggression. Some of these are probably characteristic of social life in general. Others, if not peculiar to life in a hunting society, are at least exceptionally vivid in such a society. Death is a daily presence; the means of killing are easily available, and members of every family are skilled in their use. Not only animals but also humans of all ages are perceived as vulnerable to death in a way that is not true in our own more highly protected society. Even the smallest children have often experienced the death of someone close to them, from natural causes or by accident, by suicide or, once in a while, by murder.[6] Finally, in a society in which the expression of hostility is very stringently controlled, as it is among Inuit, it is more than likely that people will project their own suppressed hostility onto others and, knowing that they themselves feel violent, will easily suspect others of murderous intent. All these things contribute to a sense that aggression is dangerous.

The fact that danger is sensed by Inuit themselves is made explicit by the Iglulik shaman quoted above. One way of coping with perceived danger is to rationalize, to argue to oneself that there is no danger, and Inuit do just that in various ways. I have mentioned that one way in which aggression can be rationalized is to consider it a nurturant act. This attitude is expressed in the rituals by which the souls of killed animals are placated or gratified. According to Birket-Smith's description of traditions, a seal, which suffers from lack of fresh water in its salty environment, is given a drink of water, and 'during the first night after the kill the harpoon must stand by the blubber lamp, so that the soul, which is still in the harpoon head, may warm itself at its flame'.

A bear is honoured with gifts, and 'a present of sole skin is good, for bears walk so much' (1959:166).

The idea that aggression – though not, as a rule, in the form of killing – is nurturant can be seen also in some of the ways in which Inuit treat one another. I think particularly of a kind of behaviour called *siqnaaq-*, which translates roughly as 'overprotection'. A parent bird protecting its young by attacking a would-be predator is said to *siqnaaq-*, and so is a human who interferes in a childish quarrel to defend his or her own offspring. But *siqnaaq-* also refers to treating a favourite child as a Cinderella: providing insufficient food, clothing, equipment or shelter, speaking unkindly, over-burdening the child with chores and giving no reward, and so on. Inuit say that this is often done to a child who has nearly died, and though one can see reasons for feeling genuine hostility under such circumstances – 's/he nearly abandoned me' – the behaviour is rationalized as protecting the child from future dangers, either by making him or her more self-sufficient, less dependent on human company and assistance; or by making others believe that this mistreated child is not one's favourite: 'If somebody wants to hurt the [child's] father, he won't dare to attack the father but he might attack the father's favourite child.'

Related to this idea that injuring a child can be nurturant is the feeling that 'a hurt baby is more lovable'. A mother who feels intensely affectionate may handle her baby in ways that look brutal to the outsider, slapping it, squeezing it tightly, or biting it until it bursts into tears. Such behaviour is called *ugiangu-* in the Cumberland Sound dialect, which literally means to 'kill without using weapons'. It refers to the way animals kill each other; but it also refers to the fierce physical expression of affection. And in view of the statement that a hurt baby is more lovable, I wonder whether *ugiangu-* behaviour is not sometimes used, unconsciously, to engender the intense love that it is said to express. In other words, one's violent actions make one feel more tenderly loving.

A third rationalization that is related, though somewhat differently, to the association between injury and nurturance is that mistreating someone one loves, as in the case of *siqnaaq-* behaviour, tests one's own psychic strength, one's ability to endure pain – because of course one feels pain when one hurts someone one loves: 'It's hard to do.' The common theme underlying all these three rationalizations is that behaviour appropriate to the aggressive value is seen as an expression of the opposite value, nurturant affection.

Lastly, one finds the rationalization that killing is necessary in self-defence – whether the victim is an angry person, a man-eating animal, or a terrified baby duck or lemming. This rationalization resonates with real feelings of fear, in the case of all the creatures mentioned. Not only do Inuit have a horror of anger, they have also been taught as small children to fear small fuzzy moving objects, whether it be a lemming or a bit of fluff tied to an invisible thread and jerked in front of them, and the resulting strong squeamish feeling seems to be very long-lasting.

To sum up so far, then, Inuit compartmentalize, but imperfectly, their aggressive and non-aggressive behaviours, and they deal with the danger that this imperfection creates by rationalizing in various ways – generally, in such a way that the behaviour that is disapproved of in the given context appears to be motivated by the approved value.

But, as I have said, valuing is an emotional activity, and feelings do not follow docilely in the trail of ideas; so rationalization does not work perfectly, either. If it did, no sense of danger would remain. To some extent the opposing values remain antagonistic, and therefore we may expect to find additional coping mechanisms and additional effects of the conflict on behaviour. I think that in the Inuit case one of the major effects and, at the same time, one of the most important coping mechanisms, is the dramatization of the conflict through interpersonal games or rituals.

These games are small exchanges, spontaneous in occurrence but highly stereotyped in form, between a child and one or more other people, who may be older children or adults of either sex. Sometimes the older person teases the child in some standardized way: 'Where's your [absent] daddy?' 'Whose child are you?' 'Do you wrongly imagine you're lovable?' 'Shall I adopt you?' 'Shall I hit your nasty old mother?' At other times the game consists in tempting the child to engage in some disvalued behaviour: 'Don't tell your sister you have that candy; it's the last one; eat it all yourself.' There are a great many such games; they are played all the time by everybody and a very high proportion of interactions with small children take this form. Most interesting is the fact that the games occur with only minor variations in Inuit groups that have no contact with one another, and their forms remain stable over generations. I think this indicates clearly their importance in creating and maintaining an Inuit style of interpersonal relations: smooth, light in tone, controlled, and, at the same time, covertly conflictful. On the one hand, these games provide a way of expressing and managing profoundly felt value conflicts; they are cathartic for both adults and children. On the other hand, the games, as dramas, create for children the plots of everyday life by selecting the stimuli that are to be attended to and interpreting them in cultural terms. By making conflicts salient to children, they help to create a sense of danger and, ultimately, commitment to the values.

The sense of danger is created partly by making children aware that contradictory and imperfectly compartmentalized and rationalized values exist, but, even more, by pointing up, or even creating, contradictory *feelings* about each of the opposed values.

The games do this in various ways. First, they help to create the identification between person and animal and provide occasions on which children can engage in contradictory behaviours toward the animals they identify with. That is, they help to destroy compartmentalization. For example, a child may be given a fuzzy duckling as a pet and admonished, in the same tender tone of voice and with the same words in which s/he is warned not to hurt a new baby: 'Don't hurt it – don't kiss it too hard – be careful.' And the child's protective feelings will be further aroused by a game in which someone pretends to attack the pet – 'Shall I hurt it?' – until the child screams and wards off the attacker. But then someone – and it may be the same person who cautioned the child not to hurt the pet – may hand the child a stick and say in a persuasive, excited voice which the child has learned to associate with other enjoyable activities: 'Kill it! Get the game! It will be a catch for you!' And the audience will watch with approval while the child slashes at the baby bird it has just been told to be gentle with. In this way, opposing and potentially conflictful feelings of protectiveness and aggression are directed toward the same creature.

Moreover, this creature is not always an animal. There are other games in which the child is urged to injure a loved human being – by punching, biting, or pebble-throwing – and while the victim cries out, 'A-aaa! That hurts!' s/he also says, smiling sweetly: 'Isn't that fun?' In one particularly dramatic form of the game which I once saw, a four-year-old was asked in the excited, persuasive tone of voice: 'Why don't you kill your baby brother? Like this!' – and the proper technique was demonstrated. Since the child has good reason to identify with the small and vulnerable or large and loved victims of this playful – and, in the case of animals, occasionally lethal – aggression, the feelings engendered must certainly be vivid.

Contradictory feelings are also aroused when rationalizations are acted on, playfully or otherwise. I have already mentioned the playfully aggressive behaviour called *ugiangu-*. This is one of many games in which children learn that love can hurt. This awareness has complex implications for the emotional structure of Inuit values. For present purposes the point is that, by such means, children acquire mixed feelings about affection, which give vivid emotional support to the cognitive association between nurturance and aggression, and which make them both want, and not want, to be loved and nurtured.

To recapitulate, emotionally charged games like those described elicit protective feelings toward animals that are to be killed and suggest, or bring into open awareness, feelings of hostility toward creatures who are to be protected. They also teach that nurturant affection can hurt and that injury can be affectionately motivated. These conflictful feelings and perceptions – which by no means end with childhood – make a person simultaneously both want and not want to conform to the approved behaviour. The sense of danger surrounding conformity stems from the person's awareness of his/her own conflict, combined with knowledge that, on the one hand, a severe sanction for nonconformity exists and that, on the other hand, one is vulnerable to that sanction.

In the Inuit case, one of the most frightening sanctions is abandonment, and – associated with it – death. A sense that one is vulnerable to that sanction is created by the everyday experiences of comings and goings, which are the stuff of nomadic life. It is also created by interpersonal games like those described above, which demonstrate to children that they can be injured, and by other games, which teach children to wonder whether their place in society is secure, whether they are loved. In one such game, an adult pretends to envy some possession of the child's and suggests to the child: 'Why don't you die so I can have it?' In another game, the child is asked repeatedly: 'Are you lovable? You *are*? Are you really? Are you more lovable than your brother? Is he more lovable than you?' and so on. The message – which is delivered with great consistency in many contexts and in many forms – is that if one is not loved, one runs the risk of being left behind: emotionally or physically abandoned or even killed.

All these playful messages are delivered in a form that is extremely vivid, personal, and larger than life, and that makes it easy for children to see the problems posed for them by their contradictory feelings, to perceive emotionally the fatal consequences of a wrong choice of behaviour, and to feel that since they have 'bad' feelings, they are themselves vulnerable to the sanctions illustrated for them. To be sure, at one level the medium of the message is just a game, and therefore a cathartic way of coping with the contradictions that trouble one in real life. But at the same time, at another level, a doubt is engendered as to whether it really is a game, and the dangerous possibility that it might not be – the resulting fear – must make children try harder to conform than they might do if they did not feel themselves vulnerable to sanction.

Moreover, the values themselves become emotionally charged as a result of the threats that surround them. A child who is asked, 'Why don't you die so I can have [your shirt]?' may start to value the shirt, and keeping it, more; and on the other hand, s/he may come to place a high value on giving, because it is difficult to give away something one wants to keep. And when s/he gives – the shirt or something else – the recipient too will value the gift because s/he knows it was hard to make. Similarly, the child who is asked, 'Why don't you kill your baby brother?' may love more strongly, and may value loving more, to compensate for the dislike s/he is made aware of feeling along with his/her affection.

It should be emphasized that what is created by these complex messages is *doubt*, a sense that the social world is somewhat unpredictable and must be closely watched and continually tested – a sense that human relations are a little fragile and that one's own position is not quite secure.[7] The games are, by and large, played in the most benign of ambiances; they contain positive messages about being loved, as well as negative ones about the possibility of losing that love. So children cannot clearly and definitely experience themselves as outcast for their imperfections, a perception which would probably cause them to reject society in turn. On the contrary, the doubt will bind them more closely to society; the fear that love may be lost – through rejection by others or through their own fear of being loved – will make them try harder to act in such a socially approved way as to obviate the fear of loss.

Clearly, this is not a straightforward way of learning values; neither does it further the neat compartmentalization of values. But these complex learning experiences do help to create at least two motives for being 'good': (1) one conforms because the consequences of not doing so have been presented in a frightening and personally relevant form which makes one feel vulnerable to sanction, and (2) they create commitment intrinsic to the values themselves by making them the focus of conflict and creating an awareness that the values might be lost. I think they may create a third motive, as well. Games like those described are played all the time, and they are rationalized in part as 'tests' of a child's development. Inuit children acquire a life-long habit of testing themselves in all kinds of difficult tasks, physical and emotional. Remember the parents described earlier who mistreat favourite children 'to see if I can do it'. So, I think testing oneself, 'to see if I can do it', may also be a motive for good behaviour.

In sum, the argument is that in the Inuit case, the existence of polar values is not simply a troublesome and unsettling fact of social life. And the contradictory emotions surrounding these values are not merely an expression of human imperfection. Contradictory values that are imperfectly compartmentalized and rationalized do create problems in the form of potentially dangerous choice situations. The choices are dangerous because one's behaviour can backfire: one can suddenly discover that one has injured when one thought one was nurturing. They are also dangerous, in terms of psychic economy, because any behaviour that expresses one value necessarily renounces the opposite but equally desired value: one nurtures when one would like to kill. And choices are made more dangerous by all the other contradictory emotions surrounding each value, which make one *want* to lose the value. However, under circumstances like those I have outlined, in which directives for behaviour are clear and the sanctions for misbehaviour are personally threatening, these dangers promote morality by motivating the members of society to defend those beleaguered values – not against outer enemies, which may never seem quite real in a society in which people often treat one another in a scrupulously benign fashion; but against the more intimately known and therefore more formidable enemy within: their own wish to violate the values. The perception of danger results in values being defended with compensatory intensity.

The sense of danger, then, signals that the cognitive devices like compartmentalization and rationalization that societies use for coping with potentially conflictful situations are not complete solutions; but, far more important, it is itself a mechanism for coping with those conflicts.

Research questions

I hope that the preceding analysis has demonstrated the need for attending, first to the overall structure of interrelationships among a society's values; and secondly to the psychological variables in the operation of those values.

Data are particularly needed on the presence, the management, and the social and psychological effects of *contradictory* values and emotions, both within societies and within individual members of those societies.

At least two sorts of value contradiction can occur. In this paper I have discussed the sort of contradiction created by a situation in which two values exist, both of which are positively valued by the society in different, but imperfectly separated, contexts. But, obviously, another sort of contradiction may also be found – one in which one of two polar values (for example, giving) is positively valued by society, while its opposite (for example, having) is valued negatively by society but positively by individuals: we ought not to want it but we do. This sort of value contradiction also exists in Inuit society. It was implicit in my mention of atttitudes toward dependency, as well as in my equally brief mention of the contradictory emotions surrounding the Inuit value of generosity. Are both kinds of contradiction found in all societies? Under what circumstances do they interact with one another to maintain values, as opposed to disrupting or changing them? And how exactly do they interact, cognitively and emotionally, to maintain values?

With regard to the nature of valuing as a psychological process, more cross-cultural data are needed on the kinds of emotion that can energize values, the kinds of experience that create and maintain those emotions, and the kinds of psychological mechanism that are brought into play in managing potentially conflicting values. These data cannot be obtained by attending solely to the ways in which valued behaviour is *directly* modelled and encouraged and disvalued behaviour discouraged by precept and example, reward and punishment. Attention must be paid to the full gamut of emotionally charged experiences that children have, which relate to the core values of the society. Only when this is done will we begin to understand the *complex* ways in which emotions become associated with values and values become related to one another. If we can learn to understand valuing at an emotional level we should be better able to answer whole series of questions to which there are at present no satisfactory answers: Why are some values of a model adopted and not others? How do children become acutely vulnerable to certain sanctions and not others? How, in a word, do values become internalized, not just as whole-cloth imitations of a model's values but in a reworked form which has strong personal meaning – in a sense, recreated by individuals on the basis of their experience with the values?

Attention to the psychological level in the study of values can tell us much about the nature of an individual's bond to his or her society. We tend to assume, I think, that people who are born into a society just 'naturally' come to feel that they belong to it – at least to some segment of it – especially if the society appears to treat its members as benignly as many hunting and gathering societies do. But the Inuit data suggest that an individual's feeling of belonging may be problematic, even in hunting and gathering societies, indeed, perhaps especially in nomadic hunting and gathering societies, where the possibility of abandonment if one is not a worthy member of the group is vividly real.

I think we also assume too often that the reasons for commitment to socially approved values are pretty much the same everywhere and are therefore not a very interesting subject for investigation. We tend to focus on discovering what a society's values *are*, and perhaps on what *causes* them to be what they are, and we are not so concerned to find out just what emotional meanings the values have for the individuals in a society, what emotional reasons people have for adhering to them. But it should be obvious that adherence to the 'same' value may be differently motivated in different societies – and probably in different individuals, as well. To take a simple example, the 'same' value of 'self-restraint' may be motivated, as in Japan, by a fear of hurting another person, who is viewed as emotionally overburdened and fragile (Nakane: personal communication); or it may be motivated, as among Beaver Indians, by a fear that the other may be waiting to pounce on whatever weakness one's self-expression may reveal (Ridington: personal communication); or it may be based, as among Inuit, on a fear that one may injure oneself by one's own emotional disequilibrium; or, again, on a wish to appear unthreatening to others, so that they will be friendly – also an important Inuit reason. In all these cases, the behaviour at a given moment may look the same, but the implications for interpersonal relations of the underlying feelings and rationales are extremely different.

Yet again, in a given case, self-restraint may not be inspired by any of the fears or wishes mentioned, all of which are intrinsically attached to that particular value, but may instead be motivated by fear of an extrinsic punishing event, or perhaps by affectionate bonds with other people, whose expectations one conforms to out of love. If morality is fear-inspired, the effects on social relations will be different, depending on what sort of fear it is: of abandonment, of starvation, of murder, of supernatural revenge. And if morality is affection-inspired, the effects will be different depending on how people feel about loving and being loved. People may fear loving and being loved as well as desiring it – Inuit do – and the quality of an ambivalent bond – its effects on behaviour – may be quite different from the quality of an unambivalent one.

Furthermore, just as similar-looking values may represent dissimilar emotional meanings, so may those meanings be inculcated by a variety of methods. But how much variation is there across cultures in the way the meanings are learned? I have mentioned that Inuit data accord very well with psychoanalytic ideas concerning the role of inner conflict as a motivator of behaviour; and conflict of one sort or another surely is a condition of life in all societies. But does it play the same role in generating values in all societies? Does one consistently find evidence that strongly suppressed negative feelings exist in conflict with positively approved behaviours which are firmly adhered to? It seems possible that any intensely and personally felt threat that a psychologically or physically essential quality or condition might be lost, or any sense that one has been injured by someone's disvalued behaviour, could make a value emotionally salient and, thus, valued, just as conflict does. Are Inuit, then, unusual among cultures in the extent to which they incorporate emotional conflict into the cultural design, playing it up and dramatizing value conflicts for children in order, consciously or unconsciously, to create life-plots for them and to facilitate the learning of the motivational scripts?

Finally, there is the question of sanctions. As I illustrated earlier, the nature of the punishment that a person fears affects the quality of his or her bond with society. That is an obvious point. Perhaps less obvious is the point that sanctions, like values, derive their power to injure from the complexes of emotionally charged meanings that surround them. We should not rest satisfied with finding out what sanctions are imposed to enforce adherence to values, nor should we take for granted that people are 'naturally' vulnerable to the sanctions with which they are threatened. Instead, we should look for the ways in which these vulnerabilities are created, so that children become intensely sensitive to some sanctions and not to others.

Only by investigating questions like these can we hope to understand in depth the differences in the emotional quality of life in the various societies we study.

Given the fact that my hypotheses concerning the nature of valuing are based on data from a hunting society, comparison with other hunting and gathering societies seems an appropriate next step in testing their generalizability. Since hunting and gathering societies tend to resemble one another in important respects, they provide a good field for controlled comparison of the operation of value systems.

One of the most striking ways in which such societies resemble one another is precisely with regard to their values. Richard Lee (1978) out-

lines these as follows: sharing, reciprocity, marrying out (as an obligation), carrying one's share of the work load, political equality, sociability (communicativeness), humility, and even-temperedness. Objections
may be raised concerning the generality of specific items on this list;
and other values – such as capacity for autonomous action – might be
added. But, such minor issues aside, the fact is that the existence of
superficially similar values in many hunting and gathering societies
makes them a most appropriate field for investigating the underlying
dynamics of these values, both the possible emotional interrelationships among them and the combinations of emotions that can underlie
any one value. For example, if, as we may assume, similar values give
rise to similar contradictory requirements for behaviour – violent and
nonviolent, self-sufficient and nurturant, self-confident and humble –
what are the various ways in which the 'same' potential opposition can
be managed, cognitively and emotionally? And what is the range of
emotional meaning with which it can be imbued?

It is obvious that, in addition to the values themselves, hunting and
gathering societies share a number of other characteristics, such as the
small size of the group, the shifting composition of the latter, its
mobility, the low population density, living arrangements that are dense
and porous within the camp, a relatively undifferentiated social structure, and, of course, the non-cumulative and somewhat erratic nature
of subsistence. Some or all of these characteristics, together with the
interpersonal style that derives from the values such societies share,
may well combine to influence what the value-charging experiences and
the socialization practices will be. It may be that hunting and gathering
societies in general provide exceptionally fertile ground for the kind of
socialization that characterizes the Inuit.[8] I have mentioned the appropriateness of the threat of abandonment as a sanction in a nomadic
society with flexible camp composition, where a child not only can *see*
the possibility of being left behind, but has actually experienced the
departure – and sometimes the permanent loss – of people s/he is emotionally dependent on. Draper (1978) mentions that, among the !Kung,
the constant presence of many monitors near at hand makes it possible
to defuse hostility before it gets out of hand, to nip misbehaviour in
the bud by the use of pleasant distraction instead of punishment. A
multitude of socializers might also facilitate a learning system that
depends heavily on interpersonal games. There is always someone there
to initiate a game; the same lessons are received from every quarter;
and perhaps some of them are less threatening, and therefore easier to

learn, when the socializer is an older child or an aunt, rather than the mother, on whom the child is most intensely dependent (Haavind 1975). One might also ask whether the development of inner conflict as a motivation for conformity might be more necessary in a society that is sufficiently nurturant that small children may not experience serious – as opposed to playful – external threats to the things they hold essential to their well-being. In Inuit society, they are generally given what they want immediately. And might not playful interventions be most appropriate in a society that places such a high value on autonomy that power is hardly ever directly asserted, even against children? Inuit children are not 'punished' in any way recognizable to the Western eye; the will to conform is thought to develop autonomously, with the help of frequent 'reminders'.

Hypotheses like these can only be checked by comparing one hunting society with another and noting the contexts of the variations in socialization practices that are found. Such comparison, if it is careful, will also tell us how profound the apparent similarities in values and in socialization patterns are, and whether subtle but important differences in emotional structure lie beneath them.

The fact that hunting and gathering societies have relatively undifferentiated social structures facilitates the study of valuing in another way, too. If a society contains no groups for whom different values and styles of socialization are appropriate, one possible source of variation and contradiction in value structure is absent. And if complex and contradictory value structures are found in societies, and in individuals within societies, which have ostensibly simple value systems, their presence will support the idea that such contradictions are essential to the process of valuing and, indeed, will show them to be a fundamental fact of human psychic functioning.

Finally – and the point is not a small one – the open life-style of hunting and gathering camps makes visible the minute details of daily interactions. The small spontaneous interpersonal dramas or rituals that play such an important role in the creation of Inuit values may be almost impossible to see in the context of a formal visit to a household where much of the interaction goes on behind doors, or where certain kinds of interaction are reserved for family audiences only. Thus, these kinds of behaviour are much harder to observe in settlements than in camps.

In short, I suggest that value conflict and emotional conflict surrounding values can be constructive social forces, not just in bringing about change but in maintaining the status quo. However, the circumstances under which this is true, and how it all works, need to be spelled out with the help of much more detailed research on the complexities of value systems and the acquisition of values by individuals. Hunting and gathering societies provide good ground for this research and, indeed, may turn out to share common features in this, as in other, respects.

Acknowledgements

The field work for this chapter was supported by the Wenner-Gren Foundation; the Northern Co-ordination and Research Centre of the Department of Northern Affairs and National Resources (now the Northern Research Division of the Department of Indian and Northern Affairs) of the Canadian Government; the National Institute of Mental Health of the US Government (Pre-doctoral Research Fellowship 5 Fl MH–20, 701–02 BEH with Research Grant Attachment MH–07951–01); the Canada Council (award from the Isaak Walton Killam bequest to the Department of Sociology and Anthropology of the Memorial University of Newfoundland); the Institute of Social and Economic Research of the Memorial University of Newfoundland; and the National Museums of Canada, National Museum of Man, Urgent Ethnology Programme.

In writing this chapter I have drawn on material that has been published elsewhere: a monograph, *Aspects of Inuit value socialization*, National Museum of Man, Mercury Series, Ottawa, 1979; and an article, 'The creation of value in Canadian Inuit society'. *International Social Science Journal*, vol. 31, no. 3, 1979. The publishers – the National Museum of Man and UNESCO – have kindly granted permission for use of this material.

For their helpful comments on the manuscript, I should like to thank Drs Adrian Tanner and Judith Adler.

Notes

1 This chapter is based on fieldwork done between 1963 and 1975 with two Canadian Inuit groups, the Utkuhikhalingmiut of Chantrey Inlet and the Qipisamiut of Cumberland Sound. Especially heavy use is made of data gathered in Qipisa in 1974 (three months) and 1975 (three months). The earlier trips were as follows. Between 1963 and 1965, 21 months were spent with Utkuhikhalingmiut, 17 in Chantrey Inlet and four in the nearest settlement of Gjoa Haven with relatives of the Chantrey Inlet people. An additional eight months were spent in Chantrey Inlet in 1968. During the next two or three years, most of the Utkuhikhalingmiut moved to Gjoa Haven, and I have visited them there three times: in the summer of 1971 (one month), in the winter of 1971–2 (one month), and in 1972 (three months). The Utkuhikhalingmiut data used in this paper are drawn largely from my Chantrey Inlet notes, and the ethnographic present refers to the period between 1963 and 1968. The study of the Qipisamiut was begun in 1970 (two months), and I also lived with them for eight months in 1971, in addition to the 1974 and 1975 trips

mentioned above. The ethnographic present refers to the whole period between 1971 and 1975.

2 In order to clarify the discussion that follows, I should explain that Inuit do not conceptualize killing versus non-violence and self-sufficiency versus nurturance as two *separate* oppositions. The Inuit concept of *nallik-* (or *naklik-*), which can be glossed, roughly, as 'nurturant affection', is a core value in Inuit culture – that is, it applies to everybody, all the time, under all circumstances, and *nallik-* behaviour defines a good person. The behaviour that is defined as *nallik-*, nurturant, covers a very wide spectrum and *includes* non-violence. *Nallik-* behaviour is, theoretically, antithetical to any form of aggression. Physical attack, verbal unkindness or criticism, even unexpressed hostile thoughts are opposed to *nallik-*. Consequently, instead of defining the opposition as killing versus non-violence, I could have set it up more broadly as aggression versus nurturance.

But self-sufficiency, too, is antithetical to *nallik-*, nurturance, since a concern for one's autonomy, one's own welfare, may generate unkind, ungenerous acts. Self-sufficiency has two opposite poles: nurturance and dependence. However, of these, only nurturance is positively valued by society. Extremely strong, dependent, possessive needs exist in Inuit and are recognized by them; and these dependent feelings help to support both the independent behaviour and the nurturant behaviour that Inuit value (Briggs 1975 and 1978), but dependent behaviour *per se* is, I think, not valued except in small children. Moreover, unlike the opposite poles of violence, one of which (nurturance) subsumes the other (non-violence), the two opposite poles of self-sufficiency are sometimes themselves in conflict, as when the wish to give nurturantly occurs simultaneously with a wish to take dependently. It is, then, clearly an oversimplification to speak of 'killing versus non-violence' and 'self-sufficiency versus nurturance'; and the fact that the situation is really more complex explains why from time to time I refer to nurturance as the opposite of killing or injuring, and dependence as the opposite of self-sufficiency. In the space of this paper it is impossible to lay out the complete paradigm of relationships among Inuit values. However, I do not think that this incomplete exposition damages the argument of the paper, which rests on the pervasiveness of contradictions in Inuit values and emotions. If the data were fully laid out, they would show the existence of far more contradictions than I can describe here.

3 This idea was suggested to me by George DeVos' discussion of Japanese tolerance for cognitive dissonance (1975:165–82, especially pp. 168–9), although he says that where affect is involved – as it is in the case of values – tolerance for dissonance disappears.

4 The same kind of analysis works for other values, too. See, for example, my analysis of the motivations underlying self-sufficient behaviour in Inuit society (1978).

5 One Eastern Arctic woman, talking about difficulties she had experienced while living in the more highly controlled Central Arctic, said: 'When I first came here, people were afraid of me. They thought that when I yelled at my kids I was angry enough to kill.' This woman's disciplinary shouts were very moderate by comparison with some Euro-Canadian yells.

6 Traditionally, Inuit killed recidivist murderers and the violently insane; and

defensive murder attempts on angry people have also been recorded (e.g., Rasmussen 1932:19–21). Murders for other, less socially acceptable, reasons such as sexual jealousy are said to have been common, also.

7 This emotional sense of the unpredictability of the social world is reflected in the Inuit world view, in which the physical world, too, is seen as uncertain and in need of careful handling – a connection that was pointed out to me by M. Godelier and A. Balikci in comments on the spoken version of this paper.

8 I share in the general assumption that these same conditions also help to determine what the values will be. Observers have recorded remarkable similarities both in values and in socialization practices and philosophies, not only in hunting and gathering societies but also in some proto-agricultural societies; and some of these observers have pointed out the importance of geographical and historical context in determining the values and practices. For a few recent examples of such studies, see the papers by Draper, Sorenson, Dentan, Berndt, and Turnbull, all in Montagu (1978); and see also Lee (1972). I have been told that Lappish child-rearing practices show some striking similarities, too.

Bibliography

Berndt, Catherine H. 1978. 'In Aboriginal Australia', in A. Montagu (ed.), *Learning non-aggression*, 144–60. New York: Oxford University Press

Birket-Smith, Kaj 1959. *The Eskimos*. London: Methuen

Briggs, Jean L. 1970. *Never in anger: portrait of an Eskimo family*. Cambridge, Mass: Harvard University Press

1975. 'The origins of nonviolence: aggression in two Canadian Eskimo groups', in W. Muensterberger (ed.), *The psychoanalytic study of society*, 6:134–203. New York: International Universities Press

1978. 'Cohesive loners'. Paper presented at the First Inuit Conference, Laval University

Dentan, Robert Knox 1978. 'Notes on childhood in a nonviolent context: the Semai case', in A. Montagu (ed.), *Learning non-aggression*, 94–143

DeVos, George A. 1975. 'Affective dissonance and primary socialization'. *Ethos* 3:165–82

Draper, Patricia 1978. 'The learning environment for aggression and anti-social behavior among the !Kung', in A. Montagu (ed.), *Learning non-aggression*, 31–53

Haavind, Hanne 1975. 'Mothers as teachers, children as learners'. Mimeographed MS. University of Troms, Norway

Lee, Richard B. 1972. 'Population growth and the beginnings of sedentary life among the !Kung Bushmen', in B. Spooner (ed.), *Population growth: anthropological implications*. Cambridge, Mass.: Massachusetts Institute of Technology Press

1978. 'Issues in the study of hunter-gatherers: 1968–1978. Paper presented at the Conference on Hunter-gatherers, Paris, June 1978

Montagu, Ashley 1978. *Learning non-aggression*. New York: Oxford University Press

Paine, Robert 1971. 'The heroic act'. Seminar delivered at Universities of Oslo and Bergen, Norway

Rasmussen, Knud 1932. *Intellectual culture of the Copper Eskimos*. Report of the Fifth Thule Expedition 1912–1924, 9. Copenhagen

Sorenson, E. Richard 1978. 'Cooperation and freedom among the Fore of New Guinea', in A. Montagu (ed.), *Learning non-aggression*, 12–30. New York: Oxford University Press

Turnbull, Colin M. 1978. 'The politics of non-aggression', in A. Montagu (ed.), *Learning non-aggression*, 161–221. New York: Oxford University Press

6. The ritualization of potential conflict between the sexes among the Mbuti*

COLIN M. TURNBULL

If humans have a seemingly limitless capacity for violence, for aggression, they have an equally great potential for nonviolence and non-aggressivity, and a notable feature of many small-scale societies is the great amount of concern shown, in a wide diversity of institutionalized forms, for the reduction of humanity's potential for aggressivity and violence to a remarkable minimum. It is not that 'primitive' people were or are any more moral than ourselves, nor necessarily more pragmatic; if they see the wisdom of minimizing violence and aggressivity, reducing hostility to a level far below their mental and technological potential, it is perhaps simply because that best answers their overall need for survival just as our own maximal development of the aggressive potential may answer our needs, if not our tastes. . . .

The Mbuti hunter-gatherers of the tropical rain forest in northeastern Zaïre accept that human nature is not angelic, and they expect, with typical pragmatism, that however divine our essence may be (and they have such a concept) our social self may stray. Therefore, by stating at the outset our potential for harm, they defuse that potential to a major extent, which allows them time to put considerable energy into averting that harm while, and by, developing their potential for nonharm. . . .

For the Mbuti there are four major principles of social organization, which correspond to the four major areas in which conflict is most likely to occur in their lives. These areas are clearly recognized by the Mbuti; the inherent potential for conflict in each is made manifest in ritual form and is further guarded against by appropriate social institutions. These areas are territory, family (or kinship), age, and sex. These areas are progressively explored in approximately that order, both as princi-

*Reprinted by permission of the author and editor from Ashley Montagu (ed.), *Learning non-aggression*, Oxford University Press.

ples of organization and as dangerous areas within which conflict can arise and violence erupt, as the newborn passes from infancy through childhood into youth. In this way he is equipped to be a part of a highly integrated, organized community, in action and belief, and the nature of his educational experience is that he is also equipped to deal with conflict as it arises without the fear that comes from individual isolation and competitiveness. On the contrary, his total experience has led him, by youth, to enter any situation of stress with the very confidence that is one of his chief weapons against stress. This confidence is well supported by a whole repertoire of specific conflict resolving skills and techniques well learned and practised throughout childhood. While he may feel a degree of uncertainty, he feels none of the fear and perceives nothing of the threat which could lead ultimately and exclusively to a violent solution to conflict. . . .

The children in the *bopi* (playground), especially the older ones, when tired of physical pastimes, have many verbal pastimes. Many of these involve jokes – ways of exploring alternative modes of behaviour, discovering those that are proper and work, and those that are improper and do not work. But often they involve the rational and verbal use of concepts such as *ekimi* ('quiet' or 'peace') and *akami* ('noise' or 'conflict') in the settlement of conflict situations. It may start through imitation of a real dispute the children witnessed in the main camp, perhaps the night before. They all take roles and imitate the adults. It is almost a form of judgement, for if the adults talked their way out of the dispute, the children, having performed their imitation once, are likely to drop it. If the children detect any room for improvement, however, they will explore that, and if the adult argument was inept and everyone went to sleep that night in a bad temper, then the children try and show that they can do better, and if they find they cannot, then they revert to ridicule which they play out until they are all rolling on the ground in near-hysterics. That happens to be the way many of the most potentially violent and dangerous disputes are settled in adult life.

Laughter, jokes, and ridicule are vital elements in Mbuti life, and I believe that together they constitute a major factor in developing the affective characteristics of the adults and in minimizing the disaffective . . .

However, around the age of eight or nine, perhaps as late as eleven, and in my case at the age of thirty, boy children enter the *nkumbi*[1] and emerge a mere three months later as adults in village eyes (for it is a village ritual) but as youths in Mbuti eyes. The Mbuti have no formal

Mbuti elder, Moke, caring for another's child (C. Turnbull)

initiation of boys, nor is there any evidence that they ever had one. There might possibly have been greater recognition given to a child who catches and kills his first game – for that is both a dangerous act, compounding his original sin, and a necessary act, for by such acts alone can he survive in this world. But for a number of complex reasons described elsewhere, and to be elaborated on by a colleague (Joseph A. Towles), who as anthropologist playing the role of villager was able to penetrate the *nkumbi* far more deeply than I was permitted to do, the Mbuti find it useful to enter the village ritual. It is of paramount importance in bringing about effective relationships between the two potentially hostile groups. Within the forest world of the Mbuti it is merely an easy way of marking the rather uncertain transition of a boy from childhood to youth. For the girls there is no such problem, their transition is clearly defined by the first flow of menstrual blood, an event acclaimed with joy by all, for now that girl has the power to become a mother.[2] At that point she will become an adult, and her mate will become her husband, and an adult also.

Following the *nkumbi*, however, there are still six or seven or maybe more years to go in the realm of youth. The village ritual, with its explicit sex instruction and moral teaching and consecration of the individual to the way of the ancestors and to the society at large, has nothing to teach the Mbuti about forest life. What remains to be learned he will learn, with his age-mates, in this next stage of life facing him. Territory, kinship, and age have all been well explored. That exploration will continue, but the main sphere explored during youth is that of sex, and while that is being explored the rational ability is further developed and refined, and the youth finds himself (and herself) in a jural rather than ritual role, in the pastime of developing interdependence. During youth, also, the Mbuti becomes more fully cognizant of that ultimate all embracing sphere, *nadura* (forest), and finds that his lingering purity (he may not kill an antelope until late in youth) sometimes places him in a role that is ritual as well as jural. . . .

The youth, in so far as he is less pure, or more contaminated, is such NOT because of his increasingly physical concern with sex, but because of his increasing proximity to the daily act of sacrilege, the hunt. If anything, his sexual activity would be a purifying element . . . In the *bopi* there was no sexual discrimination in the sharing of love among the children, to their fullest capacity. I maintain that this is the same during youth, yet not once did I come across a case of homosexual intercourse, although the existence of names for both male and female homosexuality suggests that it may exist. I came across one case of bestiality (a male youth and a female goat), which was openly acknowledged and respected to the extent that neither boy nor goat suffered any disability except that they were confined to the village. The grounds for exclusion from the forest were not uncleanliness or impurity, there was no taint of immorality, merely the practical observation that the boy's 'wife' did not know how to hunt and would quickly die if she came with him back to the forest. The boy, torn between two loyalties, finally chose the forest, pensioned his goat-wife off by presenting her to a villager whom he knew would cherish her and keep her well and alive, since the villager thought he was acquiring enormous control over the forest, the goat being well impregnated with the sperm of the forest people. That boy then married an Mbuti girl with no difficulty, he was back in the centre of the forest sphere and the goat was no longer part of the 'here and now'. I mention the incident because it says a great deal about the Mbuti concept of love, even when carried into the physical act of sex. Even when so carried, the two things remain distinct. It might well be for similar pragmatic reasons that there is no recorded instance of male or female homosexuality; one's 'wife' or 'husband' simply would not know how to gather or hunt.

By this time girls have paid increasing attention to women's activities, following them on the hunt and on their private gathering expeditions, and the boys similarly have increasingly been following the men, learning the finer points of hunting and other primarily male activities. Homosexuality is not the point, however, any more than bestiality. The point is that even when boys and girls discover the ecstasy of sex, and for whatever reason confine it to a heterosexual relationship, they continue to love each other regardless of shared sexuality and even carry something of the physical act into their relationships, as though almost regretful of being separated by it. I cannot speak for the girls, though I have seen and heard enough similar behaviour amongst them to convince me there is not likely to be much difference, but the male youths delight in bodily contact throughout youth. It becomes interspersed with more frequent formal spacing as serious heterosexual courtship begins, but it continues even into early married adult life. Male youths tend to sleep together, either in the open around a fire, or in a hut built by one of them and used by all. They sleep in a glorious bundle of young life, full of warmth and full of love. There is little sexual fondling, and what there is is due more in the form of a joke than to give any sexual pleasure. However, there is no doubt that the close hugging is more than for mere warmth, necessary though that is on any night in the rain forest. And there is no doubt that a measure of physical sexual relief, or satisfaction, is achieved in this way, with or without ejaculation. An occasional muttered comment about ejaculation may be made by an individual to himself, much as I might mutter if my shoelace broke while walking along a crowded street. Messy or bothersome to the individual, but of little or no significance to anyone else. What is significant is that the growing separation of the sexes for the physical act of copulation, augmented by the growing division of the sexes by the allocation of labour, is in a very real sense being countered, and love is being shared, to the point that even if intercourse were to take place I doubt that it would add anything to the intensity of the relationship, except possibly for that one brief moment. The sacrifice of that moment, somehow, seems to make the relationship all the stronger. Before looking at the final stage of transition from youth to adulthood, which is also a transition from unconscious, or perhaps better nonrational non-aggressivity to conscious, rational non-aggressivity, a brief summary of the lessons learned and the symbols implanted will be helpful.

Values

By entry to youth (between the ages of eight or nine and eleven) the Mbuti child has learned the major values that militate against aggressivity and violence. The following are the most important.

security: The Mbuti themselves consider that their individual life stories begin with conception and their formation as a foetus in the womb of their mother. Judging by what seems to be a high incidence of trouble-free pregnancy and childbirth, accomplished with ease and resulting in a healthy child as well as a healthy mother, such experience of life as the child may have, in the womb, should be one of total security. From the moment of birth onwards everything is done to enable that sense of security to be transferred in steadily widening and inclusive circles from the sphere that is limited to the mother's body to the *endu* (leaf hut), to other *endu*, to the *bopi* (playground), to the *apa* (camp), and finally to the most inclusive sphere of all, *ndura* (the forest). The last may be taken to include, by opposition, the nonforest world of the village, for opposition is precisely the mechanism that provides the Mbuti with this ultimate security, safe within their sacred world against the profane. This process of increasing inclusion is the same process by which other values are gradually instilled, though from the point of view of infants and children each successive stage may seem more separate than inclusive, since they tend temporarily to abandon the one sphere once they have become secure in it, and experiment with the next. It is probably only in youth that the integrated nature of their total experience becomes apparent to them.

dependence: The steps are similar. Initial dependence on their mother is shown to have validity in relationship with ever expanding circles of other 'kin', ultimately including every Mbuti in the camp, regardless of age or sex. But an Mbuti also learns the value of dependence, just as that of security, with reference to territory (*endu*, *bopi*, *apa*, and *ndura*), and with reference to four age grades: children, youths, adults and elders.

interdependence is the next value learned, and again an Mbuti sees this value as having applicability in all the areas in which conflict is likely to arise: kinship, territory, age, and sex. Children do not associate interdependence with conflict; that understanding comes with youth. But they quickly move from the security of dependence in these areas to the even greater security of interdependence, where they get their first real taste of responsibility and power.

coordination: This value was first learned as infants coordinated the movements of their various limbs and then coordinated their overall movement with that of their mothers. But they also learned coordination in and between the age groups.

cooperation: As the power of reason develops, so is the value of coordination, now well learned, transcended by an intellectual attitude that accompanies the necessity for cooperation demanded by the increasingly complex activities within the *endu, bopi,* and *apa.* Even the ultimate cooperative relationship between Mbuti and their prime (*ndura*) sphere has been amply learned, first while accompanying the hunt on their mothers' side and later by setting off on foot with the men, if a boy, or with the women, if a girl. It is at this stage that this, and by inclusion the other values already learned, are extended to the fourth area of potential conflict, the differentiation between the sexes.

ekimi/akami: still, until youth, primarily at a physical rather than rational level, children have been introduced to the positive value of *ekimi*, or quiet, as against that of *akami*, or disturbance. They have learned to associate *akami* with hunger, since noise, ill temper, lack of the proper manifestation of the other values (the lack of any of these values is described as *akami*), generally leads to an unsuccessful hunt. They have equally learned that the proper manifestation of the values learned so far results in *ekimi*, a word they now begin to use in other contexts much as we would use the word 'happiness'. They find that one of the most common occasions on which the word *akami* is used is in reference not to noise on the hunt, which is unusual, but for verbal disputes in the camp. They also learn to differentiate between 'good' sound, such as song, and 'bad' sound, such as an argument, though in our sense the song may be a great deal noisier than the argument. Similarly they learn that *suso* (wind) is generally classified as *ekimi* unless it is *kuko* (wind that does damage) in which case it is *akami*. An Mbuti's starting point with this value is sound, which applies to both *ekimi* and *akami*, but it is quickly learned, well before entering youth, that it is not sound itself that results in one value or the other, but the *effect* of that sound.

Techniques of learning

The overall technique by which all this is learned in itself contributes to the enormous confidence with which the Mbuti face their total world by the time they reach youth, which becomes a time of testing that confidence, each youth consciously challenging him or herself and putting this confidence to the test. The overall technique involves allowing the child, from infancy onwards, the safe but adventurous exploration of each successive sphere, at the child's own pace, while developing (through good use) sensory and motor abilities, the as yet nonrational sensitivity to the totality (intuition?) while consciously dealing with one segment of experience after the other. Thus the ground is laid, by youth, for rational, intellectual integration of the totality of a person's experience and confidence. The various techniques we have looked at include:

endu: suckling, rocking, listening, smelling, tasting, the mother, the father, their bed, the floor and walls of the hut.

apa: physical exploration is continued so that all the various *endu* are included, though as yet the child has little experience of the *apa* as a single unit.

bopi: the techniques here first include pastimes that develop muscular strength and coordination, and although played out in company of others, they are solitary explorations. They then develop into more complex pastimes that require cooperation of increasing numbers of children, such as climbing and bending the sapling to the ground: imitation of adult economic activities (hunting, gathering, making bark-cloth); imitation of adult domestic activities (house building, cooking, eating, sleeping, quarrelling); imitation of the political activities of youth (ridicule of each other, of youths, adults and elders; ridicule of villagers). Here the pastimes demand intellectual, rational content as well as physical, especially in the ridicule of adult disputes which calls for considerable improvization and exploration of the value system. Then there is, finally, limited imitation of the ritual role of the elders, in which they perceive some similarity to their own role as lighters of the hunting fire. But the children also imitate the role of elders as story-tellers, partly by repeating the stories, and partly by improvizing similar stories of their own. Here their intellect and power of reason are being developed in such a way as to reinforce the values learned, and to prepare the way for their entry into youth and the integrated world of the *apa*. Through their physical exploration of space after space the children have come in physical contact with the major elements that will form such an important part of their later world of symbols. It may or may not be stretching things a little to link the warmth of the womb to that of the mother's body and both consequently to fire; however, I have heard Mbuti in apparently casual conversation liken the womb to a fire. But children undeniably form close associations with the hearth of their *endu*, that of other *endu*, that of *bopi*, that of the *hunt*, and that which, even before they take part in it as youths, they will have seen in the center of the *apa*, the *kumamolimo*: the hearth (literally: vagina) of the *molimo*, a hearth lit only at times of major crisis. Similarly their contact with air might be said to have begun with the first breath they drew, before the cutting of the umbilical cord, and continued through learning to play various kinds of whistles and flutes, learning to blow a fire into life (fans are never used), learning to sing, to learning if a boy to blow the breath of life through the sacred *molimo* trumpet so that the hot coals at the far end throw fiery sparks out into the forest. Earth similarly has been a constant in their lives, from their first explorations of the ground within the *endu*, *apa*, and *bopi*, the trees that grow out of it, to the earth that again, as children, they may have been or will shortly see rubbed into the *molimo* trumpet or scattered over the *molimo* hearth when, finally, it is extinguished. And water – their first contact with water was special – the water of the forest vine. Even splashing about in the forest streams was special, because that was when they began to look at reflections and when elders might tell stories of the other world. As children they are warned away from that special part of the stream where the *molimo* trumpet is kept during the *molimo* festival, warned simply by a special barricade of forest vines. And if they have not yet seen it, by peeping out from the inside of their hunts at nighttime, they will soon as youths see the *molimo* trumpet be given water to drink. Their contact with the supreme symbol, the forest itself, has been far from restricted to the mere climbing of trees – in the same way that they have come to recognize their interdependence with all other Mbuti so have they come to realize their interdependence with the natural world of which they are an integral part. . . .

At entry to youth this educative process is continued, all the values that so effectively militate against aggressivity are strengthened by further activities, which are extended to include that area of potential conflict with which the child has had least contact, sex. At the same time youths now develop an intellectual ability to integrate the *values*, just as they can now rationally integrate their various spheres and realms of activity. In the course of this they become involved in a number of institutionalized forms of behaviour that bring them into both physical and intellectual contact with the underlying, omnipresent value of non-aggressivity.

For instance, while as children being carried on their mothers' sides or trotting along beside one or another parent they were indirectly aware of the separation and physical opposition of the sexes on the hunt; it was indirect because it was to large extent involuntary and insignificant. Now that as youths they take an increasing part in the hunt, and have their special place in it, the division, and opposition, of the sexes is very real. It has its own powerful logic as a division of labour, but its ritualization in various institutionalized forms raises it to another level. The hunting song in which the youths play a major part reproduces the physical opposition of men at their nets to women driving game towards the nets, with youths in an approximately medial position on each side. While it might be difficult to demonstrate that this song is a ritual rather than another educational, value-reinforcing pastime, there are other undeniably ritual activities that involve similar antiphonal singing techniques and which are even more directly manifestations of the need to avert conflict between the sexes. Appropriately these are activities in which both adults and youths participate, not elders or children. It is expected that the conflict will arise within the age grade of adulthood, to some extent it is their role to manifest such conflict, and it is the role of youth to resolve such conflict if they cannot avert it.

One such activity is the tug of war. This is usually initiated by adults, but is generally not very successful or prolonged unless youths join in. It most often occurs during the honey season, which is a time of general relaxation, involving the fission of the hunting band into small groups that roam the territory in search of honey, with no communal hunting to bind the band together as a corporate unit. While this season may serve an ecological function, effectively putting an end to the hunt for up to two months, it undoubtedly also serves the political function of allowing unresolved disputes and potential disputes and lines of conflict to be brought into the open. The tug of war expresses the major line of potential conflict, between male and female. Men take a vine rope on one side, women pull on the opposite side. They sing in antiphony. However, if one side or the other were to win that would resolve nothing, so when the men seem to be winning one of them will abandon his side of the tug and join the women, pulling up his bark-cloth and adjusting it in the fashion of women, shouting encouragement to them in a falsetto, ridiculing womanhood by the very exaggeration of his mime. Then, when the women begin to win, one of them adjusts her bark clothing, letting it down, and strides over to the men's side and joins their shouting in a deep bass voice, similarly gently mocking manhood. Each person crossing over tries to outdo the ridicule of the last, causing more and more laughter, until when the contestants are laughing so hard they cannot sing or pull any more, they let go of the vine rope and fall to the ground in near hysteria. Although both youths and adults cross sides, it is primarily the youths who really enact the ridicule. In this way the ridicule is performed without hostility, rather with a sense of at least partial identification and empathy. It is in this way that the violence and aggressivity of either sex 'winning' is avoided, and the stupidity of competitiveness demonstrated.

The honey season is considered a time for relaxation and enjoyment of the pleasures of life, of which honey is one of the main symbols. Sexual activity among the youths is heightened. But the association of the individual quest for pleasure, however legitimate, with conflict is brought to the fore in the honeybee dance. Again, both adults and youths participate. The males form a single-file line, armed with bows and arrows, and with fire which they have to 'steal' from the various *endu* hearths. Here is the first representation (in this particular dance) of the male/female conflict: fire is controlled by women, who are responsible for carrying fire with them on the hunt or whenever they accompany the men on any journey, and above all when moving from one camp site to another, so that the *endu* hearth never dies. The Mbuti know but eschew two traditional village techniques for making fire, and use matches (if provided) *only* for 'profane' acts such as lighting cigarettes.

The men then, have to 'steal' fire from the hearths to carry it with them, as they do on the real honey-gathering expeditions, to smoke out the bees and enable them to 'steal' (again recognizing the aggressive nature of the act, comparable to stealing the life of the game they hunt for meat) the honey, and the larvae of future life which Mbuti consume with the honey. As the men dance around the *apa*, looking upwards as if looking and listening for bees, the women form another line and follow the men, dancing behind them, or parallel with them, sometimes in front, even dancing in and out of the men's line as though invisible. Then the women change direction and dance towards the men. They also are carrying burning firebrands, but unlike the men, every woman and girl has a live brand in her left hand, whereas only two or three men may have brands with them, sheathed in phrynium leaves. As the men approach the women, who have slowed down, the women break ranks and attack the men, beating their glowing firebrands over the heads of the men, covering them with sparks and hot coals that 'burn like the sting of bees'. The men are routed, and re-form and start all over again, looking for the nonstinging kind of bee. Unlike the tug of war, this dance has a rather more definite conclusion in that the men never succeed in their attempt to 'steal' honey. One or other of the women (not a girl) may end the dance by dancing into her hut and coming out with a leaf cup of honey or a piece of honeycomb, and offer this to the men, who accept it and consume it, sharing some with the women (bees).

Hoop dancing and rope skipping are two activities particularly common during the honey season, and in certain forms restricted to older girls. Girls also spend a great deal of time, in this season, decorating their bodies with the juice of the gardenia fruit, and demonstrating their nubility by playing with the small gardenia fruits, rolling them from their shoulders onto their upstanding breasts, from which they toss them up to the air and catch them and throw them back onto their shoulders again. The camp clown, a male, will frequently demonstrate that this is one thing a boy can NOT do; but the boys have pastimes of their own such as playing a 'game' with beans, seeds, or small stones, according to rules by which both sides 'win'. This is a variant of a favourite village gambling game, and an important way in which both Mbuti and villagers socialize when Mbuti are in the village. Boys also decorate themselves during this season, with leaves and orchids and fresh cut bark clothes. These are often preliminaries to the great joint pre-marital festival, the *elima*, which ideally but not necessarily takes place during the honey season. It involves all the adult male and female youths from the *apa* as it is constituted at the moment, a few only of the elders in specific roles such as the 'mother' of the *elima* (either an old widow or a younger barren woman) and a 'father' of the *elima*, a less formal role generally taken by a widower or a cripple (both the 'mother' and the 'father' thus being in a sense sexless); the other mothers in the camp act as guards of the *bamelima*, the girls who are living in the *elima* hut. Finally, male youths form other hunting territories, near or far, visit the camp in order to participate in the festival. Adult males, children and elders (other than the 'mother' or 'father' of the *elima*) are excluded except as spectators.

As with other social institutions, the *elima* can be looked at from a number of different points of view. It is occasioned by the dramatic and unmistakable entry of any girl in the *apa* into womanhood, marked by the appearance of the first menstrual blood. Unlike many societies, African and other, this is widely publicized and acclaimed with joy and exuberance, for it means that a mother has been 'born'. A camp may wait until another girl similarly 'sees the blood' for the first time, so that the two girls can combine their *elima* festivals. A girl from another camp may be brought by her parents, under the pretext simply of joining the camp during its monthly shift from one site to another, but really so that she can join the *elima*. This is most likely if the girls are friends. The girls invite other friends to join them in the *elima* house, where they live with the *ema'abamelima* (mother of the girls of the *elima*). Effectively, then, the older youths of the camp are strictly segregated at this time into male and female, and even the younger youths follow suit, separating themselves in activities they would normally pursue together.

While the *elima* is consciously thought of as a pre-marital festival, providing an opportunity for formal courtship and sexual experimentation, it can also be thought of as a joint male/female initiation that signals the approaching advance of adults into elderhood, another impending area of conflict, of possible aggressivity if not violence. The Mbuti themselves refer to this transition period as one of *akami* for the individual concerned, whereas the transitions from childhood to youth and youth to adulthood are *ekimi*. The *elima* may be used by adults on the verge of elderhood to temporarily play the role of clown. They do this, if male, by classifying themselves one generation down, as youths, fighting their way with male youths toward the *elima* house, even into it for a brief moment perhaps. Older women more rarely opt for such a medial role; if widowed the transition into elderhood is smoother than for the men, and even if not widowed they are not barred from food-gathering in elderhood to the same extent that male elders are barred from hunting. But older adult women who feel ambivalent about the approaching change of status take advantage of the *elima* by sitting with the young girls when they emerge from the *elima* house. In this way transitional adults, by allying themselves with the lower generation temporarily, automatically identify themselves with the superior generation by the principle of alternate generation alliance, which operates strongly in Mbuti society.

The main feature of the *elima* that concerns us here is the ritual conflict between male and female youths, manifest in the battle waged with sticks, large nuts and seeds, small burning embers or even logs thrown by the women, and smaller seeds or pieces of tough skin fired from the bow by the male youths, and long supple sapling whips used by the *bamelima* girls. In order to gain access to the *elima* house and thus acquire the right to sleep with one of the girls, a male youth or medial male adult has to fight his way through the barrage of fire set up by the adult women. Once inside, or even outside, they may be met by the girls themselves, armed with their whips. The same whips are used by girls in their frequent forays into the camp, and even into neighbouring territories, to beat boys (and medial adults) as an invitation to visit them in the *elima* house. There are obviously a number of complex lessons being learned here. Apart from the intense discussions the girls have with the mother of the *elima*, and the boys with the father, which provide them with an intellectual understanding of what they are being prepared for, the very physical violence they are met with in pursuit of their individual sexual desires is a dramatic ritualization of the inherent conflict between their individual and social selves, a conflict that is one of the keynotes of the adult life into which they are moving. The fact that they have already learned that adults are *expected* to be troublemakers, that it is even one of their allotted roles, that adulthood is a time of *akami*, now for the first time becomes part of their own personal experience. Yet all the familiar symbols of security are there; the mother and father, the *endu* (of the *bamelima*) with its own hearth; the firebrands they throw or have thrown at them; the very special leaves they sleep on when they gain admittance, which leaves have to be ritually disposed of afterwards; the young saplings with which they whip or are whipped; and the songs they are expected to sing in clear antiphony, distinct from all other song in form and style. Water is used in the final ritual washing of both boys and girls, when the *elima* ends.

Youths learn, through the *elima*, that the pursuit of individual desires, although not wrong in itself, is likely to lead to *akami*, and if they wish to pursue such desires they had better temper them in such a way that they are acceptable to the rest of the society. The adult women are perfectly capable of preventing even the strongest and most aggressive youth from entering the *elima* house if they so wish; they may beat him with sticks or even with thorns, or may simply pick him up bodily and throw him in the nearest stream or river. The *elima*, which lasts a month, is obviously a disruptive time, and when it is over there are many disgruntled adults and a general time of *akami*. The very youths who were the unwitting cause of *akami* are then called upon to play what is perhaps their most important role, a role that prepares them admirably for their own inevitably disputatious adulthood. In this role they are the bearers of the *molimo madé*, the lesser *molimo*. The word *molimo*, which has to do with 'leopardness', is perhaps best translated as the soul or spiritual essence of the forest. Its visible and audible symbol is a long trumpet, traditionally made from a special tree which, when cut young, can be hollowed out with a tough abrasive vine. It is usually six to ten feet in length. Elders control the *molimo mangbo*, the great *molimo*, which is used on occasions of major crisis such as death or prolonged and serious bad hunting; the *molimo madé* is brought into action to 'quieten' a 'noisy' camp. Thus it is youth who sit in judgement and primarily on adults; youth which is called upon to rectify the harm done by the adulthood into which they will shortly pass. While the *molimo mangbo* (by youths again, but under the direction of elders) is made to sound like a leopard, and to sing like Mbuti (both symbols of *ekimi*) and is given water to drink, rubbed with earth, and made to produce fire as well as song by the breath of life, the *molimo madé* of youth is made to sound like an angry elephant, the destroyer of the forest; when it comes into camp, instead of being fed with earth, fire, water and air it is taken hold of by all the male youths and stampedes back and forth, destroying anything in its path, attacking all the *endu* in turn, perhaps but not necessarily paying rather more attention to the *endu* of the trouble-makers who caused the *molimo madé* to be 'awakened'.

Nothing the adult or even the elders can do or say has any effect on the control of the youths over the *molimo madé*. It is youth that decides not only when the *akami* is serious enough to warrant such action, or whether they should merely resort to ridicule, but it is youth that effec-tively decides *what* constitutes *akami*: youth has the power of revising the values of society, of shaping the future. Youth's wealth of experi-ence is now backed up by a well-developed intellect; youths hold long and serious discussions about adult behaviour with reference to *akami* and *ekimi*, but as concepts rather than as rigid codes of behavior. Simi-larly, although adults have no control over sexual escapades of youth outside the institution of *elima*, the youths themselves, increasingly rec-ognizing the potential of sex as a source of conflict, discuss among themselves their preferences as to when and where to have sexual intercourse with a girl. It must be a time and place of *ekimi* they say, and in their discussions they state their preferences in terms of prox-imity to water, so that they can look at it or listen to it; to earth in terms of the soft feel or sweet smell of the earth (or leaf mould) in this place as against that; to air in terms of the sound of a breeze rustling the leaves. When any pair of youths decide that they have experimented sufficiently to be able to bring this *ekimi* with them into adulthood, for without it the sexual act would be neither affective nor pleasurable, they get married. For the Mbuti this involves little formality. The male youth has to show his prowess as a hunter by catching and killing 'large' game (large enough to feed a nuclear family), either on his own or by virtue of his position at the extremities of the semicircle of hunting nets; and the girl has to be willing to go with him and build a house for them to live in. Parents have little say, though they may quietly voice their opinion; elders only intervene if they feel the marriage is too 'close', a concept that involves both kinship and territoriality.

Adulthood is entered without formality as soon as youths feel ready to undertake the responsibility of marriage. Once married the youths are classified as adults. The boy's mother gives him a hunting net, and as adults the young man and his bride set off for the daily hunt with the rest of the camp; there is no vertical hierarchy within the age grade. It is then that they begin to realize fully how full of conflict is adult life. Once a child is born the husband is expected to abstain from intercourse with his wife for three years. There is no openly stated prohibition against sleeping with other women, least of all unmarried girls, but to do so immediately places him in competition with other adult males or with youthful suitors. The adult male is also the killer of game, and so the one who perpetuates human (and animal) mortality. He has to rely on children to minimize this necessary act of violence and aggressivity, through the hunting fire. He has to rely on youths to restore *ekimi* when his unwise flirtations or jealousies cause *akami*. He has to accept that the youth of the day may redefine the concepts of *ekimi* and *akami* in ways not entirely agreeable to him. And when, usually in adulthood, he is faced with the death of his own parents the adult male has to rely on the power of the elders to invoke the *molimo mangbo* and restore *ekimi* even in the face of death. At the height of his sexual potency the adult male finds himself, socially, remarkably impotent. This is largely minimized by the values learned from childhood onwards, the value of dependence and interdependence. It is further offset by his all too recent experience as a youth, and the hostility that might result between these adjacent generations is lessened by their very proximity, and by the intensive cooperation demanded between them in hunting and gathering as in ritual/sacred song and dance.

It is the adults who are primarily involved in the most dangerous of all areas of conflict, that between the sedentary village farmers and the nomadic hunter-gatherers. Because of their economic role it is they who are expected to bring meat, mushrooms, saplings, and leaves for the house-building, and other forest products, to the village. The villagers misread this economic control of the adult Mbuti as indicative of political control, and conduct all their negotiations and disputes with Mbuti through the adults. This places adults, male and female, in a difficult position, since any attempt to implement the wishes of the villagers is likely to cause enormous dispute in the Mbuti forest camp, and failure to do so is going to create equal trouble in the village with which they have to deal if they are to succeed in keeping the villagers from coming into the forest and getting what they need for themselves. We cannot go into the village aspect of this conflict here, except perhaps just to draw attention again to the participation of Mbuti boys and their fathers in the village *nkumbi* initiation, by which the villagers believe they achieve ultimate supernatural control over the Mbuti, when political control through the Mbuti adults fails. Participation of Mbuti couples wishing to get married in village marriage rituals also serves the same end. But in the forest the adults are invariably blamed for the *akami* that results from even the most reasonable requests of the villagers. In the forest camp, then, it is usually the adults who in the guise of entertainment ridicule the villagers constantly, such as when recounting tales of their visit to the village: how they swindled the villagers or cheated them or stole from them, beat them at their own gambling games, and so forth. In such pantomimes the adults ridicule the villagers as clumsy, stupid, noisy, dirty, but also as dangerous, like the elephant.

The constant mobility of the Mbuti, who change camp sites almost every month, helps prevent conflict between Mbuti and villagers. The camps fluctuate in both size and composition as well as in location so that a villager never knows which Mbuti are where. This same process of fission and fusion is of course also a major element in conflict avoidance between Mbuti themselves, allowing potential disputants to separate themselves into different camps, temporarily, before the dispute flares up into major proportions.

More than any of the above, however, as a factor in controlling aggressivity, violence, and conflict in adult life, is the demonstrably positive value of *ekimi* that the adult has perceived at every stage of his life and which he still perceives and strives for, even in the pursuit of individual satisfaction. The *molimo* festival is demanding and exhausting. While stressing *ekimi* it almost inevitably creates *akami*. The *molimo* is always accompanied, then, by rituals that reverse *akami*. The *molimo madé* is one, the other is focused on sex. As the prime noise-makers it is not surprising that it is the adults, male and female, that are expected to perform *ekokomea*, the most formal of all the various rituals of reversal and/or rebellion. Like other rituals *ekokomea* demonstrates, rather as a controlled experiment does, the danger of alternative modes of behaviour and thought. Here again we see that underlying the diversity of ways of actively expressing and expelling aggressivity there is a constant focus on purity, or health, without which the ritual dramas would be empty and ineffective. In *ekokomea* the sex norms are all cast aside, reversed and ridiculed. Alternative modes of behaviour are experimented with and tested by mime and ridicule. In particular both as individuals and as groups women and men are able to ridicule the opposite sex, most often in terms of sexual behaviour and cleanliness. As with the tug-of-war, each individual act of ridicule adds to the general hilarity and detracts from the underlying latent aggressivity, until the ridicule goes so far beyond the realm of reason that aggressivity itself becomes unthinkable. The *ekokomea* group then collapses in hysterics, rolling on the ground, eyes streaming with tears, gasping for breath; and when they recover men and women alike resume their normal roles as though nothing has happened, other than a general improvement in their good spirits.

The *molimo mangbo*, however, is the greatest of all purificatory rites or festivals among the Mbuti, serving as a dynamic reminder to all, of any age or sex, of the value of *ekimi*, and of the vital, necessity for cooperation in order to achieve *ekimi*. It is here that the Mbuti see themselves as being united together in the centre of the most inclusive of all wombs, that of the forest. It requires cooperation on this scale to restore *ekimi* in the face of that supreme *akami* of death. The very nature of the ritual cooperation required represents the mutually complementary roles of all four age levels in Mbuti society, and in just the same way that life (and *ekimi*) would be impossible without this daily interaction and interdependence between children, youths, adults, and elders, so would the *molimo mangbo*, and the reversal of *akami*, be impossible without the cooperation of the same groups. The *molimo mangbo* integrates the age groups, the sexes, and it unites all the individual *endu* (however disunited in terms of kinship) in terms of common territoriality. Finally, the *molimo mangbo* expresses the greatest opposition of all, that between the forest and nonforest. In this one ritual every major potential source of conflict is expressed. Thus there are three periodic, constantly repetitive situations that demand the ritualization of conflict and expulsion of aggressivity. The annual honey season, during which the territorial band breaks down to its minimal segments; the *elima*, whenever a girl in the band has her first menstrual period; and the *molimo mangbo* which takes place whenever any adult or elder (sometimes a youth) dies. It is not impossible to have all three at the same time, though generally an *elima* will be delayed if there is a death *molimo*.

In the *molimo mangbo* the role of children, and some younger youths, is to 'steal' (again) the food and fire from each *endu* hearth for the central *molimo* hearth, the *kumamolimo*. That they have to mime the act of stealing focuses attention on the inherent conflict between the individual and the social good; and it is at the adult level that this conflict is most likely to be manifest. As in the *molimo madé* the youths are the bearers of the *molimo* trumpet, and it is one of them that sings into the trumpet, giving the song of the men a special power as they repeat it and echo it on into the forest, so that *ndura* will hear. But instead of the trumpeting of an elephant, they make the *molimo* reproduce the soft growls and coughs of a leopard, the symbol of death itself, but of the kind of death that leads to life, not the kind of death brought by the elephant. While the elders initiate the *molimo mangbo*, determining both its moment of beginning and its moment of ending, it is the youths who decide if and when the *molimo* trumpet itself shall enter the camp and feed at the *kumamolimo*. This is consistent with their jural role. If they decide that adults, elders, and children, male and female, are not cooperating and giving their all to the festival, if they judge that there is *akami* in the camp, then that night when they take the trumpet out of its stream, bathe it, and give it water, earth, and fire to eat and drink, and invest it with their own breath of life, they approach the camp but do not enter. And instead of sounding like the leopard, the reconciler of death, it will sound like the elephant, and early in the morning it is the *molimo madé* that might enter the camp, not the *molimo mangbo*. Once again the youths, about to enter that disputatious and noisy time of life, adulthood, are given the responsibility of restoring *ekimi*.

The adult males, who represent the first male hunter to bring death and *akami* to mankind, are the ones who suffer the most discomfort during the long and tiring festival. Even their singing, which is the loudest, does not have the necessary quality to bring the *molimo* into camp. It has to be transformed by the trumpet and transposed by the voice of youth into a sound of pure *ekimi* that the forest will surely hear. Some laxity is allowed the elders, youths, females, and children; but if an adult male as much as nods during the long nights of *molimo* singing he is threatened with death. The intensity of his singing, equally, must be greater than that of any of the others. And finally the adult male has to suffer the indignity, toward the end of the festival, of having his role usurped by the women, who come in and take over the men's song, tying the men all up with nooses made from the *nkusa* vine from which hunting nets are made, so that, as they say, the women have tied up the song, and tied the hunt. Only when the men make an appropriate propitiatory gesture will the women release them, and allow the *molimo* to continue. Even then, one old woman will in a gesture of supreme control slowly and deliberately trample right through the *molimo* fire, scattering the logs and embers to all sides, threatening to extinguish life forever. Each time the men rebuild the fire and 'rekindle' the smouldering embers with a dance in imitation of the act of copulation, the old woman dances through again, scattering it, to say that, as the giver of life, she also has the ultimate power of bringing death, through the negation of her life-giving power. After the female elder has repeated this for perhaps two or even three nights, the *molimo* comes to an end; with the very last embers of the hearth being carefully extinguished by a male elder; the *molimo* trumpet being triumphantly carried back to the depths of the forest by youths. Only at this point are the adults allowed to wash and cleanse themselves of the taint of death, and resume normal daily activities.

It will be seen that both male and female adults have been effectively educated from infancy onward to avoid conflict, avert it, divert it, or, when it erupts despite all precautions, to resolve it with a minimum of aggressivity, mental or physical. Adulthood offers the most opportunities for *akami*, and the lessons and habits acquired in infancy, childhood, and youth are not enough in themselves to avert *akami* at all times. However, adulthood is marked by a different phenomenon, that of sexual differentiation at a level not previously known. Until entry to adulthood the only age level to which the terms of address distinguish sex as well as age, is adulthood itself. To infants, children, and youths alike, all adults are separated into *ema* or *eba*, whereas amongst themselves, within their own age group, they are all *apua'i* regardless of sex. Or if addressed by someone older they are *miki*, regardless of sex. Now, as adults, however, while addressing each other as *apua'i* they find, for the first time, that when addressed they are separated into male and female. Further, although the *elima* prepared the way for a new distinction in behaviour and role, clearly giving the initiative to the female, the adult male still seems to find it difficult, at times, to reconcile himself to female dominance. He sees himself as the hunter, but then he could not hunt without a wife, and although hunting is more exciting than being a beater or a gatherer, he knows that the bulk of his diet comes from the foods gathered by the women. And while his wife shares almost every aspect of his social life, he can never share her role as a mother, except in the strictest classificatory sense. And once his wife gives birth, she seems to remove herself still further from him by refusing to have intercourse with him for three years. Open and devoted affection persists throughout all this, but in any one hunting camp tensions are always rising to the surface along these lines.

It is almost as though at this point the woman (the mother) becomes sacred and the male (the bringer of death) profane. The obligatory reluctance of the woman to contribute to the *kumamolimo*, her power to tie up (women often use the word 'to silence') the song and the hunt, her power over the fire of life, all this is consistent with her role as life-giver, as the bringer of *ekimi*. Similarly the adult male is consistent as the bringer of *akami*, and it is just as vital that he play that role as it is that the female plays hers. Tendencies to aggressivity among the males, however, are curbed throughout adulthood not only by the various rituals in which male and female must cooperate, or reverse their roles, nor even by the necessary cooperation and interdependence required by hunting and gathering, but also by their proximity at one end of adulthood to youth, and at the other end to elderhood. The young husband, newly a father, and already deprived of the right to sleep with his wife, may spend much of his time with youths whose company he has just left. He may even take part in the *molimo madé*, and so he is still to some extent acting out a jural role as well as his adult economic role, however unofficially. Even when he is too old to continue this association with youth, it is still recent enough for him to be influenced by it, and for him to be ready to accept the judgement of the *molimo madé* and the will of youth.

At the other end, when his wife has ceased to give birth to children, he is close to elderhood, and so he is that much closer to purity. The transition from adulthood to elderhood is a gradual one; for those who find it difficult a way out may be found by playing the role of clown. Others, probably most, tend to slip more easily into elderhood by embracing it at just the moment they finally let go of their last contact with youth. In this way they move from contact with a jural role to contact with the role that elders play as mediators. Thus adulthood, for the male, is in itself a medial position, marked by ambivalence. The alliance between the alternate generations of youth and elderhood is a major asset in the prevention of aggressivity during adulthood.

Once the transition to elderhood is over, the danger of aggressivity is reduced to practically nil. The elders, who are addressed as *tata* even by their adult children, are again not differentiated by sex – the sexes are joined once more. Further, because of their proximity to death they are increasingly imbued with spiritual power, and associated with *ekimi*. Their role as arbitrators is informal, by virtue of their age they merely have a wider range of experience from which to cite precedent. Or they may, wordlessly, insert themselves physically between two disputants, making the argument or fight that much more difficult to continue. But whereas in the control of aggressivity the youth, with the *molimo madé*, is dealing with the sphere of the 'here and now', and appealing by argument to reason, the elder is introducing an element of the 'other' sphere, the 'other-than-here-and-now', and is invoking spirit, not reason, through the *molimo mangbo*. If youth has power, elderhood has authority. At both levels, other than in the context of the *elima*, there is no sexual differentiation, and in this respect the two are allied to childhood, and all three differentiated from sexually differentiated adulthood.

Almost by definition aggressivity and violence are virtually impossible in Mbuti society until adulthood; its manifestation then is restricted primarily to manifestation by adult men, and this is controlled by the powerful jural and spiritual institutions adjacent to adulthood, from one of which the adult has just passed, and into the other of which he is about to emerge; a juxtaposition that in itself is an effective measure of control. Throughout this dangerous state of life the adult woman stands firm as the symbol of *ekimi*, however closely allied to adult male *akami*. The frequent ritual manifestations of her ultimate control cannot help but serve as a reminder of the ultimate security offered by the most inclusive womb/sphere of all, the forest. It is little wonder that when Mbuti die, they do so without fear, and it is only right that the songs that mark such a death are songs of the same joy in which life itself was conceived. It is the same joy with which the infant is born into the *endu*, the child into the *bopi*, and the youth into the *apa*; for all come from and return to *ndura*. For the Mbuti this joy, which accompanies them throughout life, from sphere to sphere, is *ekimi*, the antithesis of *akami*. At the very least the Mbuti experience teaches that aggressivity is politically inexpedient; *ekimi* simply is not compatible with the supreme *akami* of violence.

Notes

1 Colin M. Turnbull, 'Initiation among the BaMbuti Pygmies of the Central Ituri', *J.R.A.I.* 87:2 (1957):191–216; Colin M. Turnbull, *Wayward servants*. New York: Natural History Press, 1965
2 A girl's early menstrual cycles are usually anovulatory, 'so that usually she does *not* yet have the power to become a mother'. See Ashley Montagu, *The reproductive development of the female*. New York: Julian Press, 1957

Part II: Forager–farmer relations

7. Relations of production in band society

ELEANOR LEACOCK

Anthropologists have characterized the generally cooperative and egalitarian structure of band-organized gathering-hunting societies in various ways. Contrasting egalitarian with 'rank' society, Fried (1967) writes
of the former that as many status positions are available as there are
people capable of filling them while in the latter there are a limited
number of valued statuses. Fried also states that there are no restrictions on access to basic resources in egalitarian gathering-hunting
society. Meillassoux (1975) focuses on the direct appropriation of natural resources in band societies, where there is no investment of labour
in the land, and he also points out the ease with which a person can
change band affiliation. Hindess and Hirst (1975) stress the communal
appropriation of surplus labour through what they term 'simple redistribution'. Their formulation parallels Sahlins' (1972) definition of 'generalized' reciprocity in the distribution process in band societies as
compared with the 'balanced' reciprocity of villagers.

Phrasing egalitarianism in operational terms, Lee (n.d.:8) writes: 'The
hunting band or camp is a unit of sharing, and if sharing breaks down
it ceases to be a camp.' Godelier (1973) discusses the virtual identity of
reciprocal production relations and kinship structures among the foraging peoples of Australia, and Keenan (1977), with particular reference
to the San, notes the importance of reciprocal relations among as well
as within bands. Given the unity of the entire production process
stressed by Marx in the *Grundrisse* (1973:83–100), I add that the direct
participation of all adults in production, distribution, exchange, and
consumption obviates dyadic relations of economic dependence in
nuclear families (Leacock 1974, 1978, 1980). In terms of fundamental
structure, each individual is directly dependent on the multi-family
group as a whole.

I am not here concerned with the points of difference among these various theorists, although these are considerable when the formulation of each is stated in its totality. Nor do I intend to deal here with the question of which dimensions are the most basic to the relations of production among gatherer-hunters. Instead, I would settle with the level of agreement that exists about readily observable dimensions of egalitarianism in gathering-hunting band societies in order to emphasize an important point: that despite great generosity and collectivity among peoples who still depend in large part on the direct acquisition of wild vegetable and animal food, properly speaking a mode of production characteristic of mobile gatherer-hunters no longer exists. Corollary to this point is an admonition: before alluding to one or another society as representative of foraging cultures, it is essential to examine its history and to define the realities of its economy at the time the data being cited were collected.

In most instances, peoples with a gatherer-hunter heritage have not lived solely as gatherer-hunters for a long time. This fact is well established for the native peoples of the Canadian subarctic, where the combined impact of the fur trade, missionizing, colonization, and competition and warfare among European nations were felt from the early sixteenth century onwards (Bailey 1969). Rogers (1972) for the Mistassini-Cree and I (Leacock 1954) for the eastern Montagnais-Naskapi, along with other field workers, have documented in detail the nature of socioeconomic changes brought about in northeastern Algonkian society by native involvement in the fur trade.

Prior to dependence upon the fur trade, the basic economic unit among the Montagnais-Naskapi was the lodge group made up of several families among whom food was shared on a daily basis. Total sharing both within this group and between it and other such groups when nearby or in need meant that every individual was ultimately dependent on the collective as such, not on particular individuals within it. However, the stockpiling of furs for trade slowly replaced individual dependency upon the group as a whole with individual dependencies on an outside market. Concomitantly, new economic ties were created within nuclear families, as wives and children became dependent upon men's returns from trapping (Leacock 1955). Cooperative practices and attitudes continued to be important in the difficult north woods, but eventually the 'trading post band', a loose network of nuclear family units, sometimes with a formal head man or 'chief', superseded the previous socio-economic form. Meanwhile, the Montagnais-Naskapi blended aspects of Catholicism with their prior beliefs and practices

Marie Bastien, Montagnais-Naskapi, setting a rabbit snare (R. Leacock)

and used trade goods to develop their particular clothing styles and tool kits. They continued to have their own distinctive culture, but it was one that had been constantly changing since first described by European travellers and missionaries in the sixteenth and seventeenth centuries.

The transformations in Montagnais-Naskapi economic structure were somewhat masked by strong cultural continuities such as language, tent-living, and certain religious practices. This fact enabled some among the first generation of ethnographers that worked in the Labrador Peninsula, notably Frank Speck (1926) and John Cooper (1939), to argue that the privatized form of land use they found among some bands was aboriginal. Incorrectly defining this form of land use as 'privately owned hunting territories', Speck and Cooper argued that lands had never been communally owned among these bands, nor among other gatherer-hunters as well. Hence, they contended, individual ownership of basic resources was not limited to hierarchical society but was found in all types of cultures. Subsequently this argument was contradicted by research such as mine and Rogers' and by parallel work on Athapaskan peoples to the north and west (as, for example, Helm 1961 and Slobodin 1962). Research made clear: first, that hunting lands and all resources but furs were communally and not privately owned even into the present – only the furs of fur-bearing animals on lands a person was trapping were considered that person's property; and second, such regularization of individual usufruct rights to trapping grounds as existed had followed involvement in the fur trade and was not aboriginal.

Another example of post-colonial changes in band structure is afforded by the Paiute. Steward (1963:101) characterized Paiute society as at a 'family level of integration'. Taking issue with Steward's interpretation, Service (1962:94–7, 1975:67–8) pointed out that the fragmentation of the Paiute into isolated families became necessary in colonial times to avoid harassment and capture by their congeners, the Ute. Slaving for the Spanish had become a lucrative occupation, and, upon obtaining horses, some of the Ute pushed the Paiute from lands they had previously occupied into less-well-endowed desert areas, and raided them for slaves to sell in Santa Fé.

Others besides Service questioned Steward's concept of a family level of integration, and, in his last paper on band organization, Steward (1969:290–1) shifted his position slightly. He wrote that accumulating data showed the 'minimum band', the 'primary subsistence band', or the 'basic unit that cooperates in the tasks necessary to physical survival' to consist of

no fewer than about twenty-five persons – or some five families – because owing to its isolation during much of the year, approximately this number is necessary to ensure mutual aid in sickness, baby tending, and various cooperative activities including food sharing. Cases of one or two isolated families in aboriginal times are almost certainly abnormal . . . In recent cases of seasonal fragmentation into one or two nuclear families, the effects of firearms, commercial fur trapping, and other European influences are usually discernible.

Service (1975:68–9) has referred to the tropical forests of South America as another area in which societies fragmented for defensive reasons following colonization. Most of the peoples to whom Service referred are horticultural. However, the Aché Guayaki of Paraguay are a gathering-hunting people who have for many years lived almost constantly on the run to avoid slave raiders. According to Clastres (1972:145), danger 'incites the Indians to remain ready to flee as soon as the danger has been spotted. Within only a few minutes the women must assemble and pack up all the goods scattered around them in order to quickly disappear into the protection of the forest.'

By contrast with the Aché, the hunter-gatherers of the pampas obtained horses after colonization and became involved in expanding trade networks. Like former foragers of the North American plains, they developed more elaborated organizational forms than had previously obtained. For example, as Service (1975:68) pointed out, the Puelche and Tehuelche of central Argentina 'are well-known examples of durable large-scale federations that made strong, hence aggressive (and therefore later epitomized in ethnology as 'warlike'), predatory tribes'.

A good description of the differential impact relations with outsiders can have on the production relations and social-cultural life of gatherer-hunters is offered by Turnbull's (1962, 1972) accounts of the Mbuti of the Congo forests and the Ik of the Kenya-Uganda borderlands. Sporadic service work for and trade with a horticultural village society that was itself not wholly involved in market relations had not undermined the cooperative Mbuti, who were still subsisting largely by hunting on their traditional lands at the time Turnbull lived among them. By contrast, the Ik had been pushed into a marginal farming area; hunting on their former lands had been outlawed; and their sources of income in a situation of recurrent drought and famine were structured by competitive and individualized market relations in a community that was itself economically marginal.

At the time of Turnbull's study, the Ik subsisted largely on badly administered government relief; secret and individual hunting which had become poaching; direct prostitution as well as marriage liaisons with outsiders that were all but prostitution; work for Dodos or Turkana herders that, although institutionalized as 'friendship', called for spying, thieving, and cattle raiding; wage work for the police; and, for highly skilled opportunists, becoming 'chiefs', or go-betweens with the administration, thereby benefiting from resulting handouts. The only 'honest' occupations available to them were working on the roads or making and selling charcoal or pottery (Turnbull 1972:96, 105, 141, 159–60, 162, 176, 244, 249, 254–5, 261, 279–82). The contrast between the Ik and the Mbuti, even if exaggerated by Turnbull as some have suggested, is sharp.

Aboriginal Australia is another area where the precise nature and effects of colonial impositions have to be analysed in detail for different regions and peoples before firm generalizations can be made about aboriginal cultures. Direct European intrusion was predated by Portuguese slave raiding in northern coastal areas (Hart and Pilling 1962:97–100), and the last two centuries have seen the steady westward push of European settlement with genocide and land grabbing, widespread disease, enslavement or forced labour, brutalization in the name of the law, flight and stepped-up warfare among peoples pushed onto each other's lands, missionizing, and, recently, mission and government provisioning and community regulation (Stevens 1972).

Around the world, then, the colonial expansion of European nations has resulted in profound transformations in gathering-hunting societies. European colonialism was not, however, the only source of such transformation. After all, the entire course of history over the past 15,000 years or more has been one of transformation from gathering-hunting to agricultural society. In most cases, the adoption of agriculture spread peacefully from areas where the exigencies of geography and human history first made sedentism preferable to mobility, and domestication, based on accumulated knowledge of plant and animal life, a viable adjunct to gathering and hunting. In some cases, however, foraging peoples were harassed by agricultural peoples as were the Ainu by the Japanese. In other cases foraging peoples entered into long-term exchange relations with settled neighbours, such as the Paliyan and Birhor of India who traded forest products with nearby peasants (Gardner 1972; Sinha 1972).

Sometimes mobile foragers have a prior history of village living. During the first millennium A.D. ancestors of present-day Inuit in Alaska had much in common with other peoples of the north Pacific, the Aleuts, Ainu, and peoples of the Northwest Coast of North America who were involved in regularized exchange networks and who lived much of the time in relatively large and permanent settlements.

In sum, the reconstruction of a particular people's history through careful examination of archaeological, ethnohistorical and ethnographic materials is essential, before it is possible to assume that a particular socio-cultural pattern directly reflects the necessities and constraints of gathering-hunting economy in a specific ecological setting. Even very early reports on a culture cannot be taken at face value but have to be appraised with care. The very fact that written records of a gathering-hunting people are available means that the people have already become involved in some way with economic and/or political relations with a market society. Furthermore, such records are coloured by the prejudices of the particular European – or perhaps Chinese or East Indian – who wrote them, or distorted by the fact that the representatives of foraging peoples best known to some explorer, missionary, or trader were usually those who had broken with their kinfolk and attached themselves to the outsiders.

Debate concerning aboriginal gender roles and female–male relations in the Canadian subarctic affords a good example of problems yet to be resolved. Ethnohistorical reconstruction of aboriginal culture history in subarctic Canada has resulted in consensus on the fact that privatization of land-use followed, rather than preceded, dependence upon fur trading with Europeans. However, there remains considerable disagreement over issues like post-marital residence and female autonomy. Extensive genealogical data taken in 1950 and 1951 showed that among the Montagnais–Naskapi, matrilocality had been the ideal, but that it was being superseded by patrilocality in response to new economic and political conditions. (Leacock 1955). Recently analysed ethnohistorical data are indicating that the same may be the case throughout the Canadian subarctic (Krech 1980). However, these data are often spotty and indirect and are at present far from accepted as conclusive.

With respect to the issue of male 'dominance' versus female 'autonomy', the seventeenth-century record of women's social and sexual independence among the Montagnais-Naskapi of the Labrador Peninsula is rare in its explicitness (Leacock 1980; Leacock and Goodman 1976). The head of the Jesuit mission at Quebec, Paul Le Jeune, spent a winter in a Montagnais lodge in order to learn the language and understand the culture he sought to change, and he sent a detailed account of his experiences back to Paris. Time and again, during his subsequent years in Quebec, he made reference to the problems women's autonomy was causing him and to his difficulties in attempting to introduce principles of male dominance among the Montagnais-Naskapi.

It is my view that the egalitarianism that obtained between the sexes among the Montagnais-Naskapi also existed among other Algonkian and Athapaskan hunters. However, Ronald Cohen (1978:257–9) interprets Samuel Hearne's account of his eighteenth-century trip with a Chipewyan 'band' from Hudson's Bay to the Coppermine River as evidence that male dominance over, or at least casual brutality toward, women was aboriginal. To Cohen the late eighteenth century is too early for much culture change. However, as I (Leacock 1978:271–2) point out, the 'band' with which Hearne travelled was not a hunting band at all, but a 'gang' (Hearne's term) of middlemen in the fur trade, a group that temporarily gathered around a man by the name of Matonabbee. Matonabbee was a full-time worker for the Hudson's Bay Company, and he and the men in his gang were not only occasionally abusive toward women, but also robbed and even killed some of the people they encountered on their trip.

The behaviour of Matonabbee and his men, robbing and killing some people, although trading fairly, even generously, with others, was apparently not governed by cultural tradition as much as by what was most profitable, given the exigencies of the role they had taken on as middlemen in the fur trade (Cox 1979:416). Their middleman role did afford them access to desirable trade goods, but on the whole, according to Hearne (1911:123), yielded them no more than 'a bare subsistence', and furthermore forced them to risk starvation periodically when travelling through barren lands to reach the trading fort. By contrast, Hearne described the traditional Chipewyan as living 'in a state of plenty, without trouble or risque', and hence as happier and more independent. Matonabbee and his gang, caught in a bind between a company that was driving as hard a bargain as it could and people with whom they traditionally expected to share freely, sometimes acted with a violence that characterized colonial frontier life in general.

As for some of the abusive behaviour toward women that Hearne described, it smacks more of the attempt on the part of some men to exploit them as well as other men, than it does of culturally institutionalized assumptions of authority and superiority. Women were important as porters; Matonabbee made it his business to acquire as many tall strong wives as he could – seven at the time of Hearne's trip. Yet he could do nothing to hold them against their wishes except threaten violence. There were no established cultural sanctions to bind them. Although the women according to Hearne were generally hard working and good humoured, they had, as Cohen admits, many ways of defending their interests, and some in Hearne's (1911:320) view were 'as lofty and insolent as any women in the world'.

It is my understanding, then, that Hearne's eighteenth-century account of a Chipewyan hunting 'gang' does not contradict the import of Le Jeune's seventeenth-century account of life in a Montagnais-Naskapi lodge. However the issue of aboriginal Chipewyan practices certainly cannot be 'proved' in a formal sense. The question is thereby raised: if each statement about some aspect of social life among gatherer-hunters can be argued in this fashion, in what sense is it possible to generalize about the socio-cultural concomitants of gathering-hunting production relations? Can we arrive at agreement on the major corollaries of gathering-hunting economies? The level of agreement referred to in the opening paragraphs of this paper attests to the possibility of a positive answer. With historical questions, the accumulation of evidence pointing consistently in the same direction eventually leads to consensus.

As an example of debate resolved, take collective land ownership as an accepted characteristic of band-living gatherer-hunters. Put forth by Morgan and Engels as basic to the 'communism in living' (Morgan 1965) that once characterized human society, the principle of collective land ownership was challenged by anthropologists of the Boasian school and virtually discarded. Yet further research affirmed its reality which is now accepted. Similarly, the assumption that 'public' decisions in gathering-hunting society were made by individual leaders or 'chiefs' holding formal authority has increasingly given way to the understanding that such decisions are arrived at through discussion and adjudication. With respect to gender, studies of women's changing social roles among gatherer-hunters are beginning to contradict assumptions of male 'dominance' even among peoples where it seemed quite obvious, such as Aboriginal Australians (Bell and Ditton 1980). Detailed historical analyses to supplement field studies may soon demonstrate that such male dominance as exists in otherwise egalitarian societies is a function of changing relations of production reinforced by missionary teachings, legal systems, and European role models.

In closing, I wish to stress that accurate reconstruction of the history and the associated socio-economic changes in gatherer-hunter societies is of far more than theoretical interest. It is also of great importance on political and ethical grounds. The descendants of gatherer-hunters are peoples now fighting for land rights, if not for sheer survival, and for access to education which makes it possible for them to choose their own life-style in the contemporary world. Anthropologists have a responsibility, therefore, to be correct in describing their histories. To lump as gatherer-hunters *today* all peoples who were so at the time of European colonization, and to talk of recent social and ideological features of their cultures as uniformly characterizing a gathering-hunting mode, is to reify culture and freeze it in a timeless mould. In such a scheme, cultures cannot grow, but can only be whittled away through 'acculturation'. The centuries through which erstwhile foragers have coped with the conditions of colonization are thereby negated; the peoples concerned are robbed of both their history and their culture.

Colonization characteristically brought disruption and devastation to foraging peoples and it is necessary to point this out. However, for ethical and political as well as scientific reasons, it is equally necessary to note and to document the resiliency and creativity with which different peoples moved to survive in, cope with, and take what advantage they could of new situations in which they found themselves. In most cases, after initial disruption, peoples reorganized their economic lives in connection with trade and/or seasonal or temporary labour, accepted a modicum of formal leadership to deal with the 'outside', incorporated a measure of Christian belief and ritual into their traditional religious practices, and reinterpreted their definitions of male–female roles and relations, as they welded past and present in an ongoing way of life. They evolved new cultural forms which, although much changed from aboriginal times, continued to be distinctively theirs. In the name of 'modernization' and 'development', these cultures are now being threatened as capitalist relations are fully imposed even in the most remote hinterlands of the world.

Bibliography

Bailey, Alfred Goldsworthy 1969. *The conflict of European and Eastern Algonkian cultures, 1504–1700.* Toronto: University of Toronto Press

Bell, Diane, and Ditton, Pam 1980. *Law: the old and the new, Aboriginal women in central Australia speak out.* Canberra: Aboriginal History

Clastres, Pierre 1972. 'The Guayaki', in M. G. Bicchieri (ed.), *Hunters and gatherers today.* New York: Holt, Rinehart and Winston

Cohen, Ronald 1978. 'Comments on "women's status in egalitarian society: implications for social evolution" (Eleanor Leacock).' *Current Anthropology* 19:257–9

Cooper, John M. 1939. 'Is the Algonquian family hunting ground pre-Columbian?' *American Anthropologist* 41:66–90

Cox, Bruce 1979. 'More on women's status in egalitarian societies'. *Current Anthropology* 20:415–16.

Fried, Morton H. 1967. *The evolution of political society.* New York: Random House

Gardner, Peter M. 1972. 'The Paliyans', in M. G. Bicchieri (ed.) *Hunters and gatherers today.* New York: Holt, Rinehart and Winston

Godelier, Maurice 1973. 'Modes de production, rapports de parenté, et structures demographiques'. *La Pensée*, December, 7–31

Hart, C. W. M., and Pilling, Arnold 1962. *The Tiwi of north Australia.* New York: Holt, Rinehart and Winston

Hearne, Samuel 1911. *A journey from Prince of Wales's Fort in Hudson's Bay to the Northern Ocean.* Toronto: The Champlain Society

Helm, June 1961. *The Lynx Point people: the dynamics of a northern Athapaskan band.* National Museum of Canada Bulletin 176

Hindess, Barry, and Hirst, Paul Q. 1975. *Pre-capitalist modes of production.* London: Routledge and Kegan Paul

Keenan, Jeremy 1977. 'The concept of the mode of production in hunter-gatherer societies'. *African Studies* 36:57–69

Krech, Shepard 1980. 'Introduction to a symposium, a reconsideration of Aboriginal social organization in the North American Subarctic'. *Arctic Anthropology* 27:1

Leacock, Eleanor 1954. *The Montagnais 'hunting territory' and the fur trade.* American Anthropological Association Memoir 78

    1955. 'Matrilocality in a simple hunting economy (Montagnais-Naskapi)'. *Southwestern Journal of Anthropology* 11:31–47

    1974. 'The structure of band society, review of M. G. Bicchieri (ed.), *Hunters and gatherers today'. Reviews in Anthropology* 1:212–22

    1978. 'Women's status in egalitarian society: implications for social evolution'. *Current Anthropology* 19:247–75

    1980. 'Montagnais women and the Jesuit program for colonization', in Mona Etienne and Eleanor Leacock (eds.) *Women and colonization: anthropological perspectives.* New York: Praeger

Leacock, Eleanor, and Goodman, Jacqueline 1976. 'Montagnais marriage and the Jesuits in the seventeenth century'. *Western Canadian Journal of Anthropology* 6:3

Lee, Richard n.d. 'From foraging to farming: historical materialism and the dynamics of pre-class society'. MS.

Marx, Karl 1973. *Grundrisse.* Translated by Martin Nicolaus. Middlesex, England: Penguin Books

Meillassoux, Claude 1975. *Femmes, greniers et capitaux.* Paris: Maspero

Morgan, Lewis H. 1965. *Houses and house-life of the American Aborigines.* Chicago: University of Chicago Press. (First published 1881)

Rogers, Edward S. 1972. 'The Mistassini Cree', in M. G. Bicchieri (ed.), *Hunters and gatherers today.* New York: Holt, Rinehart and Winston

Sahlins, Marshall D. 1972. *Stone Age economics.* Chicago: Aldine/Atherton

Service, Elman 1962. *Primitive social organization.* New York: Random House

    1975. *Origins of the state and civilization.* New York: Norton

Sinha, D. P. 1972. 'The Birhors', in M. G. Bicchieri (ed.), *Hunters and gatherers today.* New York: Holt, Rinehart and Winston

Slobodin, Richard 1962. Band organization of the Peel River Kutchin. *National Museum of Canada Bulletin* 179

Speck, Frank G. 1926. 'Land ownership among hunting peoples in primitive America and the world's marginal areas'. *Twenty-second International Congress of Americanists,* 2

Stevens, F. S. (ed.) 1972. *Racism: the Australian experience,* 2, *Black Versus White.* New York: Taplinger

Steward, Julian 1963. *Theory of culture change*. Urbana, Ill.: University of Illinois Press
    1969. 'Postscript to bands: on taxonomy, processes, and causes', in David Damas (ed.) *Contributions to anthropology: band societies*. *National Museum of Canada Bulletin* 228
Turnbull, Colin 1962. *The forest people*. Garden City: Doubleday
    1972. *The mountain people*. New York: Simon and Schuster

8. The family, group structuring and trade among South Indian hunter-gatherers

BRIAN MORRIS

The important symposium on 'Man the hunter' whose deliberations were published a decade ago, raised many interesting issues relating to the ecology and social organization of hunter-gatherers. Looking again at these discussions one is struck by certain limitations; a neglect of any discussion of the socio-historical context of hunter-gathering communities, and an androcentric bias that lends to an overemphasis of the 'hunting' aspect – nevertheless the symposium constituted something of a landmark in anthropological studies of pre-farming communities. But one is equally struck by a lack of consensus in the theoretical perspectives offered by the various contributors to the symposium – which is of interest, because each of the main orientations that can be delineated in the work have been elaborated in subsequent writings.

The purpose of this present paper is both to offer some ethnographic notes on the social organization of one South Indian hunter-gathering community, the Malapantaram, and to relate this material to current debates. After initial clarification of theoretical issues in the first section of this paper, I suggest, in the second part, that there is a need to disentangle several distinct 'levels' of hunter-gatherer social organization. In the final section of the paper I outline Malapantaram group structuring, and in interpreting their organizational patterns, indicate the importance of their trading contacts.

There are I think three broad approaches to the sociology of hunter-gatherers.

The first is the well-known patrilocal band model. In spite of numerous criticisms the patrilocal-band model surprisingly still has currency and there are writers who continue to advocate that this form of social organization provides an adequate model for understanding so-called 'band' societies (Williams 1974: 18–29). What is of interest is not whether the model can be matched against empirical data – I do not think it *can*

Malapantaram woman breaking up plant stalks to extract flour, Kerala (B. Morris)

because it conflates several separate dimensions of social reality – but the fact that it is still advocated by some anthropologists. Thus it is not that the model has theoretical elegance and parsimony, as Lee suggests, which is of relevance, but rather the fact that in specific ethnographic cases the different levels of social organization are sufficiently consonant as to lend seeming support to the theory. The patrilocal-band model therefore must not simply be rejected as inadequate, but rather 'dismantled'; in the process the concept of 'band' or 'horde' must in certain cases be exorcized as conceptually redundant.

The second approach to hunter-gatherer sociology is reflected in the writings of Richard Lee (1972, 1976), and formed an underlying theme in the 'Man the hunter' symposium. Basing generalizations on the recent research among the Hadza, Mbuti and the !Kung, and highly critical of the patrilocal band model, this perspective tended to stress the bilateral and flexible nature of hunter-gatherer camp aggregates, and to see this fluid organization as having an adaptive function – in adjusting group size to resources, and in resolving tensions and conflicts within the group. Such a perspective retains many of the assumptions implicit in the earlier theory. It assumes, like Service (1962), that the subsistence mode – the technology – is a primary factor in determining hunter-gatherer social organization, and that there is therefore a close identification between hunting-gathering as a form of subsistence and a *specific* model of organization, in this instance a flexible, nomadic pattern. This second approach underplays environmental factors, and ignores the fact that culture has not only an adaptive function, but a dynamic of its own. This approach also emphasizes the 'band' level of organization, but this is viewed in residential terms – and kinship and sex groupings, marriage patterns, and ritual congregations are seen as essentially extraneous. The 'model of hunter social organization' offered seems to focus almost exclusively on patterns of residential aggregation.

An approach similar to that of Lee is provided by Claude Meillassoux (1973) in his essay 'On the mode of production of the hunting band'. Although Meillassoux noted that the model he proposes may not be generalized to be applicable in all its aspects to other hunting and gathering peoples, he clearly sees hunting-gathering as constituting a specific mode of production, defined primarily in terms of the exploitation of land. Drawing on Marx's distinction between land as the subject and as the instrument of labour, he suggests that the use of land as the subject of labour fosters an 'instantaneous' production process, in which a sharing of the produce takes place at the end of each enterprise. Once the hunter-gatherers have shared the product they are free from any further reciprocal obligations (1972: 99). Significantly he re-analyses the Mbuti material to illustrate the basic characteristics of the social organization of the hunting 'band' as he understands it – sexual equality, flexible and unstable social groupings, individual mobility, and a way of life 'tied to the present'.

What is surprising about Meillassoux's analysis, seminal though it is, is that he fails to recognize the unmistakable similarities between the agricultural mode of production he outlines (Meillasoux 1960) and the social patterns of many hunter-gatherer communities. Indeed, in a review of the 'lineage' mode of production, Dupré and Rey (1973) actually mention the Northwest Coast Indians in a discussion of the function of prestige goods – without seeing the theoretical implications of this admission. Clearly the advent of agriculture is not the 'great divide' that many anthropologists assume it to be. Technology is not everything!

The third approach to the sociology of hunter-gatherers was expressed as marginal thoughts in the 'Man the hunter' symposium, where many contributors were struck by the diversity of social patterns apparent in the ethnographic record. Two writers, Gardner (1966, 1969) and Woodburn (1976), have attempted to avoid the limitations of the first two approaches – which imply a neat correlation between hunting-gathering as a subsistence mode and a specific type of social organization– with-

out going to the other extreme and collapsing either into a vague partic-
ularism, or alternatively, engaging in typological reconstructions in
which ecological factors alone are given explanatory prominence. Gardner and Woodburn postulate that there are two basic types of hunter-
gatherers and fruitfully move the analysis away from a narrow focus on
environmental and technological factors.

Gardner develops the perspective of Service, and suggests that a crucial factor in understanding contemporary hunter-gatherer social
organization is that of inter-cultural pressure. He posits a dichotomous
categorization of hunter-gatherers; those experiencing pressure from
dominant neighbours, and those living in insular situations or in a culturally homogeneous environment.

My concern here is not with the empirical validity of this dichotomy,
which has a certain simplicity about it. But Gardner's analysis is salu-
tory in bringing cultural and historical factors into the analysis. There
are limitations and dangers of overstressing inter-cultural factors but
such limitations are not nearly as inhibiting to our understanding as
the opposite ploy of ignoring such factors entirely. The writings of Frank
(1975) and Wolf (1955) on Latin American peasantry should make us
alert to the dangers of abstracting societies, hunter-gatherers in particular, from their socio-historical context.

In suggesting a dichotomous typology of hunter-gatherers, James
Woodburn (1976) takes as his point of departure Meillasoux's analysis
of the Mbuti pygmies. Aware that complex re-distributive patterns can
develop on a hunter-gatherer base, Woodburn suggests that there is a
class of hunter-gatherers whose productive mode implies an immediate
return on labour. A lack of investment in productive technology – wiers,
traps, boats – is here seen as a primary causal factor to account for the
cultural features characteristic of certain hunting-gathering communities. An avoidance of long-term commitments, a lack of social structure
or corporate groupings, a fluid nomadic pattern, a lack of emphasis on
kinship and ritual, and an extractive technology that implies little
thought for resource conservation are, perhaps, some of the features
which Woodburn would see as characteristic of this type. Against this
are set those hunting-gathering communities in which there is a delayed
return for labour. The Ainu and the Northwest Coast Indians are cited
as examples.

What is of interest is that the theories of Woodburn and Gardner,
based as they are on quite different theoretical postulates, should agree
so closely in their dichotomous division. Equally interesting is the shift

in theoretical perspective which Woodburn makes when confronted with the ethnographic material on the Australian Aborigines, who, for some reason, have often been looked upon as having a 'unique' status among hunter-gatherers. Clearly the Australian tribal communities had a great deal of ritualization, expressed both in marriage patterns and in cosmological systems, so Woodburn shifts his theoretical ground. The social patterns characteristic of the Australian Aborigines are seen by him not so much related to labour investment in productive technology, but rather as a function of an enterprise whereby men, in their political manoeuvring, seek to gain control over a woman's potential labour.[1] This brings the analysis even closer in line with Meillassoux's model of self-sustaining agricultural society, and is an important step, for it moves the focus decisively away from technological and environmental determinism.

For some years Maurice Godelier has been suggesting that anthropological studies should emphasize the social relations of production, and he has recently (1975) offered suggestive thoughts on the relationships among kinship, demography and the labour process. What emerges from this discussion, and from the general literature on hunter-gatherers, is that we have several 'levels' of social organization, that have either been conjoined (as in the patrilocal band model) or left out of discussion altogether, through a misleading focus on residential patterns. Such 'levels' or patterns of organization (whether or not evident in specific cases) seem worth itemizing, for a 'model' of hunter-gatherer social organization must incorporate a specification of these various 'levels' and their articulation or role in the productive process.

First, there is the resource-holding group, which is variable both in relation to the resource and to the social composition of the group claiming ownership. It may be a territorial region, as among the Ainu, collectively owned by a settlement, whose core members consist of male agnates (Ohnuki-Tierney 1974:73), a group of totemic sites owned by a patriclan or a group of clans, a pattern which seems to have been common among the Australian Aborigines (see Hiatt 1965: 14–20; Tindale 1972:223), or it may be a sibling set who are acknowledged owners of a waterhole (Lee 1976:77). Equally of course there may be no group asserting ownership of resources.

Second, there is the local group or residential aggregate. This may constitute a clearly defined, even if loosely knit community who reside together, or customarily move about together, and can thus be legitimately designated a settlement or band. But frequently no such aggregates exist, and residential patterns, as among the Hadza, are loose and ephemeral. Even where such 'bands' exist there is invariably, as Lee (1976:96–7) has stressed, a pattern of dispersal and re-aggregation within or between groups. Such residential units, whether or not permanent, are usually units of production and sharing, and many even constitute political units.

Third, there are groups, clans, sections or kinship categories that serve to designate marriage classes or patterns of marriage. To what degree these classes have corporate unity, or are consonant with the other levels of organization is variable. The seminal work of Hiatt (1965) stressed both the distinction between land-owning and residential patterns, and the fact that the patriclans were not units of 'wife exchange'. A similar situation seems to have been in evidence amongst the Tiwi, where land ownership was associated with a patrilineal sibling set, matrilineages were the recognized units of marriage exchange, and residential aggregates were bilateral (Goodale 1971:69–100).

Fourth, there is the family or domestic group – a social unit that tends to get overlooked in discussions of hunter-gatherer social organization. Although Godelier's (1975:3) insistence that the family is not the basic unit, in that it is incapable of reproducing itself, must be heeded, nevertheless the crucial significance of this unit among hunter-gatherers must be noted. This becomes especially relevant when Gardner, for instance, writes that 'nuclear families constitute the only units of Paliyan society characterized by cooperation' (1966:393). This unit is variable, particularly in the degree to which polygyny is stressed.

And finally, among many hunter-gatherers the men constitute special cult groups focused around ritual activities. Where such groups exist male solidarity is seldom matched by female solidarity, and, though women may have their own ceremonies and are not necessarily excluded from the sacred rites performed by the men, the latter ceremonials are commonly seen as the essential ones necessary for community well-being. Such cult groups or lodges may also be land-owning units, but significantly there is a tendency for them to have intergroup significance, and to serve, through an elaborate system of male initiation, to give elders control over younger men. They also have an important ideological function in sustaining male secular authority.

There are no doubt other levels of organization, but these seem to me to be the five basic ones – relating to ownership of resources, residence, reproduction, commensality and male solidarity. All may have a productive function. Although Arnold Pilling (1968:142) has noted the difficulty of attempting to assess the *complexity* of social organization among hunter-gatherers, we can see that, in certain ethnographic cases, each of these levels is developed and elaborated to a degree that matches Meillasoux's conception of a 'self-sustaining agricultural society'. There is then in many instances an elaboration of the 'economy of reproduction', expressed in marriage prestations, a prestige sphere, 'chiefs' and in the attempts of older men to gain rights over the control of a woman's labour, or even that of non-kinsmen.

On the other hand there are ethnographic examples, for example the Paliyans and Kadar, where only three 'levels' of social organization are relevant, and we have a situation that corresponds to what Gardner has termed 'individualistic culture'. Given that both these two models (which may reflect ends of a continuum) are found in varied environments, and cannot be explained in terms of ecological or technological factors alone, hunter-gatherer social organization must be interpreted either by reference to external factors, or to its own internal dynamic which we have yet to explore.

To facilitate further discussion on such issues I shall present some ethnographic material on a type of hunting-gathering community that has tended to be overlooked in past discussions, namely these which have become 'encapsulated' within the environs of a pre-industrial state.

The Malapantaram (hereafter referred to as the Hill Pandaram), a tribal community of South India, are not strictly 'pure' hunter-gatherers – any more than were the Veddas, the Siriono or the Semang – for at the present time[2] they indicate varied strategies of adaptation. Their population, numbering about a thousand individuals, is centred in the forested hills south of Lake Periyar. The earlier ethnographic accounts of the community describe them as hunter-gatherers and as practising no agriculture (Mateer 1883:81; Iyer 1937) but from the earliest times they appear to have had established an important trading contact with neighbouring agriculturists, either through silent barter, or, since the beginning of the nineteenth century, through forest contractors – honey, meat, dammar and various medicinal herbs being the main items bartered. Although many Hill Pandaram are associated with a recent Government-sponsored scheme to settle them (Morris 1976a), the majority of the community are nomadic gatherers of forest produce, collecting both for subsistence and for trade. And they live in dispersed groups within the forest, continually on the move. Such groups never

Table 8.1 *Camps in the Achencoil forests*

Locality	Month visited	Number of leaf shelters	Adults		Children under 16 years		Number of commensal units	Total number of persons
Kaduwaparai	Oct	4	4	1	2	1	2	8
Vangara	Aug	5	5	4	7	5	4	21
Amerika	Sept	3	1	2	6	—	2	9
Periya Eli	Oct	5	3	3	5	4	2	15
Pallivasal	Nov	1	1	1	4	1	1	7
Amerika		1	2	1	3	1	1	7
Vangara	Aug	5	3	4	3	4	3	14
Kumbaruthi	Oct	2	3	3	1	—	2	7
Pothumeen	Dec	4	4	5	3	2	4	14
Manalar	Aug	cave	4	2	4	3	2	13
Pothumeen	Aug	4	4	1	1	3	2	9
Sarojini	Sept	cave	6	2	1	3	3	12
Pallimundan	Sept	4	2	2	4	4	2	12
Valiam	Nov	2	2	1	2	2	2	7
Pallivasal	Dec	3	2	2	2	5	2	11
Manalar	Jan	cave	1	1	3	2	1	7
Vangara	Mar	4	2	2	3	2	2	9
Manalar	May	1	2	2	2	—	2	6
Achencoil	June	2	1	1	—	4	1	6
		6	4	4	4	7	4	19
Pallivasal	July	4	3	4	3	1	3	11
Pattamile	Mar	2	2	2	8	4	2	16
		in open	—	1	2	1	1	4

contain more than about twenty individuals and are fluctuating in size and composition.

Excluding those camps which were associated with the collection of a specific resource, for example overnight camps for the purposes of collecting honey, I visited during my research a total of 43 forest encampments. The accompanying table 8.1 gives details of some of the forest camps in the Achencoil forest range, three of which were in rock shelters. Figure 8.1 indicates the kin composition of three of these encampments.

A camp (*thangel*) consists essentially of one to six small leaf shelters with typically each shelter housing a conjugal family. Each family is a separate commensal and economic unit. Although daily foraging parties are variable in composition, and may draw members from different commensal units, individuals (even children) collect vegetable foods and trade goods either for themselves alone, or for their own immediate family unit. Only meat and tobacco, and the proceeds of the collective honey-gathering expeditions (which involve two or three cooperating

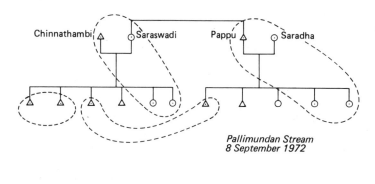

Pallimundan Stream
8 September 1972

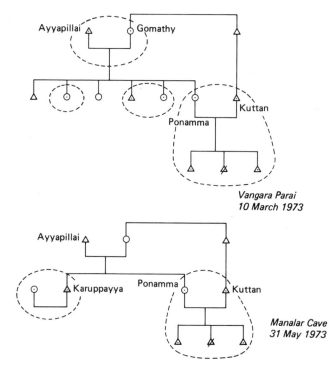

Vangara Parai
10 March 1973

Manalar Cave
31 May 1973

8.1 Kin composition of three Achencoil forest encampments

males) are shared between family units. Thus the composition of foraging parties, sleeping arrangements and commensal units vary independently of one another. Significantly an encampment has no communal fire or icons. Some 30 per cent of the camps visited consisted only of a conjugal family, but typically an encampment comprised two or three co-habiting couples and their children.

The significant features of Hill Pandaram social organization can be summarized as follows:

First, many conjugal families reside as isolated units, and frequently this separation from relatives may extend over several weeks.

Second, there is a continuing pattern of separation and reaggregation between families and individuals (even children); but significantly this is not linked to any seasonal variations in the supply of forest produce. Many of the latter of course are seasonal commodities, but the pattern of aggregation nonetheless does not indicate any fluctuation. There is no seasonal concentration of families such as we find in many other hunting-gathering societies.

Third, there are no corporate groups among the Hill Pandaram above the level of the family, and even this unit is flexible, for marriages are brittle, and couples often live apart for long periods. Thus like the Kadar, there is no unilineal descent system or ideology, nor do the men form themselves into any recognizable cult fraternity. Equally important is the fact that there are no ritual congregations, nor any other communal associations which have salience for group structuring.

Fourth, there is a pervasive emphasis on sexual egalitarianism, and women sometimes form commensal units independent of a man, though they always form a part of a wider camp aggregate. This is coupled with a normative stress on individual autonomy and self-sufficiency. However this stress on automony did not lead to a situation suggested by Friedl (1975:18) where a conjugal couple did not jointly share the food which was gathered. Among the Hill Pandaram the conjugal unit was a cooperating even if a flexible and sometimes transient unit.

Fifth, the Hill Pandaram are in fact and in sentiment nomadic and are so characterized by local agriculturalists, who denigrate this aspect of their culture – as well as their yam digging. The usual length of stay at a particular camping site (or rock shelter) is from two to 16 days, with seven to eight days being the average, though there are specific families who may reside in a particular locality for about six to eight weeks. Nomadic movements usually vary over distances of between a half and four miles, with about two miles (as the crow flies) being the average distance. On daily foraging expeditions the Hill Pandaram may range over several miles.

And finally, although specific individuals and families tend to confine their movements to a particular forest area or 'home range' there is no assertion of territorial rights. An important aspect of Hill Pandaram cosmology is the belief in hill spirits (*mala devi*) who are contacted through spirit-possession seances, but there is no direct relationship between such spirits and specific families or groupings. Significantly, the home ranges of individuals or families who aggregate together on a regular basis do not coincide, nor did I find any evidence for the existence of endogamous 'micro-castes' (cf. Yalman 1971); thus I question whether the use of the term 'local group' or 'band' to describe the residential aggregations of the Hill Pandaram has any validity.

I have elsewhere (1976b) discussed the importance of affinal ties in structuring Hill Pandaram camp aggregates, and the pervasive distrust which male siblings have for one another. This has led me to question whether hunter-gatherers live in quite the Rousseauesque state of nature, as implied by Meillassoux, coming together only for temporary productive enterprises. For, although the Hill Pandaram (unlike the Australian Aborigines) have no elaborate social mechanisms which imply that men seek to gain control over a woman's potential labour, their Dravidian kinship terminology and the focal emphasis placed on affinity, indicate that there are underlying social patterns which imply a concern for 'social reproduction'. But my concern here is not with this issue, but rather with the contrast between the Hill Pandaram and another community who lived in a similar environment – the Andamanese. I am aware of the importance of coastal fishing among the Andamanese – but nevertheless the contrast between these two communities, both living in a tropical environment of the same forest type is instructive, for it illustrates some of the contrasts suggested by Gardner and Woodburn.

The first contrast relates to the family. For a writer who regarded the family as the basic unit of kinship it is interesting to note that Radcliffe-Brown's ethnographic account of the Andamanese (1964) devotes only a few lines to this social unit, and places focal emphasis on the 'local group' which is seen not only as a land owning unit, but as having a residential locale. Although there was a pattern of seasonal dispersion, both Radcliffe-Brown and Man (1883) speak of the Andamanese as living in villages or 'permanent encampments'. This contrasts significantly with the nature of residential aggregations among the Hill Pandaram, where, as among the Kadar and Paliyan, the local group loses its corporateness and the family emerges as the focal unit. Although the family cannot be seen as the basic unit, Steward's depiction of the western Shoshoni as living at the 'family level' of socio-cultural integration

(1955:101–21) may have reflected an empirical reality – though on evolutionary and theoretical grounds his formulations are clearly misleading.

Secondly, among the Andamanese there were elaborate ceremonials focused around puberty and death. Complex initiation ceremonies were undertaken by both sexes, ceremonies which involved the ritual eating of three prestige goods associated with men – pigs, turtles and honey – and which were consonant with a complex symbolism. The funerary rituals were equally complex, and the bones of deceased relatives were preserved as sacred relics. This situation contrasts markedly with the Hill Pandaram and the Paliyan, where there is a singular lack of ritual ceremonial and an emphasis on memorate knowledge. Whether these ritual patterns among the Andamanese expressed, in embryonic form, sex and age distinctions that may have become more systematized in other pre-contact hunter-gatherers – and reach their clearest expression among cultivators like the Ndembu and Gouro – I cannot say, but importantly such patterns are absent among the Hill Pandaram. Funerary and initiation rites are not elaborate, hunting is not a ritualized activity, and there is a complete absence of corporate entities beyond the immediate family and the camp aggregate – which could be said to be a transient corporate unit.

What factors then have relevance in attempting to understand the contemporary social patterns of the Hill Pandaram? It is misleading I think to interpret these patterns as a reflection of their status as hunter-gatherers, and to view them (as Ehrenfels (1952:299) viewed the Kadar) as a 'survival' of some primeval food-gathering culture that was once widespread in southern India. Nor is it a question of interpreting their 'individualistic culture' simply as a response to intercultural pressure, although their extreme nomadism, the 'timidity they indicate in the village setting', and the 'non-violent image' they express, are clearly related to the harassment and bullying they receive from the agricultural peoples of the plains. Certainly they lack any long-term investment in productive technology, but, as what they do have is probably on a par with that of the Australian Aborigines, this factor also cannot account for the 'fragmentary' nature of their group structuring. What however *is* an important factor in their group structuring are the trade links which they have with the wider economy. Such trading contacts are mentioned by other writers on south Indian hunter-gatherers (Ehrenfels 1952; Gardner 1972:417) but their significance tends to be underplayed, and they are not deemed to have structural significance. I have elsewhere (1977) discussed the nature of this contractual trading system, but a few brief comments may be added here.

It is clear from early Tamil texts around 200 B.C. that the forests of the Western Ghats were inhabited from earliest times by tribal communities that had important trading contacts with their agricultural neighbours. It is also evident that the early Tamil kingdoms had well-developed trading relations overseas, and that this trade included many forest products – peppers, ginger, cardamom, myrobalan. Yet many writers on the hill tribes of southern India speak of these people as 'social isolates' or as 'aborigines', with the implication that they are autochthons of the forest without contact with the plains people.

An economic survey of Cochin and Travancore States made by Ward and Conner at the beginning of the nineteenth century indicates the importance of trading links between hunter-gatherers and plains peoples. Two significant features of such trading contacts are reported by the survey. First, the hill tribes were considered to 'belong' or have allegiance to specific states or petty-chieftains and the exploitation of the forest resources was organized through specific merchants. Second, forest products formed an important revenue item for these states or kingdoms.

There is essential continuity between this nineteenth-century 'rentier' system and the present situation. The Hill Pandaram, as a scheduled tribe of Kerala, come under the protection and surveillance of the Welfare Department. They have historically been considered the virtual 'wards' of the Forest Department, and like most hunter-gatherers have no land rights in the forest areas they inhabit. All forest products are deemed to be national resources, and their exploitation and extraction, as government property, is executed and controlled by the Forest Department. With respect to minor forest produce, each forest range – varying in size from 30 to 91 square miles – is leased out annually to a forest contractor who pays for the right to collect the produce on it. Thus the trading links in which the Hill Pandaram are involved are of a contractual nature. A specific merchant has a monopoly over the sale of the forest produce in any given area, and Hill Pandaram trading links are a form of mercantile barter that is geared less to local village needs than to the requirements of a wider market economy.

The Hill Pandaram situation is similar to that found among the Mundurucu and Algonkians, as described by Murphy and Steward (1956) in a now classic paper on the socio-cultural implications of trading contacts. These authors showed that as these two cultures became integrated into a wider economy, which was essentially one of mercantile capitalism – as rubber tappers and fur trappers respectively – this led to a reduction in the level of local integration. With the processes of change incumbent on a shift from a subsistence economy to one geared to external barter, the individual family emerged as a primary economic and social unit and the original structures of pre-contact times – the village and the band respectively – were drastically modified. Murphy and Steward also emphasized the importance of personal ties linking the collectors of the forest produce to individual merchants; the lack of any medium of exchange in the transactions; and the part which a system of indebtedness played in binding the primary producers to the market system. My own studies of the Hill Pandaram seemed to confirm the essential arguments of these writers; thus the 'fragmentary' nature of Hill Pandaram group structuring can be seen as a mode of organization most conducive to the dual nature of their economy, geared as it is both to subsistence production and to external trade. Richard Fox's (1969) re-analysis of the South Asian hunter-gatherers adds support to this thesis, for he sees the emergence of the 'family' as the primary unit as a direct outcome of the economic 'enclavement' of these gathering communities into a wider economic system. Moreover the pattern of highly migratory individuals, the lack of any formal kin pattern in the composition of the residential aggregates, the lack of extensive reciprocity and sharing among family groups – features which, as we have seen, are characteristic also of the Hill Pandaram – all these are seen by Fox as consonant with, as he puts it, 'the fragmentation of the society into individually competitive units each geared to external trade or barter exchange' (Fox 1969:142).

Of equal interest to this discussion is Turnbull's study of the Mbuti pygmies. In the forest setting, it would appear, the family as a social unit is almost totally absorbed into the 'band', which, though internally structured along age and sex lines, is the primary unit of economic cooperation. Yet in the village setting, although economic ties with villagers may have an individual basis, it is the Mbuti family which is the unit of economic exchange, and the 'band simply ceases to exist' (1965:228). Clearly a more permanent and structured trading relationship between the Mbuti and the external economy would seem to imply a fragmentation of this 'band' structure.

The introduction of external trade as a factor in the analysis of hunter-gathering group structuring undoubtedly complicates many of the issues I have discussed earlier in this chapter. It is a factor that has been neglected in past discussions of hunter-gatherers which, as Fox noted in referring to the writings on the Asian gatherers, have tended to ignore historical and intercultural processes. Trading contacts are certainly an important part of such processes. As our historical knowledge of hunter-gatherers increases, and the complexity of the subject-matter becomes even more evident, it is to be hoped that we will resist the temptation to construct a 'model' of hunter-gatherer social organization that gives 'technique' priority, while at the same time avoiding the equal temptation to collapse into particularistic studies.

Notes

1 Many women anthropologists have recently provided an important corrective to the assumption that women are simply 'pawns' in the political manoeuvrings of men. Nevertheless one has only to compare Turnbull's (1965) and Draper's (1975) writings on the Mbuti and !Kung respectively, with that provided by ethnographers on the Australian Aborigines (cf. White 1970:21–3) to realize that we are dealing with two very different situations. For an important and necessary corrective of Meillassoux – though aimed as a critique of Terray – see Molyneux (1977).
2 Research among the Hill Pandaram was undertaken between June 1972 and July 1973, and was supported by research grants from the Social Science Research Council and the Horniman Trust. To these agencies I am grateful. I would also like to acknowledge the help I received in the field from Sri E. N. Bhaskaran of the Kerala Forest Service, and the help and theoretical stimulus given to me by Dr James Woodburn. These summary ethnographic notes are based on my thesis on the Hill Pandaram (1975).

Bibliography

Draper, Patricia 1975. '!Kung women: contrasts in sexual egalitarianism in foraging and sedentary contexts', in R. Reiter (ed.) *Toward an anthropology of women*. New York: Monthly Review Press
Dupré, G., and Rey, P. P. 1973. 'Reflections on the pertinence of a theory of the history of exchange'. *Economy and Society* 2:131–63
Ehrenfels, U. R. 1952. *Kadar of Cochin*. Madras: Madras University Press
Fox, Richard G. 1969. 'Professional primitives: hunters and gatherers in nuclear South Asia'. *Man in India* 49:139–60
Frank, A. Gunder 1975. *On capitalist underdevelopment*. London: Oxford University Press
Friedl, Ernestine 1975. *Women and men*. New York: Holt, Rinehart and Winston
Gardner, Peter M. 1966. 'Symmetric respect and memorate knowledge: the structure and ecology of individualistic culture'. Southwest Journal *Anthropology* 22:389–415
   1969. 'Paliyan social structure', in David Damas (ed.), Contributions to anthropology: band societies. National Museum of Canada Bulletin 228

1972. 'The Paliyans', in M. G. Bicchieri (ed.), *Hunters and gatherers today.* New York: Holt, Rinehart and Winston

Godelier, Maurice 1975. 'Modes of production, kinship and demographic structures', in M. Bloch (ed.), *Marxist analyses and social anthropology,* 3–27. London: Malaby Press

Goodale, Jane C. 1971. *Tiwi wives.* Seattle: University of Washington Press

Hiatt, L. R. 1965. *Kinship and conflict.* Canberra: Australian National University

Iyer, L. A. Krishna 1937. *The Malapantaram in Travancore tribes and castes.* Trivandrum: Government Press

Lee, Richard B. 1972. 'Work effort, group structure and land use in contemporary hunter-gatherers', in P. J. Ucko (ed.), *Man, settlement and urbanism,* 177–85. London: Duckworth

1976. '!Kung spatial organization', in R. B. Lee and I. DeVore (eds.) *Kalahari Hunter-Gatherers,* 73–97. Cambridge, Mass.: Harvard University Press

Lee, Richard B., and DeVore, Irven 1968. *Man the hunter.* Chicago: Aldine

Man, E. H. 1883. 'On the original inhabitants of the Andaman Islands'. *Journal of the Anthropology Institute* 12:69–175

Mateer, S. 1883. *Native life in Travancore.* London: W. H. Allen

Meillassoux, Claude 1960. 'The "economy" in agricultural self-sustaining societies', reprinted in D. Seddon (1978) *Relations of Production,* 127–57. London: Cass

1972. 'From reproduction to production: Marxist approach to economic anthropology'. *Economy and Society* 1:93–105

1973. 'On the mode of production of the hunting band', in P. Alexandre (ed.), *French perspectives in African studies,* 187–203. London: Oxford University Press

Molyneux, Maxine 1977. 'Androcentrism in Marxist anthropology? *Critique of Anthropology* 9:55–82

Morris, Brian 1975. 'The economy and social organization of the Hill Pandaram'. Ph.D. Thesis, Univ. London

1976a. 'Settlement and social change among the Hill Pandaram'. *Man In India* 56:134–51

1976b. 'Group structure and affinal ties among the Hill Pandaram'. Unpublished MS.

1977. 'Tappers, trappers and the Hill Pandaram'. *Anthropos* 72:225–41

Murphy, R. F. and Steward, J. H. 1956. 'Tappers and trappers: parallel process in acculturation'. *Economic Develop. Culture Change* 4:335–53

Ohnuki-Tierney, E. 1974. *The Ainu of the northwest coast of South Sakhalin.* New York: Holt, Rinehart and Winston

Pilling, Arnold R. 1968. 'South eastern Australia', in Lee and DeVore (1968) 138–45

Radcliffe-Brown, A. R. 1964. *The Andaman Islanders.* New York: Free Press

Service, Elman R. 1962. *Primitive social organization.* New York: Random House

Steward, Julian H. 1955. *Theory of culture change.* Illinois: University of Illinois Press

1968. 'Causal factors and processes in the evolution of pre-farming communities' in Lee and DeVore (1968) 321–34

Terray, Emmanuel 1972. *Marxism and primitive societies.* New York: Monthly Review Press

Tindale, Norman B. 1972. 'The Pitjandjara', in M. G. Bicchieri (ed.), *Hunters and gatherers today*, 217–65. New York: Holt, Rinehart and Winston

Turnbull, Colin M. 1965. *Wayward servants*. New York: National History Press

Ward and Conner 1863. *Memoir of the survey of the Travancore and Cochin states (1816–20)*. Travancore: Sircor Press

White, Isobel M. 1970. 'Aboriginal woman's status resolved', in Fay Gale (ed.) *Women's role in Aboriginal society*, 21–30. Canberra: Australian Institute of Aboriginal Studies

Williams, B. J. 1974. 'A model of band societies'. *American Antiquity* Memoir 39

Wolf, Eric R. 1955. 'Types of Latin American peasantry'. *American Anthropology* 57:452–70

Woodburn, James C. 1976. 'Sex roles in hunting and gathering societies; some of the issues'. Unpublished Paper

Yalman, Nur 1971. *Under the bo tree*. Berkeley: University of California Press

9. Aka–farmer relations in the northwest Congo Basin[1]

SERGE BAHUCHET and HENRI GUILLAUME
translated by SHEILA M. VAN WYCK

The myth of the forest cocoon

For a variety of reasons, research carried out in central and southern Africa has long ignored the problem of contacts between the Later Stone Age populations of hunter-gatherers and the Iron Age peoples who brought techniques of food production, pottery-making and metallurgy. Recent archaeological research in Zambia, Malawi and Zimbabwe and more sophisticated methods of dating have begun to provide us with evidence on the antiquity of these contacts, dating in some cases to at least the beginning of the Christian era (Miller 1969; Phillipson 1976). The co-existence of these two modes of existence has consisted not merely in a juxtaposition, but also has involved long-term exchange relations without technological assimilation. The antiquity and persistence of these relations compel us to perceive these foraging societies in a new light. Long assumed to have been on the fringe of history, these societies now appear to have been in contact, yet have nevertheless remained distinct. If some of them enable us to observe ancient forms of social and economic organization, they are by no means fossils of a prehistoric state, magically preserved. It is highly likely that centuries of proximity and contacts have had profound influences on both sides. From this viewpoint, it is clear that we must rely heavily on the findings of archaeology, linguistics and human biology for further insight.

The case of the Aka Pygmies illustrates the extent of these contacts. It appears that the western equatorial forest fringe, where the Aka live, was penetrated by Savannah people as early as 2400–500 B.C. (N. David forthcoming). This colonization, which took the form of local and progressive migrations rather than a single massive move, was carried out by people, perhaps already Bantu, who made stone tools and pottery, and probably had techniques of food production. In David's view:

Aka Pygmy net hunters procure game in part to trade with farmers. Pygmies may have originally adopted the net-hunting technique from their farming neighbours (S. Bahuchet)

Migratory movement would have been primarily by canoe along the coast and the waterways, and settlement concentrated in riverine areas with rich alluvial soils. The economy would have been based upon yams for starches, palm oil for lipids and fish as the main source of animal protein, although goats may have accompanied the immigrants and Pygmy–Bantu symbiosis have provided the latter with game and other forest produce.   (David forthcoming)

The spread of iron from Nigeria into southern Africa probably started as early as the Christian era, and was most likely effected through the natural communications networks within the forest itself. The river system of the Congo basin provided the probable axes of diffusion. The traditional view, that iron spread through the north, along the forest edge (Phillipson forthcoming), has recently been called into question by new findings which show the progressive occupation of the area by people of the Adamawa-Oubangui family from as early as the first millennium A.D. (David and Vidal 1977). Already in possession of food production and pottery-making techniques, and having acquired metallurgy without the help of the Bantu, they would have impeded the expansion of the latter to the east. Moving in this direction themselves, some members of the Oubanguian branch went back to the south-east via forest waterways (probably from 1000 A.D. onwards).

Evidence of the antiquity of forest penetration suggests that there has been a long tradition of contact between Pygmies and the Bantu-speaking people, as well as the Oubanguian people. Several recent studies of Pygmy languages also call into question the widespread image of Pygmies living confined and isolated in their forest cocoon. The important variable of contact history, then, must not be neglected. Even if contacts were limited and occasional, they clearly contributed to the contemporary identy of the various peoples. The interest of such information to researchers is underlined in the preliminary attempt, partly hypothetical, to reconstruct historically the way of life of the Mbuti Pygmies of the Ituri in Zaire (Harako 1976).

For the moment we will limit ourselves to a discussion of oral traditions, specifically those which reveal the ideological viewpoints which Pygmies and their neighbours have of themselves and the nature of their relations. These attitudes derive from practical and economic reality of contact, and do not constitute a mere justification of the latter; rather, they are one of the conditions which shaped relations in the first place.

Civilizers, saviours and savages

The Aka (*moaka*; *baaka* or *biaka*) are related to both Oubanguian and Bantu-speaking people (Figure 9.1). They speak a language of a Bantu type not mentioned by M. Guthrie (1967–71), but which can be included in the C-10 group. C-10 also features two geographically neighbouring languages, the Ngando and the Isongo (Cloarec-Heiss and Thomas 1978). The Aka language, while obviously borrowed, is also unique and autonomous, a result of its long evolution from the source language (Thomas *et al.* forthcoming). Today, there is no mutual comprehension between the Aka and neighbouring Bantu groups. Relations between them favour the use of Bantu languages (Guillaume and Delobeau 1979), a phenomenon which reflects the more general state of domination the Pygmies live under. The linguistic affiliations of Aka, and the long process of differentiation, imply the existence of ancient contacts which must have been more extensive than mere occasional exchanges of material goods.

To understand settlement and the evolution of Aka–Bantu relations,

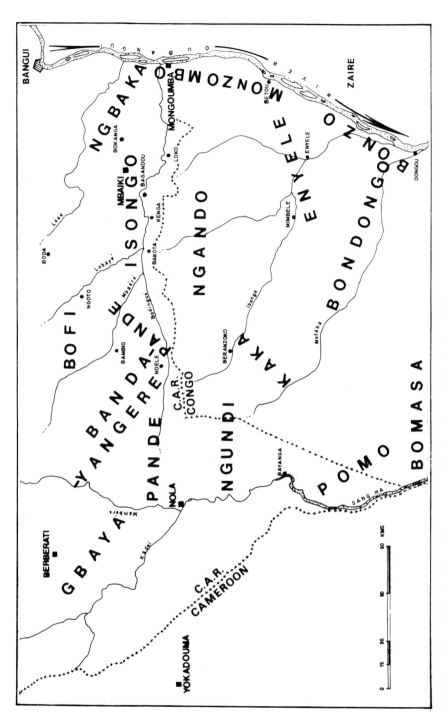

9.1 Aka settlements in the Lobaye River area and the locations of their Black neighbours

the identity attributed to each party in the consciousness of the other must be taken into account, for these contribute to the constitution of relations and the definition of their form.

Conceived of by their neighbours as a separate entity, or one that is linked to chimpanzees as related in folk-tales, the Aka (*yandenga* in Monzombo, *bambenga* in Ngbaka and in Ngando, *bakola* in Isongo) are always semantically opposed to men (*mose* in Monzombo, *yo* in Ngbaka, *moto* in Ngando, *mondo* in Isongo) or to villagers (*bose* in Monzombo, *wagba* in Ngbaka, *moto a mboka* in Ngando, *mondobo* in Isongo). The village is conceived of as a human and cultural space, as opposed to the Aka camps in the forest. They are also differentiated from animals, their links with chimpanzees perceived as having been ruptured at some point in the past when the latter were relegated to the animal world (Delobeau 1977). The Aka, then, occupy an intermediate state between the human world and the animal world, and are conceived of with considerable ambivalence by their 'Tall Black' neighbours. (The Aka call the neighbouring peoples *milo/bilo*, which is best translated as 'Tall Blacks'. The term has several connotations: racial, i.e. stranger or non-pygmy; cultural, i.e. villager, sedentary; social, i.e. master or boss.)

For the Tall Blacks, the Aka represent the Civilizing Being (*Etre Civilisateur*), who enabled men to make the passage from nature to culture through the introduction of fire, blacksmithing, cooking of food, and plant domestication. Even though this notion of civilizing capacity does grant the Aka with more than they actually introduced themselves, it does confirm their role as the first inhabitants of the country. In fact, the Tall Blacks made numerous moves in the Congolese Basin, and forged successive links with various Aka bands and other Pygmy groups (as the Baka of Cameroon). Occasionally, such links took the form of joint migrations. The Pygmy identity as Saviours, which is inherent in their function as Civilizing Beings, is thus reinforced in so far as it was the Pygmies who guided the Savannah peoples through the forest. The Pygmies initiated the Savannah peoples to a world which was previously alien and hostile to them, and provided them with necessary forest products (i.e. meat, gathered food, medicinal plants, etc.). In consequence, the Savannah peoples learned to exercise a degree of direct, if limited, control over the natural world of the forest. It should not be forgotten that some groups, such as the Kaka and the Ngando, have a long tradition of forest activity, a fact which has been obscured by the effects of French colonization, agricultural development, and recent commercialization. But it is evident among peoples such as the Ngaka, who previously led a semi-nomadic life based partially on hunting, gathering and fishing in the forest. Their agricultural activities at that time were limited to the relatively undemanding cultivation of bananas (Thomas 1963).

Settled on the forest edge, and along the waterways, the Tall Blacks occupy *cultural* space, whereas the Aka are confined to *natural* space within the forest. The separation in geographical area is considered as a reflection of a natural division of labour by the Tall Blacks; to the Aka it is a result of theft. They relate the tale that, upon returning from the forest, they were surprised to find that their villages (i.e. sedentary camps) had been taken over by the Tall Blacks, who in turn drove the Aka back into the forest. This interpretation is reiterated in a number of other legends. One is a Mbuti story, in which the Pygmies are robbed of their ability to propagate bananas; their neighbours fooled them and took the banana roots, leaving only the leaves to the Pygmies (Turnbull 1966). In another story, contained in a Ngbaka song, the 'gift' of Pygmy trapping techniques and rituals is revealed to have been forced (Arom 1970). Thus, the situation is inverted: Men who were nothing now find themselves in possession of all culture; whereas, the Pygmies who had everything are now totally deprived. This is the other side of the ambivalence.

Relegated to the forest, the land of savagery in the eyes of the Tall Blacks, the Aka (Civilizing Beings and Saviours) are equally Savages. This ambiguity underlies the Tall Blacks' view of the Aka, who are objects of scorn but also of fear. That the Aka cohabit the same territory with dreaded spirits, share in common their faculties of strength, skill and mobility, and possess the ability to contact those spirits, impresses and even frightens the Tall Blacks. They resort to the magical and therapeutic knowledge of the Aka, and their own pantheon shows the influence of their natural and supernatural world.

Deprived of culture (Savages), the Aka are bound to be dominated. The counterpart to this view, which at the same time justifies their domination, is the socialization of the Aka. In return for their services, the colonizers provide goods to the dominated people, goods which they can no longer produce themselves (forged-iron objects, cultivated plants, etc.). The supply of such items is merely the material element of a much wider socialization policy, one that implies a whole conception of the relations between man and nature. To the colonizers, the Aka are asocial beings, with a life-style characterized by laxity and absence of rules: lack of constraint in sexual relations and marriage practices, wasted natural resources, institutionalized theft, etc. Moral action favours the organization of marriages and the institution of the dowry, the construction of food storehouses, etc. Such practices assure the proper reproduction of life: of men, of animals and of plants. This point of view is inherent in the confrontation between two antithetical socio-economic systems (hierarchical organization and centralization of authority versus egalitarian organization and diffusion of power; lineal organization versus groupings of shallow genealogical distance; predatory action versus limited transformation of a forest environment). The combination 'man–villager' cannot be disassociated from the connotation 'master' (*mo* in Monzombo; *molo* in Ngbaka; *kumu* in Ngando and Isongo). Thus, 'men–villagers–masters' are opposed to 'Pygmies–foresters–dependants'. But the actual undertaking of domination, despite appearances on the part of the Aka (apparent flexibility, ease of contact, etc.), remains elusive and the justifications are still disputed.

The socio-economic relations which objectively link the two groups do not, in fact, correspond to the state of subjugation that ideological representations legitimize. For a long time, contacts have taken the form of balanced reciprocity of services, based upon complementary opposition of technologies and modes of adaptation to the natural environment. These relations do not constitute an articulation, conditioning the reproduction of either or both groups. Nevertheless, it is the beginning of a determined mutual dependence for the Aka. Constraints such as withdrawing the products of work, restricting freedom of movement, institutionalizing physical punishment (including military skirmishes), etc., are enforced upon them by their very economic need for iron, which is used in tool manufacture. More important than the supply of agricultural produce, this need for iron (which they obviously did not have previously) lends an imperative character to relations between Aka and Tall Blacks. The gap between the actual content of relations, and the representation of it in Tall Black ideology is projected into their supernatural world. By way of example, the Ngbaka represent the relations through the behaviour they attribute to the *mimbo* or trapping spirits. In fact the *mimbo* (originally given to the Ngbaka by the Aka), do not hunt for their own benefit but are content with a limited portion of game. It is this attitude which the colonizers really desire in their relations with the natives. Morphologically, physiologically, and culturally comparable to forest people, the *mimbo* appear 'not only as "the spirits of hunting and trapping" but also as a projection of "the Aka-client" in a magical appropriation process' (Arom and Thomas 1974). Thus, the

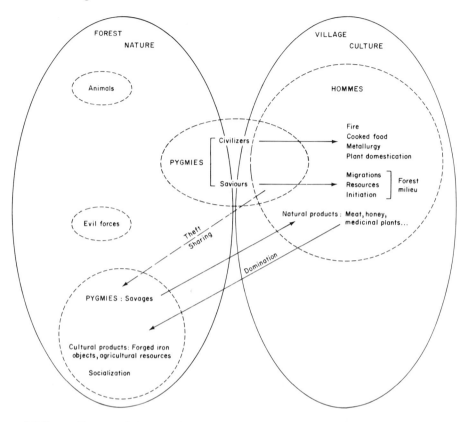

9.2 Pygmy-Farmer relations symbolically represented

ideological representation legitimizes not only existing relations – enabling the Tall Blacks to devote themselves to their essentially cultural activities (metallurgy, agriculture) by a division of labour – but also more institutionalized relations of dependence which may emerge in the future. Figure 9.2 is an attempt to simplify the status and functions of each group.

Ecology and forest exploitation

Of all the variable features of the natural environment which act as *ecological* constraints on the Aka hunter-gatherers (Bahuchet 1978a), two are primary and may account for differences in subsistence activities in various areas of the forest. On the one hand, the forest cover in the Aka area is heterogeneous in character; on the other, there are modalities in relations with agricultural groups, which are themselves influenced by the nature of the forest. We will examine both these factors from a historical perspective.

Heterogeneity in the forest milieu

Over and above the fact that the forest consists of a mosaic, a juxtaposition of micro-environments brought about by the varying life-cycles of trees (the fall of which provokes the growth of different species in the undergrowth), the nature of the soil is the determining factor in several types of plant formation. Humid soils are characterized by particular species of vegetation. In the flat areas of the Congo Basin, waterways have very wide beds which are regularly or permanently flooded, forming marsh zones. Vegetation varies according to the wetness of the soil, which is in turn a function of the rhythm of flooding: a dense, marshy forest with low shelter grows on flooded soil without drainage; a flood-plain forest with a high canopy grows on soil which is permanently wet, but also occasionally flooded with one to two metres of water; a mixed forest grows on wet slopes that are only flooded for short periods and eventually dry out. Besides the flower composition, which is different from that of solid-ground forests, wet-zone wildlife is very different: the biggest mammals (which are the most valuable to the Aka) such as the elephant and the *situtunga* antelope (*Tragelaphus spekei*) are found in marshy forest; the *bongo* antelope (*Boocercus euryceros*) inhabits the mixed forests of the wet slopes.

Solid-ground forest itself consists of several types: semi-deciduous forest, in which flower composition varies according to sub-soil type (secondary sandstone, tertiary sandstone or alluvia, quartzite sandstone, etc.); or evergreen forest of a widely dominant species (*Gilbertiodendron deweuri*, Cesalpiniaceae). Large wildlife in the semi-deciduous forest consists of several species of duikers (*Apholophus*), red hogs (*Potamochoerus porcus*) and apes (gorilla and chimpanzee); in evergreen forests, a species of duiker (*Cephalophus leucogaster*) and the bongo are common.

Thus, the primary model of the humid tropical forest is not homogeneous as is sometimes supposed, but *heterogeneous*, at both the local and regional levels.

Before European colonization, this heterogeneity appeared as a difference in varying frequency of hunting techniques and 'usual' game. Pygmies in the Lobaye region, where semi-deciduous forest is predominant, hunt anthropoids, red hogs and duikers with spear-tracking techniques in the rainy season. Motaba Pygmies, on the other hand, living in a flooded forest zone, hunt elephants and situtungas with the same techniques, but in any season. Groups living near the Motaba springs, or near the Sangha, where evergreen and semi-deciduous forests are mingled, hunt bongos. Diversity is also found in the exploitation of caterpillars for food. The northern part of the Aka territory, which has a tropical climate during the rainy season, is well provided with caterpillar trees (solid-ground forest including Meliaceae). At the south of the same zone, the flooded forest has fewer species of trees that support edible caterpillars, and the climate is of equatorial type; hence, caterpillars are relatively scarce.

It is important to acknowledge these characteristics of the natural environment and take them into account when comparing the modes of subsistence of various African Pygmy groups.

Exchange with the Tall Blacks

Today, the Aka maintain a complex system of exchange with the sedentary Tall Black farmers. In addition to working in the fields for several weeks each year, products of the hunt are the basis of reciprocal exchange (i.e. meat for metal tools, salt, and starchy foods). The use of Aka Pygmy labour on a periodic basis on the plantations is quite recent (within the last twenty years). By contrast, the exchange of meat for metal tools is very old.

In the pre-colonial situation, the exchange pattern seems to have been more-or-less identical for most forest groups. The heterogeneity of the forest environment did not influence the character of these exchanges; what varied was the animal species from which meat was produced. Neither was there any noteworthy influence from the villagers on the types of hunting practised. It was more a question of Aka exchanging surplus food products after their own consumption needs had been met.

Conditions changed with the creation of a commercial market and an external demand for products which were not traditionally used, either by the Aka or the villagers. This occurred when the Portuguese, with the help of intermediary marketing groups, undertook trade on the coasts of the Congo in the sixteenth century, i.e. long before the Europeans actually entered the Aka forest area. The first mention of this commerce is found in the 'Description de l'Afrique' by O. Dapper in 1686. He recounts that 'dwarves' living outside the forest brought 'elephant teeth' to the townspeople of the Lovango Kingdom; these ivory tusks were then sold to the Portuguese.

We lack adequate documents to analyse the importance of this trade economy in the northwest Congo Basin before twentieth-century white penetration. Some clues lead us to believe that inhabitants of this area took active part in the ivory trade (Sautter 1966), sending ivory to Stanley Pool in the south via the Sangha and Oubangi waterways, and to the northwest (Cameroon, Adamawa) with the help of Hausa traders (Bruel 1918).

At the time of colonization, the trade was imposed on the villagers, who in turn compelled the Aka to take part via their exchange relations with them. From then on, exchange acted as a constraint, modifying relations between the Aka and the forest (i.e. emphasis on hunting efforts, privileged use of certain hunting techniques, and therefore changes in group structure, etc.). However, in spite of domination, the status of the Tall Blacks as 'masters' (*konza*) would be better likened to tutors or protectors than owners. They are, in fact, 'masters' who do not own the Aka, but who make them dependent by monopolizing metallurgy, agriculture and, most importantly, the access to new economic networks. The dependence of the Aka is in no way a form of slavery, a parallel sometimes drawn by European colonizers on the basis of Tall Black interpretations of their relation to the Aka. The Aka are not 'desocialized', neither are their demographic and economic reproduction controlled by their 'masters'. The reproduction of Aka camps is achieved on the basis of the kinship system (Guillaume forthcoming).

The Colonial trade

The heterogeneity of the forest, discussed above, becomes a striking factor once the whites enter the area (1890) and divide it into concessionary companies after an 1899 decree. These companies were privileged to exploit natural products (i.e. rubber, resin, oleaginous plants, ivory and pelts) and were granted commercial monopoly (Coquery-Vidrovitch 1972).

Natural products with commercial potential were few and of variable importance. Rubber, ivory, pelts and palm nuts were products with an important and permanent market; by contrast, other minor products were only occasionally commercialized, on a small scale (i.e. copal resin, raffia, rattan and kola nuts). Some of these resources are located in marshy forest zones (copal, a resin used in the varnish industry; ivory;

raffia); others, like palm nuts, are found on the edge of the forest (particularly Lobaye). For this reason, the villagers in various regions had production activities which differed according to resource exploitation. The shifting interests of the concessionary companies, in combination with natural diversity, account for the differences.

From 1899 to 1910: ivory Right from the beginning, several foreign depots were created within each concession. Their exclusive aim was trading, especially of ivory. The whole of French Equatorial Africa exported more than 100 tons of ivory per year during this period (Bruel 1918). The villagers were responsible for the ivory market, but it is obvious that the Aka were the principal producers, as several texts maintain. As the only people with hunting skills, they were eventually provided with guns by company agents in order to improve hunting of elephants. Other groups were content to set large traps. From then on, the Tall Blacks added the intermediary role to their technological superiority; a role which has increased to the present day at the expense of the Aka.

Ivory exploitation had several consequences:

1. The development of a type of hunting which provided large quantities of meat that was not traditionally used.
2. The intensification of contacts, diversification, and an increase in volume of exchanged goods. For the Pygmies, the counterparts of ivory were iron and salt.
3. The depletion of elephant populations.
4. The reinforcement of the bases of power of the *Tuma*, the 'master of the great hunt'.

By virtue of personal qualities of strength and courage, of extensive knowledge of nature and magico-religious arts, the Tuma's intervention is indispensable for the organization of a successful hunt. Therefore, his role is primary in the acquisition of iron. But even if his participation is critical in the hunt, and he controls the exchange of ivory, he does not, for all that, widen his field of authority. Neither he nor the *Mbai-moto* (the elder of the agnatic kinship group), who centralizes the iron collected after a great hunt, attain generalized power thereby; neither do they accumulate material wealth, for goods remain the property of the whole group. Despite the increasing introduction of iron, the use of material goods remains egalitarian.

From 1908 on, due to the spread of firearms, the ivory trade dwindled in importance as the elephants dramatically diminished in number. At this point, the companies began to get interested in rubber.

From 1910 to 1940: wild rubber In 1910, the eleven concessionary companies which shared the northern Congo forest merged to create the 'Compagnie Forestiere Sangha-Oubangui' (cfso), on a 17-million-hectare concession which entirely encompassed the Aka territory. From that point on, this company was entitled to the leasing of rubber. Trading was no longer a monopoly, but nevertheless the cfso remained the only trading company.

The company employed manpower from the villages in order to collect rubber by 'bleeding' the trees in the forest. Company agents, alone in foreign depots, forced men into the forest to collect rubber. This compulsory aspect was further reinforced by the imposition of government taxes, payable only in rubber. This was to be the gruesome epoch of forced labour denounced by André Gide in his *Travels in the Congo* (1962).

Thus were men compelled to live in the forest and work without rest; women were forced to tend manioc plantations in the villages in order to feed the porters, the armies, and the road workers. In such a situation, the exhausted villagers were unable to meet subsistence requirements and relied upon their Aka 'allies' to produce meat. (In fact, the Aka were never involved in the harvesting of rubber.) The Aka, relying upon familiar spear-hunting techniques, hunted animals less dangerous and more easily caught than the elephants (particularly red hogs).

However, from 1925 on, a market for duiker skins developed in France; the skins were tanned on the spot and sent out to make coats and 'chamois leather' (*sic*). Commercialization of the skins, together with the fact that the Aka were often settled in the forests near the work camps (to provide meat and help with net hunting), resulted in a period of acquisition by the Aka of the techniques of hunting with nets, which may be traced out. That this in fact occurred is confirmed in stories and traditions of the Aka and other groups, which related that hunting with nets was a village practice unlike 'real' Aka spear-hunting techniques. Several clues confirm it, in particular the custom of sharing meat, which is not at all egalitarian compared to that of meat acquired in collective spear-hunting. (See Bahuchet 1978b for the details of sharing.)

Although rubber was by far the most important product from the company's point of view, it also organized the gathering of copal and palm nuts (*Elaeis guineensis*, the almond, or palm nut, provides an oil used in food industries – i.e. margarine – and chemical industries – i.e. soap). If the Aka did not take part in rubber collection, it has been proven that they did contribute their labour to the copal and palm nut industries in the Ibenga and Motaba areas. In the Lobaye region they only did so on an occasional basis; they were mainly suppliers of meat.

From 1940 on: duiker hunters More and more, the Aka utilized collective net hunting. To be efficient, it required the participation of numerous adults, men and women, to do the beating. The camps were then on a much larger scale than ever before (40 to 60 adults instead of 15 to 25), and became more permanent.

The slaughter of duikers increased from 1937 on, after the CFSO disappeared and the 'Sociétés Indigènes de Prévoyance' (SIP) were created. The development of saw-mills, diamond mines, rubber and coffee plantations resulted in employees being brought in from other areas. In 1949, such employees formed 22 per cent of the total population of the Boda and Mbaiki districts (Bouscayrol 1950).

The SIP aimed at developing agriculture, herding, hunting, fishing, gathering, and organizing the preparation and marketing of products (Suret-Canale 1977). After World War II there was a growing demand for raw skins. Following the decrease in European herds, the SIP got the monopoly for buying skins (by decree in 1945). In some forest zones, the market in the fifties was averaging around 27,000 skins of *Cephalophus* per year (Dongier 1953).

The decline of the great spear-hunting expeditions, linked with new motivations and a decrease in 'big game', provoked a decline in the position of *Tuma* (outlined above); whereas the *nganga* diviner–healer intervened more and more to ensure the success of rituals associated with net hunting.

Thus, the Aka devoted themselves to the search for export goods, or contributed indirectly to it by feeding the workers. In either case, their intervention implies that production activities turned outwards. This tendency responds precisely to the colonial administrative design.

The 'Taming' policy

Enigmatic figures, long classed in European thought with spirits, monsters, 'pre-men' or 'ape-men', the Pygmies only achieved the status of men shortly before the establishment of colonial structures. They were perceived as 'back-ward', 'uncultivated' beings by the administrators; they led a 'wandering' or 'roving' life in search of subsistence. Nonetheless, their primitiveness was seen as an insurmountable hindrance to the 'civilizing mission' of the colonizers. 'Naive', naturally 'quiet' and 'peaceful', the Pygmies were not elements of disorder; for the missionaries, their belief in one God simplified matters and justified their Christianization. They were seen as living testimony to the universality of monotheism, even among the most primitive populations.

The colonial enterprise itself responded to a highly humanitarian motive: to free the Pygmies from subjection by their neighbours. In the 1930s, it took the form of the so-called 'Taming Policy', which was marked with sentiments of 'softness', 'care', and 'kindness', and stressed the need for 'tact', 'caution', and 'patience'. Its purpose was to win the Pygmies' trust, to attract them and familiarize them with administrative contact, and to show them the advantages of medical care. This was accomplished with the help of gifts of iron, salt, and tobacco. The idea was that the Pygmies would thereby see the benefits of dealing directly with the Whites, and rid themselves of their traditional intermediaries.

This 'prudent' policy was explained by the 'timid', 'fearful' temperament of the Pygmies (who were always ready to flee into the forest, or cross the Oubangui River). They were not yet accustomed to the idea of 'emancipation', or resisting their 'masters', for fear of losing their privileges. This type of rationalization and behaviour is a constant feature of the colonial experience in contexts of dependency or slavery, especially in Sahelian and Saharan Africa (Guillaume 1975). Rushing the evolutionary process could lead to a chaotic, uncontrollable situation, for here too it was a matter of adjustment in the relations between traditional forces. Written works mention, for instance, how the Pygmies helped to single out and denounce Tall Blacks who were resisting the work imposed by the colonial administration. The colonial aim was to emancipate the Pygmies from their 'masters', only to make them dependent upon the administration. In so doing, their participation in 'productive work' was ensured, as was the 'development' of the colony. Pygmy collaboration led to further weakening and more effective control of their neighbours.

In fact, the Pygmies' contribution was indispensable to the exploitation of the sparsely populated areas (exploitation which, for a long time, consisted mainly of 'looting'). The labour shortage was made worse by the colonial administration itself: the result of excesses by the concessionary regime and the administrative work projects (i.e. out-migration, malnutrition, high mortality rates, etc.). Added to this was the spread of sleeping sickness; the confluence of the Ibenga and the Motaba

Rivers with the Oubangui was an important centre in this regard. The value of demographic data, based on very approximate estimates for the early period of colonization, sets a limit on extrapolation. But, 'we must note', as Coquery-Vidrovitch (1972) has put it, 'the sharp decline [in population] affecting the lower part of the Oubangui (Ibenga, Motaba, Likouala), which undoubtedly corresponded to real phenomena: that of the semi-desertion of the land which was the result of the Forest Company regime and the effects of sleeping sickness'.

As the 'taming' of the Pygmies progressed and they made repeated contacts with the administrators, a policy of 'stabilization' was undertaken. Established among other populations since 1915, it consisted of regrouping settlements along communication axes for the purpose of facilitating control (i.e. census, tax collection, marketing, labour recruitment, etc.). The Pygmies were encouraged to settle along such routes, to undertake cultivation and sell their products either at the markets or at foreign depots. In accordance with the policy of 'prudence', they were not immediately burdened with the same obligations that had been imposed on their neighbours. But the final result of the policy was to integrate the Pygmies fully into the colonial system. This objective was clearly stated in the recommendations to district officers made by the Governor-General for French Equatorial Africa in 1934, 'In the future, when they [Pygmies] are used to us and our institutions, which they will have profited from and will still want to enjoy, we may initiate the weight of taxes and other obligations. Therefore, you must not enter those you have registered on your tax lists for at least five years' (Governor-General 1934).

The commencement of this programme varied according to the level of regional administrative control. In 1933, Pygmies from the Epena area to the south of Aka country were already settled, included in the census, and were paying taxes. They served as an example for the administration to hold up to the Aka Pygmies. The Aka in the Ibenga-Motaba area were included in a fragmentary census in 1936. They took part in the exploitation of copal and palm nuts, and had begun to sell their products without recourse to their 'masters'. Some settled close to communication routes, maintained plantations, and grew manioc, corn and bananas. Their Tall Black neighbours discouraged their enterprise, and willingly furnished bad advice as to cultivating techniques.

The Aka were undoubtedly affected by the colonial economy, but the 'stabilization' policy only affected a minority of them, primarily in the riverside areas of the Oubangui. In the Lobaye district, its effects were limited. This may have resulted from later control by the administration, successive additions of territory to the region, and numerous changes in internal organization. There were camp̃s settled along the communication axes, but it was not until 1949 that the M'Baiki- and Boda-district Aka were included in a partial census. The Mongoumba groups were not covered in this first investigation. These Pygmies supplied meat, and sometimes sold it directly to the markets, a valuable consideration in view of the difficulty of feeding the labour-force.

It appears that, on the whole, the 'taming' policy proved to be ephemeral, with results that were contrary to desired aims. If profound acculturation took place among several groups in the Beton and Dongou regions, and a certain amount of economic independence was achieved, elsewhere 'emancipation' led to an aggravation of the dependence of the Aka on the Tall Blacks. By encouraging an increase in production for the external market, stimulating exchange and creating new needs, the colonial administration did not assist the Pygmies in controlling their position in a new world; rather, they reinforced the privileged position of the Tall Black intermediaries.

Aka integration into Tall Black production activities

Following the 'taming' policy, the process of dependency developed without direct outside intervention. It was not until 1974 that public interest was renewed in the Central African part of Aka territory.

In the preceding 25-year period, one determining factor emerged in the evolution of relations between the Aka and Tall Blacks. This was the increase and expansion of agriculture, the decisive threshold of which was reached in the 1960s with the commercial production of coffee among most of the Lobaye farmers. From then on, the services which the Aka were expected to provide had less and less to do with their forest skills and knowledge. Their position as suppliers of forest products (ivory, meat, pelts, copal, palm nuts) was based upon traditional collecting technology; in the new state, they were integrated into a technological milieu and introduced to production activities that were foreign to them.

The Aka became a work force primarily to be used in agriculture, a tendency which developed at the expense of their forest existence. From the initial exchange system of game and gathered products for iron and agricultural products, there developed a new basis of exchange: labour for food, manufactured goods and money. The exact nature of the exchange depended upon the type of service provided. Money, which had been introduced several years before (to some extent during the 'taming' policy), was exchanged primarily in the form of wages for agricultural workers.

Today the production activities of the Aka take various forms in accordance with the situations of neighbouring groups and villages to which they are tied. In the Kenga area where coffee production is unimportant, the Ngando hunt during several months of the year. In addition, they claim meat products from the Aka which they then sell to urban centres and large forest and coffee enterprises. It is important to note that this trade is rarely, if ever, carried out directly by the Aka; it is usually done through the villagers to whom they are linked. This contrasts to the situation of the Mbuti from Ituri, where outside traders carry on the exchange of meat (Hart 1978). Thus, the Aka maintain forest activities which are nonetheless conditioned by their neighbours. Much hunting time is devoted to producing game for the 'masters'. Furthermore, net hunting is on the increase, and the use of snares (which they recently learned from the villagers) is replacing track hunting. Such snares are made during the rainy season out of bicycle brake cables. The use of snares, and the tending of those that belong to the 'master', has provoked a notable reduction in camp mobility. The products of hunting have a comparable importance in the Ndele region which is still rich in game. There, the Aka hunt with nets for the greater part of the year in order to sell meat to the villagers (the Banda-Yangere agriculturalists). For the remaining part they work for wages on the coffee plantations.

Elsewhere (Mongoumba, Loko, Bagandou, Ngoto, Bambia), the Tall Blacks rely on Aka labour for their plantations. The development of agriculture and coffee production outstripped the labour supplies of the villages, and Aka labour is now used to reinforce the productive capacity of the Tall Blacks. In addition to supplying much-needed labour, it allows the Tall Blacks to avoid the hardest chores and attend to other matters.

Alongside their integration into agricultural production, the Aka carry on their forest exploitation, for themselves and for their 'masters'. Participation in agricultural work usually occurs at the beginning of the dry season (December–January), during the land-clearing and coffee-cropping phases. Activities are more generalized in the major part of the season (cutting of trees, burning-off, etc.). The annual cycle is thus divided into two periods: one which is increasingly determined by the economic life of the villagers; the other resting on more traditional bases. The latter period is characterized by the collection of caterpillars in the rainy season, an activity in which numerous villagers take part. Between the two extremes – forest life interrupted by several weeks' stay near the villages at the beginning of the dry season, and settlement on the edge of agricultural areas with forest camps in the rainy season (August–September) – there are a number of intermediate arrangements. The Pygmies may return to the forest for the duration of the rainy season, or in the middle of the dry season, to hunt with nets, collect honey, or fish. But the general tendency is increasing polarization around village centres.

The process of Aka integration into the Tall Blacks' economy is similar to the pattern of evolution described for the southern part of Aka territory (Demesse 1978):

1. Nomadism decreases and the time spent in settled camps on the edge of the forest, close to villages, increases. Hunting and gathering are increasingly carried on from these bases, and no longer from temporary forest camps.

2. The territory of exploitation is more and more restricted. Great hunting expeditions are slowly replaced by shorter trips of limited distance.

3. There is a decrease in natural resources and lowered hunting efficiency occurs because of over-hunting in the most frequented areas. Big game, such as elephants, bongo, and red hog are becoming scarce, and only survive deep in the forest. The most common game are duikers and other small animals: forest porcupine, mongoose, genet, rats, and squirrels. Duikers are the net game par excellence (in beats which are increasingly executed in shorter trips), but they are also trapped with snares. Snares are used for other animals in addition, small hunts are sometimes carried out by a family, or by two or three men, sometimes with the help of dogs. Snaring and small hunting parties are popular because they are so appropriate to changes in animal resources and hunting activities in general.

During this phase of disintegration of the traditional economy, the decrease in subsistence collected from the forest (due to the decline in the productivity of hunting) results in increased consumption of agricultural products (manioc, corn, bananas). Agricultural foods are no longer a welcome contribution to the diet, but form the major part of

Aka food intake. In consequence, their diet is increasingly imbalanced, and malnutrition results. Thus their former dependence is significantly increased.

Unlike the Baka Pygmies of the Konabembe (southeast Cameroon), who started their own household plantations in the 1950s (Althabe 1965), the Aka switched to farming without achieving independent production. Time spent working village fields and in forest activities, and cultural norms, constituted barriers to the development of autonomous agricultural production. These limiting factors are further reinforced by the pre-existing situation of dependency. The fields of most benefit to the Aka are the plantations (manioc, bananas, oil palm trees) abandoned, sometimes momentarily, by their 'masters'. In cases of marked sedentarization (except for groups of M'baiki that have cultivated for about ten years), they nonetheless begin by clearing small parcels of land.

Widening dependency leads to the incorporation of the Aka into other sectors of the Tall Blacks' economy: fishing for the Monzombo, crafts, porterage, construction, domestic labour, well-drilling, maintenance works, etc.

The position of the 'masters' is strengthened by the development of a credit system which ties the Aka, through indebtedness, to their creditors. The weakly developed market network exacerbates this problem, as the Aka are unable to supply themselves directly. Therefore, the money from cash wages immediately returns to its original source. The decrease in mobility, and increase in settlement near agricultural areas, places the Aka within easy reach of their neighbours; as a result they are susceptible to forced labour. During periods of settlement near to the villages, the 'masters' disrupt the camps on a daily basis. Conflict ensues, and the mood is in sharp contrast to the peace and quiet of forest camp life. The consumption of manioc and corn alcohol increases, and ragged clothing, inappropriate to the climate, is common.

The socio-economic dynamics of the Aka's situation may also be observed in neighbouring societies. The phenomena affect the internal organization of the camps, as well as relations within the bands. The acquisition of material goods is increasingly the result of individual effort, and no longer based upon group cooperation. This is obviously related to agricultural production, but also to hunting techniques which are highly individualistic, or at least require fewer and fewer participants. The process of individualization results in the disintegration of former associations between camps and lineages, or segments of lineages in the villages. Contacts are thus diversified, and even if the traditional 'master' remains a privileged spokesman, any villager is a potential employer. The development of polygamy, previously non-existent, is undoubtedly linked to the possibility of acquiring and using bride-wealth. At a band level, the decline in cooperative activity is evident in the diminishing number of great hunts, which, in any case, take place at the beginning of the dry season when demands for agricultural labour are at their height.

The disintegration of the hunting and gathering economy of the Aka and their incorporation into the economic system of the Tall Blacks, has increased in pace since 1974. At the moment, it is occurring rapidly in the Mongoumba area, where the Aka are linked to a people with little traditional orientation to the forest, the Monaombo. The decision of the authorities to develop this area is accompanied by aims to integrate the Aka. Confined, until recently, to simple invitations to settlement and agriculturalism, this project received planning impetus with the opening of the first 'school of integration'. The implementation of the integration policy is reinforced by the presence of Catholic missionaries, whose aims and objectives are more-or-less similar. The acculturation process is strikingly rapid, and is symbolized by the appearance of mud huts, based on the village model but smaller in size. It is certainly linked to the desire of the Aka to acquire material goods, and to enter fully a world which previously had been marginal to them; their entry being symbolic of the end of their inferiority. Access to it is made easier through knowledge of the national tongue: Sango. Their present evolution is conditioned by their existing relations with the Tall Blacks. To them, the Aka are folk objects to be displayed for visitors; yet, the Aka regularly hire out as farm labourers to their 'masters' and 'bosses' (words which were themselves drawn from the colonial vocabulary). The two societies have become closely interdependent; social reproduction of the Aka no longer occurs without the aid of their neighbours.

One recent phenomenon may provide us with a clue to the future: during the dry season of 1979, Aka camps moved away from village settlements and started their own plantations at the edge of the forest.

New needs are born of new values. The definition of policy with regard to the Aka, which cannot be dissociated from the policy towards the forest itself, must take into account and be based upon the combination of agricultural and forest activities.

Note

1 This article emerges from two communications to the Paris Symposium on Hunting and Gathering Societies. S. Bahuchet originally dealt with the ecological constraints of the forest environment and the social and technological influences of the peoples with whom the Pygmies are in touch. H. Guillaume dealt with the nature, form, and evolution of the relations between the Pygmies and the successive colonizers of the forest. The whole text was extensively reviewed and discussed by its two authors, and reflects common ideas. The data presented here were recorded in the northern part of the Aka foraging area (Lobaye region); some information is still available for the southern part (Ibenga-Motaba region).

Bibliography

Althabe, G. 1965. 'Changements sociaux chez les Pygmées Baka de l'Est-Camerounais'. *Cahiers d'Etudes Africaines* 20: 561–92

Arom, S. 1970. *Contes et chantefables Ngbaka-Ma'bo (République centrafricaine)*. Paris: SELAF

Arom, S. and Thomas, J. M. C. 1974. *Les mimbo, génies du piégeage, et le monde surnaturel des Ngbaka-Ma'bo (R.C.A.)*. Paris: SELAF

Bahuchet, S. 1978a. Les contraintes écologiques en forêt tropicale humide: l'exemple des Pygmées Aka de la Lobaye. *Journal d'Agriculture tropicale et botanique appliquée* 257–85

1978b. *Introduction à l'ethnoécologie des Pygmées Aka de la Lobaye, Empire centrafricain*. Paris: EHESS-MNHN

Bouscayrol, R. 1950. *Rapport politique Lobaye 1949*. Archives de la Sous-Prefecture de Mongoumba (ECA)

Bruel, G. 1911. *Notes ethnographiques sur quelques tribus de l'Afrique Equatoriale Française*. Fasc.1: 'Les populations de la Moyenne Sangha: Pomo, Boumali, Babinga'. Paris: Leroux, extrait de *Revue d'ethnographie et de sociologie*

1918. *L'Afrique Equatoriale Française: le pays, les habitants, la colonisation, les pouvoirs publics*. Paris: Larose

Cloarec-Heiss, F. and Thomas, J. M. C. 1978. *C'aka, langue bantoue des Pygmées de Mongoumba (Centrafrique) introduction à l'étude linguistique, phonologie*. Paris: SELAF

Coquery-Vidrovitch, C. 1972. *Le Congo au temps des grandes compagnies concessionaires*. Paris-La Haye: Mouton

Dapper, Olfert 1686. *Description de l'Afrique*. Amsterdam: Wolfgang, Weesekerge, Boom and van Someren (trans. from Flemish)

David, N. forthcoming 'Early Bantu expansion in the context of central African prehistory : 4000 – 1 B.C.' *Colloque sur l'expansion bantoue*. Paris: SELAF

David, N. and Vidal, P. 1977. 'The Nana-Modé village site (sous-préfecture de Bouar, Central African Republic) and the prehistory of the Ubangian speaking peoples'. *West African Journal of archaeology*, 7

Delobeau, J. M. 1977. *Yamonzombo et Yandenga: les relations entre les villages monzombo et les campements Pygmées Aka dans la sous-préfecture de Mongoumba (Centrafrique)*. Thèse 3e cycle. Paris: EHESS

Demesse, L. 1978. *Changements techno-économiques et sociaux chez les Pygmées Babinga (Nord Congo et sub-centrafrique)*. Paris: SELAF'Etudes Pygmés I'
Dongier, R. 1953. *Rapport d'inspection de la région Lobaye*. n°24/IAA 1. Archives de la préfecture de la Lobaye (Mbaiki, ECA)
Gide, André 1962. *Travels in the Congo*. Berkeley, Calif.: University of California Press (first published in French, 1926)
Governor-General of the AEF: lettre du 31 Mars 1934 aux chefs de circonscription. Brazzaville. Archives d'Aix en Provence, section Outre-Mer, série 5 D
Guillaume, H. 1975. 'Système socio-économique et pouvoir politique chez les Touaregs de l'Imannen', in: *Etudes sur les sociétés de pasteursnomades: classes sociales et état dans les sociétés*. Cahiers due CERM (Paris) 121:63–76
forthcoming. 'Les Pygmées Aka et la colonisation de lat forêt: du troc des produits à l'exploitation de la force de travail'.
Guillaume, H. and Delobeau, J. M. 1979. 'Une mosaïque ethnique et linguistique en milieu rural-enguêtes de demographie linguistique dans le sous-préfecture de Orongoumba' in: J. P. Caprile (ed.), *Contacts de langues et contacts de culture* I:11–65. Paris: SELAF
Guthrie, M. 1967–71. *Comparative Bantu*. Faruborough, Hants: Gregg International Publishers Ltd
Harako, R. 1976. 'The Mbuti as hunters: a study of ecological anthropology of the Mbuti Pygmies (Zaire), I'. *Kyoto Univ. African Studies*. X, 37–99.
Hart, J. 1978. 'From subsistence to market: a case study of the Mbuti nethunters'. *Human ecology*, 6(3):325–53
Miller, S. F. 1969. 'Contacts between the Later Stone Age and the Early Iron Age in southern Central Africa'. *Azania*, IV:81–90
Phillipson, D. W. 1976. *The Iron Age in Zambia*. Lusaka: Historical Association of Zambia
forthcoming. 'L'expansion bantoue en Afrique orientale et méridionale: les témoins archéologiques et linguistiques'. *Colloque sur l'expansion bantoue*. Paris: SELAF
Sautter, G. 1966. *De l'Atlantique au fleuve Congo. Une géographie du sous-développement*. Paris-La Haye: Mouton
Suret-Canale, J. 1977. *Afrique noire occidentale et centrale: l'ère coloniale (1900–1945)*. Paris: Editions sociales
Thomas, J. M. C. 1963. *Les Ngbaka de la Lobaye. Le dépeuplement rural chez une population forestière de la République Centrafricaine*. Paris-La Haye: Mouton
Thomas, J. M. C., Arom, S., Bahuchet, S., Cloarec-Heiss, F., Guillaume, H., Motte, E., and Senechal, C. forthcoming. *Encyclopédie des Pygmées Aka de Centrafrique et du Bord-Congo*. 3 vols. Paris: SELAF
Turnbull, C. M. 1966. *Wayward Servants. The two worlds of the African Pygmies*. London: Eyre and Spottiswoode

10. Adaptive flexibility in a multi-ethnic setting: the Basarwa of the southern Kalahari

HELGA I. D. VIERICH

The Kalahari Desert of Southern Africa has one of the largest concentrations in the world today of peoples whose economies could be characterized as dominantly hunting and gathering. Most of these people are referred to in the literature as 'Bushmen' or 'San' (Murdock 1968:15; Lee 1968:30–48; Lee 1976:5–6). In Botswana, the country with the greatest number of hunter-gatherers, they are referred to as 'Basarwa' which means 'Bushmen' in the dominant Bantu language, and it includes groups of people who are not racially Khoisan (Nurse and Jenkins 1977). A limited number of these groups have been studied so far in any detail and there has been a tendency to focus on the hunting and gathering aspects of their economy. This is because these studies have often been directed at increasing our understanding of the hunting and gathering way of life as a pattern apart from that of pastoralists and agriculturalists (see Lee and DeVore 1968).

The majority of Basarwa have lived for hundreds of years in contact with societies that grow crops and keep domestic livestock (Marks 1972; Denbow personal communication).[1] If the hunting and gathering way of life has survived in the Kalahari, it is not because of isolation. What accounts for its durability? In a sense, the answer to this question is the key to understanding the hunter-gatherer adaptation. Richard Lee (1973) has summarized part of the answer in a memorable quote from one of his informants: 'Why should we plant when there are so many mongongos in the world?' The relative ease and security of a hunting and gathering way of life means that it has remained an attractive option in many parts of the Kalahari.

The other part of the answer may be found in observing the interactions between economies based on hunting and gathering and those based on pastoralism and agriculture. Not all parts of the Kalahari are blessed with the mongongo, and even in some locations where the

Southern Basarwa roasting wild marama beans (H. Vierich)

mongongo is plentiful, hunting and gathering has given way to other economies; this has been the case along the Nata River in northeastern Botswana. The majority of Basarwa have for generations been deriving at least some of their subsistence from agriculture and livestock. They do this either by growing their own crops and keeping their own livestock, or (more often) by working for their Bantu or European neighbours as herders on cattleposts, as seasonal agricultural workers, or even as household servants. Are they forced into these positions by personal misfortune, environmental change, or political domination, or do they enter these roles by choice?

In the early period of my fieldwork among the Basarwa in Botswana, I carried out a socio-economic survey in a region of some 35,000 square kilometres lying 700 km southeast of the Dobe-Nyae-Nyae areas. This is an area of fairly typical Kalahari vegetation, soils and climate, dotted with pans and dissected with fossil river valleys. The mongongo (*Ricinodendron rautanenii*), a staple in the diet of the !Kung in the northwest, does not grow in this part of the Kalahari. Instead, two species of wild beans (*Bauhinia macrantha* and *B. esculanta*) and a number of species of melons and tubers form the staples. Unlike the Dobe-Nyae-Nyae region, there are virtually no naturally occurring permanant water sources.

Out of a multi-ethnic population of approximately 10,000, over 2,000 people were found to be doing a substantial amount of hunting and gathering. Most of these people are Basarwa, while a smaller percentage comprise poor Bantu-speaking peoples. The Basarwa are of three different language groups: several major dialects of the central or Tshukwe language, a dialect of the southern language group, and finally the newly discovered and possibly unique language, eastern ≠hûâ (Traill 1973), are all found in the area.

I assessed the degree of economic change among these Basarwa groups on the basis of data collected on livestock ownership, growing of crops, employment on cattleposts and agricultural lands, incidence of mine labour, and frequency of hunting and gathering activities. To supplement this information, I took inventories of the implements people had on hand. These included a range of items from bows and arrows and digging sticks to ploughs, hoes and saddles. I also took note of the food people were currently eating, as well as recently gathered veldfood, grain stores, recently killed game or livestock, milk, and the evidence of foods purchased at the local shop given by sugar bags and maizemeal sacs. The types of buildings and other structures gave me information on whether they were storing food, investing in more permanent structures and to what extent they were sorting out their use of living space into definite activity areas. Many of these criteria were based on discussions with Robert K. Hitchcock, who had been doing studies of the features associated with increased sedentism in the eastern Kalahari. The overall settlement pattern, in relation to the distribution of different areas of land use within the region, provided additional information on the importance of different kinds of subsistence activities for particular family groups. In terms of social criteria I looked for evidence of acculturation, such as the degree of fluency in the dominant Bantu language, and the presence of a Bantu name in addition to – or even in place of – a Sarwa name. Important also was the incidence of intermarriage and concubinage with Bantu groups. These measures of acculturation did not always coincide with the degree of economic change; the significance of this will become clear later.

What initially had appeared to be an unbroken continuum of adaptations from hunting and gathering to heavy involvement in agriculture and pastoralism emerged in this study as four clusters of adaptive strategies. These were (1) a purely hunting and gathering strategy, (2) a basically hunting and gathering subsistence supplemented by products from agriculture and pastoralism on a seasonal or occasional basis, (3) a mixed strategy involving roughly equal inputs from the hunting and gathering economy and from the pastoral and agricultural economy, and finally (4) a pattern in which agriculture and pastoralism provide the majority if not all of the subsistence.

About one quarter of the Basarwa surveyed are living primarily as hunter-gatherers (strategies 1 and 2). The minority of these, approximately 10 per cent of the total Basarwa population sampled, could be considered 'pure' hunter-gatherers. Most families in this category appear to be exploiting their traditional territories, following an annual cycle of subsistence which brings them into minimal contact with populations whose economies are based on domestic livestock and agricultural land use. In most areas of the southeastern Kalahari, the hunter-gatherers rely on gathered roots, melons, and bulbs for most of their water requirements throughout the year, and even at the height of the dry season avoid staying close to the wells and boreholes belonging to Bantu pastoralists. Thus, their settlements are usually far removed from those of Bantu-speaking peoples and more acculturated Basarwa groups. One major reason for this may be that the availability of veldfood and game declines as the intensity of grazing and population density go up.

Among those Basarwa who are primarily hunting and gathering but who have small, and generally seasonal, inputs from pastoralism and agriculture, small gardens and a small herd of goats may be owned. Both the goats and the gardens are individually owned, which has important implications for their care and usage. Goats limit mobility to some extent, and, in areas of no surface water, increase the amount of time spent in gathering water roots and melons. The goats are kept mainly for milk, which is available in small quantities for a month or so following the birth of a kid. Goats and chickens are often also bred for trade and sale to Bantu-speaking people living on boreholes and in agricultural areas in the Kalahari, or to shopkeepers in the nearest villages. The harvest from a garden might last anywhere from a few days to several weeks. Melons and beans are the most common crops. When melons are grown, they supplement the wild melons in providing a water supply, and this increases the time a group may remain sedentary. The growing of melons is, in effect, a process of cultivating one's water supply (Cashdan 1977). The most common way that people who are hunting and gathering may supplement this is by brief periods of agricultural work during the peak periods of harvest, or by casual work as herders on cattle posts. During years of drought, such employment opportunities are greatly reduced, as is the viability of their own small gardens, and the proportion of families reliant purely upon hunting and gathering throughout the year is increased.

There are a number of features associated with both 'purely' and 'primarily' hunting and gathering economies. House and storage structures are simple and residences are temporary, there is a minimal amount of bush clearance around camps, cooking is usually done by roasting food in hot sand and ashes, and the remains of veldfood and game are scattered throughout the camp. In addition, there is a lower incidence of fluency in a dominant Bantu language, fewer dual names, and a low incidence of intermarriage with Bantu-speaking groups.

For groups following a mixed strategy, in which the products of pastoralism and agriculture account for over half of the diet, there are two ways of gaining access to these products, as in the above. One way is by acquiring livestock and by acquiring seed and planting their own fields; the other is by herding someone else's animals in exchange for milk and occasionally meat, by helping others with their agricultural activities in exchange for some of the produce, and generally doing work for other people in exchange for food. Regulating the form that these relationships may take, there are certain arrangements or contracts formalized within Tswana tradition, such as *Majako*, a contract whereby work in other people's agricultural fields is done in exchange for a portion of the harvest, and *Mafisa*, an arrangement whereby cattle are loaned out and the recipient may use them for draught, drink their milk, and may be given a portion of the increase (Schapera 1970:115; 1955:246–50, 253–5; Curtis 1972:67–8, 76–8). In the past, however, and even to some extent today, the most common relationships were forms of clientage and serfdom.

On the whole, it seemed that the more dependent a family is on livestock and agricultural products, the less likely they are to actually own livestock or plant their own fields. It is a startling fact that among Basarwa of the remotest parts of the central Kalahari a greater proportion of familes own livestock than do Basarwa who live on cattleposts, yet the latter are far more dependent on pastoralism for subsistence. A few Basarwa who were heavily dependent on pastoralism and agriculture did own livestock and practise agriculture independently of the Bantu. Of this handful of cases, the majority were very acculturated and seemed to have gained ownership of livestock and access to land through kinship links resulting from intermarriage with Bantu-speaking peoples.

There are complex historical, social and economic reasons for this. Briefly summarized, there was, and still is to some extent, a system of relationships shading from patron–client to more feudal types of institutions which influence the access of different ethnic groups to various economic options. During the period between 1600 and 1900, the Tswana tribes, which were highly organized chiefdoms, dominated and incorporated, either by assimilation or by the evolution of feudal relationships, quite a large number of other ethnic groups, including the peoples of the Kalahari. The two major ethnic groups of subject peoples in the Kalahari were the Basarwa and a number of Bantu-speaking pastoral and agricultural peoples known collectively as the Bakgalagadi. The Bakgalagadi had already envolved economic relationships with the Basarwa in many parts of the Kalahari before the Tswana arrived. The Tswana superimposed their political authority over both, and generally increased economic links between the Kalahari and the surrounding areas. Under the Tswana, the Basarwa and the Bakgalagadi became essentially serfs (*Batlhanka* or *Malata*) (Schapera 1970:86–9). Serfs did not have rights to private property and were expected to pay yearly tribute to Tswana chiefs. This system of vassalage has been slow in dying out, particularly in the Kalahari, and especially with regard to Basarwa. In addition, there is evidence that there have been times when people *deliberately* opt for patron–client types of relationships, rather than invest in the full technology and infrastructure required for long-term independent pastoralism and agricultural modes of production. After all, investing in storage facilities and in the care of livestock takes time and labour away from other subsistence pursuits. In a year of good rainfall marginal agriculture and animal husbandry may be worthwhile. In a drought year however, it may be very costly to preserve breeding stock and seeds, as more and more effort must go into hunting and gathering. It seems likely that there is a critical number of animals and size of harvest which must be achieved before a family will be able to make a permanent transition to agriculture and pastoralism. The Bantu have the assistance of kinfolk and are able through wage-labour to raise the capital to finance their accumulation of livestock and the purchase of seed grain. By contrast, the hunter-gatherers rarely have kin rich in cattle and seeds and generally do not have as much access to wage-employment in towns. Thus, when trying to start a herd or to grow crops, Basarwa may very well face greater hardships than Bantu. Basarwa who try to keep animals and farm are further handicapped by the value system of hunting and gathering, which stresses generalized reciprocity. The clash of this value system with the requirement of storing grain and keeping a breeding nucleus alive through the year has been well described in Lee (1979:412–14). To become a successful pastoralist or farmer, a Basarwa must risk the rupture of sharing relationships with his relatives. It is not surprising therefore that most Basarwa in my sample were found to be *working for* pastoralists and agriculturalists rather than *becoming* pastoralists and agriculturalists. Thus, rather than undergoing a contemporary 'Neolithic Revolution' (see Lee 1975), the hunter-gatherers of the southeastern Kalahari are becoming increasingly dependent on the encroaching Bantu economy.

The study showed that dependence relationships begin as hunter-gatherers exploit the opportunity to cash in on the agricultural surplus of their Bantu-speaking neighbours. Later, with the introduction of well-digging, and then borehole-drilling technology into the Kalahari, what had been an option became a necessity in areas where there was a heavy influx and permanent settlement of pastoral-agricultural peoples.

Where grazing pressure by domestic livestock is high, game is scarce, and a relatively sedentary Bantu population competes with hunter-gatherers for veldfood, the viability of the hunting and gathering way of life has declined over time. Drought years can lead to an increase in dependency relationships in such environments.

However, even while increased dependency was developing in some areas, there were still parts of the same Basarwa community which maintained a hunting and gathering subsistence base. This does not, however, mean that the community was being broken down over time by uneven patterns of economic change. Individuals and even whole families were found to have shifted between strategies.

Virtually every family or group, no matter what their subsistence strategy, had at least one member who had been involved in another strategy in the past. In some cases entire families or larger groups had shifted from one adaptive strategy to another. These shifts occurred in both directions, although in the recent high rainfall period (from 1973 to 1979) shifts towards greater reliance on pastoral and agricultural modes of production were more common. These shifts were frequent between the less dissimilar strategies, while shifts between the extreme ends of the adaptive spectrum were relatively rare.

How do such shifts take place? This question was answered by another finding: that kinship ties cross-cut the whole spectrum. There are no families or groups without at least one member of the family branch currently involved in another strategy. These are often very close kin ties. A hunter-gatherer living in a remote part of the Kalahari might have a sister working in the household of prominent Bakgalagadi family living in some large village, or a son in the mines of South Africa. A family employed throughout the year at a cattlepost, and getting part of their livelihood from cow's milk and meat, might also have a group of relatives totally dependent on the economy of a Bantu village, and another group of relatives who depend on hunting and gathering for virtually all of their food. Members of both groups of relatives might visit occasionally. While they are at the cattlepost they gain access to the kinds of foods and other products available there through their host. If this visiting is extended and becomes a regular or seasonal event, particularly if the visitors begin to play roles in the cattle-post economy while they are there, then a shift in adaptation might be taking place. The hunter-gatherers might be shifting from strategies (1) to (2) or even to (3) depending on the frequency and length of visits. It is worth noting that a shift to (3) will very probably be accompanied by a shift in the location of their settlement closer to the well or borehole. Thus, while on previous visits the hunter-gatherer group would have set up camp several kilometres from the water point, they would now set up camp nearer to it, although not always next to the settlement of the permanent residents.

Thus, people often gain access to a different set of economic options through relatives. This is strengthened and augmented by marriage. There is a tendency among Basarwa in the southeastern Kalahari to marry a close relative; the incidence of marriage between first and second cousins is high. Given the wide divergence of strategies between closely related families, it is not surprising that many people change their mode of subsistence when they marry, as well as their residence. There is a tendency towards matrilocal post-marital residence, and this means that it is often a young husband who makes the shift in strategies.

Kinship and marriage-mediated shifts in strategies go on in both directions. The present-day patterns of adaptation indicate that shifts in modes of subsistence are undergone frequently and have been going on for generations. The present generation of Basarwa heavily involved in pastoral and agricultural economies may be the parents of the next generation of hunter-gatherers.

In the study of how a people oscillate between the world of the hunter-gatherer and that of the farmer and pastoralist, I think it is significant that we find evidence for flexibility in both directions. In an environment such as the Kalahari, with its enormous fluctuations in rainfall, investment in social mechanism for economic opportunism may have paid off much better in the long run than a uni-directional process of social and economic change. In this way, hunter-gatherer peoples have been emerging as distinct ethnic communities within Botswana, rather than undergoing wholesale economic and cultural integration.

The future of this 'Basarwa' ethnic minority now hangs in the balance. The advent of borehole drilling has led to an increase in the number of cattle and people in the Kalahari. The socially mediated opportunism of the Basarwa is becoming more and more limited as the viability of hunting and gathering declines and economic dependency on other ethnic groups increases. During the 1970s Botswana embarked on an ambitious programme of 'Remote Area Development' to aid peoples such as the Basarwa to develop their local communities on the basis of independently controlled agricultural and livestock operations, thus avoiding increased dependency and destitution. How successful these programmes will be may well be determined by the direction of development within Botswana as a whole.

Lying just north of South Africa and surrounded by politically delicate countries such as Namibia to the west, Angola and Zambia to the north, and Zimbabwe (formerly Rhodesia) to the east, Botswana faces problems of economic dependency which in many ways mirror the internal situation of her Kalahari hunter-gatherers.

Acknowledgements

This paper was prepared during field work among Kalahari peoples sponsored by the National Research Council of Canada and subsequently by the Social Science and Humanities Research Council of Canada.

Note

1 James Denbow, an archaeologist from Indiana University, is currently the National Monuments Officer in Botswana, and has been working on early Iron Age (estimated around 800 A.D.) material for many years in and near the Kalahari.

Bibliography

Cashdan, E. 1977. 'Subsistence, mobility and territories among the Gllanakwe of the northeastern Central Kalahari Game Reserve'. Mimeograph Report to the Ministry of Local Government and Lands. Gaborone, Botswana

Curtis, D. 1972. 'The social organization of ploughing'. *Botswana Notes and Records*, 4:67–80

Lee, R. B. 1968. 'What hunters do for a living, or, how to make out on scarce resources', in R. B. Lee and I. DeVore (eds.), *Man the hunter*. Chicago: Aldine
1972. 'The intensification of social life among the !Kung Bushmen', in B.

Spooner (ed.), *Population growth: anthropological implications*, 343–50. Cambridge, Mass.: MIT Press

1973. 'Mongongo: the ethnography of a major wild food resource'. *Ecology of Food and Nutrition*, 2:307–21

1975. 'The !Kungs or new culture'. *Science Year* 1976. Chicago: World Book Encyclopedia

1976. 'Introduction' in R. B. Lee and I. DeVore (eds.), *Kalahari hunter-gatherers*. Cambridge, Mass.: Harvard University Press

1979. *The !Kung San: men, women and work in a foraging society*. Cambridge: Cambridge University Press

Lee, R. B. and DeVore, I. (eds.) 1968. 'Problems in the study of hunter-gatherers', in R. B. Lee and I. DeVore (eds.), *Man the Hunter*. Chicago: Aldine

Marks, S. 1972. 'Khoisan resistance to the Dutch in the seventeenth and eighteenth centuries'. *Journal of African History* 13 (1):55–80

Murdock, G. P. 1968. 'The current status of the world's hunting and gathering peoples', in R. B. Lee and I. DeVore (eds.), *Man the hunter*, 13–20. Chicago: Aldine

Nurse and Jenkins 1977. *Health and the hunter-gatherer: biomedical studies on the hunting and gathering populations of Southern Africa*. Basel: S. Kargen

Schapera, I. 1952. *The ethnic composition of Tswana tribes*. London School of Economics and Political Science, Monographs on Social Anthropology, No. 11

1955. *A handbook of Tswana law and custom*. London: Oxford University Press

1970. *Tribal innovators: Tswana chiefs and social change 1795–1940*. London: Athlone Press

Traill, 1973. 'S4 or N6: a new Bushman language'. *African Studies* 32

11. Patterns of sedentism among the Basarwa of eastern Botswana

ROBERT K. HITCHCOCK

There are relatively few groups left in the world today which are still engaged in full-time mobile hunting and gathering. Most band societies have had their mobility restricted as a result of either internal pressures or external forces; many have suffered the effects of disease, habitat deterioration, and pacification efforts. Some national governments, under the guise of 'integration' policies, have brought about situations in which band societies have become completely dependent upon outside assistance for their very existence. In other cases, hunter-gatherer groups have been incorporated into local and national economies as specialized labourers who are often paid little or nothing for their work. There has been a world-wide trend towards settlement of nomadic peoples, not only hunter-gatherers but also pastoralists and swidden agriculturalists. This trend has been encouraged by business interests, national governments, and individuals, many of whom stand to gain in some way from the changes in the social and economic systems of nomadic societies.

Surprisingly, the process of sedentism, whereby the mobility of human groups is reduced to the point where they remain residentially stationary year-round, has received relatively little attention from students of hunter-gatherer societies. Most considerations of the consequences of settlement have been those of researchers and organizations working with pastoral nomads (see, for example, Amiran and Ben-Arieh 1963; Baxter 1975; Lewis 1975; Food and Agriculture Organization 1970, 1972; International Labour Organization 1965). The causes of sedentism,[1] on the other hand, have been dealt with not so much by ethnographers as by archaeologists, many of whom view the process of settling down as simply a byproduct of increased reliance upon food production. It is only recently that sedentism has come to be viewed as a problem in need of explanation in and of itself.

The purpose of this paper is to address the question how and why hunter-gatherer groups reduce their mobility and begin to settle in single locations. In order to illustrate some of the factors involved in the shift to a sedentary way of life I will draw upon data collected over a three and a half year period among mobile and sedentary Basarwa[2] in two areas of eastern Botswana. The paper is divided into two parts: the first is a general discussion of the causes and consequences of sedentism, while the second is an evaluation of some of the general conclusions in light of specific case material. By approaching the subject of sedentism through case-studies I hope to shed light on some of the conditions under which hunter-gatherer groups become sedentary and to elucidate some of the broader implications of the process of settling down.

Sedentism and its beginnings

The term 'sedentism' means many things to many people. To some researchers sendentism is synonymous with what V. Gordon Childe (1942, 1951) called the 'Neolithic Revolution', which supposedly heralded the rise of the 'settled arts' (Coe and Flannery 1964:650) or the 'hallmarks of sedentary life' (Flannery 1972a:23) such as permanent villages, loom weaving, and ceramics. Others, not content simply to define 'the sedentary way of life', have attempted to delve into some of the causes of sedentism. There has been a general tendency, however, to focus on the origins of agriculture rather than on sedentism itself (Harris 1977:402). The reason for the emphasis on food production was that many believed that fully settled villages could not have come about without the 'secure' resource base provided by domesticated foods. MacNeish (1964:531), for example, states: 'It is generally accepted that the development of agriculture is basic to the rise of village and urban life' (see also Braidwood and Braidwood 1953:278).

Childe, one of the most influential researchers to deal with the beginnings of food production, cautioned us not to make too much of the supposed connection between agriculture and sedentism: 'The adoption of cultivation must not be confused with the adoption of a sedentary life. It has been customary to contrast the settled life of the cultivator with the nomadic existence of the "homeless hunter". The contrast is quite fictitious' (Childe 1951:63). He goes on to note that the Neolithic Revolution was actually the culmination of a lengthy process (Childe 1951:87). Nevertheless, discussions of the beginnings of settled life

Nata River Mosarwa man carrying salt to trade with Kalanga neighbours for grain, pots, ammunition and marihuana (R. Hitchcock)

tended to be dominated by those who believed agriculture and sedentism to be intricately linked. Some of the early arguments about the origins of food production, such as those of de Candolle, Roth, and Peake and Fleure, held that a fixed settlement, or at least a certain degree of security of settlement, was a necessary precondition for the beginnings of agriculture (Wright 1969:450–51, 455). More recent discussions, however, have tended to focus on agriculture as the primary force which 'permitted' people to settle down. Kenyon makes this point very clearly when she states: 'The first steps in the long road which led man from life as a wandering hunter, as a savage, to life as a member of a civilized community, were taken when the beginnings of agriculture and the domestication of animals enabled him to establish himself in one spot, assured of an adequate food supply' (Kenyon 1959a:35). MacNeish (1972:90) sees the change from 'seasonal micro-macrobands' to 'central-based bands' as being due to (1) the development of greater specialization in collecting techniques, (2) the solving of scheduling problems, and (3) increases in agricultural productivity. Much of the work of Braidwood (1952, 1958, 1960a and b; Braidwood and Braidwood 1953; Braidwood and Reed 1957; Braidwood *et al.* 1971, 1974) was based on the assumption that 'villages' could not have existed without an agricultural subsistence base.

Historically there has been a belief on the part of a number of researchers that sedentism was the preferred way of life for human populations. Braidwood, for example, argues that, once man became sufficiently familiar with his environment, he was able to settle down and produce food. As he puts it, 'In my opinion there is no need to complicate the story with extraneous "causes". The food-producing revolution seems to have occurred as the culmination of the ever increasing cultural differentiation and specialization of human communities' (Braidwood 1960b:134). MacNeish (1972:88) makes a similar point, remarking that over time people were able to accumulate more and more knowledge of the food potential of their environment. Increased familiarity with local habitats supposedly allowed people to 'settle into' their environments 'with relatively greater intensity' (Braidwood and Reed 1957:20). Binford (1968a:322) has attacked these kinds of arguments as being 'vitalist' in nature, stating that they are orthogenetic in character and are dependent upon 'emergent human properties'. Simply citing human tendencies is insufficient as an explanation for why changes occurred. Food production and sedentism did not come about because people wanted them to; rather, they occurred in response to various pressures on human systems which necessitated organizational shifts.

Two other arguments concerning the beginnings of sedentism involve implicit assumptions about how and why cultural changes occur. The first argument is well illustrated in a remark made by Beardsley *et al.* (1956:134): 'We have taken it for granted that in general sedentary life has more survival value than wandering life to the human race, and that, other things being equal, whenever there is an opportunity to make the transition, it will be made.' This kind of statement implies that humans necessarily recognize which strategies are best to pursue and will always initiate changes to enhance their survival. From an evolutionary standpoint it is clear that natural selection operates on choices made by human groups, and the fact that population extinctions have occurred indicates that those decisions were not always the right ones. A second argument holds that cultural changes simply occur. Bender, for instance, says: 'Cultural systems do not die, they change. Why? How? Because the cultural system has self-transforming properties' (Bender 1978:207). To carry this position too far, however, would lead to a kind of intellectual complacency, lulling us into thinking that organizational changes are not in need of explanation.

There is clearly some confusion in the literature over just what sedentism is and how it might have come about. On the one hand it is viewed as a combination of features, including agriculture, permanent architecture, ceramics, and food-processing facilities, while on the other it is seen as a process. Amsden makes an important observation when he notes: 'While sedentism is sometimes perceived as a simple dichotomous variable – a population is either sedentary or nomadic – this is an inaccurate view . . . in fact, sedentism . . . was a gradual process involving many variables.' (Amsden 1977:337). He goes on to say that 'It is misleading to view the origins of sedentism as a single event; it is more productive to consider it as one extreme of a continuum, and underlying processes should be isolated and explained' (Amsden 1977:338).

Arguments about the origins of settled life can be classified according to the postulated causal determinants cited as the reason for human groups becoming residentially stationary. These arguments can be broken down into the following categories: (1) climatic change arguments, (2) resource abundance and/or diversity arguments, (3) demographic arguments, and (4) social causality arguments. In the following discussion I will deal briefly with each of these types of arguments.

Perhaps the best example of an argument for sedentism and food production involving climatic change is Childe's (1942, 1951) 'oasis' or 'propinquity' theory. In essence, Childe holds that dessication at the end of the Pleistocene epoch forced people, plants, and animals into smaller and smaller areas, or oases, where permanent water was available. This 'enforced juxtaposition' led to a kind of symbiosis, Childe argues, the result of which was the beginnings of domestication. The expansion in the food supply brought about by food production would, in turn, have encouraged people to settle down. Later research in the Middle East by Braidwood and his colleagues led them to conclude that there was little evidence of major climatic change having occurred, and it was also noted that climatic changes had occurred previously without causing cultural change leading to domestication (see, for example, Braidwood 1952).

Coe and Flannery (1964, 1967; Flannery and Coe 1968), after noting that macro-environmental changes may be insufficient as an explanation for cultural change, instead focus attention on what they call 'microenvironments'. As they note, 'It has seemed to us that only a drastic reduction of the number of niches to be exploited, and a concentration of these in space, would have permitted the establishment of full-time village life' (Coe and Flannery 1964:651). Using data drawn from research in the Tehuacan Valley of Mexico and the Pacific coast of Guatemala, they note that whereas groups were nomadic in Tehuacan long after the inception of agriculture, populations living along the coast were able to become sedentary. A combination of effective food production and exploitation of wild food resources from the lagoon-estuary system on the coast facilitated year-round occupation of villages (Coe and Flannery 1964:653). Agriculture, in itself, was insufficient to support a sedentary population, but when abundant gathered resources could be used to supplement the diet, people were no longer required to exploit a variety of ecological zones, a process which Coe and Flannery term 'microenvironment reduction'.

Several elements of Coe's and Flannery's arguments are echoed in the writings of other researchers who have dealt with mobility reduction. Sauer, for example, argues that marine resources were crucial to settlement; as he puts it: 'It may be proposed that, wherever man came from, the discovery of the tidal area was a major event . . . Primitive man could hardly find a better prospect than in beachcombing, which was also conducive to social grouping and to reduced mobility' (Sauer 1961:263–4). The correlation between marine resources and sedentism has been noted by a number of researchers in both the Old and New Worlds (Binford 1968a:332–6; Binford and Chasko 1976:139; Flannery 1973:283; Osborn 1977:179; Cohen 1977a; 1977b:160, 164; Bray 1976:83). Schalk (1977:207) points out that groups along the Northwest Coast of North America are often seen as exceptional among hunter-gatherers in that they have a relatively high degree of residential stability. Like the Ainu of Japan (Watanabe 1968, 1977) and populations along the east coast of North America (Binford 1964), the Northwest Coast groups derived part of their subsistence from anadromous, or spawning, fish. Sedentism and utilization of aquatic resources are correlated because, according to Sauer (1961:263–4), fish and shellfish are both more abundant and more predictable than terrestrial resources.

Discussions of resource abundance being a 'cause' of sedentism are by no means limited to aquatic resources. Both Birdsell (1968:239) and Bray (1976:83) point out that there are numerous situations in which food resources are concentrated. Examples cited include California, where acorns were available (Bray 1976:83), and the Near East, where there were dense stands of wild cereal grasses (Flannery 1973:278, 280). Bender (1975:4, 7, 30) suggests that sedentism may have come about in 'optimal environments' where there was a concentration of resources (see also Harris 1977:410). Osborn (1977:169–71) suggests that sedentary communities could have occurred in areas where there was ready access to several different ecological zones. A similar point is made by Watanabe (1977:27), who says that the occurrence of a number of ecological zones in close proximity could in itself encourage residential stability.

Two basic arguments are implicit in the discussions of aquatic resources and ecological zones supporting large amounts of terrestrial resources. The first argument is that resource abundance by itself can facilitate sedentism, while the second is that by locating one's residential base in a place with easy access to a variety of ecological zones, it is possible to become sedentary. In some cases researchers have elements of both the abundance and diversity arguments in their discussions of sedentism (e.g. Bender 1975:4, 30; Harris 1977:410). Binford (forthcoming) has pointed out that these kinds of simplistic environmental determinism arguments are based on what he terms the 'Garden of Eden' principle. One can legitimately ask the question: if abundance and/or diversity are sufficient causes of sedentism, why, then, do we have no evidence of sedentary habitation sites for the entire time-range of hominid populations' existence on earth? While populations utilizing 'unearned' resources such as anadromous fish or abundant resources like wild wheat and barley are frequently stationary for at least part of the year, it must be stressed that simple availability of resources in large quantities is insufficient in and of itself to facilitate sedentism. Binford and Chasko (1976:139) and Schalk (1977:231) argue that exploitation of highly nucleated resources must be coupled with a storage potential in order for groups to remain residentially stable.

An extension of the 'Garden of Eden' argument is the one which holds that agriculture is responsible for sedentism. By planting crops people were, in effect, creating their own Gardens of Eden. After remarking on the 'optimal' conditions under which people supposedly became sedentary, Bender (1975:7) states that 'food production mimicked these conditions and extended the potential for permanent settlement'. In this sense, human populations can be seen as becoming sedentary either through falling into a Garden of Eden or creating one where it had not existed previously. In a comparative study of settlements in the Near East and Mesoamerica, Flannery (1972a:23) notes that fully sedentary communities existed in the former region without evidence of domestic plants or animals, while groups in the latter region were nomadic for thousands of years in spite of the presence of domesticated foods. He points out in other publications (Flannery 1972b:402, 1973) that sedentism occurred prior to agriculture on the coast of Peru. In short, agriculture and sedentism do not appear to covary directly with one another in all cases.

Another class of arguments concerning the origins of sedentism incorporates demographic factors. Binford (1968a:328) points out that there are two main sets of conditions under which one might anticipate major organizational changes in subsistence and settlement systems: (1) a change in the physical environment such that there is a reduction in the amounts of food available; and (2) a change in the demographic structure of a region which results in the impingement of one group on the territory of another. Childe's dessication argument is an example of physical environmental change leading to cultural change, while Binford (1968a) and Flannery (1969) provide examples of population density changes leading to cultural change. The correlation between sedentism, population size, and population density has been noted by Binford (1968a:330–6) and Binford and Chasko (1976:137). Harris (1977:410) suggests that territorial confinement as a result either of environmental factors or of intergroup hostility is a possible factor in the beginnings of sedentism. Cohen (1977a:83) argues that territorial impingement and resource depletion are factors related to sedentism. Finally, Flannery (1969:75, 78; 1972a:26; 1973:276, 283) points out that the population was higher in the Near East than ever before at the time food production and settled life occurred.

The final argument for the beginnings of sedentism is what I have termed the 'social causality' argument. Flannery sets out the rationale for this argument in the following statement: 'It may be that the "demographic change" which made cultivation seem like a good idea in Southwest Asia was an increase in sedentary communities – and the latter may have begun in response to changes in sociopolitical organization which had had nothing to do with either climate or population density' (Flannery 1973:234). Bender, following Flannery's lead, suggests that too much attention has been paid to technology and demography and too little to social relations (Bender 1978:204). In making a number of important points concerning sedentism, Bender (1978:208) concludes that in her opinion: 'A techno-environmental explanation of sedentism is unacceptable.' She goes on to offer an alternative suggestion, one which holds that the establishment and maintenance of social alliances is crucial to an understanding of systemic change.

Alliances, as Bender (1978:210) points out, serve to maintain social relations, and they also function in such a way as to serve both economic and political ends. These alliances, in turn, make demands on production. In order for people to keep up their reciprocal obligations they must produce foods and goods over and above their own needs. There is thus a direct link between evolving social institutions and increasing pressure on production (Bender 1978:213). A more indirect link is that between social institutions and sedentism. 'Surplus' production often involves delays in return, and these promote sedentism since they favour residential stability and investment in permanent facilities. Group cohesion is also favoured, something which in turn requires leadership to mediate in social conflicts. Group leaders often have a monopoly of social knowledge, including knowledge of alliance rules, and by using this information they are able to reinforce their own positions. Thus, as Bender (1978:213) concludes: 'The leader both promotes and permits sedentism.'

An examination of the conditions under which sedentism has occurred world-wide, both in the past and at the present time, reveals that there are two main contexts in which mobility reduction comes about: the first I will call primary or *in situ* sedentism and the second is secondary or contact sedentism. Primary sedentism, occurring in certain parts of the world 10,000 or more years ago, came about when groups took advantage of highly nucleated and abundant resources. Simple availability of these resources, however, was insufficient to bring about residential stability for an extended period of time without techniques which could enable the extension of use-life of those resources. Settling in areas where there were abundant resources, such as along coasts and rivers or in passes where migratory herds move, can be viewed as a kind of opportunistic sedentism. Long-term residential stability comes about when a group's mobility options are restricted due to the fact that there are too many other groups occupying the habitat. Regional saturation resulting in range restriction can occur as a result of long-term slow rates of population growth or as a result of in-migration. As the number of groups in a region increases, there would be an increased trend toward localized settlement and perhaps territorial demarcation.

Contact sedentism occurs when a region is entered by a population which is technologically and organizationally more complex than those already inhabiting the area in such a way as to alter local living patterns. Lee (1972a:141) has referred to what L. R. Hiatt has called 'the magnets' of attractiveness such as trading posts, mission stations and ranches; these places often attract local groups who come to settle on their peripheries in order to gain access to food, trade goods, or perhaps employment opportunities. Outside groups often introduce technological innovations which affect the mobility or resource procurement capability of local populations; examples include the snowmobile in the north and rifles and shotguns in many areas. A sub-type of contact sedentism is forced settlement, whereby an outside agency attempts to reduce the mobility of local populations by confining them to what in effect are reservations or resettling them in new locations. Settlement efforts can take two forms: on the one hand they can be active interventionist policies designed forcibly to reduce mobility through pacification or even eradication measures, while on the other they can be development schemes set up to introduce new social and economic arrangements. Table 11.1 contains a listing of some populations which

Table 11.1 *Some ethnographic examples of societies undergoing the process of sedentism*

Country and region	Group name(s)	Researcher(s)
Zaire; Central African Republic (Ituri Forest)	Pygmies	S. Bahuchet, L. Cavalli-Sforza, H. Guillaume, R. Harako, J. Hart, T. Tanno, C. Turnbull
Tanzania	Hadza	J. Woodburn
	Sandawe	J. Newman
Zambia, southwestern part	Kwandu	B. Reynolds
Namibia (South West Africa) northern Kaokoveld	OvaTjimba	B. Grobelaar, H. MacCalman
Botswana, Namibia (northwest Kalahari)	!Kung San (Bushmen) (Zu/twasi)	M. Biesele, I. DeVore, P. Draper, H. Harpending, N. Howell, M. Konner, R. Lee, L. Marshall, P. Wiessner, E. Wilmsen, J. Yellen

Table 11.1 *(continued)*

Country and region	Group name(s)	Researcher(s)
Botswana, western Kalahari	Naron and other Ghanzi groups	A. Barnard, G. Childers, M. Guenther, M. Russell, G. Silberbauer, H. Steyn, L. Wily
Botswana, central Kalahari	G/wi, G/ /ana	E. Cashdan, P. Sheller, G. Silberbauer, J. Tanaka
Botswana, eastern Kalahari	Kūa	J. Ebert, R. Hitchcock
Botswana, southeast Kalahari	Kūa, Eastern ≠Hūa	J. Copperman, H. Vierich
Botswana, southwest Kalahari	!Xō	H. Heinz, A. Thoma, A. Traill
Botswana, northeast Kalahari	/Taise, Ganade, etc.	E. Cashdan, W. Chasko, J. Ebert, M. Ebert, R. Hitchcock
Borneo, Sarawak, Belaga District	Punan	J. Langub, J. Nicolaisen
North Thailand	Mrabri (Khon Pa)	J. J. Boeles, J. Hartland-Swann, K. Nimmanahaeminda, C. Velder
Indonesian New Guinea, Irian Jaya	Asmat	P. Van Arsdale
Philippines, northeastern Luzon	Agta	J. Peterson
Philippines, Luzon	Ebuked Agta	A. Estioko-Griffin, B. Griffin
Philippines, Palawan Island	Batak	J. Eder
Australia, Western Desert	Pitjandjara	R. Gould, A. Hamilton, N. Tindale, D. Vachon
Australia, Darling Basin	Bagundji	H. Allen
Australia, Yalata Reserve, Southern Australia	Yalata	I. White
Australia, Western Desert	Docker River groups	S. Woenne
Australia, Cape York Peninsula	Edward River groups	J. Taylor
Australia, Western Desert	Western Desert groups	N. Peterson
Australia, Western Desert	Alywara	L. Binford, W. Denham, J. O'Connell
Japan, Hokkaido	Ainu	H. Watanabe
Israel	Beduin	D. Amiran, Y. Ben-Arieh
India, Southern Bihar	Birhor	B. Williams
India, Andra Pradesh	Chenchu	C. Fürer-Haimendorf
Sri Lanka	Vedda	B. Seligman, C. Seligman
United States, Alaska, Brooks Range	Nunamiut	C. Amsden, L. Binford, J. Campbell

234 Robert K. Hitchcock

have undergone the process of sedentism in the recent past or are settling down at the present time. It must be stressed that contact in some
of these situations has taken a variety of forms. Among the Sandawe of
Tanzania, for example, the Germans introduced hunting laws designed
to force them to settle down (Newman 1970:59), while in Japan agricultural projects were started among the Ainu to encourage a shift away
from hunting and gathering (Watanabe 1968:72). One needs only to look
at the history of the United States or Brazil for examples of eradication
measures undertaken against indigenous populations.

The distinction I have drawn between primary and secondary sedentism is not always clear-cut. It is possible for a group to become sedentary in a region where no outside forces are at work but where the
indirect effects of contact are nevertheless responsible for sedentism.
An example would be a situation where the introduction of guns or
steel traps results in over-exploitation of local faunal populations, forcing people to alter their settlement and subsistence systems. A similar
contrast to the one made here is that of Lewis (1975:437) who distin-
guishes between 'natural' or spontaneous processes of settlement and
contrived or directed processes. The same kind of distinction is implicit
in Harris' discussion of sedentism, as seen in the following remark: 'I
do not minimize the significance of contact with more advanced groups
as an agent of change among hunter-gatherers, but this is a secondary
process which is not directly relevant to the central question of evolutionary change under "pristine" conditions' (Harris 1977:408). Both
Harris (1977:410) and Bender (1978:208) stress that modern ethnographic cases of sedentism should be approached with caution since
the conditions under which people are settling down today are associated with factors which did not exist previously. Harris (1977:410), for
example, points out that sedentism may have taken place more gradually in the past than today when it is encouraged or enforced by governments. Bender (1978:208) notes that contemporary populations are settling down in situations where they have access to new kinds of foods
and better medical attention. I would argue that if it is our job as
anthropologists to explain cultural variability, then our propositions
should be applicable to both the past *and* the present. Whether sedentism came about as a result of *in situ* or outside changes, the point is
that the consequences of the process are the same. Mobility reduction
in any context will result in pressures on human groups which they
must cope with.

Single factor explanations of the beginnings of sedentism such as drastic environmental change or 'environmental familiarity' are insufficient to explain how and why people began to settle down. Mobility reduction occurs in a variety of contexts. 'Sedentism', as Redman (1977:526) points out, 'can be thought of as a threshold that was difficult to attain.' It is a complex process involving a wide range of variables, all of which must be examined if we are to understand organizational changes in human adaptations.

Sedentism among Kalahari hunter-gatherers

The Basarwa of Botswana and adjacent countries in southern Africa are often taken to be representative of some of the last hunter-gatherers on earth.[3] Because of its supposedly harsh nature and inaccessibility, the Kalahari Desert is described as a 'hunting and gathering stronghold' where groups continued to maintain an independent foraging existence. In fact the contemporary Basarwa exhibit a wide variety of adaptations from hunter-gatherers, to clients of Bantu-speaking pastoralists, to wage workers, to independent farmer-herders to sedentary fishing people (Lee 1965; Harpending 1976:153). Furthermore, recent archaeological research is revealing a considerable time-depth of contact between some San groups and their farming and herding neighbours. These contacts, both recent and prehistoric, have resulted in some marked shifts in settlement and subsistence patterns among many Basarwa, perhaps the most significant of which are in the degree of residential stability and increased dependence upon domestic food sources and trade goods. These changes have been accompanied by social and political shifts which are reminiscent of changes among many hunting-gathering groups as they become increasingly sedentary.

More and more anthropologists working among Basarwa populations in Botswana are tending to focus on adaptive changes as the groups settle down. The Basarwa provide us with an almost ideal situation in which to assess the causes and consequences of mobility reduction. Attempts have been made to categorize Basarwa groups according to their degree of dependence upon other populations (e.g. Vierich 1977a:12), or according to criteria involving settlement and subsistence practices (e.g. Silberbauer 1965; Tobias 1959a, b, 1962, 1964). We must be careful, however, in seeing these categories as static; a better way to envision them is as points along a continuum from fully mobile hunter-gatherers to fully settled food-producers or dependants. A group which today is settled on a borehold, drinking milk and eating maize meal, may tomorrow be back in the bush hunting and gathering. Basarwa groups, like other hunter-gatherers, should be seen as opportunists, taking advantage of new resources when and if they decide it would be worthwhile.

Relatively little attention has been paid to the causes of sedentism among Basarwa, emphasis being placed instead on the consequences of settling down. Tobias (1957, 1962, 1964, 1970, 1975a,b,c) has provided a number of observations about changes in Basarwa lifeways. At one point Tobias (1964:67) states that 'large sections of the surviving Bushmen are absorbing elements of Neolithic culture, by the adoption of some set-tled, pastoral habits from European, coloured, and African pastoralists'. Another observation made by Tobias is as follows: 'As a result of seven consecutive years of drought, the movement of "wild" Bushmen into the water-holes has been greatly accelerated. Because the farms are on their permanent watering places, the Bushmen are acquiring new ideas, new habits of life, along with victuals and water' (Tobias 1962:808). A third point made by Tobias (1962:808; 1964:70) is that Basarwa settle on farms because there is a 'more assured supply of food'. Boreholes, according to Tobias (1970; 1975b:290), are a sign of environmental improvement or 'betterment' because they provide not only water but also food in the form of milk and domestic-animal meat, not to mention employment opportunities. Tobias (1964:82) notes that one conse-quence of the presence of boreholes is the drying up of natural springs. Thus, in Tobias' view, a combination of ecological, economic, social, and technological forces are associated with increased sedentism among Basarwa.

Lee (1972a,b,c,d, 1976, 1979) has discussed the shift toward a more sedentary way of life among !Kung, and he attributes the changes in residential stability to contact with outside groups. As he notes, 'The actual changes in land use can be accounted for by a combination of economic and political factors, although common to all situations is the introduction of an economic "magnet" and along with it an outside jural authority' (Lee 1972a:142). Cattle-posts serve to attract people because of the presence of water, food, and a 'more intense social life' (Lee 1972c). The problem with greater concentrations of people is that more work is required to support them and conflicts are more frequent. Outsiders, according to Lee (1972d:183), often mediate in disputes, thus becoming 'a crucial element in stretching the duration of the Bushmen public life beyond the few weeks or months of former years'. Thus, the two essential factors in facilitating sedentism among !Kung, according to Lee (1972c:348–9), are (1) supplementary food sources, including milk, domestic meat, and grains, and (2) the presence of outsiders who serve to adjudicate disputes.

The arguments about the beginnings of sedentism among Basarwa can be grouped into three categories, which correspond to some of the arguments in the general anthropological literature on sedentism discussed earlier. The first argument is the 'abundance' idea, which holds that ample food supplies in and of themselves encourage sedentism. Tobias' statements about the 'assured food supplies' to be found on boreholes and farms fall into this category, as does Harpending and Davis' (1977) notion of spatial clumping of resources. The second argument falls under the category of the 'oasis' idea of V. Gordon Childe, with Basarwa being forced by drought to aggregate at water sources. The third argument is that contact in and of itself leads to sedentism, since not only are new food resources available, but so, too, are conflict resolution mechanisms. There is no question that each of these ideas has merit, but by themselves they fail to account for the various conditions under which Basarwa groups have become sedentary.

Sedentism: Eastern Kalahari and Nata River cases

Ethnographic research in the eastern and northeastern Kalahari Desert areas of Botswana provides us with good examples of some of the conditions under which Basarwa have become sedentary. In this region there is evidence for all three kinds of sedentism: contact, forced, and primary. After a general discussion of the Basarwa of eastern Botswana, I will briefly consider some of the causes and consequences of reduced mobility.

The eastern and northeastern Kalahari (Figure 11.1) is an area of Botswana where large numbers of Basarwa exist. Relatively little ethnographic research has been done among these groups, in part because anthropologists have assumed the area to be devoid of people who were independent of other groups. Schapera, for example, makes the following remark about eastern Kalahari groups:

> All these tribes have evidently been long exposed to Bantu influence, and are strongly mixed with Bantu blood. Some of them still lead their traditional mode of life, but they are all to some extent subject to their Bantu neighbors, often acting as their huntsmen and cattle herds, as well as being required to pay them a regular tribute.
> (Schapera 1930:36).

11.1 The study area

A similar point is made by Tobias (1957:33), who notes that while most Basarwa are still hunter-gatherers, 'exceptions are the 9,587 Bushmen living in the Ngwato Reserve, most of whom are cattle herders . . .'. Surveys carried out in the 1930s revealed many of the Basarwa of the Ngwato District[4] to be either serfs living on cattle-posts of other groups or, in some cases, independent pastoralists and agriculturalists (Tagart 1933; Joyce 1938). Given the anthropological emphasis in the 1950s and 1960s on documenting the lifestyles of hunter-gatherers, it is not surprising that little attention was paid to the people of the eastern Kalahari.

The eastern and northeastern Kalahari Desert is an excellent area in which to carry out a regional study of processes of environmental, economic, and social change. A substantial amount of ethnohistoric and early ethnographic information exists, beginning with the writings of Livingstone (1857), Chapman (1971), MacKenzie (1871), Mohr (1876), and Holub (1881). There are twentieth-century accounts by travellers such as Hodson (1912), Schönland (1904), Vialls (1908), Schwarz (1926a and b, 1928), and Clifford (1929, 1930). Early ethnographic research was carried out by Dornan (1911, 1917, 1925), and some photographs of eastern Kalahari Basarwa were taken by Duggan-Cronin (1942).

Beginning in 1975, the University of New Mexico Kalahari Project carried out surveys of both mobile and settled Basarwa in two areas of eastern Botswana: (1) the east-central Kalahari, sometimes called the Western Sandveld region, and (2) the Nata River region (Figure 11.2). Although both regions fall within the bounds of the Kalahari Desert, they contrast with one another in some important respects and can therefore be used as testing grounds for seeking answers to questions about processes involved in sedentism.

The climate of the eastern and northeastern Kalahari is semi-arid with dry, cool winters and hot, rainy summers. As is the case with other semi-arid areas, rainfall is highly variable in both place and time. The eastern Kalahari is characterized by tree and shrub savanna dominated by acacia species. Perhaps the most important ecological feature of the region is that it totally lacks surface water except after rains. Vegetation, therefore, is well adapted to arid conditions, including plants with large roots (e.g. *morama*, *Tylosema esculenta*) or those with seed-containing fruits (e.g. melons such as *Citrullus naudinianus*). In the absence of permanent water, human and animal populations are often forced to resort to utilizing moisture-bearing plant species in the eastern Kalahari.

The Nata River region, by contrast, is characterized by a strip of riverine gallery forest along the banks of a sandy-bedded river which flows off the Zimbabwean Plateau. Unlike the eastern Kalahari, water can be obtained even in the dry season by digging pits in the sandy bed, and the river itself flows during the rainy season, which lasts roughly from October to April. Ecological diversity in the riverine area is relatively high. While vegetation and faunal species composition in the two areas are comparable, the Nata region tends to have better soils, more water, and more topographic diversity than the east-central Kalahari.

The Basarwa populations inhabiting eastern and northeastern Botswana can be divided into two major groups on the basis of sero-genetic data: (1) Khoisan groups, and (2) Negro hunter-gatherer groups (Nurse and Jenkins 1977). Both of these groups speak Khoisan languages which contain click consonants, specifically Central Bush or Tshu-Khwe lan-

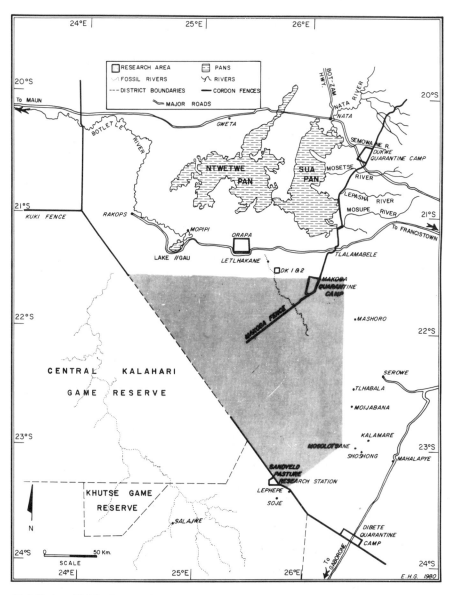

11.2 Eastern Kalahari research area

guages (Westphal 1962, 1963, 1971). Groups living in the Nata and surrounding areas, including the Makgadikgadi Pans and Botletle River,
are biologically Negro and thus differ from the San groups found in the
eastern Kalahari and areas to the west. Sometimes called 'River Bush-

men' or 'Black Bushmen', these groups contain many individuals who are relatively tall and dark-skinned. While some investigators believe these physical characteristics to be indicative of admixture with Bantu-speaking populations (e.g. Schapera 1930:36; Bleek in Duggan-Cronin 1942:13–14), sero-genetic investigations have shown that there is only a small amount of gene exchange between Negro and Khoisan hunter-gatherers (Nurse and Jenkins 1977; Chasko *et al.* forthcoming). Thus the Nata River groups are linguistically Khoisan, but biologically Negro. Culturally and economically the Nata peoples differ in several key respects from the desert Basarwa patterns. The eastern Kalahari groups, are by and large, linguistally, biologically and culturally San.

There are a bewildering number of different named groups occupying the eastern Kalahari. The Nata River groups refer to themselves as Cwa or Shuakhwe, and they note that two distinct languages are spoken there: (1) Goredum, and (2) Chira. The eastern Kalahari populations tend to refer to themselves as Kūa. Unlike the eastern groups, the Nata River populations have totemic clans, each of which has a name (e.g. the /Taise, who have a genet as their totem, or the Ganade, who have *tshuma*, or goat testicles, as a totem). Judging from the diversity of languages and groups in the northeastern Kalahari, it is possible that the Nata River represents an important linguistic and cultural ecotone, with numerous groups coming together there.

The Kūa of the east-central Kalahari are similar in many ways to the G/wi and G//ana of the Central Kalahari which have been described by Silberbauer (1965, 1972, 1973) and Tanaka (1969, 1971, 1976). They are full- and part-time hunter-gatherers living in groups of up to 42 people, most of whom continue to move about the landscape in search of food plants and game. Unlike the !Kung described by Lee (1965, 1968, 1979), Kūa groups aggregate in the wet season and disperse in the dry season. Kūa are egalitarian, with decision-making done on the basis of consensus. The /Taise, //Gwaochu, Ganade, and other Nata populations no longer live in traditional band groups but instead occupy nuclear-and extended-family compounds in a series of villages stretched along the river (Figure 11.3). Today many Nata River Basarwa work for absentee cattle owners as *badisa*, herders, in exchange for in-kind payment such as milk and grains. Some of the Nata River Basarwa households are engaged in food production, cultivating small fields with digging sticks or single-furrow ploughs. A number of households have a few cattle, while others keep smallstock, mainly goats. Fishing is done with the aid of woven fish traps and spears, and long-distance trading trips are

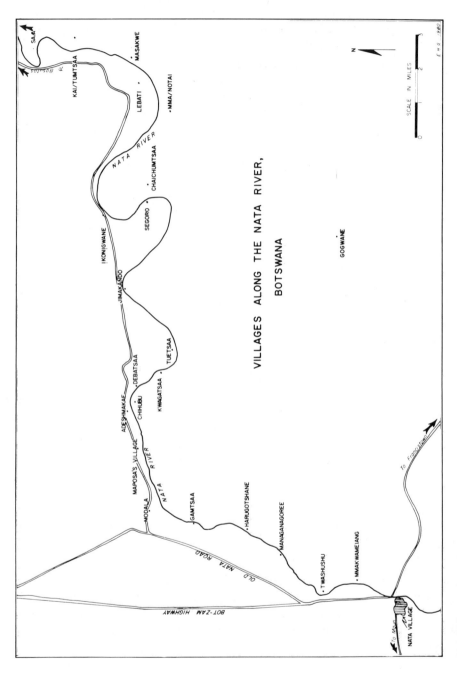

VILLAGES ALONG THE NATA RIVER, BOTSWANA

11.3 Villages along the Nata river

made, with salt and palm leaves taken to the Bokalaka region to the east and exchanged for grains, tobacco, pots, and other items. Economic and social differences are somewhat more pronounced among Nata River groups than among Kūa, with traditional doctors (*cho k'aos*) being accorded a great deal of respect, and territory owners (*//kaihas*) appearing to have more say about who can and cannot use their areas.

It is apparent from archaeological and ethnohistoric information that contact with other groups has been a regular feature of life for the Basarwa for a substantial period of time, well over a thousand years. Oral history data collected among Kalanga and Bamangwato indicate that Basarwa were often used as guides and hunters and that some Basarwa were brought to villages to help in agricultural and pastoral activities as well as household labour. By the mid-nineteenth century the Bamangwato were using Basarwa in the eastern Kalahari to watch their domestic stock (see, for example, Chapman 1971, i:52). The Bamangwato also resided in the Nata River region in the early part of the nineteenth century (Parsons 1972:140), and cattle posts were kept on the Nata even after the capital of the Bamangwato was established at Shoshong in 1850.

While a number of outside groups moved into the eastern Kalahari over the past several hundred years, it is important to stress that many different ethnic groups already resided there. Table 11.2 gives a breakdown of ethnic composition data for the Bamangwato tribal territory as a whole, the Western Sandveld region (the east-central Kalahari), and the Nata River region. The ethnic diversity of the Ngwato District is striking. There is no question that the influx of people into the Kalahari, made possible in part by the digging of wells, combined with Livingstone's 'discovery' of Lake Ngami in August 1849, resulted in major changes in the region. A combination of over-hunting and habitat deterioration, processes which picked up pace in the latter part of the nineteenth century, led to a decline in hunting and gathering and an increase in residential stability.

By the 1850s and 1860s when such travellers as Livingstone (1857) and Chapman (1971) passed through the eastern Kalahari, there were already wells at such places as Nkawane and Mmalatswai. In the past, cattle, which are water-dependent, were taken into the Kalahari only seasonally, being kept at pans during the rainy season. The expansion in the number of wells enabled livestock to be kept year-round in the Kalahari. The increased demand for meat in the 1890s reinforced a trend toward more pastoral production. Although major setbacks occurred in

Table 11.2. *Ethnic composition data for the Ngwato (Central) District,*[a] *the Western Sandveld region,*[b] *and the Nata River region*

Group name	Ngwato District		Western Sandveld		Nata River	
	Number	% of total	Number	% of total	Number	% of total
Bamangwato	17,850	18.09%	89	2.52%	76	12.14%
Kalanga	22,777	23.08%	20	0.57%	40	6.39%
Tswapong	11,237	11.39%	18	0.51%	—	—
Babirwa	9,636	9.77%	—	—	—	—
Basarwa	9,587	9.72%	2,709	76.76%	503	80.35%
Bakhurutshe	5,441	5.51%	1	0.03%	—	—
Bakgalagadi	3,963	4.02%	245	6.94%	—	—
Talaote	3,538	3.59%	—	—	—	—
Bakaa	3,055	3.10%	2	0.06%	—	—
Bapedi	2,572	2.61%	171	4.85%	—	—
Phaleng	2,409	2.44%	14	0.40%	—	—
Herero	1,013	1.03%	36	1.02%	—	—
Barotse	1,006	1.02%	2	0.06%	—	—
Bakwena	892	0.90%	9	0.26%	—	—
Seleka	889	0.90%	—	—	—	—
Nabya	844	0.86%	—	—	—	—
Koba	724	0.73%	5	0.14%	—	—
Teti	435	0.44%	16	0.45%	—	—
Subia	274	9.28%	3	0.09%	—	—
Malete	240	0.24%	—	—	—	—
Rolong	155	0.16%	—	—	—	—
Tlokwa	141	0.14%	—	—	—	—
Bakgatla	—	—	1	0.03%	—	—
Zulu	—	—	1	0.03%	—	—
Batawana	—	—	2	0.06%	—	—
Lozi	—	—	1	0.03%	—	—
Manoka	—	—	1	0.03%	—	—
Simburu	—	—	1	0.03%	—	—
Basotho	—	—	—	—	7	1.12%
'intermarriages'	—	—	182	5.16%	—	—
	98,678	100.00%	3,529	100.00%	626	100.00%

[a] 1946 Bechuanaland Protectorate census
[b] Hitchcock (1978a:219, Table 8.8)

1896–7 with the rinderpest epidemic and a series of droughts in the early twentieth century (Parsons 1974; Hitchock 1978c), cattle numbers expanded, especially with the introduction of veterinary services.

There are a number of major implications of increasing livestock numbers in the Kalahari. Fear of the spread of livestock diseases led to the construction of a series of cordon fences beginning in 1896. A cordon fence running from a point near the Botswana–Zimbabwe border south through Dukwe and Tlalamabele and then southwest through Makoba was constructed in 1954. Game migration routes were disrupted by the fences, and people were no longer allowed to pass through the fences if they were carrying animal products, something which made inroads on the trade of dried meat and leather in the Nata region. Another major outgrowth of the expansion of the livestock industry was the beginning of borehole drilling in the Kalahari. While the first borehole in the eastern Kalahari was sunk in about 1940, two major periods of drilling occurred later, one in 1958 and another in 1965. These deep wells made larger amounts of water available, thus reinforcing the trend toward larger numbers of domestic animals being kept in the desert.

Contact sedentism began to occur at wells and boreholes in the eastern Kalahari. Not only were these places attractive from the standpoint of having permanent water, occasional domestic foods, trade goods, and labour opportunities, there were other reasons for increased sedentism on their peripheries. Cattle, being tied to water sources, tend to graze and browse out edible species in the immediate environs of the water. Intense grazing pressure can lead to (1) changes in species composition of grasses, with a drop in sweet varieties, (2) an increase in shrubs at the expense of grasses, a process known as bush encroachment, and (3) a drop in the water table. Cattle tend to eat the vines which indicate the presence of particular roots of importance to humans. Browsing on the leaves of *mopane* trees results in a drop in availability of *mopane* worms (*Acanthocampa belina*). Some species, such as tsama melon (*Citrullus vulgaris*), are annuals which grow from seed every year; if they are over-exploited, they will not grow in abundance the following year. Cattle have indirect effects on food plants, as well, for example, through encouraging the spread of shrubs and trees at the expense of grasses; melons do less well, since shade inhibits their growth. Also, cattle tend to outcompete wildlife species, resulting in smaller herd sizes of some game species and changes in distribution patterns of others.

Doubt is cast on the idea that abundant resources on cattle posts attract hunter-gatherers by ethnographic data on subsistence ecology. In fact the opposite may be true. Nearly all Basarwa cattle-post residents are dependent, at least to a certain extent, on wild foods (Ebert *et al.* 1976; Hitchcock 1978a). Wages are low, and even those who get paid must still walk up to 50 miles to reach a store to buy food. Milk is available only seasonally, and cattle owners are becoming more and more restive about the numbers of people utilizing milk that might otherwise go to the calves. In-kind payment is highly irregular, and it must be shared among large numbers of people. In addition, the presence of water, by itself, is insufficient to account for the decision to settle, since many people continue their mobile lifeways even when water is available. The decision to remain mobile is not only true of hunter-gatherers; groups of Kūa keeping goats, donkeys, and even horses were observed moving independently of water, relying instead on melons and roots.

Nevertheless, ethnographic data on subsistence activities, when compared to cattle numbers on boreholes, show that the higher the number of cattle the lower the dependence upon hunting and gathering (Ebert *et al*. 1976:F2). Hunting is affected before gathering, but eventually gathering, too, is seriously reduced. The number of gathering trips drops, and the distance which people must travel to obtain bush foods increases. Labour time goes up while at the same time returns are dropping. Accepting a job on a cattle post results in labour being taken away from foraging activities, thus causing hunter-gatherer groups to become increasingly dependent upon alternative food sources. The presence of cattle posts, then, does not serve to attract people because of water or abundant resources, but rather because there is no alternative, since wild foods and labour have become less available.

It is highly significant that malnutrition among part-time hunter-gatherers living on the peripheries of cattle posts is much more common than among mobile full-time hunter-gatherer groups. Contact with outside groups has provided access to certain items that have facilitated sedentism. Donkeys in particular are important, as they enable groups to gather larger amounts of bush foods which they can store at their residential locations. Elizabeth Cashdan (personal communication) saw 'melon camps', places where melons had been collected and then placed in small areas surrounded by thorn fences. Storage of melons and other bush foods enables groups to reside in specific localities for longer periods. Horses, though not common in east-central Kalahari camps, enable hunters to extend their effective range, and some species such as giraffe can be brought down more easily with a spear from horseback. The increase in guns, too, had an effect on sedentism, since overhunting led to a reduction in the availability of certain species and an increase in the flight distance of prey, making the animals much more difficult to kill. It should be noted that agriculture, given its low returns in the Kalahari, does *not* require groups to become sedentary. Some groups were observed planting small fields and then continuing on their annual rounds, returning to the fields only when the crops had ripened. The key to sedentism in the eastern Kalahari is access to resources in periods of the year when they might otherwise not be available. Thus, storage, access to water, and access to alternative food sources gained through employment or begging can be seen as important in increasing residential stability.

The Nata River region provides examples of forced and primary or *in situ* sedentism. An incident occurred in 1943 in the Nata region which led to overt attempts on the part of the Bechuanaland Protectorate Administration to control the Basarwa. A group of Ganade hunters from Gum//gabi, a pan north of the river, had killed some large animals and were in the process of butchering them when a small plane crashed nearby. Two military fliers, wearing their military uniforms, climbed out of the plane, only to come face to face with the Basarwa. The hunters, fearful that the fliers were game scouts, speared the two men to death. The crime was learned of later through a relative of the guilty men, and the Basarwa were taken to court (BNA s.303/8/1).[5] The incident led to a large-scale effort to round up all the Basarwa north of the river, disarm them, and march them at gunpoint to places south of the Nata where they were forcibly settled.

Besides evidence of forced sedentism, there is archaeological, ethnohistoric, and ethnographic evidence that Basarwa populations on the Nata were relatively sedentary long before the Bamangwato and the British were factors in the region. Some sites indicate long-term occupation. Dornan (1925:66, 69, 98) points out that a number of eastern Botswana Basarwa, particularly those along rivers in the northeastern part of the country, resided in sedentary villages. Oral-history data collected among elderly Nata residents indicate that residential moves[6] were made once or at most twice each year. Table 11.3 contains data on the number of annual residential moves of some Kalahari Basarwa populations. The range in the number of moves is from zero to 37, with the mean falling between six and nine moves per year. It can also be seen that the numbers of moves vary not only regionally but over time as well, as is indicated by the difference between the 1975–6 and the 1978–9 Kũa data.

The Nata groups stand out as being either completely sedentary or moving only once a year. These figures should not be taken to mean, however, that groups on the Nata are sedentary for substantial periods, as most households erect new compounds every third year on the average. The Nata River region, as has been noted, has both permanent water and relatively high ecological diversity when compared to other parts of the Kalahari. But these features in and of themselves did not 'allow' sedentism. Middle and Late Stone Age archeological remains

Table 11.3. *Number of residential moves per annum among a sample of Kalahari Basarwa populations*

Group name	Period of observation	Location	Number of moves	Reference
Kūa	10/75–11/76	Eastern Kalahari	6–18	
Kūa /Taise,	7/78–10/79	Eastern Kalahari	4–9	
Ganade, etc.	9/75–11/76	Nata River	0–1	
G/wi	9/67–3/68	Central Kalahari	11	Tanaka (1969:9, 1971)
G/wi	1961–1966	Central Kalahari	9–10	Silberbauer (1972:297)
!Kung	8/63–1/65	Northwest Kalahari	5–6	Lee (1968:35)
!Kung	1/68–7/68	Northwest Kalahari	37	Yellen (1977a: 60, Table 3)

found in the area do not indicate that local hunter-gatherer groups were sedentary. It appears that residential mobility was not reduced until such time as the number of groups in the region reached a saturation distribution, reducing their mobility options. Table 11.4 contains data on range size, population size, and population density for a sample of Basarwa groups. It is interesting to note that the range size of groups in the Nata region is much smaller than that of other groups in the Kalahari. In addition, with the exception of the southwestern Kalahari populations, the population density is also higher for Nata groups. From these figures it appears that there are some regular, deterministic variables operating which relate range size, population size, and population density, much as Binford and Chasko (1976:137) have suggested.

There is no question that the mobility of human groups is affected by the distributional structure of resources in space and time. It must be stressed, however, that consideration of a single aspect of distributional variability tends to mask the full range of determinants involved in changes in mobility patterning. While it might be useful for heuristic purposes to consider spatial heterogeneity of a region, as Harpending and Davis (1977) have done, it is clear that hunter-gatherers must solve problems associated with variation over time in resource availability as well. Central-place foraging, such as that described by Wilmsen (1973), can only work if human groups have been able to solve the problem of extending the use-life of resources available for limited periods of the

Table 11.4. *Data on range size, population size, and population density for a sample of Kalahari hunter-gatherer groups*

Location of group	Size of range (km^2)	Size of population	Population density[a]
I. Eastern Kalahari (Hitchcock 1978a)			
Khwee 1	1,100	42	3.8
Khwee 2	1,370	36	2.6
Diphala	940	22	2.3
Ana-O	1,025	29	2.8
Go/to	890	19	2.1
Ramokgophane	675	23	3.4
Pulenyane	925	36	3.9
II. Northeastern Kalahari (area north of Nata River)			
Montomaganyane	195	14	7.2
Gum//gabi	325	88	27.1
Tamashanka	400	32	8.0
Ngwasha	360	50	13.9
Cheberumkwakwa	275	41	14.9
III. Central Kalahari (Silberbauer 1973 and personal communication)			
≠Xade	906	85	9.4
G!osa	457	21	4.6
Easter Pan	777	50	6.4
Kxaotwe	1,036	64	6.2
Tsxobe	725	70	9.7
Piper Pans	777	53	6.8
IV. Central Kalahari (Sheller 1977)			
G≠wi/dom, etc.	2,335	147	6.3
Dantukwe	1,825	41	2.2
Lana	1,637	116	7.1
//oege	2,791	46	1.6
Sibobane	3,415	69	2.0
//Hue	505	45	8.9
Kikao	505	152	30.1
Monatsha	2,615	167	6.4
Metse-a-monong	1,825	155	8.5
/o≠we	2,673	83	3.1
Molapo-Gyem	4,323	165	3.8
V. Southwest Kalahari (Thoma and Lawry 1978)			
N≠haite-Hukuntsi-Nwatle	2,200	315	14.3
Pepane-Lehututu-Monong	1,000	247	24.7
Hukuntsi-Tshotswa	1,800	80	4.4
Tshane-Lotlhake	1,600	65	4.1
Kang	1,700	235	13.8

[a] Persons per 100 square kilometres

year (Binford forthcoming). Harris (1977:410) suggests that one of the situations which might have resulted in sedentism was where groups adopted technological innovations, particularly those related to the processing and storage of food.[7] The Nata River populations have shifted more and more towards the use of storage as a strategy. Wild plant foods were found stored in baskets in a number of compounds (Ebert 1977), and agricultural products were kept in mud storehouses. Groups of men were observed going on long-distance hunts in the winter, and often large amounts of meat were obtained, most of which was dried or smoked for later consumption. Gathering large amounts of bush foods or killing and processing large numbers of animals necessitates an increase in work effort. Draper, working among both mobile and sedentary !Kung in northwestern Botswana, points out that a major contrast between the mobile and sedentary lifestyles is in the area of work. Work has implications for sex-role differentiation (Draper 1975a and b) and for child socialization (Draper and Cashdan 1974). Whereas children in mobile situations do little if any subsistence-related work, this is not the case for children in settled villages. In the sedentary context, labour time increases, and the tasks become more differentiated. Young girls begin to oversee their younger siblings, whereas boys' work often takes them away from home. Observations of children in Nata River compounds revealed that many of them engaged in work. Thus, children are brought increasingly into the labour-force as populations settle down.

The combination of increased dependence upon storage, the use of facilities, and organizational changes in labour resulted in mobility reduction among Basarwa populations. The most important factor in mobility reduction, however, was the increase in the number of groups in the habitat. This increase in group number resulted in competition for resource space, something exemplified in the number of conflicts over territorial access mentioned frequently by Nata River Basarwa. Both ethnohistoric and ethnographic evidence indicate that territorial conflict was not uncommon. Hodson, for example, makes the following observation: 'Bushmen in this country generally have their own well-defined territories in which they hunt, and it would be bad form for a Metsibotlhoko Bushman to hunt in the Sebanene district. They do not like leaving their districts at all, and nothing, as a rule, will tempt them to do so' (Hodson 1912:227). The marked territoriality of the Nata River groups is a good illustration of the consequences of sedentism and of the economic transformations associated with it. The Nata groups obtain the greater proportion of their subsistence from *sources* other than hunting and gathering. The ownership of agricultural lands, of herds and of fishing sites along the river as well as the evidence for crowding of settlements together on the Nata are clearly factors which favour more territorial demarcation. The Kua, by contrast, showed a lack of territoriality and an open pattern of movement similar to that described for the !Kung (Yellen and Harpending 1972; Lee 1972a).

The Nata case gives weight to the argument that with increased sedentism there is a concomitant increase in territorial identification and demarcation (see also Smith 1972:17; 1976:26; Flannery 1972a:28–9). To reinforce control over localized resource areas, an ideology might be developed which emphasizes the maintenance on land across generations (Flannery 1972a:28–9). Observations of Nata River groups reveal that lineal inheritance patterns have become more common, at least in part because of the increased value of goods owned by households. The rights to agricultural fields are passed down through the male line. Whereas among mobile hunter-gatherers in the eastern Kalahari territories (*nos*) are inherited by either males or females, rights of access to territories along the Nata are usually passed on to males.

Another consequence of sedentism concerns the range and spread of social relationships. Baxter (1975:224) argues that the range becomes increasingly restricted, while Lewis (1975:423) says that sedentism tends to expand the size of effective political units. It is interesting to note that reduced mobility did *not* lead to an increase in local group size among eastern Botswana Basarwa but rather resulted in a decrease. Table 11:5 contains data on co-resident group sizes among eastern, northeastern, and northwestern Kalahari populations. It can be seen that those groups in the Nata River region are smaller in size than groups in either the eastern or northwestern Kalahari. These figures cast doubt on the notion that sedentism necessarily leads to an increase in community size, as is argued by Redman (1977:533), Kenyon (1969:145), and Childe (1942:73). Thus, while White (1977:100–1) has observed larger groups of Australian Aborigines moving over smaller ranges, and new organizational units beginning to emerge (White 1977:102), this is not yet the case among eastern Kalahari Basarwa populations.

Wiessner (1977, this volume) has emphasized the importance of sharing among hunter-gatherers, noting that it serves to reduce risk. Maintaining social alliances is crucial in an environment characterized by spatial and temporal variability in resource availability. As competition for residential space increases, and, later, as competition for logistical

Table 11.5. *Size of group in relation to economic strategy among Kalahari Basarwa*

Area	No. of groups	Mean group size	Range
Foraging groups			
1. Eastern Kalahari[a] (1975–6)	8	29.1	12–42
II. Dobe area[b] (1963–4)	15	20.7	9–52
III. Nyae Nyae[c] (1953–5)	13	22.5	8–42
Settled groups			
IV. Eastern Kalahari cattle posts[a] (1975–6)	14	9.2	3–26
V. Nata River[a] (1975–6)	16	7.7	4–12

[a] Author's field data
[b] Lee (1965:47)
[c] Marshall (1976:157–9)

space goes up, groups are forced more and more to change their sharing patterns. Networks become more restricted, and there is a shift from generalized to balanced reciprocity. We can observe this occurring among the Nata people: most sharing was done among close kin, usually within extended families. Long distance exchange trips, on the other hand, became much more common. Changes in the size of sharing networks are correlated, at least in part, with changes in marriage rules. Along with patrilineality the Nata people have much more preferential first-cross-cousin marriage than among other Basarwa groups; in addition, there is a higher rate of polygamy. Increased residential stability may result in a reduction in the overall size of marriage networks. Evidence for such a shift has been found among the !Kung, with distances between marriage partners being greater among mobile than among sedentary groups (Yellen and Harpending 1972:248–9). Distances between marriage partners was much greater among the mobile Kūa than among the settled Nata River groups.

The rise of specialized social and economic roles with sedentism would reinforce trends toward increasing social complexity. Organizational changes in labour, especially in terms of an increase in complexity, have social consequences, including the rise of economic specialists. Along the Nata a specialized hunt leader, known as a *dzimba*, emerged. This individual gradually became more and more important in decision-making. Also, traditional medical practitioners, *cho k'aos*, have become increasingly important in group affairs among Nata River Basarwa. Dances and curings, over which doctors preside, have become large communal affairs, and there is a sense of increasing ritualization of various other aspects of life among Nata Basarwa. Leadership roles have also begun to emerge among settled Basarwa. In the mid-1970s I was able to observe a situation in which the Nata people elected their own leader. Several people were considered, including a *cho k'ao*, a *dzimba*, and an articulate, well-liked individual who had been to the mines and to both government and tribal meetings. After a great deal of discussion, the latter individual was chosen, primarily because of his acquaintance with the ways of the outside world. The newly appointed leader immediately began to adjudicate disputes, hearing cases in a *kgotla* or tribal court. Unlike the situation described by Lee (1972a, c, d; 1976) for the !Kung, Nata River Basarwa elected their own leader rather than appeal to outsiders for assistance.

The final area of change among Basarwa populations of eastern Botswana that is correlated, at least in part, with sedentism, is in demography. Demographic patterning is the area where the greatest amount of attention has been paid in terms of assessing the consequences of sedentism (Lee 1972b; 1976; 1979; Binford 1968a; Binford and Chasko 1976; Harris 1977; Sussman 1972; Hassan 1973; Wilmsen 1978; Howell 1979). There is some disagreement over the causes of changes in population growth rates at the end of the Pleistocene which were noted by a number of researchers (e.g. Childe 1942:73; 1951:36; Peterson 1960:870; Sussman 1972:258; Carneiro and Hilse 1966). Peterson (1960:870) attributes the demographic changes to the rise of food production, whereas Binford (1968a:330), Lee (1972b:339), and Sussman (1972:259) suggest that sedentism in and of itself could trigger population growth. The determinants of demographic change can be divided into two classes: (1) cultural, and (2) biological. Infanticide in particular has been mentioned as a cultural means of regulating population growth (Birdsell 1968:239; Binford 1968a:330). More recent research has tended to emphasize biological causes. Lee (1972b; 1976:186; 1979), for instance, suggests that long lactation has a contraceptive effect among !Kung, while Masnick (1979) and Saxena (1977) stress that the relationship between lactation and postpartum amenorrhoea is at best a very loose one. Knodel (1977:1111–2) also says that the contraceptive effect of prolonged breast feeding is not always reliable on the individual level.

A second major biological argument is concerned with maternal nutrition and has been called the 'critical fatness' hypothesis (Frisch 1975a, b; 1978; Frisch and MacArthur 1974). Frisch and MacArthur (1974) suggest that a minimum level of body fat is necessary for the onset of menstruation and an even higher level is required for ovulation to occur. Huffman, Chowdhury, and Mosley (1978), however, found that the duration of postpartum amenorrhoea was related only slightly to maternal nutrition. Yet another suggestion is that the mechanism which suppresses ovulation is associated with endocrine levels (van der Walt, Wilmsen, and Jenkins 1978:661–2). Konner and Worthman (forthcoming) also see hormonal factors as important in ovulation suppression, but they attribute the production of prolactin to stimulation of the nipple brought about by the suckling act. Wilmsen (1978) and Binford and Chasko (1976) see changes in conception cycles as being due largely to changes in nutrition, although other variables, such as changes in miscarriage rates and male absenteeism, are also seen as contributing to the observed patterning. These findings suggest that a combination of cultural, nutritional, and hormonal factors are related to changes in demographic patterning.

Demographic data on Kũa and Nata River groups reveal a number of differences between the two in terms of population structure. Data on completed family size for postreproductive females show Kũa with 4.2 and Nata River groups with 5.7. Duration of lactation was lower among Nata groups, with weaning foods being introduced as early as five to six months of age, and weaning occurring between ages one and two. Infanticide appears to have been slightly higher along the Nata, with 11 cases reported as opposed to none in the eastern Kalahari and six out of 500 births among !Kung (Howell 1976a:147). In contrast to Harpending's findings among Nharo and ≠Au//ei in western Botswana (Harpending 1976:158, table 7.2), infant mortality rates were higher among settled Nata groups than among mobile Kũa. Morbidity levels were also higher among settled cattle-post residents than among mobile groups. Venereal disease, according to medical personnel in Botswana, is much higher at Nata than in the eastern Kalahari, something which may affect reproductive performance and sterility rates. Impressionistically, more individuals suffering from birth defects and serious incapacitating injuries lived in settled compounds than in nomadic groups, a trend Watanabe (1968:74; 1977:31) predicts would be the case under settled living conditions.

Finally, some observations on the nutritional status of mobile and sedentary Basarwa populations in eastern Botswana reveal that nutritional problems are greater in settled situations, something noted for Australian Aborigines by Taylor (1977:147–8). Poor hygienic conditions and nutritional problems are often correlated with high rates of infective disease (Robson and Wadsworth 1977:196). Outbreaks of epidemic disease occurred in the Kalahari in 1950–1 and as recently as July 1977, when nearly half the members of a small group of hunter-gatherers died near Kedia. Dietary changes with sedentism include an increased dependence on carbohydrates and sugar and an overall reduction in dietary diversity. These nutritional changes may correlate with observed trends toward greater stature of Basarwa populations in eastern Botswana, a point noted by Tobias (1962, 1970, 1975b and c) as occurring among other Basarwa groups. In spite of the trend toward greater stature, both the health and the nutritional statuses of settled Basarwa populations were poorer than those of mobile ones, though the demographic effects of the changes were such that overall the settled populations were growing much more rapidly than the mobile populations.

Conclusions

Analysis of data on eastern and northeastern Kalahari Basarwa populations reveals that many of the ideas about how and why sedentism occurs among hunter-gatherers are in need of re-evaluation. Arguments about sedentism being the result of contact are incapable of accounting for situations where groups became residentially stationary in the absence of external forces. Resource abundance or diversity arguments fail to account for the late appearance of sedentary habitation sites in the archaeological record. Hunter-gatherers, it appears, did not settle down out of some innate desire to be sedentary; rather, they were forced to reduce their mobility by declining returns.

Demographic and technological variables are crucial in the process of sedentism. It was only when the population reached a density threshold that mobility options began to be reduced. More and more emphasis had to be placed on food storage and the construction and maintenance of facilities. Competition over resource space began to occur, with a consequent reduction in range size and more territorial demarcation. Increases in scheduling and interpersonal conflicts, both within and between hunter-gatherer groups, necessitated organizational mechanisms to adjudicate disputes. Sharing networks became more restricted, and status and wealth differences began to emerge. Family size began to grow, labour effort went up, and malnutrition and illness became more common. Considering all the problems incurred by sedentism, it comes as no surprise that hunter-gatherer groups would attempt to keep moving if at all possible.

Acknowledgements

Support of the research upon which this paper is based was provided by the us National Science Foundation (grants soc75–02253 and bns76–20373), and permission to carry out the work was granted by the Office of the President, Republic of Botswana. Some of the data were collected during the course of a consultancy survey of the eastern Kalahari sponsored by the Remote Area Development Programme, Ministry of Local Government and Lands, Government of Botswana. I wish to thank Jim Ebert, Melinda Ebert, Patricia Filteau, and Aron Crowell for their assistance in collecting some of the data reported here. I also wish to thank Lewis Binford, Richard Lee, and Patricia Draper for their help in clarifying some of the ideas in this paper. Jim Ebert and Emily Garber prepared the figures, and for this I am very grateful. The warmth and hospitality of the people of eastern Botswana is greatly appreciated. Without their cooperation and assistance, my research could never have been completed.

Notes

1 There are many terms which have been used in the anthropological and archaeological literature to denote year-round residential stability. The word found in most dictionaries is 'sedentariness', from the Latin word *sedentarius*, from *sedens*, past participle of *sedēre*, to sit. *Webster's New Twentieth Century Dictionary of the English Language* defines 'sedentariness' as (1) characterized by or involving sitting, (2) remaining in one locality, not migratory, and (3) in zoology, fixed to one spot. Some of the other terms used synonymously with sedentism and sedentariness are as follows: sedentarization (Lee 1972a:339; Amiran and Ben-Arieh 1963), sedentarism (Watanabe 1968:69), sedentariness (Watanabe 1977:27), settled village life (Braidwood and Braidwood 1953:278, Kenyon 1956:193, Coe and Flannery 1967:5), sedentary life (Flannery 1969:80, 1972a:23), full-time village life (Coe and Flannery 1964:651), settled life (Bray 1976:82, 1977:234), stability of residence (Watanabe 1977:24), perennial occupation (Braidwood et al. 1971:1238), permanent year-round settlement (Braidwood 1975:118), year-round open settlement living (Braidwood 1958:1423), fully settled life (Wright 1969:461), settlement (Kenyon 1959a:36; Bender 1975:38), sedentary living (Sauer 1961:266), sedentization (Harris 1977:410), culture of settlement (Nurse and Jenkins 1977:2), and de-nomadization (Amiran and Ben-Arieh 1963:161). Other terms I have heard in conversation include: permanence, fixity, sedentation, permanent settlement, permanent occupation, immobility, static living, and year-round residence. For purposes of this paper I use the term 'sedentism', since that is the one

used by researchers who have dealt directly with the process of settling down (see Binford 1968a; Binford and Chasko 1976; Redman 1977; Draper 1975a, b; Harris 1977; Bender 1978).

2 'Basarwa' is the term used by the Botswana Government and the people of Botswana to refer to people of hunting and gathering origin and/or practice. It is a Setswana word used for those people referred to by anthropologists as Bushmen or San. In the past the term used for Bushmen in Botswana was 'Masarwas', a word found in a number of early explorers' journals and anthropologists' writings (Holub 1881 I:345–6; II:83; Schönland 1904:313; Vialls 1908:29; Dornan 1911:218; 1917:37; 1925; Schwarz 1926a:533; 1926b:27; 1928:172–3; Schapera 1930:36; Clifford 1929:347; 1930:19; Tagart 1933; London Missionary Society 1935; Joyce 1938). As is the case with many of the terms used for Bushmen, 'Masarwa' has pejorative connotations; consequently, there is a lively debate in anthropology over the proper terminology to be applied to the people of the Kalahari, with some favouring 'San', others favouring 'Bushmen', and still others preferring 'Basarwa'. While not wanting to make the situation even more confusing than it already is, I use the term 'Basarwa' because it is the one preferred by the people of Botswana. In addition, this term applies to a broader range of people than the so-called San. Nurse and Jenkins (1977:3) point out that the hunter-gatherers of Southern Africa are divided into two major groups: Khoisan and Negro. There are no hard and fast distinguishing criteria that can be used to differentiate between the two groups, as there are overlaps in language, economy and social organization. Sero-genetically, the Negro hunter-gatherers are closer to Bantu-speaking populations than they are to the San, yet they are commonly referred to as 'River Bushmen' (Nurse and Jenkins 1977:3) since they tend to inhabit the better-watered areas of southern Angola, the Caprivi Strip, northern Botswana, southern Zambia, and western Zimbabwe. The term Basarwa, then, is more accurate than San since it takes into account those groups which are genetically distinct but are Bushmen nonetheless.

3 There is a substantial literature on the Basarwa, much of it concerned with hunting-gathering lifeways. Histories of research among Basarwa have been compiled by Tobias (1975a) and Hitchcock (1978b). General overviews of Basarwa can be found in Schapera (1930), Lee (1965), and Tobias (1956, 1957, 1964). Studies of specific groups include the following: !Kung (Draper 1975a, b; Draper and Cashdan 1974; Gelburd 1978; Harpending 1972, 1976; Harpending and Davis 1977; Howell 1976a, b, 1979; Lee 1965, 1968, 1972a–d, 1976, 1979; Marshall 1960, 1976; Wiessner 1977; Yellen 1977a, b; Yellen and Harpending 1972); !Xo (Heinz 1966, 1967, 1972; Thoma and Lawry 1978); G/wi and G//ana (Sheller 1977; Silberbauer 1965, 1972, 1973; Tanaka 1969, 1971, 1976); Nharo and others on the Ghanzi Farms (Guenther 1971, 1973, 1975, 1976, 1977; Silberbauer 1965; Russell 1976; Russell and Russell 1979); Southern Kũa and Eastern ≠Hũa (Vierich 1977a, b); and Kũa (Ebert *et al.* 1976; Hitchcock 1978a). Specialized studies include discussions of genetics (Nurse and Jenkins 1977; Tobias 1972), nutrition (Metz, Hart and Harpending 1971; Wilmsen 1978), and endocrine patterns (van der Walt, Wilmsen, and Jenkins 1978). Linguistic investigations have been summarized by Köhler (1963, 1971) and Westphal (1962, 1963, 1971). It must be stressed that some of the conclusions reached on the basis of Basarwa research findings have been challenged

(e.g. by Williams 1977) and defended (e.g. by Lee, Howell, and Harpending 1977). Some issues, such as territoriality, are being debated in the Basarwa literature (Heinz 1972; Lee 1972a). Nevertheless, research among Basarwa populations has gone a long way toward refining some of our notions about hunter-gatherer behaviour.

4 The Ngwato District, also known as the Ngwato Reserve, is the tribal area belonging to the Bamangwato, the largest of the Tswana tribes. This tribal territory was decreed in 1899 (Proclamation No. 9, Bechuanaland Protectorate). In 1966, when Botswana gained its independence from Great Britain, the Ngwato District became the Central District, the largest district in the country (147,730 km^2 or approximately 25% of the total area) and the one with the largest population (228,627 in 1971, over 36% of the total population). I use Ngwato District and Central District interchangeably in this paper.

5 BNA stands for Botswana National Archives, and the number following represents the file number in the archives.

6 A distinction must be drawn here between *residential* mobility and *logistical* mobility. Residential mobility consists of the movement of a co-resident group, including both producers and dependants, from one location to another. Logistical mobility is characterized by either the producers of a group ranging out from a location for subsistence procurement purposes while dependants stay at home, or a specialized group leaving a residential location for purposes of carrying out a specific task, visiting, or environmental monitoring. Binford (forthcoming) has pointed out that these two kinds of mobility should not be viewed as opposing principles but rather as organizational mechanisms which may be employed in different mixes in different settings. Attempts to dimensionalize mobility have been made by Binford (forthcoming), Beardsley et al. (1956), Watanabe (1968, 1977), Braidwood (1960a), and Braidwood and Reed (1957).

7 Numerous researchers have noted the correlation between sedentism and the use of storage facilities (e.g. Beardsley et al. 1956:138; Childe 1942:65; 1951:71; Braidwood and Reed 1957:22; Wright 1969:476; MacNeish 1972:76; Redman 1977:537; Cohen 1975:474; 1977a:82–3; Glassow 1972:296–8; Flannery 1969:78, 87; 1972a:26; 1973:276, 280–1; Binford 1968a:333, 335; forthcoming; Binford and Chasko 1976:111, 139; Bender 1975:7; 1978:213; Schalk 1977:231). Flannery (1969:78) notes that the development of storage facilities was one of the crucial 'pre-adaptations' which facilitated the rise of food production. Schalk (1977:231) notes that storage did not 'allow' sedentism so much as reduced mobility required increased dependence upon stored foods. Storage, according to Binford (personal communication), is a way of gaining 'time utility' from resources. It is a mechanism used by human, animal, bird, and insect populations to buffer against resource scarcity during periods of the year when resources are unavailable. Storage is also, as Flannery (1969:87) notes, a method of 'banking' surpluses. Technological changes are associated with the increased dependence upon storage. Wagner (1960:92–4) has drawn a distinction between 'facilities' and 'implements' or 'tools', noting that the former are 'stationary artificial objects whose function is to contain or restrain motion', while tools are movable objects used to transmit motion. A major change postulated to have occurred at the end of the Pleistocene, and one which is correlated at least in part with an increase in sedentism, is a rise in

the use of facilities relative to implements (Binford 1968b; Flannery 1969; 1972a:26).

Bibliography

Amiran, D. H. K., and Ben-Arieh, Y. 1963. 'Sedentarization of Beduin in Israel'. *Israel Exploration Journal* 13(3):161–81

Amsden, Charles Wynn 1977. 'A quantitative analysis of Nunamiut Eskimo settlement dynamics: 1989 to 1969'. Unpublished Ph.D. dissertation, University of New Mexico, Albuquerque

Baxter, P. T. W. 1975. 'Some consequences of sedentarization for social relationships', in Theodore Monod (ed.), *Pastoralism in tropical Africa*, 206–28. London: Oxford University Press

Beardsley, Richard K. *et al.* 1956. 'Functional and evolutionary implications of community patterning', in Robert Wauchope (ed.), Seminars in archaeology 1955, *Society for American Archaeology Memoir* No. 11

Bender, Barbara 1975. *Farming in prehistory: from hunter-gatherer to food producer*. London: John Baker

1978. 'Gatherer-hunter to farmer: a social perspective'. *World Archaeology* 10(2):204–22

Binford, Lewis R. 1964. 'Archaeological and ethnohistorical investigations of cultural diversity'. Unpublished Ph.D. dissertation, University of Michigan, Ann Arbor

1968a. 'Post-pleistocene adaptations', in Sally R. Binford and Lewis R. Binford (eds.), *New perspectives in archaeology*, 313–41. Chicago: Aldine

1968b. 'Methodological considerations of the archaeological use of ethnographic data', in Richard B. Lee and Irven DeVore (eds.), *Man the hunter*, 268–73. Chicago: Aldine

Forthcoming. 'Willow smoke and dogs' tails: hunter-gatherer settlement systems and archaeological site formation. *American Antiquity*

Binford, Lewis R., and Chasko, William J., Jr. 1976. 'Nunamiut demographic history: a provocative case', in Ezra B. W. Zubrow (ed.), *Demographic anthropology: quantitative approaches*, 63–143. Albuquerque: University of New Mexico Press

Birdsell, Joseph B. 1968. 'Some predictions for the pleistocene based on equilibrium systems among recent hunter-gatherers', in Richard B. Lee and Irven DeVore (eds.), *Man the hunter*, 229–40. Chicago: Aldine

Braidwood, Robert J. 1952. *The Near East and foundations for civilization*. Condon Lectures. Eugene: Oregon State System of Higher Education

1958. 'Near Eastern prehistory'. *Science* 127:1419–30

1960a. 'Levels in prehistory: a model for the consideration of the evidence', in Sol Tax (ed.), *Evolution after Darwin, Vol. II: The evolution of man*, 143–51. Chicago: University of Chicago Press

1960b. 'The agricultural revolution'. *Scientific American* 203:130–41

1975. *Prehistoric men*. Chicago: Scott, Foresman, and Co.

Braidwood, Robert J., and Braidwood, Linda J. 1953. 'The earliest village communities of southwestern Asia'. *Journal of World History* 1:278–310

Braidwood, Robert J., Cambel, Halet, Redman, Charles L. and Watson, Patty Jo

1971. 'Beginnings of village-farming communities in southeastern Turkey'. *Proceedings of the National Academy of Sciences* 68(6):1236–40.

Braidwood, Robert J., Cambel, Halet, Redman, Charles L., and Stewart, Robert B. 1974. 'Beginnings of village-farming communities in southeastern Turkey–1972'. *Proceedings of the National Academy of Sciences* 71(2):568–72.

Braidwood, Robert J., and Reed, Charles L. 1957. 'The achievement and early consequences of food production: a consideration of the archaeological and natural-historical evidence'. *Cold Spring Harbor Symposia on Quantitative Biology* 22:19–31

Bray, Warwick M. 1976. 'From predation to production: the nature of agricultural evolution in Mexico and Peru', in G. de G. Sieveking, I. H. Longworth, and K. E. Wilson (eds.), *Problems in economic and social archaeology*, 73–95. London: Duckworth

1977. 'From foraging to farming in early Mexico', in J. V. S. Megaw (ed.), *Hunters, gatherers, and first farmers beyond Europe*, 225–50. London: Duckworth

Carneiro, Robert L., and Hilse, Daisy F. 1966. 'On determining the probable rate of population growth during the neolithic'. *American Anthropologist* 68:177–81

Chapman, James 1971. *Travels in the interior of South Africa*. Cape Town: A. A. Balkema

Chasko, W. J., Jr., Nurse, G. T., Harpending, H. C. and Jenkins, T. forthcoming. 'Sero-genetic studies on the "Masarwa" of northeastern Botswana'. *Botswana Notes and Records*, 11

Childe, V. Gordon 1942. *What happened in history*. London: Penguin

1951. *Man makes himself*. New York: Mentor Books

Clifford, B. E. H. 1929. 'A journey by motor lorry from Mahalapye through the Kalahari Desert'. *Geographical Journal* 73(4):342–58

1930. 'A reconnaissance of the Great Makarikari Lake'. *Geographical Journal* 75(1):16–26

Coe, Michael D., and Flannery, Kent V. 1964. 'Microenvironments and Mesoamerican prehistory'. *Science* 143:650–4

1967. Early cultures and human ecology in south coastal Guatemala. *Smithsonian Contributions to Anthropology* 3

Cohen, Mark N. 1975. 'Archaeological evidence for population pressure in pre-agricultural societies'. *American Antiquity* 40(4):471–5

1977a. *The food crisis in prehistory: overpopulation and the origins of agriculture.* New Haven: Yale University Press

1977b. 'Population pressure and the origins of agriculture: an archaeological example from the coast of Peru', in Charles A. Reed (ed.), *Origins of agriculture*, 136–77. The Hague: Mouton

Dornan, S. S. 1911. 'The Masarwas and their language'. *South African Journal of Science* 8:218–25

1917. 'The Tati Bushmen (Masarwas) and their language'. *Journal of the Royal Anthropological Institute* 47:37–112

1925. *Pygmies and Bushmen of the Kalahari*. London: Seeley, Service, and Co.

Draper, Patricia 1975a. '!Kung women: contrasts in sexual egalitarianism in the foraging and sedentary contexts', in Rayna Reiter (ed.), *Toward an anthropology of women*, 77–109. New York: Monthly Review Press

1975b. 'Cultural pressure on sex differences'. *American Ethnologist* 2(4): 602–16

Draper, Patricia, and Cashdan, Elizabeth 1974. 'The impact of sedentism on !Kung socialization'. Paper presented at the 73rd annual meeting of the American Anthropological Association, Mexico City

Duggan-Cronin, A. M. 1942. *The Bushman tribes of Southern Africa*. Kimberley, South Africa: Alexander McGregor Memorial Museum

Ebert, James I., Thoma, Axel, Ebert, Melinda C., Hitchcock, Robert K., and Oabile, Malebogo 1976. 'Report and recommendations for land allocations and Basarwa development in the Sandveld region of the Central District, Botswana'. Report to the Ministry of Local Government and Lands, Gaborone, Botswana

Ebert, Melinda C. 1977. 'Patterns of manufacture and use of baskets among the Basarwa of the Nata River region'. *Botswana Notes and Records* 9:69–83

Flannery, Kent V. 1969. 'Origins and ecological effects of early domestication in Iran and the Near East', in Peter J. Ucko and G. W. Dimbleby (eds.), *The domestication and exploitation of plants and animals*, 73–100. Chicago: Aldine

1972a. 'The origins of the village as a settlement type in Mesoamerica and the Near East: a comparative study', in Peter J. Ucko, Ruth Tringham, and G. W. Dimbleby (eds.), *Man, settlement, and urbanism*, 23–53. London: Duckworth

1972b. 'The cultural evolution of civilizations'. *Annual Review of Ecology and Systematics* 3:399–426

1973. 'The origins of agriculture'. *Annual Review of Anthropology* 2:271–310

Flannery, Kent V., and Coe, Michael D. 1968. 'Social and economic systems in formative Mesoamerica', in Sally R. Binford and Lewis R. Binford (eds.), *New perspectives in archaeology*, 267–83. Chicago: Aldine

Food and Agriculture Organization. 1970. *Report on the group study fellowship tour on settlement in agriculture of nomadic, semi-nomadic and other pastoral peoples*. UNDP Report 2810. Rome: FAO

1972. *Report on the FAO expert consultation on the settlement of nomads in Africa and the Near East*. UNDP Report RP 20. Rome: FAO

Frisch, Rose E. 1975a. 'Demographic implications of the biological determinants of female fecundity'. *Social Biology* 22(1):17–22

1975b. 'Critical weights, a critical body composition, menarche, and the maintenance of menstrual cycles', in Elizabeth S. Watts, Francis E. Johnston, and Gabriel W. Lasker (eds.), *Biosocial interrelations in population adaptation*, 319–52. The Hague: Mouton

1978. 'Nutrition, fatness, and fertility: The effect of food intake on reproductive ability', in W. H. Mosley (ed.), *Nutrition and human reproduction*. New York: Plenum Press

Frisch, Rose E., and MacArthur, Janet W. 1974. 'Menstrual cycles: fatness as a determinant of minimum weight for height necessary for their maintenance or onset'. *Science* 185:949–51

Gelburd, Diane Elizabeth 1978. 'Indicators of culture change among the Dobe !Kung San'. Unpublished M.A. thesis, George Washington University, Washington, D.C.

Glassow, Michael A. 1972. 'Changes in adaptations of southwestern basketmakers: a systems perspective', in Mark P. Leone (ed.), *Contemporary archaeology*, 289–302. Carbondale and Edwardsville: Southern Illinois University Press

Guenther, Mathias G. 1971. 'Kalahari Bushmen in transition'. *Rotunda* 4(3):8–16

1973. 'Farm Bushmen and mission Bushmen: social change in a setting of conflicts and pluralism of the San of the Ghanzi District, Republic of Botswana'. Unpublished Ph.D. dissertation, University of Toronto

1975. 'San acculturation and incorporation in the ranching areas of the Ghanzi District: some urgent anthropological issues'. *Botswana Notes and Records* 7:167–70

1976. 'From hunters to squatters: social and cultural change among the farm San of Ghanzi, Botswana', in Richard B. Lee and Irven DeVore (eds.), *Kalahari hunter-gatherers: studies of the !Kung San and their neighbors*, 120–33. Cambridge: Harvard University Press

1977. 'Bushman hunters as farm laborers'. *Canadian Journal of African Studies* 11(2):195–203

Harpending, Henry C. 1972. '!Kung hunter-gatherer population structure'. Unpublished Ph.D. dissertation. Harvard University, Cambridge

1976. 'Regional variation in !Kung populations', in Richard B. Lee and Irven DeVore (eds.), *Kalahari hunter-gatherers: studies of the !Kung San and their neighbors*, 152–65. Cambridge: Harvard University Press

Harpending, Henry C., and Davis, Herbert 1977. 'Some implications for hunter-gatherer ecology derived from the spatial structure of resources'. *World Archaeology* 8(3):275–86

Harris, David R. 1977. 'Settling down: an evolutionary model for the transformation of mobile bands into sedentary communities', in J. Friedman and M. J. Rowlands (eds.), *The evolution of social systems*, 401–17. London: Duckworth

Hassan, Fekri A. 1973. 'On mechanisms of population growth during the neolithic'. *Current Anthropology* 14(5):535–40, 542

Heinz, H. J. 1966. 'The social organization of the !Ko Bushmen'. Unpublished MA thesis, University of South Africa, Pretoria

1967. 'Conflicts, tensions, and relief of tensions in a Bushman society'. *Institute for the Study of Man in Africa Papers* 23

1972. 'Territoriality among the Bushmen in general and the !Ko in particular'. *Anthropos* 67:405–16

Hitchcock, Robert K. 1978a. *Kalahari cattle posts: a regional study of hunter-gatherers, pastoralists, and agriculturalists in the western Sandveld region, Central District, Botswana*. Gaborone, Botswana: Government Printer

1978b. 'A history of research among the Basarwa in Botswana'. *National Institute for Research in Development and African Studies, Documentation Unit, working paper* 19. Gaborone, Botswana: National Institute for Research

1978c. 'The traditional response to drought in Botswana', in Madalon T. Hinchey (ed.), *Proceedings of the symposium on drought in Botswana*, 91–7. Gaborone: The Botswana Society

Forthcoming. 'The ethnoarchaeology of sedentism: a Kalahari case'. *Proceedings of the VIIIth PanAfrican Congress of Prehistory and Quaternary Studies*, Nairobi

Hodson, Arnold W. 1912. *Trekking the great thirst: sport and travel in the Kalahari Desert*. London: T. Fisher Unwin

Holub, Emil 1881. *Seven years in South Africa: travels, researches, and adventures between the diamond fields and the Zambezi (1872–79)*. London: Sampson Low, Marston, Searle, and Rivington

Howell Nancy 1976a. 'The population of the Dobe Area !Kung', in Richard B. Lee and Irven DeVore (eds.), *Kalahari hunter-gatherers: studies of the !Kung San and their neighbors*, 138–51. Cambridge: Harvard University Press

1976b. 'Toward a uniformitarian theory of human paleodemography', in R. H. Ward and K. M. Weiss (eds.), *The demographic evolution of human populations, Journal of Human Evolution* 5:25–40

1979. *Demography of the Dobe !Kung*. New York: Academic Press

Huffman, Sandra L., Chowdhury, A. K. M. Alauddin, and Mosley, W. Henry 1978. 'Postpartum amenorrhea: how is it affected by maternal nutritional status?', *Science* 200:1155–7

International Labour Organization. 1965. *Report to the government of the Republic of the Sudan on the sedentarization of nomadic tribal populations in the Buntana Region of northern Sudan*. Geneva: ILO

Joyce, J. W. 1938. *Report on the Masarwa in the Bamangwato Reserve, Bechuanaland Protectorate*. League of Nations Publications VI. B. *Slavery*. Annex 6:57–76.

Kenyon, Kathleen M. 1956. 'Jericho and its setting in Near Eastern prehistory'. *Antiquity* 30:184–95.

1959a. 'Some observations on the beginnings of settlement in the Near East. *Journal of the Royal Anthropological Institute* 89(1):35–43

1959b. 'Earliest Jericho'. *Antiquity* 33:5–9

1969. 'The origins of the neolithic'. *Advancement of Science* 26:144–60

Knodel, John 1977. 'Breast-feeding and population growth'. *Science* 198:1111–15

Köhler, Oswin 1963. 'Observations on the central Khoisan language group'. *Journal of African Languages* 2:227–34

1971. 'Die Khoe-sprachigen Buschmänner der Kalahari'. *Sonderdruck aus Forschungen zur Allgemeinen und Regionalen Geographie: Feschrift für Kurt Kayser*. Kölner Geographische Arbeiten, Sonderband, 373–411

Konner, Melvin and Worthman, Carol forthcoming. 'Nursing frequency, gonadal function, and birth spacing among !Kung hunter-gatherers'. *Science*

Lee, Richard B. 1965. 'Subsistence ecology of !Kung Bushmen'. Unpublished Ph.D. dissertation, University of California, Berkeley

1968. 'What hunters do for a living, or, how to make out on scarce resources', in Richard B. Lee and Irven Devore, (eds.), 30–48. Chicago: Aldine

1972a. '!Kung spatial organization: an ecological and historical perspective'. *Human Ecology* 1(2):125–47

1972b. 'Population growth and the beginnings of sedentary life among the !Kung Bushmen', in Brian Spooner (ed.), *Population growth: anthropological implications*, 343–50. Cambridge: MIT Press

1972c. 'The intensification of social life among the !Kung Bushmen', in Brian Spooner (ed.), *Population growth: anthropological implications*, 329–42. Cambridge: MIT Press

1972d. 'Work effort, group structure, and land use among contemporary hunter-gatherers', in Peter J. Ucko, Ruth Tringham, and G. W. Dimbleby (eds.), *Man, settlement, and urbanism*, 177–85. London: Duckworth

1976. 'The !Kung's new culture'. *Science Year 1976*. 180–95. Chicago: Field Enterprises Educational Corporation

1979. *The !Kung San: men, women and work in a foraging society*. Cambridge: Cambridge University Press

Lee, Richard B., Howell, Nancy and Harpending, Henry 1977. '!Kung ecology', *Science* 197:1234

Lewis, I. M. 1975. 'The dynamics of nomadism: prospects for sedentarization and social change', in Theodore Monod (ed.), *Pastoralism in tropical Africa*, 426–42. London: Oxford University Press

Livingstone, David 1857. *Missionary travels and researches in South Africa*. London: John Murray

London Missionary Society 1935. *The Masarwa (Bushmen): report on an enquiry by the South Africa district committee of the London Missionary Society*. Alice, South Africa: Lovedale Press

MacKenzie, John 1871. *Ten years north of the Orange River: a story of everyday life and work among the South African Tribes from 1859 to 1869*. Edinburgh: Edmonston and Douglas

MacNeish, Richard S. 1964. 'Ancient Mesoamerican civilization'. *Science* 143: 531–7

1972. 'The evolution of community patterns in the Tehuacan Valley of Mexico and speculations about the cultural processes', in Peter J. Ucko, Ruth Tringham, and G. W. Dimbleby (eds.), *Man, settlement, and urbanism*, 67–93. London: Duckworth

Marshall, Lorna 1960. '!Kung Bushman bands'. *Africa* 30:225–55

1976. *The !Kung of Nyae Nyae*. Cambridge: Harvard University Press

Masnick, George S. 1979. 'The demographic impact of breastfeeding: a critical review'. *Human Biology* 51(2):109–25

Metz, J., Hart, D. and Harpending H. C. 1971. 'Iron, folate, and vitamin B12 nutrition in a hunter-gatherer people: a study of the !Kung Bushmen'. *American Journal of Clinical Nutrition*, 24:229–42.

Mohr, Edward 1876. *To the Victoria Falls of the Zambezi*. London: Sampson Low, Marston, Searle, and Rivington

Newman, James L. 1970. *The ecological basis of subsistence change among the Sandawe of Tanzania*. Washington, D.C. National Academy of Sciences

Nurse, G. T., and Jenkins, T. 1977. *Health and the hunter-gatherer: biomedical studies of the hunting and gathering populations of Southern Africa*. Basel: S. Karger

Osborn, Alan J. 1977. 'Strandloopers, mermaids, and other fairy tales: ecological determinants of marine resource utilization – the Peruvian case', in Lewis R. Binford (ed.), *For theory building in archaeology: essays on faunal remains, aquatic resources, spatial analysis, and systemic modeling*, 157–205. New York: Academic Press

Parsons, Q. N. 1974. 'The economic history of Khama's country in Southern Africa'. *African Social Research* 18:643:75.

Parsons, Q. N. (ed.) 1972. 'Khama's own account of himself'. *Botswana Notes and Records* 4:137–46

Peterson, Max 1960. Increase of settlement size and population since the inception of agriculture. *Nature* 186:870–2

Redman, Charles L. 1977. 'Man, domestication, and culture in southwestern
Asia', in Charles A. Reed (ed.), *Origins of agriculture*, 523–41. The Hague:
Mouton

Robson, J. R. K., and Wadsworth, G. R. 1977. 'The health and nutritional status
of primitive populations'. *Ecology of Food and Nutrition* 6:187–202

Russell, Margo 1976. 'Slaves or workers? relations between Bushmen, Tswana,
and Boers in the Kalahari'. *Journal of Southern African Studies* 2(2):178–97

Russell, Margo, and Russell, Martin 1979. *Afrikaners of the Kalahari: White minority
in a Black state*. Cambridge: Cambridge University Press

Sauer, Carol O. 1961. 'Sedentary and mobile bents in early societies', in Sher-
wood L. Washburn (ed.), *Social life of early man*, 256–66. Viking Fund Publications in Anthropology, 31. Chicago: Aldine

Saxena, P. C. 1977, 'Breast-feeding: its effects on post-partum amenorrhea'. *Social
Biology* 24(1):45–51

Schalk, Randall F. 1977. 'The structure of an anadromous fish resource', in Lewis
R. Binford (ed.), *For theory building in archaeology: essays on faunal remains,
aquatic resources, spatial analysis, and systemic modeling*, 207–49. New York:
Academic Press

Schapera, I. 1930. *The Khoisan peoples of South Africa: Bushmen and Hottentots*.
London: Routledge and Kegan Paul

Schönland, S. 1904. 'Biological and ethnological observations on a trip to the
northeast Kalahari – September 1903'. *South African Association for the
Advancement of Science, report for 1904*, 308–17.

Schwarz, E. H. L. 1926a. 'Botletle river'. *Geographical Journal* 67:528–35
1926b. 'The northern Kalahari'. *South African Geographical Journal* 9:27–36
1928. *The Kalahari and its native races*. London: Witherby

Sheller, Paul 1977. 'The people of the Central Kalahari Game Reserve: a report
on the reconnaissance of the Reserve, July–September, 1976'. Report to the
Ministry of Local Government and Lands, Gaborone, Botswana

Silberbauer, George B. 1965. *Report to the Government of Bechuanaland on the
Bushman survey*. Gaberones: Government Printer
1972. 'The G/wi Bushmen', in M. G. Bicchieri (ed.), *Hunters and gatherers today*,
271–326. New York: Holt, Rinehart, and Winston
1973. 'Socio-ecology of the G/wi Bushmen'. Unpublished Ph.D. dissertation,
Monash University, Clayton, Victoria, Australia

Smith, Philip E. L. 1972. 'The consequences of food production'. *Addison-Wes-
ley Modular Publication* 31
1976. *Food production and its consequences*. Menlo Park: Cummings Publishing
Co.

Sussman, Robert W. 1972. 'Child transport, family size, and increase in human
population during the neolithic'. *Current Anthropology* 13(2):258–9

Tagart, E. S. B. 1933. *Report on the conditions existing among the Masarwa in the
Bamangwato Reserve of the Bechuanaland Protectorate and certain other matters appertaining to the natives living therein*. Pretoria, South Africa: Government Printer

Tanaka, Jiro 1969. 'The ecology and social structure of Central Kalahari Bushmen: a preliminary report', in T. Umesao, (ed.), *Kyoto University African
studies III*, 1–26. Kyoto: Kyoto University Press

1971. *The Bushmen: a study of ecological anthropology*. Tokyo, Japan: Shisaku-sha

1976. 'Subsistence ecology of the Central Kalahari San', in Richard B. Lee and Irven DeVore (eds.), *Kalahari hunter-gatherers: studies of the !Kung San and their neighbors*, 98–119. Cambridge: Harvard University Press

Taylor, John C. 1977. 'Diet, health, and economy: some consequences of planned social change in an Aboriginal community', in R. M. Berndt (ed.), *Aborigines and change: Australia in the '70's*, 147–58. Canberra: Australian Institute of Aboriginal Studies

Thoma, Axel, and Lawry, Steve 1978. *A spatial development plan for remote settlements in northern Kgalagadi*. Gaborone, Botswana: Government Printer

Tobias, Phillip V. 1956. 'On the survival of the Bushmen, with an estimate of the problem facing anthropologists'. *Africa* 26(2):174–85

1957. 'Bushmen of the Kalahari'. *Man* 57:33–40

1959a. 'The Nuffield-Witwatersrand University expedition to the Kalahari Bushmen, 1958–1959', *Nature* 183:1011–13

1959b. 'Provisional report on the Nuffield-Witwatersrand University research expedition to the Kalahari Bushmen, August to September 1958', *South African Journal of Science*, 55:13–18

1962. 'On the increasing stature of the Bushmen'. *Anthropos* 57:801–10

1964. 'Bushman hunter-gatherers: a study in human ecology', in D. H. S. Davis (ed.), *Ecological studies in Southern Africa*, 67–86. The Hague: Mouton

1970. 'Puberty, malnutrition, and the weaker sex – and two new measures of environmental betterment'. *The Leech* 40(4):101–7

1972. 'Recent human biological studies in southern Africa, with special reference to Negros and Khoisans'. *Transactions of the Royal Society of South Africa* 40(3):109–33

1975a. 'Fifteen years of study on the Kalahari Bushmen or San: a brief history of the Kalahari Research Committee'. *South African Journal of Science* 71:74–8

1975b. 'Anthropometry among disadvantaged peoples: studies in Southern Africa', in Elizabeth S. Watts, Francis E. Johnston, and Gabriel W. Lasker (eds.), *Biosocial interrelationships in population adaptation*, 287—305. The Hague: Mouton

1975c. 'Stature and secular trend among Southern African Negroes and San (Bushmen)'. *South African Journal of Medical Sciences* 40(4):145–64

van der Walt, L. Andre, Wilmsen, Edwin N. and Jenkins, Trefor 1978. 'Unusual sex hormone patterns among desert-dwelling hunter-gatherers'. *Journal of Clinical Endocrinology and Metabolism* 46(4):657–63

Vialls, C. Clements 1908. 'The Masarwa, or Bushmen of the Kalahari'. *African Monthly* 5:29–33

Vierich, Helga I. D. 1977a. 'Interim report on Basarwa and related poor Bakgalagadi in Kweneng District'. Report to the Ministry of Local Government and Lands, Gaborone, Botswana

1977b. 'Ecological anthropology: investigations among Kweneng District Basarwa'. *Botswana Notes and Records* 9:169–70

Wagner, Phillip L. 1960. *The human use of the Earth*. New York: The Free Press

Watanabe, Hitoshi 1968. 'Subsistence and ecology of northern food gatherers with special reference to the Ainu', in Richard B. Lee and Irven DeVore (eds.), *Man the hunter*, 69–77. Chicago: Aldine

1977. 'Some problems in the comparative ecology of food gatherers', in Hitoshi Watanabe (ed.), *Human activity system: its spatiotemporal structure*, 21–39. Tokyo: University of Tokyo Press

Westphal, E. O. J. 1962. 'On classifying Bushman and Hottentot languages'. *African Language Studies* 3:30–48

1963. 'The linguistic prehistory of Southern Africa: Bush, Kwadi, Hottentot, and Bantu linguistic relationships'. *Africa* 33:237–64

1971. 'The click languages of southern and eastern Africa', in Jack Berry and Joseph H. Greenberg (eds.), *Current trends in linguistics, vol. VII: linguistics in sub-Saharan Africa*, 367–420. The Hague: Mouton

White, Isobel M. 1977. 'From camp to village: some problems of adaptation', in R. M. Berndt (ed.), *Aborigines and change: Australia in the '70's*, 100–5. Canberra: Australian Institute of Aboriginal Studies

Wiessner, Pauline Wilson 1977. 'Hxaro: a regional system of reciprocity for reducing risk among the !Kung San'. Unpublished Ph.D. dissertation, University of Michigan, Ann Arbor

Williams, B. J. 1977. 'Investigations of a little-known way of life: a review of *Kalahari hunter-gatherers: studies of the !Kung San and their neighbors'*, *Science* 196:761–3

Wilmsen, Edwin N. 1973. 'Interaction, spacing behavior, and the organization of hunting bands'. *Journal of Anthropological Research* 29(1):1–31

1978. 'Seasonal effects of dietary intake on Kalahari San'. *Federation of American Societies for Experimental Biology Proceedings* 37(1):65–72

Wright, Gary A. 1969. 'Origins of food production in southwestern Asia: a survey of ideas'. *Current Anthropology* 12:447–77

Yellen, John E. 1977a. *Archaeological approaches to the present: models for reconstructing the past.* New York: Academic Press

1977b. 'Long-term hunter-gatherer adaptation to desert environments: a biogeographical perspective'. *World Archaeology* 8(3):262–74

Yellen, John E. and Harpending, Henry 1972. 'Hunter-gatherer populations and archaeological inference'. *World Archaeology* 4(4):244–53

12. Nomads without cattle: East African foragers in historical perspective

CYNTHIA CHANG

In this chapter I argue that it may be erroneous to project the present-day tribal associations of people into their past. The people with whom I am concerned are groups of hunters and gatherers presently living in the Rift Valley of Kenya and Northern Tanzania. Defined by themselves as 'Okiek', they are commonly referred to in the literature as 'Dorobo'. While some groups of Okiek may indeed constitute populations whose historical roots are distinct from surrounding pastoralists and farmers (Blackburn 1971, 1973, 1974, this volume), it is my view that present-day perceptions of tribal identity in Kenya, and the closing of tribal boundaries, are largely a product of colonial rule. Boundaries between tribal groups seem in the past to have been extremely fluid.

Available evidence suggests that a more accurate interpretation of Kenya's prehistory might be gained from examining the dynamic processes that mediated relationships between the various inhabitants of a region at given moments in history, than from focusing solely on the oral traditions, behaviour (socio-linguistic and socio-economic) and material culture of contemporary tribal entities. It is important to remember that the lives of all indigenous Kenyans were radically altered by two recent and highly disruptive developments: the trade in ivory and slaves, and colonialism.

In interpreting available sources, it is also important to consider the political and economic context in which information was gathered and diffused. The objectivity of both informant and ethnographer may be clouded by both ideological and material conflicts, and source materials should be interpreted in the light of the context in which they were written.

The names used to designate Rift Valley hunting and gathering groups have varied with the languages of the people making the distinction between themselves and these 'others'. Rift Valley hunters and gather-

A camp of 'hunter-gatherers' in central Kenya (R. Blackburn)

270

ers are most commonly referred to as 'Dorobo', a term derived from Maasai and used by both the Swahili traders and the Europeans who have written about them. In perusing the early literature on these groups, one is immediately struck by the ambiguity with which the various labels are applied. Hobley (1906), for example, informs us that the Dorobo are called 'Asi' by the Kikuyu; 'Okiek' by the Nandi; 'Il-Torobo' by the Maasai; and 'Aggiek', 'Oggiek' or 'Ogiechue' by themselves. In discussing the apparent interchangeability of these terms, Muriuki concludes that:

> The Kikuyu word Athi . . . was used to mean either an individual who practised hunting as a way of life, irrespective of ethnic grouping, or more specifically, a tribe whose economic activities were largely centered upon hunting and gathering. . . . Material collected prior to . . . 1920, as well as data I have collected recently, demonstrates without doubt that 'Athi' and 'Dorobo' are alternate names for the same ethnic group. (Muriuki 1974:38)

These various terms are often used in a derogatory sense and appear to refer to the impoverished condition of these nomads without cattle, rather than to differences in language or phenotype. Thus these scattered groups of Dorobo have in common a low socio-economic status with respect to other inhabitants of the regions in which they are found. For this reason, I have attempted to study Rift Valley Dorobo in terms of their position within a regional economy, in which the hunting and gathering mode of subsistence is but a part of a wider whole. This whole encompasses pastoralists and farmers, as well as intruders whose presence has had varying effects upon their lives. I shall argue that, at least from the mid-1800s onwards, Rift Valley hunters and gatherers have consisted largely of disenfranchised pastoralists and farmers, rather than being descendants of ancient populations who have hunted since 'time immemorial'. This viewpoint is not based upon early ethnographic sources on Dorobo, but rather derives primarily from the travel journals of the late-nineteenth-century British explorers.

Early ethnographic descriptions of East African peoples were most often written by colonial district officers and were aimed primarily towards arming the colonial government with information that would facilitate the administration of native peoples. This is especially evident in Schapera's 1949 review of anthropological research in Kenya which was prepared for the International African Institute and which contains an entire section on the practical application of ethnographic research for administrative purposes. The lack of history in most early East

African ethnography stems from the implicit assumption that Kenya's various tribes were distinct and non-overlapping populations. Indeed the concept of the 'tribe', as a discrete entity, was a necessary assumption both for tax collection and for the assignment of Africans to native reserves. It is therefore not surprising that some of the ethnographies which are concerned with hunters and gatherers, as products of the colonial period, provide only static descriptions of the Dorobo, who are presumed to be aboriginal hunters who had survived into the colonial period. Such assumptions underlie the work of Hollis (1909) and Huntingford (1951 and 1954) who wrote about the Okiek Dorobo residing in Nandi territory.

Although concerned with history, Hobley's (1903a, 1903b, 1905 and 1906) and Beech's (1915) accounts of the Dorobo are based on the assumption that the various groups that inhabit Kenya once formed a single population which fissured as the result of the intrusions of the Nandi and, at a later time, the Kikuyu. On the other hand, Dundas (1908) and the Routledges (1910) were puzzled by the complexity of ethnic identity in the Mount Kenya area. These early historians implicitly take issue with the concept of the 'tribe', since the fluid nature of tribal boundaries, as evidenced by the great deal of economic exchange and marriage *across* such boundaries, inspired their investigations. Thus Dundas states: 'Anyone enquiring into the descent of those present at a meeting of Kikuyu elders will find an extraordinary number of different tribes represented. One is Maeru, another Chaga, a third a Maasai, a fourth a Shuka, a fifth a Dorobo, and so on' (Dundas 1908:139). Both Dundas and the Routledges accept the oral traditions of the Kikuyu as historical fact. According to these traditions, Mount Kenya was occupied by two distinct groups of hunters and gatherers prior to the arrival of the Kikuyu: the Gumba (who were short in stature, lived in pits dug into the ground and had taught the Kikuyu how to work iron) and the Asi (who were the same people as the Dorobo). According to these oral traditions, however, the ancestors of the Kikuyu consisted of an admixture of displaced persons, including Asi, who were descended from a common ancestor, Digiri, and who had migrated from a region to the northeast of Mount Kenya to escape an invasion of their country of origin by Galla pastoralists. Thus the oral traditions of the Kikuyu are confusing and the term 'Asi' is applied both to the Kikuyu pioneers and to one of the populations which they displaced.

Using these data and the recollections of post-colonial Kikuyu elders, Muriuki (1974) has published a history of his people, the Kikuyu.

According to Muriuki, the ancestral immigrants to Mount Kenya consisted of horticulturalists, pastoralists and hunters and gatherers who had intermarried extensively, despite heterogeneity in both language and mode of subsistence. As this admixture of peoples (who were to become collectively known as the Kikuyu) expanded in a southwesterly direction from the Tigania Plateau towards Mount Kenya, subsequent groups of hunters and gatherers were encountered and were absorbed through intermarriage. Upon reaching Mount Kenya, an area of rich agricultural potential, the proto-Kikuyu learned iron working from the Gumba and began to practise slash and born horticulture. Thereafter additional Gumba and Asi were either absorbed into the Kikuyu economy or forced onto the plains, due to the destruction of the forest hunting habitat by swiddening. Muriuki estimates that initial contact between the proto-Kikuyu and the Gumba occurred during the mid-seventeenth century. By the time of the Kikuyu 'Cuma' ('Raiding') Generation Set (1687–1781 ± 30 years), horticultural expansion had resulted in the Kikuyu migration into the areas of northern Metumi and Gaki where additional groups of Gumba were still being encountered. The last oral traditions of the Gumba date from the last decades of the nineteenth century. Thus ethnohistorians assume that further Kikuyu expansion into Kabete either displaced the Gumba or forced their complete assimilation, through intermarriage, with the Asi Dorobo. Kikuyu expansion into Kabete was during the 'Ndemi' ('Cutters') Generation which Muriuki estimates at 1792–1826 ± 15 years.

Lawren (1968), in a study based largely upon the analysis of initiation age-set names (which are presumably derived from real events) has studied the relationship between the Kikuyu and the Maasai. He believes that it was during the 'Cuma' ('Raiding') Generation that the Kikuyu first encountered the Maasai. During the next generation, 'Mathathi', we have accounts of Kikuyu borrowing such cultural elements from the Maasai as their manner of hair-styling and the use of red ochre. The Kikuyu also borrowed their concept of 'left-hand' and 'right-hand' (alternating) initiation age-sets.

Hobley and Dundas both mention Endaramuroni clans who were Cushitic-speaking pastoralists. Dundas, Lawren and Muriuki concur in dating their arrival in the area south of Mount Kenya as a mid-nineteenth-century event. Dundas states that:

> In those days the Aikipiak Masai occupied the Laikipia Plateau, the Purko Masai were at Naivasha, the Kaputei in the Kidong Valley and the Tarosero at Iriaini. The Dorobo, who were still the dominant tribe

occupied with the Kikuyu the present Kikuyu country . . . With all these tribes the Endaramuroni (who had settlements at Nyeri, Naivasha and throughout the Kikuyu country) lived in a state of chronic warfare.   (Dundas 1908:137)

Dundas' informants advised him that the Maasai, Kikuyu and Dorobo had all joined forces in order to expel these foreign invaders.

Muriuki feels that his work largely confirms the accounts of Dundas and the Routledges. However, these earlier accounts were based upon the recollections of Kikuyu informants who were suffering considerably at the hands of the European settlers. Therefore the data gathered by the early British historians should be seen in light of the plight of their informants. They all used 'Chief Karuri' as an informant. Karuri was a Kikuyu paramount chief who had been assigned his office by the colonial government. By all accounts he was an avaricious individual who was intensely disliked by his Kikuyu subjects. Karuri claimed Dorobo ancestry which might best be understood as an assertion of primordial rights to lands which were previously acquired from Dorobo by Kikuyu and which were now being confiscated by white settlers. The obsession of early colonial documents with the issue of Kikuyu land tenure appears aimed at discrediting Kikuyu rights to remain in the region which they had converted for agricultural use. It may well have been in reaction to these efforts that so many Kikuyu were espousing Dorobo ancestry. Due to the emotions which surrounded the subject of land, it is difficult to determine the exact nature of the Kikuyu process of land acquisition, as well as their indigenous system of land tenure.

Some Kikuyu claimed to have purchased their lands from Dorobo, using goats as currency. Such statements may have been motivated by the desire to make the process of land acquisition comprehensible in European terms. Such is the nature of the debate between Mortimer (for the Commissioner of Lands) and Wade (Chief Native Commissioner) in the *Kenya Land Commission Report* of 1933, in which Mortimer states:

> So far as can be traced, no claim to outright ownership of land based on individual or family purchase has ever been advanced by any body of natives in Kenya except by one small section of the Kikuyu tribe— the Kiambu section. . . . According to C. W. Hobley (1912), heads of family paid purchase money to Dorobo and became landlords; as rent they received a biennial portion of harvested produce. . . . The Commissioner cites evidence from other areas of Africa . . . to advance the contention that private ownership (as opposed to tribal or communal ownership with individual use rights) is an alien concept to

the Kiambu of Kikuyu as well; purchase and sale of land are inconceivable to an African. Where the concept of private ownership exists, it is by European influence.

(British Colonial Government 1933 1:28–33)

In defence of African rights, Wade states:

I do not believe that any Kikuyu ever bought land from any Dorobo in the sense in which we use the words 'to buy'. It is, however, certain that individual Kikuyu did make friendly arrangements of some sort with the Dorobo under which the former were allowed to cultivate within the hunting grounds of the latter, and it is equally certain that in consideration of this permission, the Kikuyu paid considerable fees to the hunters. The effect of the whole transaction was not very different . . . from the effect of sale and purchase.   (ibid:43)

As an educated African, and spokesman for his people on the issue of Kikuyu land rights, Kenyatta (1938) described the system of land tenure as one in which the family heads who had cleared the forest had inalienable use-rights which were passed on to their offspring. The clan, however, was held to be the 'owner' of the land and was the ultimate mediator in any land disputes. There was also a system of tenant farming in which an 'ahoi' could work land belonging to another individual. His indebtedness was met through payment of a portion of his produce to the owner of the land.

Thus, in pre-colonial times, there appears to have been a system of granting access to the means of production for individuals who could not claim land tenure through clan membership. This was a strong mechanism for absorbing strangers into the Kikuyu economy. Such mechanisms were destroyed, along with the native economy, by the Europeans.

European preference for settlement in the temperate and relatively disease-free Mount Kenya highlands resulted in the alienation of Kikuyu lands. The settlers also aimed to destroy the Kikuyu's ability to subsist within an autonomous native economy in order to force them into wage-labour on European farms. The colonial period was one of such severe disenfranchisement of Africans, especially the Kikuyu, that it is on the basis of the social environment in which historical data were collected that I question the reliability of these accounts.

Perhaps the most reliable sources on social and economic processes prior to the establishment of Kenya as a colony are the travel journals of the late-nineteenth-century explorers. The explorers (Arkell-Hardwick 1903; Chanler 1896; Hohnel 1894 and 1938; MacDonald 1899;

Neumann 1898; Smith 1897; Stigand 1910 and Thomson 1885) all came into frequent contact with many groups of Dorobo. They present vivid accounts of the effects of the ivory and slave trades on the interior of Kenya and northern Tanzania prior to its usurpation as a British Protectorate.

Following are two quotations from Thomson, the first British explorer to travel through Maasailand to the Mount Kenya area. The first quote is a typical description of the radical changes which were occurring at the time, while the latter quote is a description of Dorobo:

The people (Wakwavi) of Njemps presented an interesting study to the observer as throwing light upon the origin of the various small tribes which people Africa. Unquestionably Masai in race, and only separated from that tribe through the loss of their cattle and the consequent necessity of breaking their cherished convictions by cultivating the soil, they have developed new ideas, manners, and customs in a comparatively short period . . . They lead upon the whole a very miserable life, ever threatened with destruction by the Masai, who have swept off several villages and all of their cattle.   (263)

This tribe (Dorobo) is a small race of people scattered over Masailand, who gain their entire livelihood by the chase. They neither keep cattle nor cultivate the land. The antelope, the buffalo and the elephant supply them with such meat as they may desire, while they always find neighbouring tribes, less skilful in hunting, eager to exchange vegetable food for game. The elephant, however, seems to be their staple food, and as a rule the Andorobbo are to be found only where those animals abound. . . . They are rarely found in numbers and usually in very small villages, so that there is nothing like tribal life among them.   (202)

Arkell-Hardwick, Chanler, Neumann and Thomson all describe the Dorobo as 'degenerate' Maasai who speak the Maasai language. Smith states: 'I use the term Wandorobbo to designate the poor of any tribe who live by hunting and fishing'(303). Boyes advises us that Dorobo is 'a term of contempt among the Kikuyu, as the word means a man without anything, a wanderer without possessions' (1911:213).

In summary, these journals are explicit in considering the Dorobo to be disenfranchised members of other groups, yet there are frequent references to 'true Dorobo' who speak distinct languages. Writing on the Dorobo of northern Tanzania, Maguire (1927–28) also comments on two types of Dorobo; some were linguistically and physically identical to members of the groups with whom they were associated. Maguire concluded that, in such instances, the Dorobo were, in fact, impoverished members of their associated groups who, having lost their cattle, had resorted to hunting and gathering and were thus referred to as Dorobo by their more affluent kin. He noted that the acquisition of cattle immediately converted them back to fully fledged membership in the group. He noted, however, that the Mosiro and Aramanik Dorobo possessed languages of their own, while living in close association with the Maasai. Many Mosiro were members, by adoption, of Maasai clans and received frequent rations from the Maasai. Maguire was informed that the Mosiro had helped the Maasai on many occasions in the past, particularly during the great cattle epidemic of the 1890s. In the past, when the Mosiro acquired cattle they had slaughtered and eaten them but, at the time of Maguire's visit, they were beginning to herd cattle. Yet the Mosiro were not considered to be a Maasai by virtue of cattle ownership. As for the Aramanik Dorobo, their language was distinct from both Mosiro and Maasai. An Aramanik informant advised Maguire: 'We are not Masai, but they are our brothers, and we have married their women and they ours. Now we live with our cattle, like the Masai' (249).

In light of the two types of Dorobo, it seems relevant to look at the processes involved in 'becoming Dorobo' and then to evaluate whether or not these processes could have influenced the formation of such groups prior to the mid-nineteenth century when Swahili and Arab intervention occurred in the form of the ivory trade and intensified slave-raiding.

The latter half of the nineteenth century was an era of severe disruption. Both the Chagga of northern Tanzania and the Kamba of central Kenya were engaged in capturing slaves for the coastal trade. Peoples of the interior had begun to acquire guns and to live in heavily stockaded villages. Those who inhabited areas adjacent to the trade routes, especially the Maasai, suffered from virgin exposure to smallpox while cattle populations were decimated by bovine pleuro-pneumonia. Thus, for the Maasai, reductions in the number of both productive adults and livestock had offset the delicate balance in the economically viable ratio of herders to animals, forcing large numbers of pastoralists to seek alternative modes of subsistence.

Waller (1976) discusses their alternatives. Many Maasai hired themselves out as mercenaries to despots, such as the Chagga chief, who sought to profit from the ivory and slave trades. These Maasi received a portion of the spoils from livestock raiding in return for their services as mercenaries. Other Maasai settled amongst horticulturalists, using existing kinship ties and trading relationships as an entrée into a specific farming community. Still others regrouped in order to restore the man-to-cattle ratio and to aggregate enough warriors to conduct cattle raids upon neighbouring peoples, including other Maasai clans. Thus internecine fighting was rife. These circumstances conditioned the Maasai to cooperate with the British during the first decades of the colonial era; thus they settled temporarily on missions or served in punitive expeditions which the British conducted upon people, such as the Nandi, who attempted armed resistance, and for which the Maasai received payment in livestock. Others functioned as intermediaries in supplying the trade caravans with produce grown by farmers, a mode of livelihood which the Swahili traders specifically associated with Dorobo.

In view of these severe social and economic disruptions, it should come as no surprise that the accounts of the first British explorers almost all concur in describing the Dorobo as an inferior class of Maasai. Many Dorobo explicitly stated that they *were* Maasai (or Samburu) who had lost their cattle during the epidemics. Not only were the late-nineteenth-century Dorobo the major suppliers of ivory for the coastal traders, but the early accounts also contain many comments on their role as local entrepreneurs; the Mount Kenya Dorobo delivered Kikuyu produce to the trade caravans at Mianzini, a Swahili entrepôt near Lake Naivasha. They also delivered Kikuyu produce to Maasai pastoralists, due, perhaps to a deterioration in direct trading relationships between the two latter groups as a result of intensified cattle raiding.

The appendix of Spencer's 1973 monograph is one of the few sources on Dorobo under colonial administration and it also provides an outstanding account of recent Dorobo–Samburu relationships. Spencer claims that, as individuals, the Dorobo collaborated with the administration and many entered into government service. As loosely organized and geographically remote groups, however, the Dorobo created an administrative problem with regard to tax collection and confinement to the reserves. A Dorobo reserve was established on the Leroghi Plateau, north of Mount Kenya, in order to contain both the Maasai and the Dorobo who had evaded their official removal from Laikipia in 1911 when this area was opened to European settlement. Other groups of Dorobo were sent to the Samburu Reserve and were considered to be 'Samburu' by the administration for the purposes of tax collection. These

Dorobo, however, remained socially and economically apart from the Samburu. Additionally, the Doldol Reserve, north of the Samburu Reserve, was established for a number of other Dorobo groups, many of whom were linguistically distinct from one another.

Spencer witnessed a general pattern in Dorobo migration during his period of field work in the early 1960s and assumes that this pattern probably reflects their behaviour during much of the colonial period. Dorobo groups tended to remain closely associated with their traditional hunting grounds and to adapt themselves socially to new immigrant groups. Territorial ties were important since knowledge of the area was essential to their bee-keeping economy. Whether the Dorobo were officially classified as belonging to neighbouring tribes, as illegal immigrants to their former territories or as squatters on European farms, they showed a persistent tendency to migrate back to their former territories where they lived in small, inaccessible groups. Since hunting was now forbidden to them, attempts were constantly being made to provide the Dorobo with cattle or to settle them among farmers. Although many of them had acquired stock and thus practised animal husbandry in addition to bee-keeping, they were almost always regarded as Dorobo by their neighbours, due to differences in attitude and behaviour. The Dorobo were more often monogamous than polygynous; they were endogamous by comparison to the standards of their neighbours. However, they practised a mode of subsistence that did not favour the accumulation of brideprice in cattle, a situation which enforced their exclusion from economic participation and social reproduction with their more affluent neighbours. The Dorobo played distinct roles in the rituals in which both they and their neighbours participated, supplying the honeywine for circumcisions and, in some cases, performing the circumcision operation (Cf. Blackburn, this volume). Finally, they were purported to be excellent sorcerers and were usually regarded with suspicion by surrounding peoples.

Spencer also provides a brief history of the Doldol Reserve. Since it was initially administered by the government station at Nanyuki, a considerable distance away, the authorities paid little attention to the Reserve. Thus it appeared as an unadministered 'paradise' and attracted individual pastoralists and farmers who were trying to escape overcrowded conditions in neighbouring reserves. Periodic attempts were made to return migrants to their former reserves, with little regard for the links that individuals had established with the various Dorobo groups of Doldol. In the mid-1950s, the local administration was moved to Doldol and the policy of deporting immigrants and their stock was intensified. The area was systematically depopulated of Maasai, Samburu and Kikuyu at frequent intervals. Since the administration held the misconception that Dorobo groups were specific and rigid tribes, they attempted to identify those groups which had a right to remain and those which should be expelled. The rifts between different Dorobo families and groups were greatly exacerbated by this situation. Since very few individuals could claim indigenous rights to live in the reserve, there were many allegations of false ancestry made to the administration as some people sought to establish their own rights to remain at the expense of their neighbours.

The case of Doldol draws our attention to the precise conditions which led to the intensification of ethnic differences in East Africa and to the reification of the European notion of 'tribe' in the minds of the indigenous actors.

The relationships of East Africans who have been subjected to the colonial experience stand in marked contrast to those which obtained prior to colonialism. Previously a Maasai could 'become Dorobo' through the loss of livestock but could once again 'become Maasai' through reacquisition of cattle. A landless individual could 'become an ahoi' on a Kikuyu farm. The coastal trade had provided still more options in the form of new entrepreneurial roles for those who had become alienated from their traditional modes of subsistence. Colonialism eradicated the apparent close association between ethnic identity and mode of subsistence while simultaneously destroying the social mechanisms by which people of varying modes of subsistence could participate in the social and economic life of the region. Colonialism also made the notion of 'tribe' a salient factor in African competition for rapidly diminishing resources. Therefore it is legitimate to question the degree to which the ethnographic present can shed light on East Africa's past. What the present and recent history *do* tell us is that regional processes are far more significant than are the particular life-styles of present day marginal groups.

It might be more accurate to classify the practitioners of the hunting and gathering mode of subsistence as 'nomads without cattle', rather than as populations which hunt and gather by their own preference and intent or through lack of technological development.

Bibliography

Arkell-Hardwick, A. 1903. *An ivory trader in northern Kenya*. London: Longman
Beech, M. W. H. 1915. 'Pre-Bantu occupants of East Africa'. *Man* 15:40–1
Blackburn, R. 1971. 'Honey in Okiek personality, culture and society'. Unpublished abstract of thesis, Michigan State University
    1973. 'Okiek ceramics: Evidence for Central Kenya prehistory'. *Azania* VIII:55–70
    1974. 'The Okiek and their history'. *Azania* IX:139–57
Boyes, J. 1911. *John Boyes, king of Wakikuyu*. London: Methuen
British Colonial Government 1933. *Kenya Land Commission report*, I London:HM Stationery Office
Chanler, W. A. 1896. *Through jungle and desert, travels in eastern Africa*. London: Macmillan
Dundas, K. R. 1908. 'Notes on the origin and history of the Kikuyu and Dorobo tribes'. *Man* 8:136–9
Hobley, C. W. 1903a. 'Notes concerning the Eldorobo of Mau, British East Africa'. *Man* 3:33–4
    1903b. 'Anthropological studies in Kavirondo and Nandi'. *Jour. of the Anthropological Institute* 33
    1905. 'Further notes on the El Dorobo or Oggiek'. *Man* 5:39–44
    1906. 'Notes on the Dorobo people and other tribes; gathered from Chief Karuri and others'. *Man* 6:1119–20
Hohnel, L. von 1894. *Discovery by Count Teleki of Lakes Rudolf and Stefanie*, I and II. London: Longman
    1938. 'The Lake Rudolf Region: its discovery and subsequent exploration, 1888–1909'. *Jour. of the Royal African Society*. 37:21–45; 206–26
Hollis, A. C. 1909. *The Nandi*. Oxford: Clarendon Press
Huntingford, G. W. B. 1951. 'The social institutions of the Dorobo'. *Anthropos* 46:1–48
    1954. 'The political organization of the Dorobo'. *Anthropos* 49:123–48
Kenyatta, J. 1938. *Facing Mount Kenya*. London: Martin Secker and Warburg, Inc.
Lawren, W. L. 1968. 'Masai and Kikuyu: an historical analysis of cultural transmission'. *Jour. of African History* IX(4):571–83
MacDonald, J. R. L. 1899. 'Notes on the ethnology of tribes met with during the progress of the Juba expedition of 1897–99'. *Jour. of the Royal Anthropological Institute* 29
Maguire, R. A. J. 1927–8. 'Il-Torobo'. *Jour. of the Royal African Society* XXVII:127–41; 249–68
Muriuki, G. 1974. *A history of the Kikuyu, 1500–1900*. London: Oxford U. Press
Neumann, A. H. 1898. *Elephant hunting in east equatorial Africa*. London: Rowland Ward
Routledge, W. S. and Routledge, K. 1910. *With a prehistoric people: the Kikuyu of British East Africa*. London: Arnold
Schapera, I. 1949. *Some problems of anthropological research in Kenya Colony*. For International African Institute, London: Oxford
Smith, A. Donaldson 1897. *Through unknown African countries*. London: Arnold

Spencer, P. 1973. *Nomads in alliance: symbiosis and growth among the Rendille and Samburu of Kenya*. London: Oxford U. Press

Stigand, C. H. 1910. *To Abyssinia through an unknown land*. London: Seeley

Thomson, J. 1885. *Through Masailand*. London: Samson Low

Waller, R. 1976. 'The Maasai and the British 1895–1905: the origins of an alliance'. *Jour. of African History* xvii(4):529–53

13. In the land of milk and honey: Okiek adaptations to their forests and neighbours

RODERIC H. BLACKBURN

The Okiek are a hunting and gathering or foraging people inhabiting the central highland forests of Kenya which are interspersed among open woodlands and plains inhabited by horticultural and pastoral tribes. Understanding the Okiek requires an understanding of their adaptations to both their natural and their social environments. As will be described in this paper, Okiek use of their forest and its resources and their relationships to neighbouring tribes are mutually interdependent, neither one possible or explicable without the other. The complexity of their relationships can be explained in terms of certain needs which the tribes fulfil for each other and by the fact that the Okiek are a small scattered people in close proximity to larger and more powerful tribes, yet the Okiek inhabit a distinctly different ecological niche.

This chapter is based on data derived from my field work among the Okiek of the Mau Forest in Narok District during the period 1968 to 1970, and from the writings of travellers, government officers and other anthropologists who have contacted Okiek groups throughout the highlands of Kenya over the last century. Unless otherwise indicated, the ethnographic data presented here refer to three Okiek groups with whom I had first-hand experience: the Kaplelach, Kapsupulek and Kipchorn'wonek II (see Figure 13.2).

Okiek history and identity

The Okiek have been known in the literature primarily as the 'Dorobo', a general term derived from the Swahili 'Wandorobo' which itself comes from the Maasai 'Il Toroboni' meaning a person who is so poor that he owns no cattle and thus must subsist on wild meat, a regrettable low state for anyone in Maasai eyes. The term was thus applied by the Maasai and by early Swahili traders and later Europeans indiscriminately

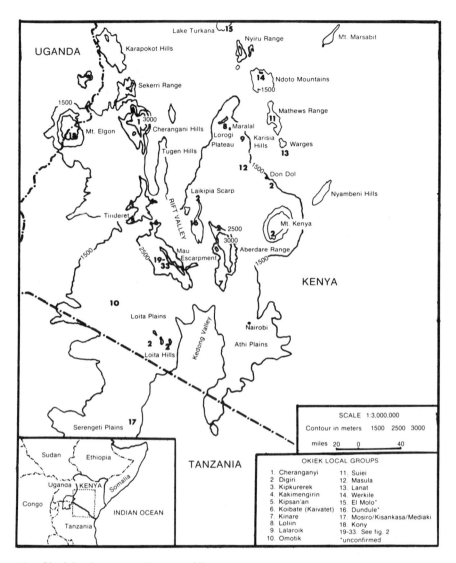

13.1 Okiek local groups in Kenya and Tanzania

to any people who lived by hunting, of which there are and have been several groups in Kenya. The subject of this paper is but one of those groups who call themselves Okiek (Okiot, sing.) and are so called by all other Kalenjin-speaking people. Because of the multiple references of the term 'Dorobo' it is important that the Okiek be distinguished henceforth by their own name.

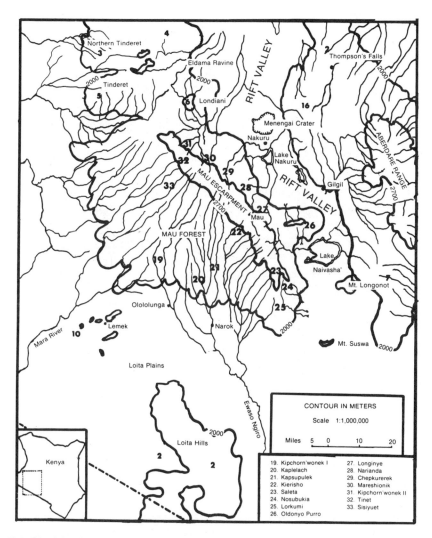

13.2 Okiek local groups in and around the Mau escarpment

The Okiek are composed of at least 33 local groups inhabiting the highland forest regions of Kenya (see Figures 13.1 and 13.2). These forests are geographically divided by valleys and plains in such a way that many Okiek local groups are so distant from each other that they have no knowledge of each other. Nevertheless, they all share, from what evidence I have seen, a number of distinctive and recognizable characteristics of culture, social organization and technology in their foraging

Two Okiek men about to leave for the forest to place a new beehive in the upper branches of a tree (R. Blackburn)

way of life. This supports their own contention that they were once a single group now dispersed for at least several hundred years. Most local groups have taken on superficial characteristics of their neighbouring horticultural and pastoral tribes, leading many early writers to the belief that the Okiek were offshoots of these larger tribes. These writers did not observe the distinctive Okiek characteristics which only a close intimacy would reveal, nor had they the chance to observe that these characteristics were common to all the farflung local groups; it is not surprising that they concluded that the Okiek were derived from these various larger tribes. All people who call themselves Okiek speak a Kalenjin dialect as their first language. Most of them live near one of the principal Kalenjin-speaking peoples such as the Kipsigis, Nandi, Tugen or Marakwet and their dialect usually is more similar to their neighbours than to other Okiek local groups. This proximity and similarity in dialect has prompted some Okiek (and others) to speak of such and such a local group as 'Okiek of Kipsigis' (or Nandi, etc.). Thus one might be led to believe that a local group of Okiek may also be genetically and/or ethnically derived from the larger group. These Okiek, and even the larger groups neighbouring them, will admit on questioning that the Okiek local group is more closely related to other Okiek than to any other group. All Okiek maintain that they are one people in origin who have separated some time in the distant past and now live in different forest regions and have 'become like' their non-Okiek neighbours in language, and to some extent in culture, social organization and technology. Apart from their Kalenjin tongue, most Okiek also speak the language of their most prominent non-Kalenjin neighbours, who in many cases are the Maasai. Apparent assimilation has gone further with some Okiek local groups than others. Thus the Digiri are to outward appearances Maasai, speaking that tongue as their domestic language and keeping herds of cattle as their main subsistence. Yet they acknowledge and are so acknowledged by other Okiek as being of common Okiek origin, they practise hunting and honey collecting in the Okiek manner. Even their pottery has the same distinctive style as that of other Okiek.

Perhaps the most interesting clue to a common Okiek history is the fact that one local group, the Omotik, who, like the Digiri, keep cattle and speak Maasai as their domestic language, not only know Kalenjin but in addition know a third language which is unintelligible to Maasai and Kalenjin speakers. This has been identified (Heine 1971:54–5) as a derivative of 'Proto-Southern Nilotic' from which 'Proto-Kalenjin' later developed (see also Blackburn 1973:57); which is to say that the Omotik language, which may or may not once have been shared by all other Okiek, split from the main Kalenjin stock as much as 1,500 years ago (estimate by glottochronology, Heine 1972), suggesting a distinct identity for these foragers of considerable antiquity. This conforms with the Okiek assertion that they were living in central Kenya prior to the arrival of any other presently existing people, an assertion which is also supported by the traditions of the other groups such as the Kikuyu, Maasai, Kipsigis, etc.

Social and political organization

The Okiek are composed of local groups each with its own name and area of residence. Each local group, in turn, is made up of patrilineally related lineages which constitute the principal units of Okiek social organization. The lineage is the corporate organization in Okiek society, as it is the ownership unit of rights to some natural resources, the social unit responsible for giving daughters in marriage, for negotiating and paying compensation in legal cases, and the unit of residence. Typically a lineage is composed of all the descendants of a common male ancestor of the third or fourth ascending generation, about 50 to 80 people, or about 10 to 15 families, the male heads of which are brothers or close or distant cousins. Cross-cutting the descent system is an age-set system which unites all men, regardless of lineage or local group, into peer-group relations for various purposes, but especially for defence and hunting. In the absence of formal positions of authority like headmen or chiefs, or even formal councils, the Okiek maintain social control through the influence of informal meetings of lineage members, the age-set system, and the internalized norms of proper social conduct.

Subsistence

To my knowledge all Okiek groups continue to hunt animals and gather wild food, principally honey. In the last century, especially within recent generations, most, but not all, Okiek have added some horticulture and/or animal husbandry to their subsistence base. Even the most pastoral or agricultural of Okiek, however, continue to hunt actively and gather food. The Kaplelach local group, with whom I did most of my field work, are probably the most conservative of Okiek, only some of them having recently experimented with domestic food subsistence.

The Okiek hunt virtually all mammals which inhabit their area. In the case of the Okiek of Mau, these include both forest and plains game, from the smallest dik-dik antelope to elephants. Hunting on the plains is a matter of individual or small-group tracking, stalking and killing with arrows, or, in the case of the largest animals, using poison-tipped spears. Hunting in the forest, on the other hand, requires dogs to bring game to bay when spears are used at close range to kill the quarry. Smaller antelope are taken in snares in the forest, as well. As for collecting, the Okiek are especially known for their collecting of honey. Indeed, honey and its derivative, an alcoholic drink like mead, are of primary importance in Okiek society, culture and personality. Honey's symbolic importance permeates all aspects of Okiek life in much the same way as do cattle in African pastoral societies. To a great extent, Okiek adaptation to a foraging way of life derives from their desire to

acquire and use honey. This is true despite the fact that honey contributes no more than 15 per cent to the Okiek diet. The Okiek are also
unusual, in comparison to other hunting and gathering societies,
because they rely heavily on meat and very little on wild vegetable
foods.[1] This reflects the fact that they live in a high altitude forest with
a relatively stable moist climate which makes possible a dependable
and abundant supply of game the year around, but with a virtual absence
of wild fruits, nuts and tubers, the type of food-encapsuled seed associated with harsher climates. Parenthetically this also means that the
Okiek subsistence is almost exclusively a male activity. All these factors
distinguish the Okiek as being unusual in adaptation compared to their
neighbours, and, indeed, unusual compared to most foraging societies.

Also unusual, and clearly related, is the elaboration of the Okiek
resource-tenure system. I use the term 'resource-tenure' instead of territoriality or land-tenure because the Okiek system, although initially
involved with land, is primarily, in their eyes, a means to allocate natural resources, especially honey, while avoiding interpersonal or interlineage competition for these resources. The following explanation
should make this clear:

The high forests of Kenya, where the Okiek live, are on the sides of
mountains, mountain ranges, or escarpments; each forest grades in
elevation from about 1,800 metres – the level of the plains and valley –
up to 2,600 or more metres. On the south side of the Mau Escarpment,
for example, the gradation begins in the south and rises over a 40-mile
slant to the north. Moving upward, from south to north, the average
yearly temperature tends to decrease and the amount of rainfall to
increase. The result is a series of parallel vegetation zones about every
150–200 metres of elevation which run east and west in bands (Figure
13.3). The Okiek recognize basically four different forest types beginning at the edge of the plains at 2,000 metres' elevation. The lowest is
the dry, fairly open forest they call *soyua*. Next comes a dense forest,
similar to the deciduous forest of the eastern United States, which they
call *sasaondet*. Next is a lush mature forest of large trees and low green
underbrush called *tirap*, or, where rainfall is heavier, a wet bamboo
forest called *sisiyuet*. These are followed in drier areas at 2,650 metres'
elevation by an open glade or moorland with intermittent mature trees
which they call *oloprigit* or *mau*. Each forest has its distinctive trees and
shrubs. Hence, trees flower, and honey is produced by bees, at different times of the year in each forest type, though especially after the
rainy seasons. This is of primary importance to the Okiek, for gathering

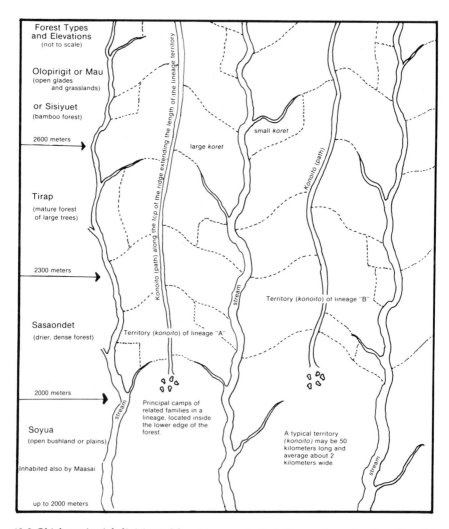

13.3 Okiek territorial divisions, Mau escarpment. Each lineage has a territory (*konoito*) bordered by adjacent streams which is made up of smaller parcels of land (*koret*). Each territory extends through four or five forest types

honey is their chief interest in utilizing the forests within which they live. A second advantage of the forest to the Okiek is the fact that, despite dry seasons, the forest holds moisture and ground water sufficient to maintain plant growth the year around, resulting in a stable population of wild game for food. Traditionally this meat has comprised as much as 75 per cent of the Okiek diet. But even though honey comprises only 15 per cent of the diet, it is honey which primarily motivates Okiek use of the forests. They expend up to 50 times more time and effort for a pound of honey than for a pound of meat,[2] a measure of how important the Okiek view honey to be for their social life, cultural beliefs, personal needs, and relations with other ethnic groups.

These four forest types run parallel to each other going east and west, with the elevation increasing from south to north. The one additional topographical feature is a series of parallel streams running from north to south, cross-cutting the forest types. The strips of land between the streams – about a mile and a half in average width and over 30 miles long – are each, in a particular sense, 'owned' by separate lineages. These lineage 'territories', which they call *konoito* (*konituek*, pl.), are actually rights to exclusive use for the purpose of gathering honey either from natural beehives in hollow trees or from hives which the Okiek make themselves from hollowed-out, 5-foot sections of logs placed in the branches of high trees. This should clearly be distinguished from our own notion of land tenure. Indeed, the Okiek may do anything they want in any *konoito* – hunt, live, collect berries, etc. – except gather honey, place hives or use forest products to make hives in any *konoito* but their own. Why not restrict hunting to one's own *konoito*? The Okiek say, 'that is silly – there is plenty of game for everyone – and besides, since these animals wander all over the forest, how can you say one animal is yours when tomorrow it may be in someone else's *konoito*?'[3] But you make ask: bees also go here and there, how can you claim that bees in your *konoito* are yours alone? To this the Okiek concede you are right, but they feel that the honey, being in hives, is stationary and its supply is limited and that if others take honey from natural hives there will be less for oneself. Secondly, they admit that the desire for honey is so great that there is too much temptation to steal from others' hives. Thus, excluding others from your own *konoito* will militate not only against loss of honey, but, importantly, against the interpersonal friction and fighting which would result. In this respect, the Okiek have always had a problem with social control in the absence of authority figures. Interlineage feuding was, until recently, a major problem, resulting in retaliatory killing of men, women and children, even to the extinction of at least one lineage in the area where I worked.

The resource-tenure system is even more complex. Each lineage *konoito* is divided into as many as two dozen smaller areas each called a *koret* (*korosiek*, pl.), and even a large *koret* will be subdivided. Each *koret* may be a mile to ten square miles in size. In the larger lineages these korets (to anglicize the Okiek word for convenience henceforth) are assigned to individual families, thereby replicating the same separation of people in terms of rights to honey as is found in the larger *konoito* system. The manner in which the *konoito* system has developed over time, and the way korets are sometimes sold or given to others, even between lineages, is a complex and fascinating subject which can be only briefly alluded to here. Korets are economically important for the opportunities they provide for collecting honey. They are the single most valuable commodity that an Okiek man will inherit from his father. Korets are almost as important socially as they are economically because they are used to satisfy a wide range of social indebtedness. A man can give his korets to another person or lineage as he pleases. These types of transfer include giving a koret(s) in marriage, or in gratitude to a kin relation of importance, or as an outright sale. A lineage can give a koret(s) to another lineage. This is usually done as compensation for interlineage homicide. This type of payment usually takes place after an extended period of feuding in which deaths on both sides have exhausted the survivors to the extent that both lineages agree to cease hostilities, hold a peace ceremony (*tumdo op ngaungisto*, lit.: ceremony of (removing) the curse) and settle the deaths by paying out korets and sometimes honey, ivory and money.

Looking at the Okiek use of their resources and land through a period of time, we typically find members of a lineage living about half the year in scattered camps in the low elevation forest of *soyua*, with ready access to the open plains for hunting, but still hidden within the forest for protection from other more powerful neighbours like the Maasai. The rest of the year is spent going to and from the various forests to collect honey as different trees flower. This is the natural advantage of a lineage *konoito* extending uphill through all the forest types – it gives each lineage equal access to all types of forest resources. Individual families alone or the families of brothers together tend to compose the units which camp and travel together. Much of the time spent in various forests is devoted to collecting honey from one's own hives, repairing old hives, making new ones, and placing them in suitable trees, high out of reach of the forest scourge, the honey badger. Hunting is a by-product of going from one hive to the next. On the way, dogs usually catch the scent of an animal, chase it, bring it to bay and the men spear it. It is usual to get one animal sometime during the day. If one is staying in camp for a period of time then snare traps can be set up in the area providing an adequate supply of meat without having to hunt.

Although the Okiek are adapted to a high forest environment primarily because of their interest in honey, it is evident to me that at least two other necessities for survival are forest-related. Clearly they cannot live on a honey diet alone, and are thus largely dependent on meat. Forest hunting is feasible, however, only because the Okiek have dogs. Without dogs to bring game to bay, that is, within sight and range to kill, the Okiek could probably not live in the forest for long. Interestingly, the Okiek procure most good dogs from the Maasai, who make little use of them. The second important aspect of the forest for the Okiek is the necessary protection it affords to this relatively powerless tribe. The Maasai have for centuries been the terror of the plains – defeating, driving off, even annihilating any group that got in their way – groups much larger and more powerful than the Okiek. The Okiek, however, have survived, even prospered, despite their propinquity to the Maasai and, elsewhere, several other large tribes. Why? There are a number of reasons, a discussion of which will explain not only how the Okiek survive, but also the ecological distinctions which help clarify the differences between, and hence, identity of, the Okiek and their neighbours.

Intertribal relations

Like the Mbuti Pgymies the first and most important factor in Okiek life is the forest. The Okiek, in part, survive because they are able to hide from danger in the forest. They know the forest and don't get lost in it and have successfully adapted to it. The Maasai, on the other hand, are a plains-dwelling pastoral people who don't know the forest and would very quickly lose themselves in it if they followed the Okiek there. Secondly, cattle are grazers and cannot forage in the forest. This, plus the fact that the Maasai don't know how to collect honey or hunt (even if they would eat game meat, which they despise) preclude them from ever entering the forest. In fact, the Maasai fear the forest and harbour all sorts of unfounded suspicions about the dangers of the forest and of the Okiek, to whom they impute certain malevolent supernatural powers. An aggressive people, the Maasai tended to want to treat the Okiek as they have treated other tribes; but there were and are critical differences. The Okiek, unlike other tribes, do not hold the things the Maasai covet most: cattle, sheep and goats. Furthermore, the Okiek, with nothing to lose or gain, would not stand and fight. The Okiek were and are wisely passive and slip back into the shadows of the forest when confronted by Maasai warriors.

The Okiek on the Mau have been in contact with the present Maasai since the latter invaded the area, nearly 100 years ago. Before that, other Maasai-like pastoralists had been living around the Mau. Today, most people find it impossible to distinguish Okiek from Maasai, as their appearance, ornamentation and dress are very similar. This is an outward expression of the influence Maasai have had on these Okiek. Virtually all Okiek people speak Maasai and have adopted many Maasai words into their own Kalenjin dialect. This is especially true of words for places, trees, age-set names, personal names, and forms of greetings. In Okiek society and culture, Maasai influence is most obvious in clans and the age-set system and its attendant ceremonies. The Okiek children go through a series of scarifications and operations marked by small ceremonies in a manner similar to those of the Maasai. The Okiek now share the Maasai values on possession of cows and 'richness' and, as best they can, try to accumulate stock, pointing with pride to their 'wealth'. At the same time, the Okiek still conceive of themselves as being rich if they have many hives.

The Maasai of Narok District are traditionally only pastoralists, though intermarriage with the agricultural Kikuyu has begun to change this, especially on the fringes of the forest where most Kikuyu live. As the dominant tribe, the Maasai control the local county council and section chiefships.

Pastoralism, like hunting and gathering, is essentially a passive adaptation to an environment. Instead of reworking the land for his livelihood like cultivators, the pastoralist accepts the natural conditions and moves in response to them from place to place, seeking the best water and grass for his stock. Hunters and gatherers are essentially similar, a difference being that it is their 'stock' (wild animals), and not they, who decide when and where to go. This passive responsiveness to nature, and the migrations it entails, contribute to the Maasai attitude that 'progress', e.g. development, building, and its necessary base – education – is irrelevant and also inconsistent with their need to change residence seasonally. If others wish to come and build or to cultivate a few acres here and there, it is no great threat to the Maasai, as a few acres lost to grazing in one place is minuscule compared to the hundreds of miles of plains. If the Kikuyu, for example, wish to clear forests for gardens, there is no loss at all to the Maasai, who have no use for forests. The Maasai can afford to be tolerant of the incursions and development of other non-pastoral groups, as they feel little threat to their own lives. Even the Kikuyu admit, and would like to emulate, the wealth and ease of living that the Maasai enjoy. Since children herd the stock and women milk them, a Maasai man's day is pretty much his own. It must appear silly to many a Maasai man to send children he needs as herd boys to school to learn facts unrelated to pastoralism, so they can get a job and work all their lives, when at home they can be rich and 'permanently retired' most of their lives.

Retirement, however, is relative. The Maasai, in the past, have filled the void of inactivity with an organized warrior age-grade in an age-set system. These warriors, or *morans*, as they are now called even in English, have been involved in cattle raiding and the protection of home against counter-raids. Cattle raiding, the Maasai 'natural sport', is the quickest, yet most gloriously dangerous way of becoming richer.

Both the environmental passiveness and personal aggressiveness of Maasai life are two themes which directly affect Okiek life. The third aspect of Maasai–Okiek relations derives from mutually complementary needs which can be satisfied only by material trade between the two tribes. The combination of these three factors has resulted in a complex relationship between Maasai and Okiek. Anthropologists, with some exceptions (Leach 1954), have ignored the study of intertribal or inter-ethnic group relations, despite the practical and theoretical importance of them, especially when projected on an international level. A small group like the dispersed Okiek compels such a study because relations with other groups are a major part of day-to-day living.

The fundamental reason the Okiek, as a people, have survived the waves of pastoral invasions in central Kenya, when all previous groups have been decimated, scattered, or merged with their conquerors, is that pastoralists have no use for forests. In fact, unequipped with the knowledge to live in the forest, they avoid them, and consequently the forest-dwelling Okiek have generally been unmolested. The corollary to this is that the Okiek had no stock, so the Maasai had little reason to be actively aggressive toward the Okiek. It is this reason, plus the desir-ability of Okiek women as wives, and of their honey based beer, that accounts for the tolerance the Maasai have toward the recent incursions of Kikuyu into Narok District. In contrast to the Kikuyu, the cattle-owning Kipsigis have had a more difficult time getting into Narok. In 1965 the Maasai defeated the Kipsigis, forcing most of them back into the Kipsigis Reserve. Since then, the Kipsigis have begun to infiltrate again, with a resulting series of raids and counter-raids in 1969.

While the Maasai are tolerant to Okiek as a whole, the relationship on an individual level is more ambivalent. Maasai warriors view their role as essentially aggressive and, therefore, have vented their aggression on individuals or small groups of Okiek that they meet by chance along the way. Thus one occasionally hears how Maasai beat and abuse the Okiek into doing things for them, such as slaughtering and cooking a cow for Maasai warriors, or making a shield. The Okiek, aware of their numerical weakness, have been chary about retaliating for fear of far worse retribution. An exception was an age-set of the Maresionik, who had a reputation among Okiek for beating the Maasai. The fact that the Maresionik live on the outer fringe of Maasai territory and outnumber the Maasai in their area, may help explain this apparent anomaly.

Maasai conceptions about the Okiek help to explain their ambivalent attitude toward them. The dominant attitude is that the Okiek are an inferior class of people. They are inferior because they are different, especially in their poverty as they have no cows and must eat wild animals to get meat. To the Maasai this means that the Okiek are without the sense to develop and care for possessions. The Maasai are confirmed in this belief by the fact that in the past any cow they have sold to Okiek has been slaughtered for food. To the Maasai this is tantamount to killing the proverbial golden-egg-laying goose. To Okiek, however, there are at least three good reasons for doing this. One, they cannot care for cattle if they live in a forest. Secondly, if they attempted to keep cattle, the cattle would undoubtedly be stolen from them by Maasai. Third, what few cows they could afford would tend to be those which they would have to purchase for specific ceremonies at which the cattle must be slaughtered for food (and for fat, which is symbolically important). Though Okiek desire as much as do the Maasai to be rich, they do not find the Maasai any more likeable for it. One day I was driving up the Mau when some Maasai were walking home and waved to me for a ride. A resentful Okiek riding with me sternly said, 'Go on. Don't pick them up. They give no thanks. They are rich.'

Many of the Maasai I talked with about Okiek were not candid, reflecting their assumption that I had a vested interest in the Okiek and their real opinion of them would not please me. When I did get some comments out of Maasai, their actual knowledge of Okiek was slight, compared to their opinions and misconceptions. In fact, Okiek life is a mystery to the Maasai. They know Okiek kill animals and collect honey and that they are similar to Maasai in appearance and in some ceremonies. Maasai are, however, curious about the Okiek. They feel there is something mysterious, unknowable about them. They brought up the subject of the Okiek more in hopes of learning some dark secrets from me than to divulge anything themselves. No doubt the fact that Okiek life is largely hidden by a forest the Maasai fear to enter in part accounts for the curiosity and exaggerated misconceptions the Maasai have about Okiek.

According to Jacobs (1965, and personal communication) the Maasai view the Okiek as being poor because they are gluttonous and stupid. They 'eat the heifer', that is, they are profligate. They are such gluttons that they eat foul meat. Also, they say that the Okiek easily lose their tempers and 'get physical', fighting among themselves and beating their wives – behaviour the Maasai find shameful. The Maasai say the Okiek have no sense of honour, that they will do things for aggrandizement, such as sorcery, without any sense of shame. In the presence of Okiek, Maasai will act brave, as they respect an Okiot's ability to fight with another, but, unlike Maasai, the Okiek are not organized for large-scale combat.

Spencer (1965:285) reports similar attitudes about Okiek among the Samburu (actually Il Kitoip, a branch of pastoral Maasai): 'They are Dorobo; they have no sense of respect; their girls make notoriously bad wives, and marriages with them generally do not last. And, above all, the Dorobo know the secrets of sorcery and will not hesitate to use it against their personal enemies.' 'The Dorobo make honey-beer and drink it regularly; this frequently leads to quarreling among them and this, possibly more than anything else, confirms the Samburu view of them that they have no sense of respect.' 'They are people who are prepared to use any mystical powers at their disposal for their own ends.'

In the Maasai origin myth, an Okiek man figures prominently as annoying God by his profligate behaviour (some versions say jealousy of Maasai) resulting in no more cattle being lowered from heaven. This denied Maasai more cattle. At the same time, however, God condemned the Okiek to live only by wild animals thereafter. The story, with various forms, both rationalizes Maasai hostility to Okiek and also confirms a feeling that Okiek are neither capable nor deserving of keeping cattle.

Okiek relations with Maasai, however, do not consist entirely of begrudged tolerance or active abuse. The Maasai, in a number of ways, are dependent on the Okiek. The most obvious way is the fact that Maasai use honey and do not get enough from occasional natural hives to satisfy their needs. Honey is useful as food, and especially as wine. It is also a necessary part of ceremonial ritual, much as it is among the

Okiek. The Okiek barter honey directly with the Maasai or, these days, usually sell it to the shops in trading centres, from which Maasai and others subsequently purchase it as needed.

There is another way by which some Maasai get honey, and this is by relations of friendship between individual Maasai and Okiek, one of the principal mechanisms of exchange between the two peoples. Most Okiek men have at least one Maasai, usually of their own age-set and often of the same clan (in either case they are already terminologically 'brother'), with whom they have a convenient, sometimes close, personal relationship. The Maasai establish friendship relations by giving a heifer or cow to another, the value of the present influencing the type of friendship. This in turn is acknowledged by use of one of three grades of terms of address between the two friends. The origins of these friendships is most fortuitous. Thus one Okiot has made friends with a Maasai who happened along when other Maasai were about to beat him. His soon-to-be friend took pity on him and managed to extricate him from his misfortune. Since then, as the Okiot told me, whenever his friend has slaughtered a cow or sheep, he brings a leg to him while he, in turn, brings him some of the honey he gets each season. The Okiek recognize that the usefulness of these relations can extend beyond occasional gifts of meat. If a man, for example, has to hold a ceremony, such as an initiation for his child, he can go to his friend for a gift or credit for a sheep to slaughter, if he is without one then or has no money to buy one. If a cow dies of disease, a Maasai is as likely to call on his Okiek friend to see if he wants it for eating (Okiek believe that the disease will not be transmitted to the consumer). If either is holding a ceremony, he will invite his opposite to come and enjoy the liquor and food. Occasionally, having a Maasai friend, especially if he is of the same clan, is politically useful for gaining a favour or dismissing a complaint. Thus one lineage of Okiek of the Lugumoi clan used their 'relationship' with an influential Maasai chief of the same clan to help them deal with Maasai who had stolen some of their property. This type of relationship, however, is not primarily based on friendship and exchange of goods, though it may be reinforced by such transactions. Rather, it is a fictive kin relationship, connoting 'brotherhood' in the same clan. In fact, within memory, various Okiek lineages have adopted Maasai clan names, primarily, they say, to cement friendship relations by making them kin relations and thus transferable through generations. Thus current kin relationships had their beginnings as friendships originating when the present Maasai came to this country about

100 years ago. Though the kinship remains, the original friendships are fading in memory. Maasai would comment to me that those Okiek of such and such a place are related to them, 'somehow', and indeed the Maasai feel some sort of bond with those Okiek, addressing them as 'brother' or 'sister'.

Trade between Maasai and Okiek can involve an astonishing number of items that are produced by both groups in excess of their needs. Honey and domestic stock are the two most important items. In addition to these, I have heard of or seen the Okiek trading the following items: shields of buffalo hide, tobacco containers of ivory and buffalo horn, fly whisks of giraffe and wildebeest tail hair, lion manes, ostrich feathers for headdress, colobus monkey skins for leg bands, kudu horn for trumpet, rhino horn and ivory for chief's club, eland skin for leather thongs, eland meat in extreme necessity for food, ivory to trade with caravans, various animal hides, sword sheaths, and decorative skin necklaces (the latter two are currently manufactured by Okiek in considerable numbers). On occasion, I have seen an Okiot fashion house poles and thatch a house for a Maasai who desired a Kikuyu-type house. Arrows and bows have been actively traded recently, as more Maasai see their utility in defence and for hunting (less traditional Maasai now eat the meat of antelope and the fat of most wild animals).

In addition to trading goods, the Okiek perform services, the most important being that of circumcising Maasai boys. The Maasai and Okiek both say that Okiek have been the circumcisers of Maasai for as long as they can remember. Despite the importance placed on circumcision and the payment of a heifer for the labour, it is not an esteemed position and Maasai will almost always seek out the inferior 'Il Torobo' or Arusha to perform the operation. There is also a certain amount of personal risk to the circumciser, for if he performs a faulty operation he can be beaten (Jacobs, personal communication). Some Okiek suggest that their prominence as circumcisers is a result of the Maasai's first learning of the ritual from the Okiek and, not knowing how to perform it, they had Okiek do it for them. Maasai don't agree with this. Interestingly, most sources credit the Cushites with having 'given' circumcision to the Nilotes (Murdock 1959:337). In view of the apparent fact that the Okiek were the earliest Nilotic speakers to enter central Kenya at a time when Cushites still predominated there, it is quite possible they adopted the rite before the Nilotic Maasai entered the area.

Up until recent years, Maasai warriors would forcibly impress an Okiot into their service to slaughter and cook for them a Maasai ox in the bush. What meat might be left over the Okiot would get, but the abuse he received clearly indicates that his services were involuntary. The Okiek rarely speak of the abuses they have suffered, indicating that the experience must have been quite ego-deflating. Another service, ostensibly voluntary, was for a young Okiot to attach himself to a Maasai family as a herd boy, for which he received his keep and an annual heifer (Jacobs, personal communication). These services, though more dramatic and hence more often spoken of, are less important in Maasai–Okiek relations than the more frequent and more substantial exchange of goods. In return for the wide variety of items traded to the Maasai, the Okiek receive fewer but usually more substantial items, especially cows, sheep and goats. The Okiek have no use for Maasai donkeys. The Maasai use donkeys for transporting household goods when migrating. They are not eaten, even by Okiek. Both Maasai and Okiek, especially the more fastidious warriors, have generalized the Maasai taboo against eating donkeys to not eating zebras. I have never received a consistent rationalization for this, but one explanation is of particular interest to understanding Okiek feelings about animals and people. One day a man replied to this question, saying that zebras are not eaten because they are like donkeys, and donkeys are not eaten because they are beasts of burden. Since donkeys carry things as do women, the two appear to be equated, and since women are not eaten, the idea of eating a donkey, and hence a zebra, is repulsive.

Okiek have always purchased domestic stock for food. They have also adapted it for use in ceremonies. Thus, a cow supplies meat for visitors, since the supply of wild meat is sometimes unpredictable in the lower *soyua* forest near their base camps. A cow or sheep also supplies fat, a highly valued energy food, especially for children. It commands from Maasai and Okiek four times the price per pound of honey or meat in the Narok market place.

The Okiek maintain that they have always made use of domestic animals for these reasons, at least for as long as memory recalls. In the use of these animals, the Okiek have followed similar Maasai traditions, apparently adopting Maasai concepts of the medicinal and supernatural value of meat, and especially of fat. This would not deny, however, the equivalent belief in and use of wild animal meat and fat for these same purposes. Even today, animal fat is eagerly sought, even if it comes from animals otherwise untouched for food, such as cats, birds and snakes.

Domestic animals are the principal items of trade sought from the

Maasai, in large part because the Maasai produce little else. They are not a craft tribe, and in fact, despise such work as the only means by which lesser people, not fortunate enough to have cows, have had to make their living. Occasionally, Okiek will get milk from Maasai, as milk is valued by all ages as a healthful food alone or mixed with 'tea' (made from tea leaves, burned sugar or, traditionally, blood and honey). The Okiek use the thin throat tissue of cows to make their unique scented necklaces. Impregnated with little cups tied in this skin are small amounts of the *sokomik* plant, a sweet-smelling forest plant which Okiek warriors like to wear to be alluring to the girls. The Maasai warriors feel the same way and so pay one shilling and 50 cents per necklace in Narok. In this transaction, the Maasai have sold throat tissue, which comes back to them in the form of a necklace. Okiek, at least those who happen to be camped in *soyua*, will buy, for a few cents, the hoofs and lower legs of butchered Maasai cows. There is some edible fat therein, but also there is marrow for eating and thick leg tendon, which is chewed and then tied on arrows as a binding for holding the arrow head in the shaft. Okiek will also buy cow heads which they boil to make, they say, a delicious soup. Head soup has also been a European and American delicacy, at least up until recently. Cow horns are made into drinking cups, and head skin is used for making sword sheaths which, like necklaces, are actively traded to the Maasai. In recent years cowhides are bought from Maasai, both for making sheaths and for making a sleeping skin – that is, the dried and stretched skin is used in Okiek (and Maasai) homes as a sleeping mat.

All of these items received from Maasai, however, are not essential, as all can be duplicated from wild-animal products. Fat is found especially on the large animals, and skins of eland, bongo and buffalo closely approximate that of cow, while skins of bushbuck, red duikers and yellow-back duikers resemble those of sheep and goats. Milk is only essential for babies and is usually available from the mother. What this means is that the Okiek, in their traditional manner of living, are not dependent on Maasai for specific goods or services. They have traded with Maasai because they can make use of Maasai stock. They may also trade with Maasai for the purpose of creating friendly relations, that is, encouraging Maasai economic dependence on them (at least for honey), in the hope that the Maasai would become emotionally dependent on the Okiek. Certainly, I found that the Okiek are clever manipulators, in that they know the ways of pleasing people in order to get them to do what they want. After the initial distrust of me wore off, I became a frequent object of manipulation for all sorts of things, but especially rides. The Maasai get 'conned' in the same way, usually being invited as an honoured guest to partake of some wine. Following the Maasai's statement of thanks, the host would carefully slip in a request for this or that. In fact, one of the most important functions of honey in social relations is the use of wine to create rapport and facilitate manipulation. Individual Okiek–Maasai friendships may be created, and are certainly encouraged, by wine in this manner. From the Maasai view, on the other hand, Okiek may not need to trade for domestic stock, but undoubtedly the Okiek must see the value of stock and desire it very much, especially as it is the essence of Maasai wealth and prestige. Therefore, an Okiot who wanted to be able to buy a cow would have to be especially considerate to his Maasai acquaintance, in order to have the opportunity to purchase the cow. Hence the need for courteous hospitality and respect deservedly due a rich Maasai.

The Maasai like wine. It is sweet and an effective alcoholic drink. The Okiek drink far more than the Maasai (hence, in part, their reputation among Maasai as 'hot-tempered and physically belligerent'), but this, in part, probably reflects the greater supply available to the Okiek. Certainly the Maasai I have observed express as much desire to drink as the Okiek, perhaps the more so because they get less of it. In this sense, the Maasai are more dependent on the Okiek than the Okiek are on any product of the Maasai. Though Maasai can make themselves do without all other Okiek trade articles, they cannot substitute for Okiek honey. It is true that they occasionally find bees living in the ground out on the plains, or in trees in *soyua*, but, if that honey were enough for the ritual use in ceremonies, it is not enough for the very important use of honey as wine for hospitality in ceremonies, in meetings, and among friends. It should be borne in mind that these are the conditions I found in Narok District. It is quite possible that these generalizations do not hold for Maasai in other areas, especially those not living adjacent to Okiek. For example, in Kajiado District, where no Okiek live, the Maasai manufacture their own sheaths and necklaces. I am not aware of what they do for honey.

There is a good deal more to Okiek–Maasai relations than stated here, especially relations between members of the same age-set, marriage between Okiek women and Maasai men, politics of land-claim controversies, and relationships to animals, but this brief account of the role of honey in their relations, especially trading, should indicate that the intersocietal relations are more complex than the usually blithe generalizations 'servitude' and 'overlords' would indicate. Furthermore, I have tried to indicate that Okiek–Maasai relations are not only affected by honey trading, but that these relations are important conditions affecting Okiek adaptation in general, that the conflicting needs and dispositions in Maasai society are as important 'technical facts' in Okiek adaptation as the natural environment. To a lesser extent, this can be said of Okiek relations to other ethnic groups and organizations in Narok.

Summary

From the example of the Okiek it would appear that where hunting and gathering societies are small in size and contiguous to other more powerful groups, whether or not they may compete within the same ecological niche, the nature of their social and cultural relationship may have a significant impact on their adaptation. Therefore, to study only their natural ecology, as some ethnographers have tended to do, may be misleading. My own field observations among three local groups of Okiek in the Mau Forest of Narok District in Kenya confirms the intricate interdependence of a web of relationships between the Okiek and their natural environment and neighbouring groups. This brief description of this interrelation could be expanded to include other groups which affect Okiek life: the Kikuyu, the Kitonik (a caste of blacksmiths), and various agencies of the central and local governments as well as some other more peripheral groups. Further analysis would support the above point. In situations such as the Okiek are in – and few ethnic groups do not have boundaries with others – it is more accurate and informative, if not heuristically convenient, to study adaptation, in terms not simply of preconceived concepts of 'adaptation to a natural environment' or 'intertribal relations', but of both and more. All the influencing factors should be taken together, no one *a priori* assumed to have greater theoretical prominence.

Acknowledgements

Field work upon which much of the material in this chapter is based was carried out between 1968 and 1970 in Narok District, Kenya, and was supported by a grant from the National Institute of Mental Health. I especially wish to express my appreciation to Richard Lee for his helpful suggestions on the content of this paper which, at his suggestion, was rewritten as an expanded version of a paper presented at the African Studies Association in November of 1978.

Notes

1 Information on the relative dependence now and in the past on food derived from hunting, collecting and trade is based on three sources: earlier historical and ethnographic accounts, informants' statements made to me, and my own observations. Now, as in the past, the ratio of food types changes with certain conditions: residence, personal preferences for certain foods, age or inability to hunt or gather food, drought or rain which affect food supply and location, proximity of cultivating or pastoral groups who could provide other foods, successful or unsuccessful adoption of some cultivation or animal husbandry by some Okiek, etc. All of these factors make anything but the most gross generalization about relative food dependence inaccurate no matter how carefully one might measure daily intake for individuals. For example, while in the forest, principally to collect honey and repair and make hives, an Okiek family heavily depends on freshly killed animals for about 75 per cent to 85 per cent of their food intake, while honey will amount to 10 per cent to 20 per cent and occasional wild berries for a little more. On the edge of the forest where the Okiek have their base camps, there is now a high intake of cultivated foods, especially maize meal, either from their own gardens or purchased from adjacent tribes. The Okiek maintain that, even in the past, they traded for considerable amounts of maize meal as well as domesticated animal meat and milk. How much of these domesticated foods was traded, in the past or even now, is difficult to estimate for the reasons stated above. My own experience was that in a base camp as much as 60 per cent might be domestic foods.

2 The remarkable difference in energy expenditure per pound of meat and honey collected is worth commenting upon. Hunting in the forest usually involves one or more men and their dogs walking along the top of a ridge until the fresh scent of an animal, usually a giant forest hog, bush pig or similar large animal, is picked up by the dogs and followed, bringing the animal to bay in a few minutes, at which time it is speared. Perhaps one to four hours has gone by between setting off and returning to camp with anywhere from 100 to 300 pounds of meat. Honey, on the other hand, requires a much longer effort: it may take one to two days to make and place a hive in a tree; months later it is visited and what honey is found therein is removed (between five and 30 pounds). Thereafter, one may wait a year to get more honey from this hive. The hive may have been repaired during this time as well, requiring another trip to the forest. Thus a man may spend three hours to get 200 pounds of meat, but he may expend the equivalent of two days to get 20 pounds of honey. It is also possible to go a day without killing an animal, but one is just as likely to go a year without any honey accumulating in a hive.

3 This is the rule among the Okiek with whom I spent most of my time: those on the south side of the Mau Escarpment, who have a large forest in which to live. An interesting contrast exists with the Marashionik Okiek on the north side of the Mau Escarpment. They have far less land and years ago much of it was timbered and planted in large strands of single species trees. With the lack of diverse vegetation, game does not thrive and the Marashionik can get relatively little meat. The rules of their resource tenure system include a provision that one can only hunt within one's own lineage territory,

the implication being that there isn't enough meat to go around for everyone. This variation from the Okiek practice on the south side of the Mau Escarpment supports the hypothesis that restricted access to resources applies to scarce resources, that is, objects of real competition which, if unregulated, would lead to problems of social control in a simple society not otherwise equipped to handle this problem effectively.

Bibliography

Blackburn, R. H. 1971. *Honey in Okiek personality, culture and society*. Unpubl. Ph.D. thesis, Michigan State University
    1973. 'Okiek ceramics:evidence for Central Kenya prehistory'. *AANIA* VIII:56–70
    1974. 'The Okiek and their history'. *Azania* ix:139–57
Heine, B. 1971. 'Kalenjin glottochronology – preliminary hypotheses'. *Mila* ii(2)
    1972. 'Nilotic glottochronology'. Unpubl. seminar paper, University of Nairobi
Jacobs, A. H. 1965. *'The traditional political organization of the pastoral Maasai'*. D. Phil. thesis, Oxford University
Leach, E. R. 1954. *Political systems of highland Burma: a study of Kachin social structure*. G. Bell and Sons, Ltd:London
Murdock, G. P. 1959. *Africa: its peoples and their culture history*. McGraw-Hill Book Co., Inc.:New York
Spencer, P. 1965. *The Samburu*. University of California: Los Angeles

Part III: Contemporary political struggles

14. Utter savages of scientific value

RENATO ROSALDO

In 1970 hunter-gatherers captured banner headlines in the popular press. The occasion was the 'discovery' of the Tasadays in the forested backlands of Mindanao, Philippines. Early reports described a frightened group of 'stone-age' refugees from the dawn of human life on earth, and claimed that studies of these primeval beings could reveal the ultimate core of human nature. Are pristine beings aggressive, self-seeking brutes, or generous loving souls? When I shopped for groceries or went out for a hair-cut, people who learned that I was an anthropologist with research experience in the Philippines immediately asked: 'Are the Tasadays for real? I mean are they really from the stone-age?' Their wonder at living cave-dwellers quickly led to questions about whether civilization had tamed or corrupted human nature.

Official answers to these questions came remarkably quickly. In a book tellingly entitled *The gentle Tasaday* John Nance quoted the excited reaction of Manuel Elizalde (head of a government agency for supporting Filipino cultural minorities) to his first encounter with the Tasadays:

> Listen. These are incredible people. We can learn from them. They are simple, absolutely honest people who have found a way to live happily in their environment . . . no greed, no selfishness. Everyone goes around talking about people being bad because that's human nature. Well, I say that is crap. When you see these people, you have got to say, 'No, man is not basically evil.' At Harvard, for instance, I never heard it said that man was basically good. No. (Nance 1975:75)

Although Elizalde's ecstatic message reached an international metropolitan public, the agony of the Tasaday encounter was passed over in relative silence. Nance briefly depicted the visible terror with which the Tasadays greeted their discoverers: 'The forest men's trembling worsened into uncontrollable shaking. They sat or stood awkwardly, darting peeks out of the corners of their eyes' (p. 11). He went on to describe how members of Elizalde's party reacted: 'Felix scanned the edge of the forest for sign of an ambush. Dudim was worried. He grew increasingly nervous as he moved toward the men. They are weird, he thought. He remembered the tales of Blit hunters mysteriously disappearing in the forest.' That the Tasadays should shake before a helicopter-load of giants armed with .45-calibre pistols and an automatic rifle is perfectly intelligible. But what made the giants quaver? Surely they had nothing to fear.

The ambivalence toward the Tasadays was quickly resolved. Elizalde's word won the day and the mysterious 'wild men' of the rain forest officially became more Noble than Savage.[1] But no sooner were the Tasadays dubbed refugees from a stone-age Garden of Eden than they became the beneficiaries of powerful protectors. Indeed the massive publicity campaign about their discovery was in part intended to inhibit land-grabbers from invading them. Officials evidently believed that the curious fascination of international onlookers could prove a life-preserving kind of surveillance (not unlike that enjoyed by 'endangered species'). Not so naive as to rely solely on public opinion, the Philippine government also used armed guards to protect the threatened Tasadays.

Perhaps the need to protect the Tasadays was self-evident. They were, after all, few in number and poorly equipped to confront the modern world. But what threat could have required such extraordinary measures as armed guards and a world publicity campaign? More puzzling yet was the fear with which Elizalde's party first confronted the naked, trembling Tasadays. How could a tiny band of foragers even for a moment terrorize men armed with the most up-to-date weapons of modern civilization? One wonders whether the armed men thought they had intruded on the forest primeval or an outlaw haven. The actions of Elizalde's party in any case were extreme and contradictory; initially they feared beyond reason, and then turned around and mounted an enormous effort to protect the people who had so frightened them.

More peculiar yet, the state emissaries, for all their helicopters and modern weapons, conducted themselves in an unsettlingly archaic manner. Their dramatic apparition among the 'forest men' displayed more nineteenth- than twentieth-century themes. Consider the romantic adventure of heroic exploration, uncharted terrain, stone-age people and human origins. At the same time the Tasaday episode's worldwide notoriety indicated the extent of public craving for scientific dis-

A Negrito woman with an American colonial administrator, Bataan, Philippines, 1901 (Dean C. Worcester Collection, University of Michigan, Museum of Anthropology)

coveries about the primeval human condition. This flamboyant quest for the 'missing link' probably captured the imagination of popular science and headlines in the mass media more because of than despite its incongruity with modern times.

The strange vicissitudes of the Tasaday encounter require recognition for what they were: ideological barriers that have long confronted hunter-gatherers, at least in the Philippines and probably more widely, in their meetings with emissaries of the state. Through the distorting lenses of official versions the scientific value of the Tasadays became inflated by the promise that they held the secret of ultimate human nature. Little wonder that their presence inspired both excessive fear and tender love. The various versions of the Tasaday discovery emanated from a zone, as critical as it is often overlooked, at the intersection of living hunter-gatherers, their juro-political administration, and the practical uses and abuses of anthropology. Indeed an anthropology narrowly concerned with the nature of hunter-gatherers or the history of science risks ignoring the political context and applications of its investigations.

The urgency of studying the uses and distortions of anthropological lore in the administration of tribal Filipinos only increases when considered in historical perspective. Like other discursive practices, civilized notions about foragers can best be understood over a series of incidents, for they are never fully articulated in a single episode. Rich in precedents, the Tasaday incident particularly recalls relations between American colonial officials and so-called Negritos in the first decade of this century. Resemblances between policies toward Tasadays and Negritos include inflated claims about primordial humanity, ideological invocations of anthropology, and nineteenth-century views of the world. In this case the benevolence of Elizalde becomes more intelligible when juxtaposed with the benign neglect of earlier colonial officials.

Ultimately, precedents for the Tasaday encounter could be sought in the beginnings of the Spanish colonial enterprise in the Philippines (1565–1898). Called *negros*, *negrillos*, or *negritos* by the Spanish because of their relatively short stature, their dark complexions, and their tightly curled hair, they were viewed during that colonial era as brutish, short, nasty, and black. A late-sixteenth-century source, for instance, described them as follows:

> There are also some Negroes, ancient inhabitants of the island [Panay] who occupied it before the Bisayans did. They are a little less black and ugly than those of Guinea, smaller and frailer but in the hair and the beard perfectly similar. They are much more barbarous and wild than the Bisayans and the other Filipinos, for they have no homes like these, nor any permanent settlement. They neither plant nor reap, and seek their livelihood only by roaming like beasts, half naked, through the mountains with their wives and children. They hunt the deer or the wild boar, and while the meat lasts they tarry only long enough to eat it wherever they may have killed it. They have no property other than the bow and arrow. Out of sheer compassion they have not been exterminated by the Bisayans, with whom they have no enmity but also very little contact.   (Chirino 1969:261)

Negritos were regarded as the most savage among those who had never become civilized *indios* living within the jurisdiction of a town and its

Roman Catholic church. 'Ancient inhabitants of the island', they were both primordial and the Other, the oldest and most marginal form of humanity.

Though longer continuities could be traced, a more strategic focus is the initial decade of the American colonial period (1899–1946) when policies toward Negritos reached a peak of explicit conceptualization and systematic application. By this time the Negritos emerged more sharply than ever as a racial category that also included the Andaman islanders and groups on the Malay peninsula (with more distant affinities to central African pygmy groups). They were seen by many, most notably the *Kulturkreislehre* school of ethnologists, as being survivors of the most primitive cultures on earth. But by then the best-known Negrito hunter-gatherer groups had gone beyond pure foraging to include limited horticulture and the use of steel tools. (In retrospect it becomes evident that the stage was set for the entrance of the Tasadays who racially resembled other Filipinos but – lacking horticulture and steel tools – technologically stood out as even more 'primitive' than Negritos.)

The administration of the Negritos became the preserve of Secretary of the Interior Dean Worcester and a governmental agency called the Bureau of Non-Christian Tribes. Initially, the task of colonial rule was simply to control the 'wild tribes' (as they were named in the 1903 census). But even the earliest policy statements extended beyond establishing order to encompass the increasingly dominant American Civilizing Mission. In its founding statement, for instance, the Bureau of Non-Christian Tribes was:

> charged with the duty of conducting systematic investigations, in order to ascertain the name of each tribe, the limits of the territory which it occupies, the approximate number of individuals which compose it, their social organization and their languages, beliefs, manners, and customs, with especial view to learning the most practical way of bringing about their advancement in civilization and material prosperity.　　　　　　　　(Taft *et al.* 1901 1:38)

With a view to eventually setting up schools and uplifting economies American colonial officials began a concerted effort to establish order by codifying more loosely organized Spanish notions about the wild tribes. From the start Americans established separate governmental mechanisms for the administration of the non-Christian tribes (see F. and M. Keesing 1934:21–33).

Dean Worcester himself attributed much confusion in earlier reports to the multiple names by which single groups were known, and he found twenty synonyms for Negritos (1906:805–6). In his view the proliferation of names for unified racial and cultural groups, even for those geographically dispersed like the Negritos, simply created confusion, increasing the difficulty of their efficient administration.

Worcester, it should be stressed from the outset, was a man of remarkable vision, talent, and energy. A former Assistant Professor of Zoology and specialist in ornithology, he was the main architect of American colonial policy toward the non-Christian tribes from his appointment to the first Philippine Commission in 1899 until his resignation in 1913 (Hutterer 1978). His career path from university professor to Philippine Secretary of the Interior indicated the close links between the formulation of colonial policies and evolutionary ideas popular among natural historians and social thinkers of the day.

Nonetheless, Worcester and other officials still regarded the Negritos as more savage than noble, and mentally incapable of being educated to live in civilized society. Perhaps the baldest statement of this view is one of the earliest: 'They [the Negritos] are, physically, weaklings of low stature, with black skin, closely curling hair, flat nose, thick lips, and large clumsy feet. In the matter of intelligence they stand at or near the bottom of the human series, and they are believed to be incapable of any considerable degree of civilization or advancement' (Taft *et al.* 1900 1:11; cited and attributed to Worcester in Hutterer 1978:138). In their savagery and their inability to be uplifted by education Negritos occupied a peculiar and extreme position in the perceptions of officials.

The unique position of the Negritos beyond the outer reaches of a frontier more ideological than spatial begs for explanation as a rationalization of the crude material interests of colonists. What first comes to mind along these lines is the possible interplay between the Negrito's political weakness and the colonist's insatiable land-hunger.

So long as they retained their lifeways Negritos tended to be widely scattered over the landscape, enjoying a low population density. Being few in number and inordinately – as measured in hectares per capita – wealthy in land, they could have made easy marks for land-hungry colonists. But the Philippine situation in the first decade of this century never led to pitched battles between relatively powerful but landless squatters and weak but land-rich Negritos. To begin with, lands inhabited by Negritos lacked mineral resources and were far from the roads and sources of labour needed for profitable logging. Their territory was marginal from the viewpoint of colonial extraction. And Negritos knew full well that to stand and fight was to engage in losing battles likely to cost them both their land and their lives. Hence they simply retreated before the irrepressible advance of civilization as they tried to find haven in the more remote forested regions of the Philippine island world.[2]

Negritos, in short, were no threat to land-hungry colonists. Perhaps the perception of Negritos as less than human relieved colonists of the burden of guilt for taking their ancestral lands. But this convenient notion was more an incidental consequence than an explanation for the formation of an ideology. Because they used neither overt force nor judicial procedures, colonists never needed to regard Negritos as sub-human in order to legitimate grabbing their lands.

Evidently I have moved too quickly from ideology to the world. Though ideas often rationalize practices, these notions require further investigation in their own terms. When asking how ideology works one must also understand what it says (Geertz 1964). Thus the meanings of ideological statements should be unpacked as fully as possible in studying problems of rationalization, distortion, and mystification.

In the case of early American colonial practices toward non-Christian tribes this methodological caution is particularly compelling. Long before the American colonial enterprise began in the Philippines its funda-mental ideas and institutions had already been well developed in other times and places. Worcester and his fellow officials were more the heirs than the inventors of their administrative techniques. Whether ideol-ogy, practice, or their interplay should be the entry-point depends, among other things, on whether a study concerns a late, early, or mid-dle point in an unfolding colonial process.

Let us listen for a moment to the ideology. What in fact did Worcester say about Philippine Negritos at the beginning of the American colo-nial era? The systematic ordering and classification of non-Christian tribes coupled with the peculiar position of Negritos were nowhere more evident than in the following passage of a *National Geographic* article by the Secretary of the Interior:

> In this regard there are wide differences between the several tribes. The Negritos are not far above the anthropoid apes, and the Ilongots and the Mangyans have advanced but little beyond the Negritos. The Bontoc Igorots are filthy, and while Governor Pack, of the Mountain Province, insists that the Benguet Igorots are just naturally dirty rather than filthy, I venture to disagree with him. The Ifugaos are compara-tively clean. The Kalingas are more so. The Tinguians are one of the cleanliest peoples in the world.   (Worcester 1913:1251)

At this time, in the heyday of American imperialism, the 'Negritos' were located at the bottom of a hierarchical ordering of human types ('not far above the anthropoid apes').

Worcester's rank order of tribes on Luzon reflected widely accepted scientific views of the day about social evolution. Visibly manifest (to official eyes) in varying degrees of cleanliness and filth, the social hierarchy was based on a combination of subsistence modes and a now-dated theory of distinct racial migrations. Wet-rice agriculturalists (putatively the most recent migrants to the islands) ranked highest; dry-rice horticulturalists (the next most recent migrants) ranked in the tier below them.[3] Ranked lowest were the Negrito forager-horticulturalists dating from the most ancient wave of human migration to the Philippines. Not surprisingly, Negrito racial character was seen as inferior to the rest because they remained the shortest, blackest people on the islands. Worcester's scale could have been constructed by any Social Darwinist of the time (Hofstadter 1955).

The early period of American rule in the Philippines, however, twisted received social evolutionary ideas in a peculiar way. Most of the people under the jurisdiction of the Bureau of Non-Christian Tribes occupied a contradictory position, at once privileged and inferior to that of their Christian Filipino brethren. Although their level of civilization was seen as lower than that of Christian Filipinos, non-Christian tribes enjoyed the advantage of not being Catholic. Better a pagan than a Catholic because pagans were more likely to convert to Protestantism and become educated in a manner compatible with the American way of life.

Thus the position of former savages underwent a metamorphosis in the shift from the Spanish to the American colonial era. The most loyal Spanish subjects, the Catholic *indios*, became uneasy allies whereas the savages who had effectively resisted Spanish dominion became potential friends. This special relation with the wild tribes, though genuinely subscribed to by Dean Worcester most prominently among others, conveniently fitted the time-honoured colonial policy of divide-and-rule in which Filipinos, as under the Spanish, were pitted against themselves.

Nonetheless, the position of the Negritos remained anomalous. They alone stood as an exception to the rule of favouring former savages. In relations with American officials they rarely shared the privileged status of their fellow non-Christians. Indeed they often were simply overlooked and relegated to a null position beyond the reach of even the most humane policies. In effect, for many administrative purposes they did not exist.

The decision to make Negritos invisible and place them on the social evolutionary ladder's lowest rung derived more from received wisdom of the day (itself in part based on earlier colonial ventures and late-nineteenth-century imperialist fervour) than from American colonial experience in the Philippines (compare Saxton 1979). Social thought already well developed by the late nineteenth century simply cannot be explained by attempting to ground it in colonial practices of the early twentieth century. The American imperialist venture in the Philippines, after all, began only in the twilight of four centuries of Western colonial domination. In learning the tools of their trade officials could and did turn to the lessons of the American West, the Dutch in Java, and the Spanish in the Philippines. Their problem by this point in colonial history was less to invent than to apply an available ideology and set of administrative techniques. The issue thus shifts from explaining the origins to delineating the applications of the scale of human types during the first decade of this century.

Consider the American colonial regime in its best light: humanitarian imperialism. A historian of the Philippines describes this stance as follows:

> Those Americans who came to serve (to say nothing of those who were more selfishly motivated) considered the Filipinos unsuited for self-government in the foreseeable future because of their alleged racial and cultural incapacities. And yet they came to educate, to convert, to uplift the 'native' (insofar as they believed this was possible), to reform Philippine society along Western lines – in sum, they were there to shoulder the White Man's burden.   (Clymer 1976:497–8)

By and large contemptuous of their Spanish predecessors, especially the Roman Catholic friars among them, the Americans – at least those among them driven by the ideal of service – felt duty-bound to provide Filipinos with a sound, secular educational system. The need to enlighten the populace, as they saw it, was enormous, for the 'natives' had only deteriorated under Spanish Roman Catholic dominion.

Humanitarian imperialism was perhaps best exemplified by the colonial career of David Prescott Barrows (Clymer 1976). Barrows, as he recalled in his memoirs (1954:72), received his initial appointment as head of the Bureau of Non-Christian Tribes (1901–3) directly from Worcester. Like Worcester, he enjoyed a dual career as colonial official and university professor. A Chicago Ph.D. in anthropology, Barrows served in the Philippines until 1909 when he became Professor of Education and later President of the University of California at Berkeley.

Once again, the connections between current social thought and colonial practices were evident in the education and positions held by key
colonial officials. These officials, to play a moment on their scales, stood
well above the gifted amateur anthropologist and somewhat below the
full professional.

Early in his colonial career, in 1902, Barrows entered the following
dialogue with chairman Henry Cabot Lodge of a US Senate Committee
on the Philippines:

THE CHAIRMAN. You have lately taken charge of the bureau of wild
tribes?

MR BARROWS. Yes, sir.

THE CHAIRMAN. What sort of people compose those wild tribes?

MR BARROWS. There are three or four elements there. To begin with
we have the oldest in the islands, the little black dwarfs, the Negritos.
They of course are a diminishing factor. They are utter savages and
they have no political significance.

THE CHAIRMAN. They are in the lowest state of savagery?

MR BARROWS. They are in a very low state of savagery. They are
exceedingly interesting from a scientific point of view, but they have
no political significance in the problem.   (Barrows 1902a:719–20)

Barrows then described in sequence the 'wave of immigration' represented by 'wild primitive Malayans', a 'more powerful and more
advanced Malay race', and the 'vigorous, industrious, Christianized
Filipino'. Like Worcester in his inclination to rank human types, Barrows saw the people under his jurisdiction arranged on rungs of an
evolutionary ladder where later migratory waves ranked higher than
earlier ones.[4]

What stood out in Barrows' testimony was his flat dismissal of
Negritos. He believed that they stood at the bottom of the evolutionary
hierarchy. They represented – according to scientific views of the time
– the earliest wave of migration to the Philippines and their racial stock
was therefore the most inferior found on the islands. Negritos, for Barrows, were 'utter savages' with 'no political significance'. And in any
case they were a 'diminishing factor' (presumably he meant diminishing in population).[5]

Robbed of their Spanish infidel status, Negritos no longer threatened
the state. Instead they became passive, though 'exceedingly interesting', objects of knowledge that became significant only when under
scientific surveillance.[6] Their human worth was deflated at the same
time that their value for human knowledge was inflated. They almost

seem to have been granted scientific significance in compensation for the unilateral declaration that their conduct had no conceivable political meaning.

Whereas Worcester downgraded Negritos for filth, Barrows flunked them for sloth. Though not saying so directly, Barrows spoke of Negritos' laziness by implication in discussing other Philippine racial stocks. His views on racial vigour and the capacity for cultural advancement became evident, for instance, in his assessment of the most 'advanced Malay race' among the non-Christian tribes:

> THE CHAIRMAN. You think by judicious management and protection their districts can be opened to trade and they can be advanced?
>
> MR BARROWS. I think so, Senator. I think they are hopeful because they have already made a considerable economic advance. They are industrious. They are agriculturalists. They are raising a variety of agricultural products. They live in cooler altitudes.
>
> THE CHAIRMAN. They are a stronger race than the Malayans on the coast?
>
> MR BARROWS. Certainly; they are more vigorous. They will do much more work. (Barrows 1902a:721)

Race, culture, and labour capacity were so conflated by Barrows that one simply reflected the others, and all together were but visible indices of a population's level of civilization.

In this context Negritos' reputed lack of aptitude for disciplined labour became a moral as well as an evolutionary failing. Hard work was equated with virtue and sloth with vice.[7] Cleanliness and industriousness, the virtues Worcester and Barrows invoked to justify their evolutionary scales, were of course closely related. Both exemplified the Protestant Ethic as described by Max Weber.[8]

The consequences of colonial administration were mixed. In many cases Negritos were simply left to their own devices – benign neglect in a strict sense. In a letter to Worcester, for example, the Chief of the Division of Ethnology recommended that Negritos be left alone because 'they are so scattered and enjoy their free life so well that it seems difficult at present to do anything for them beyond protecting them from abuse' (Miller 1906:16). But the final phrase – 'protecting them from abuse' – hints at their becoming fair game for their neighbours. The absence of administrative policy created a void at times filled by spontaneous local efforts at eradication. And indeed pockets of Negritos did disappear during the American colonial era. The Negrito presence, as Barrows said, did diminish.

Negritos were even judged incapable of improvement through education. They did not enjoy the privileged position of their fellow non-Christians who could readily make the great step forward into American favour. Early reports of provincial governors, for example, were laced with such remarks as: 'There are many groups or families of Negritos in this province, but as this tribe has no future I refrain from dwelling on it' (Villamor 1906 1:302). Early colonial assessments of Negritos' potentialities were more fully evident in an official statement by Barrows' predecessor as Head of the Bureau of Education:

Hitherto no attempts have been made to reach, by any educational process, the feeble and declining tribes of Negritos, who lead the wandering life of wild men in the mountains of some of the provinces. They are comparatively few in number and are very near the bottom of the social scale. They are apparently a hopeless fragment of humanity, not sufficiently advanced to establish and maintain for themselves permanent abiding places, and are therefore ignored in the system of education which embraces the other people of the islands.   (Moses 1902 2:883–4)

Some six years later Barrows (then Head of the Bureau of Education, 1903–9) reversed earlier official views, including his own, concerning Negrito intelligence and ability to learn. He wrote:

Two statements made in regard to these little blacks have been widely repeated; first, that they are rapidly disappearing; second, that they are quite incapable of cultural improvement. Both of these statements I consider to be untrue. While the Negrito has disappeared from many places where he was found in the past, at the present time he appears to be holding his own; and in defiance of the second assertion, in many communities he is making really notable progress considering his primitive condition of savagery . . . In many places the Negritos have partially or entirely ceased their nomadic wandering and settled down in well-established small communities. Here they have built houses, or at least permanent huts, and they have learned from the Malayans their method of forest cultivation, and to plant crops of mountain rice, maize, beans, taro, yams, and tobacco.

(Barrows 1908:45–6)

Negritos, in other words, had demonstrated their ability to clean up and work hard, thereby improving themselves.[9] But they could do so only by ceasing to be what they were and yielding their hunter-gatherer lifeways to a more horticultural and sedentary mode of existence (compare Rosaldo 1978). Foraging as a legitimate way of life remained as unrecognized as before. Even this apparent exception once again proved the rule that, for the American colonial regime, Negrito foragers did not exist.

Perhaps a more precise expression of this peculiar relation is that American officials restricted the grounds for confronting Negritos. In administrative terms the presence of Negrito foragers was diminished for lack of political significance, mental capacities for education, and moral fibre for hard work and cleanliness. Deprived of any legitimate voice in the colonial administrative arena, Negritos took on a narrower, more passive, and more precious significance: they became valued objects for scientific scrutiny.

The Negrito presence justified American policy toward non-Christian tribes on the grounds of discriminating ethnographic judgement rather than blanket favouritism. Had Negritos not existed perhaps they would have been invented to define that marginal point hopelessly beyond administration but perhaps invaluable for human knowledge.

My brief reconnaissance of Negritos' situation in the first decade of American colonial dominion in the Philippines has now ended. But the point of departure was how a sketch of a bygone slice in time could illuminate the Tasaday situation. In what sense can the current situation of Philippine hunter-gatherers be best understood in relation to the legacy of American policies toward non-Christian tribes?

Recall that the Tasaday encounter contained a deep paradox. Elizalde's party initially feared the trembling Tasadays and then about-faced to mount a massive effort to protect them in the name of scientific significance. Their initial fear was more a reaction to the unknown than a realistic estimation of objective danger. Indeed relations between foragers and government emissaries remained uncharted territory from the early American colonial period to the present. From the colonial era onward Negritos and by implication hunter-gatherers were denied their existence as political actors and educated citizens.

The massive campaign to protect the Tasadays was rooted in earlier decisions that placed Negritos beyond the reach of colonial policies. The absence of policy long allowed unofficial practices of abusing Negritos whose only defence was to retreat or perhaps change their lifeways. When Elizalde mounted his campaign of protection he was correct in thinking that, left to their own devices, the Tasaday could simply be eradicated by encroaching settlers and loggers. The Tasaday encounter, for all its flamboyance and good intentions, revealed that the colonial legacy cannot easily be cast away.

Vulnerable to their neighbours and unknown to the state as political actors, the Tasadays entered the public vision above all as objects of scientific scrutiny. Worcester and Barrows would surely have joined Elizalde in declaring that the Tasadays' true significance was scientific – a matter bearing on human origins rather than the politics of the present. These perceptions, I have argued, can best be understood in the context of early American policies toward the non-Christian tribes.

The timeless curiosity of ethnography, official pronouncements on ultimate human nature, and silence about the political aspirations of hunter-gatherers are all of a piece. Anthropologists, officials, and foragers inhabit overlapping political realms and confront, from divergent angles, the same ideological inheritance. Hence the significance of understanding why utter savages have been endowed with inestimable scientific value.

Acknowledgements

I am grateful for the comments of Harold Conklin, Eleanor Leacock, Patrick Menget, Arturo Pacheco, Michelle Rosaldo, and Sarah Stapleton. This chapter developed from studying colonial policies toward Ilongots in northern Luzon (Rosaldo 1978 and 1980, especially chapter 8).

Notes

1 Perceptions of foragers in the Philippines partially derived from Western European conceptions of the Noble Savage and Wild Man. These conceptions, dating from at least the medieval period, are treated at length in Bernheimer (1952) and in the collection edited by Dudley and Novak (1972).
2 Jean Peterson's recent work (1977, 1978) suggests that hunter-gatherer groups in the Philippines have long inhabited the 'edges' between the monsoon forest and land cleared for cultivation. Often bordering on grassland, secondary forest, and primary forest, these edges are ecologically diverse and thus favoured feeding sites for wild game. Foragers as a result rarely move directly into the deeper forest, but instead tend to retreat more gradually along the advancing edge between cultivated and forested land. In other respects, however, my account of Negrito relations with their more powerful neighbours could be generalized to include many frontier conflicts between Filipino groups with differing modes of exploiting (for example, dry-rice versus wet-rice) the same habitat.
3 Worcester's scale of upland peoples in Luzon requires further elucidation beyond the scope of this paper because certain of his distinctions at the upper end of the scale fail to correlate with subsistence differences. Perhaps this issue can be taken up on another occasion.
4 Barrows' Darwinist views are described at some length in Clymer (1976: 505–7). Although Barrows accepted the notion of a racial hierarchy, he was

humanitarian in advocating the betterment of putatively inferior racial stocks.

5 The notion of Negritos diminishing in population occurred throughout American reports of the period. A representative statement was: 'The number of Negritos in the Philippines can hardly exceed 25,000, and it is constantly diminishing from purely natural causes. In many regions their birth rate is known to be materially below their death rate, and in my opinion they must be regarded as a "link" which is not now missing, but soon will be. Within my own recollection they have disappeared from Cebu, Masbate, and Sibuyan' (Worcester 1912:849).

6 On another occasion, for example, Barrows wrote: 'While the vast bulk of the population is unquestionably of Malayan origin, the aboriginal race of the archipelago is the dwarf, black people known as "Negritos", or little negroes. This race is almost the smallest on the globe, and while suggestively negroid in their dark color and frizzly mops of hair, they have neither the prognathism nor the dolichocephaly of the African and Melanesian . . . The number of problems presented to the ethnologist by these little blacks is almost bewildering. What place have they in the evolution of man?' (1902b:680). Compare the later, more subdued professional tone of Barrows' article in the *American Anthropologist* (1910).

7 Although recent researchers have persuasively demonstrated that hunter-gatherers spend so little time meeting their subsistence needs that they could be called the 'original affluent society' (Sahlins 1972; Lee and DeVore 1968), these writers are less convincing when they assert that prior to the 1960s anthropological wisdom affirmed that hunter-gatherers constantly work in an unending struggle for survival. The classic early American Negrito ethnography says: 'The Negrito can not by any stretch of the imagination be called a worker. His life for generations has not been such to teach habits of industry. But for the fact that he has to do some work or starve, he would spend all his days in idleness except that time which he devoted to the chase' (Reed 1905:42). Moreover, Barrows and Worcester held views similar to those of recent researchers, for it is but a short step from the lazy savage to the affluent hunter-gatherer. This observation does not refute current anthropological views, but rather warns against letting earlier ideological notions creep into present theories.

8 Although the American colonial ethos can be characterized as diffusely Protestant, the connection in this case was rather more specific. Worcester's old New England family included a number of clergymen, and his missionary uncle devoted his life to the Cherokee (Hutterer 1978:130, 151). Barrows' New England family had deep Congregationalist attachments, and he himself affiliated with the YMCA (serving briefly as president) during his Philippine years (Clymer 1976:500).

9 Barrows' 1908 views had precedents in more professional ethnography. Reed, for example, said that the Negrito's 'knowledge of things other than those pertaining to his environment is, of course, extremely limited, but he is possessed of an intellect that is capable of growth under proper conditions' (1905:63). At the same time Barrows failed to persuade all his fellow officials. Even in 1912, for example, Worcester wrote that Negritos 'are wonderful woodsmen and display great skill in taking fish and game and in still-hunting their enemies; but here their proficiency ends. They are good at nothing else, and their intelligence is of an exceptionally low order' (1912:841 and 847).

Bibliography

Barrows, David P. 1902a. 'Statement of David P. Barrows'. Senate Committee on the Philippines, *hearings on affairs in the Philippines*, 57 Cong., 1 sess. 679–728

1902b. 'Report of the chief of the Bureau of Non-Christian Tribes for the year ending August 31, 1902'. *Report of the US Philippine Commission*, 1902. Part 1. 679–88

1908. *Eighth annual report of the director of education*. Manila: Bureau of Printing

1910. 'The Negrito and allied types in the Philippines'. *American Anthropologist* 12:358–76

1954. 'Memoirs of David Prescott Barrows, 1873–1954'. Bancroft Library: University of California, Berkeley

Bernheimer, Richard 1952. *Wild men in the middle ages*. Cambridge, Mass.: Harvard University Press

Chirino, Pedro, S. J. 1969. *The Philippines in 1600*. Manila: MDB Printing (First published 1604)

Clymer, Kenton J. 1976. 'Humanitarian imperialism: David Prescott Barrows and the white man's burden in the Philippines'. *Pacific Historical Review* 45:495–517

Dudley, Edward, and Novak, Maximillian (eds.), 1972. *The wild man within: an image in western thought from the Renaissance to Romanticism*. Pittsburgh: University of Pittsburgh Press

Geertz, Clifford 1964. 'Ideology as a cultural system', in David Apter (ed.), *Ideology and discontent*, 47–56. New York: Free Press

Hofstadter, Richard 1955. *Social Darwinism in American thought*. Boston: Beacon

Hutterer, Karl L. 1978. 'Dean C. Worcester and Philippine anthropology'. *Philippine Quarterly of Culture and Society* 6:125–56

Keesing, Felix M., and Keesing, Marie 1934. *Taming Philippine headhunters*. London: George Allen and Unwin Ltd.

Lee, Richard, and DeVore, Irven (eds.), 1968. *Man the hunter*. Chicago: Aldine

Miller, Merton L. 1906. Letter of 25 June 1906, to Secretary of Interior Dean Worcester, in H. Otley Beyer (ed.), *The Itneg-Kalinga papers*, (60). Peabody Museum, Harvard

Moses, Bernard 1902. 'Report of the Office of the Secretary of Public Instruction'. *Report of the US Philippine Commission, 1902*, 2. 867–1049

Nance, John 1975. *The gentle Tasaday: a Stone Age people in the Philippine rain forest*. Cambridge, Mass.: Harvard University Press

Peterson, Jean 1977. 'The merits of margins', in William Wood (ed.), *Cultural ecological perspectives on Southeast Asia*, 63–73. Athens: Ohio University

1978. 'Hunter-gatherer/farmer exchange'. *American Anthropologist* 80:335–51

Reed, William Allen 1905. *Negritos of Zambales*. Manila: Bureau of Printing

Rosaldo, Renato 1978. 'The rhetoric of control: Ilongots viewed as natural bandits and wild Indians', in Barbara Babcock (ed.), *The reversible world: symbolic inversion in art and society*, 240–57. Ithaca: Cornell University Press

1980. *Ilongot headhunting, 1883–1974: a study in society and history*. Stanford: Stanford University Press

Sahlins, Marshall 1972. 'The original affluent society', in *Stone Age economics,* 1–39. Chicago: Aldine

Saxton, Alexander 1979. 'Historical explanations of racial inequality'. *Marxist Perspectives* 2(2):146–68

Taft, Wm Henry, Worcester, Dean, Wright, Luke, Ide, Henry and Moses, Bernard 1900. *Reports of the Taft Philippine Commission.* Washington, DC.: Bureau of Printing

 1901. *Reports of the Taft Philippine Commission.* Washington, DC.: Bureau of Printing

Villamor, Blas 1906. 'Report of the governor of the Province of Isabela'. *Report of the us Philippine Commission, 1906.* 1:293–304

Worcester, Dean 1906. 'The non-Christian tribes of northern Luzon'. *The Philippine Journal of Science* 1:791–863

 1912. 'Head-hunters of northern Luzon'. *The National Geographic Magazine* 23:834–930

 1913. 'The non-Christian peoples of the Philippine Islands, with an account of what has been done for them under American rule'. *The National Geographic Magazine* 24:1157–256

15. From foragers to fighters: South Africa's militarization of the Namibian San

RICHARD LEE and SUSAN HURLICH

> We know SWAPO. They won't kill us. We'd share the pot with SWAPO.
> — a !Kung elder at Chum!kwe[1]
>
> If we go, the Bushmen will go with us.
> — South African commander of !Kung army base[1]

Generations of students in anthropology and social science classes have been introduced to the Kalahari San (Bushmen) as examples of hunter-gatherer societies. They are told that the hunting or foraging way of life was once the universal mode of human existence. Many of the case studies anthropologists use to illustrate their lectures were carried out 10 to 50 or more years ago before the penetration of European colonialism and capitalism. Too often, what they are *not* told is what these hunter-gatherers are doing today.

Several of the papers in this volume document the political mobilization of the foraging peoples in the face of threats to their land base and cultural identity.

The !Kung San of Namibia have not yet mobilized and the threat they face is not to their land but to their very lives. Since the early 1970s, some of the !Kung have been drawn into the military orbit of the South African Defence Forces. Their militarization, ostensibly to fight against the freedom fighters of SWAPO (South West African People's Organization) illustrates in graphic terms the techniques used by South African imperialism to preserve at any cost the interests of capital in southern Africa.

The goal of this paper is to document this militarization and to show that just as history does not stand still, neither does the subject matter of anthropology come to an end when the last hunter-gatherer lays down his bow. The challenge to anthropologists is two-fold, to understand

San soldiers of South African Defence Forces, 36 Battalion (Armed Forces Magazine, June 1980)

the dangerous realities facing native peoples, and also to do something about them.

The San as hunter-gatherers

The devastating impact of European 'civilization' on the small-scale societies of the non-western world is well known. The Aborigines of Tasmania and the West Indies, the Beothuk Indians of Newfoundland, and the Xam Bushmen of South Africa were all exterminated by land-hungry European settlers before 1900. Hundreds of other aboriginal societies in Canada, the United States, Australia, and South America, having survived the initial onslaught, have continued into the present but with reduced numbers and a shrunken land base. In a very few parts of the world favoured by extreme isolation, hunting and gathering peoples managed to survive into the mid-twentieth century with their numbers, social organization and economy essentially intact.

The interior !Kung San of the northern Kalahari of Botswana and Namibia (South West Africa) were one such people. Living at a ring of pans and natural springs around the Aha Mountain range and surrounded by a belt of waterless uninhabited country 50–150 kilometres wide, the 1,000 interior !Kung San were almost entirely unknown to outsiders until the 1950s.

In late 1950, an anthropological team led by Lorna and Laurence Marshall entered the area from the east and over the next two decades produced a superb series of ethnographic studies and films of the Nyae Nyae !Kung (L. Marshall 1976, J. Marshall 1980, E. M. Thomas, 1959). A decade later another group of anthropologists led by Irven DeVore and Richard Lee initiated a fifteen-year programme of studies among the closely related Dobe area !Kung in Botswana (Lee and DeVore 1976, Howell 1979, Lee 1979, Yellen 1977).

As a result of these two long-term projects involving over thirty scientists from a variety of fields, the interior !Kung San of Nyae Nyae, Dobe, and /Xai/xai are now among the best-documented hunter-gatherers in the history of social science.

Far less well known to the world, however, are the traumatic events that have overtaken the !Kung in the 1970s *after* the bulk of the anthropological studies were completed. Starting out as the most isolated hunter-gatherers in Southern Africa, the !Kung San have been drawn by the South African Army into the middle of a shooting war. Having survived for thousands of years in the desert the !Kung's very physical survival is now threatened by the South African military machine.

The San and apartheid

The mineral-rich territory of Namibia, also known as South West Africa, has an area of 318,000 square miles and a population of 1.5 million. Its major exports include copper, nickel, uranium, diamonds, fish and karakul sheep furs. Germany ruled South West Africa from 1885 to 1915. After the First World War, South Africa took over the colony under a League of Nations Mandate. During the 1920s and 30s South Africa moved thousands of White settlers into South West Africa and developed a thriving economy based on the abundant natural resources and a plentiful supply of cheap black labour. Following World War Two when all the mandate powers turned their mandates over to the jurisdiction of the United Nations Trusteeship Council, South Africa alone refused to relinquish its control over South West Africa. It continued to administer the colony as if it were a fifth province of the Union. With the complicity of a number of multi-national companies including Canada's Hudson's Bay Company and Falconbridge Nickel, South Africa continued to exploit the mineral, fishery and agricultural wealth of South West Africa.

Throughout the 1950s and 60s the people of the country petitioned the UN, the World Court and international public opinion for redress for their intolerable situation. Only token support for their struggle was given by the West, while inside the country peaceful protests were met by more and more violence and repression.

In the isolated border regions, however, peoples such as the !Kung were only peripherally involved in these events. Until the 1930s the !Kung San were a single people moving freely from east to west in search of food and friends. In 1965 a fence was built along the Botswana–Namibia border dividing the population into what the !Kung themselves called the 'Boer San' and 'British San'. As was the case with so many African peoples, the imposition of colonialism led formerly united groups to follow different historical paths.

As its claim to South West Africa (SWA) was increasingly being called into question at the UN, South Africa sought to strengthen its grip on the border regions and to establish a colonial infrastructure where none had existed before. South Africa built a series of government stations in northern SWA in the period 1960–5 and all the !Kung in Nyae Nyae were summoned to come and settle at a station called Chum!kwe with the promise of free rations and medical care.[2] In the first few years of the settlement some 700 people were gathered in, far more than had been expected, and the South Africans were faced with the problem of whom to accept and whom to exclude. The neighbouring Botswana Blacks were rigidly excluded and their cattle and other livestock were shot on sight if they were caught straying across the border from the Botswana side. But how were they to distinguish between !Kung from SWA and !Kung from Botswana when in their eyes all !Kung looked alike, were related by kinship, and all moved freely back and forth?

The South West African Department of Native Affairs had compiled data on !Kung geographical place names in Botswana (BP) and SWA. The administrators hit upon the idea of using these data to determine who was a bona fide SWA !Kung and who was not. When !Kung men and women reported to the settlement's office for their weekly ration of maize meal, the clerk looked them up in these data; if they qualified as a resident of a waterhole on the SWA side of the border they were issued a metal dog-tag; each was stamped with a unique number and had to be presented each time food was handed out. If their place did not happen to fall in SWA, they were told, in the words of one informant: 'You are not our Bushmen. Go back to BP side; the British will take care of you.'.

The strong !Kung institutions of sharing and gift exchange initially foiled this crude attempt at Divide and Rule. A lively trade in dog-tags sprang up on both sides of the border. Dog-tags bearing specific numbers were frequently passed from hand to hand as Chum!kwe residents offered their BP relatives a month or more of Boer hospitality at the settlement scheme.

Gradually the South Africans instituted a system of payments for wage-labour and phased out food hand-outs; the traffic in dog-tags declined but visiting and sharing of food rations continued despite the ban on BP !Kung.

In the mid-1960s other techniques of domination were introduced by the South Africans. A Dutch Reformed Church missionary-linguist was sent to Chum!kwe. To gain the confidence of the !Kung at first he simply handed out food and medical care. Later he began to preach the gospel in the !Kung language and to be openly hostile to !Kung traditional healing dances, calling them the work of the devil. Next a school was opened offering instruction in the lower primary grades. !Kung was the language of instruction with Afrikaans, but not English or Oshiwambo, offered as a second language (Oshiwambo is the majority language of Namibia). The exclusive use of !Kung and Afrikaans was part and parcel of the system of domination. (1) It opened up an exclusive channel of communication for ruling-class (i.e. Afrikaner) ideology. (2) It limited communication between the !Kung and their Bantu-speaking neighbours in other parts of South West Africa. (3) It limited the !Kung ability to listen to radio broadcasts in English or in African languages from the countries of Black Africa which offered alternative political viewpoints to those of Afrikanerdom.

Once the full apartheid apparatus was in place other developments followed quickly. Religious instruction for adults and children became part of the programme of the Chum!kwe school and some of the gospels were translated into !Kung. Christian ideas were a long time in taking root among the !Kung, but in September 1973 the Windhoek newspapers reported mass conversions at Chum!kwe, as many !Kung renounced the old ways and embraced Jesus Christ as their saviour.

Economically the !Kung were introduced to the 'value' of wage-labour and the importance of consumer goods. Transistor radios, Western clothing, powdered milk and commercial baby foods became popular items in the Chum!kwe store. With the new consumerism and exposure to racist advertising, the !Kung rapidly grew to be contemptuous of their own personal appearance. The Chum!kwe storekeeper reported to Lee that hair-straightening and skin-lightening creams had become the most popular items and the store could barely keep them in stock because of the great demand. Much of the remaining !Kung income went into ingredients for brewing home-brew beer. The Chum!kwe settlement in the late 1960s became the site of marathon drinking bouts, brawls, and absenteeism and child neglect caused by drinking. (It was the devastating effect of the drinking that the !Kung claimed drove them to religious conversion; a good example of the capitalist system providing both the cause of the corruption and its 'cure'.)

The full apartheid system also made provision for political 'leaders' to be appointed from the native community. The traditional !Kung had lacked all forms of chieftainship or headmanship; what leaders there were exerted their influence in subtle and indirect ways; in a strongly egalitarian society they could persuade but not command. The new leaders appointed by the Native Affairs Department therefore had little credibility with the people and there was a rapid turnover of the occupants of these positions.

The San inhabitants of Chum!kwe enthusiastically took to the ideas of free food and medical care but remained, in general, suspicious or uncertain about the security of their new life and about the Afrikaners' long-term intentions. An indication of this reserve was the continuing importance of the SWA !Kung attached to maintaining links with their hunting and gathering relatives across the border in Botswana. Rarely a month passed when there weren't 40 or 50 Chum!kwe residents paying visits to their kin at the Dobe area waterholes.

The struggle for liberation

The !Kung San are only one of a dozen ethnic groups in the territory of Namibia. The bulk of the population is made up of Bantu-speaking peoples such as the Ovambo, Kavango, Kwanyama, and Herero, as well as the Khoikhoi-speaking Nama, Damara and other groups. San people like the !Kung in fact constitute only about two per cent of the black population of the country. And in many ways the fate of the !Kung under the apartheid system was vastly different from that of their compatriots.

While the !Kung enjoyed some material benefits from the South African occupation, the great majority of the people of Namibia were moved into overcrowded reserves from which they were forced in ever-increasing numbers to migrate out in order to find work in the mines and ranches of the territory. The low pay, harsh working conditions and lack of political freedom, coupled with the illegality and intransigence of the South African regime, drove the working people increasingly towards militant nationalist political organizations as their main salvation. After years of unsuccessful peaceful appeals to the South African regime, it became clear to the bulk of the people that armed struggle was the only way that Namibia could become free. In 1966 SWAPO[3] – the liberation movement representing the vast majority of the Namibian people and recognized as their authentic representative by the UN and the Organization of African Unity (OAU) – initiated an armed liberation struggle with a series of attacks on South African military installations in the Caprivi Strip. Since then SWAPO has won the support of the great majority of the people in the urban centres and larger reserves. Most Western observers agree that if a free election were held in Namibia SWAPO would get between 70 and 90 per cent of the vote.[4]

With the opening of the resistance movement South Africa's occupation tactics entered a new phase. In many parts of the Third World European powers have tried to hold on to colonies and neo-colonies by force. From the British experience in Malaya, the French and later American experience in Indo-China and the Portuguese in Angola, Guinea and Mozambique, the Western powers gradually have built up a textbook of counter-insurgency warfare techniques to attempt to stifle or forestall the coming to power of progressive and popular revolutionary movements in the Third World. This kit of techniques now came into play with the South African occupation forces of Namibia. The story is eerily reminiscent of the use that the American Special Forces units (Green Berets) made of the Montagnard tribesmen of the strategic central highlands of Vietnam.

Paramilitary tracking units.

After a decade of experience administering the San settlement at Chum!kwe the South African Police, (SAP), around 1970, began the wholesale incorporation of some of the bands into paramilitary tracking units directly involved in the anti-guerrilla war. The SAP chose the most isolated and politically least sophisticated of the bands, and they set these units up in isolated border posts where they are 'protected' against outside influences, and are virtual prisoners of the army, dependent on them for their water and their weekly rations and for other supplies.

These units are spaced at camps, 40–60 kilometres apart along the border fence and they follow a regular routine. Every morning two trackers set out from each post, one to the north the other to the south, scanning the sand for fresh tracks. Two trackers meet in the middle of the sector, compare notes, and may spend the night camped on the road. The next day they return to their respective posts, and another set of trackers set out. Thus any incursion into the territory is reported to the Police within hours.

The duties of the trackers also include frequent visits to !Kung villages inside Botswana. The South Africans have instructed them to tell nothing of what they may know of troop movements on the Namibian side but to observe closely any unusual behaviour on the Botswana side. The result is that the Namibian San exploit their kin ties, and the trust explicit in them, to feed information to the South Africans. This is bizarre behaviour by !Kung standards; they expect other !Kung to engage in greetings and share fully news of what they have seen of interest along the way. Just as the !Kung and other hunter-gatherers place a high value on sharing and reciprocity of food, so do they emphasize sharing and reciprocity of information. When this is interrupted the fabric of !Kung society is threatened.

The final solution? the military takes over

The second phase of militarization has been the actual recruitment of the San into the South African Defence Forces. This has been accompanied by a virtual replacement of civilian by military administration as the whole of northern Namibia has been declared 'an operational' zone.

1975 marked a turning point for South Africa. Its colonial rule of Namibia was doomed and it sought to 'Africanize' its regime by creating puppet institutions of government through 'elected' black leaders from the ten non-white homelands into which Namibia had been divided. This resulted in the Turnhalle negotiations for independence under the Democratic Turnhalle Alliance (DTA).[5] The puppet nature of the Turnhalle leaders is very apparent and this internal settlement attempt, bypassing SWAPO, has never achieved any credibility outside South Africa, except in the Reagan administration in the USA.

South Africa also sought to Africanize further its anti-guerrilla war by training puppet troops to do more of the actual fighting themselves. After 1974 !Kung soldiers were recruited directly into the South African Defence Forces. Although paramilitary tracking units continued to exist, the bulk of the !Kung recruits were put into regular army units at special bases where they were issued automatic weapons and taught to use them. As a result the !Kung have begun to die in increasing numbers in skirmishes in the Caprivi Strip and in incursions into Angola.

Two South African battalions are manned largely by 'Bushman' troops. Battalion 31 was set up in the Caprivi Strip in 1974, composed of both !Kung and Barakwengo, or River 'Bushmen'. And in 1978 Battalion 36 was created with headquarters at Chum!kwe, in the heart of the Marshalls' Nyae Nyae area. In 1980, 31 Battalion (also known as Base Omega) had a strength of 600 Bushmen soldiers and 250 white officers. In addition 700 women, 1,200 children and 200 older dependants also live on the base (Poos 1980:47). 36 Battalion's numbers are lower and instead of a single base, the soldiers and their dependants are spread out at 20 smaller camps at boreholes dotted throughout Bushman land (Heitman 1980:14).

For a number of years South Africa's secret war and its manipulation of the San and other ethnic groups was unknown to the outside world. In late 1977, however, the South African Defence Forces made known for the first time the existence of their secret Bushman military bases in the Caprivi Strip and took South African newsmen on a tour of some of them. The picture presented provides a chilling account of forced acculturation and how it is packaged by the media:

> Deep in the dense Caprivi bush a colony of Bushmen are being taught a new culture and a new way of life by the White man. More than a thousand Bushmen have already discarded the bow and arrow for the

R1 rifle and their wives are making clothes out of cotton instead of skin.

Gone are their days of hunting animals for food and living off the yield. They now have 'braaiveis' and salads with salt and pepper while the men wear boots and their ladies dress in the latest fashions. Their children go to schools and sing in choirs.

A handful of South African soldiers started the Colony some time ago, attracting the children of the veld to a secret Army Base where they are teaching them the modern way of life.

'The most difficult thing to teach them is to use a toilet,' the Commander of the Base said. Money and trade is something completely new to them but they are fast learning the White man's way of bickering.

In their small community they now have a store, hospital, school and various other training centres.

The men are being trained as soldiers while their womenfolk learn how to knit, sew and cook.

Well built wooden bungalows in neat rows are their homes although some of them still prefer to erect shanties next to them.

Medicine is also something new to them. It is estimated that Bushmen in the area were dying at a rate of 35 a month whereas they now have an average of three deaths a month.

Most of them died of disease and by the hands of witchdoctors.

It is an open camp and the people may come and go as they please, but most of them prefer to stay.

(*Windhoek Advertiser*, 19 September 1977)

Analysis: counter-insurgency warfare for the eighties

This account – and many others like it (e.g. Poos 1980; Heitman 1980) – shows clearly that the South African Army is embarked on a major overhaul of the social, economic and cultural life of the San. It is also clear (according to the UN Council for Namibia) that the transformation of the San is part of a much larger South African plan: to create loyal malleable allies for South Africa out of indigenous ethnic groups of northern Namibia. The main means for achieving this goal is to combine civil and military action so that the army becomes the main agent for social change. By militarizing large segments of the population, the South African army becomes at once the government of the area, the main employer, the main or sole source of health care and education and the dominant source of ideology. The pattern among the San has been repeated elsewhere in Namibia. Under the rubric of 'Namibianization' battalions of soldiers along the lines of 31 and 36 have been set up in East Caprivi, West Caprivi, Kavango and Ovambo ethnic areas and the techniques used are remarkably similar to those employed among the !Kung (IDAF 1979). The overall goal of the South Africans will be all too familiar to those who lived through the Vietnam era. In the words of one South African correspondent:

Winning the trust and the 'hearts and minds' of the local population [in Namibia] is the most demanding task of the South African Defence Force, but it is winning. The army also has the support of 2,000 Bushmen, experts in bush survival, the support of the SA Air Force when needed, and an elaborate and well-equipped war machine.

(Fischer 1977)

Let us look at the South African strategy in more detail. Drawing a leaf from the Maoist and Leninist theories of revolutionary warfare, counter-insurgency planners seek to turn the techniques of mobilization and political education to their own advantage. It is recast under the heading of psychological warfare. Anthropology (unfortunately) plays a major role in this activity. In 1977 *Die Suidwester*, a Windhoek newspaper, reported that

Major Van Niekerk has been leading a team of 16 ethnologists in the South African Army in the research of cultural aspects of the people of the Kaokaoveld, Ovambo, Kavango and Caprivi to develop better understanding among the members of the South African army of the traditions of these groups.   (UN Council on Namibia 1977:23)

A 90-page psycho-war kit for the Army was drawn up partly based on Major Van Niekerk's findings. It was entitled 'Guide for Psychological Action', and its use was restricted to senior officers. Another kit was issued to enlisted men. Dennis Herbstein of the *Sunday Times*, examining the psycho-war guide kits, writes:

The manual for national servicemen says the 'insurgents' are trying to set up a communist regime – disregarding the fact that SWAPO's main internal support comes from the Anglican and Lutheran Churches. Young soldiers are warned that in the developed countries the communist technique is to soften up morals and values from within by 'enslaving the youth to drink, drugs, pornographic literature and pop music; by encouraging free sex, even across the colour line, and discouraging attendance at church'; and 'by cultivating an unnecessary guilt feeling towards the black man'.

The 'psych-ac' officers watch for tell-tale signs of 'communist' influence and send regular reports to headquarters on the psychological situation of the troops.

Not surprisingly, soldiers mixing with the locals should be prepared to answer delicate questions like: 'who are the terrorists, SWAPO or the whites?' and 'why do they (the whites) assault us?'

Senior officers are told in their guide to 'retain or regain the support of the Africans'. For example, they should protect 'spirit mediums' and provide sporting facilities. 'Ceremonies and martial music in the operational area . . . raise the morale of the population and demonstrate continuing presence.'

In more sinister vein, it suggests 'the display of deceased insurgent leaders' bodies to the population, among whom they had built up a reputation for invincibility. Care should be taken, however, not to create martyrs.'

The guide recommends a 'regard and surrender policy, which has proved a success even among the most sophisticated black tribesmen'. It is a vital weapon in the armoury of psychological warfare.

The guide says all attempts to influence the locals must be based on the truth, 'insofar as the population can appreciate the truth'. It also recommends the 'planned rumour' spread by undercover agents. 'Even if its authenticity is sometimes doubted by the target, and its origin is impossible to fix', the guide says, 'the rumour will rapidly spread if it was well chosen and put out at the right time.'

(*Sunday Times*, London, 3 April 1977 as quoted in UN Namibia Bulletin No. 2. 1977)

Because the San population is relatively small and isolated compared to the other Namibian groups, the South Africans can excercise an even more total control over every aspect of the lives of the San.

The military bases function as 'total' institutions. San women and children are brought into the camps along with the men and are given a comprehensive package of programmes ranging from sewing and cooking lessons to weapons training and martial arts. In their isolation these camps are closed societies like the 'protected villages' or 'strategic hamlets' set up by the Americans in Vietnam, or more recently by the Ian Smith regime in pre-1980 Rhodesia. The ostensible purpose is to 'protect' the inhabitants from the guerrillas but in reality the goal is to prevent the inhabitants from giving support to the freedom fighters. The nature of one camp, Omega, as a total institution is ominously spelled out in a report in the 'South African Digest', an official government publication:

Omega, the Greek word meaning 'last', is an appropriate choice of name as it is here that the Bushmen community has finally found a permanent, secure home.

Much more than just a military training centre, the base is the centre of a large-scale *development programme* for the whole Bushman community, instigated by the Defence Force. [emphasis added]

(Fourie 1978)

As part of this 'development programme', Omega Base has been equipped with a school, and child care and personal hygiene are taught at the local hospital to San women. Instruction in farming methods, occupational skills and religion are provided. For recreation there are sports and film shows. South African Defence Force personnel are involved in this programme, though Omega Base Commandant Piet Hall is quick to point out that 'it is not their idea to fully Westernize the Bushmen so that they lose their identity. The children are regularly taken into the bush to encourage them to retain their natural instinct and acumen, and their culture and ancient customs are kept intact.'

This 'humanitarian' stance of the South African forces towards the San – wanting to introduce them to Western practices while simultaneously preserving certain San customs – does not mask the explicitly military purposes to which the San are put. The article continues:

It seems only natural . . . that the SA Defence Force should apply the Bushmen's age-old talent for survival warfare to the task of outmanoeuvring the enemy at short range – quietly, ruthlessly and efficiently.

Only the times have changed, with the bow and arrow having been replaced by rifles, mortars and other modern weapons of an infantry unit. But their approach stays the same, and the setting is still the familiar wilderness of the border zone, where their acute sense of direction, tracking ability, knowledge of the bush and far sight make them perfect guerrilla fighters. (Fourie 1978)

The parallels to Vietnam should be spelled out. In the central highlands of Vietnam and in Laos entire tribes of Montagnards numbering thousands of people were wooed by the Special Forces and by CIA operatives during the 1960s. Some, like the Mnong Gar studied by the French anthropologist Georges Condominas (1957), were badly displaced by the war and their forest environment repeatedly bombed. Others were herded into refugee camps in the Kontum area and were attacked first by the Viet Cong and later by their American protectors during and after the 1968 Tet Offensive (Fitzgerald 1972). In both the Montagnard and the San cases whole communities of women and children are brought into the war zone; thus not only the men of fighting age, but entire societies faced and are facing the threat of injury and death.[6]

The parallels to Vietnam were not lost to the American mercenary magazine *Soldier of Fortune*. In a leading article on the 31 Battalion they called the Bushman the 'Montagnards of South Africa' (Poos 1980).

The containment and subsequent militarization of the San is basically a continuation of the policy of Divide and Rule at a more sophisticated level. The 'development programme' at the San settlements and bases stems from the apartheid policy of Separate Development based on strictly enforced ethnic lines, and is simply another example of what South Africa is doing elsewhere in Namibia. In the case of larger more settled groupings like the Ovambo or Herero, this separate development assures, among other things, a steady supply of labour out of the reserves and into the foreign-owned mines, industries and farms. It is worth noting that the militarization process of the San also represents a systematic drawing in of their labour power – as trackers, landmine detectors, and counter-insurgency forces. In earlier times, because of their small numbers and nomadic way of life, it was difficult to incorporate the San into colonial labour patterns with any reliability. Now, with the South African-monitored programme of settlement and containment, the San become a valuable – and predictable – source of labour.

SWAPO has been highly critical of South Africa's use of the San and has protested against their actions at the United Nations.

Mr Theo-Ben Gurirab, SWAPO Chief Representative at the UN, accused South Africa of using the San as 'landmine sweepers' against their will. He went on to say:

The Bushmen being traditionally hunters are being used by South Africans as trackers. In the process they become victims of landmines and guerrilla ambushes. It is really tragic that South Africa has to go so low as to use people who are not conscious of what they are doing for her war efforts of aggression in Namibia.

These ancient people . . . are lured with tobacco, dagga (marihuana), the meat to do the dirty job . . . Since they always walk in front of patrolling soldiers in most cases they receive much of the punishment intended for the racist soldiers. Their population being small, our concern is that they might be exterminated.(Gurirab 1977)

In the field SWAPO has paid particular attention to the problem of the San and has tried to avoid injuring them. In July 1980 one of us (Lee) interviewed San of the Dobe area of Botswana. At least 20 Botswana

San had crossed the border and joined the SADF (an unfortunate fact in light of Botswana's staunch support of SWAPO and the liberation struggle),[7] yet informants could not name a single San killed by SWAPO.

On the other hand seven cases of homicide were reported in the period 1978–80 in which !Kung killed other !Kung in the camps, usually in drunken brawls. The weapons used were army-issue bayonets, knives and guns. The homicide rate generated by these figures is about five times as high as the homicide figures for the same !Kung during the period 1920–55 (Lee 1979:397–8). This is compelling evidence for the brutalization of the San; the South African military training teaches hand-to-hand combat and strongly encourages 'macho' behaviour in the recruits.[8]

While SWAPO has been careful not to injure the San, they have also not been particularly successful at educating the San about their goals. Most !Kung Lee contacted in 1980 said they had never seen or talked to a SWAPO. They reported only one encounter. A unit of San soldiers had captured a SWAPO militant in an attack, and as they were guarding him he spoke to them (in Herero):

We are not after you Bushmen. We are only after the South Africans. We don't want to hurt you because you and we should be working together. This country belongs to us all.

But it looks like the South Africans have put all of you to work for them. There are so many of you how will it be possible for us to avoid killing you when we attack the Boers?

Under the expanding conditions of the war and South Africa's increasing use of puppet troops it is clear that the relatively low San casualty rates must give way to a much more deadly form of combat in the future.

But it would be a mistake to think of the San as simply victims of South African guile. Nor are they all involved in South Africa's counterinsurgency forces. There are San who have joined SWAPO, though as SWAPO members their identity is based on national and not ethnic divisions and they are Namibians rather than Barakwengo or !Kung. SWAPO, as a political as well as a military organization, has extensive educational campaigns throughout the country and among all sectors of the population. As difficult as it is to penetrate the contained settlements of the San, there is every reason to assume that SWAPO is also present here. John Marshall's film, *N!ai: The Story of a !Kung Woman*, filmed in mid-1978, graphically portrays the militarization of the San and shows the actual formation of 36 Battalion. But in one scene, a !Kung elder speaking in !Kung tells Marshall 'We know SWAPO. They won't kill us. We'd share the pot with SWAPO.'

What's to be done

Anthropology came into its own largely in the late nineteenth century, when Western industrial nations were beginning to administer colonial empires in their search for new sources of raw materials, cheap labour and markets. Early anthropological studies provided colonial administrations with valuable information they could turn to their own use in controlling local land use, labour supplies and commodity production. As a child of imperialism, anthropology's intellectual and ideological underpinnings are much the same as the Western tradition of which it is a part – a tradition which has been concerned with the politics of domination and control, and with the ideological concealment of this fact. As an example anthropologists and sociologists have always been more comfortable with the study of *ethnicity* than with the study of *class*, and with the concept of *acculturation* than with the concept of *capitalist penetration*. On the other hand many individual anthropologists have grasped the larger issues and have put their energies to work on behalf of oppressed Third and Fourth World peoples.

The South African regime, in pursuit of its policy of Apartheid and Separate Development, is attempting to channel and 'freeze' local communities in ways which keep them artificially divided. To the extent that anthropologists continue to respond to the San (or Ovambo or Herero) merely as San (or Ovambo or Herero), tacit support is given to the South African policy of Apartheid.

The people of Namibia, under the leadership of SWAPO, have made it clear that they are fighting as Namibians for control of their nation, and not as San for control over their San communities or as Herero for control over their Herero communities.

SWAPO's commitment to national unity rather than ethnic divisions is clearly expressed in its Constitution, adopted by the meeting of the Central Committee, August 1976 in Lusaka, Zambia. Among the ten basic aims and objectives which SWAPO espouses, the following are of special note here:

> 2. To unite all the people of Namibia, irrespective of race, religion, sex or ethnic origins, into a cohesive, representative, national political entity;

3. To foster a spirit of national consciousness or a sense of common purpose and collective destiny among the people of Namibia;
4. To combat all reactionary tendencies of individualism, tribalism, racism, sexism and regionalism.   (SWAPO 1976)

The theoretical challenge posed to anthropologists is also a contradiction. With our use of the culture concept we claim our expertise in the study of *specific* cultures. Yet to advocate the preservation of a specific culture places us on a politically shaky footing. We can only begin effectively to use our knowledge and skills on behalf of our 'cultures' if we learn the lesson that the late Amilcar Cabral sought to teach to the people of Guinea Bissau, a lesson summed up in the phrase, 'die a tribe to be born a nation'.[9] Only then, by supporting the *national* political struggles of peoples in Namibia and elsewhere can we regain our role as students of humanity for the party of humanity.

Notes

1 Quoted from *N!ai: the story of a !Kung woman*, a film made by John Marshall, and shown on US Public Television April 1980.
2 A different rationale for the settlement station at Chum!kwe is offered by Lorna Marshall (1976:60–1).
3 Prior to the formation of SWAPO on 19 April 1960, the anticolonial activities of the Namibian people were largely uncoordinated localized strikes and petitionings. During the early half of the 1960s the main task of SWAPO was to establish its presence throughout the country with the formation of local branches. The launching by SWAPO of an armed struggle was accompanied by an intensification of political mobilization of the people with the creation of mass-based organizations for women, youth and workers. Throughout the 1970s and into the early 1980s, the struggle has escalated with stepped-up military operations by SWAPO in the north, nationwide worker and student strikes and massive public rallies. The political work of SWAPO is discussed in more detail in Hurlich and Lee (1979).
4 See for example *Christian Science Monitor*, 25 September 1980. Recent developments in Zimbabwe provide an instructive parallel to the Namibian situation. After seven years of armed conflict, the first genuinely free and fair elections were held in late February 1980. With a strong voter turn-out, the ZANU and ZAPU wings of the former Patriotic Front – the internationally recognized liberation movement in then Rhodesia – received 88 per cent of the vote, leaving no doubt about where the support of the majority of the people had been all along. Given the massive support which SWAPO enjoys inside Namibia, there is every reason to anticipate a similar outcome should free elections be held.
5 The DTA takes its name from the old Turnhalle gymnastics hall – built in the early days of German SWA – in which these negotiations took place. The DTA

is at base a continuation of South Africa's policy of enforced ethnicity, as from its inception it focuses on 'population groups' in Namibia rather than on unifying national interests. In addition to the whites, the ten other 'population groups' correspond to the ten homelands or reserves established by the South African regime: the Damara, Bushmen, Nama, Tswana, Caprivi, Kavango, Basters, Coloureds, Herero/M'banderu, and Ovambo.

6 Studies of the impact of the military on the life of the Montagnards are not easy to find. Two such studies are *The Montagnards of South Vietnam* (Minority Rights Groups, 1974), and the massive US Army Compendium *Minority groups in the Republic of Vietnam* (Schrock et al. 1966).

7 In December 1980 the government of Botswana passed the Foreign Enlistment Bill, a piece of legislation expressly designed to prevent recruitment of Botswana citizens into South Africa's armed forces. For other recent developments see Poulton 1981.

8 Another form of brutalization is the systematic mutilation of the corpses of SWAPO combat victims by white officers for the edification of their San recruits. One soldier's relative gave Lee the following account:

> On one patrol the soldiers ambushed a SWAPO unit. The white officer shot and killed the leader. The rest escaped. The officer then made the three !Kung soldiers fire into the body of the dead man. Then the officer cut off the dead man's penis and stuffed it into his mouth. After photographing this the whites and the San went back to camp.

9 Cabral's ideas deserve careful study by anthropologists. For good introductions to his writings see Cabral 1969 and Cabral 1973.

Bibliography

Cabral, A. 1969. *Revolution in Guinea*. New York: Monthly Review Press
   1973. *Return to the source*. New York: Monthly Review Press (and Africa Information Service)
Condominas, G. 1957. *Nous avons mangé la forêt*. Paris: Mercure de France
Fitzgerald, F. 1972. *Fire in the lake*. New York: Vintage
Fischer, J. 1977. 'South West Africa: tightrope walking in a terrorist war'. *To the Point* 6(38): 56–7
Fourie, L. 1978. 'Ancient breed of new soldiers'. *South African Digest* 28 April 1978:16–17
Gurirab, T.-B. 1977. 'Bushmen being used as landmine sweepers'. *Namibia in the news*, office of the Commissioner for Namibia 23 Sept. 1977:1–2
Heitman, H.-R. 1980. '36 (Bushman) Battalion'. *Armed Forces* June 1980:13–15
Herbstein, D. 1977. 'Psycho-war kit for South African Army'. *Sunday Times of London* 3 April 1977
Howell, N. 1979. *Demography of the Dobe !Kung*. New York: Academic Press
Hurlich, S. 1975. 'Up against the Bay: resource imperialism and native resistance in Namibia and Canada'. *This Magazine* 9 (4):3–8
Hurlich, S. and Lee, R. B. 1979. 'Colonialism, apartheid and liberation', in D. Turner and G. Smith (eds.), *Challenging anthropology*, 353–71. Toronto: McGraw-Hill Ryerson
IDAF-International Defence and Aid Fund 1979. *The South African war machine*.

London: International Defence and Aid Fund. Fact Paper on Southern Africa No. 8

Lee, R. B. 1979. *The !Kung San: men, women and work in a foraging society*. Cambridge and New York: Cambridge University Press

Lee, R. B. and DeVore, I. (eds.) 1976. *Kalahari hunter-gatherers: studies of the !Kung San and their neighbors*. Cambridge, Mass.: Harvard University Press

Marshall, J. 1956. *The hunters* (film). Somerville, Mass.: Centre for Documentary Educational Resources

   1980. *N!ai: the story of a !Kung woman* (film). Somerville, Mass.: Centre for Documentary Educational Resources

Marshall, L. 1976. *The !Kung of Nyae Nyae*. Cambridge, Mass.: Harvard University Press

Minority Rights Group 1974. *The Montagnards of South Vietnam*. London: Minority Rights Group, Report No. 18

Murray, Roger 1977. 'South Africa sets up "Namibia National Army" '. *New African* Nov. 1977:1123

Poos, B. 1980. '31 Battalion Bushmen: their SWAPO kill ratio is 36:1'. *Soldier of Fortune* May 1980:44–50, 84

Poulton, T. 1981. 'A race against time and assimilation: Canadian anthropologists are concerned about the fate of the African Bushmen'. *Macleans: Canada's Weekly News Magazine* 13 April 1981:49–50

Schrock, J. L., Stockton, W. Jr, Murphy, E. M. and Fromme, M. 1966. *Minority groups in the Republic of Vietnam*. Washington: Department of the Army Pamphlet No. 550-105, Ethnographic Study Series:ix and 1163

SWAPO 1976. *Political program of the South West Africa People's Organisation* (SWAPO) *of Namibia*. Lusaka: SWAPO Department of Publicity and Information

Thomas, E. M. 1959. *The harmless people*. New York: Knopf

United Nations Council on Namibia 1977. *Namibia Bulletin* 2/77

Windhoek Advertiser 1977. 'New Life for the Bushmen: secret army base of education'. *Windhoek Advertiser* 22 Sept. 1977

Yellen, J. 1977. *Archaeological approaches to the present: models for reconstructing the past*. New York: Academic Press

16. Dene self-determination and the study of hunter-gatherers in the modern world

MICHAEL I. ASCH

> Hunting is real. Hunting exists and hunting and gathering econom-
> ies exist and this is to me a new fact in the modern world because
> twelve years ago at the Man the Hunter conference we were writing
> an obituary on the hunters. (Richard Lee 1978:30)

The purpose of this paper is to discuss the political and economic realities facing the Dene. Usually, such a subject conjures up in the minds
of anthropologists an exposé of the desperate conditions of once-
independent but now marginalized native peoples and is therefore not
a subject of hope but rather of despair. Such, as I will demonstrate below,
is not the case here. That fact in itself, I presume, makes the Dene situation of great relevance and interest to the students of hunting-
gathering societies.

Who are the Dene? Anthropologists know them as the Northern
Athapaskan-speaking peoples of the Mackenzie River Valley who live
in what is now called the Northwest Territories in Canada's western
sub-Arctic. They are usually referred to in our literature by their regional
or 'tribal' designations such as Slaveys, Dogribs, Chipewayans, and
Hare. They are probably known best to students of hunter-gatherers
through the extensive research of Professor June Helm and, perhaps
most especially, by her pioneering discussion of the composition of
Dogrib bands (Helm 1968).

But, unfortunately, they are best known to the wider anthropological
audience – both student and scholar alike – from the 'awkward' char-
acterization made of them by Professor Elman Service in his 1962 book
Primitive social organization – a statement he repeats in his 'revised' second edition published in 1971 (Service 1962, 1971) that: 'The initial
shocks, depopulations, relocation, and other disturbances in the early
contact period . . . produced refugee-like groups of unrelated families

even before the time of the American Revolutionary War' (Service 1971:77) and that the 'Athapaskans who survived the early disasters became employees (or, more accurately, debt-peons) of the European fur-trading companies almost 200 years ago' *(ibid*:77ff.). Well, those people whose social organization 'disintegrated' two centuries ago and who became refugees and debt-peons dependent on the fur-trade have not disappeared. No, they are still among us and are demanding for themselves the right to continue and develop their own way of life, their right to self-determination within Canada; their right, in short, to status as a nation. That is, to put it in their words:

> We the Dene of the Northwest Territories insist on the right to be regarded by ourselves and the world as a nation . . .

> Our plea to the world is to help us in our struggle to find a place in the world community where we can exercise our right to self-determination as a distinct people and as a nation . . .

> What we seek then is independence and self-determination within the country of Canada. (Indian Brotherhood of the Northwest Territories 1977:3ff.)

Excerpted from the 'Dene Declaration', this statement was passed at the Second Annual Joint Meeting of the Indian Brotherhood of the Northwest Territories and the Metis Association of the Northwest Territories on 19 July 1975.

What, then, do the Dene mean by self-determination? Does it, in fact, have any 'reality' two hundred years after the supposed decimation of their social fabric? In this paper, I wish to address these questions and to discuss the role anthropology can play in answering them. Then, I will briefly turn the subject around and ask how the Dene experience can help anthropology improve its theories of change – especially as they concern hunter-gatherers in the post-contact period. Finally, in my conclusions, I will make a few remarks about the economic and political realities facing the Dene and the place of anthropology – even in its least-engaged form – in their struggle.

Dene self-determination

The Dene position on national self-determination has been developed primarily through a series of struggles with the Canadian state and multi-national corporate interests. There are a number of mile-posts in this development. Not the least of these was the creation in the 1960s

The traditional stick game played at Dene National Assembly Meeting, Fort Good Hope, Northwest Territories, Canada 1980 (M. Asch)

of a national political organization called the Indian Brotherhood of the Northwest Territories and now appropriately renamed the Dene Nation. This organization was formed, among other reasons, to coordinate the land claims of the various regional groupings of Dene and to act on their behalf in negotiations with the Federal Government of Canada. Their first major battle was a court test in which they obtained legal recognition that Treaty number 11 which was signed in 1921 and 1922 did not, as appears in the written version, cede any land to the Canadian state. The decision in this case was based in large measure on the testimony of witnesses who were present at the Treaty signings and, in some cases, whose 'signature' appears on the document itself.

However, there was another event which was even more significant in the development of the Dene's political position on self-determination and in the unification of the various regional groupings behind it. It is the Dene's struggle to halt the construction of a natural gas pipeline through their lands. As I believe that a description of this struggle is the best way to further clarify the Dene's position on national self-determination, at least for an anthropological audience, let me begin with an account of it.

In 1974, after years of planning, a consortium of multinational petroleum corporations filed an application with the National Energy Board of Canada to construct an $8-billion pipeline to ship Alaskan and Canadian arctic gas to markets in southern Canada and the United States. The proposed pipeline was to be routed along the Mackenzie River Valley and hence through Dene lands.

Normally, the decision-making process for such projects would be limited to the National Energy Board and the Federal Cabinet. The decision itself normally would be based exclusively on the assessment of whether the project was in Canada's national interest and would not include the interests or even the input of local residents. However, due to a unique combination of circumstances, not the least of which was the successful assertion by the Dene of the unsettled land claim mentioned above, normality did not apply. Instead, the Federal Government of Canada was compelled to strike a commission of enquiry to examine, among other things, the potential impact of the pipeline on the social and economic life of the native people of the Valley and to advise Cabinet on how to proceed.

Entitled the Mackenzie Valley Pipeline Inquiry, but commonly known as the Berger Inquiry, after the name of the Commissioner Mr Justice Thomas Berger, the Inquiry held hearings for a period of over two and a half years. During this time, the Commissioner heard the testimony of over 300 expert witnesses who included environmentalists, geologists, economists, sociologists, and anthropologists. In addition to these formal hearings held at Yellowknife (capital of the Northwest Territories), the Inquiry conducted what it called 'community hearings' both in major southern Canadian centres and, more significantly to us here, in all the native communities that would be affected by the proposed pipeline. It is from an examination of the evidence provided by the native people themselves at these community hearings that a clearer picture of what the Dene mean by national self-determination emerges.

In order to set the context for this position, I will start by briefly outlining the argument provided by the consortium. At heart, this argument was intended to demonstrate that the construction of the pipeline was in the interests of the native people of the Valley. To this end, they hired a consulting firm to do an analysis of the economic 'realities' facing the native population (Gemini North 1974). According to this assessment, the 'traditional' economy (in other words the hunting-gathering and trapping economy which characterized the fur-trade period) was moribund. That is, while 'the bush' still held a sentimental attachment for native people, it no longer provided any significant economic benefits. Furthermore, they argued, it appeared that this attachment would decrease even more significantly as the younger native people – the first generation to acquire a western education – grew up. In short, the view they conveyed was that the Dene were undergoing the inevitable process of acculturation and assimilation which is often said to characterize change among hunter-gatherers, especially in North America, in the post-contact period (Murphy and Steward 1956, Woods 1975).

Following this line of reasoning, the consortium argued that what the Dene needed at this point in their history was a means to fulfil the expectations of the younger generation and the older people who had 'given up' bush life. What they needed, to put it concisely, was jobs.

Without the pipeline, they continued, there would be little development in the region and hence few full-time jobs. The result would be growing impoverishment and despair. On the other hand, with the pipeline would come development and thus much employment. And, in order to ensure that native people would be prepared to take these jobs once they came on-stream, the consortium, with the aid of the Federal and Territorial Governments, began a major job-training programme. Hence, in their view, the result of the pipeline, if all went according to plan, would be beneficial for the Dene for it would ease the process of transition from the traditional to the modern way of making a living.

The proposition was not seen in the same light by the Dene. In the northern community hearings, the Commissioner listened to over 1,000 native witnesses. Of these virtually all, regardless of age or sex, spoke in opposition to the project.

Although no rigorous analysis of these data has yet been published, all who have carefully read the transcripts would agree that one reason for this opposition stands out clearly. It is that the pipeline, primarily because of its potential environmental impact, would do serious harm to the continuation of Dene traditional life in general and their reliance on the bush in particular. In other words, in contrast to the evidence presented by industry, the Dene did not see themselves as in a period of transition from one way of life to another, but rather as continuing in the present their traditional life-style.

This is not to say the Dene witnesses denied that in the present day their traditional means of making a living was in a period of decline. Indeed, they often asserted in consort with industry that, in the first instance, this was due to their movement into town and the western-style education of their children. However, they differed greatly with the consortium as to the nature of the ultimate cause. This, they argued, was not due to some inevitable process of change, but was rather caused by the coercive effect that external powers in general and the Federal Government in particular was having on their lives.

In short, the Dene argued that the pipeline, with or without jobs, was not in their interests. Indeed, it represented to them merely another intrusion into their lives. They organized both in the north and in southern Canada to oppose the project and received much sympathy and support among members of the public in Canada. Ultimately, it was a resistance that succeeded in that the pipeline route was shifted to the Yukon Territory and hence off Dene lands.

Although it is impossible to capture the true sense of this testimony by citing a few examples, perhaps the flavour and the strength of their sentiments can be glimpsed at by the following two illustrations. The first is by Mr Robert Clements of Fort Norman who said (1976:5):

I remember a few years ago, people lived in their own houses, they got their own wood and hauled their own water. People were happier then. When they didn't have to depend on the Government all the time, we were happier then and we could do it again. But look at what has happened. Now the Government gives the people every-thing, pays for the water and the fuel and the houses, the education. It gives the people everything, but one thing. The right to live their own lives. And that is the only thing we really want, is to control our lives, our land.

The second is by Chief Frank T'Sellie of Fort Good Hope (1977:16ff.):

Our Dene nation is like this great river [the Mackenzie]. It has been flowing before any of us can remember. We take our strength and our wisdom and our ways from the flow and direction that has been established for us by ancestors we never knew, ancestors of a thou-sand years ago. Their wisdom flows through us to our children and our grandchildren and to generations we will never know. We will live out our lives as we must and we will die in peace because we will know that our people and this river will flow on after us.

We know that our grandchildren will speak a language that is their heritage, that has been passed on from before time. We know they will share their wealth and not hoard it or keep it to themselves. We know they will look after this land and protect it and that five hundred years from now someone with my skin colour and moccasins on his feet will climb up the Ramparts [near Fort Good Hope] and rest and look over the river and feel that he too has a place in the universe; and he will thank the same spirits that I thank, that his ancestors have looked after his land well, and he will be proud to be a Dene.

It is for this unborn child, Mr Berger, that my nation will stop the pipeline. It is so that this unborn child can know the freedom of this land that I am willing to lay down my life.

In sum, then, from the evidence presented at the Berger Inquiry, the Dene position on national self-determination can be seen as arising out of these perceptions about contemporary reality. The first is that their traditional way of life is still, in their view, both of practical import and highly valued and that it ought to continue to be so in the future. The second is the realization that, despite their desires, this way of life is being seriously eroded in the present day. The last is their attribution of this erosion not to some inevitable process of acculturation or to some 'voluntary choice' mechanism, but rather to the coercive influence that external powers are exerting over their lives.

In a series of proposals made to the Federal Government and, through them, to the Canadian public, the Dene have begun to specify how they would act to preserve the present situation. The key to this process would be the establishment of an autonomous self-governing region within Canada. Called the 'Dene Nation', its territorial base would include virtually all traditional Dene lands – an area which amounts to approximately 450,000 square miles. Within this jurisdiction, the Dene would assert complete control over such governmental functions as education, trade, taxation, and the regulation of the exploitation of nature resources.

Using these powers, the Dene would act to direct their society towards a future which remains consistent with their traditional institutions and values. For example, they assert that a Dene-controlled economy would not be developed, as is the case at present, to suit the need in southern Canada and the United States for the non-renewable resources found on Dene lands. Instead, they argue, 'our purpose is to bring an end to such colonialism and to re-establish a process and experience of development for the Dene Nation as a whole' (Indian Brotherhood of the Northwest Territories 1976:8). This, specifically, means development based on the continued reliance primarily on the exploitation of renewable resources. Thus, they state (*ibid.*: 7ff.):

> Clearly, we must develop our own economy, rather than depending on externally initiated development. Such an economy would not only encourage continued renewable resource activities, such as hunting,

fishing, and trapping, but would include community-scale activities designed to meet our needs in a more self-reliant fashion. True Dene development will entail political control, an adequate resource base, and continuity with our past. It will be based on our own experience and values. In accordance with our emphasis on sharing, Dene development will not permit a few to gain at the expense of the whole community.

As well, the Dene would replace the parliamentary system of representative government now being promoted in the region with one which emphasizes the traditional Dene mode of decision-making based on consensus and face-to-face dialogue. Thus, they state (Dene Nation 1979:2):

> Rather than representative government, we would encourage government by the people. Instruments through which people could not only be consulted but be a part of decisions on major policies would be the right of the people . . .

> The constitution that would govern the Dene homeland would define the power of Dene government in a manner to limit the powers of elected leaders on many important issues affecting the lives of the population.

In sum, what the Dene are asserting is this. In spite of the erosion which exists in the present day, their society still has the potential and the will to develop in a manner which strengthens rather than diminishes their traditional institutions and values. What they require to effect such an end is merely the power to control their own destiny. Seen in this context, national self-determination becomes a key objective for, by removing the locus of decision-making away from others and returning it to the Dene themselves, it provides them with the means both to check the further erosion of their traditions and to base their future on a continuation with rather than a transition from their present way of life.

Dene self-determination: An evaluation

It is clear from the above that, in Dene perceptions at least, their society still has the potential for their objective to be realized. It is certain as well from the evidence presented at the Berger Inquiry that the will to succeed is also present. But will alone is not enough. The basic question is whether Dene perceptions of the state of their society have a factual basis. If not, then, despite their strong will and fine rhetoric, their plans are merely self-delusions and hence are, almost certainly, doomed to failure. What is needed at this point, then, is a scientific evaluation of the Dene's assertions and it is to this task I now turn.

Space constraints preclude a detailed presentation of this subject. I will therefore limit my discussion in two ways. First I will focus solely on one area of concern: the economic. It is hoped that, by analogy, this evidence will be extendable to other areas of social life. Second, I will be able merely to summarize evidence on this subject in the text. However, I will refer in this discussion to the relevent supporting literature upon which these are based.

The issue to be addressed is divisible into two parts. The first and prior one is whether, as the Dene assert, their traditional way of life in general and the hunting-gathering economy in particular remains viable in the present day. The second and contingent question is whether the Dene have the potential to construct a future society based on these traditions, should they prove to retain their viability.

There are two aspects to the assessment of the continuing viability of the traditional Dene hunting-gathering economy. One concerns the import to the contemporary Dene economy of subsistence obtained through these activities; the other, whether the institutional and value framework within which these productive activities take place in the present still bears the stamp of Dene traditions and values.

How important is subsistence obtained through hunting-gathering activities to the Dene economy today? During the course of the Berger Inquiry, much evidence on this subject was provided by expert witnesses not associated with the pipeline consortium. Key testimony was provided by Scott Rushforth, an anthropologist who spent the period from May 1974 to June 1975 among a group of Dene who live in the region of Great Bear Lake. During this field work, Rushforth collected detailed information on hunting-gathering subsistence activities. From this he concluded that, based on conservative estimates, the Bear Lake people still derive between 27 and 42 per cent of their food requirements through hunting-gathering activities, an amount that translated to a cash equivalent of between $200,000 and $250,000 for the community or between $3,200 and $3,500 per household (Rushforth 1977:42ff.). As well, he found that 'almost the entire area of land which was occupied by their ancestors is still used by the Bear Lake people today' (Rushforth 1976:48) and that, using comparative figures from 1970–1, there has been no downward trend in participation by Bear Lake people in hunting-gathering activities in recent years (*ibid*.:48). He found also that 'a significant percentage of Bear Lake people still engage regularly in traditional land-use activities' (*ibid*.:48). Hence, he concluded, 'in spite of the fact that these people no longer make their entire living from the land, this land remains economically important to them . . .' (*ibid*.:48).

Rushforth's conclusions were corroborated by briefs submitted by other anthropologists who had recently worked in Dene communities. These included Joel Savishinsky on Colville Lake (Savishinsky 1976) and David Smith on Fort Resolution (Smith 1976a). Support for Rushforth's assertions concerning the Dene region as a whole was forwarded by June Helm (Helm 1975, 1976).

Support for Rushforth's position also came from a most unexpected source – the evidence of the applicants. An examination of their analytic procedures led to the conclusion that their results were based in large measure on the use of faulty methods of valuing bush production and in establishing the percentage of total income derived from it: methods which led to a consistent underestimation of the value of this production (Asch 1976a:33, Berger 1977a:104). When a re-analysis of the data was done using more valid procedures, the results actually conformed quite well to Rushforth's finding.

The ultimate confirmation of this claim, however, came from the Report of the Berger Inquiry itself. After a detailed investigation of all available data, the Report concluded that, at minimum, resource collection activities, excluding fur production and gathering, netted the Dene at least 3.36 million lb of food or roughly 240 lb *per capita*. Based on the costs of imported foods which the Dene would have to buy if they did not produce this themselves, this amounted in dollar terms to nearly $10.2 million or $726 *per capita* (Berger 1977b:32ff.). It is an amount which represents approximately 39 per cent of their total income. Thus, the Commission concluded (*ibid*.:7) 'The evidence before this Inquiry has clearly established the importance of renewable resources to the Northern economy. This sector of the economy has provided and must continue to provide native people with employment and income.'

The other aspect of the question to be considered here concerns the institutional framework and value system within which Dene hunting-gathering production takes place. Specifically, the issue is whether, after two hundred years of contact, Dene institutions and values still remain vital.

At the outset, let me state that the position held by Service cited above is not shared by most students of Dene society and is rejected most particularly by virtually all who have had a long-standing appreciation of the field. Rather, their carefully accumulated historic and ethnographic evidence tends to support the Dene claim that no fundamental disruption in their social life occurred until the end of the fur-trade era; that is, until roughly the end of the Second World War (Helm 1975, Helm forthcoming, Helm and Leacock 1971, Janes 1976, Sharpe 1977, Smith, D. 1976b, Smith, J. 1976).

My own research into the economic history of the Dene who live in the lakes region to the north of Great Slave Lake and to the east of the Mackenzie River strongly corroborates this finding (Asch, 1976b, 1977, forthcoming). Elsewhere (Asch 1977), I have provided an explanation which well accounts for its appropriateness. This I will briefly summarize below. First, however, let me outline what the research of Athapaskanists indicates are the central characteristics of 'traditional' Dene hunting-gathering institutions and contrast these with the institutional framework of hunting-gathering today.

In the interests of brevity and clarity, I will limit this description in two respects. First, I will discuss only one grouping of Dene – those regional bands of Slavey speakers who resided in the area which is the focus of my own research. Nonetheless, as the economic history of the region is not a-typical of the Dene as a whole, the characteristics outlined here have a much more general applicability. Second, I will describe 'traditional' hunting-gathering in one time-period alone. It is the fur-trade florescence period which begins, depending on local conditions, by at least 1914 and ends approximately in the mid-1950s. It is, in short, the period immediately prior to the contemporary one.[1]

In the period of fur-trade florescence, the primary unit of production and consumption was the local band which consisted of perhaps 20 to 30 kin-related individuals. In winter, these bands oriented themselves along the shores of the larger lakes where the small game and fish, which constituted a primary food staple, as well as the fur-bearers collected for trade were found in the greatest and most constant supply. In summer, however, for a period of perhaps two months, the local bands would venture to a central location, usually a trading post, where they would mingle together to form what is known as a regional band (Helm 1968:118).

Labour within the local band was organized solely on the basis of age and sex. To capture game, the Slaveys relied mainly on subsistence technology associated with snaring, netting, and trapping. However, by this date, local materials used in producing these tools had been replaced by goods such as wire, steel traps, and fishnet strings, obtained through trade. As well, while big game was occasionally captured by means of snaring (made from heavy cable), most often it was hunted using a high-powered rifle. Nonetheless, most hunting-gathering production, including big-game hunting, was a labour-intensive activity which required collective effort.

While productive technology appears to have been owned by individuals, the fruits of production were shared collectively on the basis of reciprocity among local band members. Yet, it would be wrong to conclude from this that the local bands owned or even held exclusive use rights in the resources found in its zone of exploitation. Rather, the evidence suggests the existence of a tenure system in which ownership of land as a means of production was vested in a collective larger than the local band. In practice, this unit was probably the Dene who lived in a particular regional marriage isolate. But in principle it suggests that ownership of land was held collectively by the Dene as a whole.

In contrast to the period of fur-trade florescence, most Dene, by the mid-1970s, had shifted their primary residence from the bush and into towns. These settlements ranged in size from a minimum of under 100 Dene to a maximum of over 600. As well, although some of the smallest settlements were virtually all Dene, most did contain large non-native populations.

The evidence indicates that, while living in the bush, the Slaveys of the region sustained themselves, even at the peak of the fur-trade florescence, primarily through the consumption of local resources which were produced through hunting-gathering activities. In the present day, however, as the Berger data attest, there has been a significant decline in the quantity of goods obtained through them. Yet, it is important to stress that this does not imply a shift in economic focus for, except in the largest centres, the data indicate that bush production still provides the central pivot for all Dene regardless of age or educational background. Rather, this decline can be attributed, on the one hand, to the fact that the towns are located at distances far removed from the lakeshore regions which represent the zones of highest productive potential and, on the other, to the fact that, due to the sedentary nature of residence, the bush resources in the area immediately surrounding the settlements have been virtually played out.

Another major change which has taken place since the move is the shift in the primary unit of production and consumption from the local band to the 'household'. This typically consisted of an older adult couple, their juvenile offspring, and their adult married children – a grouping of perhaps 10 to 12 individuals.

However, in most other respects, the traditional institutional and value framework of Dene hunting-gathering remained little changed well into the 1970s. For example, within the primary unit of production and consumption, labour was still organized solely on the basis of age and sex. As well, hunting-gathering still relied on methods of game capture that are labour-intensive and required collective action. Further, reciprocity still obtained within the household and, indeed, where surpluses existed this practice was routinely extended to other households in the community which used to form a local band and, whenever possible, even to the community as a whole. Finally, traditional rules concerning the ownership of land as a means of production remained in place.

Nonetheless, for reasons which I will summarize below, Dene traditional institutions and values, as the Dene assert, are becoming eroded in the present day. However, the evidence indicates that, at least in the mid-1970s, this erosion had not progressed to the point that these institutions were no longer significantly vital in Dene society.

In short, then, the evidence supports the Dene contention that hunting-gathering remains vital to their society. The question, now, is whether the Dene have the potential to construct the kind of economy they expressly desire on the basis of these traditions. This is a question which, once again, can be best addressed by dividing it into two component parts: the practical and the 'institutional'. Let me begin with the former.

On the practical side, what the Dene are calling for is an economy which is based primarily on the exploitation of traditional bush resources. The Report of the Berger Inquiry speaks directly to this possibility (Berger 1977b:Ch. 2). The evidence in this document tends towards this position and hence it concludes that the potential for such an economy *does* exist. That is, it specifically suggests that there is on Dene land a renewable resource base of sufficient size to provide the present Dene population with virtually all their subsistence needs including food, clothing, shelter, and fuel; and, as well, to provide, through the sale or trade of bush products, for all the goods they cannot produce themselves.

This result, the Report continues, can be attained by means of a combination of these strategies. First, there is the potential to increase greatly the production of bush products. For example, fur production could be sustained at twice the current volume, while fish production could be increased from its present volume of seven million pounds to twenty. There is also the possibility of increasing the production of big and small game especially by exploiting areas which are now not easily accessible. Second, value could be added to these products by processing them in the Dene Nation rather than exporting them in their raw form to southern markets. Among the most promising possibilities in this regard, according to the Report, are fur-tanning, garment manufacture, fish-processing, and handicraft production. A third strategy would be the development of fur-farming using fish as feeder stock, while a final one would be to promote the increased use of the region for sporting activities and tourism in general.

On the practical side, therefore, the primary question is how to build the infrastructure necessary both to increase production to maximum sustainable yields and to maximize the potential to process raw materials locally. As well, given the fluctuations inherent in markets for the commodities the Dene would produce for trade (and especially furs), there probably would be a need as well for funds to be available to support prices in lean years. The question, in other words, reduces to one of capital.

Under the present political arrangement, the Dene have very limited sources to draw upon for these funds. However, were the Dene to gain, along with political autonomy, the right to levy taxes and procure rents and royalties, the situation would change dramatically. Now in place on lands within the proposed Dene Nation are a large number of major non-renewable resource operations. These include four major mines which produce lead-zinc, gold, silver, and tungsten; crude-oil production; and natural gas. According to Arvin Jelliss, an economist who appeared at the Berger inquiry, surplus profit – that is, profit in excess of the reasonable 15 per cent over costs of production – on these operations was, in terms of 1975 dollars, an amount in excess of $51 million (Jelliss 1977:64ff.). Thus, just by taxing the non-renewable industries now in place, the Dene, could recover enough capital to easily provide the funds necessary to finance this development programme and run most, if not all, government services in their jurisdiction. Further, once the Dene had created such an infrastructure and found other means of raising revenues within their Nation (something which some observers say would take perhaps a decade), they would have the power to curtail or even phase out these operations completely.

It thus seems clear that the Dene have the practical capability to develop a modern economy based primarily on the exploitation of traditional renewable resources. It now remains to evaluate whether, even if the Dene had self-determination, the structure of this economy would continue to reflect Dene traditional hunting-gathering institutions and values.

Here, the evaluation is more problematic. Today, the Dene hunting-gathering economy has a simple and non-specialized division of labour. And it seems reasonable to infer that in large measure Dene institutions and values such as reciprocity, egalitarianism, and collective ownership are associated directly with this reality. However, it is equally the case that, if the renewable-resource-based economy proposed by the Dene is to be viable, it must have a highly developed infrastructure. This means, of course, that the division of labour within the economy will be complex and specialized. Thus, the central question becomes whether the Dene can translate their traditions and values into this new and more complex institutional setting.

The little evidence that exists on this subject, such as that concerning the organization of native-controlled cooperatives and sawmills, does give some grounds for cautious optimism (Asch 1977:58). Yet, the information is too scant to be considered reliable. Hence, at present, the answer to this question remains unknown. Indeed, I would go further and suggest that, given the potential problems in this area, both anticipated and as yet unanticipated, success, in this aspect of the proposition at least, is most doubtful.

On the basis of these evaluations, then, the following conclusions can be drawn. In the first place, the Dene proposals cannot be seen merely as empty rhetoric or self-delusions which are devoid of substance. Rather, they must be taken as serious propositions based on an accurate factual assessment of real conditions. As well, while it is clear that the task facing the Dene is, to say the least, extremely difficult, the evidence indicates quite strongly that both the practical prerequisites for success and the will to make a serious attempt at attaining their goals exist. Finally, I think it is reasonable to argue that without self-determination these objectives cannot be achieved.

Hence, what remains is to evaluate whether, as the Dene believe, the granting of self-determination will make a significant difference to the success of their enterprise. That is, whether given the state of their society today and the potential for development within it, self-determination would be the key which would enable the Dene to create in their homeland a modern economy and polity which is based on the strengthening of their traditional institutions and values.

The answer to this question is not now known and, I submit, will forever remain unknowable, at least in the abstract. Indeed, I would argue, this in the final analysis is the essential historical question which – given the opportunity – must be answered by the Dene themselves.

The Dene and anthropological theories of change

Before launching into my conclusions, it is essential to look at the implications of the Dene experience to the anthropological understanding of the process of post-contact change among hunter-gatherers particularly in North America. To this end, I will return briefly to a subject alluded to above: the exposition of an analytical framework which helps to account on the one hand for the stability of Dene traditions in the fur-trade period and, on the other, their much more rapid erosion in the present day. It is, perhaps, a framework which has a wider applicability.

Although at first blush the hunting-gathering and trapping economy of the Dene during the fur trade era appears as a single unity, in fact it consisted of two analytically distinct economic structures or modes of production. The first was the bush subsistence mode of production. From it, as the description above details, the Dene provided for themselves through locally produced and finished goods virtually everything they needed to survive, and did so within an institutional framework in which cooperative labour, collective responsibility, communal land tenure, and reciprocity were emphasized.

The second was capitalism, a mode of production in which individual ownership, private accumulation of goods and individual responsibility were stressed. Through trade of primary resources, and in particular furs, the Dene obtained from this mode of production certain dietary staples such as flour, sugar, and tea; motors for their boats; clothing; and, significantly, much of the productive technology they used in harvesting bush resources. As traders in primary products, the Dene participated in the capitalist mode of production in the role of small-scale commodity producers – a role, it should be noted, which makes them somewhat similar to small, independent subsistence farmers.

While Dene society came to rely on industrially made goods, even in the critical area of productive technology, the social relations of production of capitalism never intruded into the fabric of Dene social life. Thus, for example, as late as 1947, Slobodin (1962:50–3) describes that while pelts were considered to be the possession of an individual, bush foods were shared by the local band on the basis of reciprocity. Indeed, even in the post-fur-trade period, it has been my experience that while the furs themselves are owned individually, the western goods for which they are exchanged, including for example tinned foods, are distributed on the basis of reciprocity as, I should add, is the flesh of the fur-bearer.

How, then, can the continuing dominance of the institutional framework and values associated with the bush subsistence mode of production be explained? To my mind, this can be traced to two primary factors. The first concerns the unique nature of the central resource of the period – the fur bearer. Obviously the pelt of the animal was crucial to the Dene for it was the primary means by which they could gain access to industrially made products. As well, as I have indicated here, the fur bearer was significant in the bush subsistence mode of production for its flesh often provided a source of nutriment and its fur, when not traded, an important material in the manufacture of certain locally finished goods. Furthermore, it must be remembered that, in many regions, fur bearers were found in the same locales as other game animals and therefore could be harvested with them. As a result, participation in trapping for trade did not necessitate a change in economic orientation away from a hunting-gathering focus.

The second factor concerns the fact that the fur trade, particularly in the north, was a capitalist enterprise of the *mercantile* variety. This meant that, unlike an *industrial* capitalist enterprise which would seek to increase profitability by re-organizing production along more 'efficient' lines, the traders relied primarily on differences between buying and selling prices of goods produced by others for their profits. Thus, for example, little was done to interfere with traditional production methods – even in the period of high competition which came to the region by the beginning of the First World War. Rather, the traders still relied primarily on price and choice of goods as inducements to increase production. Hence, no external pressure was placed on the Dene to reorient their economy away from its bush subsistence rationality.

As a result of these factors, the Dene economy was able to operate on the ground as if trapping were merely an extension of activities associated with hunting-gathering production. Hence, the dominance of the institutional framework associated with the bush subsistence mode of production could maintain ascendency.

Clearly, however, the success of this economic formation was dependent upon a particular set of economic conditions. Of these, the central one was the ability of the exchange value of furs alone to provide the trader with profitability and the Dene with enough credit to fulfil all their trade-good needs. This, of course, remained the case throughout the period of fur-trade dominance.

However, in the period immediately following the Second World War, an abrupt change in economic conditions emerged. While the cost of industrially made goods used by the Dene sky-rocketed, prices paid for furs fell into a deep and prolonged decline. As a result, trapping alone could no longer provide the credit necessary to fulfil their trade-good needs and thus, the Dene were forced to seek cash income from other sources.

The solution for some Dene was to take on full- or part-time wage-labour. As a result, for the first time large numbers of them came into direct contact with the institutional framework of industrial capitalism. In the main, however, most Dene have sought to overcome this cash crisis by obtaining their income in ways, such as family-allowance payments, old-age pensions, and welfare, which do not require direct labour input. As a result, they are reasonably free to spend their labour time in hunting-gathering and trapping pursuits and hence outside of industrial capitalist institutions. Nonetheless, this group as well comes under the influence of the social relations of production of industrial capitalism for this is the economic rationale under which these grants are administered by the Canadian state.

Elsewhere (Asch 1976a:20–5) I have provided much detail on this; here let me illustrate the point with a single example: welfare. Like the other grants, welfare is paid to individuals or to individual households. As such, it tends to emphasize the separateness of these units as against the larger collective. Furthermore, in the case of welfare, this form of payment tends to isolate poverty and create a division between 'rich' and 'poor'. As a result, on the one hand, it relieves the community of its traditional responsibility to share on the basis of reciprocity and, on the other, it provides the opportunity for something new to be introduced – social differentiation based on wealth.

In short, unlike in the fur-trade era, the institutional framework of the bush subsistence mode of production does not retain total dominion over Dene economic life. Rather, as the above example illustrates, the Dene, even when they wish to avoid direct contact, are still enmeshed in their daily lives in the institutional framework of industrial capitalism. And it is this entanglement which is creating the context in which erosion can take place.

This process, however, has been significantly accelerated by another factor: a policy of directed culture change initiated by the Canadian State in the post-war fur-trade depression era. This policy, based on the presumption that the poor economic conditions signalled the end of a way of life, has been working to prepare the Dene for their eventual proletarianization. To this end, the state has initiated programmes, such as the erection of cheap housing in town and the provision of a western education for all Dene children, to ease the transition. Aside from making bush production more difficult, the main consequence of this policy has been to interfere directly in the normal enculturation process by which traditional skills as well as social relations of production were reproduced. This has set the pre-conditions in which the young – no longer able to provide skilled labour for bush production – would be more willing to accept the institutions and values of industrial capitalism. The result has been an acceleration of the erosion process.

On the basis of this discussion, it is possible to formulate these tentative hypotheses about the process of 'erosion' or change towards dependency which is said to take place during the periods of contact between hunting-gathering peoples and the industrial systems. In the first place, it seems reasonable to conclude that the mere adoption of new technologies, even when they represent improvements over traditional ones, does not in itself produce 'erosion'. Nor, it would seem, does mere contact with other and perhaps more highly developed modes of production. Rather, the key factor in the process appears to lie in the area of social relations of production in general and their reproduction in particular. That is, I would argue that the Dene case indicates that as long as a society is able to maintain the dominance of their traditional mode of production and to control the reproduction of its institutional framework, it is able to accommodate much change in the technological area without undergoing a transformation. Once, however, the ability to reproduce these skills and social relationships becomes disrupted, as happened to the Dene with the advent of western-style schooling, then the society begins to undergo a rather rapid process of erosion which leads first to the subordination of the traditional institutional framework and, unless checked, ultimately to its demise.

Conclusions

Whether the Dene will get the chance to establish an autonomous, self-governing region within Canada is open to serious doubt. Nonetheless, the Dene have a realistic proposal and, as well, certain political advantages which give them an opportunity unequalled by any other aboriginal population in North America, save, perhaps, the Inuit of the Canadian Arctic. Indeed, I would venture that if there is a region on this continent where the recent colonists would seriously consider making some accommodations to the aspirations of native peoples, it would be in the political jurisdiction within which the Dene (and the Inuit) reside.

There are many anthropologists around the world who are lending their expertise directly to help peoples such as the Dene get that chance. Some of what we are doing to support the Dene's proposal has been presented in this paper. Some of what anthropologists are doing to aid other hunting-gathering groups is addressed in other papers in this volume. It is a type of work that is both important and, speaking from my own experiences, intellectually challenging. It is a kind of work that I am sure will continue and will broaden as other anthropologists get drawn directly into these struggles.

It should be clear that there are many kinds of contributions anthropologists who wish to become engaged even indirectly in these struggles can make. One of these would be to help to establish a data-bank on the various ways in which the economic and political relationships between hunting-gathering peoples and the nation-states within which they are contained are expressed. This proposition, put forward by Professor Megan Biesele and myself, could assist hunting-gathering groups in many practical ways, not the least of which would be to demonstrate to various national governments the world-wide nature of the problem and the urgency for a solution. It is an endeavour which would also help anthropological theory-building for it would provide a data-base upon which we could test our notions about the processes of change among hunter-gatherers in the post-contact period. We have asked that any information on this subject be forwarded to Professor Biesele at the Department of Anthropology, Rice University, Houston, Texas, USA.

In closing, however, I wish to address the more general question of how anthropologists who do not wish to become involved in these struggles can, nonetheless, contribute to them. The area of concern which I have in mind relates to public knowledge of the nature of hunting-gathering.

The problem is this. If hunting-gathering peoples such as the Dene are to realize their objectives, their proposals must first gain the acceptance of the national governments within whose territory they now reside. In the Canadian case (and this is typical) there has been much opposition on the part of state authorities to the kind of proposal put forward by the Dene. Thus, if the Dene and other such groups are to be successful, they must find ways to overcome this resistance. A primary strategy in this regard could be to gain widespread public support for their proposals both in Canada and in the world community.

Tremendous sympathy already exists for the conditions of aboriginal peoples, at least among the Canadian public. Indeed, it is a sympathy which, when tapped successfully as it was in the case of the Mackenzie Valley gas pipeline debate, is potent enough to influence the Canadian state authorities to take account of native aspirations in their decision-making process. It is a sympathy which must once again be tapped if the Dene are to be successful. But it is a public response which is most noticeable by its absence.

One central reason for this absence is the firmly held belief among members of the general public that hunting-gathering is a mode of subsistence which is too 'primitive' and 'simple' to be viable in the modern world; that it is, in effect a 'stage' of evolution which must eventually disappear. It is, as I have shown, a notion which is shared by decision-makers in both government and industry.

Now, such a notion does not necessarily act as a barrier to generating mass support in cases such as the Mackenzie Valley gas pipeline; for, to sympathetic members of the general public, there is an implication that what peoples such as the Dene need is time to develop the skills necessary to participate fully in modern society. However, it certainly should be clear that the adherence to this notion does act to block support in the present struggle. Indeed, I can state from my own experience that non-natives who hold this view, even when they are predisposed to be sympathetic to the Dene, are unable even to consider their proposal in rational terms.

On the other hand, as this paper has demonstrated, the popular notion is falsified by the Dene experience. Instead, the facts indicate that hunting-gathering exists among the Dene because it remains rational *even* in the modern world. And I have found that once people begin to understand this truth, their preconceived notions about hunting-gathering are quickly dispelled. Furthermore, this is not difficult to do. For example, when explaining the Dene position, I often make the following analogy between hunting-gathering and agriculture:

Agriculture, like hunting-gathering, can be identified as a stage of human evolution. Yet, no one would seriously assert that agriculture has no place in the modern world because the 'industrial' stage of evolution has been reached. Rather, it is considered to be an economic sector which must continue to exist if an industrialized society is to obtain necessary subsistence. But is the situation different for the Dene? The answer is no. There is no possibility for agriculture on their lands. Hence they have only two options. Either they can all become engaged in industrial activities and import all their food at high costs from agricultural areas which are hundreds of miles away or they can maintain and develop an economic sector based on hunting-gathering activities. It is clear that the Dene have chosen the latter and, it would seem when viewed from this perspective, the more rational course. For historical and cultural reasons the form within which these activities, as well as industrial ones, will take place will be different from those we would develop for ourselves, and it must be understood that their proposition is based on a form of reasoning we can all comprehend.

Based on my experiences, I am convinced that if the notion that hunting-gathering exists because it is rational even in the modern world were common knowledge, this would go a long way to creating the intellectual atmosphere in which proposals such as that of the Dene could be judged rationally and on their own merits. This, of course, can only represent an improvement over the present state of affairs. The immediate question, then, becomes how to encourage the dissemination of this concept to the general public.

Today, many anthropologists are doing this through direct means such as writing newspaper articles, giving public lectures, and testifying at public enquiries. And, as the results of the Berger Inquiry attest, this is having a positive affect.

This concept could, as well, be fostered indirectly by the anthropological community. It is clear, for example, that, as the world-wide existence of societies which use hunting-gathering attests, the Dene are not alone in concluding that this mode of subsistence remains viable even today. Yet, there is little in our own literature which reflects this aspect of hunting-gathering. Rather, we tend to portray hunting-gathering as an entity which exists in but is not part of the modern world. It is, in short, studied as a part of the *ethnographic* but not the *historical* present.[2] As a result, we project an image of hunting-gathering to the general public which is, to say the least, irrelevant to the issue at hand. Furthermore, we occasionally lapse, especially in our more popular writings, into 'awkward' phrasings which tend to reinforce, albeit unwittingly, the public's prejudiced notions. In short, I would submit that the anthropological literature has for the most part not made a positive contribution to the necessary process of information dissemination on this subject.

With this in mind, I would urge that we begin to focus more in our research, articles, and, especially, introductory textbooks on the study of hunting-gathering as a part of the contemporary world. From my own research, I am convinced that such a shift in orientation will make a positive contribution to the science of anthropology. But it would have another effect as well. It would tend to reinforce the notion that peoples who use hunting-gathering are not our 'contemporary ancestors', but are, rather, equal participants in the modern world community. Hence, an emphasis in our own work on this orientation would help to develop the intellectual atmosphere the Dene and other hunting-gathering societies struggling for self-determination so sorely need if they are to broaden their base of political support. As such it is, given the nature of the political realities faced by hunter-gatherers in today's world, a potential contribution of the anthropological discipline to their struggle which must not be discounted.

Notes

1 My reasons for choosing this period are simple. To begin with, there are substantial data for it and therefore interpretations do not vary greatly. Further, it is quite easy to trace the institutional characteristics of hunting-gathering found at this time back to the early fur-trade era. Thus it is possible to assert with some certainty that what is described here is in fact characteristic of the whole fur-trade era. This means that, even excluding the aboriginal horizon, what is to be described here has existed for over 200 years and thus demands to be called 'traditional'. Finally, I chose the period because it is the one which the Dene themselves refer to as 'traditional' and as well is the one against which they measure the situation today.
2 This turn of phrase I learned from my late colleague Professor Richard Frucht.

Bibliography

Asch, Michael I. 1976a. 'Past and present land use by the Slavey Indians of the Mackenzie River District'. Evidence presented to the Mackenzie Valley Pipeline Inquiry. Yellowknife. *Records of the Mackenzie Valley pipeline Inquiry* 148:22674–737
1976b. 'Some effects of the late nineteenth-century modernization of the fur trade on the economy of the Slavey Indians'. *Western Canadian Journal of Anthropology* 6(4):7–15

1977. 'The Dene economy', in M. Watkins (ed.), *Dene nation: the colony within*. University of Toronto Press: Toronto

forthcoming. 'The Slavey Indians', in J. Helm (ed.), *The handbook of North American Indians volume VI: the sub-Arctic*. Smithsonian Institution: Washington, D.C.

Berger, Mr Justice Thomas 1977a. *The report of the Mackenzie Valley pipeline Inquiry: volume I*. The Queen's Printer: Ottawa

1977b. *The report of the Mackenzie Valley pipeline Inquiry: volume II*. The Queen's Printer: Ottawa

Clements, Robert 1976. Untitled. Testimony of Robert Clements, in 'The people speak'. Unpublished manuscript

Dene Nation 1979. Press release. Dene Nation Office: Yellowknife

Gemini North Limited 1974. 'Social and economic impact of proposed Arctic gas pipeline in northern Canada, 7 volumes'. Unpublished manuscript, Canadian Arctic Gas Pipeline Limited, Calgary

Helm, June 1968. 'The Nature of Dogrib socioterritorial bands', in R. Lee and I. DeVore (eds.), *Man the hunter*. Aldine Publishing Company: Chicago

1975. 'Summary of overview testimony'. Evidence presented to the Mackenzie Valley Pipeline Inquiry. Yellowknife. *Records of the Mackenzie Valley pipeline Inquiry*. 12:1228–323

1976. Untitled. Brief submitted to the Mackenzie Valley Pipeline Inquiry. Yellowknife. *Records of the Mackenzie Valley pipeline Inquiry* exhibit no. 644

forthcoming. 'Indian dependency and Indian self-determination: problems and paradoxes in Canada's Northwest Territories', in E. Schusky (ed.), *Political organization of native North America*. University Press of America: Washington, D.C.

Helm, June, and Leacock, Eleanor 1971. 'The hunting tribes of the Subarctic', in E. Leacock and N. Larie (eds.), *North American Indians in historical perspective*. Random House: New York

Indian Brotherhood of the Northwest Territories 1976. *Agreement in principle between the Dene Nation and Her Majesty The Queen in right of Canada*. Dene Nation Office: Yellowknife

Indian Brotherhood of the Northwest Territories and the Metis Association of the Northwestern Territories 1977. 'Dene declaration', in M. Watkins (ed.), *Dene nation: the colony within*. University of Toronto Press: Toronto

Janes, Robert 1976. 'Culture contact in the nineteenth-century Mackenzie Basin, Canada'. *Current Anthropology* 17(2):344ff.

Jelliss, Arvin 1977. 'The loss of economic rents', in M. Watkins (ed.), *Dene nation: the colony within*. University of Toronto Press: Toronto

Lee, Richard 1978. Quote from transcript of session on contemporary political struggles at the Hunter-Gatherer Conference, Paris, France, July 1978

Murphy, Robert, and Steward, Julian 1956. 'Tappers and trappers: parallel processes in acculturation'. *Economic Development and Cultural Change* 4:393–408 (Bobbs-Merrill Reprint 39)

Rushforth, Scott 1976. 'Recent land use by the Great Bear Lake Indians'. Evidence Presented to the Mackenzie Valley Pipeline Inquiry. Yellowknife. *Records of the Mackenzie Valley pipeline Inquiry* 148:22632–72

1977. 'Country food', in M. Watkins (ed.), *Dene nation: the colony within*. University of Toronto Press: Toronto

Savishinsky, Joel 1976. Untitled. Brief submitted to the Mackenzie Valley Pipeline Inquiry. *Records of the Mackenzie Valley pipeline Inquiry* exhibit no. 645
Service, Elman 1962. *Primitive social organization.* Random House: New York
1971. *Primitive social organization:* Second edn. Random House: New York
Sharpe, Henry 1977. 'The caribou-eater Chipeweyan: bilaterality, strategies for caribou hunting, and the fur trade'. *Arctic Anthropology* 14(2):35–40
Slobodin, Richard 1962. 'Band organization of the Peel River Kutchin'. *National Museum of Canada Bulletin* 179. Department of Northern Affairs and National Resources: Ottawa
Smith, David 1976a. Untitled. Brief submitted to the Mackenzie Valley Pipeline Inquiry. *Records of the Mackenzie Valley pipeline Inquiry* exhibit no. 646
1976b. 'Cultural and ecological change: the Chipeweyan of Fort Resolution'. *Arctic Anthropology* 13(1):35–42
Smith, James G. E. 1976. 'Local band organization of the caribou-eater Chipeweyan'. *Arctic Anthropology* 13(1):12–24
T'Sellie, Frank 1977. 'Statement of the Mackenzie Valley Pipeline Inquiry', in M. Watkins (ed.), *Dene nation: the colony within.* University of Toronto Press: Toronto
Woods, Clyde 1975. *Culture change.* William C. Brown Company: Dubuque, Iowa

17. The future of hunters within nation-states: anthropology and the James Bay Cree

HARVEY A. FEIT

The revolution in anthropological thought of the last decade brought about by the 'discovery' that the productive activities of hunting and gathering peoples are relatively reliable, abundant, and efficient has stimulated the re-examination of a series of anthropological models and explanations. Among the most important areas of revision are the anthropological models of how hunting and gathering societies change and undergo transformation. This paper raises several questions concerning anthropological and popular ideas about the future of hunting and gathering societies, and it suggests some orientations for discovering and/or creating answers.

The central question that arises from the developments occurring within the hunting societies of the Canadian north today concerns the nature and diversity of the transformations which occur when hunting and gathering societies become less isolated and must increasingly relate to and respond to nation-state political and bureaucratic structures and to international economic structures. These questions are relevant to a wide range of the surviving societies of hunters and gatherers. It is not simply a question of the transformation of hunters and gatherers into something else: farmers, pastoralists, slum dwellers, ethnic minorities, proletarians, specialized labourers, or welfare recipients. It is also a question of the transformation of hunting societies into new and potentially viable forms of hunting societies, with diverse productive organizations, consumer goods, complex imported productive technologies, and extensive state intervention and relationships. In these societies hunting and/or gathering is no longer the sole productive activity, but hunting and/or gathering still is significant economically, and it is often the key productive activity with essential reticulate linkages to cultural, ecological and social conditions. In order to understand these contemporary hunting and gathering societies it is essential to understand the directions of their change.

The study of change, however, is not a matter of just recording transformations. Change in the current context must be analysed with new tools because it is becoming more and more clear that significant components of the changes are self-conscious. In increasingly diverse ways the hunting peoples themselves are actively trying to play a determining role in the transformations they themselves are undergoing. They are not just trying to survive. At least in some regions the hunting peoples have adopted new means by which to seek to restructure their relationships with macro-institutions in terms of their own cultural systems. These include protest movements, public information campaigns, legal actions, drafting legislation, and direct negotiations. In the process, the hunters have not only modified the means, they have set out to redefine the ends, namely their own futures.

This is a situation in which the anthropologist may be a participant and an observer, but in a sense that is wider than the usual anthropological meaning of those terms.

Anthropologists are being called upon, in such situations, to play new roles, roles that often require them not only to criticize the societies in which their own professional work is embedded, but to go beyond such critiques to evaluate/discover/create means by which other societies can achieve their own futures in the face of world political and economic interventions. The scope of the task is delimited on the one hand by the real and fundamental, but not universal, conflicts of interest between hunting societies and industrialized nation states and economies, and it is delimited on the other hand by the relative improbability of fundamental short-term transformations in nation-state and international economic structures. It is a situation in which anthropological understanding and theory must be both applied and developed in the same process.

These problems are discussed here primarily on the basis of examples and data drawn from recent research on the hunting peoples of the Canadian north, and particularly the Eastern Cree Indian communities of the James Bay region of Quebec. Much of this recent Canadian research has focused on the interaction of societies of hunters with the political institutions of the nation state and with the international economy (see Salisbury et al. 1972a; Salisbury 1976a, 1976b, 1977, 1979, forthcoming; Paine 1971, 1977; Freeman and Hackman 1975; Asch 1979; Savard 1979; LaRusic 1970, 1979; Chance et al. 1970; Charest 1975;

Cree children displaying ducks killed during a summer hunting trip, Waswanipi, James Bay, northern Quebec (H. Feit)

Recherches Amérindiennes au Québec 1971, 1979, 1980; Inuit Studies 1979a, 1979b; Tanner 1979; Scott 1979; Usher and Beakhust 1973; Feit *et al*. 1972; Feit 1972, 1973b, 1979, forthcoming).

    This paper is composed of four parts: (1) a brief résumé of recent developments in the Canadian north; (2) a critical analysis of previous anthropological assessments of the changes being undergone by hunting societies in the light of recent data on Cree hunters in Quebec; (3) an account of the nature of the dependences encountered by the Cree in interaction with the state; and (4) an account of some new and innovative responses initiated by the Cree, and designed to enhance their autonomy in the face of present changes. The paper concludes by indicating some implications of these developments for the theoretical orientations and the practical activities of anthropologists who study hunting peoples.

Hunters and anthropologists: recent developments in the Canadian North

Hunting and gathering societies have continued to exist in the northern parts of Canada despite 150 to 350 years of involvement with the international fur-trade, despite 25 to 75 years of administrative involvement with national and provincial governmental structures, and despite governmental policies that have frequently been based on the assumption that hunting was a dying way of life. In the last decade several developments have simultaneously brought these facts into the forefront of both public attention and anthropological interest. New plans have been put forward for the 'development' of the resources of northern portions of Canada by the national and provincial governments, and by international economic interests. These plans and projects have been a stimulus for significant changes in the consciousness both of the hunting peoples and of the anthropologists and other social scientists who are familiar with the region.

The native peoples have increasingly sought to stop and/or prevent these developments, because aspects of such development conflict with their interests, particularly their interests as hunters, and because they have been undertaken without their consent and participation. They have been using legal means, and particularly recourse to claims for legal recognition of their 'aboriginal rights' to accomplish this goal. Across much of the Canadian north aboriginal rights have some *prima facie* recognition within the legal system and have not been extinguished or clearly defined. This fortunate circumstance provides a legal resource with potential political and economic influence for many northern hunting peoples.

The native position has not been a simple opposition to development, but rather an insistence that aboriginal rights must be recognized before development can proceed. Although it has taken many forms, this has been interpreted by all the groups of native peoples to mean the negotiation and establishment of land-claims agreements between themselves and the appropriate levels of government. Such agreements would recognize their rights, clearly define them, and afford legal protection to such rights. All native groups have sought a comprehensive agreement that would include a definition of the rights as well as specific benefits and actions. These would touch on many areas of activity, including as a minimum: (a) protection and development of their hunting and gathering economies including protection of the environments and biotic resources on which they depend; (b) expansion of the local economies; (c) increased control and/or involvement in the local economic projects of regional, national or international institutions; (d) maintenance and expansion of community self-determination; and (e) new social and political institutions to articulate the local and regional native interest with the larger political systems up to the national level. While the means by which each group seeks to accomplish these general goals varies, and the relative values they put on each goal vary, the native groups have all sought such goals with increasing clarity and with a determination not to be satisfied with mere tokenism (see Cumming and Mickenberg 1972; Cumming 1977; McCullum and McCullum 1975; McCullum, McCullum and Olthuis 1977; Usher 1971, 1976a, 1976b; Watkins 1977; O'Malley 1976; Richardson 1972, 1975; Weinstein 1976; Brody 1975; Berger 1977; Sanders 1973; Rouland 1978; Peterson and Wright 1978; Keith and Wright 1978; Penn 1975; Feit 1979, forthcoming).

The last decade has thus led to the threshold of a series of significant and widespread new transformations that will be occurring in the hunting societies of the Canadian north during the last quarter of this century, and beyond.

In this context social scientists, and anthropologists in particular, have been called on to take up some relatively new roles. At least four general demands have been made upon the social scientists: (1) to document the aboriginal and contemporary ways of life of the native peoples, and the transformations that have already occurred, especially in systems of land use and subsistence economies; usually in order to provide evidence for use by the native peoples in their legal, para-legal and political confrontations; (2) to advise the native peoples on the detailed formulations of their goals and the means of attaining them in the light of present social-science theory and knowledge of the interactions, processes, and transformations of hunting societies and national and international institutions; (3) to help present and articulate such policy as is adopted by the native people to the public, to the government, and to the courts; and (4) to do problem-oriented research on present conditions and by this and other means help to implement the changes sought.

Such developments provide an opportunity to link anthropological thought and action in a way that fulfils the claims for the ultimate usefulness of anthropological knowledge, while at the same time making possible significant advancement of that knowledge. There is therefore an opportunity both to be useful and to do theoretically significant research on the interaction between local populations and the larger political and economic systems in which they are irrevocably enmeshed.

An early example of the study of this interaction was the pioneering work of cultural ecologists and acculturation theorists following the Second World War, which specifically touched on the question of the future of hunting societies. This work stands out in the anthropological literature because, contrary to many studies which have either viewed hunting societies as static, or studied hunters from the perspective of the abstract evolution of modes of subsistence, the acculturation theorists effectively located hunting peoples in the modern world and attempted to analyse the processes of change actually occurring. These formulations have been so out of keeping with the main trends in hunting studies during recent years that they have not generally been submitted to a critical evaluation and revision in over two decades.

As the ongoing processes of change in hunting societies become a renewed focus of attention in anthropology, it is appropriate to return to these early formulations and examine them in the light of the new data now available. A review of this work in the present context provides an opportunity to suggest some of the changes which have occurred in the last decades in both the local and the macro-level settings. And it will set the stage for a discussion of more recent developments and responses.

Initial assessments of the future of hunters in northern Canada

In 1956, Robert F. Murphy and Julian H. Steward proposed a general and explicitly theoretical analysis of the transformations occurring under certain specified conditions in hunting and gathering societies. They formulated certain cross-cultural regularities in processes of acculturation (1956), basing their analysis in part on the field research of Eleanor Leacock in northern Quebec (1954) and of Murphy in Brazil. In addition, they went boldly beyond a synthesis of existing data on historical change and, under the conditions specified, predicted the likely future of specific hunting and gathering societies, defining a 'final cultural type' which was then emerging among such populations (Murphy and Steward 1956:335).

Murphy and Steward argued that in the geographically diverse cases cited, 'outside commercial influence led to reduction of the local level of integration' (1956:335–6) and resulted in a culture type that was similar, in each case, because the local culture core contained 'the all-important outside factor of almost complete economic dependence upon trade goods which are exchanged for certain local produce and because the functional nature of local production, the family, and other features were directly related to this new element' (1956:336).

This shift from a subsistence economy to dependence upon trade is 'evidently irreversible', they claimed, so long as there is continued access to trade goods. 'It can be said, therefore, that the aboriginal culture is destined to be replaced by a new type which reaches its culmination when the responsible processes have run their course' (1956:336).

This final phase, under the conditions specified, is 'characterized by assimilation of the Indians as a local sub-culture of the national socio-cultural system' and eventually it may result in the 'virtual loss of identity as Indians' (1956:350). Murphy and Steward identify six features which characterize this phase of convergence and culmination in northern Quebec: (1a) fur-trapping is predominant over subsistence hunting and (1b) winter provisions are purchased; (2) economic interdependences shift from group to trader; (3) winter groups are not necessary as family or individual hunting is more efficient and permits resource conservation; (4) the nuclear family is the basic unit at all times of the year; (5) hunting territories develop which are exploited only by a trapper and his family; (6) chiefs emerge as intermediaries with administrative institutions. These features may be broadly considered as falling into two groups: the economic criteria, items 1 and 2, and the social criteria, items 2 to 6.

This provocative summary of acculturation processes and prediction of future outcomes involving disintegration, dependence and assimilation of hunting peoples has been used to describe historical changes among native people of northern Quebec by several other researchers (Pothier 1967; Samson 1966; Désy 1968). While some criticisms and revisions were suggested, predictions respecting the end product of acculturation processes were not generally revised (for partial exceptions see Balikci 1964 and Bernier 1968).

However, despite this initial support, more recent, intensive and long-term studies have tended to contradict rather than confirm the predictions. Significantly, much of the latter research cited below owes its inception and execution to needs generated by the native responses to development projects and by their claims for recognition of their aboriginal rights. One result has been much more comprehensive data on the economies, culture and social organization of native communities than were previously available. Drawing on data from my own research among the Waswanipi Cree, an Indian band which is adjacent to one of the groups on which Leacock provided extensive historical data, and on other recent research among closely related Eastern Cree bands,[1] it is possible to subject the specific criteria offered by Murphy and Steward to a detailed review.

With respect to the relative importance of trapping for furs to sell and hunting for subsistence foods, Knight has argued (1965: 35) that fur-trapping is not incompatible with various hunting activities, as had been assumed. Certain intensively harvested animals, such as beaver, lynx and muskrat, are important both for the commercially saleable pelts they provide, and for the substantial quantities of food they provide. Certain other species which are hunted primarily for food, such as moose, are harvestable at times and places that are compatible with trapping for fur bearers, while other species hunted primarily for food, such as geese, are harvestable at seasons when fur trapping is relatively less productive. The consequence is that as fur trapping becomes important it need not replace hunting for subsistence.

The data now available from recent studies in fact indicate that fur-trapping has not become the predominant productive use of wildlife, and that subsistence hunting, which includes the trapping of such fur-bearing animals as are used as components of the normal diet, remains the predominant use. In terms of labour inputs to wildlife harvesting, a sample of Waswanipi hunters, whom I studied in the autumn, winter and spring of 1968–9, the main fur-trapping period of the year, spend 31 per cent of harvesting man-days hunting moose, small game and waterfowl, and fishing for food, whereas they spent 7 per cent of man-days trapping fine-fur-bearing animals other than beaver, some of which were eaten. But, they spent 62 per cent of harvesting man-days hunting and/or trapping beaver (Feit 1978:839). Beaver was both the most important source of subsistence foods and the most important source of fur sales income, accounting for 54 per cent of all calories available from winter food harvests and 84 per cent of the cash value of all fur pelts sold.

Data on the community-wide patterns of production indicate fur-pelt sales provided $36,149 of income in 1968–9, whereas subsistence production accounted for 206,453 lb of butchered food, which I estimate would have cost $185,902 to replace with commercially produced meats, fish and poultry at local prices (1978: 78 and 91).[2] The comparable fig-

Table 17.1. *Comparison of incomes derived from fur-pelt sales and subsistence-food harvest, Eastern Cree communities, various years*

Year	Communities	Fur-pelt sales	Cash value of subsistence foods
1968–9	Waswanipi[a]	36,149	185,902
1969–70	Waswanipi[a]	27,585	169,694
1970–1	Eastern Cree[b]	300,000	3,864,300
1971–2	Fort George[c]	20,180	526,487
1973–4	Fort George[d]	72,413	782,299
1971–2	Paint Hills[c]	16,238	162,636
1971–2	Eastmain[c]	14,962	66,769
1974–5	Eastern Cree[e]	384,340	3,632,713

[a]*Source:* Feit 1978
[b]*Source:* Salisbury et al. 1972a
[c]*Source:* Salisbury et al. 1972b
[d]*Source:* Unpublished data from the Fort George Resource Use and Subsistence Economy Study, Grand Council of the Crees (of Quebec), Montreal
[e]*Source:* Fur-pelt sales from James Bay and Northern Quebec Native Harvesting Research Committee 1976; cash value of subsistence harvests from Grand Council of the Crees (of Quebec) 1977

ures for the following year were $27,585 in fur-pelt sales and $169,694 worth of subsistence foods. The value of subsistence production was therefore about six times the value of fur-pelt production.

Comparative data on fur production and subsistence production from other Eastern Cree communities during the 1970s indicate a similar predominance of the value of subsistence products (Table 17.1). The most recent published figures for the Eastern Cree region as a whole are for 1974–5, for which fur-sales income was $384,340 (James Bay and Northern Quebec Native Harvesting Research Committee 1976: 198) and the subsistence-food value calculated on a basis similar to that used above was $3,632,713.50 (Grand Council of the Crees (of Quebec) 1977: Table 8c). Subsistence hunting has therefore remained the predominant use of wildlife resources and the predominant harvesting activity.

As these figures would suggest, the importance of local subsistence products, called 'bush food', also remains high in relation to the quantity of commercially purchased foods. In a sample of winter hunting camps at Waswanipi in 1968–9, bush foods provided 78 per cent of the calories available for human consumption from all foods during the winter period, 93 per cent of the available protein, and 90 per cent of available fat (Feit 1978:624). In the neighbouring community of Mistassini Adrian Tanner estimates that in the winter of 1969–70 bush foods provided 573,400 lb of foodstuffs, while commercially bought foods provided 140,000 lb, or 20 per cent (cited in Salisbury *et al.* 1972a:46).

The data therefore also contradict the predicted dependence of the hunters on commercially purchased provisions.

Nevertheless, the proportion of total food requirements provided by bush foods would be much lower than 80 per cent if accurate data were available for the entire year and the entire community. Only estimates of these parameters are available. The percentage of annual community-wide requirements that are provided by bush foods is estimated to range from 50 to 55 per cent for all Eastern Cree communities by weight (Salisbury *et al.* 1972a:50), to 25 per cent of calorific needs (Berkes and Farkas 1978:162). My own estimate for Waswanipi is 45 to 50 per cent of calories (Feit 1978:82). The bush food available to the community can however provide between 50 and 100+ per cent of the mean adult recommended daily intake of most other nutrients (Feit 1978:84; Berkes and Farkas 1978: 162–3). In the bush camps, from which the most intensive hunting takes place, there is a clear predominance of bush food, and at Waswanipi about 40 per cent of the bush food produced there is brought back to the settlements either for later consumption or for wide distribution (Feit 1978:696).

The reason for the discrepancy between figures for bush camps and those for the community as a whole is primarily due to the fact that not all Cree adults now participate intensively in hunting activities. Wage employment and transfer payments have become sources of significant incomes, and they provide opportunities for some adult males to work on a permanent or on an intermittent basis.

Virtually all able-bodied men still participate in some hunting activities, but the degree varies from individual to individual, and from time to time. Intensive hunters often work during the summer period, when hunting is least productive, and when employment is often available in the 'bush' where their hunting activities can be conducted daily around flexible working schedules. As LaRusic has shown, Cree choices of involvement in employment often emphasize those factors that best facilitate an integration of wage-labour with hunting activities (1970:B40). On the other hand, those who work often have wives and children who fish or snare small game, while workers themselves often hunt on weekends and take holidays to coincide with a particular productive hunting season; and, since wage employment for many is often temporary, many men hunt between periods of work.

The effectiveness of these methods as means of retaining a significant subsistence harvest is substantial, although it varies depending on the kind of biological resources available, especially near the settlement where workers must harvest most of their catch. Recent data from the James Bay Cree communities indicate that those who do not intensively hunt as their primary winter activity harvest an average of 41 per cent as much subsistence food by weight on an annual basis as those who do hunt as their primary winter activity (James Bay and Northern Quebec Native Harvesting Research Committee 1978:222). Thus, while winter employment does reduce subsistence harvests, it does not completely eliminate hunting activities as might have been expected. Indeed, in 1975–6 the harvest taken by non-intensive hunters accounted for 27 per cent of the total community harvest by weight.

In 1968–9 and 1969–70 surveys of Waswanipi men indicated that 55 and 50 per cent hunted during at least five months of the productive seven-month autumn–winter–spring season, two-thirds of whom also worked during part of the year; and 30 and 37 per cent of Waswanipi men worked or looked for work during all seasons, all of whom also hunted. The remaining 12 and 13 per cent were aged, sick or indigent, and did relatively little work or hunting (Feit 1978:62).

Thus, it is wage employment, rather than trapping, which has become an important alternative to intensive hunting; but it is also, as I will show below, an important support for hunting activities. On a community-wide basis incomes derived from employment accounted for 33 to 40 per cent of total incomes, whereas incomes from the sale of furs accounted for only 8 and 6 per cent in the two years. By comparison, incomes in kind from hunting bush foods accounted for 40 and 37 per cent of total incomes. Transfer payments account for the remaining 18 and 17 per cent (Feit 1978: 81). Figures for other communities in the Eastern Cree region are generally similar, although the relative importance of incomes from hunting, transfer payments and employment varies among sectors of the population, and from community to community, and from year to year (Table 17.2). Fur-pelt sales income is uniformly less than 10 per cent of total incomes.

Even for those men who hunt intensively in winter, and who only work in summer, the percentage composition of annual incomes indicates the relatively smaller contribution of fur incomes than transfer payments and wages. At Waswanipi in 1969–70, those who hunted intensively derived 55 per cent of total incomes from subsistence foods, 19 per cent from employment, 14 per cent from transfer payments, and 12 per cent from the sale of fur pelts (Feit unpublished data).

Table 17.2. *Percentage of total incomes derived from employment, fur sales, subsistence harvests and transfer payments, Eastern Cree communities, various years*

| | | Percentage of total incomes derived from | | | |
Year	Communities	Employment income	Fur-pelt sales	Cash value of subsistence foods	Transfer payments
1968–9	Waswanipi[a]	33	8	40	18
1969–70	Waswanipi[a]	40	6	37	17
1970–1	Eastern Cree[b]	25	8	50	17
1971–2	Fort George[c]	61	1	25	12
1973–4	Fort George[d]	50	2	25	24
1971–2	Paint Hills[c]	18	3	30	49
1972–2	Eastmain[c]	11	6	32	51

[a]*Source:* Feit 1978
[b]*Source:* Salisbury et al. 1972a
[c]*Source:* Salisbury et al. 1972b
[d]*Source:* Unpublished data from the Fort George Resource Use and Subsistence Economy Study, Grand Council of the Crees (of Quebec), Montreal

These data uniformly indicate that trapping has not become the primary source of total or cash incomes, and that hunting has continued to hold a decisive place among economic activities. While employment has become a significant economic activity, it has not become the predominant form of productive activity. Although fewer men hunt intensively now, those who continue to hunt intensively appear to have increased per hunter harvests sufficiently to offset the modest declines incurred by those who work, so that total food harvests appear to have remained about stable over a 10-to-15-year period (Feit 1978:83). The intensive hunters harvest foods over and above the nutritional needs of themselves and their families in order to provide a net exchange of food gifts to those who hunt less intensively. It is estimated that a net 20 per cent of their production flows to the families of men who do not hunt intensively (Feit 1978:696).

Thus, production and sharing of food, and economic interdependences among Cree themselves, remain central to Cree economic and social life. Although hunting and wage employment provide roughly equal contributions in dollar value to the total economic outputs at a community level, hunting is the more highly valued activity, it is the more stable activity, and it remains most closely and reticulately linked to the local social and cultural structures that are central to Cree life and that the communities clearly desire to maintain.

With respect to the social organization of hunting, Waswanipi hunters in 1968–70 did not pursue intensive hunting individually and without their families. They typically established winter hunting camps with their wives, their non-school-age children, and often some of their school-age children. In total about one-half of all children, or one-quarter of the school-age children, were in winter hunting camps in any year (Feit 1978:474; and Salisbury *et al.* 1972a: 178).

The family, or commensal unit, which generally cooks separately, eats together and keeps a distinct but not exclusive larder, is the social unit with the greatest economic cooperation and the greatest social solidarity. It is the basis of both productive activities and consumption activities, although it is not the only important socio-economic unit. At Waswanipi, no hunter stayed in the bush without being attached to a commensal unit,[3] and each commensal unit was built around an adult-male and adult-female pair, with an interdependent division of labour. In 75 per cent of the cases, the commensal unit was a nuclear family (Feit 1978:460). Waswanipi hunters did not, therefore, go to the bush hunting camps individually but as families.

Nuclear families, on the other hand, were the most basic of the social units through the year as Murphy and Steward predicted, but, in intensive hunting especially, they were not the only important units nor were they self-sufficient.

The commensal groups that go to winter bush camps to hunt form larger social groups – hunting groups. The hunting groups are winter co-residential groups comprising one or more commensal groups that live together at the same camp site. Thus the 42 commensal groups hunting in the winter of 1968–9 were organized into 18 hunting groups, and the 41 commensal groups in 1969–70 were organized into 21 hunting groups. Over the two years 67 per cent of the hunting groups comprised more than a single nuclear family. This pattern is consistent with those reported earlier for Waswanipi in 1964–7 (Bernier 1968) and for the neighbouring community at Mistassini, by Rogers in 1953–4 (1963), Pothier in 1964 (1967), and Tanner in 1968–70 (1979).

Within the hunting groups there is extensive sharing of bush-food harvests, of equipment and of purchased food. Furthermore, hunting units are important units of economic cooperation not only with respect to consumption, but for production as well. Hunters typically work on a daily basis in pairs, and in many cases the hunters' teams comprise hunters from different commensal groups within the hunting group. Furthermore, the hunters who make up a hunting group generally follow a consistent hunting strategy under the direction of the head of the group who has special rights with respect to the hunting territory on which the group resides.

Hunting groups use specific delimited areas, or hunting territories, but these are not exploited exclusively by a trapper and his family. In the present Waswanipi system of hunting territories each territory is identified with a specific 'owner' whom I define, on the basis of discursive statements by the Waswanipi, as a person with a claimed and acknowledged right to take long-term decisions respecting the ongoing relationships between human beings and the animals and spirits inhabiting an area. In more etic terminology the owner is a person with a right and an obligation to manage and use the animal resources of an area (1978:948–9). While Waswanipi statements about rules emphasize these rights and obligations with respect to fur-bearing mammals, less formal statements and actual practices indicate that these rights and obligations extend to intensive use of all the most important wildlife resources (1978: 947–8).

The owner, or a hunter he chooses, is the head of the hunting group which uses his hunting territory in a given year or season. In addition to the rights and obligations of the owner, there are three other key kinds of recognized interests. First, there is a recognized right of any person for short-term access and use of the animal resources of the territory, such as occurs in normal travel or in abnormal emergencies. Any individual hunter may take game animals whenever in serious need of food, and any hunter may take smaller game animals anywhere on an occasional basis, that is, during a brief period. However, any intensive hunting of the major 'big game' wildlife species and therefore, in effect, any sustained or long-term hunting in an area, is always assumed only to be proper under the direction of the hunting territory owner or his delegate.

Second, there is a recognized right of most hunters who are not owners to use one or more specific hunting territories for intensive hunting under the general decision-making authority of the owner. These men, who have typically hunted with the owner of a given territory over a period of years, are often, but not always, related to the owners of the hunting territories to which they have such rights. I call this a long-term right of access, and a person with such a right to a given territory is normally assumed to be able to join the hunting group using a given hunting territory whenever the owner decides to use, or permit the use, of a hunting territory in a given year (Feit 1978: 950).

Third, in contrast to rights of ownership and access, there is a recognized privilege to use intensively a particular hunting territory which is given by the owner of a hunting territory for a defined or assumed period of time (1978:952). Owners appear to be under obligation generally to grant such privileges where this is consistent with expected harvests, although they are not under obligation to each particular individual request. Nevertheless, obligations do frequently develop between individuals on the basis of more or less extended series of exchanges of privileges.

As a result of this system of rights and privileges the number and composition of the group of hunters using a hunting territory varies considerably from year to year.

There were 40 Waswanipi hunting territories in 1968–70, of which 13 were not used in either of the two years of the research. Most of these owners, and intensive hunters with long-term access rights to unused territories, were exercising privileges to gain access to other territories. In only 22 per cent of the cases did the hunters actually using a hunting territory in a given year exactly correspond to the hunters with long-term rights of access. Furthermore, only three cases of the same hunters using the same hunting territory in both years occurred, about 19 per cent of the cases (1978: 1055–6).

Privileges therefore play an important role in allocating use of hunting territories among hunters, and the granting and exchanging of such privileges comprises an important dimension of economic, social and spiritual interdependence within the community. Waswanipi hunting territories are not therefore exploited exclusively by a single trapper, nor are they typically used exclusively by a stable group of closely related kinsmen.

Furthermore, this hunting territory system is an effective means of conserving wildlife, more effective in fact than a system in which hunters were less flexible, because it permits a management of wildlife populations by a single individual, while also permitting a fluid redistribution of hunters to resources. This provides a complex series of strategies for changing the demand for harvests of particular wildlife resource populations in accordance with the changing conditions of the wildlife. The distribution of hunters and dependants can be changed from year to year, territories can go unused so game populations can recover from declines, the 'mix' of wildlife resources used to meet subsistence needs can be varied, and the actual level of production of subsistence foods can be modified within certain limits (Feit 1973a, 1978: 1000–76). The success of this system is demonstrated by the stability of the harvests over periods of a decade or more, and by certain critical indicators of the conditions of the intensively utilized wildlife populations (Feit 1978:870–8 and 893–9).

This culturally distinctive set of beliefs and rules about the order and meaning of the world and about the rights and responsibilities men have towards each other and towards the land, which they use to distribute men, land and harvests, is clearly not dependent on either the new administrative positions or external institutions. I do not, of course, claim that there have not been changes and cross-cultural influences, as I will indicate later, but the end product is not a simple individualized possession and ownership of land or resources. There has not been a breakdown of effective group cooperation in these areas, nor has change led to the degree of individualized control of resources predicted with the acculturation model.

While it might be argued that such results do not preclude the future predicted by Murphy and Steward, because the processes of transformation are ongoing and the final stages have not as yet been reached, there are reasons for rejecting such a conclusion. As I have indicated already, there are data for an extended period of time and from a series of studies in a number of communities which now indicate that, in general, neither the economic nor the social trends are as predicted. A similar conclusion appears to have been recently reached by a group of researchers working on new data on Brazilian conditions (Gross et al. 1979:1048–9).

Given that the historical trends have generally not been as predicted, what conclusions may we then draw about Murphy and Steward's basic theoretical orientations? If their bold and innovative analysis is not correct it may be because several factors were omitted in their analysis, either because they were not perceived, or because conditions have changed since they wrote. And, if there are key elements omitted, then we may find that their theoretical framework is itself not adequate for a contemporary analysis.

I think that two basic elements have been omitted in their analysis. First, the variety of the types and complexity of the interactions hunting societies have with external institutions need to be expanded, especially to include relations to nation-state institutions as opposed to only considering economic-sector institutions. Second, the varieties of conscious control of such interaction now being actively sought by hunters need to be considered, thereby reducing the relatively simple determinism implicit in their predictions of future trends. In the next two sections of this paper I will explore each of these factors in turn, indicating both the origins of the pattern of Cree hunting described above, and then the response of the Cree themselves to recent conditions.

The intervention of the nation-state in northern Quebec, new dependences

Murphy and Steward consider the world economy, operating through the traders, as the major external factor determining the course of development in the local societies. The external political condition, particularly in the form of nation-state institutions, policies, programmes and action, do not explicitly enter their analysis. While this may have been true over much of the period they were considering, it has clearly not been the case in recent decades throughout most areas occupied by hunting peoples.

Since at least the 1940s in northern Quebec, the nation-state and its subsidiary governments have become major interveners, affecting the conditions of the native populations. They have intervened both as developers of resources or promoters of that development, as in the James Bay hydroelectric scheme, and as a source of programmes affecting incomes, health services, education, employment and community infrastructures available to local societies. The specific effects of these latter interventions on the lives of people in the north of Canada cannot simply be analysed as coincident with the interests of world economic institutions, although the governmental actions may precisely coincide with and assist these interests on specific occasions. It is clear that in addition to economic interests, governments are motivated by a range of specifically short-term political, social, and bureaucratic interests, that often lead to policies and programmes whose impacts need to be analysed rather than assumed.

This is especially so because the impact of government interventions, given political and bureaucratic interests, often is to initiate significant changes in the lives of people living in local societies, changes which notoriously often are unforeseen. As a result, the changes often both conform to and conflict with state interests as well as with local interests, producing a pattern of policy failure and local crises accompanied by a growing pattern of local dependency and reduced local autonomy.

Murphy and Steward clearly foresaw the critical issue of increasing dependence, but they failed to note the political components which are now often key elements in the increases in dependence.

The origins of the recent changes in the economic and social pattern of Cree communities, described in the previous section of this paper, are closely linked to the nature of governmental programmes and administration. The active involvement of government agencies in aspects of Cree hunting activity began in the 1930s and 1940s, when the governments of Quebec and Canada instituted programmes in response to the decimation of the beaver populations in the Cree territory. This near-extermination was caused primarily by pre-emptive hunting by the Cree, in response to the intrusions of Euro-Canadian trappers who were extending their trapping activities during the period of high world fur prices. These trappers sought to clean out beaver populations in specific areas, including parts of the Cree territory, and then move elsewhere in successive years. The Cree hunters, despite the indigenous system for management of wildlife, found themselves left with little choice other than taking the beaver before the Euro-Canadians got to them, thereby decimating the populations (Feit 1978:1117–25). The government programmes were designed to: give legal recognition to the traditional system of Cree hunting territories, now called traplines; improve beaver populations; exclude non-native trappers from the region; prevent excessive harvests; and improve the Cree trappers' cash return from the sale of fur pelts. The governments were concerned to prevent the Cree from becoming completely dependent on government support.

In addition to these responses, the government of Canada started giving out limited transfer payments to Cree hunters in the 1940s, in response to the economic crisis in subsistence and incomes caused by the decimation of beaver populations during the preceding decade. The government provided incomes first in the form of welfare in kind or credit and later also from universal-transfer-payment programmes in cash. This income helped the Cree hunters meet subsistence and cash needs during the period of low beaver harvests.

When beaver trapping recommenced in the early 1950s, after joint government and Cree restocking, fur prices were high and the combination of incomes from the sale of pelts and government assistance provided an adequate income. Furthermore, the incomes were well integrated with the specific scheduling needs of hunters, the welfare ration was given out monthly in summer, when hunting is more limited, and in a lump sum in the autumn, and the fur income came in winter and in spring. The autumn lump-sum payment was needed to facilitate purchasing the goods – food, supplies and equipment – for the six to nine months of living in isolated bush camps between September and June. The welfare payment complemented and partially replaced the credit given by the fur trader in the autumn, which was traditionally repaid when the pelts were sold in winter and spring. With fewer beaver, and with stricter debt policies imposed by the main trading firm, the Hudson's Bay Company, credit was limited and welfare rations took up the slack in the autumn. By giving out a lump-sum autumn ration, equivalent to about 3 months of welfare payments, the government kept people productive in the bush in winter, and off welfare for part of the period from September to June.

The cash available was used by many hunters to reduce some of the most onerous aspects of the heavy work load required of intensive hunters, living in a highly unstable, relatively unproductive, and rigorous sub-Arctic environment. While certain components of this work could not be reduced, given the nature of the animal distributions and abundance, and given the technology available, there were other components which could be eased.

Most important for present purposes were the possibilities of more extensive use of chartered bush aeroplanes as a means of improving transportation to and from those winter camp locations which were not readily accessible from the summer settlements by waterway or by the new but limited road network. Air transportation eliminated the need to carry families and winter supplies to bush camps by canoe. Travel by canoe usually involved paddling one or more heavily packed canoes, and then frequently portaging the supplies and canoes between water bodies. While the time saved by flying varied widely, the more isolated hunters could save two to four weeks of travelling time, and the more than 100 portages needed to reach winter camps. Given this situation, the practice of chartering bush aircraft rapidly became commonplace, and it had ramifications creating other new labour-saving uses of cash incomes.

Use of chartered aircraft made possible the transportation of larger quantities of supplies to the bush, including the liquid fuels needed for more extensive use of equipment such as outboard motors and snowmobiles. These changes involved significant new annual cash expenditures, both as capital investments and for operations and maintenance.

The period of adequate funding therefore led to the kind of transformations which have been found in subsistence societies, the use of available cash to improve labour efficiency, to possibly improve productivity, and to improve security and comfort through a limited use of consumer goods.

But these desired improvements brought with them an increased, but possibly not yet apparent, dependence, not only on the world fur market, but also on the governmental welfare system. This dependence existed despite the fact that the Cree themselves often perceived the welfare payments as compensation for past profits by Canadians at Cree expense, and therefore as 'due', and despite the fact that the actual levels of cash incomes being received were modest by the standards of an affluent nation-state.

During the middle and later 1960s the consequences of these increased and new dependences became apparent as conditions changed. First, the income from fur-pelt sales declined. Second, the credit system was curtailed by the Hudson's Bay Company. The growing Cree demands for consumer goods made it more profitable for the Hudson's Bay Company to shift its emphasis, in much of the region, from running fur-trading posts to becoming general merchants. This, plus the growing Euro-Canadian presence which brought in competition among merchants, made them less willing and able to issue large credit amounts in many communities.

The Cree, in general, attempted to use the growing opportunities for summer employment to increase their incomes, and to offset these other restrictions on access to cash, because summer wage-labour could be integrated with the maintenance of winter hunting and trapping. Summer employment however also increased expenses because less fishing was done, and more foods were purchased to meet family needs during the summer itself. To meet their winter needs many Cree would therefore work later into the autumn when possible, almost until freeze-up, and then fly to the bush. And they would come out of the bush earlier in the spring as well. Changing world economic conditions therefore initially forced many Cree into a more intensive involvement in wage-labour, although it did not force them out of hunting (Feit 1978:44).

These changes led the government of Canada's representatives in the southern part of the region to decide the Cree were on the way to abandoning hunting and becoming wage-labourers. As a result they started cutting off lump-sum payments to hunters in the autumn, and offered a standard monthly welfare cheque, while introducing various make-work programmes to reduce the apparent unemployment (see Feit 1978:52–3).

This change of policy deprived many hunters in some communities of the cash to charter aircraft in the autumn, and it encouraged people to stay near the towns to pick up their monthly cheques. The final result was that many hunters were in fact within a few years forced by the shifts in government policies to abandon intensive hunting from isolated bush camps. It should be noted however, that the numbers of intensive hunters did increase somewhat later, after a Cree initiated reorganization, but it has not yet returned to previous levels.

These problems were accompanied by other changes related to the cost of hunting. The lack of fur-trade posts in some areas meant that the specialized goods needed for hunting were often unavailable. Similarly, changes in the demand for air services often meant that planes were not available when needed. And, the increased services available in the settlements increased demands for improved services available in the bush camps, but these had to be funded by the individual hunters because there were no provisions for bush services under existing government policies.

While quantitative data for the early decades are not available, the data for the 1970 to 1975 period indicate the problems. In 1969–70, Waswanipi hunters owned hunting equipment with an average replacement value of $848 per hunter, and they incurred expenses each year of some $175 for winter food purchases, $79 for hunting and trapping supplies, and an estimated $85 for travel costs (Feit 1978: 529, 541, 535). By 1975–6, Waswanipi hunters had equipment valued at a replacement cost of $2,685 (Feit 1978: 533–4, 529 and unpublished data), and they were spending $1,274 on food and hunting and trapping supplies, and an estimated $134 for travel (Bearskin *et al.* 1977:14). In 1969–70, fur income averaged $619 (Feit 1978: 547) and in 1976 it averaged $671. By 1976, the Cree regional average value of hunting equipment owned by hunters was $2,328, and the average annual costs of intensive hunting included an estimated $761 for supplies of food and goods and $284 for transportation. The maximum possible fur-sale income averaged $617 for the year (Bearskin *et al.* 1977: 14, 15, 16).

Thus, the Cree were trying to maintain a subsistence economy in the midst of an increasing interaction and dependence on cash, goods, services and employment in the regional market economy. The results were mixed, and a significant number of people were being driven out of intensive subsistence production in the process. The external factors affecting the Cree during this period included market conditions for both the sale of products and the provision of needed goods and services, and also government policies concerning social assistance and community infrastructure.

These problems were exacerbated during the period by the accelerating pace of change in the regional resource use and environmental conditions, which also put Cree hunters in an increasingly difficult situation. Although these problems had their origins in the increasing physical intrusion of Euro-Canadians into Cree territory, the problems were intimately linked to the development policies and the accompanying expansion of the administrative and political structures of the nation-state.

Mining centres were opened in the 1950s bringing roads and rail communication links into the southern portion of the Cree territory, and opening the well-forested southern portion to commercial forestry operations. Along with the generally adverse impacts this activity had on the wildlife and the ecological systems of the territory, the new communication links made the region significantly more accessible to Euro-Canadian sportsmen. Competition for those wildlife species of interest to sport hunters and fishermen rapidly developed, and as a response to this problem the government of Quebec implanted conservation officers, then called game wardens, in the southern portion of the territory.

The conservation officers began to impose provincial game laws, regulations and policies on the Cree hunters for the first time, as part of their response to the wildlife conservation and management problems. These policies were based on a recognition that standard game laws could not be inflexibly applied to Indian populations, who hunted and fished for subsistence, who extensively depended on the food of the animals they harvested for nutrition, and whose whole culture and society were integrated with and by hunting activities. The government did not however recognize a basic right to hunt, and it viewed the special exclusions from the laws of general application as a privilege granted by the government to the Crees. The government therefore reserved entirely to itself the formulation of the extent of special privileges to be accorded indigenous peoples. While the Cree resisted these new policies, largely by passively or surreptitiously ignoring them, some of the new regulations which were imposed had the effect of limiting Cree hunting in the areas most accessible to sportsmen.

The government programmes of this period can be contrasted with those which had been introduced in the 1930s and 1940s. The latter were distinguished by the fact that: they excluded Euro-Canadian trappers and protected Cree interests; the entire system was cooperative, encouraging Cree inputs; and, in so far as it involved Cree compliance, it was self-regulated. In fact, the system had as its model the indigenous Cree system of hunting-territory organization and wildlife management. The involvement of the Quebec government in the 1960s was therefore a radical break with previous practice because: the existence of an aboriginal right to hunt was explicitly denied; the government acted to protect the interests of Euro-Canadian hunters and restricted some Cree activities; and the Cree no longer participated in the formulation of new policy nor were they involved in its implementation.

The dependence of Cree on government regulations concerning developmental and sporting activities by Euro-Canadians thus became as important as their dependence on government-issued welfare and transfer payments. During the 1960s, dependence on nation-state programmes and institutions was apparent to the Cree as it had not been in the 1940s and 1950s. A critical step in this course of events came with the announcement that the provincial government was going to build a massive hydroelectric project on Cree lands, without consultation or forewarning. This threat eventually provided the context within which the Cree initiated an autonomous new local response to these growing crises.

Dealing with dependence, the Cree approach to enhancing autonomy

The Cree response to the crises of growing dependence was greatly facilitated by using the leverage provided by their opposition to the James Bay hydroelectric project, and their claim for settlement of their aboriginal rights. The Cree response to the project was to try to stop it, but when it became clear how difficult this would be the Cree progressively moved towards negotiations that would moderate the impacts of the project, while providing measures necessary significantly to enhance the Cree ability to maintain their way of life and reduce their dependence. These negotiations resulted in the first comprehensive aboriginal-rights settlement in Canada.

The negotiation of a comprehensive aboriginal and land-claims settlement during 1974 and 1975 not only provided the Cree people with the first opportunity to deal with the general problems of hunting, it permitted them to do so in a relatively extensive and coordinated fashion. It was one of their objectives during the negotiation of the agreement to establish the conditions necessary to sustain the central core of Cree life and society, and to ensure that in the future they could build a society based on a balance among the population of participation in subsistence activities and in economic enterprises and employment. Furthermore, they explicitly sought to reduce both the economic and the administrative dependences.

The James Bay and Northern Quebec Agreement (JBNQA) was signed in 1975 by the James Bay Cree, the northern Quebec Inuit, the government of Canada, the government of Quebec and the James Bay Corporations after two years of detailed negotiations. The Agreement provided for the extinguishment of any aboriginal rights or claims the approximately 11,000 Cree and Inuit might have in Quebec, in exchange for the specific rights and claims spelled out in the 30 sections and over 400 pages of the agreement. The agreement was comprehensive, covering the questions of hunting, fishing and trapping, land allocations and regimes, local and regional government, education, health and medical services, economic and social development, income security, police and justice, environmental protection, modifications to the James Bay hydroelectric project, compensation and eligibility (Anonymous 1976). In each of those areas the JBNQA provided for specific rights, benefits and responsibilities of the parties and for the mechanisms thought necessary for successful exercise of those rights, benefits and responsibilities.[4]

A major component of the settlement concerned the protection and enhancement of the hunting activities of the Cree. The range of hunting problems the Cree addressed during the negotiations had five focuses for which the Cree sought solutions: definition and recognition of aboriginal hunting rights; effective involvement of the Cree in management of wildlife and the environment; regulation of the allocation of wildlife between indigenous hunters and sportsmen including priority allocation to the former; regulation of the environmental impacts of developmental activity; and reduction of the dependence of the hunters on world-market conditions and on government policies and programmes.

The specific provisions designed by the Cree negotiators and their scientific and legal advisers in order to meet the first four of these objectives have been described in detail elsewhere (Feit 1979), and only a brief review of these can be offered here.

With respect to hunting rights the JBNQA provides for a right to 'harvest', which includes the right to pursue, capture and kill all species of fauna at all times over the entire territory where the activity is physically possible and where it does not endanger the safety of others. The generality of the right to harvest is limited by the operation of the principle of conserving endangered wildlife species and habitats, but this conservation is specified as being for the primary purpose of maintaining the traditional pursuits of the native people, and it is implemented in the first instance through traditional Cree measures for conservation and management. The right to harvest and the principle of conservation are an attempt to codify an aboriginal hunting right in modern terms and to give it a legal force that is binding on government. The right and the associated principles are intended to stop the unilateral redefinition of native hunting rights, and the *ad hoc* encroachments on Cree hunting activities by governments.

Effective involvement of Cree in the management of wildlife and the environment is established through a joint and balanced Hunting, Fishing and Trapping Coordinating Committee which is the permanent, exclusive and mandatory forum in which native authorities and the responsible governments formulate regulations, supervise administration, and manage the regime. The powers are predominantly consultative, but the consultation is mandatory, and in a limited number of key areas the committee has major decision-making authority.

The allocation of wildlife resources between Cree hunters and sportsmen was a critical area, and the Cree established a binding principle for those allocations which gave priority to Cree hunters. They also established an operational procedure for implementing the principle. This procedure involves the establishment of the present levels of wildlife harvests by Cree peoples over a specified seven-year period by a joint research team (see James Bay and Northern Quebec Native Harvesting Research Committee 1976, 1978, 1979). This present level then determines the allocation of permissible harvests for those species populations which are under careful management for conservation purposes. If these populations permit a kill exceeding the number presently harvested, then the Cree hunters are allocated the present harvest level automatically, and the balance of the permissible harvest is divided between Crees and sport hunters according to need and the principle of priority to Cree harvesting. If the populations only permit a kill equal to or lower than present harvest levels, then the entire permissible kill is allocated to Cree hunters.

This operational procedure assures priority to Cree hunters, and minimizes the impacts on them of declines in animal populations. In addition, certain areas of land, and certain species which are not of primary interest to sportsmen, are reserved for the exclusive use of the Cree.

In total, these provisions are intended to assure that, although the nation-state and its subsidiary governments exercise most wildlife-management authority, they will do so only within certain limits, according to rules and procedures that protect Cree interests, and on the advice of the Cree themselves; and that the Cree will have a legal recourse against the governments if they violate these terms of the agreement.

The protection of the environment from the adverse effects of development, and the minimization of negative impacts on Cree hunting, economies, societies and culture, were the subject of a series of parallel principles, procedures and consultative and participatory mechanisms. These have a similar intent to those directly related to hunting, both limiting the exercise of state authority and assuring Cree participation in decision-making. In addition a number of specific programmes and organizations, to be described below, were designed to provide the economic means whereby the Cree could adapt their hunting patterns to the changes created by resource-development activity in their territory.

This first group of procedures made up an integrated package designed to reduce Cree dependence resulting from the political, legal and administrative activities of the Canadian and Quebec governments in relation to the environment, wildlife and hunting in the Cree area.

The second range of problems the Cree set out to deal with in the JBNQA were related to the growing difficulty of meeting the economic costs of hunting and the resultant dependence.

The economic problems of hunting were addressed primarily in the JBNQA sections dealing with an Income Security Program for Cree Hunters, Trappers and Fishermen (ISP), and related programmes for a Cree Trappers' Association (CTA), and the provision of a corporation to undertake remedial works relevant to the impacts of the first stage of the hydroelectric development (SOTRAC). ISP was the key provision, intended to provide sufficiently generous cash payments to Cree hunters effectively to reduce their dependence on fur prices in the world economy, on wage employment and on government transfer payments. The explicitly stated objective of ISP is: 'The program shall ensure that hunting, fishing and trapping shall constitute a viable way of life for the Cree people, and that individual Crees who elect to pursue such a way of life shall be guaranteed a measure of economic security consistent with provisions prevailing from time to time' (JBNQA, Section 30.1.8).

With development of the natural resources of the Cree region accelerating, the ISP was justified as a way of providing individual Cree hunters with the means to maintain, modify or expand hunting activities in the face of the more difficult hunting conditions. The improved funds available to hunters could be used to pay for transportation to more distant or isolated wildlife resources, to improve hunters' equipment which could improve the efficiency of hunting at a time when other factors might lead to declines in efficiency, and to improve the levels of security experienced in the bush during a time of disruption caused by development. The programme and its form however were generally designed to respond to the dependences native people perceived were being created for their hunting activities and economy during the previous decades.

Since the main reasons cited for abandonment of hunting were instability of the available cash and insufficiency of the total cash actually available, the ISP was designed to provide a stable cash income for those who practised intensive hunting, sufficient to meet current needs taking into account other earned incomes.

The ISP provides an annual guaranteed income to Cree hunters who meet the basic requirements. Requirements for participation are, generally: (a) that more time be spent each year in hunting and related traditional activities than is spent in paid employment; and (b) that at least four months be spent in hunting and traditional activities of which 90 days are out of settlements 'in the bush' (Anonymous 1976). In fact, 80 per cent of all participants spend over 150 days 'in the bush', and 50 per cent more than 200 days, almost seven months (LaRusic 1979). Eligibility for any year is based on the activities of the previous year.

The main payment in 1979–80 was $16.64 per day for the head of household, and a similar amount for the consort, for up to 240 days each spent 'in the bush' in hunting and related traditional activities, paid four times a year. This amounts to 75 per cent of the total paid under the programme, and it is guaranteed to all beneficiaries. In addition a basic amount is calculated for each family based on the composition and size of the family. From this amount 40 per cent of all family cash income including daily payments is deducted, and the balance paid to the family. This amount, which is approximately 25 per cent of the total paid, goes primarily to families that have a large number of dependants and to those with relatively few days 'in the bush'.

At the beginning of 1979–80 year, the fourth year of operation, there were a total of 841 beneficiary units, single individuals 18 years of age or over, or heads of families. The average payment was expected to be about $7,683 per year to bi-parental families, and $3,265 to single individuals and the few mono-parental families. The overall average was expected to be about $5,900. It is difficult to compare this with welfare payments, but welfare would maximally amount to 60 per cent of what beneficiaries receive from ISP all year. However, because of the time spent in the bush, few hunting beneficiaries get the maximum welfare in a year, so ISP is probably more than two times what beneficiaries would get from welfare if they maintained their hunting patterns.

Beneficiaries also receive other universal transfer payments such as family allowances and old-age pensions, but are not eligible for social aid or welfare. The amounts paid under the programme are indexed annually to the cost of living.

At the time of negotiating the programme the Cree negotiators were aware that the control of transfer payment programmes at the provincial and national levels was creating a real dependence on those institutions by hunters. There was therefore concern that although ISP benefits could meet immediate needs, the programme still could increase dependences. The incorporation of ISP into the framework of the JBNQA claims settlement made it possible for ISP to be structured in a way that could limit some of the dependences inherent in usual transfer payment programmes. The programme was therefore designed to differ from other transfer payments in several respects.

First, ISP exists through Quebec legislation which is to give force to the terms of the claims agreement. But, because this legislation does not replace the agreement, and because the agreement provides that the implementing legislation must reflect the provisions of the JBNQA, any change in the government legislation or in the programme must involve changes in the agreement, and this can only be done with Cree consent. This was intended to ensure, in effect, that ISP is not treated as a standard government programme, which could be unilaterally changed by the government. It is intended to ensure, with certain specific exceptions, that changes to ISP require the approval and consent of the Cree. If this principle is violated, the agreement provides a base for the taking of legal recourses against the government by the Cree.

Second, unlike most welfare recipients, the beneficiaries of ISP have the right to benefit from ISP, so long as they meet the fixed criteria for eligibility in the programme, and based on fixed criteria for calculating the size of the benefits to be paid. And, they can appeal or take legal action if those rights are violated.

Third, ISP is not administered by the government that funds it, but by a separate corporate entity, the Cree Income Security Board, made up equally of Quebec and Cree appointees, with a rotating chairmanship. The Board hires and employs its own staff, although those hired may be civil servants if the Board so decides. The legal obligation of Quebec is to transfer the funds needed each year to the accounts of the ISP Board. In practice, the Board members and the staff are either closely associated with the Cree or with the Quebec government, but a balance is and has been maintained. The Board is therefore not bound by the full range of government administrative norms, and it is given considerable authority to implement, and where necessary interpret and review, the programme and its operations, consistent with the agreement and the legislation.

Fourth, the Board operates out of a regional office, but it must also maintain staff and offices in each community to assure access of the beneficiaries to the administrators of the programme.

Furthermore, the incorporation of the negotiations over ISP within the framework of the comprehensive aboriginal and land-claims negotiations permitted ISP to be integrated into a package of regimes, programmes, organizational structures and benefits thought to be necessary to assure the viability of hunting as a way of life (see Feit 1979). To review, then, the negotiation of ISP established a programme that: although funded by government, was significantly independent of changes in government policy and politics; was jointly controlled and administered by the government and the representatives of the beneficiary population; and it also provided the opportunity to legally encode the specific rights of the beneficiaries.

Several researchers at McGill University are presently studying the initial responses of the Cree hunters to the programme but our results can only be indicated here (Scott 1977, 1979; LaRusic 1979; Scott and Feit 1981). A major available indicator of the response is the history of enrolment. During the initial registration there was a provision to admit people who wanted to try hunting as a way of life, but who were not currently doing so. Approximately 300 beneficiary units were admitted under this provision, approximately 43 per cent of 700 already hunting as their main source of livelihood. After one year of operation about 75 dropped out, and the remaining 225 stayed. These people have effectively returned to, or begun hunting as their major productive activity, apparently as a result of the establishment of the programme. In fact, the great majority of these people were former intensive hunters and their families, who had been driven out of intensive hunting under pre-ISP and pre-JBNQA conditions.

Other preliminary results suggest that hunters stay away longer in the bush, and most of those who had not taken their families to the bush in the recent past because of the costs involved have begun to do so. In some communities more isolated geographical areas have begun to be used because of the additional funds to cover travel costs, and significant new capitalization has occurred to increase the ease and efficiency of hunting, skidoos especially being purchased in large numbers. Data on harvests are still only available for a few communities, but it appears that individual harvests may not have increased, although the increase in people hunting may have increased the total harvest proportionally.

These data are too limited, and cover too short a time, to permit final conclusions concerning whether the Income Security Programme will continue to meet its stated objectives in the longer term. The general experiences with the provisions of the James Bay and Northern Quebec Agreement are just beginning to accumulate, and it will be several years in my view before it will be possible to evaluate the provisions of the agreement in general. One aspect is already clear: subsistence production has been maintained during the first half-decade following the agreement, despite increased development activity in the region. This continuing subsistence production may itself be a significant factor in the levels of autonomy or dependence experienced by the Cree.

While it is too soon to say whether the provisions of the agreement will meet the expectations of the Cree, the process has clearly demonstrated how a hunting people can undertake to define their own futures, and how they can take innovative local initiatives aimed at achieving these objectives. It will be important to see whether the particular provisions included in the structure and organization of the James Bay and Northern Quebec Agreement are effective to prevent or limit the extent of local dependency on international markets and provincial and federal governments that have been characteristic of recent Cree history. And this will provide one of a number of fundamental tests of the assumption made during the negotiation of the agreement, namely that local populations can develop specific institutions and benefits, closely linked to national institutions, and still retain and enhance local autonomy.[5]

Conclusions

The responses of the Cree to the conditions of increasing dependence on macro-level economic and political institutions emphasize the possibilities for responses to these conditions generated at the local level.

This indicates a second type of inadequacy of the theoretical formulation provided by Murphy and Steward. The acculturation model, and indeed many other anthropological theories of change, involves the assumption that micro-level changes originate primarily externally, and more particularly that local-level responses are simply reactive, the local population having neither the power nor the means to generate unique or effective responses. Thus Murphy and Steward predict the course of local-level change entirely from an account of macro-level interventions and local patterns of material production given the currently existing environment and technology (see Murphy 1970).

The data on James Bay Cree history indicate that there may be important local-level initiatives taken, and that the impacts of macro-institutional interventions in a given community cannot be assumed to be generally and simply determined externally, given the local productive organization, and independent of: (1) the economic and political resources of that community; (2) the specific cultural values of that community; and (3) the specific decisions and actions taken by the local population.

It is clear from the above data that hunting societies have not been simply passive in the face of external changes, and that many have sought to set and meet their own objectives. In the Canadian context it is clear that native groups in general have tried specifically to retain their ties to the natural environment, their subsistence production, their social and community ties, their languages, and their belief systems, in the face of those changes whose origin lies totally, or in part, in the macro-institutions. And it is also clear that many native societies have had, under conditions found in developed nation states, a substantial measure of success to date. The data on the James Bay Cree specifically indicate that under certain conditions, hunting people are able to maintain significant parts of the communal fabric of their society and culture in the face of significant externally initiated changes and at least some dependences on international economic institutions and nation-state structures.

The reasons for this degree of success are complex. The data indicate that when hunting peoples in developed states are able to mobilize some political/economic leverage in the macro-arena then it may be possible for them not only to resist external pressures leading to a restructuring of their own social fabric, but they may also be able to restructure the relationship between themselves and the impinging macro-institutions. The extent of such restructuring is variable, and the means of reorganizing relationships between a hunting society and macro-societies necessarily involve the creation and introduction of new institutions. While it is clear that the particular legal and political leverage which the Crees were able to exercise is not universally available to hunting peoples, these and other significant forms of leverage are available in much of the Canadian north, and to many other hunters in developed nation states. Therefore, it is plausible that when such political leverage can be mobilized organizational forms and local control can be developed that will both be responsive to local conditions and goals, and at the same time effectively accomplish those local objectives in macro-level arenas and institutions. In short, local societies may have and exercise effective power, in the sense of being able to accomplish their own objectives.

These conclusions indicate that local values and knowledge play a central part in the process, and that a singular focus on material resources, work organization and material production is insufficient, because indigenous peoples are increasingly seeking to choose for themselves and the particular 'mix' of values and institutions with which they want to make their lives. The extent of local success is and will be variable, but nevertheless one cannot adequately describe or account for the actual course of change without taking into account the values and knowledge that inform people's decisions and actions.

Following from this then the Cree example also indicates that the course of change can only be accounted for by examining the consequences of both local and macro-level actions, and the ways in which these consequences are interpreted and inform later action at all levels. This emphasizes the need to link macro- and micro-levels of analyses.

In addition to revising our theories of change so as to better account for local-level power, belief, decision and action, we also need theoretical frameworks that provide us with a more complex and sophisticated analysis of the macro-system itself. We need a framework from which to analyse and evaluate the inconsistencies and impotencies of nation states and international markets, as well as their powers. That is, we need a critique of developed nation-states that does not fall into the structural trap of seeing them as all-powerful and hyper-integrated. The Cree data emphasize again the very commonplace finding that government policies often fail, and that governments often do not control the effects or the outcome of their actions.

Therefore we need, given a critical analysis of nation-state political and international economic structures, to be able to analyse these both from the perspective of their constraints on autonomous local action, and simultaneously from the perspective of their intended or unintended potentialities for effective local initiatives informed by local knowledge and values. We might say that we need to move from the single-focus study of dependence, to a wider framework that, without abandoning such study, also includes study of the means of action by which autonomy may be created among the constraints causing dependence.

The creation of means to such autonomy, and the critical evaluation of the effectiveness of their implementation, is a significant task for local populations and for anthropological research. If anthropologists are to analyse and to assist in this process, the challenge will be to develop and apply theoretical orientations which enhance the capacity of local populations to determine their own futures. These will have to involve, in my view, analyses of local beliefs and knowledge, of possible sources of local power, and of the effectiveness of decisions and actions at all levels. This will require the linking together of analyses of both the logic and the incoherence of macro-level structures with comprehensive decision-making analyses of the micro-level knowledge, power, imagination and initiative.

We need a social analysis that has a macro-view but that also can account for and contribute to the process by which groups of men and women may make their own futures within the constraints determined in their interactions with the nation state and international economies. Such research holds the unique promise of both being theoretically informed and contributing to the efforts of hunting peoples to avoid extinction or assimilation and to create new, viable and relatively autonomous forms of hunting societies.

Acknowledgements

An earlier version of this paper was presented at the Conference on Hunters and Gatherers held June 27–30, 1978 in Paris. I want to thank Richard F. Salisbury, Colin Scott and Alan Penn for comments on the earlier version, and for many discussions over recent years. In addition, I would like to similarly thank Ignatius LaRusic, Philip Awashish, Peter Hutchins and Rick Cuciurean for stimulating and valuable conversations that have clarified my understanding of many of the issues raised herein. Attendance at the Paris conference was made possible by a grant from the Gouvernement du Québec, Ministère des Affaires Intergouvernementales. This expanded paper was prepared during Killam Postdoctoral Research Scholarship from the Canada Council, and it draws extensively from this ongoing research on 'Socio-political Implications of Native Land Claims in Canada: The Case of the Negotiation and Implementation of the James Bay and Northern Quebec Agreement'. Data on the land-claims negotiations were also gathered while serving as a consultant to the Grand Council of the Crees (of Quebec) and to the Cree Regional Authority. Additional data cited in this paper on Waswanipi Cree hunting were collected during the term of a Canada Council Doctoral Fellowship; and data on the Income Security Program for Cree Hunters, Trappers and Fishermen were gathered in part during a research grant from the Gouvernement du Québec, Ministère des Affaires Sociales, Comité de la recherche socio-économique.

Notes

1 I am including among the Eastern Cree the bands of: Great Whale River, Fort George, Old Factory (Paint Hills), Eastmain, Rupert House, Nemaska (Champion Lake), Mistassini and Waswanipi.
2 For a general discussion of the methodology of establishing the cash value of subsistence food production see Peter Usher 1976a. It may be worth emphasizing here that the Waswanipi do not consider commercially produced foods to be the equivalent of locally produced foods, in terms of nutrition or spiritual origin.
3 Although adult all-male hunting camps have occurred at other Eastern Cree communities at certain periods, such camps have not become common in the region, and tend to be declining for reasons now related to the structure of the income security programme to be discussed later in this paper.
4 Since December 1973 I have served as an adviser to the Cree Indian organizations, the Grand Council of the Crees (of Quebec) and the Cree Regional Authority, first in their court fight against the hydroelectric project with respect to the social implications of the James Bay development, and later in the negotiations, on the social aspect of the James Bay and Northern Quebec Land Claim Agreement. For a discussion of the process of negotiating the agreement, see Feit forthcoming.
5 A wide range of research on the James Bay and Northern Quebec Agreement, its implementation, and its impacts on regional development have been and are being undertaken by researchers in the Programme in the Anthropology of Development, at McGill University (see Salisbury 1976a, 1976b; LaRusic 1979; LaRusic et al. 1979; Scott 1977, 1979; Scott and Feit 1981; Feit 1979, forthcoming).

Bibliography

Anonymous 1976. *The James Bay and Northern Quebec Agreement*. Quebec: Editeur Officiel

Asch, Michael I. 1979. 'The economics of Dene self-determination', in David H. Turner and Gavin A. Smith (eds.), *Challenging anthropology: a critical introduction to social and cultural anthropology*, 339–52. Toronto: McGraw-Hill Ryerson Ltd

Balikci, Asen 1964. *Development of basic socio-economic units in two Eskimo communities*. National Museum of Canada: Bulletin no. 202

Bearskin, Steven *et al.* 1977. 'Report on feasibility of forming a Cree Trappers' Association and developing a wild fur harvesting and marketing program for the James Bay Agreement Area, Province of Quebec'. Val d'Or: Grand Council of the Crees (of Quebec)

Berger, Thomas R. 1977. *Northern frontier, northern homeland: the report of the Mackenzie Valley pipeline Inquiry*. Vols I and II. Ottawa: Minister of Supply and Services Canada

Berkes, Fikret, and Farkas, Carol S. 1978. 'Eastern James Bay Cree Indians: changing patterns of wild food use and nutrition'. *Ecology of Food and Nutrition* 7:155–72

Bernier, Bernard 1968. *The social organization of the Waswanipi Cree*. Montreal: McGill University, Programme in the Anthropology of Development, McGill Cree Project, Research Report

Brody, Hugh 1975. *The people's land: Eskimos and Whites in the eastern Arctic*. Harmondsworth: Penguin Books

Chance, Norman A. *et al.* 1970. *Developmental change among the Cree Indians of Quebec (Summary Report)*. Ottawa: Queen's Printer for the Department of Regional Economic Expansion

Charest, Paul 1975. 'Les ressources naturelles de la Côte-nord ou la richesse des autres: une analyse diachronique'. *Recherches Amérindiennes au Québec* 5(2): 35–52

Cumming, Peter A. 1977. *Canada: native land rights and northern development*. Copenhagen: International Work Group for Indigenous Affairs. Document 26

Cumming, Peter A. and Mickenberg, Neil H. 1972. *Native rights in Canada*. Second Edn. Toronto: The Indian-Eskimo Association of Canada and General Publishing Co. Ltd

Désy, Pierrette 1968. 'Fort George ou Tsesa-sippi: contribution à une étude sur la désintégration culturelle d'une communauté indienne de la Baie James'. Thèse de doctorat, Université de Paris

Feit, Harvey A. 1972. 'The Waswanipi of James Bay'. *Canadian Dimension* 8(8): 22–5

1973a. 'The ethno-ecology of the Waswanipi Cree – or how hunters can manage their resources', in Bruce Cox (ed.), *Cultural ecology: readings on the Canadian Indians and Eskimos*, 115–25. Toronto: McClelland and Steward Ltd

1973b. 'Twilight of the Cree hunting nation'. *Natural History* 82(7):48–57, 72

1978. 'Waswanipi realities and adaptations: resource management and cognitive structure'. Ph.D. dissertation, Department of Anthropology, McGill University

408   Harvey A. Feit

1979. 'Political articulations of hunters to the state: means of resisting threats to subsistence production in the James Bay and northern Quebec Agreement'. *Etudes/Inuit/Studies* 3(2):37–52

forthcoming. 'Negotiating recognition of Aboriginal rights: the context, development, strategies, and some consequences of the James Bay and Northern Quebec Agreement'. *Canadian Journal of Anthropology* 1(2)

Feit, Harvey A. *et al.* 1972. 'A case study in northern Quebec', in Fikret Berkes *et al.* (ed.), *Environmental aspects of the pulp and paper industry in Quebec*, 165–87. Second edn. Montreal: Terra Nova, STOP

Freeman, Milton M. R., and Hackman, L. M. 1975. 'Bathurst Island NWT: a test case of Canada's northern policy'. *Canadian Public Policy* 1:402–14

Grand Council of the Crees (of Quebec) 1977. 'Position of the Grand Council of the Crees (of Quebec) and the James Bay Crees respecting the possible imposition of a 150,000 man/day limit on the Income Security Program for Cree Hunters and Trappers established by section 30 of the James Bay and Northern Quebec Agreement'. Restricted Manuscript at Grand Council of the Crees (of Quebec), Montreal

Gross, Daniel R. *et al.* 1979. 'Ecology and acculturation among native peoples of central Brazil'. *Science* 206:1043–50

Hunt, Constance D. 1978. 'Approaches to native land settlements and implications for northern land use and resource management policies', in Robert F. Keith and Janet B. Wright (eds.), *Northern transitions: volume II: second national workshop on people resources and the environment north of 60°*, 5–41. Ottawa: Canadian Arctic Resources Committee

Inuit Studies 1979a. 'Revendications autochtones/native claims'. *Etudes/Inuit/Studies* 3(1)

1979b. 'Quart monde nordique / northern fourth world'. *Etudes/Inuit/Studies* 3(2)

James Bay and Northern Quebec Native Harvesting Research Committee 1976. *Research to establish present levels of harvesting by native peoples of northern Quebec: part I: a report on the harvests by the James Bay Cree*. Two vols. Montreal: James Bay and Northern Quebec Native Harvesting Research Committee

1978. *Interim report for phase II, year 1, research to establish present levels of harvesting by native peoples of northern Quebec: part I: harvests by the James Bay Cree*. Montreal: James Bay and Northern Quebec Native Harvesting Research Committee

1979. *Harvests by the James Bay Cree, 1976–77. third progress report (phase II, year 2): research to establish present levels of harvesting by native peoples of northern Quebec*. Montreal: James Bay and Northern Quebec Native Harvesting Research Committee

Keith, Robert F., and Wright, Janet B. (eds.) 1978. *Northern transitions: volume II: second national workshop on people, resources and the environment north of 60°*. Ottawa: Canadian Arctic Resources Committee

Knight, Rolf 1965. 'A re-examination of hunting, trapping, and territoriality among the northeastern Algonkian Indians', in Anthony Leeds and Andrew P. Vayda (eds.), *Man, culture and animals: the role of animals in human ecological adjustments*, 27–42. Washington: American Association for the Advancement of Science, Publication No. 78

LaRusic, Ignatius E. 1970. 'From hunter to proletarian', in Norman Chance (ed.), *Developmental change among the Cree Indians of Quebec*. Ottawa: Queen's Printer for Department of Regional Economic Expansion

1979. *The Income Security Program for Cree Hunters and Trappers: a study of the design, operation, and initial impacts of the guaranteed annual income programme established under the James Bay and Northern Quebec Agreement*. Montreal: McGill University, Programme in the Anthropology of Development

LaRusic, Ignatius E. *et al.* 1979. *Negotiating a way of life: initial Cree experience with the administrative structure arising from the James Bay Agreement*. Montreal: Social Science, Development and Cultural Change, Inc.

Leacock, Eleanor 1954. *The Montagnais 'hunting territory' and the fur trade*. American Anthropological Association, Memoir no. 78

McCullum, Hugh, and McCullum, Karmel 1975. *This land is not for sale: Canada's original people and their land: a saga of neglect, exploitation, and conflict*. Toronto: Anglican Book Centre

McCullum, Hugh, McCullum, Karmel and Olthuis, John 1977. *Moratorium: justice, energy, the north, and the native people*. Toronto: Anglican Book Centre

Murphy, Robert F. 1970. 'Basin ethnography and ecological theory', in E. H. Swanson, Jr (ed.), *Languages and cultures of western North America*, 152–71. Porcatello: Idaho State University Press

Murphy, Robert F., and Steward, Julian H. 1956. 'Tappers and trappers: parallel process in acculturation'. *Economic Development and Cultural Change* 4: 335–55

O'Malley, Martin 1976. *The past and future land: an account of the Berger Inquiry into the Mackenzie Valley pipeline*. Toronto: Peter Martin Associates Ltd

Paine, Robert (ed.) 1971. *Patrons and brokers in the east Arctic*. St John's: Memorial University of Newfoundland, Institute of Social and Economic Research

1977. *The white Arctic: anthropological essays on tutelage and ethnicity*. St John's: Memorial University of Newfoundland, Institute of Social and Economic Research

Penn, Alan F. 1975 'Development of James Bay: the role of environmental assessment in determining the legal rights to an interlocutory injunction'. *Journal of the Fisheries Research Board of Canada* 32(1):136–60

Peterson, Everett B., and Wright, Janet B. 1978. *Northern transitions: volume 1: northern resource and land use policy study*. Ottawa: Canadian Arctic Resources Committee

Pothier, Roger 1967. *Relations inter-ethniques et acculturation à Mistassini*. Quebec: Université Laval, Centre d'Etudes Nordiques, Travaux Divers 9

Recherches Amérindiennes au Québec 1971. 'La Baie James des amérindiennes'. *Recherches Amérindiennes au Québec* 1(4–5)

1979. 'Autochtones: luttes et conjonctures I'. *Recherches Amérindiennes au Québec* 9(3)

1980. 'Autochtones: luttes et conjonctures II'. *Recherches Amérindiennes au Québec* 9(4)

Richardson, Boyce 1972. *James Bay: the plot to drown the north woods*. San Francisco: Sierra Club

1975. *Strangers devour the land: the Cree hunters of the James Bay area versus*

Premier Bourassa and the James Bay Development Corporation. New York: Alfred A. Knopf

Rogers, Edward S. 1963. *The hunting group – hunting territory complex among the Mistassini Indians*. National Museum of Canada: Bulletin 195

Rouland, Norbert 1978. 'Les Inuit du Nouveau-Québec et la convention de la Baie James. Québec: Association Inuksiutiit Katimajiit et Centre d'Etudes Nordiques, Université Laval

Salisbury, Richard F. 1976a. 'Transactions or transactors? an economic anthropologist's view', in Bruce Kapferer (ed.), *Transaction and meaning: directions in the anthropology of exchange and symbolic behavior*, 41–59. Philadelphia: Institute for the Study of Human Issues

1976b. 'The anthropologist as societal ombudsman', in David Pitt (ed.), *Development from below: anthropologists and development situations*, 255–65. The Hague: Mouton

1977. 'A prism of perceptions: the James Bay hydro-electricity project', in Sandra Wallman (ed.), *Perceptions of development*, 172–205. Cambridge: Cambridge University Press

1979. 'Application and theory in Canadian anthropology: the James Bay Agreement'. *Transactions of the Royal Society of Canada* IV(17):229–41

forthcoming. 'The north as a developing nation', in *At the turning point*. Proceedings of the Eighth Northern Development Conference, November 1979

Salisbury, Richard F. *et al.* 1972a. *Development and James Bay: social implications of the proposals for the hydroelectric scheme*. Montreal: McGill University, Programme in the Anthropology of Development

1972b. *Not by bread alone: the subsistence economies of the people of Fort George, Paint Hills, Eastmain, Great Whale, Fort Chimo, and the Nitchequon band from Mistassini*. Montreal: Indians of Quebec Association, James Bay Task Force

Samson, Marcel 1966. 'Economic change among the Cree Indians of Waswanipi'. Montreal: McGill University, Programme in the Anthropology of Development, McGill Cree Project, Research Report no. 2

Sanders, Douglas Esmond 1973. *Native people in areas of internal national expansion: Indians and Inuit in Canada*. Copenhagen: International Work Group for Indigenous Affairs. Document 14

Savard, Rémi 1979. *Destins d'Amérique: les autochtones et nous*. Montreal: L'Hexagone

Scott, Colin H. 1977. 'The income security program for Cree hunters, fishermen and trappers – an initial field report on impacts and reactions in four James Bay coastal settlements'. Manuscript. Montreal: Grand Council of the Crees (of Quebec)

1979. *Modes of production and guaranteed annual income in James Bay Cree society*. Montreal: McGill University, Programme in the Anthropology of Development

Scott, Colin H., and Feit, Harvey A. 1981. *Income security for Cree hunters: initial socio-economic impacts and long-term considerations*. Montreal: McGill University, Programme in the Anthropology of Development

Tanner, Adrian 1979. *Bringing home animals: religious ideology and mode of production of the Mistassini Cree hunters*. St John's: Memorial University of Newfoundland, Institute of Social and Economic Research

Usher, Peter J. 1971. *The Bankslanders: economy and ecology of a frontier trapping community.* 3 vols. Ottawa: Canada, Department of Indian Affairs and Northern Development, Northern Science Research Group, NSRG 72(2)

1976a. 'Evaluating country food in the northern native economy'. *Arctic* 29: 105–20

1976b. 'The class system, metropolitan dominance and northern development in Canada'. *Antipode* 8(3):28–32

Usher, Peter, and Beakhust, G. 1973. *Land regulation in the Canadian north.* Ottawa: Canadian Arctic Resources Committee

Watkins, Mel 1977. *Dene nation – the colony within.* Toronto: University of Toronto Press

Weinstein, Martin S. 1976. *What the land provides: an examination of the Fort George subsistence economy and the possible consequence on it of the James Bay hydroelectric project.* Montreal: Grand Council of the Crees (of Quebec)

18. Hydroelectric dam construction and the foraging activities of eastern Quebec Montagnais

PAUL CHAREST

Introduction

As we know, the domination of the capitalist mode of production over previous modes of production means fundamental transformations which lead in the long term to the extinction or to the total dependence of the former modes. The aim of this chapter is to illustrate how such a process of destruction of a former communal mode of production has occurred among the Montagnais of northeastern Quebec.

Like other Algonkians of northeastern North America, the introduction among the Montagnais of mercantile relations by European conquerors generated the development of a certain form of private appropriation of hunting resources by subdivision of the community territory into family hunting territories (Leacock 1954). In spite of the penetration of mercantile capitalism in the whole of Algonkian territory through the fur trade, hunting activities and new production relations could be maintained in a relatively stable way for several centuries, in fact until very recently. Like many other marginal areas of the world – the Amazon and Congo forests, the Australian and Kalahari deserts, and the Arctic tundra – the vast boreal forests of northeastern Canada had constituted for a long time a barrier to the expansion of industrial societies. This is no longer the case and since the Second World War all these areas – even in socialist countries – have witnessed an accelerated penetration of industrialization, especially in the mining, forestry and hydroelectric sectors.

In Quebec, this industrialization process in the remote areas has corresponded to the second phase of industrial expansion. Starting in the 1940s, it has affected most of the Montagnais bands, through either forest exploitations (bands from Ouiatchouan, Bersimis, Sept-Iles-Maliotenam), mining developments (bands from Schefferville, Sept-Iles-Maliotenam), or hydroelectric establishments (bands from Ouiatchouan

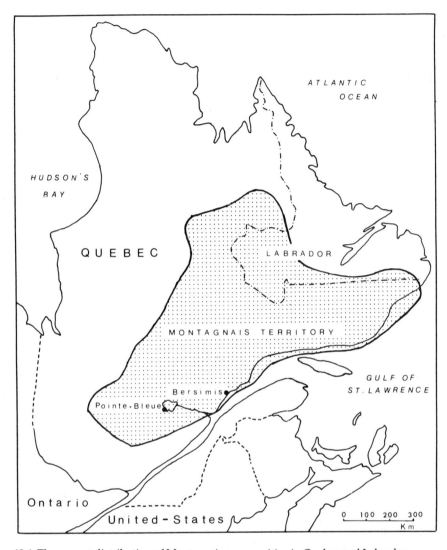

18.1 The current distribution of Montagnais communities in Quebec and Labrador

and Bersimis). The combined effects of these three types of industrial production have been considerable and have led to the sedentism and proletarianization of former nomadic groups of Montagnais hunters-trappers. However, due to its central role in the industrial development of the Quebec periphery, it is principally hydroelectricity with construction of giant hydroelectric plants and immense reservoirs in Montagnais territory which will receive our attention here. The data used to

A Montagnais family in northeastern Quebec, circa 1905 (Collection du Conseil Attika-mek – Montagnais)

illustrate my argument have been collected during research conducted in 1977 for the Montagnais-Attikamek Council, a regional association which has regrouped all of the Indian communities from those two eth-nic groups.

The production of hydroelectricity and the industrialization of Quebec

As the economic historian J. H. Dales (1957) has demonstrated, the industrialization of the province of Quebec has been closely associated, from its beginning, with the production of hydroelectricity. The absence of other energy resources, such as coal and oil, in Quebec territory and the favourable topographical hydrographical conditions have naturally oriented capital investments towards the production of this constantly renewable and non-polluting source of energy. However, the relatively late development of hydroelectric technology partially explains the delay in Quebec's industrialization by comparison with neighbouring Ontario and New England.

At first confined to the more densely populated areas of the valley of the St Lawrence and easily accessible tributary rivers, such as Out-aouais and St Maurice, the hydroelectric development of the immense hydraulic basins of Quebec later progressed towards more peripheral areas, such as Saguenay-Lake St John, the North Shore of the St Lawrence and, more recently, James Bay. Thus, the hunting territories of the Montagnais, already affected by decades of agricultural colonization and forestry, have been heavily disturbed since the early 1940s by the setting up of 13 plants and five hydroelectric reservoirs of major importance, along with other installations of minor importance. A multinational corporation, the Aluminium Company of Canada (ALCAN), and a provincial corporation, Hydro-Québec, have been the principal managers of these gigantic works. Moreover, since the nationalization of electricity by Quebec in 1963, the latter has had a quasi-monopoly in the production and distribution of electric energy. Nevertheless, ALCAN company has maintained an important network of five privately owned electricity plants in the hydrographic basin of Saguenay-Lake St John, which continue to provide very cheap and abundant hydroelectric energy for its Arvida and Ile-Maligne aluminum plants. Within the Montagnais territory, two other multinational corporations operate hydroelectric plants in the basin of the Manicouagan river (McCormic and Hart-Jaune).

Consequently, after the construction of the great Hydro-Québec projects in the basins of the Bersimis, Aux Outardes and Manicouagan rivers, and the current construction on the La Grande river at James Bay, Quebec has gained worldwide fame in the domain of production of hydroelectricity. With an actual capacity of about eighteen million kW and a yearly production reaching nearly one hundred billion kWh, Quebec ranks first in the world for the production of hydroelectricity *per capita*. A low proportion of that production (10–15%) is exported to the neighbouring province of Ontario and to the state of New York. Quebecois hydroelectricity is used, therefore, to satisfy, above all, local industrial and domestic needs. Pulp and paper and metallurgical –

mostly aluminium – industries are the principal industrial consumers of hydroelectric energy. These industries are precisely located in the peripheral areas near the abundant sources of hydroelectricity and raw material, particularly the pulp and paper mills. Thus, eight plants utilizing wood fiber and three aluminum plants have been built in territories which were more-or-less recently hunting areas for the Montagnais.

The multiplication of electrical appliances and the oil crisis have caused the economists to predict that the demand for electricity will double each decade from now until the year 2000. Starting from that – doubtless exaggerated – prediction, Hydro-Québec has conceived projects to dam all the hydraulic basins of Quebec, even those of the most remote areas, in the Arctic tundra zone. So, the industrialization process actually going on in a part of the Montagnais territory could eventually extend to the ensemble of the hunting territories still used by the native populations of Quebec.

In his paper (this volume), Harvey Feit reviews the political and legal struggles of the Cree Indians to resist the Hydro-Québec projects at James Bay and outlines some parts of the agreement that they have reached with the government of Quebec. All of these debates concerning what was supposed to be the 'projet du siècle' (project of the century), as expressed by Quebec's former prime minister, have given way to many studies on the ecological and socio-economic impacts of the hydroelectric works pertaining to James Bay, of which a good part of the results are still unknown. While so much effort is being invested there, the analysis of the longer-term effects of the already existing dams in the basins of the Saguenay-Lake St John and Upper North Shore river have been almost totally neglected. It is only very recently that the Montagnais themselves have taken the initiative to carry out an enquiry into the socio-economic impacts on the two Indian communities most directly affected by hydroelectric development: the Ouiatchouan and Bersimis.

Hydroelectric works in Montagnais Territory

In the hydroelectric basin of Saguenay-Lake St John, there are actually six major hydroelectric plants and three big reservoirs. Four of these plants and two reservoirs built by the Alcan company date from 1940. The erection of three of these plants on the Péribonka river, in territory still occupied by the Montagnais, directly affected many family hunting territories that had been successfully exploited until then. The main

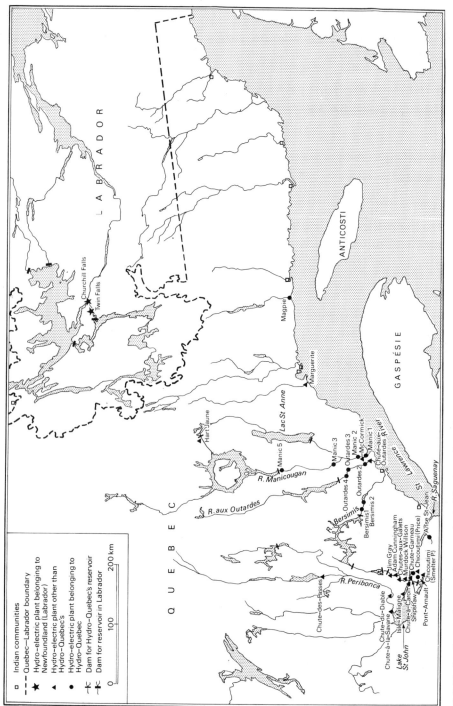

18.2 Hydroelectric dams and reservoirs in Montagnais territory

Table 18.1. *Hydroelectric plants in the areas occupied by the Montagnais Indians*

	Opening year	Area (of Reservoirs)	Power (of Plants) hp	kW
Saguenay area				
Plants				
Chute-du-Diable	1952		275,000	187,250
Chute-à-la-Savane	1953		285,000	187,250
Chute-des-Passes-Danger-				
euses	1959–60		1,000,000	742,000
Reservoirs				
Manouane	1941	122 m²		
Passes-Dangereuses				
(Péribonka)	1942	151 m²		
North Shore area				
1. Bersimis River Basin				
Plants				
Bersimis 1	1956–9		1,200,000	912,000
Bersimis 2			900,000	655,000
Reservoir				
Pipmuacan-Lac Cassé	1956	340 m²		
2. Aux Outardes River Basin				
Plants				
Outardes 2	1978		621,000	453,900
Outardes 3	1969		1,034,000	765,200
Outardes 4	1969		864,000	632,000
Reservoir				
Outardes 4	1969	250 m²		
3. Manicouagan River Basin				
Plants				
McCormick	1951–65		452,000	—
Manic 1	1967		240,000	184,410
Manic 2	1967		1,360,000	1,015,200
Manic 3	1976		1,608,000	1,183,000
Manic 5	1972		1,768,000	1,292,560
Hart-Jaune	1960		66,000	48,450
Reservoirs				
Lac St Anne	1958	95 m²		
Manic 5	1972	750 m²		

Source: Hydro-Québec (1975)

features of these plants and of the reservoirs that feed them are shown in Table 18.1.

The overall hydroelectric power produced during the last 25 years in these basins exceeds ten million kW, representing more than half of

Quebec's production of electric power. The Montagnais' hunting territories have then been used as the main water-works for the rest of Quebec and have consequently been strongly disturbed by these giant hydrographic rearrangements.

Ecological Effects of Dams and Reservoirs[1]

The ecological effects of these works on the Montagnais hunting territories are multiple and have affected both the aquatic and the terrestrial ecosystems. In the case of the aquatic environment, major hydrological modifications have resulted in the creation of vast artificial lakes and important annual variations of their water level, regulation of the downstream flow and an increase in the annual average flows. The aquatic fauna has manifested repercussions concerning the location of spawning grounds, feeding and migratory habits, species' distribution, interspecific relations of predation, etc. Certain important species have locally disappeared: this is particularly true of the ouananiche or freshwater salmon (*Salmo ouananiche*) in the Péribonka river and the Atlantic salmon (*Salmo salar*) in the Bersimis river.

Concerning the terrestrial ecosystems, bordering habitats – that were the most propitious to fur mammals such as beaver, muskrat, otter, mink and marten – have been flooded by the reservoirs or became useless due to the modification in the flow of the dammed rivers and of the reduced flow of their principal tributaries. The habitats of the beaver and the muskrat were the most seriously affected. The grazing locations of the moose and the nesting location of the wild ducks were also affected, but less severely.

The creation of the reservoirs has also flooded several hundred square miles of forest territory. In most cases, the trees of commercial value were cut beforehand and used for industrial purposes. However, the work of cutting the wood and clearing the wastes was not always completed in time; as a result the reservoirs are choked today with huge amounts of dead wood.

Economic Effects of Dams and Reservoirs

Knowing the importance that the hydrographic network has in the traditional hunting and fishing activities of the Montagnais, we can conclude immediately that the ecological effects of the dams and the reservoirs could not but affect very negatively these productive activities.

Partially flooded or affected by the modifications in the water level, most of the hunting territories have been abandoned by their users. In the basin of the Péribonka and Manouane rivers, only two of the seventeen hunting territories were still producing furs by the 1975–6 season. For the Bersimis community, 47 territories out of a total of 87 were affected by the situation of the dams and reservoirs. Of that number, 24 had not produced any fur in 1975–76. The other 23 territories produced only 302 beaver pelts. The production of other furs – otter, fox, mink, marten, muskrat, lynx – roughly follows the same downward trend.

Despite the abandoning or the low productivity of the hunting territories affected directly by the dams and the reservoirs, trapping in some areas holds its economic position as indicated by the number of marketed skins and by the income generated. In 1975–6, 102 trappers from Ouiatchouan (Pointe-Bleue) sold by auction 5,313 skins for a total value of $104,567 while 91 trappers from Bersimis sold 1,933 skins for a value of $66,703.45. The average income from the sale of furs approaches $1,000 per trapper in the first case and a little over $700 in the second. In both cases, however, the income from trapping accounts for only a small percentage of the domestic units' total income. Temporary or permanent paid jobs and transfer payments from various sources – unemployment insurance, family allowances, old-age pensions, social security – constitute in most cases at least three-quarters of the income. Consequently, the number of individuals for whom trapping and hunting remain the principal occupations is limited to about twenty per cent in each of the two communities. The moment and the length of the sojourns in the hunting territories are also determined by the scheduling of wage-earning jobs: the hunting trips usually occur in the autumn, between the months of October and December, and last for a maximum of six to eight weeks in most cases. In the still-recent past, the hunters and their families were spending over 40 weeks a year in the bush and barely 6 weeks at the trading post before returning inland at the end of August.

The total or partial abandoning of the hunting territories for fur trapping has induced at the same time a decrease in the hunting and fishing activities for subsistence. I do not actually have precise statistical data on this matter but the proportion of meat and fish in the diet of the Montagnais of Ouiatchouan and Bersimis is most probably well below the 50 per cent average for the Cree communities of western Quebec (Salisbury *et al.* 1972:44).

Let us consider now the presumably positive consequences of the hydroelectric works, for example the obtaining of wage-paying jobs by the Montagnais in the plants. Unfortunately only a few dozen Indians were hired, and these jobs were for limited periods of time and for below-average salaries. Indian workers have mostly been hired as guides, canoemen, woodcutters and workmen in the preliminary phases of the construction of the dams and as unskilled workers during the heavy work of drilling and concrete casting. From 1956 to 1958, some 50 Indians from Bersimis worked on the erection of the Bersimis 2 plant. Very few amongst them, however, were hired for the subsequent projects of the Aux Outardes and Manicouagan rivers. Thus, the projects undertaken by certain government organizations to integrate Indian labour-power into the work force used for the realization of major capitalist investments in the north of Quebec for the years 1956 to 1961 have failed (see Ministry of Citizenship and Immigration, *Annual Reports*).

However, the use of the Indian labour force *did* prove crucial during the early exploration phases as the hinterland was little known and inaccessible except by boat through the waterways network or by hydroplane. The very precise knowledge that the Indian guides had of the territory and of the hydrographic network was very useful to the engineers who conceived the great hydroelectric works. Thus in a largely unconscious way, by their knowledge the Montagnais have contributed to their own dispossession.

Combined Effects of Industrialization

Even if its progress was less spectacular, logging on the Montagnais hunting territories preceded by many years the installation of the great hydroelectric works. It started in fact a little before the middle-nineteenth century with the opening of the King's Post – then a trade monopoly of the Hudson's Bay Company – to agricultural colonization from 1837. From then on, the Montagnais hunting territories have not ceased to become stretched and distorted by outside forces (Vincent 1975:4–6). With the encroachment of logging the Montagnais from Saguenay-Lake St John have had to abandon successively the trading posts of Tadoussac, Chicoutimi and Metabetchouan to settle on the Ouiatchouan reserve. An identical process of retreat has led the Montagnais from Papinachois and Betsiamits to settle on the reserve of Bersimis.

Limited at first to the mouth of the rivers, logging progressed steadily towards the interior of the Indian land with the increasing demand for raw materials for the pulp and paper mills established in the area of the

Saguenay-Lake St John at the beginning of the century. Currently the demand of the eight pulp and paper mills in that area and in the North Shore area is such that dozens of square miles of coniferous forest are cut every year. The Montagnais hunting territories located near the mills are devastated by the forest operations and have been made partially or totally useless for a period of from ten to twenty years.

The great mining developments, built in Quebec since 1950 and mainly the work of American capital, have spared most of the hunting territories of the Montagnais from Ouiatchouan and Bersimis, except for a limited part of the latter exploited for some fifteen years by a branch of US Steel, the Quebec-Port Cartier mining company. After the company abandoned the project, the affected territories and those neighbouring, reverted to use by Indian trappers.

Finally, the industrialization and the urbanization of these raw-material-producing areas have developed the need for the white population to use the forest territories for recreational purposes. Private hunting and fishing clubs and summer cottages have thus multiplied in Montagnais hunting territory. The increased pressure on the hunting and fishing resources has reduced proportionately the possibility for the Indians to hunt and fish for their own subsistence. This recent trespassing on the territories has been greatly facilitated by the presence of several penetration roads built for the purpose of logging and construction of dams and reservoirs. When the competition with the white men on their territory becomes too strong, the Montagnais hunter-trappers finally go to hunt elsewhere or become progressively uninterested in carrying on their traditional activities.

If we add to the negative ecological and socio-economic effects of the dams and reservoirs the effects from logging, mining exploitation and the recreational hunting and fishing of the non-Indians, it is clear that the pursuit of the traditional trapping, hunting and fishing activities by the Montagnais is considerably compromised. In fact, what is surprising is that, in spite of all the constraints, the nearly two hundred trappers from the communities of Ouiatchouan and Bersimis continue to produce more than 8,000 fur pelts per year.

Consequences: Sedentarization and proletarization of the Montagnais

The settling-down process of the nomadic Montagnais trapper-hunter groups has followed the same rhythm as that of the penetration of industrial capitalism into their territories. Slow at the beginning of the agricultural colonization and the forest exploitation by commercial saw-mills, it accelerated progressively with the introduction of pulp and paper mills and aluminium plants, reaching its final phase in the last 30 years with the installation of many hydroelectric works whose effects have just been described. The Ouiatchouan community, whose reserve is located near a small industrial and commercial city, has been affected more profoundly than the more isolated community of Bersimis because, in the former, 20 production units have been permanently engaged in agriculture since the beginning of the century. In the case of Bersimis, sedentarization has been more recent and more rapid. Forest exploita-tion in the territory and in the vicinity of the reserve as well as uninter-rupted dam building since 1950 have been the major causes.

Besides the possibility of obtaining paid jobs, the other causes of sedentarization were the following: (1) the judicial status of the reserves as defined by a legislation of the Canadian government in 1951 accorded to the Indians fairly efficient protection against the many enterprises of Euro-Canadians; (2) the existence of commercial establishments; (3) the permanent presence of missionaries and religious buildings; (4) the compulsory schooling of Indian children for the last 20 years; (5) the organization of health services such as dispensaries, presence of nurses, periodical medical visits, etc.; (6) the construction of more permanent and comfortable housing; (7) the mail service and periodic distribution of various social-security payments. Tradesmen, missionaries and gov-ernment agents have thus joined industrial promoters to force the Mon-tagnais to settle on fixed locations at the margins of their hunting terri-tories. More-or-less consciously, their combined actions have led to the same result: the liberation of the Indian lands and of their abundant natural resources to the profit of state and private capitalism.

Being hardly able to resist the pressures coming at them from all directions, the Montagnais have progressively neglected their traplines and their ancestral hunting activities for salaried jobs that could pro-vide them with needed additional income during difficult periods brought about by the dropping production of, and/or prices paid for furs. The qualifications of the Montagnais labour force still do not cor-respond to the various requirements of industrial society, despite the compulsory schooling of the young Indians. The Indian workers consti-tute an underpaid reserve of labour hired for seasonal tasks, in contin-uity with the traditional occupations, such as guides, canoemen, fire-marshals, etc., or for the jobs of unskilled workers principally in the forest zone. These workers are hired as a last resort when nobody else is easily available, and seasonal or permanent unemployment constantly awaits them when the national economy slows down. From the independent producers that they were in their hunting territories, the Montagnais trapper-hunters have rapidly become proletarians in the frame of capitalist production relations.

Conclusion

As we have just seen, the destruction of the old social and economic structures of the Montagnais groups from Ouiatchouan and Bersimis under the impact of industrial capitalism is very advanced. Until now, the Montagnais had few means of resisting this destruction caused first and foremost by the occupation of their territories and the exploitation of their resources by industrial enterprises. The recently organized association with their Attikamek neighbours under the name 'Conseil Attikamek-Montagnais' is trying to tackle the most pressing problems and at the same time to answer the numerous demands coming from 13 different communities and to prepare for the next round of negotiations with the government of Quebec over their territorial rights. Politically, they are not yet very sure which road to follow, but it seems that they will diverge from the model of the James Bay and Northern Quebec agreement which still weighs very heavily on their shoulders.

Effectively, the government of the Province of Quebec represented by its prime minister recognized on 18 September 1980 the principle of the non-extinction of the aboriginal right of the Attikamek and the Montagnais as a basic principle for future negotiations. It remains to be seen if, once this principle has been accepted by the provincial authorities, the outcome of the negotiations will be the same as or different from the outcome of the James Bay case. There remains the fundamental question of who will have the control of the future development of the natural resources in the Attikamek-Montagnais hunting and trapping territories.

Note

1 For more detailed information on the ecological and socio-economic impacts of the dams and reservoirs as seen by the Montagnais hunters, see Paul Charest (1980).

426   Paul Charest

Bibliography

Charest, Paul 1980. 'Les barrages hydro-électriques en territoire montagnais et leurs effets sur les communautés amérindiennes'. *Recherches Amérindiennes au Québec* 9(4):323–37

Dales, John H. 1957. *Hydroelectricity and industrial development: Quebec 1898–1966*. Cambridge, Mass.: Harvard University Press

Feit, Harvey 1982. Contribution to this volume

Hydro-Québec 1975. *Répertoire des réservoirs et des centrales électriques en service*. Montréal: Service équipement de production

Leacock, Eleanor 1954. *The Montagnais 'hunting territory' and the fur trade*. Washington: American Anthropological Association

Ministry of Citizenship and Immigration, Division of Indian Affairs. *Annual Reports* 1950–66. Ottawa, Canada: Queen's Printer

Salisbury, Richard *et al.* 1972. *Le développement et la Baie James: l'impact socio-économique du project hydroélectrique*. Montréal: McGill University

Vincent, Sylvie 1975. 'L'espace montagnais, non pas pays mais peau de chagrin'. *Recherches Amérindiennes au Québec* 5(2)

19. The outstation movement in Aboriginal Australia

H. C. COOMBS, B. G. DEXTER and L. R. HIATT

During the last decade large numbers of Aborigines have been leaving mission stations and government settlements in order to establish small villages on their traditional lands. These hamlets have come to be generally known as 'outstations', though some authorities consider they are more aptly described as 'homeland centres'. Today they number some 200, with a total population of about 6,000. Most of them (180) are in the Northern Territory, but they occur also in South Australia, Queensland, and Western Australia.

Political background

Ten years ago most Aborigines in northern and central Australia were living in, or near, European settlements: townships, cattle stations, church missions, or government outposts on Aboriginal reserves. There were exceptions, like the 'Pindan mob' who just after the war had walked off pastoral stations in Western Australia and since have lived independently; and, more recently, the Gurindji stockmen who had not only withdrawn their labour but occupied and claimed part of the Wave Hill pastoral lease as their traditional homeland. A few small communities in Arnhem Land had decided not to move into the nearest mission station. But everywhere else it seemed that Aborigines were being steadily drawn into the vortex of white society.

In 1969 Aborigines at Yirrkala (a mission in northeast Arnhem Land) took out a writ in the Northern Territory Supreme Court seeking to restrain the Federal Government and a company called Nabalco from mining bauxite on their clan territories. Their case was rejected, and mining began at Gove Peninsula. Shortly afterwards, the Yirrkala Village Council wrote to the Federal Government's recently formed Council for Aboriginal Affairs, expressing the desire of some residents to move out of the mission in order to protect their sacred places in the countryside. The letter said: 'We want to have land to ourselves that the mining company or its workers can't come on without our permission.'

At the time the Council for Aboriginal Affairs was trying to devise ways of helping the Yirrkala people to withstand the shock of large-scale mining in their neighbourhood. The idea of decentralization offered a possible or partial solution; furthermore, it had the merit of being proposed by the people themselves.

The wish to return to the homelands, although given a sense of urgency by events at Gove Peninsula, was neither new nor peculiar to Aborigines at Yirrkala. Mission stations and government settlements, being of limited size, were inevitably situated on the territory of merely one or two clans among many; accordingly, mission and settlement communities characteristically contained many tribesmen living on land that traditionally did not belong to them. Friction between co-resident owners and aliens was not uncommon. The latter occasionally returned to their homelands, not only for reasons of nostalgia and ritual responsibility, but to ease tensions within the black community and also to escape temporarily from institutionalized white control. Always, however, the availability of European commodities and comforts drew them back to the settlement or mission. For many, there seemed to be no way of simultaneously enjoying modernity, autonomy, and autochthony.

In 1970 the Council for Aboriginal Affairs embarked on the task of persuading the government to offer assistance to groups wishing to establish their own outstations. At this stage, pending the adoption of such a policy and the availability of funds, the Council's support was moral rather than material. Early movements occurred at the widely separated centres of Yirrkala and Maningrida in Arnhem Land, Amata in northwest South Australia, and Derby in the Kimberley region of Western Australia. In 1973 the new Labor government in Canberra decided to support decentralization both in principle and in practice, and the exodus began in earnest. A factor of particular importance was that large numbers of Aborigines on reserves and pastoral stations began to receive social-service benefit in cash (old-age pensions, family allowance). This enabled people to pool their financial resources and utilize them, if they wished, towards establishing and servicing their own communities. In 1974 the federal government initiated a system of establishment grants up to $10,000 for groups in the Northern Territory with a demonstrated commitment to decentralization. Some provision

Kopanga Outstation at Blyth River, Arnhem Land, Australia in 1975 (L. Hiatt)

was made for wages for Aboriginal labour, though voluntary effort was encouraged.

In the aftermath of the NT Supreme Court's decision on the Yirrkala application, the Whitlam government appointed a Commission under Mr Justice Woodward to advise on the best method of recognizing Aboriginal land rights. Ensuing discussions may have intensified, rather than allayed, fears among traditional owners of intrusion and alienation and, at least in some areas, acted as an additional stimulus to leave the settlements and missions and re-occupy the homelands.

An earlier and more significant factor, however, was an increased availability of alcohol, consequent upon the lifting of previous restrictions in 1964 and the introduction of a cash economy. Alcohol consumption, often on a grand scale, aggravated long-standing tensions on settlements and missions, and brawling became commonplace, with attendant injury and loss of life. To make matters worse, petrol-sniffing emerged in the 1960s as a serious form of delinquency among the young in some communities, exacerbating (and to some extent caused by) incongruities of outlook and behaviour that had arisen between western-oriented youths and their more conservative parents. These developments undoubtedly strengthened the resolve of the old and middle-aged to leave: the settlements had become places of danger and demoralization to themselves and even more to their children.

Federal policy towards decentralization continued to be sympathetic throughout the 1970s, despite a change of government in 1975. In 1976–7, the new Liberal-National Country Party government granted $358,183 towards the establishment of outstations, and this figure rose to $2,645,500 in 1979–80. (All sums $A.) Nevertheless it would be misleading to suggest that the attitude of the federal government and its officers has been one of uniform and unqualified enthusiasm. Misgivings and reservations are felt and expressed at top levels, most notably in the area of education. Furthermore, at the points where policy is supposed to be translated into practice, the bureaucracy has on occasion proved slow to move in the required direction (for instance, instructions to pay social-service benefit on the reserves were initially obstructed). Officials in some areas expect Aborigines to demonstrate in advance a high-level of 'commitment' in order to qualify for an establishment grant, and in general white control over purposes and expenditure is tighter than it was in the mid-1970s. On the other hand, many white officers (community advisers, mechanics, craftwork intermediaries, teachers, etc.) have played, and continue to play, vital supportive roles, often out of a sense of personal commitment to the concept of Aboriginal self-determination. The outstation movement will continue to depend very much on their dedication for some time to come.

The Queensland State government is notoriously at odds with the federal government on Aboriginal policy and remains unrepentantly paternalistic in outlook and practice. Its opposition to decentralization came to a head during the Aurukun – Mornington Island crisis of 1978. Although the federal parliament now has legislative powers in Aboriginal affairs throughout the Commonwealth, it has been unable or unwilling to use them effectively in Queensland in pursuit of its own stated policies. It remains to be seen whether the Queensland government's opposition to outstations will influence future policy and practice in other states, particularly the Northern Territory.

Outstation communities

Outstation communities average about 30 residents. Movement of people between the outstations and the settlement or mission centre is common, and fluctuations in size occur frequently throughout the year depending on seasonal climatic conditions, ceremonial activity, school holidays, and the level of supplies.

In general, the movement back to the homelands has been led by adults in the upper age range. Often the permanent core of an outstation contains a preponderance of old people. With temporary or permanent increases in size, the age distribution approximates more closely to that of the major settlements. But in many cases young married couples, teenagers of both sexes, and younger children of school age tend to be under-represented. Conversely, in areas where the outstation movement has reached substantial proportions, these categories tend to be over-represented on the mission or settlement.

In the majority of cases the outstation community speaks in a single Aboriginal tongue. The unaccustomed diversity of languages spoken on some large settlements appears to have been a cause of disaffection. But many outstation people previously lived in centres where, in fact, only one main language was spoken. And linguistic diversity is accepted as normal on some outstations (e.g. in areas where it is traditional for a man to marry outside his language group).

The composition and location of decentralized communities depend upon metaphysically defined rights, obligations, and expectations with respect to land. In addition to the traditional owners and their spouses, the community may include other close relatives such as men linked to the outstation country through their mothers. An ethic of hospitality, coupled with enjoyment of travel, news, and gossip, also guarantees that outstation communities frequently include visitors.

The main source of cash income for the outstations is social-service payments (family allowances and pensions for old people, widows, and invalids). The opportunities for obtaining remuneration for work are severely restricted. Many outstations produce craftwork for sale, and a few individuals receive wages for schoolteaching, medical work, and storekeeping. Other sources of occasional or limited income include mining, cattle-station employment, public works (roads, airstrips, piers, buildings, etc.), vegetable growing, and fishing. In general, unemployment benefits are not paid. Figures available suggest that the average *per capita* weekly cash income on outstations (not including government grants) is around $20.

Most outstations depend in varying degrees on hunting and gathering. In some instances, practically the entire flesh component of the diet is produced by the people themselves, using a combination of traditional methods and modern materials (e.g. steel spikes for fish spears, nets, guns). Because carbohydrate can be purchased relatively cheaply in the form of flour and sugar, women nowadays concentrate more upon obtaining flesh foods (reptiles, shell-fish, grubs, etc.) and less upon the arduous task of collecting and preparing wild vegetables. The diet on most outstations is thus a combination of traditional and European foods, the latter normally being bought through the nearest main centre. Some outstations cultivate gardens and raise animals for domestic consumption.

Many observers, including medical personnel, have reported that outstation communities are healthier than settlement communities. Among the improvements mentioned are fewer infectious diseases, increased weight of children and loss of excess body fat in adults. Some observers have noted a reduction in psychosomatic complaints (headaches, insomnia, tension). The main reasons suggested are better diet (more nutritious and varied), smaller numbers of people, and relative isolation (less infection, less tension, less alcohol).

All outstations can be reached most or all of the time by some form of mechanized transport. Many have road links with the nearest service centre, though in wet weather they may be impassable. A number of outstations have airstrips for light aircraft, and some can be reached by boat. Many outstations now have two-way radios, enabling contact with other outstations as well as the main centre.

A provision service runs to most outstations, and outstation people make trips into the settlement to shop, visit relatives, and attend to various personal and outstation affairs. All outstations are visited periodically by medical personnel, some of whom are Aborigines. Some outstations have resident Aboriginal schoolteachers, with varying degrees of training and experience; and most, though not all, are visited from time to time by white schoolteachers. In rare instances, schoolteachers travel daily to the outstations.

The decentralization movement derives much of its strength from beliefs in immortals who created particular parts of the landscape and continue to live there. In recent years there has been an extensive reaffirmation of traditional religion in northern Australia, especially on outstations, as witnessed in increased ceremonial activity and custodianship of sacred sites. This has not necessarily been accompanied by a rejection of Christianity; in some cases outstation residents with a mission background have held their own prayer meetings and Bible readings, and have otherwise kept up their links with the church. There is little evidence of any increase in such practices as polygyny and marriage bestowal, as compared with the situation on neighbouring settlements and missions. In general the outstation movement is not so much a return to the past as an attempt to select and integrate elements of both Aboriginal and European traditions in a context free from white domination.

Probably the most frequent and consistent observation made about outstations is that they are more peaceful than the settlements and missions, and that morale is better. In some cases an initial euphoria has been followed by a degree of frustration and dissatisfaction (notably with regard to the supply of goods and services); and some disputes over land ownership, leadership, and property (typically vehicles) have arisen. But the general impression is that outstation people are more cheerful, contented, energetic, and relaxed than their counterparts on the settlements.

Numerous observers have remarked upon a dramatic change in bearing and manner that occurs when men leave the settlements and missions and return to where they feel they belong. This has frequently been consolidated by a sense of pride in building an outstation (instead of having it built by Europeans). Last, but not least, there is the stimulation of the natural environment itself. As one white female observer has put it: 'When I went "hunting" with the women, I was always impressed by the interest displayed in the environment; sky, grass, water and sand all had messages to be read and discussed. This source of stimulation is largely missing in settlement life and nothing appears to have replaced it . . . It is my impression that settlement dwellers are bored.'

Members of some decentralized communities have formally banned liquor on or near the outstation. Elsewhere consumption is less than on the settlements, and consequences are less damaging. Figures for outstations in northern Arnhem Land show an average *per capita* expenditure on liquor of less than $20 per annum (in the same year the average Australian *per capita* figure was $212). Outstation residents, especially younger males, from time to time use neighbouring settlements and towns as places to have a binge (conversely, settlement residents occasionally use outstations as places to dry out).

Outstations vary considerably in the amount of modern equipment they possess. There are some whose borrowings from western technology go little beyond corrugated iron to supplement bark as a building material. At the other end of the range, the inventory includes trucks and cars, dinghies and outboard motors, a tractor, two-way radio, prefabricated houses, store, school building, airstrip and hangar. The most common possessions are vehicles (usually four-wheel drive) and housing materials (corrugated iron, tarpaulins, tents). In arid zones, many (though not all) outstations have mechanized water supplies (windmills, engine pumps).

The priorities of outstation communities depend largely on existing possessions. Some relatively well-equipped outstations are now thinking in terms of an electricity supply, while others would be happy in the first instance to have a truck. Environmental differences are obviously important: a bore may be the *sine qua non* of an outstation in central Australia, whereas groups with homelands in inaccessible parts of Arnhem Land may give top priority to the building of an airstrip. Many outstation communities are torn between a desire to acquire European amenities and a wish to avoid re-creating the circumstances from which they are escaping.

Beyond a commitment to autonomy, there is no evidence in decentralized communities of an underlying hostility towards whites, nor of any outright rejection of their material culture. Outstation people are keen to maintain harmonious relations with Europeans, and to enjoy some of the benefits of European technology. They are aware that their strivings for independence depend upon white cooperation and goodwill. They want a helping hand, but at an arm's length.

Local white opinion tends to be divided. Some people see the outstation movement as retrogressive, or at best a short-term solution to current problems on settlements. Others regard it as a foundation for successful long-term adjustments and co-existence with the dominant white majority.

Prospects

Historically the official conception of Aboriginal settlements and missions has gone through a number of phases. Until the Second World

War they were regarded largely as places to protect the remnants of a dying race, both from themselves and from coarser elements in the society that had brought about their downfall. After the war, when government policy changed radically from protection to assimilation, they were supposed to become springboards into western civilization, Pygmalion training centres whose job would be done not when the last Aboriginal passed away but when he passed into the ranks of white society. By the late 1960s official thinking in Canberra (shaped to an increasing extent by the Council for Aboriginal Affairs) was shifting away from assimilation towards self-determination, at least for traditionally oriented central and northern people. When fully crystallized, the new policy appeared to visualize the settlement and mission as the unit of self-government, a permanent, more or less all-Aboriginal township, conducting its own domestic affairs as well as its relationship with the wider society.

It now remains to be seen whether governments will modify this latest conception to accommodate the decentralization movement. Current thinking about how this could be achieved is far from clear. One possibility might be to define the unit of local government as a federation of hamlets (outstations) grouped around an administrative and service centre (often, but not necessarily, the old mission station or government settlement). Each unit would be governed by a council made up of representatives of the constituent hamlets as well as of the central township itself. An unsatisfactory aspect of contemporary Aboriginal councils is that the tribe or clan on whose land the settlement or mission happens to be situated is often accorded a privileged position in the affairs of the whole district. Some constitutional provisions might therefore be needed to guarantee equitable representation.

It should be added that centralization of power, even in the form of a council drawn from a federation of communities, may run counter to at least some of the objectives of the decentralization movement; and it would not be surprising if outstations of the future sought to protect their own hard-won autonomy against intrusions from such councils. From this point of view, it may well be that the existing Commonwealth Aboriginal Associations legislation, with its emphasis on the council as the incorporated body, needs to be amended. Despite some legal difficulties the incorporation of the community would seem both more logical and likely to be more effective. In particular, it seems important that decentralized communities should be in a position to receive funds directly and exercise control over them. As far as possible, responsibilities of any council of a federal character outside the administrative centre itself might need to be confined to wider tasks of general benefit (e.g. road and airstrip maintenance, hygiene), and to that end it may be desirable or necessary for hamlets to share such central costs.

It is hard to visualize rapid or radical changes in the economic basis of decentralization, though it is expected that moneys will eventually flow directly to increasing numbers of outstation communities from mining royalties. It is reasonable to assume that Aborigines will continue to receive most social-service benefits. The question of eligibility for unemployment benefit needs to be examined, as well as the related issue whether it is possible and/or desirable to convert individual entitlements to such benefits into community-development employment grants (an alternative that is being tested in some locations). Employment opportunities for Aborigines in education, health, and community administration should expand; as also may the market for craftwork and the products of cottage industries based on such crafts. The outlook for commercial agriculture, stock-raising, and horticulture is not good in the areas inhabited by most outstation communities, and in any case their practice is often incompatible with Aboriginal lifestyles and values. However, the planned application of existing and new technology could lift the level of domestic subsistence production (breeding and selection of native flora and fauna, introduction of appropriate exotic species).

An interesting possibility is suggested by negotiations for the administration of National Parks and Wildlife sanctuaries like those at Kakadu and Tanami. As Aboriginal title to land is acknowledged over wider areas, it is possible to conceive a chain of such parks and sanctuaries in the regions of scenic and cultural significance, from which Aborigines could derive not merely opportunities from employment and contract work related to the management of the parks, but income in the nature of rent and royalties for access to them.

Although outstation Aborigines are for the most part traditionally oriented, they are keenly aware of their need for some components of white education. Present indications are that they will favour pragmatic selections from the European curriculum, while trying to reserve the inculcation of value orientations and social behaviour for traditional socialization processes. Thus we may find an emphasis on providing basic skills of literacy and numeracy within a shortened school day, so as to leave scope for traditional instruction and to minimize assimilationist influences; a shift from concentration on the child to greater involvement of family groups and adults; and an increasing emphasis on apprenticeship-type training in the nearest Aboriginal centre for skills needed on the outstations. In this context the white teacher becomes an educational adviser to the community, a mobilizer of resources and a support for Aboriginal parents as well as Aboriginal teachers and aides from within the community.

A similar approach is becoming apparent in the medical sphere, with white professional and para-professional health personnel being regarded as a resource to be drawn upon from a distance or during periodic visits. There is also a growing interest in asserting the right and capacity of homeland communities to administer law and order, with white law enforcement and judicial agencies being brought in only in the event of serious trouble or when the community feels the need for external support. This aspiration is likely to express itself in the application of traditional dispute settlement procedures, modified and perhaps formalized in community courts.

The reaffirmation of Aboriginal religion and ceremonial life is likely to continue on the outstations into the foreseeable future. Indeed, with a secure economic base and improved communications between communities, ritual activity may well become more frequent, elaborate, and large-scale than before the arrival of Europeans. It has been noted that in recent years traditionalists have been attempting to reactivate ceremonial life in communities where it has declined as a result of white contact. But there is another point. As parochialism breaks down through easier travel, Aboriginal rituals of the future may focus upon universal conceptions in traditional metaphysics and iconography, at the expense of idiosyncrasies and local allegiances. In other words, there may be a shift in the direction of a 'pan-Aboriginal' pattern of belief and ceremonial, which in turn might open up avenues of rapprochement with (as distinct from conversion to) so-called world religions.

For the time being, however, the homeland movement is to be regarded as an attempt by Aborigines to regain a physical, social, and spiritual environment in which traditional components will be more dominant and the influence of the alien culture more marginal. In such a context the task of adaptation to the modern world would, they hope, become more manageable. It would be easier for the community as a whole to proceed from the known to the unknown, to find in its own traditions elements with which the new influences could be linked or in terms of which they could be interpreted. Only if this can be done will social transformations be achieved without devastating dislocations – in particular, the polarization of generations that demoralizes the old and deprives the young of the security and support normally conferred by membership of an integrated community.

It is unlikely that this attempt will be uniformly successful. In any event the young of the outstations will respond to it in a variety of ways. Some will break their links with their community of origin wholly and permanently; others will choose to remain entirely within it; the majority perhaps will be between these extremes. We can expect that almost all will visit white towns and cities as well as their own and other Aboriginal centres. Many will at times seek employment and residence, perhaps for years, away from home, but keep in touch by visits exchanged and with the intention of returning permanently in due course. The balance is impossible to predict. But an interesting pointer is the frequency with which the ablest young adults nowadays are choosing to remain with their own people instead of pursuing jobs in white Australia. It may be that, in the opportunities offered by self-management and political action, they are finding a more effective stimulus and challenge than white society is able or willing to offer them.

Acknowledgements

This chapter is based on a longer document prepared in three sections for the Australian Institute of Aboriginal Studies during 1979: at the request of the Principal (P. J. Ucko) 'The Historical Context of the Outstation Movement' by B. G. Dexter; 'The Present State of the Outstation Movement' by L. R. Hiatt; and 'The Future of the Outstation Movement' by H. C. Coombs. These papers may be obtained from the Institute (Box 553, Canberra, Australia).

The section of the present paper entitled 'Outstation Communities' is based on personal communications from ten people with first-hand knowledge of particular outstations: David Biernoff, Peter Brokensha, Vicky Burbank, Richard Moyle, David Nash, Joe Reser, Ushma Scales, Gary Stoll, Peter Sutton, and Noel Wallace. We thank them warmly for their cooperation.

Bibliography

Altman, J. and Nieuwenhuysen, J. 1979. *The economic status of Australian Aborigines.* Cambridge University Press: Cambridge
Australia, Aboriginal Land Rights Commission 1974. *Second report, April 1974.* Parliamentary Paper no. 69 of 1974. Australian Government Printing Service: Canberra
Borsboom, A. 1978. *Maradjiri.* University of Nijmegen: Nijmegen
Brokensha, P. 1979. *'Conservatism and change'.* M. A. Honours thesis. University of Sydney

Brokensha, P. and McGuigan, C. 1977. 'Listen to the dreaming: the Aboriginal homelands movement'. *Australian Natural History* 19(4):119–23

Coombs, H. 1974. 'Decentralization trends among Aboriginal communities'. *Search* 5(4):135–43

1978. 'Australia's policy towards Aborigines 1967–77'. *Minorities Rights Group Report no. 35.* London

1978. *Kulinma.* Australian National University Press: Canberra

Coombs, H. and Dexter, B. 1976. *Report on Arnhem Land.* Australian Government Printing Service: Canberra

Coombs, H. and Stanner, W. 1974. *Report on visit to Yuendumu and Hooker Creek.* Australian Government Printing Service: Canberra

Gillespie, D., Cooke, P. and Bond, D. 1977. 'Maningrida outstation resource centre 1976/77 report'. Unpublished. Australian Institute of Aboriginal Studies: Canberra

Gray, W. 1977. 'Decentralization trends in Arnhem Land', in R. Berndt (ed.), *Aborigines and change: Australia in the 70s.* Australian Institute of Aboriginal Studies: Canberra

Kesteven, S. 1978. 'A sketch of Yuendumu and its outstations'. Master of Environmental Studies thesis, Australian National University, Canberra

Meehan, B. forthcoming. *Shell bed to shell midden.* Australian Institute of Aboriginal Studies: Canberra

Meehan, B. and Jones, R. forthcoming. 'The outstation movement and hints of a white backlash', in R. Jones (ed.), *Northern Australia: options and implications.* Australian National University: Canberra

Morice, R. 1976. 'Women dancing dreaming: psychosocial benefits of the Aboriginal outstation movement'. *Medical Journal of Australia* 2 (25–26):939–42

O'Connell, J. 1979. 'Room to move'. *Mankind* 11(2):119–31

Reser, J. 1977. 'Aboriginal dwelling circumstances in north central Arnhem Land'. Unpublished. Australian Institute of Aboriginal Studies: Canberra

Rowley, C. 1971. *The remote Aborigines.* Australian National University Press: Canberra

Sutton, P. 1978. 'Wik: Aboriginal society, territory, and language at Cape Keerweer, Cape York Peninsula, Australia'. Ph.D.thesis, University of Queensland

von Sturmer, D. 1979. 'Report on Kendall river (*empadha*) and Holroyd river (*pu'an*) outstations, west coast, Cape York Peninsula, Queensland, June – November 1978'. Unpublished. Australian Institute of Aboriginal Studies: Canberra

Wallace, N. 1977. 'Pitjantjatjara decentralization in north-west South Australia: spiritual and psycho-social motivation', in R. Berndt (ed.), *Aborigines and change: Australia in the 70s.* Australian Institute of Aboriginal Studies: Canberra

20. Aboriginal land rights in the Northern Territory of Australia[1]

NICOLAS PETERSON

It is no accident that land rights became a major issue simultaneously among the indigenous peoples of Australia, Alaska and Canada during the latter half of the 1960s. Those boom years made it clear that the future demand for oil and minerals would be at a level where it was profitable to invest millions of dollars prospecting even the most remote and difficult regions. A new phase of exploration quickly got under way and just as quickly started to disrupt the life of many indigenous peoples who until then had been living in relative social, economic and political isolation. It was an isolation that gave few of them cause to reflect on their belief that they were the unquestioned owners of the land in which they lived. Granted there were whites who did many things without consulting them, but nevertheless most were government servants ostensibly there to help and few stayed long. If some did have doubts about the recognition of their ancient rights, others may have been reassured by the existence of treaties or the reserve status of their lands. It did not take long under the impact of the new phase of exploration for the people to realize they were wrong.

The realization led to developing legal and political battles for recognition of their rights and has begun to result in legislation: in Alaska the Alaskan Native Claims Settlement Act of 1971; in Quebec the James Bay Agreement as outlined in 1975; in Australia's Northern Territory, the Aboriginal Land Rights (Northern Territory) Act, 1976; and in all three countries continuing negotiations for settlements covering other regions. It is important to emphasize that these agreements, which are seen as such a positive step by many whites, are in reality a final acknowledgement of defeat for the indigenous people. For in every case they consolidate the loss of land to whites and grossly reduce the rights associated with the land they have managed to retain.

The Aborigines of the Northern Territory, unknown to them, lost all right to their land in European law on 26 January 1788 when Captain Phillip hoisted the British flag and annexed the land to the west of Sydney as far as 135° longitude east (see Blackburn 1971:147).[2] The complete arbitrariness of this legal view is underlined by the fact that it was 183 years before lawyers were reasonably convinced it was correct, although it has always been evident that the vast majority of whites had assumed this from the first days of settlement. A declaration that can have taken no more than a few minutes dispossessed the Aboriginal occupants of 40,000 years' standing, a people whom we know to have a complex and elaborate system of land-ownership deeply integrated into their religion. Behind the legal decision lay the philosophical position that the whole earth was open to the industry and enterprise of the human race, which had the duty and the right to develop the earth's resources. The more 'advanced' peoples were therefore justified in dispossessing, if necessary, the less 'advanced' (see Blackburn 1971:200).

From the earliest days of settlement in the Northern Territory, Aborigines protested about the invasion of their country. This was usually in physical terms but as early as 1889 the Government Resident of the Northern Territory reported what a cattle station manager had told him of an old Aboriginal man who had said, 'I say, boss, whitefellow stop here too long with him bullocky. Now time whitefellow take him bullocky and clear out. This fellow country him blackfellow country' (GRR 1889). And the Resident himself stated that: 'After careful inquiry I'm of the opinion that this is the attitude of the aborigines towards Europeans. Entrance into their country is an act of invasion. It is a declaration of war, and they will halt at no opportunity of attacking the white invaders.' He recommended reserves to which the Aborigines were given absolute rights and sole control.

Reserves were declared from the 1890s onwards but the majority were small areas on the fringes of settlements bearing no relationship to the Aboriginal pattern of land holding or subsistence requirements and, needless to say, absolute rights and control were not placed in their hands. Between the early 1920s and the late 1950s, larger reserves were declared, within which it was possible for some people to continue a traditional life on their own land. By 1973, approximately 18 per cent of the Northern Territory was reserved for the 25,300 Aborigines who make up 25 per cent of the population (see *Northern Territory Statistical Summaries*), but by then no Aborigines were living completely off the land.

Despite the reserve status given to some Aboriginal land in the Northern Territory, this did not make it immune to invasion by mining

Mr Justice Toohey, Aboriginal Land Commissioner, hearing evidence in the Limmen Bight claim, Northern Territory, Australia, May 1980 (H. Morphy)

companies. One of the most notorious cases of invasion was on the Gove Peninsula of the Arnhem Land Aboriginal Reserve. In the late 1950s, there was a revival of interest in exploiting the long-known deposit of bauxite close to the Yirrkala Methodist Mission. The mission had only been established in 1935, and it was not until after the war that the majority of the Aborigines living in the surrounding bush moved to settle there. Their religious ties to their land, with its many hundreds of sacred places, were, and are still, very strong. Like other Aborigines they believe that the world was created in a series of local founding dramas in which heroic ancestors emerged from the subterranean spirit world, liberating life-giving forces. In many forms, at once human and non-human, the heroic ancestors created regional landscapes and established the pattern of life. Although it was a time of marvels the ancestors led a life much like their descendants today, until wearied from toil they sank exhausted back into the earth. This marked the end of alteration of the landscape but the power of the ancestors remains in it eternally. Thus today by re-enacting the local founding dramas in song and ceremony, the people can continue to draw on the creative powers of the ancestors in times of sickness, death, need or simply to maintain and celebrate the continuity of life.

It was in the context of these beliefs that the Aborigines at Yirrkala became increasingly upset at the damage caused by prospectors to the countryside in general and the sacred places in particular. By 1963, when it was clear that the prospectors were not going to go away, but instead stay and open a large mine that would bring an influx of several thousand whites, the people, assisted by a member of the Federal House of Representatives and the mission superintendent, objected to the granting of a mining lease over the Yirrkala area in the Warden's court. They also sent a petition painted on bark to the Federal Parliament which led to the establishment of a parliamentary committee to look into their grievances, but did nothing to prevent the development of the mine. However, it is significant that in anticipation of the mine the government had established the Aboriginal Benefits Trust Fund in 1960, into which it planned to pay royalties due to the Commonwealth Government where they came from mines on Aboriginal reserves. The standard rate was 1¼ per cent only, but it was doubled on Aboriginal reserves. Until 1977, these monies were entirely under the control of whites advised by Aborigines.

Whilst the negotiations over bauxite mining on the Gove Peninsula were going on, the Arnhem Land Aboriginal Reserve was also under threat from another quarter. In this case, the mineral resource at issue was a manganese deposit on Groote Eylandt. With a piece of initiative completely atypical for any missionary or government agency, the Church Missionary Society, which ran a mission on the island, obtained a permit to prospect over the manganese deposit in the name of the Aborigines just before Australia's largest mining company moved into the area. As a result of this recognized property right an agreement was signed in June 1963 giving the Aborigines of Groote Eylandt a 1¼ per cent royalty paid directly to them in addition to the 2½ per cent statutory royalty paid to the Aboriginal Benefits Trust Fund.

By the early 1960s, the Aborigines were becoming increasingly belligerent in pressing for their rights. The Australian public was made aware of this following a case brought before the Conciliation and Arbitration Commission in 1965. Although Northern Territory Aborigines had been granted citizenship in 1964, it was still permissible to pay those working on cattle stations less than white stockmen. To rectify this situation, a test case was brought before the Commission. It was not the Aborigines themselves who brought the case forward and, characteristically, no Aboriginal was called upon to give evidence. The Commission awarded equal wages to the Aboriginal workers but delayed implementation of the decision for three years to enable the employers to adjust to the new conditions. Angry at the delay, the black stockmen of Newcastle Waters station went on strike on 1 May 1965 (see Hardy 1968:14). Three other groups took strike action in the following year. Then in March 1967, the Gurindji on Wave Hill cattle station moved to set up their own camp at Wattie Creek on a different part of the station and demanded their ancestral lands back. A great deal of public sympathy and financial support from Australians in the south was forthcoming for the Gurindji in the following years, but even when in 1970 the company indicated its willingness to yield 500 square miles, the government opposed it. For most Australians, the Gurindji's demand for land was the first they had heard of land rights. Their demands gained much publicity and support, not only because of the obvious justness of their cause, but also because the cattle station was owned by a multinational company headed by an English peer, Lord Vestey.

Meanwhile, the mining operations on the Gove Peninsula were developing rapidly with huge areas of the landscape being desecrated. Again with the assistance of members of the Methodist Church, this time based in Victoria, the clan leaders at Yirrkala took the mining company, Nabalco, and the Commonwealth Government to court in 1968 to try to stop the whole development on the grounds that they owned the land and had not granted permission for the mining to go ahead. It was the first and only case of its kind. Three years later, they learnt that they were not the owners of the land in European eyes.[3] The decision shifted the land-rights issue unequivocally into the political domain and served to consolidate the national and international circumstances that were creating a new political awareness among Aborigines generally. The Federal Liberal – Country Party government was under strong moral and political pressure to act, but when it did there was great disappointment.

On 26 January 1972, Australia Day, the Prime Minister announced a new government policy. In some ways it was an important step forward with its emphasis on self-determination and the right of Aboriginal people to choose their own life-style, but on land rights it was as negative as ever. The only gesture was that legislation and money would be provided to protect the sacred places of Aborigines throughout the nation. This was totally unsatisfactory for many reasons, but principally because the whole landscape is sacred to and owned by the Aborigines, not just the isolated rocks and trees which it was proposed to fence and protect. It was tokenism at its worst.

The reaction of a small group of urban Aboriginal activists was swift and brilliant. They set up an Aboriginal Embassy on the lawn opposite the front steps of the federal parliament in a small green tent. The impact was immediate; few people could ignore the shameful fact that Aborigines were aliens in their own land. Although many people did not think the move would last long, they were wrong. Tens of thousands of visitors to the parliament, many foreign politicians and journalists as well as Australians, became aware that the issue could not be ignored.

With the Liberal – Country Party in politically poor shape during 1972 and the Labor Party going from strength to strength, it became increasingly clear that there might be a change of government at the next election. As part of its preparations for the election, the Labor Party re-stated its policies and its leader, Mr Whitlam, then as later, gave high priority and prominence to granting land rights. The Labor Party victory in December 1972, led to immediate action. In February 1973, Mr Justice Woodward, who had been the barrister acting for the Yirrkala Aborigines against Nabalco and the Commonwealth Government, was given a Royal Commission to inquire into Aboriginal land rights (see Woodward 1973).

Two points need to be made about the background to the Commission. First, that when people speak of land rights in Australia, they mean primarily the handing over, to complete Aboriginal control and ownership, of the lands that have already been reserved for Aborigines. While in the Northern Territory this was about ninety thousand square miles, in NSW and Victoria it was only a few thousand acres, so the peoples in these latter areas are also demanding cash compensation for loss of land. Nowhere were serious claims advanced for the return of alienated land. The other point relates to federal politics. From 1911 until 1 July 1978, the federal government had complete control over the Northern Territory and could, therefore, act freely there with respect to land rights and all other matters. But in the states it was different. Although a national referendum in 1967 had overwhelmingly given the federal government the right to make laws about Aborigines in the states, political realities have made it unequivocally clear that granting land rights in the states is an entirely internal matter. Thus the Commission focused exclusively on the Northern Territory but formulated its recommendations with a clear eye to their being workable in the states.

In April 1974, Mr Justice Woodward submitted his second and final report to the Government. The main recommendations of the two reports were:

that all reserved lands except the reserve within the municipal area of Darwin be made Aboriginal land, plus two cattle stations owned by Aboriginal companies financed by the Government and the Cobourg Peninsula and Tanami Desert wildlife sanctuary areas;

that a Northern and a Central Land Council be established to help the Aboriginal traditional owners administer their land and protect their interests. These would be entirely Aboriginal bodies, financed by 40 per cent of the statutory royalties from mining on Aboriginal land;

that Aborigines should be able to make land claims to unalienated land in the NT on the basis of traditional ownership before an Aboriginal Land Commissioner;

that no new permits for mining exploration be granted on Aboriginal land without Aboriginal agreement. This needs some explanation. Under Australian law all minerals are owned by the Crown (with a few minor exceptions) and prospectors are granted the right to prospect by the Government, the landowner having no interest in the minerals. The Aborigines sought ownership of minerals primarily because they wanted to be able to refuse absolutely the entry of miners onto their lands with the consequent damage to their sacred places and swamping of their way of life. But as white Australians did not own minerals, Mr Justice Woodward recommended that the Aborigines should not either but that unlike the great majority of Australians they could refuse entry to prospectors. Not only does this allow the people to keep miners out, provided the national interest, as agreed to by both houses of parliament does not overrule it, but it gives the Aborigines a right with which to negotiate.

(Woodward 1974)

It took a year for the legislation to be drafted in a form that implemented the recommendations almost directly, but during that period the fortunes of the Labor Party began to slip and the Liberal – Country Party opposition prepared for an election. In re-writing their policies both opposition parties agreed to implement the recommendations of the Woodward report thus completely reversing their 1972 stand on land rights. This proved to be of great significance, for the Labor bill introduced into the House in November 1975 never got past the first reading because the Labor government was ousted from power. With the election of the Liberal – Country Party government there were some doubts about the speed with which they would move to fulfil this election promise about which the Country Party was never happy. But, to many people's surprise, they took it up immediately. A great deal of political pressure to radically emasculate the bill was brought to bear on the government by the Country Party both within the coalition and in the Northern Territory, as well as by the Australian (and foreign!) Mining Industry Council, especially in view of another election promise made by the Government of the Northern Territory for independence within five years. To the dismay of the Aborigines some major concessions were made, mainly in the form of allowing the Northern Territory Legislative Assembly to make complementary legislation on the day-to-day working of land rights. Specifically, the Northern Territory was enabled to make ordinances concerning the protection of Aboriginal sacred sites, the control by Aborigines of people entering their land, the closure of coastal waters adjoining Aboriginal land up to two kilometres from shore and the conservation of wildlife, by agreement, on Aboriginal land. The dismay had its source in the open and racist hostility of senior Country-Liberal Party politicians to the Aborigines of the Northern Territory.

The Aboriginal Land Rights (NT) Act 1976 became law on 26 January 1977, but drafting defects, in the section dealing with the Land Trusts that hold the land, meant that it was not until 1978 that any land was actually transferred into Aboriginal ownership. The delay proved frustrating to certain mining interests who were pushing for a quick clarification of title to the large uranium province discovered on the western fringe of the Arnhem Land Aboriginal Reserve in the late 1960s. This province extends into adjacent unalienated Crown land and, under the terms of the Act, Aborigines had the right to place claims to all unalienated land before the Aboriginal Land Commissioner. This caused great concern to the mining industry, already frustrated by long environmental impact studies, a Government Inquiry led by Mr Justice Fox and the nationwide debate on whether to exploit the uranium deposits at all. The Land Rights Act itself did nothing to dispel the uncertainty over who owned the lands where the deposits were located. Only the Aboriginal Land Commissioner could do that and, in 1976, no one had been appointed to the post. So, in order to clarify the situation, the Fox Inquiry was empowered to make a finding on whether there were any traditional Aboriginal owners of the unalienated Crown land at issue. In addition to the miners and the Aborigines, a third major interest group was the conservationist lobby who had been pressing to establish a national park in the region of the proposed mine since 1965 and who had received a certain degree of government support for their scheme.

The Northern Land Council proved that there were traditional owners in the terms of the Act for a large region, including the Ranger uranium deposit. They made it absolutely clear that the Aboriginal owners were opposed to any mining on the grounds of the damage it would do to their sacred places and the vast influx of whites it would bring with it, despite the possibilities of great financial rewards. The government made it equally clear, however, that the findings of the Inquiry, in their eyes, gave the green light for exploiting the deposits. But the conservationists, the anti-uranium lobby and all the more radical supporters of the Aborigines believed that if the Northern Land Council had forcefully opposed the development of the mines, and had joined forces with those unions opposed to uranium mining, instead of accepting that it was inevitable that the mining would go ahead, they could have prevented any mining at all. This was unrealistic given the government's extraordinary keenness to encourage mining without fetters – most recently evidenced by the astounding decision not to levy a resource tax on the mining industry – and its 72½ per cent contribution to the capital of the Ranger Uranium Mines Company.[4] Adopting the view that the government could not be stopped on the Ranger mine, the Northern Land Council proposed an astute deal to the Inquiry. If Aboriginal ownership of the land were recognized, they would hand it back to the nation as a huge national park, many times larger than that originally proposed by the conservationists, on a long lease. This proposition was made in recognition of the outstanding environmental and recreational importance of the area to whites and also because they realized that, with the Australian National Parks and Wildlife Service running the park on terms agreed with the Northern Land Council, the people would have much greater control over white use of the region than they would ever have been able to exercise themselves.

Although the government had stated that the Aborigines could not stop the mine, because prospecting was already well under way before it became Aboriginal land, they did acknowledge that the Aborigines should be able to negotiate financial and social conditions under which the mining could go ahead. It is not clear what the government expected the Northern Land Council to come up with, but it was certainly not one of the better mining agreements seen in Australia. The Australian (and foreign) Mining Industry Council, caught unaware by the proposal, conducted a vicious campaign against the Aborigines and brought all its very considerable political influence to bear, particularly through its advocates in the Country Party. What they objected to was the idea of a resource tax on super-profits, which all agree the mine will generate within a few years.

Not unexpectedly, the Mining Industry Council succeeded in opposing the resource tax and, because the Northern Land Council had nothing to bargain with, since the government had made it clear the mine would go ahead, only a small 1¾ per cent royalty, on top of the statutory 2½ per cent, was gained along with some safeguards to features of Aboriginal significance and the environment. Nevertheless, even this level of royalty payments will generate, at a very conservative estimate, over \$A 8 million a year by 1985 in addition to the \$A 3 million a year already being received from the mines at Gove and Groote Eylandt.[5]

Since the Ranger claim, five others have been heard, and four more are before the permanent Aboriginal Land Commissioner, Mr Justice Toohey. At least a further 27 claims are likely to be brought before him in the two years 1978–80. Although there is no time limit to when claims may be made, a shaky understanding between the Federal and Northern Territory governments freezing the leasing of all unalienated land under claim until August 1980 is a strong incentive to bring claims on as soon as possible.

So far each claim has proved remarkably different in its legal and anthropological aspects. The common feature has been that despite the Northern Territory government's alleged support for the principle of Aboriginal land rights, it has opposed every claim except that by the Alyawarra-Kaititja. Opposition has been based not on questioning the anthropological evidence of ownership, but on legal points. Either the jurisdictional competence of the land Commissioner has been challenged or reliance has been placed on Section 50 of the Act. This requires the Commissioner in making his recommendations on a claim to the Federal Ministers for Aboriginal Affairs and the Northern Territory to have regard to, and comment on, among other things:

> the detriment to persons or communities including other Aboriginal groups that might result if the claim were acceded to either in whole

or in part and the effect which acceding to the claim either in whole or in part would have on the existing or proposed patterns of land usage in the region. (Section 50:3b and c)

The detriment argument was used with some effect by the Northern Territory government and Mount Isa Mines Ltd in the Borroloola claim to secure the exclusion of an island acknowledged as being owned by Aborigines in terms of the Act and for an easement corridor across the mainland area claimed, on the grounds that they might be required in the future for railway and port facilities by the company.

The detriment argument was also raised in the Warlpiri and Kartan-garurru-Kurintji claim, which covered a massive 95,000 square kilometres. Acceding to the claim, the Northern Territory government argued, would mean the loss of the Tanami Desert Wildlife Sanctuary, itself a huge wilderness of 37,500 square kilometres.[6] This objection was not successful, and the whole area was returned to the Aboriginal owners.

Jurisdictional points have been argued in three cases and are foreshadowed in others. The Lake Amadeus claim originally included Australia's best-known tourist attraction, Ayers Rock, which a Labor government had promised to return to its Aboriginal owners, but the Northern Territory government successfully made their point. Ironically, they used a Federal Conservation Act against the Federal Land Rights Act, thus underlining both the conflict within the federal government about how strongly to support its own land rights legislation and, more generally, that although conservationists claim to support Aboriginal land rights principally because they believe Aborigines will prevent mining on their land, Aboriginal ownership is obviously only second best to outright conservation status for the land.

The foregoing claims were all in remote parts of the Territory, but others are close to the major towns of Darwin and Katherine. Showing its true colours, the Northern Territory government recently expanded the Darwin municipality boundaries to make them the world's largest in order to frustrate the claims nearby, by taking advantage of the section of the Act which prevents such municipal lands from being claimed. The legitimacy of this extension is still being fought out in the courts.

A jurisdictional point was also argued unsuccessfully by the Northern Territory government to frustrate the conversion of the seven Aboriginally held pastoral (ranch) leases to freehold land. White pastoralists, who can only hold land under lease, oppose the conversion for a range of reasons, but the government has a problem since their objection affects the Gurindji's (Kurintji) lease at Wattie Creek. For most Australians Wattie Creek is the symbol of land rights, and the failure of these people to secure their land will rally much opposition. The high level of opposition by the Northern Territory government is further reflected in the fact that only one of the federally granted land titles was actually registered in the Territory between 1976 and June 1980.[7] Before it would register the titles, the Territory government wanted to have all the major bush tracks in the Arnhem Land Trust area, in particular, declared public roads, thus opening up the area to whites and initiating the erosion of Aboriginal control over it. A partial resolution to this problem was reached just prior to the territory election in June 1980 by the Federal Government amending the Act so that the titles did not need to define which roads were public. This has been left to negotiation or litigation.

With 25.9 per cent of the Northern Territory now owned by Aborigines, most of the 76,000 Whites feel the Blacks have enough land. This feeling, already strong, will increase during 1980, as the first applications are heard for the closure of coastal waters adjoining Aboriginal land up to two kilometres out to sea. Aboriginal groups seek the closure of the waters not only to keep whites away from their communities, but also because many are dependent on the sea for their subsistence protein (e.g. see Meehan 1977). Since, however, more than 60 per cent of the Territory coastline is Aboriginal land, not only professional fishermen but recreational groups are likely to oppose each application strongly. It needs to be emphasized that most of this coastline is remote from the main centres of white population and was never open to whites when the Aboriginal lands were reserves administered by the government, just as entry to these reserves has always been by permit only.

There can be no doubt that whatever the limitations of the Aboriginal Land Rights (NT) Act 1976 or the problems posed by the Northern Territory government's attitudes, it is the most important advance in the status of Aborigines since European colonization. No policy – from turning a blind eye to murder in the early days, through benign neglect, to welfare institutionalization from the 1930s onwards – has done much to eliminate the Territory's 'Aboriginal problem'. Past policies failed because they did not open the way for Aborigines to become part of the social, economic and political fabric of the Territory. Without endorsing everything that has happened since the passing of the Act, nobody can fail to be impressed by the extent to which Aborigines have since been drawn into the political life of the Territory, the impact that negotia-

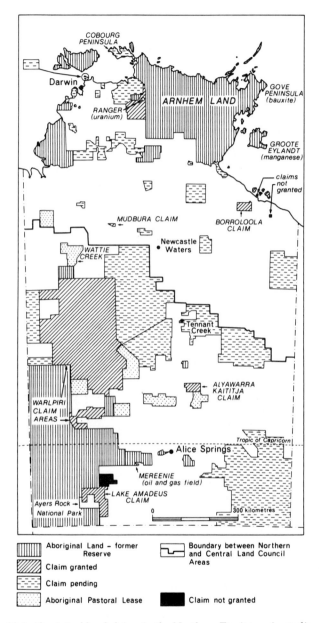

Within the map:

COBOURG
PENINSULA

Darwin

ARNHEM LAND

GOVE
PENINSULA
(bauxite)

RANGER
(uranium)

GROOTE
EYLANDT
(manganese)

claims
not
granted

MUDBURA CLAIM

BORROLOOLA
CLAIM

WATTIE
CREEK

Newcastle
Waters

Tennant
Creek

ALYAWARRA
KAITITJA
CLAIM

WARLPIRI
CLAIM
AREAS

Tropic of Capricorn

Alice Springs

MEREENIE
(oil and gas field)

LAKE AMADEUS
CLAIM

Ayers Rock →
National Park

0   300 kilometres

Legend:

Aboriginal Land – former
Reserve

Claim granted

Claim pending

Aboriginal Pastoral Lease

Boundary between Northern
and Central Land Council
Areas

Claim not granted

20.1 Aboriginal land claims in the Northern Territory, Australia

453

tions with government and mining companies have had on the development of Aboriginal leadership and the motivation which real property rights have provided for public and private bodies to consider Aborigines at the very outset of their planning. In the past, it has been easy to forget them as the majority live out of sight in isolated areas where there are few, if any, productive enterprises. Mining is changing that. Although most Aborigines are still actively opposed to mining, because of the damage it does to sacred places and the overwhelming number of whites it brings in its wake, royalties from mining are central to the success of the land-rights legislation. All of the major mines and oil and gas fields in the Territory are so far on Aboriginal land. Income from these mines, currently around $A3 million annually, will run into tens of millions by the late 1980s providing Aboriginal people with substantial funds basically independent of government control. It is these monies that are financing the land councils and the lawyers to fight the land claims, and which in future will give the Aborigines the power to negotiate their place in Territory society on their own terms.

Many white residents are bitter about the royalties Aborigines will receive for their collective benefit, when, in their opinion, they have too much already and spend it all on drink. Yet the *per capita* income of Aborigines in the Northern Territory is only $800 a year as opposed to the gross domestic product of $3,769 for the nation as a whole: infant-mortality rates are 4.5 times higher than for white Australians and Aboriginal unemployment runs at 50 per cent against a national average of close to 6 per cent. Aborigines are poor (see Altman and Nieuwenhuysen 1979); but, without the heavy overheads of a middle-class Australian way of life, their income is entirely for spending on consumer and luxury goods which largely accounts for the views of the whites. As they move into European houses and have their poverty-level incomes eaten up by fixed overheads and outback prices inflated by transport costs, they can only become poorer. It is poverty that will be aggravated by population increase at twice the national rate and the fact that, although a minority of the population, they make up 64 per cent of the rural residents among whom unemployment is highest. Territory whites forget, too, that the royalty payments to Aborigines are the only share of the profits of the companies kept in the Territory.

Most Aborigines are not fully aware of the economic and political problems of the future. For the middle-aged and older, the overwhelming issue is the spiritual and religious significance of the land itself and the need to protect it. As they have perceived the threat to their lands, and as the government policy of self-determination has made it possible for them to gain access to basic necessities beyond the villages, many hundreds of people, particularly in the north and the more hilly parts of the desert, have moved back on to their own lands. There they lead a semi-traditional life in small groups of 20–50 people, supplying their own protein from the bush and purchasing most of their carbohydrate with social-service cheques from travelling shops. This homeland centre or outstation movement allows them not only to protect the land, but to return to something of the self-planned, self-directed lives they led before institutionalization. It reflects and reinforces a long and strongly held respect for personal autonomy among adult males which often poses a political problem in dealing with whites effectively and in accepting such new political structures as the Land Councils with their in-built, although flexible, need for representation.

The Aboriginal Land Rights (NT) Act 1976 has demanded and will continue to demand changes from both Aborigines and Europeans. For the Aborigines the Act has sought to minimize those problems that would have arisen from a straight codification of traditional practice with all its consequent rigidification and irrelevance to the future.[8] But in creating new institutions and laws for new problems, it has inevitably created new stresses as well as possibilities. Apart from grappling with representation, the need to rely largely on white technical advisers in the absence of Aboriginal lawyers, economists and managers is a sensitive point that Blacks (and Whites) use on occasion to their own individual political advantage but collective disadvantage; the complexity of the legislation means that many Aborigines will not fully understand for a while what it does and does not do; and there are some Aborigines who remain landless, or for whom the emphasis on 'traditional owners' in the Act may lead to long-term inequalities. Whether it does or not partly depends on the personal views of the white advisers implementing the legislation about such fundamental matters as the nature of property and human rights.

As far as Aborigines in the rest of Australia are concerned, the greatest weakness of the legislation is that it only covers the Northern Territory which has less than 16 per cent of the nation's Aboriginal population (see Table 20.1).[9] Queensland with over 25 per cent of the Aboriginal population stands in marked contrast, with an openly racist government, discriminatory legislation, outdated assimilation policies, complete rejection of land rights and government-organized cultural destruction. Western Australia is little better, although a former Labor

Table 20.1. *The Aboriginal population at the 1971 and 1976 censuses*

State or territory	1971	1976	State or territory Aboriginal population as a percentage of the total 1976 Aboriginal population	Aboriginal population as a percentage of the total Australian population by state or territory in 1976
Northern Territory	23,381	25,300	15.5	24.9
Western Australia	22,181	26,126	16.1	2.2
Queensland	31,922	41,345	25.4	1.9
South Australia	7,299	10,714	6.7	0.85
New South Wales	23,873	40,450	24.9	0.82
Tasmania	671	2,942	1.8	0.72
Victoria	6,371	14,760	9.1	0.43
Australian Capital Territory	255	827	0.5	0.41
TOTAL	115,953	162,464	100%	

government did create an Aboriginal Land Trust to control and manage the 49 million acres of Aboriginal Reserve Land held by the Crown. However, the Trust is little more than an advisory body which does not even have final control over who enters Aboriginal land, nor any rights to minerals. Indeed only $A50,000 a year *in toto* from this vast area may be paid to the Land Trust by way of rents or royalties. It is significant that both Queensland and Western Australia seek mining development at any cost and see Aborigines only as an obstacle to such development. South Australia is the other state with a substantial proportion of its Aboriginal population tradition-oriented. Although South Australia has had an Aboriginal Lands Trust since 1966 and the reputation for being in the vanguard in terms of enlightened policies towards Aborigines it is only in 1981 that the huge 28,310 square miles North-West Reserve, home of the Pitjantjatjara peoples, will be handed back to them. Under a Labor government in 1979, it looked as if they would regain this area with absolute ownership of minerals, on the basis of the Cocks Report (1978) and the bill put before parliament that was based on it. However, a snap election in 1979 put the Liberal (conservative) Party into office before the bill was passed.

After a year of political activity the Pitjantjatjara Council and the Liberal government have reached the first negotiated land-rights settlement in Australia which will become law in 1981. Under the terms of the passed, but not yet gazetted, Pitjantjatjara Land Rights Act not only the North-West Reserve but three neighbouring pastoral leases and an area of Crown land, totalling over 100,000 square km, all become Aboriginal land. Minerals remain the property of the Crown but the land-holding body to be established by the Act, the Anangu Pitjantjatjaraku (the Pitjantjatjara People), can impose conditions on mining companies or refuse them permission to prospect. In the event of refusal the mining company may take the matter to arbitration by a judge whose findings are binding on all parties. One third of statutory royalties will be payable to the Anangu Pitjantjatjaraku who may negotiate further payments with the mining companies. Like the land in the Northern Territory, it may be neither sold nor taxed.

Although Victoria was the first state to hand back reserves to their occupants in 1971, only two small areas were involved. Assimilation of the Aboriginal population is superficially well advanced in Victoria but the dramatic rise in the census figures is clear warning that the Aboriginal people of this state will be looking for a better deal in the future. The same is true of Tasmania. In 1977 a Committee of Inquiry into Land Rights for Tasmanian Aborigines was established. As yet their recommendation that a Lands Trust be established and the three islands of Cape Barren, Babel and Great Dog (all off the northeast coast) be transferred to it, have not been acted on. However, the Aboriginal Land Fund Commission, established in 1975 to purchase land on the open market for Aboriginal groups on the basis of economic or social need, rather than traditional attachment, has recently bought Trefoil Island, off the northwest coast. This island is an important mutton-bird rookery and an economic resource that the people of the area have been working for Whites for many years.

Despite the existence of an Aboriginal Lands Trust in New South Wales since 1974 many Aborigines have been dissatisfied with the situation. This dissatisfaction led to the establishment of a Parliamentary Committee to investigate the situation in 1978. In August 1980 they published their recommendations which have yet to be acted upon.

The 4,299 hectares of land currently held by the Lands Trust is made up mainly of small plots of land on the outskirts of country towns to which people had been moved in the first half of this century, but which are now regarded as home by many. Although an Aboriginal body, the Lands Trust is subject to criticism for two main reasons. First, the Trust's main day-to-day work is as landlord to the 9,000 Aborigines who live in the 949 dwellings on its land. Second, the title to the land is held by the Trust, and although it is prepared to lease the land to the communities many communities want to hold the title themselves.

The recommendations of the Parliamentary Committee begin by proposing that the New South Wales parliament acknowledges the Aborigines' just claim to land based on prior ownership, tradition and needs, and further that the people have a right to compensation. This totally reverses the view of the previous Parliamentary Committee twelve years before.

The report details a completely new structure for land rights based on community title. The land-owning communities would be grouped by regions and for each region there would be an Aboriginal Land Council whose functions would be to assist the communities in the management, development and acquisition of land. Representatives from each Land Council would form the membership of the Aboriginal Land and Development Commission. This Commission would supply funds to the Regional and Community Councils. The source of funding would be from 7.5 per cent of state land tax revenue for 14 years and then 3.75 per cent for the final fifteenth year. Fifty per cent of the funds would have to be invested to create a capital fund. In 1981–2 it is estimated that 7.5 per cent of state land tax would amount to $a10.9 million.

In 1988, Australia celebrates its bicentenary. Already it is clear that the taint on the nation's title to the continent may cast a long shadow on the celebrations. Stimulated in part by this, a group of influential white Australians has called for a treaty between the federal government and the Aboriginal population, and set up a committee to help this come about (see Harris 1979). At the moment, the government is actively preparing for such negotiations.

On the other side, the population figures tell an important part of the story. In the five years between the 1971 and 1976 censuses, the Aboriginal population increased by a biologically impossible 40 per cent. These were the years in which Aboriginal political consciousness was raised throughout Australia and land rights became the crucial issue. Thousands of people of Aboriginal descent who previously kept a low profile became openly proud of their background during this period with a consequent impact on their self-identification on the census form. This is most dramatic in Tasmania, New South Wales and Victoria (in the ACT, the increase is by immigration), the areas from which the leading radicals come, but it is happening throughout the continent among people of part-Aboriginal descent. The demands for land rights and compensation for lost land from these people in the densely settled southeast of the continent are certain to be strong and persistent, just as they may be difficult to meet and politically explosive. As less than one per cent of the population of these states, their political weight obviously does not come from their numbers. Only in the Northern Territory will Aborigines ever be a substantial proportion of the population, although in the Kimberley region of Western Australia and in Queensland in Cape York, they are a regional majority. It seems likely that the governments of these two states, currently set against land rights, will eventually have to give some recognition to the preponderance of Aborigines in these regions, although what form it will take is hard to foresee.[10] At the moment, both these governments have moved against the federal government's compensatory strategy for giving these people access to land where they are living. This has been through the Aboriginal Land Fund Commission (now incorporated into the Aboriginal Development Commission) which has been provided with money to buy back land on the open market. However, after the Fund had bought two properties in Queensland and twelve in Western Australia, both governments blocked further purchases by refusing to register the titles of any properties bought by the Fund.

The view of most outback whites on land rights is accurately reflected by a comment in the Alice Springs newspaper published to celebrate self-government in the Territory. It spoke of being saddled with a liability, 'which many see as the most divisive and politically destructive law ever made' (*Centralian Advocate*, supplement 29 June 1978, p. 1). Yet, in essence, all that the Act has done in the Northern Territory is to hand over to Aboriginal control land designated as Aboriginal Reserve and areas of unalienated Crown land which, virtually by definition, were not suitable for pastoral use or they would have been taken up by whites. Further, the rights Aborigines now have in this land are no greater than those that have been exercised at one time or another by white Northern Territory officials on their behalf. It is a tragedy for the legislation that no sooner was it passed than the Northern Territory became self-governing and has been left to implement a highly innovative piece of legislation it does not want. Until such time as the other states move towards settlements similar to those in the Northern Territory, a moral taint will remain on their title, and Aboriginal people will be unable to break out of the crippling dependence created by white colonization.

Notes

1 This is a substantially updated version of a paper originally written for *Survival International Review* 1978 (with a new map, kindly drawn by Joan Goodrum) that summarizes the situation to January 1981. Developments are

fast and frequent in the Northern Territory at present and are likely to remain so for the next two years by which time most claims will be over. Shortly after this paper was completed, the Northern Territory government produced a draft bill entitled, The Aboriginal Land and National Parks Act 1980 which has since been redrafted eight times mainly to incorporate Northern Land Council suggestions. Its main purpose is to provide Aboriginal claimants whose land currently has park or conservation status (especially the traditional owners of the Cobourg Peninsula) with an alternative to making a land claim under the Federal Act which they might lose or win on less advantageous terms, particularly in the light of the emphasis being placed on the 'detriment to other interests' sections of the Act. The draft bill offers Aborigines strong use and occupancy rights without any claim, and offers the government a way to stop opposing all land claims and thereby alienating Aboriginal voters in six of the 19 Northern Territory Assembly seats. Naturally, for such certainty traditional owners lose something: public access to the areas would be guaranteed; and the Northern Territory Legislative Assembly can disallow any plan of management for the parks drawn up by the board on which the Aborigines have the majority vote.

2 For bibliography on land rights in Australia see Peterson 1981

3 A consequence of this has been that because there is no legal recognition of a primary Aboriginal title to Australia there has been no concern in granting land rights in the Territory to extinguish traditional title. Thus, unlike the Alaskan and Canadian settlements, there is no exchange of recognition of some rights and return of some land for the extinction of title to the rest. The consequence in the Territory is that currently whenever land becomes vacant Crown land the traditional owners, if any, may lay claim to it. However the Minister for Aboriginal Affairs is currently considering a report on the workings of the Act prepared by Mr B. Rowlands Q. C. This report examines the concerns of the mining and pastoral industry and it is possible that it may be used as an excuse to introduce a cut-off point for land claims.

4 In 1979 the Federal government put its share in the Ranger project up for sale and announced late in the year that it would be sold to Peko-Wallsend Pty.

5 It is difficult to estimate the amounts accurately in advance since mineral prices and production levels wax and wane, but these figures indicate the general range.

6 Such massive areas are an entailment of recognizing traditional rights in land among desert dwellers where population densities may range from 20 to 80 square miles per person. Among the Warlpiri the average density was about 40 square miles per person.

7 Apparently the significance of this failure to register title was largely symbolic. It meant that leases on Aboriginal land were not recognized under Northern Territory law.

8 Nevertheless there are many and complex problems in this area which are only now becoming apparent.

9 These population figures warrant extended comment for which this is not the place; however, some brief remarks are necessary. Many Torres Strait Islanders, who number around 10,000, and live mainly in Queensland, are included under Aborigines in the census. The Bureau of Census and Statis-

tics believes that the massive increase in the Victorian Aboriginal population is due to 3,000 non-English-speaking migrants filling the form out wrongly, although some knowledgeable research workers feel that for the first time this is a reasonably accurate count of Victorian residents who identify themselves as Aborigines in daily life. The actual Northern Territory figure was 23,751 but the census workers filling in forms for non-literate Aborigines in one region failed to fill in the racial identification section of the form. The figure 23,751 is obviously wrong since it is a mere 370 greater than the 1971 figure. It is interesting that people partly of Aboriginal descent are not identifying themselves on the census forms as Aboriginal in the Territory at anything like the rate they are in the states. The total Australian figures are still an underestimate and a best guess is that there are approximately 200,000 people who could identify themselves as of Aboriginal descent, or 1.4 per cent of the total Australian population.

10 The ballot box will be important but there are still considerable obstacles to be overcome. Voting is not compulsory for Aborigines, unlike whites. In Western Australia the government, well aware of the potential voting power of Aborigines in the Kimberley region – enhanced by a general rural gerrymandering – passed legislation in 1979 aimed at preventing enrolment and disenfranchising others. Enrolment was made more difficult so that in practice Aborigines have to approach the local police – feared local authority figures – to secure voting rights. The government is reliably reported as systematically going through the the rolls seeking to remove people with distinctively Aboriginal names on technical grounds by writing and asking them if they are still at the listed address. Since many Aborigines do not read, few letters find their way back to the electoral office with the consequence that people get struck off. Lack of reading skills is also used against Aborigines by restricting the use of how-to-vote cards. Although it has not yet been tested in court it is thought that non-reading non-writing voters must list the first three people they wish to vote for, in Australia's complex preferential voting system, before instructing the person assisting them to fill in the form to follow the how-to-vote card.

Bibliography

Altman, J., and Nieuwenhuysen, J. 1979. *The economic status of Australian Aborigines.* London: Cambridge University Press

Blackburn, J. 1971. *Milirrpum v. Nabalco Pty Ltd and the Commonwealth of Australia (Gove land rights case); Judgement of the Hon Mr J. Blackburn.* Sydney: The Law Book Co. 17 FLR 141–294

Centralian Advocate (weekly newspaper, Alice Springs, N. T.)

Cocks, C. 1978. *Report of the Pitjantjatjara land rights working party of South Australia.* Adelaide: Government Printer

Fox, R. W., Kelleher, G. G. and Kerr, C. B. 1977. *Ranger uranium environmental inquiry, second report.* Canberra: Government Publishing Service

GRR 1889. *Government Resident's report on the Northern Territory.* Adelaide: South Australian Parliamentary Papers

Hardy, F. 1968. *The unlucky Australians.* Melbourne: Nelson

Harris, S. 1979. *'It's coming yet . . .': an Aboriginal treaty within Australia between Australians.* Canberra: Aboriginal Treaty Committee

Meehan, B. 1977. 'Man does not live by calories alone: the role of shellfish in a coastal cuisine', in J. Allen, J. Golson and R. Jones (eds.), *Sunda and Sahul*, 493–531. London: Academic Press

Northern Territory statistical summaries. Canberra: Australian Bureau of Statistics

Peterson, N. 1981. 'A selective and annotated bibliography on land rights', in N. Peterson (ed.), *Aboriginal land rights: a handbook.* Canberra: Australian Institute of Aboriginal Studies

Woodward, A. E. 1973. *Aboriginal land rights commission: first report, July 1973.* Canberra: Australian Government Publishing Service

   1974. *Aboriginal land rights commission: second report, April 1974.* Canberra: Australian Government Publishing Service

21. Political consciousness and land rights among the Australian Western Desert people

DANIEL A. VACHON

Introduction

During the past 15 years, land-rights issues have taken an increasingly central role in the political lives of Aborigines throughout 'colonial Australia'.[1] This is not to say that Aboriginal interests in the religious and economic significance of their land is recent but rather that the new social relationships brought on by the British and extended by Australian capitalism and foreign imperialism have given an entirely different content to indigenous people – land relations and conceptions. In particular, conflict of interest no longer has a parochial, 'tribal' flavour. Political battles are fought in the courts, in legislative assemblies and through mass demonstrations. The actors are lawyers and politicians, representatives of mining associations, pastoral boards, labour unions and legally incorporated Aboriginal organizations. Positions are defended on moral, legal and economic grounds in the press and in the bush. The peculiarities of Walbiri and Pitjantjatjara land tenure are debated by lawyers and anthropologists in seminars devoted to land-claim work. Aboriginal men discuss Dreaming tracks and political candidates while hunting kangaroo in Land Rovers.

Since the end of World War II, the many and varied struggles for Aboriginal rights in the cities as well as in the bush reflect the growing trend of national liberation throughout the world. The Australian state can no longer isolate her indigenous native population from international scrutiny; in Basle, Switzerland, the federal government was condemned recently for its treatment of native Australians.[2] Increasingly, Aborigines are being made aware of the conditions and struggles of peoples both within and without Australia in meetings and through visual and printed media. In the North-West Reserve of South Australia, it was not uncommon to listen to Aboriginal men discussing the

A meeting of the Pitjantjatjara Council, northwestern South Australia (P. Toyne)

Mantjiltjara of the Pilbara and the Dene of the Mackenzie Valley in Canada in the same afternoon.

In Australia the federal government however, does not hold a monopoly on all aspects of Aboriginal policy making. Although the 1967 referendum placed formal control over Aboriginal welfare in the hands of Canberra, state agencies retain the effective administrative and executive bodies which originally were established before Federation in 1901. Moreover, state legislation regarding Aborigines has not been superseded by, but instead often contradicts, federal legislation. For example, with regard to the 'doctrine of communal native title' (Little 1974:93–9), pre-contact communal rights to the land are explicitly recognized in the Northern Territory Land Rights Act 1976, and finds its strongest expression in the proposed Pitjantjatjara Land Rights Bill of South Australia, while Western Australia and Queensland have never recognized native title to the land. Commonwealth – state politics are constantly coloured with conflicts over the 'Aboriginal problem' which, significantly, often centre on the question of which government will control access to primary resources (see Middleton 1977:126–7).

Within this context, it is little wonder that the historical processes leading up to the present conditions of Aborigines in the various states display wide disparities, despite the fact that, in all states, Aboriginal rights have always been recognized after the interests of small, and now, large capital have been considered.

For the Pitjantjatjara, Yankuntjatjara and Ngaanyatjara people of the northwest portion of South Australia, and in the eastern sector in particular,[3] the question of legitimate control of access to the wealth of their land by pastoralist and mining interests has become the major political issue. How this came about and how the land issue is expressed are the major subjects of this chapter. A detailed examination will be made of Aboriginal responses to successive stages of settler/capitalist development in the region as these have been affected, on the one hand, by the specific nature of the productive process contacted and, on the other, by the mediation of two disparate ideologies: the one reflecting Western Desert social organization and the other legitimizing capitalist commodity relations of the South Australian state.

Aspects of Western Desert social organization and ideology

The Western Desert 'culture bloc', which would include Pitjantjatjara, Yankuntjatjara and Ngaanyatjara people,[4] has been described by Berndt (in Turner forthcoming: 36) as extending

eastward from Kalgoorlie, Laverton and Leonora as far as Oodnadatta and south from the central mountainous core . . . to the Trans-Australian line. . . . In addition, there is a further stretch extending from the Rawlinsons north-west . . . to Wiluna and to Jingalong near the great northern highway and bounded on the north beyond the Canning Stock Route by the southern and eastern Kimberleys.

The region covers an area of approximately 250,000 square miles (Berndt 1972:180) with a pre-contact population of about 10,000 persons, yielding a man/land ration of one person for every 25 square miles. As late as 1972, Berndt estimated the Aboriginal population of the Western Desert to be less than 3,200 (*ibid.*:180).

Reports made by early observers (Basedow 1904; White 1915) described the Western Desert people of the northwest portion of South Australia to be engaged in economic activity little different from Aborigines throughout Australia. Although conditions were inhospitable in comparison with other areas, early reports give the impression that people experienced no obvious deprivations (except during drought) but preserved a favourable balance of nature similar to hunting-gathering societies throughout the world (cf. Lee 1968).

Berndt (1966:40–1; 1972:181), Elkin (1938–40:204) and Turner (n.d.:37) point out that all local groups from the Western Desert share one broad cultural pattern and display 'striking similarities . . . in terms of social organization, behavioral patterns and ideology in general' (Berndt 1972:181). Throughout the region, the tracks of mythological beings or *tjurkurrpa* directly or indirectly link all people (*anangu*) into a vast 'brotherhood grouping' (Turner forthcoming:38). As will be shown, it is in reference to this brotherhood group that *anangu* behave politically with respect to land rights. Added to this fundamental unity on one level is a complex organization of diversity on others. A number of ideologies, defining 'kinship' and ceremonial associations for instance, not only reproduce a generalized equivalence among *anangu* in their relationship to the land and its resources but also provide the mechanisms whereby individuals are recruited to various other groups, both named and un-named. Production units, foraging groups or 'hordes' are formed as the result of alliances between other groups or '*ngurra* groups' which are identified with a constellation of named sites – waterholes, hills, ridges, claypans and camping grounds (*ibid.*:181). Thus, all individuals work within one unit and identify themselves with individuals who collectively form at least one other. Membership in the latter '*ngurra* group'[5] gives an individual unqualified rights, depending on age and sex, to forage on a particular area of land and to 'care for' the sacred objects and sites found therein.

A more complete discussion of Western Desert social organization can be found elsewhere in this volume (see Hamilton). However, as the analysis proceeds, several aspects of Western Desert ideology, particularly the *tjurkurrpa* and the role of labour in a pre-capitalist context will be considered. The above serves as the barest of introductions to a highly complex and only partially understood socio-economic formation.

First stage of European settler contact

From the very beginnings of settlement in the fertile southeastern regions of South Australia, treatment of Aborigines was to take a course different from the genocidal practices of convicts and settlers in Tasmania, Victoria and New South Wales. In 1834, the Colonization Commissioners proclaimed that existing rights of Aborigines would be protected while patient gestures would be made to win them over to the 'comforts of civilized men' (Rowley 1972:74). Thus began a tradition in South Australia of reconciling the effects of 'progress' with humanistic principles or, as one writer has put it, devising ways 'to appear radical and be conservative' (Clark 1969:84). Attempts to reconcile settler and, later, capitalist interests on the one hand and Aboriginal interests on the other in South Australia therefore bore the stamp of a 'humanistic-radical' tradition which would result, from the Aboriginal point of view, in some real gains later on.

During the early days of settler expansion in the southeast, however, the very nature of incipient capitalist development meant that Aboriginal victories were few, if any. From the outset, with the formation of the South Australian Land Company in 1832, practically no restrictions were placed on the occupation of land for a minimum price (see Rowley 1972:74–5). Within a short time enough settlers had established themselves in the new colony to enable them to gain provincial status from the Colonial Office in 1834. New legislation fitted the needs of a pastoralist and agricultural community with expansionary desires limited only by geography. The need for a class of wage-labourers to make this expansion possible was not urgent, and the Act of 1834 explicitly rejected the transportation of convicts to the new colony (Clark 1969:81).

In other words, the new provincial legislature functioned to administer a rapid expansion of settlers into 'waste and unoccupied lands' (Clark 1969:81) with policies which were 'systematic' only in the sense that the least number of restrictions were placed on a community of self-interested private-property owners. As early as 1844, there were a number of stations along the Murray River to the north well beyond effective control from Adelaide (Rowley 1972:80). The pastoralists initially saw Aborigines as a potential danger to the lives of their stock and themselves. In Cockburn's *Pastoral Pioneers of South Australia* (1925), the 46 references to Aborigines invariably describe Aboriginal attacks on overlanders, shepherds etc.

It soon became apparent to the administration that it was powerless to halt the expansion which it had helped to create. With regard to the native population, original ideals had to be modified. Promises to safeguard native rights to the land were negated either by executive impotence or by a lack of determination and commitment. In 1836, a Protector of Aborigines was appointed, under whom 'native affairs were dealt with other than as central to the objectives of governments. The pietistic phraseology and the objectives of Aboriginal welfare were not necessarily insincere; but it was assumed that the land could be settled and the Aborigines compensated and satisfied at small cost' (Rowley 1972:76). The Protector's office steadily declined in function until, only a few years after its inception, it was reduced to issuing rations and setting up small reserves in order to separate Aborigines from the more brutal effects of settler contact. By 1856, the Commissioner of Crown Lands had replaced the Protector's office (ibid.:81). Aboriginal rights were now seen as the rights of a dying people who were to be given the paternal protection and institutionalized improvement afforded by government agencies.

Four years after the Point Macleay and Point Pearce Missions were established in 1868 to preserve what was left of Aboriginal society in the southeast, Ernest Giles first explored the Everard and Musgrave Ranges in the far northwest. He reported the conditions of the arid semi-desert to be largely unsatisfactory for successful pastoral expansion from the southeast, and for several decades the remoteness of the region served to discourage all but the hardiest of pioneers. A number of expeditions failed to locate mineral deposits and, except for a few lone prospectors, mining was not to be developed seriously until the 1950s.

Evidence of Aboriginal occupation was recorded by a number of explorers and surveyors. The Yankuntjatjara people were contacted in the Everard Range by Carruthers (1892:2), Basedow (1904) and White (1915). Aboriginal people were found to be inhabiting the Musgrave Range by Carruthers (1892:2) and Hubbe (in Hilliard 1968:56) in 1895 and in the Mann and Tomkinson Ranges, or what is generally referred to as 'Pitjantjatjara country',[6] by Hann (ibid.:59–60) in 1906–7. For the most part, contact was either established to satisfy mutual curiosity or initiated by Europeans in their search for water. On occasion, hostilities would break out but, apparently, these were rare and seldom resulted in killings (ibid.:55–62).

The first European-inspired economic activity in the area was 'dogging' and it is not surprising that the first economic relation between Aborigines and Europeans was an exploitative one. The Anti-Vermin Act of 1886 had set a bounty on wild-dog scalps and enterprising 'doggers' would 'trade' tea, flour, sugar and clothing for the scalps collected by native people. The industry seems to have been well organized, and recognized rounds to native camps were established by individual entrepreneurs (Love 1937:10). It is impossible to estimate the number of Europeans and Aborigines engaged in this activity but the trade continued until the latter part of the 1930s and dingo scalps soon came to be the recognized currency in the region. In some cases, the dogging trade afforded Europeans with the necessary capital to establish small pastoral properties and early pastoralists would sell the scalps to supplement their otherwise meagre income.

In addition to the government bounty on dingo scalps, the Pastoral Act of 1922 provided a number of initiatives[7] to settlers willing to take up leases in the area. However, the leases which were granted east of Oodnadatta and south of the Northern Territory border to Coober Pedy were small. Few exceeded 300 square miles, and the scale of capital investment could not ensure a marketable surplus large and regular enough for continued expansion.

The few reports available from this period reveal that properties were not fenced and herds of cattle and sheep roamed at will. Lease-holders worked collectively during mustering periods along with some Aboriginal trackers. Occasionally, small groups of Aborigines served as shepherds in exchange for food and other commodities but, for the most part, the demand for Aboriginal labour was small (*Report of the Chief Protector of Aboriginals* 1929). The most serious conflicts between pastoralist and Aborigines resulted from the spearing of stock, especially during periods of drought. In response to this threat to private property, the state set up a police camp at Indulkana Station in 1916. Offenders were either punished by the pastoralists themselves or force-marched to the nearest gaol in Oodnadatta (see Hamilton 1972:40–1).[8] Incidents of stock killing continued to be reported to the Protector until the late 1930s.

By 1937, Love (1937:7) reported that 'all the country between Oodnadatta and the Aboriginal reserve [which had been gazetted in 1921] is now leased for pastoral purposes'. However, at the same time, leases along the reserve were being cancelled (*Report of the Chief Protector of Aboriginals* 1939:1). Of the settlers who remained, many suffered heavily from the long drought of the 1930s and sold their leases during the land consolidation period at the end of the war.

At the same time that the first hesitant steps into the northwest were being made by settlers, several Aboriginal groups were also migrating – a trend which would have important consequences. The Western Desert people were involved in at least four major migrations which resulted in more-or-less permanent residence away from their *ngurra*. A number of reasons have been suggested for these movements: 'European pressure', drought, the attraction of European food and indigenous conflict.[9] Several authors (*Report of the Chief Protector of*

Aboriginals 1918, 1920; Bates 1938:172; Berndt 1941:1–5) observed that people from the Everard and Musgraves began a movement to Ooldea in 1917 which continued for approximately ten years (*Report of the Chief Protector of Aboriginals* 1925). A large number of the present population of Yalata are the descendants of these people who moved from the northwest.[10] A second movement about a decade later involved the Ngaanyatjara of the Warburton Ranges and others of the central desert regions of Western Australia who settled in Laverton and Mt Margaret in the southwest of that state (Elkin 1938–40:295–7, Berndt 1941:5).

The two migrations which are most relevant to this discussion are the movements of the Yankuntjatjara people of the Musgrave and Everard Ranges to the east and beyond to Oodnadatta (Berndt 1941:5; Hilliard 1968:82; Elkin 1938–40:204) and those people of the Mann and Tonkinson Ranges who migrated eastward.

It appears that the people known as the Antikarinya had been moving eastward to Oodnadatta since the turn of the century (*Report of the Chief Protector of Aboriginals* 1902). By 1921, a great number of people were living there (*ibid.* 1922) although the large number recorded (700–800) might be partially the result of ceremonial activity. Yankuntjatjara people from the Everards also migrated east, setting up camps along the Alberga River and as far north as Finke Siding (Elkin 1938–40:204). Finally, came the Pitjantjatjara from the Mann and Tomkinson Ranges into the area previously occupied by the Yankuntjatjara, and today the majority of the combined populations of Amata, Ernabella, Fregon, Mimili and Indulkana settlements refer to themselves as Pitjantjatjara. When asked, these people will claim that their *ngurra* is far to the west and that they are 'caring for' the land that they are now occupying on behalf of both their wives' brothers (*marutju*) who have died and the people who have left their country to reside in Oodnadatta and Coober Pedy. This situation has important implications for an understanding of Western Desert land tenure as will be discussed later.

The South Australian government, through the Aborigines Protection Board, was intent on pursuing a policy in the far northwest which would prevent the dramatic failures of the past. There was little difference in the content of the policy which, as in the southeast, was biased toward assisting early capital accumulation. The crucial difference lay in the conditions of its application. The region presented obstacles to the production of beef and minerals, and until the necessary infrastructure and knowledge of resources were made available, incentives made by the state would, at best, only attract small capital to the northwest.

For many of the Pitjantjatjara and Yankuntjatjara people, the rigorous conditions of the desert and immaturity of the infrastructure necessary for stable commodity production acted to minimize the negative effects of private interests. However, even the relative isolation of the Western Desert people was not enough to prevent the steady decline of their numbers[11] mostly as a result of influenza and measles epidemics. For many years the Protector's Board simply saw this as being the inevitable result of 'white contact' but by 1921, the policy of separation was instituted.[12]

The policy led initially to the establishment of the Northwest Reserve in 1921 and to the extension of the reserve to Ernabella Mission in 1949. By 1941, the Aborigines Protection Board (*Report of the Aborigines Protection Board* 1941:1) agreed that

> as far as possible, all tribal Aborigines living under natural conditions should be protected from being detribalized, inasmuch as experience shows that such detribalization, in spite of all efforts, leads inevitably towards extinction of the race through lack of interest in life, miscegenation, the introduction of European diseases, and under nourishment.

Protection was to be offered through the 'operations of stations by religious organizations' (*ibid.*:1) as 'preferable to control exercised exclusively by the government' (*ibid.*:1). Ernabella Mission was established by the Presbyterian Church in 1937 and sanctioned by the government to act as a 'buffer' between the settlers to the east and the Aborigines migrating out of the reserve (see Hilliard 1968:91–8). For the moment, the failure of early expansion and the policy of separation which grew out of this failure both combined to establish some form of workable humanism.

Second stage of European capitalist contact

Although reliable accounts are scarce,[13] it is generally admitted by field officers, missionaries and, occasionally, station owners themselves that the Pitjantjatjara and Yankuntjatjara people provided the bulk of the labour for the building of the post-World War II pastoral industry in the northwest of South Australia (see *Report of the Aborigines Protection Board* 1943:1; 1947:3). The plain fact is that no other source of labour was available; the roads, the bores, the fences, the yards and the homesteads were all built with Aboriginal labour-power. Furthermore, until the development of new roads and railways, the introduction of mechanized transport to rail-heads and the influx of labourers from the southern cities, Aborigines were engaged in most of the stock work such as droving, branding, mustering and general maintenance. And yet, even if recent government reports are too 'liberal' to suggest it, past reports repeatedly complained of the refractory nature of the Aboriginal work force, and the slow process of 'assimilation'. 'Primitive or near-primitive natives [will require] possibly some generations [before they] can be developed to a standard where they can be integrated and eventually assimilated' (*Report of the Aborigines Protection Board* 1956–62). It appears that over thirty years of Aboriginal station work (longer in the south) was insufficient 'proof' to allow the Board to conclude that 'spear-carrying nomadic people living under tribal conditions' (*Report of the Aboriginal Affairs Board* 1963:1) were 'integrated' and successfully 'assimilated' into the wider community.

An analysis of the exact nature of Aboriginal work (including state intervention in the 'proper' expenditure of Aboriginal labour-power on pastoral stations) is essential for an understanding of current developments in land rights. The nature of work relations and their effects on Western Desert ideology provided the basis for the development of political consciousness among the Pitjantjatjara, Yankuntjatjara and Ngaanyatjara. The analysis will consider three important elements: (1) the class nature of the state's policy of 'assimilation'; (2) the necessary conditions for pastoral commodity production in the northwest and the specific role of Aboriginal labour; and (3) the resultant changes in Aboriginal conceptions of work, particularly of labour as a commodity.

From the earliest contact with Aborigines, British colonial agents, such as Macquarie, expressed a concern with protecting them 'against the aggression of the white man' and teaching them the 'habits of industry and decency' (Clark 1969:46). However, there was never any doubt that assimilation was to be, in practice, the transformation of Aboriginal communal labour to wage-labour (see *ibid.*:46; Hamilton 1972:35; Middleton 1977:106).

In 1961, all Australian governments agreed that the policy of assimilation meant

> that all Aborigines and part-Aborigines are expected eventually to attain the same manner of living as other Australians and to live as members of a single Australian community enjoying the same rights and privileges, accepting the same responsibilities, observing the same customs and influenced by the same beliefs, hopes and loyalties as other Australians.   (In Hamilton 1972:36)

The allusion to bourgeois ethics and morality contained in the policy was clarified three years later when it was slightly but significantly changed to read: 'seeks that all persons of Aboriginal descent *will choose* to attain a similar manner and standard of living' (*ibid.*:36): a more moral and rational *class* position on a policy which, for the majority of Aborigines, was not working. Economic 'rights' for Aborigines meant primarily the right to sell their labour-power after attaining the ('single'?) culture of the Australian community, by unburdening themselves of communal (native) ties and being transformed into self-seeking individuals economically compelled to find a job, a 'privilege' accorded to all Australian workers. If Aborigines *chose* to retain their own culture and the poverty which went along with it, legally the decision was theirs to make and morally they only had themselves to blame for their irrationality. That such 'freedoms' should be given *after* their destruction was well under way is perfectly consistent with the granting of bourgeois freedoms and, from the Aboriginal point of view, only emphasizes the hypocrisy of state policies generated by bourgeois values and mentality in the interests of the ruling class.

In the northwest of South Australia, which aspects of 'aboriginality' were to be protected and which were to be assimilated shifted with the emphasis placed on protection versus assimilation by the makers of native policy. This emphasis, in turn, shifted with the unpredictable needs of capital. During the first four decades of the twentieth century, petty-commodity production operated outside a regular capital – labour relation. In fact, early pastoralists operated outside regular relationships to Aborigines except for the dogging trade and the taking of Aboriginal women as 'wives'. After the end of the war, leases to the pastoral land of the north, east of Todmorden Station near Oodnadatta, gradually became consolidated into large holdings controlled by a few interests,[14] and development of the productive base began with the sinking of bores, the grading of tracks and the erection of station homesteads. Cattle replaced sheep in response to market demands. Miles of fence were needed not only to separate new breeds but to protect one's investment. Raw materials, such as wood and stone, were easily found in order to build fences; yards and buildings and natural water supplies could either be modified[15] or serve as a supplement to stock demands. Above all, a cheap source of labour was conveniently available.

Small Aboriginal camps had been constantly forming and reforming near early settler homesteads since the turn of the century. The usual practice of the Protector's Office was to supply rations to settlers and missions for distribution to Aborigines who would congregate at the depots, especially during times of drought, and disperse again when the rains came. Government rations had been distributed by the Presbyterian Mission at Ernabella since 1937 and the Australian Inland Mission at Oodnadatta even earlier. By 1945, partially as a response to increased Aboriginal migrations from the west into the eastern pastoral area, additional depots had been set up at Granite Downs, Everard Park and Mabel Creek Stations and continued until 1965.

When control over rationing was placed in the hands of employers of Aboriginal labour, this 'social service' became little more than a government subsidy ensuring the uninterrupted reproduction of Aboriginal labour-power. Wages could be kept down[16] and still a healthy supply of labourers would be assured. Medical care and, later, social security were seen to be the responsibility of the state. Little government supervision either in the distribution of rations and welfare cheques or in the conditions of work was felt to be necessary by the Board of Protectors (see Stevens 1974:104). Incidentally, even today, older Aboriginal men who worked or lived on the stations will respond with surprise when it is suggested that rations were supplied by the government and not as an expression of the good will of the pastoralists themselves.

Protection was breaking down not only in practice but in official policy as well.[17] Ernabella, the erstwhile 'buffer' mediating so-called black/white contact, was to become an official training centre for Aborigines since 'the time has now arrived . . . to prepare the people for an earlier contact with the outside world than had been anticipated. This is due to the steady development of the pastoral industry in the surrounding areas, with the resultant opportunities in employment' (*Report of the Aborigines Protection Board* 1950:5). In their zeal to assist early capital accumulation as much as possible in the area, native policy makers went as far as to specify the kind of labour required by noting that 'while older people will still maintain themselves by hunting, the younger people are wanting to take up work which is both useful and remunerative' (*ibid.*:5). Apparently the work that these people had been engaged in for nearly 50,000 years was 'useless' or, rather, labour was only useful if it served the requirements of capital.

In 1946, the South Australian government agreed to the establishment of the Woomera Rocket Range and a number of regulations were suggested by the Aborigines Protection Board to 'protect' Aborigines from personnel who entered the reserve in the northwest. One patrol officer was recommended to supervize an area which would easily contain England and Wales. Nine years later the mines department was given permission to enter the reserve 'to make a geological survey in view of the importance of uranium' (*Report of the Aborigines Protection Board* 1955:2). The Board continued to note in the report that no uranium had been found but nickel deposits had been. In the same year, the Board promptly agreed to the leasing of an area near Mt Davies to the Southwest Mining Pty Ltd. No regulatory supervision of these activities was provided and the construction of roads and the drilling of bores were permitted 'in such places as determined by the Board' (*ibid.*:2). Finally, in response to pastoral interests, a request made by the Pastoral Board to carry out 'an inspection and investigation of the North-West Reserve in regard to the possibility of establishing a cattle industry' (*Report of the Aborigines Protection Board* 1956:7) was granted. But, again, the Pastoral Board was not impressed with the prospects. Unlike the policy maintained with regard to Aboriginal employment on pastoral stations, the state disallowed any Aboriginal participation in mining and related activities[18] due to their concern for the effects of 'white contact'.

However, even for those who were involved in developing the pastoral industry, Aborigines did not follow the scenario of assimilation suggested by the policy makers. Apparently, Western Desert people did not enter into a capital – labour relationship as isolated individuals who, driven by economic necessity were intent on finding work. As one author has put it, they were truly a 'people in between' (Hilliard 1968), as they are today, with a different relationship to the capitalist economy.

Within communal property relations, according to Marx (1979:85), 'individuals behave not as workers, but as owners . . . and members of a community who also work'.[19] Within a production process where an individual shares with others the dual status of communal owner and worker, the purpose of work is 'the maintenance of [both] the individual owner and his family as well as the communal body as a whole' (*ibid.*:85). In the Western Desert, communal relations can be induced most easily when people are observed to act with reference to the 'brotherhood group', and not only in economic and ceremonial life. At the risk of anticipating the argument, it is particularly significant that the land-rights issue should be interpreted by *anangu* as the struggle to ensure the recognized rights to the land for *all anangu* as '*walytja*' or 'kin'. That is, land rights can be seen to be the exceptional political activity of *anangu* to ensure the uninterrupted maintenance of the 'communal body as a whole' or, in this case, the brotherhood group.

Apparently, the *essential* equivalence of *anangu* as communal owners is not contradicted, given the present level of productive forces or external pressure, by the exercise of exclusive rights and obligations held by all individuals as members of various *'ngurra* groups'.

During the period of Aboriginal involvement in the pastoral industry, communal relations, as these are reflected, maintained and reproduced by a complex of ideological mechanisms, became doubly complex since 'work' was now being performed within both 'old' communal relations and wage-labour – capital relations. The assumption, in line with assimilationist policy, that an individual Aborigine's conceptions of himself and his labour would automatically change as a result of working for a wage, is questionable at best.

That Western Desert people were engaged in pastoral work through communal interest and not individual self-interest is suggested by their pattern of work. For example, during the fifties and sixties, according to one field officer's reports, approximately a hundred people were living in camps near Granite Downs Station; 50–60 at De Rose Hill; 20–30 at Lambina; and 90–100 at Everard Park. Often the size and location of such groups were determined either by the site of the next ration 'dump' or by the demand for labour by the pastoralists. Either Aboriginal people would leave the main camp for several days, going back to work in small groups building fences, or younger men would be gathered by the station manager to perform stock work, dig bores or clear tracks.[20] If no work was available, if rations were low, or game and firewood scarce, or if a ceremony was being held elsewhere, the entire group would move. As one observer pointed out during the fifties, large numbers of people would leave Ernabella and move west collecting dingo scalps and native food, while others would join their kin living near the stations. Whatever the specific factors which led Aborigines to work on the stations, such as the attraction of a more assured supply of food or the lure of other European commodities, these were based on *collective* desires or responses to certain conditions and not based on individual motivation (see Hamilton 1972:42).

Furthermore, the use-values exchanged for labour-power were not considered to be a means to satisfy individual needs and desires. In terms of Western Desert economic relations and ideology, that which is gained as a consequence of a particular social status (e.g. elder, or, today, welfare recipient) or as a consequence of work is not the *property* of individuals, just as their labour is not theirs to expend as they see fit. There is no evidence to be found either in Western Desert ideology or

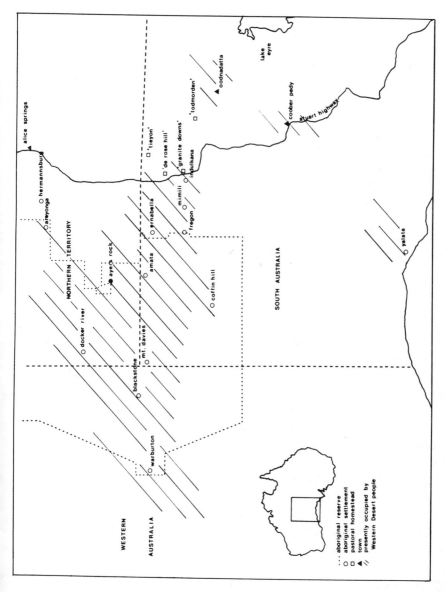

21.1 Western Desert Aboriginal communities in Australia

in social practice which suggests that *any* social status or expenditure of productive energy provides a benefit which is *exclusive* to an individual who either held the position or did the work. Individuals do not own their labour to expend, much less sell, as they themselves choose. If anything, the rights people have to their own labour (including ceremonial labour) are at the same time the rights they have to the collective labour of others, whatever the collective may be during the period of work. In other words, an individual's purpose for working is the collective's purpose for working. Individual labour must not contradict social interest, and, indeed, it would not be in the individual's interest to do so.

Although traditional economic (foraging) activity has been modified, work is seen in the same way today as it was in the past and as it was during the period of pastoral employment. In the settlements of the northwest, the people who work for the school, the hospital or the community receive a wage which is distributed to a wide range of kin, far wider than the immediate nuclear family (*Report of the Pitjantjatjara land rights working party* 1978:26). Social-security cheques are distributed in the same manner. Also, during 20 months of field work, no evidence of incipient entrepreneurial activity was recorded.[21]

The nature of pastoralist production, Aboriginal involvement in the productive process and, finally, the intervention of the state combined to affect Western Desert communal relations and ideology remarkably little. Firstly, pastoral production does not necessarily interfere with foraging activities as has been previously suggested and, in fact, it was in a pastoralist's interest that some hunting and gathering should continue. Along with a number of government subsidies, foraging was an added assurance that labourers would be reproduced at no expense. Often the people would return to their *ngurra*, as they still do today (see Wallace 1977:129–30), so that attachment to the land, not only in an emotional sense but in an economic sense as well, was to some extent maintained. Certainly, a modification in Aboriginal patterns of consumption with a reliance on European foods has altered the emphasis placed on hunting and gathering activities. However, the fact that Western Desert people may eat more flour than mulga seeds is likely to have a greater effect on their health[22] than on social relationships and conceptions. Secondly, and more importantly, the separation of Western Desert people from the means of production (i.e. the land) was not a precondition necessary for capitalist production in the area. By the very fact of selling their labour-power, the people were alienated from the pastoral productive process, but their consciousness of this objective fact was of small significance to the Pitjantjatjara and Yankuntjatjara who continued to retain effective control over the land as an element of their own social-productive processes. In particular, the ceremonial cycles and sacred sites through which these people reproduced communal relations and exercised 'control' over natural processes were not altered or destroyed by pastoralism to any great degree, unlike mining, for instance.

Finally, Aborigines were involved in an obvious contradictory process which tended to weaken and finally break down the relation between capital and wage-labour. No matter how well various traditional aspects of behaviour fit with the pastoral industry's needs, the emphasis placed on using Aboriginal labour to build the productive base meant that the people were, in essence, building themselves out of jobs. And, indeed, after 25 years, all the bores were dug, the fences built and the roads cleared; there was little left to do. Furthermore, the changes occurring outside the industry, such as the introduction of roads, trains and the influx of non-Aboriginal labour from the south, released most of the younger men from heavy employment in stock work. The resultant problems generated by a large number of Aborigines living near the stations with nothing to do left the government with no choice but to respond to the complaints of pastoralists and intervene. The Aboriginal Affairs Board requested and received funds to build government settlements such as Indulkana and Amata which served either as welfare depots or as training centres for non-existent pastoral work.[23] In other words, the state had been forced to interrupt the process of freeing Aboriginal labour, and again offered a modified programme of protection along with increased economic dependency.

While the state was proposing old solutions to new problems created by capitalist development, young Aborigines once more embraced the old men, the Dreaming and the land which had continued to be a living part of themselves.

The rise of land rights

In the previous section, it was shown how the state's policies of assimilation and protection as well as the character of pastoral development in the northwest and Aboriginal involvement in the industry both combined to effect superficial changes on Western Desert social organization and ideology while leaving the fundamentals intact. In particular, the central attitudes of Pitjantjatjara and Yankuntjatjara people toward labour and the land are seen to be essential components in the dialectic of a specific syncretic process of 'communal – capitalist' interaction. It was suggested that the conceptions of work held by Aboriginal people are based on collective rights to the main means of production. Rights to labour in the social processes found within communal relations, as in the Western Desert, are not individual rights but communal rights. Furthermore, collective rights determine an attitude toward the land which has nothing in common with the ideology of the market. Land is inalienable within Western Desert communal property relations; land is not an object for sale.[24] In this case, alienation of the main means of production could only have been brought about by outside forces. Neither state intervention nor capitalist production had destroyed those social processes and relations (e.g. recruitment principles to land-owning local groups, ceremonial processes) necessary for the reproduction of communal relations of production and distribution. On the other hand, Western Desert people were beginning to realize the economic benefits gained through commodity-based economic activity, such as working on pastoral stations and selling precious stones to miners. As Rowley (1972a:173) suggests, 'contact with the cash economy also led to appreciation of the cash value of the lands taken over'. At the very least, Western Desert people could begin to realize both the value of the land in acquiring European goods and the land's value to others, whose use of it could have disastrous effects on Aboriginal interests.

The dual nature of Aboriginal interests, as these relate to both communal and commodity relationships, is an essential ingredient in Aboriginal *political* consciousness today. It now remains to consider the development of Western Desert people's political activity, its expression and possible outcome in their attempts to regain legitimate control over the land.

In 1965, the South Australian government, in an unprecedented step, established the Aboriginal Lands Trust under the Aboriginal Land Trust Act 1966 (see Rowley 1972a:181) by which freehold title could be proclaimed for any Crown lands or reserve lands with the exception of certain areas, such as the North-West Reserve (s. 16.1). Apparently, the people of the northwest did not comprehend the Trust and thus were unable to decide when or whether to enter it.[25] In respect of land occupied by Western Desert peoples, the Yalata Reserve was transferred to the Trust in May 1975, as was the 42 square km Indulkana lease in October of the same year. The Crown, however, retained control over all minerals[26] on these lands vested under the Act. Although such lands could not be sold without the consent of the Minister and both Houses, there was no provision for entrenchment, that is, land was not to be held by Aboriginal groups in perpetuity and, therefore, could be alienated from them without their consent. Still, in terms of practical politics, the South Australian government had explicitly recognized native title arising from prior occupation: a necessary condition if future concessions were to be won later.

Meanwhile, by 1968, the process of transferring Aboriginal people from the cattle-station camps to church- and government-administered settlements had been completed, with the exception of Everard Park Station, which was acquired for Aboriginal use in 1972. At this time, most Western Desert people in the northwest of South Australia were living at the settlements of Indulkana (established, 1968), Fregon (established, 1961, as an outstation of Ernabella), Ernabella and Amata (established, 1961). Along with this movement away from the stations, another movement of significance was taking place. In 1971, a small group of people from Amata established a camp at Puta Puta, 193 km west of Amata (Wallace 1977:131). Although Puta Puta has since been abandoned, it became the first of many settlements, referred to as 'homeland communities', to be formed in the North-West Reserve. Unlike previous centres which had been established by outside agencies, homeland communities were the result of Aboriginal initiative born of the desire to return to one's *ngurra*, a process which had been occurring, with brief interruptions, for some time (see Wallace 1977). The re-establishment of a physical connection to a person's or a group's socially recognized 'country' provided an important impetus for the political demand for legitimate control of the land. Today, there are about 13 to 15 of these communities varying in size from 20 to 150 persons and, in settlements from as far east as Indulkana, groups of people are constantly discussing the ways and means to leave the larger community and to set up 'a tank, a shed and a garden' in their own 'countries'.

A second important factor which directly led to the land-rights debate was the rapid increase in the northwest in mining activity which, unlike pastoralism, has always been interpreted by Aboriginal people as a threat to secret/sacred sites.[27] The control of mining is a crucial element in the land-rights debate but from the Aboriginal point of view compensation through royalty payments was never seriously considered as an important issue. Although South-West Mining's operations had been discontinued, miners are constantly prospecting, particularly in the

Western Australian side of the Central Desert and, to the east, in the Indulkana-Mimili area. Whereas the South Australian government has made some restrictions on mining activity in order to prevent the wholesale destruction of sites, the Western Australian government has provided no guarantees. The increasing likelihood of the destruction of sites along with the migrations of Pitjantjatjara people back to their countries have led the Western Desert people to draw on their wide-ranging social ties to all others in the 'brotherhood group' and to organize themselves into a single *political* unit to express common interest.

In July 1976, through the efforts of the Aboriginal people and some European advisers, a meeting of Pitjantjatjara, Yankuntjatjara and Ngaanyatjara people from nearly all communities in the northwest of South Australia as well as Blackstone in Western Australia and Docker River in the Northern Territory was organized and held at Amata. At that meeting, the Pitjantjatjara Council was formed[28] and it was agreed that the Council would be open to all Western Desert peoples living in the Central Desert areas. Furthermore, control of the land was expressed as being the foundation of Pitjantjatjara culture and it was stated that the Council's main aim in this respect was to gain full title to those lands still available to them. Since the first meeting, the Council has met bi-monthly at various Aboriginal communities in the Centre and, although a number of issues have been raised, such as attempts to restrict circulation of publications considered to be offensive and the establishment of a 'homelands' health service', the land question has remained as the central focus.

In a submission made to the government of South Australia by the Council, it was noted that

> Membership of the Council rests on the fundamental oneness of the people, 'walytja' or family, which links the people to each other and to the land irrespective of European state borders. Dreaming lines (iwara) link communities separated by the borders. Communities only a few miles apart are administered, funded and controlled by governments and departments widely separated, with significantly different attitudes and policies.   (February 1977)

This 'fundamental oneness' was no better stated than by an old man during the Select Committee Hearings (see note 29):

> The Laws come from our grandparents. It is a strong Law and we want to keep it strong. We want to keep the land, hold the land, that is our strongest desire. It is our land, it cannot be changed. We have been holding it forever. We wish to do so. It comes down through the

generations to be passed on from one generation to the other. We cannot change the Law every year: it is one Law and it is there forever.   [Translated from Pitjantjatjara.]

With the passage of the Northern Territory Land Rights Act in 1976, the Western Desert people began to think seriously of the possibilities of forming a separate Pitjantjatjara Lands Trust. During the Council meeting at Amata, January 1977, the men expressed their resolve, as a unified group or brotherhood of *all* Western Desert people, to work towards a distinct land-holding entity (see *Report of the Pitjantjatjara land rights working party* 1978:63–4, 66). The meeting, which was attended by representatives of every Pitjantjatjara, Yankuntjatjara and Ngaanyatjara community in the Centre, also expressed the desire for 'freehold title', interpreted as communal, inalienable title including the absolute right to all on and below the ground (see note 25). With regard to the South Australian Lands Trust, the people apparently felt that 'their needs cannot be met by the State-wide Trust in Adelaide, predominantly run by southern Aborigines with little understanding of the needs or views of their tribal brothers'.[29] In response to several demands made by the Pitjantjatjara Council, a sympathetic South Australian Labor government called for the formation of a working party which would

> examine the feasibility of establishing by legislation a separate Pitjantjatjara lands trust to cover the North-West Reserve, Everard Park, Indulkana, Ernabella, Fregon, provided that the inalienability of the land is firmly established and that arrangements proposed do not contravene the wishes of any of the Pitjantjatjara communities.
>
> (*Report of the Pitjantjatjara land rights working party* 1978:2)

After making two trips to the northwest and consulting with a number of experts in Aboriginal affairs, the working party was obviously impressed with the fact that 'many Pitjantjatjara still have an alternative, adult and fully fledged culture which needs land to uphold it' (*ibid.*:21). It recommended that a Pitjantjatjara Lands Trust be formed giving Western Desert people in South Australia freehold title to a number of lands, including the North-West Reserve and Ernabella leases, and that title should include 'the control of mining and mineral extraction . . . shared by the Pitjantjatjara peoples and the Government' (*ibid.*:8). The recommendations of the working party formed the basis of the Pitjantjatjara Land Rights Bill, 1978. However, victory was not to be gained easily. The Labor government failed to have the bill passed through both Houses. When a more conservative Liberal government took power in September 1979, the bill was tabled.

At the time of the completion of the working party report, two important events were occurring, independently, which added to the intensity and scope of the land-rights debate.

In the latter part of 1977, miners began to occupy an area 30 miles south of Indulkana in the old opal fields known as Mintubi (the name of an important site which has been all but destroyed by mining activity). The area developed rapidly and by mid-1978 over 150 miners resided there, investing a wide range of capital in the operation of a variety of machinery, including bulldozers. Although Mintubi lies within the Granite Downs pastoral lease and not on an Aboriginal reserve, the people of Indulkana became alarmed when it was discovered that miners were prospecting on sacred/secret sites. In particular, the sites associated with 'man-making' ceremonies were felt to be in danger; these sites linked the people of Indulkana to Western Desert people living in the northwest and elsewhere. It is interesting to note that although many other sites and tracks in the area are known by the Pitjantjatjara people of Indulkana, the sites associated with 'man-making' were of prime importance. Indeed, other places along other tracks not associated with 'man-making', with a few exceptions, appeared not to have been visited in years. It was claimed by the Pitjantjatjara men that the old people who once cared for these, prior to Pitjantjatjara migration into the area, were all dead.

With the support of the Pitjantjatjara Council, the Indulkana and Mimili people began a struggle with the South Australian government over the control of mining activities. The issue received southern press coverage; and, most importantly, with the financial support of a number of labour unions, a public meeting was held to discuss South Australian land rights at Trades Hall in Adelaide, November 1978.

As a further indication of the support given to the Aboriginal people by the organized working class, the Trades and Labour Council of South Australia passed a resolution at its meeting on 24 November 1978, which called for

the State Government to stop all further exploration and prospecting for precious stones and minerals outside the 6-mile Mintabie opal field until the Pitjantjatjara Land Rights Bill of 1978 becomes law and until a government enquiry has examined the impact of mining on the environment, Aboriginal land claims, sacred sites and Aboriginal communities in the area.

Due to the pressure from these Aboriginal and working-class organizations, as well as others,[30] the South Australian government confined opal mining to a 50 square mile area around Mintubi, although, as in the past, these restrictions were weakened by limited policing of the area. Consequently, the effective control of prospecting is problematic, an illegal liquor outlet continues to operate at Mintubi (as of 1980); and Aboriginal contact with miners has led to violence.

The Ayers Rock land claim carried out under the Northern Territory Land Rights Act also received the encouragement of the Pitjantjatjara Council and the claim gave many Western Desert men important experience in the political arena. Without entering into a detailed discussion of the claim, it is worthwhile to note that the support given by the Pitjantjatjara and Yankuntjatjara of South Australia again reaffirmed the essential unity of all Western Desert people, particularly if one considers that the Ayers Rock claimants had been living at Hermannsburg in Aranda country for many years and, therefore, were not a part of either the ceremonial activity or the political issues of the south.

It appears that, for the Pitjantjatjara, Yankuntjatjara and Ngaanytjara throughout the Centre, the main purpose in wresting control of their land from the three state governments is to develop the land along lines which would be considered, from a modern capitalist point of view, as not being development at all. The working party (*Report of the Pitjantjatjara land rights working party* 1978:27) recognized this charge of 'collective indolence' with respect to 'proper land use' and countered by claiming that 'at the core of the Pitjantjatjara demand for land rights is the desire on the part of individuals to strengthen clan life'. Certainly, the emphasis placed by the Pitjantjatjara themselves on the religious aspects of their lives, particularly those important places scattered throughout the desert, has been a central element in their political demands and activity. However, it is unlikely that these demands related to the assured control of their ceremonial cycles and sites would be an issue today if the people did not consider it *socially* necessary to respond, again not as individuals but as collectives, to the encroachment of capital and the state, when acting as the agent of capital. As is often the case, the very sacredness of the sites precludes any public discussion, especially if uninitiated men are present.

The fact that the religious component of Pitjantjatjara land rights does not replace the economic component has important implications for individuals and organizations supporting the Pitjantjatjara case. From the point of view of the Western Desert people, the ideological level is not seen to be a domain separate from the economic and social. New ways of using the land, at least for the immediate future, rest on the assurance that, for the Western Desert people, communal relations will be reproduced through and within indigenous processes and relations.

There are many examples of groups of people in the Centre attempting to engage in new economic activities managed and controlled by the people themselves. Aboriginal pastoral stations are successfully operating at Fregon, Mimili and Kenmore Park, and Indulkana men have always added, to the demand for the protection of sacred sites, the need for more land so that jobs will be made available. It is difficult to imagine Indulkana men operating their own station on their own land *unless* the Dreaming was secure, if not in their own minds then in the minds of others. At Pipalyatjara and Wingellina, Aboriginal-controlled mining activity has resulted in mixed success but attempts are being made to work out difficulties arising from the lack of funds for development. On a smaller scale, people in the homelands communities often engage in gardening activities along with hunting and gathering.

The emphasis on religion, to the *exclusion* of economic issues, has the effect of elevating Pitjantjatjara 'culture' to a place where the problems that this 'culture' is facing are to be found nowhere else, thus producing tendencies towards an isolationist philosophy in the minds of the people and, particularly, their well-meaning advisers (see Middleton 1977:156). While the Western Desert people are constantly struggling in their own interests, they are always aware of political issues elsewhere in Australia. Moreover, the attitude that 'all whites are bad whites' does not seem to be widespread. In fact, it can be argued that the 'expansionist tendencies' of Western Desert society which have resulted in the into their Law create a consciousness which works against isolationism.

The form of the political struggle, the strategies and tactics, especially as these relate to the formation of alliances with other sectors of the Australian social system (particularly those whose political goal is also control of the main means of production), depend to some degree on the advice of Europeans working in the area. For many of these Europeans, the pervasiveness of the Black/White model of social conflict along with a paternal 'loving the oppressed' type of attitude militate against the formation of alliances. If anything is to be learned from the current outcome of the Pitjantjatjara Land Rights Bill 1978, it is the fact that the weakness of mass support, particularly from the organized working class and its allies, assures unsympathetic governments that concessions to land rights can be either refused or negated with impunity. It is essential for potential allies to recognize not only that the 'fit' of Western

Desert social relations and ideology has to meet the needs of capital, as in the past, but that these can today provide the Pitjantjatjara with the organizational weapons necessary for effective political action.

Notes

1 The term 'colonial Australia' is used here in a geographical and not strictly an economic-political sense. The area 'roughly demarcates the desert and sparsely settled pastoral country' (Rowley 1972a:1) of Australia.

2 This is in reference to the World Conference for the Eradication of Racism and Racial Discrimination held in May 1978. See *The Socialist*, May 1978.

3 A discussion of the precise meaning of Pitjantjatjara, Yankuntjatjara, Ngaanyatjara and Antikarinya is beyond the scope of this paper. Briefly, these terms denote different dialects spoken by Western Desert people and seem to have some territorial referent. See Hamilton, in this volume.

4 This region refers to the land east of Amata to the Stuart Highway in the northwest of South Australia.

5 The term *ngurra*, which is often used with a variety of qualifiers, seems to have a range of meanings. Without entering into a full discussion of Western Desert land tenure, briefly, *ngurra* can refer to one named site or a constellation of named sites. Furthermore, *ngurra* can denote current place of residence, a foraging area, a complex of sites along interconnected tracks of the *tjurkurrpa* or, in this case, the site or constellation of sites associated with a person's birthplace or a person's cognates (i.e. father, mother, father's father, mother's father, father's mother, mother's mother) and, at times, other kin as well (e.g. 'wife', 'brother-in-law').

6 Pitjantjatjara informants in Indulkana and Mimili settlements associated the Mann and Tomkinson Ranges with 'Pitjantjatjara people' while the region east of Amata was identified as 'Yankuntjatjara country'.

7 The Pastoral Board provided an advance of £200 to settlers who sank a well which could produce 4,000 gallons of good water per day. In addition, rent for the leased land was often waived by the Board and reduced to a 'peppercorn'.

8 Older men at Indulkana would often recite tales of men being marched in chains from the area – a distance of over 300 km.

9 Several older men in Indulkana claimed that, long ago, Pitjantjatjara people from the west attempted to settle in the Everards but were driven away by the Yankuntjatjara people living there. After the encounter, the former moved south to Ooldea.

10 During my field-work period, a small group of people from Yalata passed through Indulkana on their way to 'visit' and 'clean up' their *ngurra* in the Mann-Tomkinson Ranges.

11 This trend seems to have reversed itself by the fifties.

12 For many years, however, the policy of separation did not prevent the Protector's Office from removing half-caste children from their mothers, who were living in a number of rural locations, and placing them in institutions in the northeast (see Hamilton 1972:36).

13 Most of the evidence for this period is taken from interviews with patrol officers, missionaries and station managers.

14 By 1953, for example, the Granite Downs Station was made up of a number of small leases which totalled 6,000–7,000 square miles. This was one of the larger stations but not exceptionally so.

15 Many of the names of bores found on pastoral leases are taken from the original Aboriginal site names, for example, Utah Bore (Yutanya), Indulkana (Intalkanya).

16 In the mid-sixties, approximate Aboriginal wages on the stations were as follows (weekly rates): Stockboys – $6.00 to $10.00 plus food; or, depending on the wage, clothing and a blanket; Fencers and post cutters – $10.00 plus food; Housegirl – $2.00 to $6.00, depending on the amount of food and clothing supplied. The unpublished Patrol Report went on to state, in reference to one station: 'food here consists of beef to the approximate value of $2.00 per week per man, plus food to the value of approximately $3.00. This is still a government ration station so issue is supplemented with Government supplies!'

17 Actually, soon after the establishment of Ernabella in 1937, a sheep station was begun on the 500 square mile lease. One of the purposes of the station was to train young Aboriginal men in pastoral work. Also see Middleton (1977:68).

18 Rowley (1972:214–15) points out that it was the South Australian government's policy to discourage the use of Aboriginal labour in the goldmines in the late nineteenth century, preferring to import Asian labour instead. There was no need to import labour for the mining industry of the northwest, at least not on a large scale. Still, Aborigines were not used for any mining work which was available. Except for fossicking for opal near Coober Pedy (and, today, Mintubi), the Aboriginal relationship to the mining industry of the northwest has been mostly peripheral. One possible exception is the small-scale chrysoprase mine near Mt Davies operated by the Aboriginal people living in the area.

19 The precise meaning of 'family' and 'community' was not discussed by Marx in his 'Pre-capitalist economic formations', probably owing to the fact that detailed ethnographic accounts of hunter-gatherer social systems were not available at that time. However, his comments on the nature of the individual and the purpose of individual labour within generalized communal relations is the point here, while an analysis of the nature of collectives found in Western Desert society, such as 'hordes' and 'ngurra groups' (or more contentious terms such as 'family' and 'community'), is more properly contained in a discussion of land tenure.

20 Some observers who were interviewed noted that young Aboriginal men (*nyiinkas*), who were segregated from the station camp during initiation stages, would often be used in stock work.

21 One example of 'incipient entrepreneurial' activity was recorded at Indulkana. One Aboriginal man ordered quantities of soft-drinks and potato chips from Alice Springs to sell, as he put it, 'for my profit'. The scheme fell through, however, when he gave away much of the goods (and his profit) to his kin.

22 See Hamilton, Annette 1971. 'Socio-cultural factors in health among the Pitjantjatjara – A preliminary report', unpublished.

23 For a critical appraisal of the Amata settlement, see Summers, John n.d. 'Colonial South Australia'. Unpublished.
24 This position is contained, for example, in the Pitjantjatjara Council Submission to the Government of South Australia on Land Rights, 14 February 1977. Unpublished.
25 See the Pitjantjatjara Council Submission to the Government of South Australia on Land Rights, 14 February 1977. Unpublished.
26 Rowley (1972a:181) notes that the government attempted to have mineral rights vested in the Trust, but it was defeated by the legislative council.
27 This conclusion is based on evidence in the minutes and transcripts of meetings of the Pitjantjatjara Council and personal research. See also *Report of the Pitjantjatjara land rights working party* (1978:34, 72–4).
28 Unless otherwise indicated, the following information on the early formation of the Pitjantjatjara Council is contained in the Minutes of Evidence of the Select Committee on the Pitjantjatjara Land Rights Bill 1978, held on 9 March 1979, as well as unpublished Council minutes.
29 See the Pitjantjatjara Council Submission of 14 February 1977.
30 Support was also given by the Australian Workers Union, Amalgamated Metal Workers Union, Seamen's Union, Aboriginal Legal Rights Movement and Action for World Development.

Bibliography

Basedow, H. 1904. 'Anthropological notes made on the South Australian Government north-west prospecting expedition'. *The Transcripts of the Royal Society of South Australia* 29:12–37
Bates, Daisy 1938. *The passing of the Aborigines*. London: Murray
Berndt, R. M. 1941. 'Tribal migrations and myths centring on Ooldea, South Australia'. *Oceania* 12(1):1–20
    1966. 'The concept of the tribe in the Western Desert of Australia', in I. Hogbin and L. R. Hiatt (eds.), *Readings in Australian and Pacific anthropology*. London: Melbourne University Press
    1972. 'The Walmadjeri and Gugadja', in M. G. Bicchieri (ed.), *Hunters and Gatherers today*. New York: Holt, Rinehart and Winston
Carruthers, J. 1892. 'Triangulation of the north-west portion of South Australia'. *South Australian Government Parliamentary Paper 179.*
Clark, Manning 1969. *Short history of Australia*. New York: New English Library
Cockburn, R. 1925. *Pastoral pioneers of South Australia*, 2 vols. Adelaide: Lutheran Publishing House
Elkin, A. P. 1938–40. 'Kinship in South Australia'. *Oceania* 10:197–234
Hamilton, Annette 1972. 'Black and white: the relationships of change'. *Arena* 30:34–47
Hilliard, Winifred 1968. *The people in between: the Pitjantjatjara people of Ernabella*. Adelaide: Rigby Ltd
Johnston, T. Harvey 1941–5. 'Some Aboriginal routes in the western portion of South Australia'. *Proceedings of the Royal Geographical Society (South Australian Branch) of Australia*. 42–6:33–65
Lee, Richard B. 1968. 'What hunters do for a living or how to make out on scarce resources', in R. Lee and I. DeVore (eds.), *Man the hunter*. Chicago: Aldine

490 Daniel A. Vachon

Little, J. 1974. 'Land rights', in Garth Nettheim (ed.), *Aborigines, human rights and the law*. Redfern: Hogbin, Polle Pty Ltd
Love, J. R. B. 1937. *Ernabella*. Board of Missions of the Presbyterian Church of South Australia
Marx, Karl 1979. 'Pre-capitalist economic formations', in K. Marx and F. Engels, *Pre-Capitalist economic formations: a collection*. Moscow: Progress Publishers
Middleton, Hannah 1977. *But now we want the land back*. Sydney: New Age Publishers Pty Ltd
Report of the Aboriginal Affairs Board. 30 June 1963 to 30 June 1967. Adelaide: Government Printer
Report of the Aborigines Protection Board. 30 June 1940 to 30 June 1962. Adelaide: Government Printer
Report of the Chief Protector of Aboriginals. 30 June 1867 to 30 June 1939. Adelaide: Government Printer
Report of the Pitjantjatjara land rights working party of South Australia. June 1978
Rowley, C. D. 1972. *The destruction of Aboriginal society*. Ringwood, Victoria: Penguin Books Australia Ltd
1972a. *The remote Aborigines*. Ringwood, Victoria: Penguin Books Australia Ltd
Ryerson, S. 1975. *Unequal union*. Toronto: Progress Publishers
Silberbauer, G. B. 1971. 'Ecology of the Ernabella Aboriginal community'. *Anthropological Forum* 3(1):21–36
Stevens, Frank 1974. *Aborigines in the Northern Territory cattle industry*. Canberra: Australian National University Press
Turner, D. H. forthcoming. *Australian social organization*
Wallace, Noel M. 1977. 'Pitjantjatjara decentralization in north-west South Australia: spiritual and psychosocial motivation', in R. M. Berndt (ed.), *Aborigines and change: Australia in the 70s*. New Jersey: Humanities Press
White, S. A. 1915. 'Narrative', in S. A. White, 'Notes on the expedition into the northwest regions of South Australia'. *Transactions of the Royal Society of South Australia* 39:707–25
Yengoyan, A. A. 1970. 'Demographic factors in Pitjandjara social organization', in R. M. Berndt (ed.), *Australian Aboriginal anthropology*. Perth: University of Western Australia Press

Indexes

Index of peoples and places

(References to groups and bands *not* discussed in detail will be found listed under country or region of origin: e.g. Ainu under Japan; G//ana under Kalahari. Groups discussed in greater detail, e.g. !Kung San, Pitjantjara, are listed under their own names with cross reference to related groups and areas. For ease of reference all entries relating to Australian Aboriginal groups are listed under Aborigines.)

Index of authors

(The authors listed are those to whom direct reference has been made, or who have been quoted, in the text. A complete bibliography may be found at the end of each paper.)

General index